As You Like It
FROM 1600 TO THE
PRESENT

SHAKESPEARE CRITICISM
VOLUME 17
GARLAND REFERENCE LIBRARY OF THE HUMANITIES
VOLUME 1662

SHAKESPEARE CRITICISM
PHILIP C. KOLIN, *General Editor*

TWELFTH NIGHT
edited by Stanley Wells

ROMEO AND JULIET
Critical Essays
edited by John F. Andrews

CORIOLANUS
Critical Essays
edited by David Wheeler

TITUS ANDRONICUS
Critical Essays
edited by Philip C. Kolin

LOVE'S LABOUR'S LOST
Critical Essays
edited by Felicia Hardison Londré

THE WINTER'S TALE
Critical Essays
edited by Maurice Hunt

TWO GENTLEMEN OF VERONA
Critical Essays
edited by June Schlueter

VENUS AND ADONIS
Critical Essays
edited by Philip C. Kolin

AS YOU LIKE IT
FROM 1600 TO THE PRESENT
Critical Essays
edited by Edward Tomarken

As You Like It
FROM 1600 TO THE PRESENT
CRITICAL ESSAYS

EDITED BY
EDWARD TOMARKEN

GARLAND PUBLISHING, INC.
NEW YORK AND LONDON
1997

Library of Congress Cataloging-in-Publication Data

As you like it from 1600 to the present : critical essays / [edited by] Edward
   Tomarken.
        p.   cm. — (Garland reference library of the humanities ; v. 1662.
Shakespeare criticism ; v. 17)
    ISBN 0-8153-1174-5 (alk. paper)
    1. Shakespeare, William, 1564–1616. As you like it. 2. Comedy.
I. Tomarken, Edward, 1938–   . II. Series: Garland reference library of the
humanities ; vol. 1662. III. Series: Garland reference library of the
humanities. Shakespeare criticism ; v. 17.
PR2803.A93   1997
822.3'3—dc20   96-33284
                                        CIP

Printed on acid-free, 250-year-life paper
Manufactured in the United States of America

GENERAL EDITOR'S INTRODUCTION

The continuing goal of the Garland Shakespeare Criticism series is to provide the most influential historical criticism, the most significant contemporary interpretations, and reviews of the most influential productions. Each volume in the series, devoted to a Shakespearean play or poem (e.g., the sonnets, *Venus and Adonis*, the *Rape of Lucrece*), includes the most essential criticism and reviews of Shakespeare's work from the seventeenth century to the present. The series thus provides, through individual volumes, a representative gathering of critical opinion of how a play or poem has been interpreted over the centuries.

A major feature of each volume in the series is the editor's introduction. Each volume editor provides a substantial essay identifying the main critical issues and problems the play (or poem) has raised, charting the critical trends in looking at the work over the centuries, and assessing the critical discourses that have linked the play or poem to various ideological concerns. In addition to examining the critical commentary in light of important historical and theatrical events, each introduction functions as a discursive bibliographic essay that cites and evaluates significant critical works—essays, journal articles, dissertations, books, theatre documents—and gives readers a guide to the research on a particular play or poem.

After the introduction, each volume is organized chronologically, by date of publication of selections, into two sections: critical essays and theatre reviews/documents. The first section includes previously published journal articles and book chapters as well as original essays written for the collection. In selecting essays, editors have chosen works that are representative of a given age and critical approach. Striving for accurate historical representation, editors include earlier as well as contemporary criticism. Their goal is to include the widest possible range of critical approaches to the play or poem, demonstrating the multiplicity and complexity of critical response.

In most instances, essays have been reprinted in their entirety, not butchered into snippets. The editors have also commissioned original essays (sometimes as many as five to ten) by leading Shakespearean scholars, thus offering the most contemporary, theoretically attentive analyses. Reflecting some recent critical approaches in Shakespearean studies, these new essays approach the play or poem from many perspectives, including feminist, Marxist, new historical, semiotic, mythic, performance/staging, cultural, and/or a combination of these and other methodologies. Some volumes in the series even include bibliographic analyses that have significant implications for criticism.

The second section of each volume in the series is devoted to the play in performance and, again, is organized chronologically, beginning with some of the earliest and most significant productions and proceeding to the most recent. This section, which ultimately provides a theatre history of the play, should not be regarded as different from or rigidly isolated from the critical essays in the first section. Shakespearean criticism has often been informed by or has significantly influenced productions. Shakespearean criticism over the last twenty years or so has usefully been labeled the "Age of Performance." Readers will find information in this section on major foreign productions of Shakespeare's plays as well as landmark productions in English. Consisting of more than reviews of specific productions, this section also contains a variety of theatre documents, including interpretations written for the particular volume by notable directors whose comments might be titled "The Director's Choice," histories of seminal productions (e.g., Peter Brook's *Titus Andronicus* in 1955), and even interviews with directors and/or actors. Editors have also included photographs from productions around the world to help readers see and further appreciate the way a Shakespearean play has taken shape in the theatre.

Each volume in the Garland Shakespeare Criticism series strives to give readers a balanced, representative collection of the best that has been thought and said about a Shakespearean text. In essence, each volume supplies a careful survey of essential materials in the history of criticism for a Shakespearean text. In offering readers complete, fulfilling, and in some instances very hard to locate materials, volume editors have made conveniently accessible the literary and theatrical criticism of Shakespeare's greatest legacy, his work.

Philip C. Kolin
University of Southern Mississippi

FOR ANNETTE
IN SICKNESS AND IN HEALTH

TO THE MEMORY OF
HODGIE, RHEA, AND RUMBA

CONTENTS

ACKNOWLEDGMENTS

A project of this length is only possible with the help of others. I am pleased to thank David Wheeler for suggesting me as an editor to the general editor, Philip Kolin, who has been patient and helpful throughout the process of producing this book. Friends and colleagues have read various portions of the manuscript and made constructive suggestions: in particular, Fran Dolan, Charles Forker, and Scott Shershow. Jay Halio gave me some helpful advice about selections to be included. Part of the manuscript was completed at Le Moana, thanks to the generosity of Bernard and Monique Labbé. And Stephanie Wilds Shea remained a stalwart friend. Tom Montgomery and his staff helped with computer technicalities. Scott Clute and Trudi Nixon worked long, extra hours to prepare the manuscript for publication. Special thanks to William Rauckhorst of Miami University, Office of the Advancement of Scholarship and Teaching, for a small grant to help with the technical aspect of the manuscript. Phyllis Korper has been a kind and considerate editor and Laurel Stegina has been an astute proofreader.

Family members have once again tolerated rooms of cluttered papers and a regularly preoccupied academic. Pamela Porter has welcomed me to her home every summer, thus facilitating regular access to the British Library. Martin, Elizabeth, Anthony, James, and Christopher Porter provided regular entertainment and garden therapy. Ali, Candace, Dana, Jason, Peter, and Kathleen Tomarken provided western-style humor. The family sadly lost Rumba, Rhea, and Hodgie but has gained Bess, Jas, and Sam. Most important of all is the loyalty and love of my daughter Emma and my wife Annette.

As You Like It
FROM 1600 TO THE
PRESENT

AS YOU LIKE IT FROM 1600 TO THE PRESENT:
CRITICAL ESSAYS
Edward Tomarken

In keeping with the general policies of the Garland Shakespeare Criticism series, this survey seeks to reproduce whenever possible complete documents rather than excerpts, except when the material forms part of a full-length study or of a long introduction to an edition of *As You Like It*. Although criticism and theatre reviews are presented separately as documents, they will be discussed together because my research continually indicates that these two kinds of response or critical genres are interrelated, even if, as is often the case, that relationship is one of difference. Some other accounts of the critical and stage history of *As You Like It* that have proved to be particularly useful are as follows. Agnes Latham's Arden edition of *As You Like It* contains a brief but incisive history of criticism and of stage productions up to 1975. The New Variorum edition of *As You Like It* (1977) also provides a longer history of criticism as well as a somewhat more extensive account of the staging of the comedy. For a helpful account of criticism and theater presentations that includes material from the past two decades, see Alan Brissenden's Oxford edition. Jay L. Halio and Barbara C. Millard's *"As You Like It": An Annotated Bibliography, 1940–1980* is a careful and complete summary of four decades of twentieth-century commentary. The present essay attempts to give a more in-depth coverage to the history of criticism and staging than is provided in the introductions of scholarly editions. Unlike the Variorum editor, I intermingle criticism and stage history while differing from the annotated bibliographers in providing a historical framework, a conception of tradition and innovation. The result of my method is a sort of historical dialogue between critics and theater people, reviewers, actors, actresses, producers, and directors, that demonstrates how all interpretive insights have vantage points and blind spots. *As You Like It* becomes a prism of theatrical and literary criticism of the past four centuries.

FROM THE RENAISSANCE TO THE EARLY EIGHTEENTH CENTURY: ADAPTATION AND VARIATION

As You Like It has remained a popular play for the past two and a half centuries: in fact, productions have been presented almost every year since 1740. The earlier period, from 1599/1600, the generally accepted date of the first production, until 1740, is a mystery: for over a century after Shakespeare's death, there is no record of any performance. Circumstantial evidence suggests that *As You Like It* may have been staged at Wilton, the seat of the Earl of Pembroke, in 1603 (Latham, ix-x). And some have speculated that during Shakespeare's lifetime the play was withheld from the stage and publication because the character of Jaques alludes to John Marston, who was out of favor with Queen Elizabeth (Brissenden, pp. 3–4). In any event, from 1603 onward, we have no record of any version of it appearing on the stage until Charles Johnson's adaptation, *Love in a Forest*, of 1723. How do we explain this hiatus for over a century of performances of the comedy, particularly when it has proved so stageable and popular for the last two centuries? I have no ready answer to this question but have reproduced Charles Johnson's adaptation because it may shed some light on this question.

Love in a Forest has been regularly excoriated as an unholy mixture of Shakespeare's comedies with a bit of *Richard II*: The Arden editor calls it a "travesty" and the Oxford editor refers to it as a "gallimaufry" (Latham, lxxxvii; Brissenden, 52). Charles Johnson cuts Touchstone and the courtship of Phoebe and Silvius, changes the wrestling match into a sword fight, replaces Oliver with Jaques who becomes the wooer and eventual husband of Celia, and concludes with *Pyramus and Thysbe* from *Midsummer Night's Dream*, to mention only the major alterations. I include this drama, not in an attempt to make a case for it as a great work of literature, but as an important document in the history of *As You Like It* criticism. Charles Johnson removes Shakespeare's subplot concerning Phoebe and Silvius, the element of the play generally regarded as most pastoral, at a time when the genre of pastoral, fading from favor, was soon to be attacked by Samuel Johnson. The concept of the genre and genres of *As You Like It* will be a constant concern in the commentary on this comedy. In fact, I would suggest that the single most important and dominant issue in over 300 years of commentary on *As You Like It* is the question of genre.

Another important critical issue raised by *Love in a Forest* is the treatment of Jaques. While this most famous of melancholy ironists is allowed to keep his best known speeches, he courts and marries Celia. During the Restoration and early eighteenth century, that is, the period immediately following the Civil War, irony and satire were carefully monitored as possible forms of political subversion. Does Charles Johnson present the satirical observer Jaques as firmly integrated into the society by way of marriage in order to assure the audience that his irony is not intended to be politically subversive?

Over forty years later, in 1765, Samuel Johnson concluded his remarks on *As You Like It* by pointing to a moral/political matter that Shakespeare had neglected: "By hastening to the end of the work Shakespeare suppressed the dialogue between the usurper and the hermit, and lost an opportunity of exhibiting a moral lesson in which he might have found matter worthy of his higher powers" (II, 108). Perhaps we in the present are so far removed from the Civil War of the seventeenth century and the resulting trauma that lingered throughout much of the eighteenth century that we lose sight of the fact that *As You Like It* could have been perceived, in the day of Charles and Samuel Johnson, as a drama about political usurpation. The subject of political usurpation, particularly in the stark and brutal terms as it is presented in *As You Like It*, may have been too dangerous for the stage from 1660 until 1723, when Charles Johnson's adaptation removed any possible suggestion of subversion. Even the much scorned conclusion of *Love in a Forest* involving the play-within-the-play from *Midsummer Night's Dream* may bear upon this problem. Shakespeare, it will be recalled, shows Bottom and his fellow actors receiving indulgent treatment from their dramatic audience, the Duke and his retinue, because the rustics' crude attempt at entertainment does not detract from their good intentions. Charles Johnson may have been hoping that the political establishment of his day would respond with similar tolerance to his drama about ducal usurpation.

This political consideration could also explain another alteration that began with *Love in a Forest* and that persisted in stage productions of *As You Like It* until 1842 (Latham, lxxxviii). Shakespeare's First Lord's account of Jaques's response to the death of the deer (II, 1, 25 ff.) is in Charles Johnson's version spoken by Jaques himself, who introduces the tale as follows: "Indeed, my Lord, it grieves me very much, And in that Kind, I swear you more usurp, Than does your Brother, who hath banish'd you; Mark well my story and you'll find it so." Then follows the account of the tearful dying "Stag" (22–23). Does this alteration allow Charles Johnson to demonstrate that Jaques is opposed to usurpation? If so, why was this alteration maintained into the nineteenth century well after the time when Jaques's kind of satire would be seen as politically subversive? I shall return to this question when discussing nineteenth-century views, where it will become clear that Jaques taking over the First Lord's speech serves not a political goal, as in the eighteenth century, but one appropriate to the period of the rise of individualism, namely, a psychological purpose.

Furthermore, in order to understand the function of this alteration in the eighteenth century we need to keep in mind that stage productions cannot be separated from dramatic criticism. Here, it is pertinent that in 1710 Charles Gildon selected the "Old Duke's speech preferring the Solitude to the World" (365) for special praise: an exiled Duke who is so reconciled to his loss of power that he takes no action to reinstate himself is unlikely to be seen as an instance of political subversion. *Love in a Forest*, following thirteen years later, may be understood as a stage manifestation of a concept similar to that of Gildon. For Charles Johnson, Jaques is presented as joining the others at the end in marriage in order to demonstrate that his satire is not directed at establishment institutions. In the nineteenth century, productions of *As You Like It* continue to include elements of Johnson's adaptation that help establish that Jaques's irony is a reverse or disillusioned form of affection so that although he does not end up married he shares with the others the capacity to love. Thus *Love in a Forest* contributes to the stage tradition of *As You Like It* for over a century after its modest six performances in 1723.

In 1739, James Carrington published *The Modern Receipt or a Cure for Love*, another eighteenth-century adaptation of *As You Like It*, which was never presented on the stage. This drama keeps many of Charles Johnson's changes with the notable exception of the inclusion of the playlet, "Pyramus and Thysbe." In place of the play-within-the-play, Carrington expands the part of Jaques, who is taught, after some initial reluctance, how to court a woman and finally marry her. Carrington's drama demonstrates that the "Modern Receipt" for curing men of the desire to debauch women is courtship ending in marriage. During this period—Fielding's essays of the 1740s and his *Amelia* are prime examples—adultery and other violations of marriage were seen as detrimental to the orderliness of society as a whole. Perhaps one reason why Carrington's version never appeared on the stage was that it was first published within a year of the revival of Shakespeare's *As You Like It*. By 1740, when political stability seemed more certain than in the Restoration or early eighteenth century, Jaques could be presented in Shakespeare's version, particularly since Charles Johnson, in a stage version, and James Carrington, in a printed version, had already demonstrated that Jaques's satire need not be seen as politically subversive. Thus, whatever we may think of the adaptations from an artistic point of view, they have an important effect upon the critical tradition of *As You Like It*.

THE LATER EIGHTEENTH CENTURY: THE RETURN TO SHAKESPEARE'S COMEDY OF MARRIAGE

The next critical milestone is Samuel Johnson's commentary of 1765. Instead of presenting Johnson's notes apart from his text, as in the standard edition, I reprint Johnson's notes in their original context because the juxtaposition of the text of *As You Like It* with Johnson's comments as well as with those that he chose to include of his predecessors constitutes a critical document different in kind from a mere compilation of Johnson's notes. A number of critical issues are obscured by severing Johnson's notes from the remainder of the text. First, Johnson points out in his Preface that notes by other commentators reprinted in his edition without qualification represent remarks with which he agrees. Clearly, Johnson regarded these notes as important enough to be included for the reader's edification, yet, because not written by Johnson, they are omitted in the standard edition. Second, in the notes Johnson proposes emendations that he seldom includes in the text: these alternative wordings function as suggestions to help the reader understand what Johnson takes to be the meaning of the original. Subsequent editors who consult the notes alone have taken as emendations what are alternatives to be found only in the notes, not in the unchanged text. In fact, Johnson makes few textual changes and rejects many made by his predecessors, a point of particular interest concerning the speeches of Phoebe and Silvius. The words of these pastoral figures are treated with respect by Johnson. Laboring to restore the text to its original integrity, Johnson seems to have understood how the pastoral element of *As You Like It* is ironized in the context of rustic realism. He therefore makes no objection to the genre that he characterized, with reference to *Lycidas*, as "easy, vulgar and therefore disgusting" (*Life of Milton*). Once again, the manner in which pastoral is tempered by its relation to the other genres in the comedy is an issue. Third, Johnson regularly juxtaposes and combines remarks of previous commentators with or without his own comments to produce an effect upon the reader different from the intent of the individual commentators. This variorum technique is analyzed in detail in a previous work (see Tomarken, 47–8, 51, 79, 145–46, 158). For our purposes here, Johnson's edition is at once a compendium of the most important comments from previous editors and itself an interpretative document.

Moreover, it is important to keep in mind that from 1740 *As You Like It* was regularly performed on the stage. George Odell believes that from 1742 to 1817 productions became more frequent as the century progressed. (I, 338; II, 20). Neil Schroeder reports that "from 1751–1800, *As You Like It* ranked eighth out of the twenty-nine plays produced, with a total of 179 performances" (5). Hence Samuel Johnson as well as a number of his predecessors may well have seen performances of *As You Like It*. What sort of production they might have witnessed or heard about from friends who attended can be inferred from scattered theatre reviews and other accounts of performances.

Michael Jamieson, in an essay published for this first time in this volume, gives the following description of a performance in 1740: "There was a strong cast and three of Shakespeare's songs were given new settings by Thomas Arne. The Rosalind was Hannah Pritchard, then twenty-nine, who got off to a bad start. In those more boisterous days, when the auditorium remained illuminated, a performer's 'points' were applauded. It was only when Pritchard, given an unbecoming gown by the management, reached the line "Take the cork out of thy mouth that I may drink thy tidings" that she was applauded loudly for her spirited delivery. The performance not only brought her to the top of her profession but created a vogue for other Shakespearean comedies" (628).

All the great actresses of the eighteenth century played the part of Rosalind, and Bell's edition of *As You Like It* (1773) explains how the part was best played: "To do Rosalind justice, there should be an elegant symmetry of person, free deportment, remarkable vivacity of speech, and features somewhat of the arch cast" (see Schroeder, 10). Even Mrs. Siddons, the great tragedienne, tried the part but was not given the universal acclaim she achieved in tragedy. Anna Seward felt that "the playful scintillations of colloquial wit, which must strongly mark [the role of Rosalind], suit not the dignity of the Siddonian form and countenance" (see Schroeder, 11). *The Morning Post* admitted that Siddons was applauded but was not satisfied: "Mrs. Siddons, however, received very great applause; and who would not shew their judgment in applauding so great, so eminent an actress? But she was acting Comedy; she was delivering some of the most witty conceits of Shakespeare.—Did the audience laugh? Were they diverted? No. They were too much wrapped up in admiration at the extraordinary refinement of the actress; applause they gave in abundance; but reserved their laughter for Mrs. Wrighten [Audrey]" (see Schroeder 12).

We do not know why Garrick gave the part of Rosalind to the great tragic actress: was it merely because of her fame and ability to draw large audiences or was it because the comedy was seen as bordering on tragedy? Seward does report that Siddons achieved a triumph at the end of the play: "One of those rays of exquisite and original discrimination, which her genius so perpetually elicits, shone out upon her first rushing upon the stage in her own resumed person and dress; when she bent her knee to her father, the Duke, and said— 'To you I give myself—for I am yours;' and when falling into Orlando's arms, she repeated the same words,—'To *you* I give myself—for I am *yours'*. The marked difference of her look and voice in repeating that line, and particularly the last word of it, was inimitably striking. The tender joy of filial love was in the first; the whole soul of enamoured transport in the second. The extremely heightened emphasis on the word *yours*, produced an affect greater than you can conceive would result from the circumstances without seeing and hearing it given by that mistress of the passions" (165–66). Here we see manifest on the stage the eighteenth-century emphasis on family and marriage, an interest that Charles Johnson and James Carrington had made more obvious by altering Shakespeare's conclusion. This moment of triumph for "that mistress of the passions" provides us with an insight into one version of the eighteenth-century staging of *As You Like It*: Rosalind's reunion with her father, itself a moving event, gives rise to the even more intensely felt moment of forming a new family with Orlando. If this scene impressed Anna Seward, also called the Swan of Lichfield, the remarks of another resident of that city come to mind. Samuel Johnson's comment that Shakespeare neglected a moral moment in suppressing a conversation between the usurper and the hermit is usually assumed to be a typical instance of didacticism, a desire for a moral sermon that has at best only a tangential relation to the action and themes of the drama. But the restoration of family, in this instance of father and daughter, was perceived at this time as a microcosm of the political restoration of 1660. Johnson sees the marriages at the end of *As You Like It* as symbolic, a point I shall return to after completing a summary of the eighteenth-century staging tradition.

It should also be kept in mind that the eighteenth-century adaptations of *As You Like It* had other effects upon the stage productions, effects that endure to the present. Schroeder enumerates the following stage conventions, derived from Charles Johnson, that have no basis in Shakespeare's text: "The speeches of the 1st Lord in II, i . . . were given to Jaques and were to remain his for over a century. . . . In I, i, Orlando lays 'his Hand on [Oliver's] Collar' and shakes him during their quarrel. In the Forest of Arden, while 'Duke Alberto, Amiens, and Nobles [are] at a Banquet', Orlando enters, 'his Sword drawn.' During those scenes in the third act when he 'mars' the trees of the forest with verses honoring Rosalind, Orlando enters, 'a Paper of Verses in his Hand, which he fixes to a tree while delivering his lines. Later, Rosalind enters, takes the paper down, and reads it" (3). Our appreciation of modern productions is enhanced by understanding that many of these traditions that have no basis in Shakespeare's text nevertheless persist presumably because they continue to serve the purposes of producers and directors. Equally important are stage conventions that did not persist. Mrs. Siddons' dress as Ganymede was much criticized and was not imitated again until the present day. "Her dress was the most unaccountable we ever witnessed upon the stage. It was not that of either man or woman. Her Hussar boots with a gardiner's apron and petticoat behind, gave her a most equivocal appearance, which rendered Orlando's stupidity astonishing, in not making a premature discovery of his mistress. What causes Mrs. Siddons to innovate upon the former representations of this character in the article of dress we cannot guess; but we are certain that she could not appear to less advantage in any other habiliment whatever" (Schroeder, 16). Although not successful or of long duration, this experiment with "an ambiguous vestment that seemed neither male nor female" calls to mind modern performances. How is Mrs. Siddons rendition of Rosalind related to these late twentieth-century versions? How does the ambiguous vestment on the eighteenth-century stage relate to present-day gender experimentation?

In addition to Rosalind, the other important eighteenth-century role was that of Jaques. We have less evidence here. Clarity of voice and careful enunciation of the famous speeches seem to have been valued: "Quinn outdid his usual outdoings. I never heard anything spoke with such command of voice and action as the 'seven ages of man,' from the rough bass of the good Justice, 'whose round belly with good capon lined,' till he sunk to the childish treble; it was really prodigious" (Schroeder, 13). It would appear that Jaques's melancholy irony was considered as important as the romances leading to marriage.

Finally, to correct any impression that eighteenth-century staging of *As You Like It* was particularly heavy and overly serious, I have included a review of a dance performed during a 1741 production of *As You Like It* to suggest that the period, 1723–1765, that resulted in the return to the stage of Shakespeare's version of the drama, involved a recognition of the musical aspect of the play. This review from the *Gentleman's Magazine* combined with Johnson's attention to the songs in the text indicate that for eighteenth-century critics, editors, and directors music and dance provided a transition between and means of combining different modes and genres that together constitute *As You Like It*. In fact, the association of dance with *As You Like It* seems more marked in the eighteenth century than in the next century, particularly as dance was a form of entertainment often included during this period with drama and operatic presentations. In this respect it is pertinent that the new variorum editor's collaborator, Evelyn Joseph Mattern, reminds us that "Clarke considers the 1740 Drury Lane revival operatic because of Thomas Arne's incidental music and his settings for three songs" and that "Francesco Maria Veracini's opera *Rosalinda,* based on a libretto by Paolo Rolli, was produced during the composer's visit to London in 1744." "This opera," Mattern continues, "links the forest of Arden with the eighteenth-century pastoral convention of aristocratic swains maskerading as shepherds" (676). While there were operatic versions of *As You Like It* in the nineteenth and twentieth centuries, the song in these more recent versions dominates, with little dance or even the plot action of opera. Is it possible that during the eighteenth century, dance and opera, both of which involve movement rather than the static music of song, predominate because dramatic action, like the courtship and marriage of Jaques, has a political significance that it ceases to have in later ages?

To summarize, the eighteenth-century dramatic rendition of *As You Like It* emphasized the archness of Rosalind but was also able to relate her to tragic counterparts and to present her sexual ambiguities. Humour and lightness of touch were provided by music, dance, and such characters as Audrey, who was played as a country wench. Jaques's famous speeches were taken seriously and were considered more important than the character. "All the world's a stage" would take on a special meaning in the eighteenth century: the theatre of the day, marked as it was by overt stage conventions and clear concepts of acting decorum, underlines the conventional nature of the roles and rituals of eighteenth-century society. Although melancholy and ironical, Jaques can be seen to be commenting aptly upon the courtship rituals of the romantic couples even if he is unable to grasp or partake of their joy and pleasure. Rosalind's sexual ambiguity thus reflects less upon the character of Rosalind and more upon the context that fosters such a spectacle. Finally, a constant of productions for this period that will continue through the next century is the presence of pastoral, as real and ideal, Audrey and Ganymede. The relationship between these two sides of pastoral interested critics at the time. Lastly, it should be recalled, as Jamieson reminds us, that the first production of *As You Like It* in the United States was in New York City in 1786 and that during this period "it was more frequently performed there than in London" (630).

THE END OF THE EIGHTEENTH CENTURY: THE CIVIC RESPONSIBILITY OF MARRIAGE

Before turning to the considerations of pastoral at the end of the eighteenth century, we may now be able to understand the cryptic remarks of the greatest critic of this age, Samuel Johnson: "Of this play the fable is wild and pleasing. I know not how the ladies will approve the facility with which both *Rosalind* and *Celia* give away their hearts. To *Celia* much may be forgiven for the heroism of her friendship. The character of *Jaques* is natural and well preserved. The comick dialogue is very sprightly, with less mixture of low buffoonery than in some other plays; and the graver part is elegant and harmonious. By hastening to the end of his work *Shakespeare* suppressed the dialogue between the usurper and the hermit, and lost an opportunity of exhibiting a moral lesson in which he might have found matter worthy of his highest powers" (II, 108). Johnson applauds the balance of *As You Like It*; the equilibrium between the serious and the comical lends the play more dignity without detracting from the fact that it is entertaining, or what he calls "pleasing." Jaques alone receives unqualified praise because presumably he exemplifies humor that avoids buffoonery, and Celia's "heroism of friendship" lends stature to this witty comic character. The problem presented by the play for Johnson is that the "ladies" might find Celia's and Rosalind's marriages overhasty and that the conversion of the usurper is suppressed. From what we now know of the staging of *As You Like It* during this period—and although we have no certain evidence Johnson ever attended a performance of *As You Like It*, he must have conversed with those who did—these comments take on new meaning. If Jaques functioned to emphasize the conventional nature of social behavior, particularly the staginess and role-playing of the courtship ritual, the end of the play would need to make plain that these artificial and arbitrary "rites" serve an important purpose. For those of Johnson's era who viewed family and the body politic as microcosm and macrocosm, a hasty marriage could be as dangerous, in local familial terms, as a ducal usurpation. In this sense, Johnson's remarks should not be dismissed as mere didacticism: nor should it be assumed that because at a certain point in his life he ceased to frequent the theatre he was therefore out of touch with the theatrical conventions of his day.

Even Johnson's cryptic reference to the "fable" as "wild and pleasing" suggests an awareness of the pastoral element that interested other critics of this period. Francis Gentleman calls *As You Like It* a "pastoral comedy" while praising Corin's speech, "I am a true labourer," reminding us that during this period attempts were made to revive the pastoral by making it more realistic and genuinely rural, that is, more like the georgic. Yet Gentleman records his puzzlement concerning the scenes involving Touchstone, Audrey, and William: "we laugh we know not why" (473). The eighteenth-century georgic had made the farm an appropriate topic for literature, but satire of the subject matter is troubling to Gentleman. The problem is not that satire is indecorous for romantic comedy. Gentleman points out that in this play with its "very romantic air," Jaques's humor is now so well known that the "seven ages of man" speech is traditionally cited (468). Indeed, the earliest critical commentary that we have on *As You Like It* is Nicholas Rowe's admiration for this speech. "The melancholy of Jaques, in *As You Like It*, is as singular and odd as it is diverting. And if what Horace says, 'Difficile est proprie communia dicere' 'twill be a hard task for any one to go beyond him in the description of several degrees and ages of man's life, though the Thought be old, and common enough." After citing Jaques's most famous speech, Rowe concludes that "his Images are indeed every where so lively, that the thing he would represent stands full before you, and you possess every part of it" (xx-xxii). In 1709, Rowe describes Jaques's brilliance as so dazzling that it almost seems to defy description. Gentleman, writing in the second half of the eighteenth century, is still unable to resolve this generic problem raised by Jaques's satire set in pastoral. Nevertheless, Gentleman concludes that "with all its faults no more agreeable piece [appears] on the stage" (475). Charles Johnson and Richard Carrington converted the melancholy ironist into a bridegroom, but critics of Shakespeare's version must face in starker terms the question of how ironic melancholy is related not only to romance but also to pastoral.

Melancholy and pastoral are conspicuously intermingled in the scene of the dying stag. William Richardson focuses on Jaques's response to the dying stag. Characterizing this scene as "very romantic," Richardson, it should be noted, follows not contemporary productions but the printed text in attributing this speech, as do most modern editors and producers, to the First Lord and not to Jaques himself (142). Since Jaques is not seen as the speaker of these lines, he cannot be assumed to add his characteristic ironical tinge to them. They thus represent a serious side of Jaques, one involving sympathy, not satire. Richardson explains that Jaques here shows "sensibility" that is usually linked to a "social disposition" (143). Yet the melancholy romantic prefers to be alone and ends without a wife. How, Richardson asks, do we explain the fact that the social sensibility of Jaques does not manifest itself in any of his actions? Richardson explains that the social affinity can be thwarted by disappointment which, in general, can take two forms, misanthropy, like that of Swift, or melancholy, like that of Jaques. Although mixed with a bit of misanthropy, Jaques's disposition is seen as less extreme than that of Swift. A reformed "dissipated and sensual libertine," Jaques is portrayed as fond of music, which would suggest that he is at least susceptible to some pleasure. But Richardson believes that this particular pleasure is indicative of dejection that saps up all passion. Richardson concludes that Jaques serves as a warning against despondency, a "social disposition" that may render us "unsocial and morose" (169). Jaques is seen as a threat to social sensibility, a danger that Richardson warns against: "Let us love mankind; but let our affections be duly chastened. Be independent, if possible; but not insensible" (169). In fact, the famous speech beginning "All the world's a stage" is seen as an expression of disillusioned social sensibility, of a "heart, sorrowful and dejected by the repulse of an ardent passion [that] is averse from pleasure of every kind" (159). Jaques's behavior is distinguished from the content of his speeches. He tells us that he sympathizes with the dying stag as, according to Richardson, should all sociable beings. But in the end, isolating himself from the young lovers, Jaques alienates himself from the animal side of man and loses any opportunity for love. In this sense the tearful stag scene permits Jaques to expatiate on both aspects of pastoral, the animal and the romantic, while himself violating both. During this second half of the eighteenth century, following the deaths of Pope and Swift, literate people were familiar with satirists whose behavior was at variance with their precepts.

Mrs. Griffith, one of the first female commentators of the eighteenth century, reinforces the distinction between Jaques and the others by noting that his humor is different from that involving Audrey, William, and Touchstone. While the coarse humor of the subplot is, for the most part, left without comment, Mrs. Griffith focuses upon Jaques. After reminding her readers that *As You Like It* begins with a reflection on "the *principal* concern in life, the education of children," Mrs. Griffith explains that satire need not spring from cynicism but can have a social function: "As there are many vices in morals that are injurious to society, and which the laws have not stigmatized, or possibly cannot sufficiently provide against, the reprehensions of Satire, under proper restrictions, may perhaps be deemed a necessary supplement to legislation"(69–71). In illustration of this principle of functional social satire, Jaques's reply to the Duke is characterized as "a good defence made for general satire" and the seven ages of man speech is cited as "a fine picturesque and dramatic description of life and character" (79–81).

During this same period when Gentleman and Griffith are unable to account for the coarse comedy of the subplot, Edward Capell objects to the inclusion of the masque of Hymen in *As You Like It*. "The foolery of masques" is, for Capell, a fault of Shakespeare's age, but the dramatist's editors are blamed for "bringing in Hymen in *propria persona*," thus making Rosalind a "magician indeed" (69). Capell believes that the desire to retreat from "the haunts of 'ambition,' to enjoy the blessings of heaven" is satirized by Jaques's song containing the term "Ducdame" (58–9). By means of this kind of irony Capell implies that Shakespeare is able to portray his heroine Rosalind as combining Jaques's kind of humor with an earthiness and worldliness to balance the romantic aspect. The masque of Hymen, highlighting romantic fantasy, must not, for Capell, be identified with Rosalind, who subsumes romance within her complex personality.

Near the end of the eighteenth century, Walter Whiter reinforces this position and provides further details. The earthly and physical side of love is seen in the explanation of the word "overthrown," which has application to the wrestling match and to Rosalind's effect upon Orlando (15). By contrast, the Duke, according to Whiter, consoles himself for his banishment from "the paradise of a Court" by considering Arden as representing "a philosophical retirement of ease and independence." This view isolates the Duke from the love games that involve, in addition to a philosophical aspect, a physical element (18). For the exiled Duke, like Jaques, remains aloof from the realm of "Ducdame," which Whiter explains as "the usual cry of the Dame to gather her Ducks" (22). The barnyard realm of physical coupling is for Whiter an essential element of human love, a position made clear in the lengthy explanation of "content" (45–50). Although sharing with Capell the belief that Jaques debunks any Platonic or idealized concept of love and of the idyllic quality of the traditional pastoral scene, Whiter suggests that integration of the physical content of romance runs the gamut from the coarse Audrey to the refined Rosalind. Instead of following Capell in objecting to the masque of Hymen, Whiter devotes his longest note, on "Atalanta's better part," to demonstrate that Rosalind combines the refinement of idealized love with humor, modesty, and earthy awareness (29–43). In this way, Whiter is able to accommodate within his view of *As You Like It* what he sees as the pastoral (the banished Duke), the anti-pastoral (Jaques), and the masque of Hymen.

The reviews of stage versions of *As You Like It* from the 1780s reinforce some elements found in the critical commentary while raising some new issues. As the critics have maintained, Rosalind and Jaques are both complicated multi-faceted characters seen as a challenge to even seasoned actors and actresses. Rosalind must be not only beautiful but also express herself with vivacity and move about the stage with "the elegance and ease of a woman bred in the high fashion of court" (*The Times*, 7 February 1786. See also *The Times*, 23 September 1789 and *London Gazette*, 18 February 1786). In short, the heroine must be at ease with the most sophisticated and most elemental of conventions and modes of behaviour, enabling her to move between the main plot and the subplot with ease and grace. Similarly, Jaques is a difficult and complex part because he also has his place in the various plots, groups of people and genres of the comedy. Hence one actor is criticized for playing Jaques in too brutal and rough a manner so that his laugh seems strained. Jaques's melancholy is, as a number of our critics have pointed out, satiric but not tragic. Or if it does occasionally approach the depths of tragedy, Jaques must be at ease and join in with the laughter of the others. In short, the stage reviewers agree with the critics in seeing Rosalind and Jaques as versatile characters who belong equally in romance and anti-romance, in pastoral and anti-pastoral.

The theatre reviewers, however, give more attention to Touchstone than do the critics. And the reason for this attention is not merely because the clown makes the audience laugh. In fact, the reviewers see Touchstone as more than merely amusing. One reviewer characterizes one actor's rendition of Touchstone as having "magnetism"; another actor is so necessary in the part that the performance is "deferred on account of his absence." Still another reviewer considers the question of "chastity" appropriate to the part of Touchstone, and, even more surprisingly, attention is regularly given by reviewers to Audrey, Touchstone's partner. Here, it is well to keep in mind that, as Odell points out, Sir Oliver Martext, the priest who marries Touchstone and Audrey, is omitted from productions between 1773 and 1817 (II, 21–23). Since Martext is a Puritan, his suppression from the stage may be related to the laws during this period against dissenters. Also, because a marriage performed by Martext was of questionable legality, as Jaques implies to Touchstone, the question of the clown's chastity has a direct bearing upon it. Presumably during this period, Touchstone's importance on the stage, his "magnetism," was furthered by cutting this marriage that could be seen as a mere subterfuge to satisfy Audrey's sexual scruples. But, as one reviewer remarks, the pure side of Touchstone may have been overdone: "we have our doubts if a little *outre* colouring is not proper ornament to a court jester wearing a pied fool's coat" (*The Times*, 7 February 1786). On the stage, Touchstone is clearly used to give some authority to an earthy alternative to the idealized pastoral romance, epitomized, for instance, by Orlando's decorating trees with his love poems. This aspect of *As You Like It* did not receive in the eighteenth century the full attention of critics. Finally, it is important to notice the sardonic remark about Amiens: "*Johnstone* laughed heartily in Amiens,—and in return, the audience laughed as heartily at his singing" (*The Times*, 21 November 1789). We can infer from this satirical comment that by the end of the eighteenth century renditions of the songs had become commonplace in performances of *As You Like It* and that frequenters of the theatre had acquired some discrimination about the quality of musical performance.

The eighteenth-century commentators grew increasingly sophisticated about the interaction of genres in *As You Like It*. At first, the problem was to ensure that the usurpation plot did not suggest political subversion. As the century progressed and the distance from the Civil War increased, the banished Duke was seen to represent not political exile but philosophical retreat, a notion that related to the courtship action by way of Jaques's philosophical cynicism. The banished Duke was understood less in relation to the other Duke and more as a foil for Rosalind. He represents over-refinement, a position only suitable for those, like Jaques and the exiled Duke himself, who seek retirement and avoid marriage. The turning point in this century was, not surprisingly, Samuel Johnson's final remark that Shakespeare had missed a wonderful opportunity to show his abilities by neglecting to present the usurper reflecting on his final conversion from political ambition to rustic retreat. Here hermeneutics and history merge.

In 1765, a century after the Civil War, it was first possible to raise the previously avoided question of usurpation, leading to an implicit interpretation of *As You Like It* as a comedy about the process of creating a family, the courtship rites that lead to marriage, which is the basis and the result of stable government. This view of the drama, however, neglected the element of romance and caprice as Charles Johnson's *Love in a Forest* makes manifest in omitting Touchstone, Audrey, and William, as well as the courtship of Phoebe and Silvius. Samuel Johnson was probably the first editor to attend carefully to the humor of the language of these characters. But Johnson is of his age in showing little interest in how Touchstone's humor relates to Orlando's and Phoebe's capriciousness. Each subsequent period, as we shall see, neglects some generic aspects of *As You Like It* and focuses upon others. We note here that *As You Like It* is such a mixture of genres that interpretation takes the form of highlighting or neglecting genres. Thus the eighteenth-century view of *As You Like It* as a drama about the civic significance of marriage neglects not merely Orlando, Touchstone, and Phoebe but also romance. In the eighteenth century, romance was reduced to courtship leading to marriage, leaving out of account the sheer flights of fancy, epitomized by Orlando's marring trees with his poetry. The history of criticism of *As You Like It* will thus be, to some extent, an account of the rise and fall of genres.

ROMANTICISM: *AS YOU LIKE IT* AS A ROMANCE OF CHARACTER

Turning now to the nineteenth century, we see the move to Romanticism clearly represented in the commentary on *As You Like It*. In the romantic tradition of closet drama, Mrs. Inchbald prefers reading to seeing the play. "This comedy has a high reputation among Shakespeare's works, and yet, on the stage, it is never attractive, except when some actresses, of very superior skill perform the part of Rosalind." Although Mrs. Jordan's Rosalind receives high praise, Mrs. Inchbald is more interested in Jaques and his retreat from the court: "Shakespeare made the inhabitants of the forest appear so happy in the banishment, that, when they are called back to the cares of the work, it seems more like a punishment than a reward. Jaques has too much prudence to leave his retirement; and yet when his associates are departed, his state can no longer be enviable; a refined society was the charm which seemed here to bestow on country life the more than usual enjoyments." Jaques is of particular interest because he adopts the posture of the romantic poet, retirement to his solitude in order to commune with nature and articulate poetry for "civilized" readers.

Nathan Drake views this "most delightful of dramas" as "destitute of plot" but containing "wild and interesting" characters and scenery, the latter of which reminds him of the landscape painters, Ruysdale, Claude and Rosa. Here we see two new concerns, character in and of itself apart from dramatic context, and dramatic scenery as a form of landscape painting. The relationship between character and scenery is clear from the characterization of Jaques who although a "Timon" is nonetheless a disillusioned kind of romantic "whose ideals are brought out by Arden" (431–34). For Drake it would seem that the background scenery of Arden must be sufficiently picturesque to explain how as a location it converts Jaques's cynicism into melancholy disillusionment. We note that Jaques the satirist of the age of Pope and Johnson has become a lyricist in the era of Wordsworth and Coleridge. Furthermore, the action of the play, the plot, such as it is, the progress of the various courtships, is neglected in favor of a series of tableaux, characters set against a landscape-like background.

William Hazlitt is the first critic who also engages in theatre review. As a critic, Hazlitt points out that once we enter Arden we enter a world of imagination: "Caprice and fancy reign and revel here, and stern necessity is banished to the court." Having established the nature of the setting, Hazlitt turns to the characters. Beginning significantly with Jaques, Hazlitt emphasizes that "Jaques is the only purely contemplative character in Shakespeare. He thinks, and does nothing." Moreover, he resents Orlando's love because it seems to disparage his own "passion for abstract truth." Rosalind, by contrast, is "made up of sportive gaiety and natural tenderness: her tongue runs the faster to conceal the pressure at her heart." Indeed, so intensely in love is Rosalind that Celia's wit provides welcome relief. And the characters in the subplot are foils for the love of Rosalind and Orlando. "The unrequited love of Silvius for Phoebe shews the perversity of this passion in the commonest scenes of life. . . . [while] Touchstone is not in love, but he will have a mistress as a subject for the exercise of his grotesque humour, and to shew his contempt for the passion" (Howe, 4, 338–41). Romantic love so pervades Hazlitt's view of *As You Like It* that he concludes by citing as his favorite passage in the drama Phoebe's description of her infatuation with Ganymede.

As a theatre reviewer, Hazlitt, although a great admirer of Mrs. Siddons, not surprisingly preferred Mrs. Jordan as Rosalind: "She was all gaiety, openness, and good-nature. She rioted in her fine animal spirits, and gave more pleasure than any other actress, because she had the greatest spirit of enjoyment in herself" (*Examiner*, 22 October 1815). The contrast between the eighteenth-century *As You Like It* and that on the early nineteenth-century stage is illustrated by Hazlitt's description of John Kemble as Orlando: "In the early acts there was nothing extraordinary, but in the interview between Orlando and Rosalind in the forest, the easy wit, and sprightly vivacity of the sentiments, were delivered with such true comic spirit, archness, and grace, that the audience, who seemed quite taken by surprise, expressed their delight in loud and long tokens of approbation" (*Dramatic Magazine*, II (1830–31), 347). And during this same period, Coleridge devotes one of his few notes on *As You Like It* to Orlando's reply to Oliver's addressing him as "boy": "The word 'boy' naturally provokes and awakens in Orlando the sense of his manly powers; and with the retort, 'elder brother,' he grasps him with firm hands, and makes him feel that he is not *boy*" (I, 93). This note is followed by Coleridge's longest comment on *As You Like It,* which is concerned with Oliver's unaccountable malignancy in encouraging Charles the wrestler to murder Orlando. By contrast, we scarcely know who played Orlando in the eighteenth century; clearly, it was then not a major part. Now with the emphasis on the capriciousness of romance, Orlando becomes important on the stage, much as Hazlitt singles out Phoebe's whimsical love of Ganymede for special praise.

Interestingly, Kemble also played Jaques, a part for which he was even more famous than his Orlando. From an eighteenth-century point of view no two characters could be more distinct; one a lover, the other a cynic. But, as Hazlitt reminds us, Jaques is a completely passive person who occupies himself with his imagination, precisely the faculty of mind usually associated with the emotional excesses of Orlando and Phoebe. Romance then in the early nineteenth century served as a background for certain dramatic roles that were selected out of an interest in character.

THE EARLY VICTORIANS: THE GENERIC CONTEXT FOR ROMANTIC CHARACTERS

By 1832, however, Rosalind as a character is firmly placed in the genre of pastoral. Anna Jameson characterizes Rosalind as a "princess of Arcady" surrounded by the "purely ideal, " which is pastoral and picturesque. In this way Jameson is able to distinguish Rosalind from similar Shakespearian characters, Beatrice, Portia, Isabella, and Celia. Less eloquent than Portia, less wise than Isabella, Rosalind, according to Jameson, has more display of wit than Celia but is not, like Phoebe, "an Arcadian coquette." By this means, Jameson concludes, Shakespeare has anticipated all the beauties of "Italian pastoral" (76–87). Thus the genre question returns even in "character criticism," especially when the character being examined is compared to other characters of Shakespearian drama. But Charles Brown, in *Shakespeare's Autobiographical Poems* (1838) asserts that *As You Like It* is not a pastoral, a genre which is more realistic than this "privileged" magical Arden that is a "poetical" forest (283). Brown's remarks are too cryptic for us to understand them fully. What, for example, is unrealistic about William and Audrey? But Brown's comment makes clear that during this period attempts at biographical accounts of Shakespeare had difficulty integrating into their conceptions Shakespeare's use of sophisticated dramatic conventions like those of pastoral.

At this point in our history, a clear split occurs between the staging and the criticism of *As You Like It*. In 1838, Thomas Campbell complains that the story has nothing "dramatic in it," yet a review of a production four years later provides little grounds for such a complaint. This review of Macready's production approaches the drama in terms of characters but leaves one with little doubt that the overall effect is dramatic in a positive sense. Even the scenery is related to dramatic action, in this instance, the wrestling match (*The Times*, 3 October 1842). But while the reviewer of this production complains that Audrey is not rustic enough, a critic, J. Payne Collier, writing in the same year, insists that in spite of the fact that Shakespeare added Jaques, Touchstone, and Audrey to Thomas Lodge's tale, *As You Like It* is a "play about love with Rosalind as the main character" (III, 4). We note that the reviewer of the stage production faulted Mrs. Nisbett's Rosalind for its lack of "humanness of heart," suggesting that overemphasis on the wit of Rosalind can obscure characteristics of her personality that were at the time associated with romantic love. The Romantic period of *As You Like It* criticism is a time when critics turn with increasing interest to the characters, particularly Rosalind and Jaques, probably because they are the most complex and fully developed of the dramatis personae. At first, these characters are examined apart from their dramatic context, but as the character description becomes more refined and stage productions have their effect, it is necessary to distinguish these dramatic personae from similar ones in other plays by Shakespeare. The result is that genre reappears now in the form of a context for characters.

In the 1840s, two important German critics (both of whom were translated into English within a decade of their first appearance in German) debated about genres in *As You Like It.* G. G. Gervinus characterizes the play as a "pastoral drama" and cites Thomas Heywood's description of pastoral drama in Shakespeare's day: "If we present a pastoral, we shew the harmless love of shepherds, diversely moralized, distinguishing between the craft of the city and the innocency of the sheepcote" (565). Pastoral for Gervinus is a means by which Rosalind and Orlando, and even Celia and Olivia, are taught to master their passionate love: "violent passion [is] to be mastered; how she may master it, is afterwards the problem, which she has to solve in her subsequent meeting with Orlando" (552). But first Rosalind must be freed from the oppression of the court, "the intricate and manifold oppression of a rude and intriguing society" is contrasted to Arden where good humor is released that "hitherto had been fettered" (554). Here Rosalind without violating her morality can give "free scope to her love." Indeed, Gervinus believes that Celia's hasty marriage to Oliver reinforces Shakespeare's point: "the speedy marriage is a preventitive against unchastity" (556). Phoebe and Silvius as well as Audrey and Touchstone are seen as foils to the pairs of the main characters. Silvius has a "violent and importunate love" while Phoebe's "coyness" indicates her "hatred of love" (560). The marriage of the "ugly" Audrey and Touchstone, on the other hand, is "only pretended," a subterfuge whereby Touchstone is able "not to avoid immorality, but to indulge in it" (561). And Jaques is, for Gervinus, a dissipated melancholiac of relatively little importance. At the end of the play Oliver and Orlando, according to Gervinus, understand the moral mystery that is the function of the pastoral experience. When Rosalind faints at the sight of Orlando's bloody handkerchief, Oliver does not believe that her behavior is counterfeit: "We must assume that Oliver imparted his discovery to Orlando" (559). The final masque becomes then, according to Gervinus, a masquerade for Orlando as well as Rosalind where the mutual counterfeiting shows how the pastoral conventions lead to marriages that master passion.

Hermann Ulrici, however, complains that "Gervinus in his moralising tendency burdens even this light creation of Shakespeare's humour . . . with a highly important and dull moral." Such a view, according to Ulrici, neglects the poetry of Shakespeare, "what is humorous, fantastic, and romantic" (17). Ulrici begins by focusing upon Jaques and Touchstone, as two fools, a melancholy and a merry one. This initial observation leads Ulrici to argue that in *As You Like It*, we have not an ordinary world but a "fantastic reflex of life in the mirrour of caprice and humour" (13). Most of the characters, the good Duke, Orlando, Rosalind, Celia, Jaques and Touchstone, are figures that "the realistic mind would call oddities" (13). Their peculiarity stems from their acting in extreme ways that are "thoughtless, capricious and arbitrary" (16). But these extremes balance one another, as is manifest in the character of Jaques. "In reality he only acts the misanthrope, the world despairing hermit. He is himself unconscious of the part he is playing, is not conscious that he is wearing a mere mask behind which lie concealed his old love of life, his old caprices, inclinations, and sympathies. . . . Thus he is always his own counterpart" (18–19). Touchstone, on the other hand, loves Audrey just because he loves her, thus representing the arbitrariness and obstinacy of "love in its full force. . . . He the expressed Fool may frankly be declared the most rational person of the whole curious company, for he alone invariably knows his own mind; in regarding everything as sheer folly, he, at the same time takes it up in the humour in which it is meant to be understood" (20).

Touchstone is for Ulrici at one with the drama, as arbitrary, capricious and loving "*as you like it*." Even Rosalind does not, according to Ulrici, match up to Touchstone: "in spite of her brilliant, inexhaustible wit, she nevertheless does not possess a spark of that knowledge of the world which is able to grapple with the affairs of common life" (22). Like Rosalind, the other characters have a "noble frankness and candour" tarnished by "strangeness, thoughtlessness, and perversity." Ulrici concludes that this two-sided quality of the main characters is in "keeping with the meaning of *as you like it*, which is the fundamental theme of the whole. The fantastic capriciousness which shows itself either as the inner motive or the outward impulse to their resolves and actions, rules the best and noblest, as well as the worst and lowest characters in the most manifold modification" (22–23). Gervinus's moralized pastoral for Ulrici neglects the capricious humor of the drama, a caprice that Ulrici believes accounts for love itself and the appeal of *As You Like It*. In generic terms, Ulrici is not denying the pastoral element of the comedy but arguing, by implication, that pastoral is subsumed by what might be called a sort of romantic realism. We note here a division that will be continued throughout the nineteenth century between those who, like Gervinus, favor Rosalind as the center of interest and those, following Ulrici, who favor Jaques, though whether these characters are seen as moral, satirical, pastoral or romantic will vary with the particular critic.

A review from this period (*The Times*, 3 October 1842) again shows continuity and discontinuity with the dramatic criticism. Macready's Jaques seems to have given a general heaviness to the production which the reviewer sees as appropriate to the "seven ages of man" speech but not to the remainder of Jaques's part and not at all to the role of Rosalind: "Mrs Nisbett's Rosalind, though agreeable enough, and great applause was conceded to it, did not certainly fulfill every requisite of the character. Joyous indeed she was and merry, it was not the joy and merriment of the banished Duke's daughter; it betrayed an inward heaviness of heart, it was thoughtless when it should have been thoughtful." Macready's production suffers from a lack of lightness and delicacy that, according to this reviewer, is the hallmark of his version of Jaques. The reviewer requires in Rosalind "graceful sensibility," a requirement that probably would have pleased Ulrici. At the same time, the reviewer strongly criticizes Touchstone for his lack of "pompous fluency and oracular pedantry," suggestive of the moral aspect of the drama, although in a humorous mode, emphasized by Gervinus.

The most innovative element of this particular production was probably the "scenery and 'get-up,'" which made every scene into a "picturesque study" and was particularly noticeable in the wrestling scene: "the new effect was introduced of including the space where the wrestlers encounter with ropes and staves round which the courtiers and spectators stand pressing eagerly forward, watching every movement of the combatants. The effect of this was most vivid, and the natural manner of the two wrestlers through every vicissitude of the struggle elicited shouts of applause." The action of the wrestlers is balanced against the other more static scenes of speeches set against a picturesque background. The audience is drawn in by the wrestling scene of Act One—and here the reviewer's account of the tumultuous applause of the audience for Macready is apt—in the hope that they will settle down and listen to the words of Rosalind, Jaques, and Touchstone. Finally as a reward for their patience the evening concludes with a farce. (For a more detailed account of this production, see Jamieson, particularly pages 630–33.) Although *As You Like It* has often been described as a comedy without a plot, the early Victorian emphasis on character seems to have slowed the play down and made it heavier: scenery and song are skillfully employed to add lightness and verve. Moreover, although critics at this time tended to favor the character that promoted what they saw as the prevailing genre, productions made use of the contrast between characters since reviewers expected that contrast, in this instance, the difference between Jaques and Rosalind, to be readily apparent.

THE MID-VICTORIANS DEBATE GENRE: ROMANCE VERSUS PASTORAL

But in spite of the emphasis on character, the generic issue is now taken as central. In the United States, for example, at midcentury, an editor reminds his readers of this matter in clear, succinct terms: "Our poet has improved upon his model [Lodge] and has constructed one of the most exquisitely finished Pastoral Poems extant in our language" (John Hows, 111). But at this middle point in the nineteenth century moral concerns are also important. In 1851, Hartley Coleridge's comments are more reminiscent of Samuel Johnson than of his namesake. Celia's change at the end, her marriage to Oliver, "baffles all credulity of imagination" because it makes Celia more imprudent than her cousin Rosalind, which is, according to H. Coleridge, the "worst defect of the play" (II, 141). On the background scenery of the comedy, H. Coleridge is also in disagreement with his romantic predecessors: Shakespeare is said to be able to communicate all of pastoral without "ever sinking . . . [to] landscape painter" (141–42). Finally, H. Coleridge points out that the subplot involving the wooing of Phoebe functions as a play-within-a-play, recalling Charles Johnson's replacement of it with the playlet from *Midsummer Night's Dream*. At the same time it should be kept in mind that H. Coleridge considers this material of slight significance: he compares it to the appearance of "doggerel in poetry" (144). The focal point remains on the characters. We sense here a reanimation of *As You Like It*. For most Romantics character was of more interest than action. Indeed the dramatic personae became static, situated against backdrops that resembled landscape paintings. The Victorians began to understand character as a function of dramatic action; personality was reintegrated within an unfolding process. The dénouement of drama accordingly took on more significance because it helped the audience understand character as a combination of personality and action.

By the middle of the nineteenth century, the focus upon character produced surprisingly diverse views. William Birch, for instance, described *As You Like It* as Shakespeare's most subversive drama, questioning not only romance and pastoral but also religion. *As You Like It*, according to Birch, shows us that Shakespeare's views were "not those of the orthodox standard." Jaques was seen as the "philosopher of the play" along with Touchstone, but even Rosalind was characterized as marked by "profanity." Shakespeare was identified with Marlowe and Milton, and it is pointed out that the "famous 'seven ages' speech concludes without a single reference to religion" (36–7). Birch concluded with scorn for those like Samuel Johnson who did not understand why a speech on the bad Duke's conversion was omitted. By contrast, within two years of Birch's subversive view of Shakespeare's characters in *As You Like It*, James Halliwell described all the characters as neither unorthodox nor profane but delightful and romantically adventuresome. Focusing upon Rosalind and Celia, Halliwell took a previous critic to task for criticizing Shakespeare's female creations. "Rosalind and her sweet cousin, the amiable Celia, who in obedience to the promptings of her heart, gives up her father's love, her rank as princess, all the attractions and fascinations of a court, and crowd of titled admirers, to follow into solitude her dear playmate and bosom friend" (304). The nonconformity of personality that for Birch suggested religious scepticism and questioning of authority, for Halliwell indicated a commitment to love in friendship and marriage, a respect for traditional institutions. Clearly character criticism was unable to resolve some serious questions.

But in this period character is not the sole interest of critics. B. G. K. examines the versification of the comedy and is able to date it by comparing its "state of metre" with others like it, such as *Much Ado About Nothing*. B. G. K. goes on to point out that the seven ages of man speech has become well known, a fact borne out by the proliferation during this period of slim volumes devoted exclusively to this speech. These books usually contain seven illustrations each, along with the appropriate words from the speech. I have seen fourteen different versions of these kinds of books, from the period 1799–1896, all using essentially this same format, some of the volumes containing commentary on the speech and others only reproducing the text with illustrations. (See illustrations at the end of the introduction for an example.) Thus, for nearly a century a new sub-genre of *As You Like It* was born, thrived and faded away, providing a vivid example of how this comedy is more than a mixture of what Alistair Fowler calls "modes," that is, elements of a genre that can be included within another genre without altering the host genre. On the contrary, elements of *As You Like It* can be separated from the drama and stand on their own, demonstrating that the original play contains whole genres which at different periods of history emerge to be eventually dominated by others. This kind of juxtaposition is illustrated by Schroeder's description of a production derived from Macready's promptbook: "Duke Frederick, Oliver guarded by two attendants, and other Lords and attendants are discovered in the first scene of the third act, a room in the palace. Duke Frederick paces about the stage in anger during the scene, at the end of which Oliver is 'forced' out, right, by the guards. Orlando is discovered 'reading the paper [of verses] which he fastens on the tree' in III, ii. It is 'summer evening, [the] moon [is] seen faintly in the sky'" (67–8). If these two scenes seem only to illustrate the opposite excesses of romance, anger and infatuation, then consider the following combination from the same source of pastoral, satire or anti-pastoral, and romance. "Rosalind and Celia enter . . . for scene ii (Folio IV, iii), 'A Sheep-fold near. Sheep bells heard.' Silvius enters left, crosses to deliver Phebe's letter to Rosalind, and then returns center. On 'Call you this chiding?' (line 65), Silvius crosses to stage left in a gesture of despair; Rosalind follows to berate him. Silvius exits left as Oliver enters right. When Celia tells Oliver where the sheep-cote is, she points off stage-left to indicate the direction; and while Oliver is telling of Orlando's encounter with the lion, Celia puts her arm around

Rosalind's neck as a comforting gesture. Rosalind, of course, faints, and all exit left" (70).

Indeed, the Macready version of *As You Like It* presented radical genre juxtaposition even in its scenery, providing a critical suggestion that will not be pursued for over a century. The following is a reviewer's description of the final scene as it appeared in 1842: "In the last scene of wood and hill, and dale with hill and vale, all with green verdure clad, the effect was beautiful and picturesque in the extreme; a fine Maypole rears its flowered crest in proud superiority in the centre of the stage, the groves and trees echo the chirruping of the feathered songsters of the adjoining woods, the rippling of the babbling streams, the flowing dash of the spraying waterfall, meet the ear, and the hunter with his living brace of blood hounds hieing to the chase, with groupings of joyous peasants and forest nymphs chorussing the hymns of pastoral joy, in every variety of rich costume, greet Hymen with his love-lit torch to commemorate the vows connubial of sweet Rosalind and Orlando, and the votaries attendant at the festive right" (*Theatrical Journal and Musical Intelligencer*, III (1842), 322). The pastoral tradition is interrupted by the baying of hounds intent more upon blood than marriage, and the maypole is as appropriate for the courtship games of Rosalind and Orlando as it is for Touchstone's raucous humor and Jaques's irony.

THE LATER VICTORIANS: THE ATTEMPT TO INTEGRATE AND SURPASS ROMANCE AND PASTORAL

During the second half of the nineteenth century, critics publishing in the United States continued and extended the interest in character. Henry Hudson begins his introduction to *As You Like It* by pointing out that Arden is a place where characters are free to grow. Here we see Orlando add wit to his natural sense of decency, the banished Duke reconcile himself to exile and even Touchstone develop a good side of his character. But the "universal favourite," according to Hudson, is "Jaques the juicy," who, in spite of his "self-love" and melancholy has a better side that bubbles over and encourages him to engage in social interchange. Jaques is seen as competing with Rosalind, who outshines him with her wit and humor in adversity (18–19). Hudson concludes that the success of the play resides in such complex characters who prevail in spite of the improbability of parts of the play, such as the appearance of a lion in the forest of Arden, because love is blind to improbability. *As You Like It* achieves its balance and equilibrium from its characters.

But for Denton Snider, another editor from this period published in the United States, *As You Like It* is balanced by way of structural principles. The drama sets up a contrast between the actual and the idyllic, which in the imagination takes the form of the ideal. Shakespeare recognizes, according to Snider, that the idyllic or ideal must remain unreal lest it collapse in comedy. The drama thus progresses through three stages: 1) the real world of Wrong with Orlando and Rosalind as the chief victims. 2) the idyllic realm of "simple pastoral" represented by the banished Duke, the shepherds, Orlando, Celia and Rosalind. 3) Restoration of the Real World of "Right" (42–43). But Jaques shows, Snider admits, that even in the idyllic sylvan realm of pastoral there are "injustices." So the drama concludes "not as pastoral" but with love which is only central in a world without "business." Love in turn leads to marriage, and family loyalty results in "Right" being restored to the State (52–56). We note here the progress from character to characters in relation to one another, in the form of marriage and family, that is seen as more important than the individual in isolation. In this way Snider is able to explain what Hudson could only assert, that Jaques is outshone by Rosalind because she marries, thereby aiding her father in the recovery of his dukedom. Snider's notion of the progress of character development employs the genre of pastoral as a stage or place (Arden) that permits freedom of development.

In 1884, Robert Raffles, Assistant Master of Boudon Prep School in Cheshire, advises his students to study Shakespeare rather "than even the very prince of Encyclopaedias" to learn "philosophy of life" and "elevation of soul and understanding" (4). *As You Like It* in particular is a drama about how individuals are forced from the real world to the ideal realm. But this ideal, the forest of Arden, is, according to Raffles, a bubble burst in a comedy in which the pastoral is idealized. Moreover, it is not a love play. Arden, a realm of love and pastoral, is a place of remediation, a means of restoring the individual back to the "real" (53–56). Raffles is perhaps the first to deny that *As You Like It* is about love, even though what he means by the alternative to love, the "real," is enigmatic. Perhaps Raffles believes that romance, the love aspect, is undermined or surpassed as is the pastoral, in order for the drama to achieve the status of philosophy, the basis of his recommendation of it to his students.

This interrelation between the ironizing of pastoral and surpassing of romance is borne out by a theatre review of 1885. The *Athenaeum* reviewer asserts that for *As You Like It* the old conventional style of acting is more appropriate than the new style: dramatic conventions and conventionality are part of the subject of the comedy. On the other hand, vivid and "realistic" scenery is helpful, possibly because it contrasts with the artifice of the stage conventions. The scenery suggests that Arden is a place where individuals may move beyond the traditional postures of pastoral and romance. But the actress taking the part of Rosalind is seen as too one-sided. Mrs. Kendall is arch and witty but lacks poetry, magic, and rhapsody.

It would appear that Mrs. Kendall was better at debunking pastoral than at integrating and surpassing romance. Indeed, the presentation of Jaques who becomes "more reasonable and less pragmatic" suggests that the social drive many critics saw beneath the surface of Jaques's seemingly self-satisfied satire is not present. This dramatic version of the play then lacks passion, from Jaques's contempt to Rosalind's rhapsody, suggesting that passion, in its various forms, fuels the move beyond pastoral and romance, or what Raffles calls the move to the "real." At this point W. E. Henley's remark that Rosalind finishes the play reciting the epilogue—and we should keep in mind that it was unusual during Shakespeare's day for a principal female character to present an epilogue—takes on added significance (26). Rosalind, not Jaques, is seen as the goal of the drama. In the end she outshines the melancholy ironist not merely because she marries and he does not but because she articulates the principle of the play symbolized by marriage, namely, the desire to bring pleasure to others.

This position is reiterated most forcefully by Helena Faucit, who played the part of Rosalind, first under Macready's direction in 1839, and continued to assume the role until 1879. Evelyn Mattern asserts that Faucit "was the most famous and influential Rosalind of the century" (636). In her letter to Robert Browning, first printed in 1884, Faucit gives not only her view of the play but also a vivid portrait of how she played the part of Rosalind and of Macready's production of *As You Like It*. Jaques, as we would expect, ceases to be an important role: "in colloquy with Jaques, [Rosalind's] intellect alone is called into play, and the cynic comes off second-best in the encounter" (267). For Faucit the central focus of the play is love, and Jaques's cynicism and melancholy are of marginal interest. Indeed, love in *As You Like It* is too serious for the ordinary comic actress: "Those forest scenes between Orlando and herself are not, as a comedy actress would be apt to make them, merely pleasant fooling. At the core of all Rosalind says and does, lies a passionate love as pure and all-absorbing as ever swayed a woman's heart. . . . To me, *As You Like It* seems to be essentially as much a love-poem as *Romeo and Juliet*, with this difference—that it deals with happy love" (236–37). Faucit's first task is to communicate to her audience her capacity to love without expressing it overtly. In the first scene between Rosalind and Orlando, "Rosalind has not much to say, but she has to make her audience feel by subtle indications the revolution that is going on in her heart from the moment her eyes fall upon her future lover" (246). At the same time Rosalind must, according to Faucit, maintain her composure and demeanor: "Not for the world would she have Orlando recognize her in her unmaidenly disguise" (257). We can perhaps now begin to understand why Macready was probably the first to take the "Cuckoo" song away from Rosalind, since the cuckoo is associated with illicit sexual desires and Faucit's rendition avoids any such suggestions of unmaidenliness.

Indeed, one sees the stereotypical Victorian posture in Faucit's account of her performance of Rosalind in breeches: "I need scarcely say how necessary it is for the actress in this scene, while carrying it through with a vivacity and dash that shall avert from Orlando's mind every suspicion of her sex, to preserve a refinement of tone and manners suitable to a woman of Rosalind's high station and cultural intellect." In fact, so female is this part that Faucit asserts that those are mistaken who "maintain that Shakespeare was governed, in drawing his heroines, by the fact that they were acted by boys" (262–63). Still, Rosalind must have sufficient self-possession to deceive Orlando, and even when she faints at the sight of the bloody handkerchief, "Oliver has no suspicion of her sex" (277). By contrast Jaques is a "self-complacent egotist," a formulation that may help us understand why Macready was the first to follow Shakespeare's text in giving the account of the dying tearful stag, not to Jaques, but to the First Lord. In a drama of love, it is important to show that even the most cynical of characters is capable of feeling and caring for something. But if Jaques himself presents the evidence we can be left in doubt as to its accuracy, particularly if he presents it with his characteristic languid irony. The First Lord can offer an account of Jaques without the complications of the defensive postures of Jaques. In this way, all of the characters can be included in what Faucit characterizes as a "love-romance," a generic conclusion that is confirmed by Macready's decision to restore to the stage the masque of Hymen "keeping up to the last the film of glamour which [Rosalind] has thrown around her lover and the other strangers to her secret" (280). Faucit's critical position, important in itself, is much more significant as an articulation of how she acted the role of Rosalind, because, as Schroeder demonstrates, Faucit's version of the heroine of *As You Like It* dominated the stage from the 1840s when she first came to prominence until well after her last performance in 1879.

By contrast, a female critic, Grace Latham, writing during this same period, sees Rosalind as more passionate than loving, and views *As You Like It* as a drama less about love than friendship. Latham focuses upon the relationship between Celia and Rosalind, explaining that *As You Like It* was written at a "turning-point in [Shakespeare's] life's history . . . [when he] found himself deserted by [a friend] for the very man on whom he had fixed his supreme belief and affection" (285). (Samuel Schoenbaum, in *Shakespeare's Lives*, demonstrates that many such nineteenth-century biographical accounts are without factual foundation.) "Endowed with infinite humour and excellent sense [Rosalind] sees everything and every body by their light, and as a rule it is people's weaknesses and peculiarities which arrest her attention" (296). Straightforward and sensible, Rosalind tests Orlando's love and finds it genuine but at the same time treats Silvius with "scorn and indignation" and contemplates this "strange bit of natural history" called Jaques: "his pretence of wisdom, his causeless melancholy, which he seeks her acquaintance to display, his conceit and self-absorption are patent to her at once, and rouse only laughter and contempt." In conclusion, Latham suggests that "Rosalind loathes all that is false, and has an innate delicacy and modesty" but the "most womanly . . . is the gentle, loving, unselfish Celia" (317–18).

The contrast here between Faucit and Latham is subtle but important. For Faucit, the most famous and influential of nineteenth-century actresses who played the part, Rosalind is at the center of a love romance in which she must use her female powers in disguise, as an actress playing an actress, that is in disguise, to communicate her love and evoke that of others. For Latham, a female critic, Rosalind is surrounded by more pseudo- and anti-romance than real romance; accordingly, she must use her wits and belief in friendship to unmask and reject false romance. During the nineteenth century character criticism prevails. The result is a series of critical disagreements about which character(s) predominates and why. On the stage, on the other hand, *As You Like It* when presented with either one dominant mood or one personality type was remarked upon for its stasis and lifelessness, a problem compensated for in various ways, such as music and scenery. Alternatively, productions that gave a balance to the various strands and types of character in the drama risked being seen as lightweight, lacking in moral fiber.

G. B. Shaw's theatre reviews at the end of the century are very revealing in this respect. Shaw believes that the search for characters in *As You Like It* is a mistake that credits the comedy with more profundity than it deserves: "Rosalind is not a complete human being: she is simply an extension into five acts of the most affectionate, fortunate, delightful five minutes in the life of a charming woman. And all the other figures in the play are cognate impostures. . . . This is not human nature or dramatic character; it is juvenile lead, first old man, heavy lead, heavy father, principal comedian, and leading lady, transfigured by magical word-music" (23). Since these "figures" are not characters, stage illusion for Shaw is the key message: "Nothing is more significant than the statement that 'all the world's stage.' The whole world is ruled by theatrical illusion. . . . The great critics are those who penetrate and understand the illusion: the great men are those who, as dramatists plan the development of nations, or as actors carry out the drama" (25). Nevertheless, Shaw asserts that the fascination of *As You Like It*, which he admits is "still very great," resides in the character of Rosalind. Her popularity for Shaw has three main causes. Rosalind seldom speaks blank verse, "only wears a skirt for a few minutes," and "makes love to the man instead of waiting for the man to make love to her" (27). Shaw is poised on the edge, denying that Rosalind is a character but fascinated by her as a character. As a fine playwright and keen theatre reviewer, Shaw seems aware that fullness of personality in *As You Like*

It never quite happens on the stage, but he is unable to decide how much that is Shakespeare's fault and how much it is to be attributed to the actors, actresses, and producers. His witty insights suggest to us a moment in the history of criticism when critical perceptions move beyond critical precepts: Shaw's analysis of stage productions of *As You Like It* requires an alternative to the nineteenth-century conception of character, one that is not developed until the next century.

But first I turn to a contemporary of Shaw's writing in the critical not dramaturgical tradition. Georg Brandes believes that Jaques is the most important character in *As You Like It* because his position is closest to that of Shakespeare, who will develop his comic ironist, Jaques, in tragedy, into Hamlet. According to Brandes, Shakespeare when writing *As You Like It* had reached a stage in his life when he longed to leave the court and city for a simpler country life, "a life of hunting and song, and simple repasts in the open air." But he recognized that such a life would not satisfy him: "he creates the figure of Jaques, unknown to the romance, and sets him wandering through his pastoral comedy, lonely, retiring, self-absorbed, a misanthrope from excess of tenderness, sensitiveness, and imagination." Yet Jaques, unlike Molière's Alceste, is not a misanthrope; he is a witty ironist, who is "the mouthpiece of the poet." So Jaques becomes a representative of the poet, "an advocate for the freedom which poetry must claim." Brandes admits that there is also the sunnier side of the drama, represented most noticeably by Rosalind and Celia who share "gaiety without a sting," which is seen also at moments in the other characters. The result is "the piece is bathed in a sunshiny humour." But in the background lurks something more profound, to be pursued by Shakespeare in tragedy. "This is the melancholy which haunts the thinker and the great creative artist; but in Shakespeare it as yet modulated with ease into the most engaging and delightful merriment" (1, 258–69).

Here at the end of the nineteenth century we see a last vestige of Romanticism. Shakespeare/Jaques is the romantic poet whose wit permits moments of merriment, similar to that of *As You Like It*, but only at the expense of repressing a deep melancholy that will lead to tragedy, because the poet is quintessentially alone, a commentator upon not a participator in life. Brandes illustrates how the Victorian critical tradition pressed further than the Romantics while continuing to honor the premises of Romanticism, in this instance, that *As You Like It* is a romance in a pastoral setting and that the center of interest is in the characters. Faucit's Rosalind was celebrated because she created a character who demonstrated how most elements of the drama could, within the personality of the heroine, be made subservient to romantic love. But the dramaturgical critics, the people of the theatre like Shaw and others, recognized that something more complicated happened on stage.

Successful realization of roles on stage of *As You Like It* did not necessarily produce full-fledged characters or personalities, and when the complete character was produced, as in Faucit's Rosalind, a price was paid; the other "figures," to use Shaw's term, became less interesting, less important. Moreover, the method and terms used by Brandes, writing in the last decade of the nineteenth century, make clear why Shaw, writing and reviewing at the same time, did not have the method or terminology at hand to clarify his own insights.

THE EARLY TWENTIETH CENTURY: PEOPLE OF THE THEATRE VERSUS THE CRITICS

Turning now to the twentieth century, we begin with a typical introduction in a relatively inexpensive edition of *As You Like It*, probably designed for the general reader and for students. Alfred Cann explains that "the play appeals to us by its brightness and cheeriness, and we like it as we like a bright and cheery companion" (25). Although the play opens with "two discords, in which the two pairs of brothers are concerned. . . . At the close of the play perfect harmony prevails" (26). The drama is a moment in the sunshine that suggests that although relief from the darker side of life is temporary "it is good for us to get away at times from the unrealities and formalities of our artificial surroundings and commune with Nature" in the way that Wordsworth does in *Tintern Abbey* (27). The climax of the play is, accordingly, the romantic moment when Rosalind and Orlando discover their love. The subplot is concerned with "types of pastoral lovers, and their extravagances of language serve as an effective contrast to the greater restraint of Rosalind and Orlando" (29). One means of distinguishing between the elements of the play is by way of the different kinds of humor: Rosalind's humor reflects the "oddities of things in general" while Jaques's satire is peculiar to himself: "He is a cynic, and cynicism is not usually the product of a healthy life" (30). Rosalind's two-sided personality, witty and vivacious but also tender-hearted and "womanly," reveals a world less morbid and woeful than that of Jaques. Rosalind and Orlando avoid the extremes on both sides, the excess cynicism of Jaques and the extravagances of the pastoral lovers. Romance, for Cann the genre of *As You Like It*, in the form of the marriage of Rosalind and Orlando, is the result of maintaining in Arden's green world of extremes a 'golden' mean.

By contrast, Austin Brereton, a man of the theatre rather than a literary critic, edited a kind of volume similar to that of Cann during this first decade of the twentieth century. Brereton labels *As You Like It* a "serene pastoral play" which begins "with what might easily have been a tragedy [and] concludes in an atmosphere of soft beauty, forgiveness, and peace" (v). Since tragedy is very close to this comedy, Brereton gives as much attention to Jaques as to Rosalind.

The melancholy cynic is characterized as the only "purely contemplative character in Shakespeare," who has no other function or ambition but "for reflection" (vii-viii). Rosalind, on the other hand, combines "joyousness" with "sincere attachment . . . passionate love and devotion" (viii). Bolstering this balanced view of the tragic in the comic, Brereton points out that most of the great actresses who have portrayed Rosalind have been tragediennes, including Mrs Pritchard, Sarah Siddons, and Peg Woffington. And Brereton concludes his remarks by narrating the story of Woffington collapsing at the end of *As You Like It* and dying within a year. This difference of opinion between literary critics and that of the people of the theatre becomes more marked. While the critics debate as to which character and, by implication, what element of the drama, predominates—pastoral or anti-pastoral, romantic or satiric—the theatre people insist that both elements are present, particularly in successful productions.

The difference between the critical and the theatrical positions develops as the century progresses. Ellen Terry, a well-known actress, gives a brief account of Helen Faucit as Rosalind: "Her Rosalind, when she came out of her retirement to play a few performances, appeared to me more like a *lecture* on Rosalind, than like Rosalind herself: a lecture all young actresses would have greatly benefited by hearing, for it was of great beauty. I remember being particularly struck by her treatment of the lines in the scene where Celia conducts the mock marriage between Orlando and Ganymede. Another actress, whom I saw as Rosalind, said the words, 'And I do take thee, Orlando, to be my husband,' with a comical grimace to the audience. Helen Faucit flushed up and said the line with deep and true emotion, suggesting that she was, indeed, giving herself to Orlando. There was a world of poetry in the way she drooped over his hand" (188–89). It would seem that by Terry's day the "romping" Rosalind had gone too far and was in need of being reminded that she was also the delicate and lovable wife of Orlando.

In the year of Terry's account of Helen Faucit, John Masefield commented on the plays, giving special emphasis to Jaques. While the "gifts of fortune" affect all of the other characters, Jaques alone remains constant throughout, the still point of the turning wheel: "Jaques, the only wise one, is the only one not moved by Fortune" (129). "The best known character of the cast," Jaques, like the wisest of Shakespeare's characters, remains aloof from the action of the play because "wisdom has no place in the social scheme" (130). Jaques looks upon the "delightful" people of the drama, dismisses "them to their fates with all the authority of wisdom, gives up his share in the game to listen to a man who has given up his share of the world" (132). This view of Jaques as the observer apart, almost a reclusive reader, is markedly undramatic and would be difficult to render on the stage without making the entire drama a play-within-the-play for Jaques's benefit.

For this reason Charles Herford, who also believes Jaques is of central importance, asserts that the "the great public has never taken very kindly to the play" because it lacks action and suspense. Although Touchstone along with Jaques contribute nothing to the plot, together they suggest the wisdom of the fool in King Lear. "Jaques is the disillusioned man of the world, bitter as Touchstone is dry" (55–56). Rosalind and Orlando remain untouched by these fools: "cynicism and sentimentality are equally foreign" to the lovers (56). The alternative to the cynical satire of the 'fools' is, according to Herford, a love relationship that within the confines of Arden is never seriously threatened by rival lovers or anything more sinister, surely not a promising dramatic spectacle.

Continuing with this critical position that views *As You Like It* as relatively undramatic, Brander Matthews asserts that the play has an "underplot [that] scarcely ever attains even the semi-tragic" (156). In fact Jaques's part seems almost separate from the main plot. "It may not be fanciful to suggest that Jaques was possibly written into the play on purpose to supply a part for some important actor who was a good elocutionist, perhaps for Burbage himself. Certainly Jaques does nothing but stand and deliver speeches; he exists only to talk; he has no function to perform in the plot" (160). Jaques sounds here more like a character in a novel than part of a staged drama. Victor Freeburg theorizes this division between the staging and printing of drama by considering the question of Rosalind's disguise as a man. "A play differs essentially from a story, which is merely to be imagined. Consequently we have two kinds of probability. One is the probability of the plot as we see it in the mind's eye, and the other is the probability of the action as we actually see it represented physically with mechanical aids on a fixed spot and within a limited time. It is conceivable that a real Rosalind might deceive a real Orlando in a real forest of Arden. That is at least one aspect of the question of probability. But that a hundred and sixty pound, well-molded actress should deceive a hundred and thirty-five pound, slender, fifteen year younger actor into believing that she is a sentimental shepherd boy is preposterous" (17). This conceptualization makes clear that the critics during this period who argue that important aspects of *As You Like It* are undramatic while admitting that stage conventions differ from those of "life" assume that onstage "reality" alludes to offstage "reality."

Yet the theatre reviewer from *The Athenaeum* of 1890, is not troubled by the problem of credible reality and makes little mention of Jaques. Instead his chief interest is in Miss Rehan's Rosalind. In place of the previous "ethereal"

Rosalind, possibly a reference to Helen Faucit's rendition, Rehan is "bright, mirthful, and bewitching," and although "comedy prevails," her "lures" prove irresistible to Orlando and the audience. Accordingly, the "mise en scène" has reverted from Macready's enlivening innovations to an "average English representation" (198). It would seem that once the lightness of comedy is restored to the part of Rosalind there is little need of the relief provided by picturesque background scenery and an actual wrestling ring.

But by 1919, according to the reviewer for *The Times*, the interest has shifted from Rosalind to a "realism" of setting: "the basis of the staging is obviously some illuminated manuscript of the early 15th century" which is complemented by "brilliant" and "exciting" fifteenth-century costumes, and "Elizabethan music performed upon stringed instruments by players in appropriate costumes." The reviewer makes clear that this presentation is designed with the tourist trade of Stratford in mind. The visitors are to be regaled with a genuine British production of *As You Like It* that attempts to reproduce as closely as possible the original Elizabethan stage production. Indeed, Lovat Fraser's stage artistry with its use of "dim lighting . . . certainly throws up the player against the scene." The overall effect is now quite different from Macready's scenic innovations of the 1840s when, it will be recalled, a more serious Rosalind and thus a more static drama were compensated for by picturesque scenery and an actual wrestling ring to provide action on stage of interest to the audience. Lovat Fraser's presentation, unlike Macready's scenery and props that were clearly distinguishable from the actors and actresses, is an amalgam of foreground and background, actors, actresses, action and scenery. While Macready used the wrestling match and picturesque background to create sufficient interest in his audience so that it would attend to the speeches of the characters, particularly Rosalind, Lovat Fraser seems more interested in the overall effect of historical realism, a production designed to convince the audience that it was witnessing a close approximation of what was put on in Shakespeare's day. Ironically, as Michael Jamieson demonstrates, "Stratfordians" were more shocked by the break with stage tradition than with the attempt to use "modern" techniques to reenact the Elizabethan context (635).

Thus, the theatre by 1919 had responded to the critical concern about the probability of the plot of *As You Like it* by providing an historically accurate "Elizabethan" production of the play, with the implication that if it was credited by Shakespeare's audience it should have a similar effect upon the present audience. John Trewin suggests how innovative was this production, particularly for Stratford: "in 1879 Barry Sullivan had borrowed for the first Stratford Festival a stuffed stag, and in every revival since then the animal, killed originally at Charlecote, had been borne solemnly through the stage

Arden: by 1919 it was a trifle moth-eaten. Ignoring the stag and all other traditions, Playfair produced the comedy without cuts and chose Claud Lovat Fraser's scene and costume designs based upon mediaeval tapestry and illuminated Missals. These bewildered a Stratford in which *As You Like It* had to be smothered in fern and leaf with (as in Benson's production across the years) 'solid ivy for Orlando to nail in the opening scene to a very shaky canvas wall.'" Trewin remarks in a footnote that John Gielgud remembered visiting in 1913 a production where "'the terraces of Duke Frederick's garden were ingeniously transformed into forest glades by covering them with autumn leaves, which the actors had to plough through for the rest of the performance'" (86). Playfair and Lovat Fraser began the evolution from props of doubtful authenticity to an overall Elizabethan atmosphere. History and attempts at historical accuracy were perhaps important issues immediately after the Great War, which is obliquely referred to twice by "Our Special Correspondent" in *The Times*. The one nationality omitted in 1919 after World War I "which used to be represented here years ago" is clearly Germany, as opposed to the "American officers quartered in Stratford for some time" who fought on the other side (*The Times*, 23 April 1919). During the latter part of the nineteenth century and the first quarter of the twentieth, realism became an issue on the stage while critics were still, for the most part, treating *As You Like It* as a romance at one remove from representations of reality. Why people of the theatre were affected by this concept of realism before literary critics is a matter for speculation. I suspect that the moth-eaten stag is an important clue. Originally an actual stag had been donated to lend some aura of realism to the hunt, but with age it, and presumably the rendering of the rustic world, had become utterly conventionalized and trite, a spectacle particularly tawdry during a period just after so many young men had lost their lives in the fields of Flanders. Whatever the reason, by the second quarter of the century the literary critics joined in the clamor for realism. But this particular period of our history serves as an illustration of the fact that however closely related are the traditions of the staging and critical commentary on *As You Like It*, they are not identical. Their independence permits them to comment upon one another, not unlike the remarks of Jaques and Touchstone.

THE SECOND QUARTER OF THE TWENTIETH CENTURY: CRITICAL THEATRICAL REALISM

In 1923, Richmond Noble published probably the first full-length study of Shakespeare's songs. Noble explains that songs are particularly apt to *As You Like It* because "it is the comedy of romantic unreality, of the Arcadian existence of the sort we have a glimpse of in the canvases of Watteau" (71). Moreover, since the plot of this play is "lazy," it is not surprising that the songs do not forward the action. On the contrary, they function to convey "colour of scene and sense of atmosphere to make good the lack of the assistance of a scene painter" (72). In particular, Amiens' two songs in *As You Like It* are important "in the history of English dramatic song, for they are the first wherein the temperament of the singer is reflected in the lyric" (72). Both songs "are charged with poetic emotion tinged with misanthropy" and thus are related to Jaques. In fact, the interchange between Amiens and Jaques is explained by Noble in relation to the songs: "Jaques finds the singing so pleasing that he importunes Amiens for a second stanza, in which all are required to join. Then Jaques turns round and parodies the whole theme of the song. . . . Unfortunately, when this scene occurs on the stage, it is usual for Jaques to recite his parody, whereas it were more effective were he to make an effort in some sort to sing it" (73). We see here a continuation of the interest in historical accuracy, particularly when Noble points out that Amiens' songs "are songs to the other characters on the stage, and therefore the singer is prohibited from advancing to the footlights as he is far too prone to do in modern practice" (74). While Noble shares with Lovat Fraser an interest in historical realism, there is clear disagreement about the means to that end. Noble believes that the songs served in place of scenery, and he objects to actors who cannot sing reciting Jaques's song and to singers who address the audience when they should be singing only to the other characters.

It is not surprising during this period immediately after the First World War that Jaques and Touchstone become of more interest. In 1925, J. B. Priestley lyrically describes the British critical landscape: "As the sunlight filters through the leaves of Arden, scattering gold along its paths and deep into its glades, and the persons of the company there who 'fleet the time carelessly, as they did in the golden age,' pass and repass, hardly distinguishable, in their travel-stained russet and green, from the background of forest, we notice that two figures stand out in sharp relief. One is the sad-suited Jaques and the other is Touchstone, bright in his motley" (18). Touchstone is seen as the first of the important 'fools' of Shakespeare: "certainly for us he is no mere butt, for we laugh with him and not at him" (19). Jaques recognizes the worth of Touchstone, according to Priestley, and pursues him "through the greenwood as the lovers pursue their ladies" (21). But Jaques is less well received by the critics: "Ever since the delighted commentators have made the discovery that Jaques is not merely the poet's mouthpiece but a distinct character like the rest of the personages in the comedy, they have pressed hard upon him and abused him without stint. He is almost regarded as the villain of the piece. One would suppose that critics are themselves men of thought rather than men of action . . . yet, oddly enough, the very sight of a contemplative character, such as Jaques, always sends them into a rage" (21–22).

Nonetheless, Priestley recognizes the limitations of Jaques: "Tasting life is not living any more than dabbling a hand in the water is swimming. Jaques has never waved farewell to pride and secure self-possession and dived into experience, there to discover real sorrow and joy, genuine bitterness, and, perhaps, lasting contentment" (23). Yet he and Touchstone function as "the critics" at one remove from the others, noting insincerity and mocking sentimentality. But there is a difference between the two: "Motley is a better critic than Melancholy" because the clown does not completely detach himself from the others and enters into the courting ritual (24). Of course, Touchstone is not heeded by Rosalind and Celia, for "two romantic young ladies, grappling with the problem of lovers and fathers, are no audience for a humorist of Touchstone's metal." Rosalind's humor is different from Touchstone's; she "does not try to lay bare the tangled twisted roots of the Tree of Life, but plays, like a wavering gleam of sunshine or a cluster of bright birds, in its high foliage" (26). Priestley concedes that Touchstone's pairing with Audrey is not on the same level as that of the main characters, but that is because he "cannot worm his way into the idyll" (33). Granting even that Touchstone is not seriously in love, Priestley explains that is because he is not wholly serious about anything. In the end, Priestley believes that Touchstone provides a more accurate view of the world than anyone else in the drama: "This world being what it is—and how well Motley knows the world—it describes with more accuracy than all the honeyed golden speeches of the Romeos and Antonies the actual feelings that men and women, not poets and born lovers, . . . but workaday men and women, have for one another" (37). The term 'accuracy' brings us back to some version of realism, though now 'reality' has become a much more somber affair than a generation ago, and the term 'workaday' suggests a new emphasis on class distinction.

By 1930, we can see from the two selections included in this survey both continuity and discontinuity with past commentary. Continuing in a mode that is now familiar, Rosa Grindon sees *As You Like It* as a drama of sunshine but one that finally yields to solid reality. Darkening the scintillating light of Arden, Touchstone and Jaques take tenable positions on many issues but are themselves both flawed. Touchstone would have "deceived the innocent rustic maid, Audrey, with a false marriage," but for Jaques. Jaques himself "has not gone to the forest for pure love of the Duke," and as he tells us, "not for love had he left wealth and ease, and any man who does so turns ass" (67). Moreover, his melancholy "provokes a smile, . . . good testimony to the fact that his melancholy is not real" (70). Grindon therefore concludes that "a study of this play must enlarge our own outlook on life. Chiefly it shows us that, wherever we be, in town, court or countryside, in cottage or in ease, we are what we are, irrespective of our surroundings" (72).

Frederick Kolbe, writing in the same year, presents an alternative to the traditional approach by identifying the genre of *As You Like It* as neither romance nor pastoral. We are reminded that Shakespeare was in the company that first presented *Every Man in His Humour* and may well have performed in it himself a year before he presented *As You Like It*. Both plays are, Kolbe claims, about stereotypical or humorous characters: "Rosalind is the very embodiment of Caprice. Celia has unselfish and incalculable impulses which make her the most gracious figure in the play. Touchstone says: 'A poor humour of mine, sir, to take that no man else will.' Jaques is a mass of affected cynical melancholy. Orlando and Silvius are 'slaves of love.' . . . Phebe affects the airs of a Lady Disdain. Oliver is as freakish in his hatred as afterwards in his love. Adam nobly exaggerates 'the constant service of the antique world.' Sir Oliver Martext is a caricature. Corin is the only perfectly normal character, and he is so self-conscious about it that it almost becomes a pose" (82). This interest in various forms of Caprice as a humor is, according to Kolbe, how Shakespeare adapted Ben Jonson-like characters to Lodge's story *Rosalynde*, which, is about "*Fortune*, with her uncertain and unstable *gifts*, the goddess of *caprice*, upsetting the order of *Nature* in a topsy-turvy *world*" (83). This rather capricious analysis of *As You Like It* is of particular historical interest because it is an early instance of a self-conscious attempt to alter the generic terms from romance and pastoral to humours comedy, one which bases its position not on a close reading of the play, but upon historical evidence. Kolbe argues that Shakespeare knew the work of Ben Jonson and Thomas Lodge before writing *As You Like It* and combined the two by intermingling their respective themes. Grindon and Kolbe share a belief in the historical-realist premise: we can discover essential historical facts because we share a human nature. But they arrive at contrary positions—the one seeing a sunny, romantic comedy and the other a Jonsonian, humours satire—because one applies the premise to the characters in the play and the other applies it to the playwright. Here is a vivid example of how discontinuity can arise out of continuity, a principle that is borne out in perhaps less overt instances throughout this history.

During this same period, two theatre reviews set up an interesting contrast because they refer to different productions that each had Edith Evans as Rosalind and Michael Redgrave as Orlando and were presented in London within a year of one another. The earlier of the two, dated 10 November 1936, the most positive, applauds Edith Evans for a Rosalind at once romantic and witty. Indeed, at the end, we are told, "the audience is made one Orlando" (*The Manchester Guardian*). By contrast, *The Times* reviewer of 12 February 1937 faults Evans in the same part for being not an "Elizabethan Rosalind" but an eighteenth-century version of her, something closer to Congreve's Millamant. We may attribute this difference of opinion to the variations of taste, but it is important to note that there is also here a difference about the criteria of excellence. The more negative reviewer assumes that historical realism is better and therefore negatively describes the production as an eighteenth-century version of what should have properly been Elizabethan. The more positive reviewer, however, has no problem with the eighteenth-century scenery: "The costumes are more in keeping with the play, and it is not at all unhappy to begin on a note of Watteau with the ladies embarking for Arden as if it were Cythera, and Touchstone in very likeness of the famous Gilles in the Louvre." Moreover, even historical consistency is not required by this reviewer who characterizes Evans as a "Meredithean Lady," thus placing a nineteenth-century heroine in an eighteenth-century setting. It is not clear from this brief account what precisely is this reviewer's criterion of excellence, but certainly it must be something other than a literal version of historical realism.

Nevertheless, contemporary history is an important interest on the stage during this period. John Trewin describes a production in terms suggestive of the concerns of the 1930s: "Arden came indoors during a West End *As You Like It* at the Phoenix in the autumn of 1933. . . . They were lucky in Fabia Drake's Rosalind, from Stratford; Randle Ayrton's Touchstone, also from Stratford, and a man of diverting gloom; and Stephen Haggard's Silvius, work by a young actor of whom Barry Jones told Christopher Hassal: 'How he rehearsed! What absorption!'" (147). One cannot help but wonder if Touchstone and Silvius, the less privileged, become a new focus of interest during this period of the Great Depression. Did contemporary history prevail over interest in historical reconstruction of the past? On the other hand, as World War II neared Trewin suggests that escapism became the popular mode. Concerning a film version of *As You Like It* in 1936 Trewin records the following entry in his diary: "'What do I remember? Elisabeth Bergner as the archest Rosalind-Pan. A flock of sheep, another flock of sheep. The voice of Henry Ainley [Banished Duke]. Laurence Olivier's Orlando stopped at every turn by this coy and romping Rosalind. . . . A sugary, tea-gardenish, Epping-on-Bank Holiday setting, an over-populated forest" (172–73). (For an account of foreign productions during this period, see Michael Jamieson, particularly pages 638–39.)

In the next two decades, selections included in this volume suggest that some scholars persisted without questioning the old assumptions. George Gordon writes of the generic constraints of Shakespearian comedy. "In this climate of Romance, it is, of course, the rule that all the lovers shall love at once, and love absolutely. Nothing else, in this world, is to be permitted. . . . Is *Romantic* comedy then impossible?" Gordon assures us that Shakespeare complies with the rules of genre: "In Romantic Comedy, therefore, the laughers and the sighers live side by side, like good neighbours; on only *one* condition: that neither shall commit excess, or compete for attention at the expense of the other" (48–9). Similarly, Cecile De Banke outlines the limitations imposed upon Shakespeare by his acting company. De Banke points out that when Will Kemp left the troupe and was replaced by Robert Armin, Shakespeare was free to create fools like Feste and Touchstone. Moreover, the children of the company who at first played merely walk-on parts had to be trained to play the roles of women, so that dramas with parts like that of Rosalind could only be composed later in the history of the company when these young boys had learned how to play such sophisticated roles.

Both of these essays are illustrative of the perils of prescriptive realist criticism. Shakespeare is viewed as bound by rules of genre and subject to the physical limitations of his company, as if both of these matters were firmly written in stone and not subject to modification *by* or the influence *of* Shakespeare or any other artist of the day. Moreover, another buried assumption is that we in the twentieth century have direct access to the reality and essential truths of Shakespeare's day. Questions that are avoided by these critics are important. Did Shakespeare's own dramas have no effect upon what was considered romance, pastoral, or any other genre associated with *As You Like It* in the Elizabethan period? Is it not possible that Burbage remained and Kemp left because Burbage, like Shakespeare, was a shareholder in the company? The prescriptive excesses of realist criticism can be seen by De Banke's instructions to producers of Shakespearian comedy: "Since the parts of the heroines were written for boys, Shakespeare was particularly careful to avoid over-emphasis on sex in these parts. Furthermore, such restraint would help to avoid detrimental criticism from the Puritan element in London. So the heroines were acted simply and directly without individual mannerisms or self-conscious display. Always keeping in mind the boy actor, *for whom the part was written*, the young actress of today should allow only so much of her own femininity to emerge as her artistic integrity allows, and in the scenes where she is disguised as a boy, as she is in many of the comedies, should subdue even that little" (117). The italicized portion of this quotation establishes the basis of this kind of authority. It almost sounds as if De Banke were present at the original Elizabethan production (if there was one) of *As You Like It*. But we cannot be certain that Shakespeare taught his young boy actors not to mock these strict conventional rules. Nor do we know whether the Elizabethan authorities and Shakespeare's audience were as committed to rules of genre and gender as are De Banke and Gordon. The present introduction is itself an attempt to pursue a genre theory that avoids such prescriptive rules. At this point it is important, if not surprising, that in practice the essentialist assumptions concerning reality and genre were already being questioned, as is apparent in the previously mentioned 1936 theatre review.

1940–1957: THE RISE OF NEW CRITICISM: FORMALIST THEMATICS

The period 1940 to the present will be considered in an abbreviated fashion for a number of reasons. The amount of critical material on *As You Like It* reaches a new level of vastness; the annotated bibliography for the period, 1940–1980 contains 1584 entries and is over 700 pages in length. Since every entry in this work receives at least a paragraph of description I shall be particularly selective and focus upon those positions that, in my view, alter the course of the history of commentary on *As You Like It*. Some important material from the past fifty years has been omitted because of difficulty or expense in obtaining permission to publish. Lastly, I decided that given the space limitations it was more useful to include more of the older and less accessible criticism and to be more selective with regard to recent work that was generally available.

William Empson's *Some Versions of Pastoral* gives the genre of pastoral new vitality. Empson demonstrates that pastoral has a long tradition of presenting two opposed worlds, rich and poor. While the classical convention related these two within a harmonized whole, by Shakespeare's day this conception was subject to satire, if not parody. Silvius and Phebe are used as examples of a satirical view of pastoral because the lower class man is unable to woo Phebe even if he adopts the classical pastoral tradition. For Empson this satire functions to suggest how the sheer earthiness of the country life, illustrated by the rusticity of not only Silvius but also William and Audrey, is related to upper class pastoral courtship conventions. Touchstone mediates between the two worlds, and Empson analyses the clown's pun on "fain"/"feign" to demonstrate that what Silvius would 'fain' is related to what Touchstone would "feign," that the most elemental desires are related to the 'feigning' associated in the Renaissance with pastoral poetic conventions and, in general, with poetry (132).

This understanding of the two-sidedness of pastoral, its earthiness and etherealness, leads to a number of analyses in the 1940s and 1950s concerned with the balance between these two 'versions' of pastoral. James Smith, for instance, argues for a tragic undertone present in pastoral, which is seen in the figure of Jaques and in the subplot involving Silvius and Phebe. Since Jaques's ironical attitude does not permit him any personal gain, he is considered by Smith superior to Touchstone, whose scepticism is used in order to court Audrey. But Rosalind is superior to both because she combines the awareness of both Jaques and Touchstone to serve not merely her own personal goals but also the interests of others. For this reason, Smith concludes that *As You Like It* is an "unromantic" form of pastoral.

C. L. Barber, writing during both the 1940s and 1950s, places *As You Like It* in the romantic tradition in that Arden is a place that permits the entire personality to have free expression. For Barber, this comedy partakes of an ancient folk tradition of saturnalian rites, something similar to what Bakhtin calls the carnivalesque, where traditional authority is temporarily flouted for the purposes of purging the people of its opposition to the establishment. Barber sees the courtship in the subplot of Silvius and Phebe and of Audrey and Touchstone as examples of excess, either of idealism or self-indulgence, that are corrected by Rosalind and by the example provided by the marriages in the main plot. Mediating between the extremes, Rosalind comprehends both "holiday and everyday perspectives" (239).

What begins to become clear during the 1940s and 1950s is that although there is general agreement that *As You Like It* achieves balance between its extremes of self-indulgence and idealism, the thematic purport of that point of mediation is described in very diverse, sometimes contradictory ways. Even the "Seven Ages of Man" speech that in the nineteenth century had been taken to represent Shakespeare's position is now seen in more measured terms. Samuel Chew demonstrates that Shakespeare's audience would have been familiar with a long tradition of "The Voyage of Life" motifs in many of the arts since the time of the morality plays. Chew suggests that once we realize that the content of Jaques's speech is commonplace we should then keep in mind the speaker's mood and decide whether or not melancholy is appropriate to the entire play (146). At the same time, others, like Hardin Craig, stress the fact that Jaques begins a long line of choric characters in Shakespeare. Craig recognizes that *As You Like It* can accommodate the combination of zaniness and common sense of Touchstone, but believes that Jaques's part as commentator emerges in the great tragedies and late comedies in the parts of Hamlet, Macbeth, Timon, Enobarbus, and Prospero (51–6).

While a number of these thematic analyses were based upon speculation about Shakespeare's audience, Ivor Brown reminds us that we have no record of performances of *As You Like It* during the period 1600–1740. Brown infers from this lack of evidence that the play was ahead of its time and was not well liked by the Elizabethans. Whether or not we accept Brown's conclusion, he does make clear that what critics asserted concerning Shakespeare's audience for *As You Like It* were often not based upon historical evidence but were rather projections of their own interpretations of the drama.

The kind of differences that at this time divided critics over the nature of this golden mean between the extremes of real and ideal is illustrated by two essays that appeared in 1949. E. C. Pettet believes that Orlando's Petrarchan mode of courtship is mocked as much as is Silvius's extravagant language. In this way Shakespeare is, according to Pettet, showing his dissatisfaction with the conventions of romantic courtship. And although Rosalind is the clear mediator even her final indulgent attitude is not to be equated with

Shakespeare's realism. Donald Stauffer, on the other hand, believes that the earthiness of the mockery, particularly that of Touchstone, signals an attitude of reconciliation and acceptance of romantic love. Jaques becomes for Stauffer a focal point: his melancholy satire is shown by the unfolding of the drama to be excessive. Instead, Shakespeare concludes that "Nature is good, and good nature is natural" (80).

Harold Jenkins attempts to take into account both of these sorts of positions, what might be called the romantic and the realistic, in an essay of 1955 that was reprinted in Jay Halio's edition of *Twentieth Century Interpretations of "As You Like It."* Jenkins argues that *As You Like It* is a sophisticated comedy because it entertains satire of the same ideal that it seeks to maintain. The irony of Jaques and Touchstone serves to qualify each position for the audience, and, in fact, the play progresses by way of paradoxes, different views that are never completely contrary. In this way, the comedy refers to life in and outside of Arden, accommodating various perspectives and philosophical positions. In conclusion, Jenkins points out that Touchstone and Jaques are kept for the most part away from Silvius: the clown sees him only once and the melancholy satirist never confronts him. Jenkins leaves us to infer why for him Silvius is central to *As You Like It*: presumably Silvius finally wins Phebe because he has learned from Rosalind to temper his idealism with some realism. But we are left to wonder how Silvius becomes more important than or differs from, in terms of thematic purport, his instructress Rosalind.

1957–1967: THE RELIGIOUS AND SECULAR ASSUMPTIONS OF NEW CRITICISM: THE RISE OF IDEOLOGY

By 1957, Northrop Frye had fully developed an alternative to the thematic approach. Frye proposed generic archetypes that form the basis of a tradition of comedy dating back to the work of Plautus and Terence. Certain character types recur regularly: impostors, self-deprecators, and buffoons. These types manifest the extremes of comedy, irony and romance. But in the end structure prevails over any theme because the goal of comedy is social inclusion, which in *As You Like It* is exemplified by the marriages. For Frye, Arden is a green world, a post-lapsarian Eden, where love can triumph over the mundane world outside. By implication—for what is only implicit here becomes explicit in Frye's later writings—religious faith enables one to transfer this spirit of love and forgiveness to the world outside of Arden, what Frye calls "the wasteland" (164–86). Frye's analysis with its religious implications makes clear that the thematic or formal analysis of the 1940s and 1950s evaded deep differences, often involving religious versus secular views, but also other kinds of conflicting beliefs, or to use current terminology, differences of ideology.

For instance, the secular alternative to Frye's view is most articulately represented by Helen Gardner's influential essay of 1959 that is also reprinted in *Twentieth Century Interpretations of "As You Like It."* Gardner believes that Arden is unlike the forest in *Midsummer Night's Dream*. Instead of magic, Arden is ruled by a kind of realism: it borders on the edge of tragedy, reminding us of the heath in *King Lear*. But in comedy it functions as a "place of discovery where the truth becomes clear and where each man finds himself and his true way." Since we are in comedy not tragedy, good fortune, a sort of "bawd" for the lovers, does prevail (17–32). In the end, in place of Frye's spirit that with faith can rejuvenate the wasteland, Gardner sees individuals who find one another by discovering the truth about themselves.

On the stage at this time, Glen Byam Shaw's production of 1957 with Peggy Ashcroft as Rosalind is described by Rosemary Anne Sisson as follows. Ashcroft's Rosalind is "gentle and affectionate rather than high spirited [which] results, perhaps, in the loss of some of the spring-tide gaiety of the play, but in compensation many moments rise to new and natural life" (*Stratford-upon-Avon Herald*, 5 April 1957). Orlando, on the other hand, is played as "very much the country boy" but is "likeable." Touchstone's "zest" is equalled by a "shrewd" Audrey, both of whom are successful at keeping the audience amused. Here we see again the balance of romance and realism that has been the hallmark of the criticism of this period.

But Jaques proves a problem for Sisson and, it would seem, for the Byam Shaw production. "The most difficult part in the play is that of Jaques, and one whose nature, I confess, has never been entirely clear to me, either in reading or seeing the play. Do we laugh with or at Jaques? Does he reveal follies in the world, or is he, like Malvolio, perversely out of step with approved merriment? Robert Harris does not paint a clear picture, either of cynical commentator or misguided melancholic." The comments on the other elements of the production may help clarify this problem. Phebe and Silvius are, we are told played "prettily," but the mask of Hymen lacks "grace and resonance." The songs are "pleasantly romantic," especially when "assisted by Touchstone and his penny-whistle" (25–32). Clearly, irony and satire are at a minimum, particularly if Touchstone at the penny-whistle is to be taken seriously, as Sisson suggests he is. Jaques's satire, as it is more penetrating than that of Touchstone, is out of place in this thoroughly secularized, romantic production. This production exemplifies the position of Gardner or Barber, where lovers find each other by finding themselves. Jaques's irony can only be attributed to his self-indulgence. Up to this point, the stage has yet to render Frye's spiritual conception where Jaques functions to remind us of the alternative to the green world that remains to be redeemed.

By 1961, however, the presentation has altered markedly. The most innovative element of this production—and one which contrasts with that of

Byam Shaw—is the staging of the hunting of the stag. Bamber Gascoigne, in the *Spectator* (14 July) approves: "Michael Elliot's direction is crisp and intelligent. He knows precisely the pulse of Shakespeare's changing perspectives, and he adds one particularly telling touch: he stages the implied hunt which leads up to Jaques's question, 'Which is he that killed the deer?' In the excitement of the chase these courtly foresters show a streak of savagery which is out of keeping with the spirit of Arden" (59–60). This last phrase could have come from Frye's view: the hunt here functions to remind us of the world of savagery in the background of Arden and most likely in the foreground outside of Arden. The *Sunday Times* reviewer of the same production gives a vivid description of Vanessa Redgrave as Rosalind: "Miss Redgrave . . . smiles away all problems, striking a silver note unheard on our stage for years; a note which sings of radiance without effort, of an unstrained charity." A Rosalind who faces problems and is herself part of a society that has its moments of "savagery" is not surprisingly in need of "charity." Here Jaques finds his place. Gascoigne explains that "Max Adrian plays Jaques with the calmest precision" and the *Sunday Times* reviewer is more specific, relating melancholy and savagery: "Mr. Elliott gives point to Jaques's wincing—and suggests a reason for his melancholy: the old nightmare of the horns" (31) Jamieson provides us with an illustrative anecdote about this production: "Peter Hall, head of the RSC, recalled in his memoirs taking a reluctant playgoer Jean Renoir to the theatre and placing him for few minutes at the back of the stalls: 'After a short time I took his arm to show him the way out, but he resisted and stayed, his eyes alight. On stage was a girl like a rush of sunlight. He was watching the twenty-four year old Vanessa Redgrave playing Rosalind, her first unqualified triumph'" (641).

By the 1960s the stage productions indicate that to account for Jaques, not to mention the sardonic side of Touchstone, it is necessary to suggest that *As You Like It* is not merely a romantic romance and that Arden itself is, if edenic, at best a post-lapsarian paradise. Early in the decade Richard David stresses the close relationship between Shakespeare's comedies and his tragedies as well as his history plays. Richard demonstrates that the comedies and tragedies have a common method: a less direct, more allusive style in comedy permits Shakespeare to present "sober reality, . . . the hallmark of Shakespearian comedy" (93). And Frank Kermode reminds us that all of Shakespeare's mature comedies are "problem" comedies, that of *As You Like It* being "courtesy" (221–27).

Reflecting the more sober approach to *As You Like It* of this decade, Roland Frye presents a Christian interpretation, focusing upon Duke Senior and Adam. The Duke, according to Roland Frye, speaks eloquently of the difference between flattery and counsel, of the "uses of adversity" and gleans wisdom from the "book of nature," all ideas that are reminiscent of Richard Hooker and John Calvin. When Adam prays in the second act, he reflects "the framework of Christian meaning which informs the thinking of most of Shakespeare's characters" (112). If Roland Frye makes explicit the implicit spiritual element in Northrop Frye's position, some existentialists pursue a secular version of Northrop Frye's archetypal analysis. Jan Kott focuses upon the sexual implications of Rosalind disguised as Ganymede and asserts that the myth of Ganymede was associated with androgyny and that the myth of Arcadia, or lost paradise, is associated with Arden. These two myths are connected, according to Kott, by way of Adam, who was an androgynous figure before the creation of Eve. Rosalind as Ganymede is therefore seen as androgynous, which "personifies the same longing for the lost Paradise where there had as yet been no division into male and female elements" (342). Kott implies that Rosalind is able to integrate pre-sexual desires into the existing world of sexuality.

David Horowitz's existential interpretation, on the other hand, is not archetypal. Instead, he associates the end of Jaques's "Seven Ages of Man" speech with the doctrine of nothingness, representing in *As You Like It* the extreme satirical view that is tempered by Rosalind's more romantic perspective (39). But Maynard Mack compares *As You Like It* and a tragedy, *King Lear*, without arriving at an existentialist position. The pastoral pattern in both plays involves an exiled ruler along with companions, a wise fool, episodes with "rustic primitives," good and evil brothers, and the final reuniting of father and daughter. Viewing the comedy as pastoral and the tragedy as anti-pastoral, Mack points out that in *As You Like It*, "everyone meets, as in a glass, reflections of what he is" and finds his or her counterpart of just reward, whereas in *Lear* this pattern appears in the distance but is never realized (64–5). Another instance of how *As You Like It* skirts tragedy is pointed to by Arthur Sprague who characterizes the episode when Oliver delivers the message from Orlando to Rosalind and produces the bloody handkerchief as one of the "flashes of high seriousness" (240–47). And Stanley Wells suggests that tragedy seems close to comedy because of the contrived nature of Shakespeare's comic conclusions. "A normal pattern for the end of a Shakespearian comedy is a point of extreme entanglement, sometimes involving the possibility and even the fact of real suffering . . . then a disentangling of the knot, followed by a celebratory passage . . . and concluding with a more subdued rounding off, a return to normality" (110).

1967–1980: GENDER ON STAGE AND CRITICAL UNEASE WITH SECULAR AND RELIGIOUS RESOLUTIONS

The somber critical views that became common during this period caused some difficulties for those presenting *As You Like It* on the stage as a comedy.

Some producers were able to maintain in the background the philosophical import of the comedy while highlighting gender and sex. In 1967, the interest in the androgynous aspect of Ganymede and of the serious side of comedy is apparent in the Clifford Williams all-male production of *As You Like It*. The *Sunday Telegraph* reviewer describes Rosalind as follows: "Ronald Pickup's Rosalind, willowy and breastless, is the one most clinically drained of sensuality. This duke's daughter radiates the lanky, coltish, androgynous sweetness of a young Garbo, sex without gender, a platonic readiness to accept love as an emotion not yet awoken into physical passion. Curiously enough, with darkly widened eyes and generously pinked mouth setting off a cheeky beak of a nose, Mr. Pickup looks more feminine in the white simulated-leather of his Ganymede disguise than in his floor-length knitted dress at court." By contrast, sex is most overt in the subplot: "The two lesser women's roles demonstrate the extremes to which male actors can go in travestying their own masculinity. Anthony Hopkins's Audrey is completely butch: a beefy, bass-voiced rugger captain in drag parodying almost any muscular sixthformer dragooned into a dress for the school play. Richard Kay, on the other leg, is the complete female personator as Phebe, curvaceous, pretty, husky-voiced and flirtatious, far more of the randy rustic nympho than any actress I can remember." Since the main plot emphasizes the mythic dimension of the courtship ritual, the subplot is free to play up (and with) sexuality. Interestingly, this production accommodates both Jaques and Touchstone in serio-comic roles: "Robert Stephens's Jaques is a scholarly eccentric from some, probably Germanic, university: a lean and slippered pantaloon with a withered arm, a bookish stoop and a sour line in pedantic sarcasm which alternately irritates and delights his hearty companions in exile. 'All the world's a stage' comes out a pessimistic lecture, ending with a burst of self-pitying near-hysteria on 'sans everything.'" His excess is matched on the other side by Touchstone: "Derek Jacobi as Touchstone is a defensive, campy, professional comedian in the Frankie Howard vein who takes all the hoaxes and traps of fortune with a Jewish shrug and a Cockney smack of the lips. It is a perverse but triumphant interpretation which embodies the only moments of music-hall effeminacy in the entire evening." But, as if to maintain its independence from the critical establishment, the setting varies from what Northrop Frye calls the "green world." "The trees of Arden become glass tubes and plastic roofings in punched-out patterns like computer tapes. The clothes are pastel uniforms tricked out with gold and silver PVC capes and boots. Visually, it is a cross between a Pierre Cardin shopwindow and 'The Shape of Things to Come'" (*Sunday Telegraph*, 8 Oct. 1967). Perhaps sci-fi can represent a spiritual dimension in either a secular or religious context; at least this Arden can no longer be taken as literally a rustic paradise. The 1960s manifest the opposing ideologies that lay behind the thematic balance and paradox of the new criticism or formalism of the 1940s and 1950s. But this discovery and uncovering also opened the way for ideological confrontation between religionists and secularists and various versions of that division, such as historical purists or absolutists versus cultural and historical relativists.

At the end of the 1960s some critics expressed restiveness and unease with the artificiality of thematic conclusions. Stanley Wells admits that Shakespearian endings have been criticized for excessive ingenuity and for being overly inclusive, what another critic calls the "Noah's Ark" conclusion. But Wells nevertheless defends the end of *As You Like It* where cloying sweetness is avoided by the melancholy farewell of Jaques (122). Sylvan Barnet, by contrast, argues that artificiality is deliberate on Shakespeare's part. Barnet begins by pointing out that it must have been as apparent to Elizabethans as to us that Shakespeare's comedies are full of improbabilities. Hence when we come to the end of a play full of improbabilities that concludes in an artificial way, we should look for the function of this artificiality. For Barnet, Shakespeare is deliberately distancing the audience from a literal acceptance of the conclusion so that closure is understood in spiritual terms: "In Jaques's statement that he hopes to learn 'much matter' from the convertite, we may hear, very faintly, a voice like that of the jailer who asked Paul and Silas, 'what must I do to be saved?' . . . The implication is, I think, that his dissatisfaction with things as they are prepares him for the possibility of conversion of the sort experienced by Frederick and Oliver and by the lovers." Barnet goes on, after citing Northrop Frye, to indicate that for her the ending "lifts us into a higher world" (119–31). By the 1970s a number of critics were satisfied neither with Wells's assertion that *concordia discors* is achieved in *As You Like It* nor with the belief that the ending directed the audience to experience something like a religious conversion.

In 1972, Anne Barton placed *As You Like It* at the center of her analysis of Shakespearian comedy. A "classical comedy," *As You Like It* maintains a perfect balance that is on the wane and will be lost in *Twelfth Night* when Malvolio exits at the end unable to be contained within the traditional comic conclusion. The fact that Touchstone is contained in *As You Like It* makes the drama a sort of poignant autumnal paen to traditional comedy (160–80). Yet in the same year Ralph Berry attacks Northrop Frye's conception of comedy and offers an alternative interpretation of *As You Like It*. Berry has little use for Frye's comic pattern, because the most important elements for Berry at the end of Shakespearian comedy are the problems and unanswered questions. Moreover, seeing the end of *Twelfth Night* or *As You Like It* on a higher level does not help resolve these problems.

Berry's own position continues in the existentialist mode, as is suggested by his title, "No Exit from Arden." Berry believes that even Arden cannot escape the personal struggles for power within a framework that involves as much anti-romance as romance. The characters in *As You Like It* are divided into sets of debaters who do not so much disagree as compete with one another because of their likeness to one another. Jaques and the Duke Senior are, for instance, both incorrigible moralizers. The Duke "sees the exterior world as a series of emblems. But this is precisely the bent of Jaques's mind. Independently he and the Duke arrive at the same metaphor; they perceive the natural kingdom of Arden as a power struggle where man usurps the beast's place, just as he himself is the victim of usurpation" (180). Even Rosalind is seen as involved in a power struggle: "Phebe voices the antiromantic viewpoint so necessary to the play; and she administers a well-deserved beating to a ninny who, it seems, thrives on the diet. Why, then, the excited interruption of Rosalind? . . . Because . . . Phebe is a domineering woman who, reversing the sexual roles, has mastered her man; so is Rosalind" (183). And although Touchstone, a measure of and observer upon the behavior of others, cannot himself escape the contest, "we can only take Touchstone's action at face value, the ironic acceptance of a slut by a man who will always be her superior. In the context of Touchstone's other relationships, it is a likely guess that the certainty that he will remain the dominant partner is uppermost in his mind" (191). In conclusion, Berry sees little resolution of these conflicts: "There is little true accord in Arden, prior to the final scene; and the audience is entitled, if it wishes, to its reservations even then. The idyll of Arden is an idea as much under fire as the denizens of the forest; and the final path that leads away from forest to Court is a change of milieu, not a way out of those problems" (195).

D. J. Palmer characterizes this competitive spirit as a form of play, as the term is employed in Huizinga's *Homo ludens*. Palmer points out that even before we reach Arden, in the disagreement between Oliver and Orlando and in the wrestling match, "we are given some anticipation of the nature of play, and of the equivocal relations between fiction and reality, game and earnest, folly and wisdom." Play, according to Palmer, can be reduced to barbarism, as when the wrestling match becomes an arena of attempted murder, or can take the form of "ritualized conflicts that exist in wit-combats and games of mockery." The most sophisticated form of *homo ludens* in the drama is that played between Orlando and Rosalind/Ganymede: "Her game with Orlando is a lesson in awareness for each of them, a rehearsal for encountering with resilience the adversities that lie ahead." Games, Palmer suggests, help prepare the characters for the real or non-game world. For this reason the final marriages, the entry into reality, are preceded by Touchstone's game: "Before the lovers are united in Hymen's bands, . . . it is Touchstone who rounds off the comedy of pastimes with his account of how a quarrel may be translated into a courtly game. . . .

Like the Lie Direct, the confusions of make-believe are finally resolved with an IF. . . . In the world that now lies before them, subject to time and the stubbornness of fortune, there is indeed much virtue in vows made with an IF" (234–45). Games and the ability to recognize and play them are seen as preparation for the world outside of Arden. Why? Because, as Berry has demonstrated, power struggles are everywhere, even in Arden, and games provide legal and 'fair' means of negotiating political or power differences.

During this period even pastoral was reformulated as a form of conflict. David Young describes it as follows: "To be a credit to art, however, pastoral had to avoid the limited accomplishments of escape and wish-fulfillment, and had to face the issues it raised. In its function as an alternative it was to be dialectical, a kind of discourse between reality and the imagination. This process quite naturally called for continual recourse to antithesis, a favorite stylistic device, and it should be obvious, even to the most casual reader of pastoral, that it is founded on a series of tensions and oppositions" (27–33). Agnes Latham, in the introduction to her Arden edition of *As You Like It*, pursues this notion of pastoral. "Were [the Duke and his retinue] more perfectly pastoral they would do even less, for they would not even hunt. Contemplation was possible in their circumstances and was esteemed. It is one of the great pastoral values. That Jaques enjoys his melancholy is made abundantly clear." Clearly for Latham both pastoral and anti-pastoral are modified to serve purposes of individuals. Concerning Jaques, we are reminded by Latham that as the Duke points out to him "thou has been a libertine." Touchstone, on the other hand, is, according to Latham, not a fully developed character, which gives rise to an important innovative critical idea. "Touchstone never fully develops a character and tends to remain a theatrical convenience, though a very delightful one, to whom a skilled actor can give an illusion of life. . . . His creator's intelligence, not his own, is always putting Touchstone in an advantageous position." Latham is the first critic in this survey to explain why a character in *As You Like It* may not be fully developed for deliberate purposes on the part of Shakespeare. What the creator's purpose was with Touchstone is provided in Latham's description of Audrey, who is seen as another partially developed character. Audrey, one of the "true clowns, awkward and ignorant" is, Latham reminds us, treated indulgently by her creator. Moreover, not wholly true to her stereotype, she is "an obsessively moral girl," which enables Latham to explain that "it was surely she who insisted on the wedding" (xliv-lvi). Latham suggests that Audrey's part was manipulated by Shakespeare in order to indicate that Touchstone, but for Audrey's insistence, would not have married her legally. Decency, in short, is not one of Touchstone's virtues; the clown's moral cowardice is devised by Shakespeare to qualify Touchstone's view of the world. Thus Latham implies that for Shakespeare the opinions and conceptions voiced by the characters were more important than that they be totally consistent and fully developed as characters. By 1975 the interest in the power struggles in *As You Like It* led to an analysis of the power positions and postures of the characters in the drama, which in turn fostered the discovery that character consistency and development were, at times, sacrificed by Shakespeare for purposes of advancing, modifying, or undermining an ideological position.

On the stage during the 1970s we first see the influence of game theory. In 1977, B. A. Young is charmed by Trevor Nunn's Musical Production at the Royal Shakespeare Theatre. The rendition of Rosalind and Orlando is illustrative of *homo ludens*: "This Orlando is still young enough to have no beard, to rush off spontaneously after new ideas like a chicken after corn, and to play silly games with the teenage kid Ganymede that he meets in the forest" (42). Peter Thompson notes a similar element in a production at the same theatre four years earlier. "Is Touchstone's modern equivalent a rather brash seaside comic, likely to make a song-and-dance act out of his Rosalind rhymes? The suggestion didn't offend me, and I enjoyed the magnificent pattern of his 'quarrel on the seventh cause' set-piece as much as any of the other people who applauded it." We also see in this production evidence of the power struggle Berry articulated. "I was much impressed by the reticence with which a tensely loving relationship between Jaques and Duke Senior was indicated" (149–50).

But by the end of the decade some theatre reviewers objected to 'academic' theories that had undesirable effects upon stage presentations. In 1979, two reviews of Colin Dexter's production of *As You Like It* at the Olivier Theatre in London complain about the heavy-handed use of Fraser's *Golden Bough*. Ian McEwan, in the *New Statesman* describes this element of the production with more equanimity of temperament than others. "From then on it is spring. Not Vergil's spring, nor Lodge's (Shakespeare's source), but that of a more recently expounded version of pastoral; a *Golden Bough* season of pre-Christian English country lore, lusty, blood-daubed, drunken, erotic and, of course, fertile, a time of holiday misrule and mating. An anthropologist's Tree of Life sprouts and blossoms center stage, garlands and entrails of stags are hung, the bad men become good men as winter becomes spring, and by the end Dexter is in a position to mount an imposing masque on a scale that is bound to remind his audience that he is also a director of operas" (*New Statesman*, 10 August 1979: 200–11). Fraser's *The Golden Bough* seems to permit Dexter to place blood lust, sex and competition, the various forms of human difference and conflict, into a pastoral context. John Elsom, in *The Listener*, is more overtly condemnatory: "quotations from *The Golden Bough* . . . may explain why Dexter stresses fertility rituals at the expense of young love; and Dexter perpetuates another great academic cliché, by imposing the pastoral calendar—

autumn, winter, spring and summer—on the play, so that Orlando is first discovered binding up the sheaves of corn on his brother's land. The danger with such academic insights is not that they are necessarily wrong, but that they are footnotes to the text which, if taken too seriously, can overwhelm the play itself." In addition to Fraser another academic culprit cited is Jan Kott, whose view that Arden is not a place of the golden age but of "capitalist laws of hire" is a further unhealthy influence upon Dexter's production. The problem derives from the fact that Elsom, as he explains, views *As You Like It* as "a play about instant romance, and one of its chief delights is to see gorgeous youngsters falling in love as if there were no tomorrow." Hence the tragic, conflictual side of *As You Like It* is seen as "academic" (844–46). This difference between Dexter and Elsom may be a matter of personal taste or ideological beliefs, the reviewer harkening back to early days when the play was seen as a kind of romance and the producer in harmony with contemporary critics who stress the darker side of the comedy and its political import. But two negative reviews should give us pause. Quite apart from differences between the responses of Elsom and Dexter, the production was probably not a success, or at least not well received by reviewers. Does that suggest that art and ideology cannot be easily equated, or, to be more specific and to keep in mind the terms of both reviewers, that imposing ideological conceptions upon dramatic genres, here that of pastoral, needs reconsideration?

THE 1980s: CRITICS, STAGE SCHOLARS, REVIEWERS, ACTORS, AND ACTRESSES: DIFFERENCES IN THE GENRES OF IDEOLOGY

The 1980s are marked by clear differences between critics who focus upon the ideological implications of *As You Like It* and, for want of a better phrase, people of the theatre, actresses, actors, producers and directors. Indeed the very fact that during this decade we have access in print to more remarks from actors, actresses, producers, and directors suggests that some scholars believed that this other side of drama, the point of view of those involved in staging the play, more urgently needed to be heard. As we have seen, in the past accounts about or by actresses who have played Rosalind appeared in print, but these works usually date from well after the performances or at least not until the actress has become well established in the role. During the 1980s accounts are available not only of those who played Rosalind but also by players of Celia, Orlando, and Jaques within a year of the first performance. This relatively new phenomenon of writings by theatre people appearing at the same time as those by reviewers and critics sets up a new dynamic. But the matter is further complicated by the fact that some productions seem dominated by 'academic' interpretations and others react against or remain independent of this scholarship.

In 1980, Linda Kelly published *The Kemble Era*, a work that contained a brief account of Mrs. Siddons, the great tragic actress, as Rosalind. "Mrs Siddons' attempts at comedy were almost always unsuccessful and seldom more so than when, late that season, she followed her Lady Macbeth with Rosalind in *As You Like It*. Henry Bate had been enchanted when he saw her playing the part as a girl of twenty, but Mrs. Siddons was thirty now and the mother of four children. She had grown too stately for comedy; though possessed of a fund of quiet humour in private life she lacked vivacity on stage. . . . Decidedly comedy was not Mrs. Siddons' genre. . . . By 1785 redress was close at hand: Dorothy Jordan, as dazzling a star in her way as Mrs. Siddons, was waiting in the wings" (53–54). Judging from this account of Mrs. Siddons, interest in emphasizing the tragic elements of *As You Like It* by using a tragedienne risked violating certain minimal requirements of the genre of comedy.

In the same year, Charles Forker suggests that the themes of *As You Like It* involve a series of perspectives that converge in Rosalind, not merely as a character, but as a stage presence: "She is both natural and gracious, strong and frail, virtuous and full of mischief, divinely beautiful and humanly earthy all at once. She is conscious of time at the very moment that she seems to occupy and irradiate a world of timeless contentment. She is an activist without being too crudely or obviously aggressive. She is both a lover and a mocker of love, by turns both a subjectivist and an objectivist." Here we see that the thematic tensions developed during the 1970s have become transferred to the dramatic spectacle: "Rosalind is the very symbol of theatre as they liked it at the Globe in 1599, and as we continue still to like it" (78).

But the 1983 production at Stratford, Ontario in Canada seems, at least by one account, to have completely disregarded the tensions of themes and the constraints of genre. "*As You Like It* was, by far, one of the worst Shakespearean productions I have ever had the misfortune to suffer through. From start to finish, it was a perverse mutation of pastoral—a most un-English romance, misdirected as a sinister east European political satire, with heavily cloaked soldiers in dark glasses and a court that would not have been out of place in a Hollywood melodrama of Nazis and Fascists. Obviously indebted to Jan Kott's vision of a bitter Arcadia, where 'the air is stuffy and everyone is afraid,' where the new prince is distrustful, suspicious, jealous of everything and everybody, unsure of his position, sensing the enemy is everyone, Hirsch started the play with wintry chill and smog in a Victorian setting. The court was stuffily officious, and the colours glittered with black and silver portents. But the trouble with Frederick's court is not a twentieth-century barbarity. Although 'breaking of ribs' is considered a sport for ladies, and wits like Touchstone are suppressed, the oppression (as Alexander Leggatt suggests) 'is not a matter of whips and jackboots, but something more attuned to the spirit of the play—a stifling of genuine fun, and a crude idea of what constitutes sport.'" Having suggested that the general atmosphere is not comic but oppressive, the reviewer goes on to point out that the acting also lacks appropriate verve: "This Rosalind's comic sense was neither freewheelingly extravagant, nor sensuously arresting. It was forced out with little music. Of wit there was little, and of androgyny none" (*Journal of Canadian Studies,* 18 (1983–84), 150–51). The harshness of these remarks—at one point Rosalind is referred to as "mustachioed, . . . which did everything for the cause of depilators but nothing for Shakespeare's witty heroine"—indicate the reviewer is offended. This overtly political or ideological production runs contrary to the reviewer's belief as to what is appropriate for *As You Like It.*

But political and ideological interests are not always at war with the interests of histrionics. Jeanne Addison Roberts sets out to demonstrate that comic actresses of the eighteenth century have been neglected and over-shadowed by actors and male-centered scholarship. On the contrary, Roberts asserts: "I will argue that the emergence of first-rate actresses who were neither dependent courtesans nor social pariahs but affluent and respected professionals was an unprecedented development in the social history of women: that these actresses, truly extraordinary individuals, would have found in the spirited, self-reliant heroines of Shakespearean comedy roles that expressed their characters much more fully than did the limp tearful ladies of popular comedies. These actresses unquestionably had the power to influence repertory choices: and, in both private and stage roles, their influence on the theatre public, male as well as female, was significant" (213). Roberts selects Hannah Pritchard, Ketty Clive, and Peg Woffington to illustrate her position. These women as well as others appeared regularly in Shakespearian roles throughout the eighteenth century that were not marked by familiar female stereotypes: "Shakespeare's heroines combine goodness with aggressive intelligence and wit. For eighteenth-century as for Elizabethan audiences, they continued to bridge both class and sex barriers. They pleased the aristocrats with their wit and high spirits, but they also gratified the middle class with their lack of aristocratic pretension" (219). Moreover, Roberts explains, these women playing breeches roles such as Rosalind/Ganymede were recognized as "revolutionary": "I would not deny the [sexual] attraction, but I suggest that a different fascination must have exerted itself far more strongly, not only especially for the female audience, but indeed for all—the revolutionary prospect of actually witnessing a sort of female emancipation acted out with applause in a public place" (223). Peg Woffington as Rosalind is used as a particularly vivid example: "Woffington seems to have found a way, particularly in comedy, of joining her own personal freedom of spirit with projections of stage character so intriguing and irresistible to her audiences that her name virtually guaranteed financial success. . . The winning androgyny of Rosalind suited Woffington well. It seems especially appropriate that her last lines on the stage were the epilogue of *As You Like It* " (225–26). Roberts's analysis of actresses from the eighteenth century implies that these women were able to suggest a kind of female freedom that was revolutionary. Yet, as we have seen, the productions of *As You Like It* during this period were clearly in the pastoral/romance mode, unlike the overtly political version presented in Stratford, Ontario in 1983, the same year as Roberts's essay. How, we are left to wonder, did these eighteenth-century actresses express their revolutionary female views within traditional productions of *As You Like It*?

But not all productions of the 1980s flouted tradition. Orlando's (Alan Rickman) account of Terry Hands's production is quite conventional in many respects. "*As You Like It* was to be a fairy tale. A boy, Orlando, meets a girl, Rosalind, and each falls instantaneously in love with the other" sounds more like what the severe reviewer of the Stratford, Ontario productions would have found more to his liking. In addition to romance, this production seems to have emphasized male physical strength. As the actor who assumed the role of Orlando explains, "the wrestling scene was vital to the production and to my character. Losing weight and visiting a gym three times a week paid dividends. . . . In keeping with the fairy tale idea we had a fight that was reminiscent of professional wrestling at the local town hall between opponents grossly mismatched. It had moments of hilarity mixed with moments of alarming brutality. It was generally at this point that audiences loosened up and sometimes joined in. There were often boos, cheers and rounds of applause. At my suggestion we incorporated a move in which I was hurled headlong into the front row of the audience. This often took me out of the vision of upper circles and invariably brought them all to their feet, a reaction an actor rarely achieves in a long career. The front row into which I was hurled often produced reactions most actors never see. Old ladies wielding handbags yelled abuse at Charles and pin-stripe stockbroker types bemoaned the fact that, now the leading actor had killed himself, their ticket money and evening out were lost." This overtly physical element is balanced by one of quiet pathos. "Returning home from the wrestling I was confronted with this tiny old man [Adam] loaded down with several pieces of luggage and a huge two-handed sword, . . . the only weapon the old man could lay his hands on, but one he could hardly lift." The fairy tale element is continued even when Rosalind/Ganymede schools Orlando on courtship conventions. Not for a moment does Orlando recognize Rosalind or believe in her cure for his love: "he doesn't think for a moment that this boy can cure him of his love, but these games may pleasingly pass the time" (*Players of Shakespeare*, 2, 70–74).

Yet Louis Montrose, perhaps the first critic to devote an entire essay to Orlando, does not see romance as the important issue. Montrose begins by distinguishing his approach from the prevalent one at the time. "Harold Jenkins, in his influential essay on the play, writes of 'the inconsequential nature of the action.' . . . If we reverse Jenkins' perspective, we will do justice to Shakespeare's dramaturgy. . . . What happens to Orlando at home is not Shakespeare's contrivance to get him into the forest; what happens to Orlando in the forest is Shakespeare's contrivance to remedy what has happened to him at home." In this way, Montrose announces that an important topic of the play is Orlando's being a victim of primogeniture. Montrose goes on to remind us that a large proportion of the Elizabethan population was made up of younger sons of the gentry and aristocracy who would have identified with the dilemma of Orlando. Furthermore, Shakespeare changes his source, according to Montrose, in order to focus upon the problem of the younger son: "Shakespeare sets himself the problem of resolving the consequences of a conflict between Orlando's powerful assertion of identity—his spiritual claim to be a true inheritor—and the social fact that his is a subordinated and disadvantaged younger son." In *As You Like It* this problem can only be remedied in the forest of Arden where Orlando and Rosalind develop from "an initial situation of oppression and frustration to the threshold of interdependent new identities." In both instances, Shakespeare brings about this change by way of reform of character, the bad Duke amends his ways and the inconsiderate brother rekindles love for his sibling. Montrose emphasizes that Shakespeare skillfully interweaves these two family problems, so that Orlando's reinstatement permits him to marry Rosalind, who can accept his offer now that her father has been restored to his political position. Montrose concludes that Shakespeare did not, as Jenkins and many others of his day assumed, merely use the social and political situation as a pretext for a comedy about romance. On the contrary, Shakespeare, Montrose believes, concludes with a position of social and political significance: "Shakespeare's play neither preaches to youths nor incites them to riot. In the world of its Elizabethan audience, the form of Orlando's mastery of adversity could also provide support and encouragement to the ambitious individuals who identified with his plight. The play may have fostered strength and perseverance as much as it facilitated pacification and escape" (29–53). While Montrose attempted to demonstrate that in *As You Like It* Shakespeare both reflected and shaped Elizabethan social and political doctrines, stage productions during the 1980s did not use Orlando to portray this point.

Even the more innovative productions that appeared along with traditional, romantic productions like Hands's version did not pursue the social, political dilemma of Orlando. For instance, Nicholas Hytner's 1986 production is assessed in terms of charm: "Di Seymour's designs are ably seconded by Jeremy Sams' music when it comes to charm; and charm there certainly is" (*Plays and Players*, No. 390, 35). But in the same journal Adrian Noble's production staged at the Royal Shakespeare, Stratford is taken to task for rewriting the text: "*Does thou think, because thou art Jungian, there shall be no more lakes and dales,*" David Nathan asks at the outset and then goes on to explain: "They may talk of country matters in Adrian Noble's production but it is the forest itself that is banished. Where the text says trees there are no trees; where the text avers that Rosalind is taller than Celia who is, in fact, smaller, where the text declares that there is no clock in the forest one stands there, greenly mouldering among the rest of the court furniture in the ducal attic that stands in for Arden. For Arden is a state of mind, the director has discovered, quoting Jung to prove it; and the wicked duke and the banished duke are played by the same actor. . . . But it was the state of Shakespeare's mind that they reflected, a state that a director may augment, clarify or interpret, but which brooks no replacement." For Nathan the most telling violation of the text is in the rendering of Rosalind in breeches: "No Rosalind has ever looked masculine since actresses were invented and probably not before either. This is a good thing. But, oh the lost ambiguity when Rosalind is not given even the chance of make-believe and Juliet Stevenson's costume of white slacks and red braces gives the lie direct to her talk of doublet and hose" (*Plays and Players*, No. 380, 24).

Here for the first time we have appearing in print within a few years of this review Juliet Stevenson's own assessment of her role as Rosalind. A brief comparison may prove constructive. In conversation with Fiona Shaw (Celia) that was published in 1988, Juliet Stevenson begins by explaining that the casting of Celia as taller than Rosalind was part of an attempt to force "the audience to abandon any preconceptions about [such feminine stereotypes as] 'the tall skinny one and the little dumpy one.'" For this same reason, Stevenson continues, modern dress was chosen: "To liberate Shakespeare's women from the confines of literary and theatrical tradition requires an analysis of the nature and effects of those social structures which define and contain them." As the two female leads studied the play in these terms they discovered that the dominance of fathers and no mention of mothers presented a "world totally dominated by the male principle and its attendant values, a world in which we are shortly to see that the prevalent idea of a good time is to watch a wrestler bashing hell out of three young men and going for his fourth when he's killed them." Arden is accordingly seen as a metaphor: "The play is so clearly not a rural *romp*, and Shakespeare's description of the forest bears no relation to the familiar or recognisable—it is a 'desert' and 'uncouth'" While unable to articulate precisely what this version of Arden is meant to represent, the core of the drama remains for these actresses a form of love. Rosalind's falling in love before Celia causes some difficulty for the friends but not for long because love is seen as a form of education: "if love is an education then [Rosalind's] is now informing her with insight, wisdom, and a capacity to measure the inner person, as illustrated in her scene with Jaques." Once Celia has found her love, Rosalind is free to take over the conclusion of the drama, becoming a kind of ring-master, who unites the couples and the various elements of the comedy: "She is now both man and woman, in a way, and as such can transcend reality to become a creature of magic who brings a god to her wedding" (57–70).

In some respects, the contrast between the reviewer and the actress could hardly be more polar, yet both seem to accept that the play resolves itself with the notion of the power of love. The problem for the reviewer is not Stevenson but Arden: "Miss Stevenson battles valiantly to impose her will upon the play as she is entitled, indeed, required to do, but the production is against her" (*Plays and Players*, No 380 [May 1985], 24). For Stevenson, the fact that Arden is not literal but metaphoric provides her with the freedom to create her own being and in the end to control the play by way of the mask of Hymen. While Stevenson endorses Noble's removal of a traditional Arden and of female stereotypes, the reviewer believes that this constitutes what he calls violation of the text. Yet the text, particularly that of *As You Like It*, which, so far as we know, took its present form after Shakespeare's death, is always elusive. I would suggest that the question raised here is more appropriately formulated in generic terms. Does Stevenson's Rosalind, a woman who educates herself by way of courtship and then at the end takes over the courtship ritual of her companions, belong in this kind of play—whatever we call it, pastoral or anti-pastoral, romance or anti-romance, or anything else? Or did Noble in altering Arden actually change the genre of *As You Like It*?

In this regard, it is interesting to consider that the actor, Alan Rickman, who played Jaques in this same production was unable to answer the following question about his role: "the ex-head of the English department at my old school . . . had sent a card saying 'How are you getting on with Jaques? I always thought he was an old bore.' He was coming to my dressing room at the same time as a young 'A' level student who wanted me to answer questions for her theatre-studies project. 'Did I see Jaques as anything more than a self-indulgent cynic?' There must be fifty years between those two questions but Jaques seems to have been imprisoned by teachers', pupils' and audiences' preconceptions as much as by those of Duke Senior. I just wanted to let him out" (79–80). This Jaques either cannot or will not resolve the seeming contradictions in Jaques as a character. For Rickman as an actor the character seems to work on the stage if the actor is given the freedom to express him. Ironically, this position is reminiscent of nineteenth-century critics who took the opposite view but for the same reason, preferring to read the drama rather than to witness the stage presentation in the belief that acting constricted the free expression of character. Judging from the responses of Fiona Shaw, Juliet Stevenson, and Alan Rickman, Noble's production removed all restrictions on the free expression of Celia, Rosalind, and Jaques. Nevertheless, the question of the previous century returns but now in a somewhat modified form: are the characters of the play more important than the play itself, particularly when character is developed from the point of view of the individual's position in the gender and political/social hierarchy?

Ironically, although the actresses of Noble's production playing the roles of Celia and Rosalind feel a freedom from the conventional gender hierarchy, Peter Erickson, writing also in 1985, believes that in the end *As You Like It* reasserts a traditional, conservative position. The editor reprinting Erickson's essay points out that the "older tradition" that viewed *As You Like It* as the quintessential "romantic comedy with a charming, witty heroine and handsome hero escaping the pressures of an oppressive court and finding, after a suitable maturation, true love and marriage," still persists alongside a newer position. "The pastoral mode was (and perhaps remains) the fantasy of an urban ruling class, unwilling to give up its power but aware of destroying something seemingly more natural in the process." Erickson argues that the undermining of the gender hierarchy in *As You Like It* has been exaggerated. When Rosalind/Ganymede teases Orlando about the wife's power to cuckold her husband it is only teasing and nothing more. "It is clear to the audience, if not yet to Orlando, that Rosalind's flaunting of herself as disloyal wife is a put-on rather than a genuine threat. She may playfully delay the final moment when she becomes a wife, but we are reassured that, once married, she will in fact be faithful." Here and elsewhere in the disguised courtship, "Rosalind," according to Erickson, "submits not only to two individual men [the Duke and Orlando] but also to the patriarchal society that they embody. Patriarchy is not a slogan smuggled in from the twentieth century and imposed on the play but an exact term for the social structure that close reading reveals within the play." Erickson goes on to point out that Orlando's rightful place in the society is provided by a male and that if females have had any power it is temporary, a moment in what Barber called the celebration of "Saturnalian" misrule. In conclusion, Erickson asks, "what is Shakespeare's relation to the sexual politics of *As You Like It*? Is he taking an ironic and critical stance toward the patriarchal solution of his characters or is he heavily invested in this solution himself?" Erickson replies by affirming that some subversion is present in Jaques's commentary, but it is outweighed by the "defensive action against female power" and the "idealized vision of the relationship between men" (22–37). Given this view of the drama as a whole as being conservative on the matter of gender hierarchies, it is not surprising that Noble discarded Arden in order to give free rein to Fiona Shaw and Juliet Stevenson. But then again we are left to wonder how did eighteenth-century actresses, as Roberts demonstrates, feel a similar sense of liberation within a traditional presentation of Arden?

During this period, a scholar examined theatre in the provinces. We now know that *As You Like It* was popular not only in the second half of the eighteenth century but also throughout the nineteenth century and, thanks to the research of Arnold Hare, not only in London but also in other large British cities. Since a major portion of the audience during the Victorian period was female, what did they appreciate in the play? Hare demonstrates that by the mid-Victorian period provincial audiences were becoming more sophisticated because of regular visits from London companies and because the local productions were improving. In Bath, for instance, during the 1836–37 season Charles Kean arrived and played Richard III, Othello, Hamlet, Macbeth, Shylock, and Lear. In fact, the "only totally local company production in that season was *As You Like It*" (261). In short, it was so popular that, although no visiting star took any role, the local talent decided to take its chance against London names like Kean and Dowton in a production of *As You Like It*. Are we safe to assume that the women in the audience continued to insist upon and enjoy performances of this comedy that reaffirmed their subordinate position in the gender hierarchy?

But even the issue of the gender hierarchy is not agreed upon by the audience of Noble's production. While Anne Marie Drew finds it quite clear that "Rosalind's transformation represents the split-self that results when women are forced to live in a world dominated by men" (101), the *Shakespeare Survey* reviewer sees something else: "Juliet Stevenson's Rosalind was touching in her vulnerable moments but desperately unsure when she was required to be witty, flirtatious or high-spirited. It may be that this gifted actress is (like so many gifted actresses) not a comedienne" (200). It is possible that the difference between these two reviewers is attributable to gender: the female sees Rosalind's dilemma as a function of a sexist culture while the other, presumably a male, finds fault with the actress. But once again we see the question of genre, whether or not Stevenson is a comedienne, in the context of the issue of gender ideology.

Gender was also a consideration in an essay on crossdressing. Jean Howard demonstrates that the authorities of Shakespeare's era were concerned about crossdressing, an interest that related to issues pertinent to gender. "I suggest that these worries about the unruly crossdressed woman, as well as the various means of control devised to contain the threat she constituted, are signs . . . that early modern England was not only permeated by well-documented social mobility and unsettling economic change, but by considerable instability in the gender system as well." Howard focuses in *As You Like It* upon Rosalind's epilogue and its complicated gender masks and allusions. After admitting that Rosalind's crossdressing in the main body of the comedy ultimately reinforces the traditional gender hierarchy, particularly Rosalind's fainting at the sight of the bloody handkerchief, Howard sees the epilogue as making a different point. "If a boy can so successfully personate the voice, gait, and manner of a woman, how stable are those boundaries separating one sexual kind from another, and thus how secure are those powers and privileges assigned to the hierarchically superior sex, which depends upon notions of difference to justify its dominance? The Epilogue playfully invites this question" (425–35). Howard believes that this role-playing represents an "enabling" act for women, but it is not clear in the context of *As You Like It* what it enables Rosalind and the other women in the comedy to do. Leah Marcus, in *Puzzling Shakespeare*, identifies this procedure with Queen Elizabeth. "The dramatic construct of a boy clothed as a woman, an altogether credible woman, who then expands her identity through male disguise in a such a way as to mirror the activities which would be appropriate to her actual, hidden male identity—that construct precisely replicates visually the composite self-image Queen Elizabeth created over and over again through language. She showed herself a woman on the stage of public life—and she liked to call it that—but with a male identity, her princehood, underlying her obvious femininity and lending her authority, offering the subliminal promise of growth into kingship as a boy actor would grow into a man" (101). But what enabled Queen Elizabeth to cross genders may not have been extended to her subjects; indeed, such freedom could have been closely guarded as the exclusive prerogative of the sovereign. Rosalind is clearly constricted by her context; crossdressing as an enabling act would have to be located in that specific situation.

And even those involved in the staging of *As You Like It* who continue to believe that Rosalind is the center of the comedy admit that the situation surrounding Rosalind is crucial. An interesting document of this sort, concerning the staging of *As You Like It* appeared in 1988, Harcourt Williams's *Four Years at the Old Vic*. His remarks on *As You Like It* help us see and understand how the Old Vic Company presented the play during this period. "This play stands or falls by Rosalind. Martita Hunt's capacity for making what she says ring true was admirably suited to the part, and, to my thinking, she gave an altogether delightful, boyish performance. But she just lacked that touch of the pretty-pretty which the sentimental like to see in the part." Williams implies that audiences of the 1980s shared with Victorians the belief that Rosalind should have certain traditional or stereotypical feminine characteristics. Arden also, according to Williams, is subject to audience limitations. "The Forest of Arden is something of a problem to the designer. The 'realistic' wood is bound to be a failure, and yet a decorative set made out of 'stock' presents considerable difficulties. Gielgud suggested that we should have a triangular scene, and with the assistance of low rostrums and few tree-trunks Paul devised a very pleasant set with distances of undulating country not entirely uncultivated; the assumption being that Messrs. Corin, Silvius, Audrey, William and Co., Farmers, did not limit their activities to love-making and gossip, but occasionally indulged in agricultural pursuits. An open air, fresh atmosphere was certainly achieved" (58–59).

A compromise between the literal and the metaphoric seems to work well on the stage. In fact the problem with a more realistic wood is demonstrated by an account of an earlier production that included a herd of deer. The deer were controlled by "a sinister-looking half-caste . . . with a paper-bag of bread." The director decided that he would like to have the deer surrounding Orlando, who was played by Williams. "The curtain rose, but unfortunately the beasts took my crackly paper of verses for another paper-bag of bread and began to chase Orlando, looking as heroic as he could in the circumstances, round the stage. His heroism was further strained when a stentorian voice reached him from the wings: 'Mind the big beggar don't bite ye.' And the word was not 'beggar'" (191–92). Clearly the evolution to the modern stage version of Arden has its practical side, as it must on the stage. The set needs to signify a pastoral, fresh-air atmosphere without making the actors and actresses look ridiculous. Indeed, Noble admitted in an interview that his controversial sheet used to suggest a highly metaphoric form of Arden also caused a practical problem: "We wanted something that was genuinely plastic, that would change shape according to what the actors did, according to the moment in the play, because the Forest of Arden in *As You Like It* changes shape, dimension, character, according to the perception of each person. At one point it's a friendly place with bunny rabbits, at another point it's a dangerous place with lions. And we thought we had the solution. The problem was that while physically it was a bit dangerous, the actors would never know what it was going to do next, which meant that you would walk into the wings during that production and continually see the actors anxiously peering on to the stage to see how they were going to make their entrance. Not how they were going to do that scene or what their character was feeling like, but physically how they were going to get downstage, which is the kind of worry you don't want" (see Philips, 163–64). The practical element cannot be avoided by those interested in Shakespeare's artistry at any level, for an actress or actor tripping on a sheet can do little to further either a metaphoric or realistic Arden.

But the practical limitations of the stage do allow for wide differences of presentation even for a single producer. In this respect, Robin Philips speaks perceptively to Ralph Berry about his second staging of *As You Like It*. His first production had been one of the few of his own productions that he had liked; hence there was much anxiety about trying to do it again. In the earlier version, Maggie Smith played Rosalind with "aching beauty and wisdom" to a younger Orlando who was taught and guided towards love. Fortunately, in the new production an entirely different relationship emerged. Nancy Palk "discovered freedom in disguise . . . [and] stepped into her own enlightenment and self-discovery" (153). The practical limitations of the stage still permit a wide latitude of interpretation.

Nevertheless, pastoral presents particular difficulties, as J. C. Bulman reminds us in an account of the making of the 1979 BBC television version of *As You Like It*. "In principle, pastoral poses problems for producers of Shakespeare. In both ethos and form, pastoral is highly artificial: it signifies retreat to an ideal; it is a state of mind. At its most romantic . . . the green world is a world of play and game, not a place where shepherds tend sheep and maidens milk goats; at its most political, . . . it depicts an allegorical world of good government" (174–75). And television made special demands, relating to the person in charge, Cedric Messina, who characterized the audience as "unused to modern theatrical productions and nurtured instead on films shot 'on location' [and] skeptical of stage conventions." Since Messina insisted on the use of Glamis Castle, the producer, Basil Coleman had to resort to "alienation" effects in order to avoid such literalist questions as how could Orlando beat a professional wrestler or why is Orlando unable to see that Ganymede is really Rosalind. Coleman, according to Bulman, uses a number of devices that strain our credulity. "Orlando, for one thing, is rather slight and understated: his defeat of the wrestler Charles is patently absurd. And Helen Mirren's Rosalind, buxom and beautiful, is clearly no male Ganymede." And while there are real sheep in this version, when Touchstone answers the question "how like you this shepherd's life," he steps in sheep dung. Finally the mask of Hymen is deliberately contrived: "Hymen is neither god nor rustic. He is a fey figure dressed in gossamer—a ballet skirt, with a laurel wreath about his temples— who looks vaguely like a young man painted on a Greek vase" (177).

Bulman finally gets to the point of Coleman's production when he discusses Jaques: "Jaques's satiric perspective sets the tone for much of the production. Take as a final instance, his farewell in Act 5. . . . He then [after the mask] begins a slow exit up the hill that Hymen has earlier descended; and the camera, placed where the group of lovers stand, follows him up. But when the Duke bids the couples to 'proceed, proceed' with their dance, the camera suddenly spies them from atop the hill—from the very position in which Jaques has just stood. We regard them as he does, looking down on them as they form a circle" (179). These fools in love intent on "love and game," by implication, are unaware of the other side of Arden, the problem of "good government." Yet Bulman admits that he does not regard this version of *As You Like It* as a successful production: "it is far too dark and self-conscious to do justice to the spirit of festive comedy" (179). Thus even an apologist for this politically aware, if not correct, television production is not satisfied with this interpretation of the play. Ironically Arden literalized with a herd of deer is as much of a problem as Arden metaphorized with Adrian Noble's sheets. A herd of deer chasing Orlando is too much but so too is an actress tripping on the sheets.

Nevertheless, scholarship and stage experience are not always distinct. Glynne Wickham argues that *As You Like It* is the most likely candidate for the sequel to *Love's Labour's Lost* on the evidence of both scholarship and stage experience. Based upon a scholarly analysis of the source for *Love's Labour's Lost*, Wickham believes that the comedy was presented at the beginning of the twelve-day feast of Christmas, a belief confirmed by his experience as director of a production. "Directing [*Love's Labour's Lost*] for a third time this summer (1986) in an open air production at the University of the South, Sewanee, Tennessee, I was struck by other peculiarities in this text that, once again, help as I believe to unravel the mystery of how this highly sophisticated play first came to be written and performed" (210–211). This play's emphasis upon the contrast between winter and spring strongly suggests, to Wickham, the need to link this festive comedy with another one. "If this premise is granted, then the Princess's choice of a year and a day as the penitential period to be imposed upon Navarre before he may challenge her by his gift of diamonds to marry him not only ceases to be arbitrary and whimsical but fixes the date of the calendar festival in question as New Year's Eve, of Twelfth Night" (211).

Moving on then to speculation about the sequel, the supposed *Love's Labour's Won*, Wickham again combines scholarship and stage experience: "This is a view I have reached while directing [*As You Like It*] for the Hartke Theatre in Washington, D.C. Both *Love's Labour's Lost* and *As You Like It* share predominantly woodland settings. In the latter, here again most strikingly we find the four girls and four young men . . . all . . . love's victims and love's prisoners, [and] love's labors are finally won for all eight of them" (214). As a producer and scholar, Wickham assumes that *As You Like It* is a play about love, and seeing it as a sequel to *Love's Labour's Lost* and performed with it at the same Christmas festival obviates one of the major difficulties of the end of *As You Like It*. Since 1765 when Johnson first complained about the speed with which Celia and Oliver seal their love pact, directors and critics have contemplated this question, but Wickham believes that the original audience was not troubled with this question because they understood that Shakespeare (although using different names for his characters and varying the story and situation) was referring to a relationship begun in *Love's Labour's Lost*.

THE 1990S: GENDER AND GENRE: SELF-CORRECTIVE CATEGORIES

Traditional productions based upon assumptions, like that of Wickham, continue but do not prevent some important innovations of the 1990's. For instance, at Stratford, Ontario during the 1990/91 season a version of *As You Like It* was set in Quebec: "The program gave the time as "the late fall of 1758" and the place as "in and around Quebec City and on L'ile d'Orleans outside Quebec City. . . . In those days, moreover, the slippery treachery of the seat of government had not yet seeped into the woods. In unlogged Arden, amity prevailed not only among the outlaws themselves but in the association with the natives of the place. One would hardly expect the stage picture to accommodate representatives of the two thousand old 'panis,' or Indian slaves, owned by the colonists of New France at the time, but the production's decorative use of 'Indians' was excessively trite" (*Journal of Canadian Studies*, 25 [1990–91]: 131). The reviewer goes on to complain that the "big parts" have been ruthlessly pared down in order to focus upon the political dilemma of the Canadian indigenes. Since the reviewer makes plain that he regards this production as heavy-handed, it is not clear whether or not a subtler version of this alteration of the subject from love to politics would have been acceptable.

During this period, a female critic questions whether the comedy warrants a politically subversive interpretation. Camille Paglia points to generic constraints in distinguishing between Shakespeare's portrayal of androgyny in the sonnets and in the comic dramas: "Shakespeare's transvestite comedies address a public issue and take a liberal position on it. Unlike Botticelli, who allowed Savonarola to destroy his pagan style, Shakespeare never yielded to Puritan pressure. In fact there is a turn toward decadence rather than away from it in his Jacobean plays. Shakespeare continued to believe in sexual personae as a mode of self-definition. This theme is treated in different ways in his two principal genres. His sonnets circulated in manuscript among an aristocratic coterie of Apollonian exclusiveness. But the plays were for the mixed social classes of the Globe Theatre, the democratic 'Many' whom Plutarch identified with Dionysius. Hence the psychic metamorphoses of Shakespeare's androgynes were in analogy to the rowdy pluralism of his audience" (207). In the public situation of the theatre, Shakespeare was unable to be subversive without thwarting his audience's expectations. So Rosalind is a conservative woman: "Her own darting wit is this gusty draft in the closed household of Renaissance womanhood" (208–09). Even at the end when Rosalind takes control, Shakespeare avoids subversion of gender and other hierarchies: "Her hierarchically most commanding moment is paradoxically the one where she ritually lays aside her hermaphroditism to take up the socialized persona of obedient wife to Orlando" (211). Yet, Paglia concludes, "Shakespeare's view of woman is revolutionary. Unlike Belphoebe or Britomart, Rosalind has a jovial inner landscape . . . [which] is airy and pleasant, full of charm and surprise. . . . [Her] eye is truly perceptive: it both sees and understands. Shakespeare's great heroine unites multiplicity of gender, persona, word, eye, and thought" (212). Paglia implies that Rosalind is an advancement over Spenser's Belphoebe in that while the demonic eye of Spenser's female burns and seeks power, "the fascism of nature," Rosalind sees in order to understand. The liberty in intelligence advocated here by Paglia is not wholly clear, but what is clear is that Rosalind's ability to manipulate within established norms is valued as educational.

By contrast, Susanne Wofford and Michael Shapiro specify more clearly the implications of Rosalind's gender roles. Wofford argues that "the erotic performance of Rosalind/Ganymede as Rosalind seems to ward off several threats to her promised union with Orlando. Given the allusion to the Ganymede story in her self-naming as male, readers have responded to the not-so-submerged homoerotics of her performance as marking one such threat. The enactment of a homosexual wooing scene . . . may thus seem to ward off, by representing it, the danger that either lover might actually be attracted to the 'wrong' sex and thus make the comic conclusions of marriage impossible" (156). Shapiro believes that "once Rosalind is in male attire, the play makes many . . . references to her concealed feminine identity. . . . On Shakespeare's stage, these oscillations became even more dazzling in the light of spectators' dual consciousness of the boy actor producing all of these abrupt shifts. These multiple layers of identity and the swift movements from one to another produced a theatrical vibrancy that engaged audiences in the illusion that an amalgam constructed of multiple and discrete layers of identity represented a unified character" (126). While not overtly subversive, both of these analyses suggest how gender role-playing can threaten the traditions and institutions of the political establishment.

In their increasing interest in the staging devices of Shakespeare's day, theatre people seem to join with Paglia in feeling sceptical about or lacking interest in subversive politics in *As You Like It*. Alan Dessen analyzes simultaneous staging in the Elizabethan period, a technique which suggests that Shakespeare's audience might have seen at once the courtly feast and the thirsty Adam. This spectacle would deemphasize the social and political differences here, since the audience knows that help is literally at hand (152–53). And Susan Willis interviews a producer who points out that some modern versions often are "more about Mother Nature than about Rosalind, Orlando, or the dukes" (188). In 1991, Jan Kott pointed out in an interview with Charles Marowitz, itself an intermingling of critic and producer/director, that present-day audiences distrust ideology. "In my lifetime, that's to say since about the end of World War II, there was an ideological and philosophical emphasis on contemporary interpretation in Shakespeare; an emphasis on thematic content, on what these plays mean and should mean to modern audiences. And now because of a certain distrust or disenchantment with ideology, a certain boredom with politics, there is this return to a Shakespeare which is apolitical, non-philosophic, non-ideological" (103).

This position is perhaps clarified in a female reviewer's positive articulation of a cinematic version of *As You Like It* directed by a woman. Arden has been thoroughly modernized but not completely deprived of love: "Christine Edzard's *As You Like It* convincingly places the play in a contemporary context by turning the Forest of Arden into an urban wasteland in Rotherhithe and the Court into a generic City institution. . . . It undermines contemporary 'back to nature' nostalgia just as the original mocked the idealising conventions of pastoral drama. On the other hand, the film shows with relish the easy ability of the banished duke and his courtiers to adjust to their enforced exile and to enjoy the benefits of this new outlook on life." The reviewer goes on to juxtapose love and the wasteland by pointing out that Celia's part is expanded so that her capacity to engage in witty repartee is in evidence in her "putting love to the test with tomboyish abandon," all within sight of a city setting of "the ethos of post-Thatcherism." Jaques is given his part but it is only part of a larger whole: "offering the familiar speech, 'The world's a stage,' unaccented, as a prologue, Edzard signals that the film will work through doubles and reflections." The conclusion, not surprisingly, is also doubled: Edzard "juxtaposes the 'happy ending' of the lovers' embrace with Jaques's departure and the question of the forest, as she began with Jaques's arrival and the question of roles. . . . Jaques—who worries about defacing trees and hunting animals, who observes the harmony of the lovers with wistfulness and admires Touchstone, 'the fool'—walks away over the bridge in the background, continuing to seek in exile the home of the self" (*Sight and Sound* NS 2 (Oct. 1992), 45). Individual liberty is understandably limited in this world of corruption and yuppiedom: the dilemma of the wise and witty females, like Celia and Rosalind, is not different in kind from that of Jaques. Both are seriously limited, although the women are capable of love and being loved. The problem of female personal freedom is only one manifestation of the dilemma of any wise and caring person in this cultural context.

In 1993, research on performances of Shakespeare in Birmingham between 1913 and 1920 revealed that the provinces were more sophisticated as audiences than had been anticipated. The dramatic critics writing for the *Birmingham Daily Post* called for a balance between wit and affection in Rosalind and between satire and melancholy in Jaques that is now coming back into favor. In 1914, for instance, Jaques was commended for "an effective middle way between rhetoric and melodramatic bitterness" (Cochran, 52). And the balance required of the female leads is suggested by the fact that Sophie Thompson who had earlier played Celia now was cast as Rosalind in John Caird's production at the Royal Shakespeare Theatre in 1989 and at the Barbican in 1990.

Sophie Thompson, in *Players of Shakespeare 3,* relates her experiences in the role of Rosalind and how it was affected by her previous rendition of Celia. In this particular production Rosalind explains that Arden, although a "fairy-tale place," has "an edge to it": lovely leaves fall to the soft piano music but they are dead leaves. This doubleness is maintained by Rosalind who "knows about her double nature—as Ganymede and herself" even though Orlando is operating on one level taking she/he as she presents herself. Again Jaques shares a doubleness with Rosalind: "Rosalind had a strong sense of melancholy in her" (83). The experience of having played Celia before suggests how many possibilities the play contains, different paths that could be pursued, like the distinction between the production in which Thompson played Celia as opposed to the present one. And to leave the audience with the manifold possibilities in the drama, Rosalind delivers the epilogue, as if Orlando were about to speak, but choked up, and his wife comes to his aid. The audience should "understand now that love isn't all romance, and that you have to work at it every single day" (85). Thompson suggests that equal but different forms of self-expression resulted from her roles as Celia and Rosalind, for the sense of self and of a distinctly female self results from doing the most with one's limited resources and from within a context, the drama as whole, that imposes other limitations. (For a more detailed account of productions during the period 1991–1995, see Jamieson, pages 645–47).

I conclude this survey with an essay of Margaret Maurer's that has not been published before. Maurer demonstrates how Charles Johnson's *Love in a Forest* forecloses upon some of the various possibilities that are richly embedded in *As You Like It.* Understandably in an eighteenth-century context, particularly in view of Pope's recent edition of the comedy, restricting the variousness of *As You Like It* enabled the playwright to clarify a number of difficult matters, both from a critical and staging standpoint. But in the end Maurer returns to her own childhood and by extension to that of her daughter to explain how she was first drawn to Shakespeare's play, as a scholar and as an amateur actress. Recognizing that attempts to represent the drama as a women's liberation document must neglect important aspects of the drama, those historical and gender constrictions that were the mark of the British Renaissance, she nonetheless still feels drawn to *As You Like It* for reasons that she can now articulate: "the play's essential conceit . . . is usually open to anything those who play with it can imagine, finally all but indifferent to what is or what should be" (509).

Feminine and feminist criticism have helped us to see that gender constraints are no different from generic constraints: we must struggle against them and do change and modify them but could not express ourselves without resort to a radical of presentation. *As You Like It* plays such sophisticated games with genres, intermingling them in delightful and surprising ways, and at the same time developing characters who continue to fascinate us as much now as at any other time in its nearly four-hundred-year critical history. If we can now accept that there is no essential Rosalind, Celia, Jaques, Touchstone, and Orlando and that with the loss of the essence of being goes the old sexual and gender categories, then we need to keep in mind that such a radical concept is represented and communicated in a comedy, a genre that itself is changing and historicized. Genre then becomes not an essentialized category or set of absolutized rules, but a means of questioning all absolutes including theories of generic essence, or what one philosopher has called the law of genre. Doesn't *As You Like It* succeed, as it has for nearly four centuries, because it flouts and satirizes by making us laugh at such laws, even such a concept as the law of genre?

WORKS CITED

Athenaeum. January 1885; July, 1890.

Barber, C. L. *Shakespeare's Festive Comedy: a Study of Dramatic Form and Its Relation to Social Custom.* Princeton: Princeton U Press, 1959.

Barnet, Sylvan. "'Strange Events': Improbability in *As You Like It.*" *Shakespeare Studies,* 4 (1968).

Barton, Anne. "*As You Like It* and *Twelfth Night*: Shakespeare's Sense of an Ending." *Shakespearian Comedy*, Eds. David Palmer and Malcolm Bradbury. Stratford-upon-Avon studies 14. London: Edward Arnold, 1972.

Berry, Ralph. "No Exit from Arden." *Modern Language Review*, 66 (1970), 11–20. Reprinted in *Shakespeare's Comedies: Explorations in Form.* Princeton: Princeton U Press, 1972.

Birch, William J. *An Inquiry into the Philosophy and Religion of Shakspere.* London: C. Mitchell, 1848.

B.J.K. *Remarks on Shakespeare's Versification.* London: C. Mitchell, 1857.

Brandes, Georg. *William Shakespeare: a Critical Study.* Tr. William Archer, Mary Morison, & Diana White. London, 2 vols. 1898. (Orig. Danish ed., 3 vols, Copenhagen, 1895–6).

Brereton, Austin. *The Stage Shakespeare: "As You Like It."* London: William Collins, 1904.

Brissenden, Alan. Ed. *The World's Classics: "As You Like It."* Oxford: Oxford U Press, 1994.

Brown, Charles A. *Shakespeare's Autobiographical Poems.* London: James Bohn, 1838.

Brown, Ivor. *Shakespeare.* New York: Doubleday, 1949.

Bulman, J. C. *"As You Like It:* and the Perils of Pastoral." in *Shakespeare on Television*, Eds. J. C. Bulman, and H. R. Coursen. Hanover, N.H.: University Press of New England, 1988.

Campbell, Thomas. *The Dramatic Works of William Shakespeare.* London: W. S. E. Moxon. 1838.

Cann, Alfred L. *Shakespeare's "As You Like It."* London. 1902.

Capell, Edward. *Notes and Various Readings to Shakespeare.* London, Vol. 1, 1779.

Carrington, James. *The Modern Receipt or a Cure for Love,* London, 1739.

Chew, Samuel. "This Strange Eventful History." *John Quincy Adams Memorial Shorts.* Washington, D.C.: The Folger Library, 1948.

Cochran, Clare. *Shakespeare and the Birmingham Rep Theatre: 1913–1929.* London, 1993.

Coleridge, Hartley. *Essays and Marginalia.* Ed. Derwent Coleridge. London: Edward Moxon, 2 vols., 1851.

Coleridge, Samuel Taylor. *Coleridge's Shakespeare Criticism.* Ed. Thomas Middleton Raysor. 2 vols. London, 1960.

Collier, J. Payne. *The Works of William Shakespeare.* London: Whittaker, 1842. Vol. 3.

Craig, Hardin. "Shakespeare's Bad Poetry." *Shakespeare Survey* 1 (1948).

David, Richard. "The Comedies." *The Living Shakespeare.* Ed. Robert Gittings. London: Heinemann, 1960, pp. 84–98.

De Banke, Cecile. *Shakespeare and Stage Productions Then and Now.* London: Hutchinson, 1954, pp. 106–21.

Dessen, Alan. "Taint Not thy Mind—Problems and Pitfalls in Staging Plays at the Globe." in *New Issues in the Reconstruction Of Shakespeare's Theatre.* Ed. Franklin J. Hildy. New York: Peter Lang, 1990.

Drake, Nathan. *Shakespeare and His Times.* London: T. Cadell. 1817. Vol. 1.

Dramatic Magazine, II (1830–31).

Drew, Anne Marie. in *Theatre Review.* Vol 39 (1987).

Elsom, John. "Theatre: Rosalind's Lib." *The Listener.* 89 (June 1973).

Empson, William. *Some Versions of Pastoral.* London: Chatto and Windus, 1935.

Erickson, Peter. *Patriarchal Structure in Shakespearian Drama*. Cambridge: Cambridge U Press, 1985.

Examiner, 22 October 1815.

Faucit, Helena. "On Some of Shakespeare's Female Characters: by One Who Has Impersonated Them. VII.—Rosalind." *Blackwood's* 136 (Oct. 1884).

Forker, Charles R. *Fancy's Images: Contexts, Settings, and Perspectives in Shakespeare and His Contemporaries.* Carbondale: Southern Illinois U Press: 1990, pp. 71–8. This chapter first appeared as an essay in the *Iowa State Journal of Research,* 54 (1980), 421–30.

Fowler, Alastair. *Kinds of Literature: An Introduction to the Theory of Genres and Modes.* Princeton: Princeton U Press, 1982.

Freeburg, Victor. *Disguise Plots in Elizabethan Drama. A Study in Stage Tradition.* Columbia University Studies in English and Comparative Literature. New York, 1915.

Frye, Northrop. *Anatomy of Criticism: Four Essays.* Princeton: Princeton U Press, 1957.

Frye, Roland. *Shakespeare and Christian Doctrine,* Princeton U Press, 1963.

Gardner, Helen. "'As You Like It.'" *More Talking of Shakespeare.* Ed. John Garrett. London, 1959.

Gascoigne, Bamber. *The Spectator.* July 14, 1961.

Gentleman, Francis. *The Dramatic Censor; or, Critical Companion.* London, 1770, Vol 1.

Gentleman's Magazine, London, 1741.

Gervinus. George. G. *Shakespeare Commentaries.* Tr. F. E. Bunnett 1875 (1st Ger. ed. Leipzig, 1849–50; 1st ed. of tr., 2 vols, 1863).

Gildon, Charles. *Remarks on the Plays of Shakespear.* In supplementary vol. 7 (1710) of Nicholas Rowe, ed., *The Works of Shakespeare,* London, 6 vols, 1709.

Gordon, George. *Shakespearian Comedy and Other Studies.* Oxford: Oxford U Press: 1944.

Griffith, Mrs. [Elizabeth]. *The Morality of Shakespeare's Drama Illustrated,* London, 1775.

Grindon, Rosa. *Shakespeare & his Plays from a Woman's Point of View.* Manchester: The Policy-Holder Journal Company, 1930.

Halio, Jay. Ed. *Twentieth Century Interpretations of "As You Like It."* Englewood Cliffs, N.J.: Prentice-Hall, 1968.

Halio, Jay L. and Barbara C. Millard. *"As You Like It": An Annotated Bibliography, 1940–1980.* New York: Garland, 1985.

Halliwell, James. *The Complete Works of Shakespeare Illustrated.* London, 1850.

Hare, Arnold. "Shakespeare in a Provincial Stock Company." in *Shakespeare and the Victorian Stage*. Ed. R. Foulkes, Cambridge: Cambridge U Press, 1986.

Hazlitt, William. *Characters of Shakespeare's Plays*. 1817.

Henley, William E. *The Graphic Gallery of Shakespeare's Heroines*. London: Sampson Low, 1888.

Herford, Charles. *Shakespeare*. London: The Peoples's books, 1912.

Horowitz, David. *Shakespeare: an Existential View*. New York: Hill and Wang, 1965.

Howard, Jean E. "Crossdressing, the Theatre, and Gender Struggle in Early Modern England." *Shakespeare Quarterly* 39 (1988).

Hows, John W. S. *As You Like It*. French's Standard Drama, New York, 1846.

Hudson, Henry. *Shakespeare's As You Like It*. Boston: Ginn and Heath. 1867. Vol. 1.

Inchbald, Mrs. [Elizabeth]. Ed. *British Theatre*. London, 1808, Vol 2.

Jameson, Anna B. *Characteristics of Women, Moral, Poetical, and Historical*. 1832.

Jamieson, Michael. "'As You Like It'—Performance and Reception."

Jenkins, Harold. "As You Like It." *Shakespeare Survey* 8 (1955).

Johnson, Charles. *Love in a Forest. A Comedy As it is Acted at the Theatre Royal in Drury-Lane*, London, 1723.

Johnson, Samuel. *The Works of Shakespeare,* London, 1765, Vol. 2.

———. *Life of Milton*, in *The Lives of the Poets*, Ed. George Birkbeck Hill. Clarendon: Oxford University Press, 1905, Vol. 1.

Journal of Canadian Studies. 18 (1983–84); 25 (1990–91).

Kelly, Linda. *The Kemble Era*. London: Bodley Head, 1980.

Kermode, Frank. "The Mature Comedies." *Early Shakespeare*. Eds. John Russell Brown and Bernard Harris. Stratford-upon-Avon Studies, 3. London: Edward Arnold, 1961, pp. 221–27.

Knowles, Richard, Ed. *A New Variorum Edition of Shakespeare: "As You Like It." With a Survey of Criticism by Evelyn Joseph Mattern, IHM*. New York: · The Modern Language Association of America, 1977.

Kolbe, Frederick. *Shakespeare's Way: A Psychological Study*. London: Sheed and Ward, 1930.

Kott, Jan. Interview with Charles Marowitz. *Regarding Shakespeare*. London: Macmillan, 1991.

Kott, Jan. *Shakespeare Our Contemporary*, Tr. Boleslaw Taborski. London: Methuen, 1964.

Latham, Agnes. Ed. *The Arden Shakespeare: "As You Like It."* Routledge: London and New York, 1975.

Latham, Grace. "Rosalind, Celia, and Helen." *New Shakspere Society's Transactions*. 1887–92. [1892].

London Gazette, 18 February 1786.

London Mercury, Vol. 35 (1937), 498–99.

Mack, Maynard. *King Lear in Our Time*. Berkeley: University of California Press, 1965.

The Manchester Guardian, 10 November 1936.

Marcus, Leah S. *Puzzling Shakespeare: Local Reading and Its Discontents*. Berkeley: University of California Press, 1988.

Masefield, John. *William Shakespeare*. London: Williams and Norgate, 1911.

Mattern, Evelyn Joseph. See Knowles, Richard.

Matthews, Brander. *Shakspeare as a Playwright*. New York: Charles Scribner, 1913.

Maurer, Margaret. "Playing the Music in Arden: "'Twas I, But 'Tis not I."

McEwan, Ian. "In Season." *New Statesman*. 98 (10 August 1979).

Montrose, Louis. "'The Place of a Brother' in *As You Like It*: Social Process and Comic Form." *Shakespeare Quarterly* 32 (Spring 1981).

Noble, Richmond. *Shakespeare's Use of Song*. Cambridge: Cambridge U Press, 1923.

Odell, George. *Shakespeare from Betterton to Irving*. New York, 1920, 2 Vols.

Paglia, Camille. *Sexual Personae*. New Haven: Yale University Press. 1990.

Palmer, D. J. "*As You Like It* and the Idea of Play." *Critical Quarterly* 13 (1971).

Pettet, Ernest C. *Shakespeare and the Romance Tradition*. New York: Staples Press, 1949.

Philips, Robin. Interviewed by Berry, Ralph. *On Directing Shakespeare*. London: Hamish Hamilton, 1989.

Plays and Players, no. 380 (May 1985), 24; 390 (March 1986), 35.

Players of Shakespeare. Ed. Philip Brockbank. Cambridge: Cambridge U Press, 1980.

Players of Shakespeare 3. Eds. Russell Jackson and Robert Smallwood, Cambridge: Cambridge U Press, 1993.

Priestley, J. B. "Touchstone." *The English Comic Characters*. London, 1925.

Raffles, Robert. *Introductory Questions on Shakespeare's "As You Like It."* London, 1884.

Richardson, William. *Shakespeare's Dramatic Characters*. London, 1818 (original 1774).

Rickman, Alan. in *Players of Shakespeare, 2*. Eds. Russell Jackson and Robert Smallwood. Cambridge: Cambridge U Press, 1988.

Roberts, Jeanne Addison. "Shakespearean Comedy and Some Eighteenth-Century Actresses." in *Shakespeare: Man of the Theater*. Eds. K. Muir, J.

Halio, D. J. Palmer. Newark: University of Delaware Press, 1983.

Rowe, Nicholas. Vol. 2. See Gildon.

Schoenbaum, Samuel. *Shakespeare's Lives.* Oxford: Oxford U Press, 1991.

Schroeder, Neil R. *"'As You Like It' in the English Theatre 1740–1955."* Yale Univ. Diss., 1962 (DA 29 [1968], 239A).

Seward, Anna. *Letters of Anna Seward.* Edinburgh: 1811, vol, 1, 165–66 (letter dated July 20, 1786).

Shakespeare Survey. Cambridge: Cambridge U Press. 1986. Vol 39.

Shapiro, Michael. *Gender in Play on the Shakespearean Stage: Boy Heroines and Female Pages.* Ann Arbor: University of Michigan Press, 1994.

Shaw, George Bernard. in *Shaw on Shakespeare.* Ed. Edwin Wilson. London: Casell. 1961.

Sight and Sound NS 2 (Oct. 1992), 45.

Sisson, Rosemary Anne. "Glen Byam Shaw's Production and with Peggy Ashcroft's Rosalind." *Stratford-upon-Avon Herald.* 5 April 1957.

Smith, James. "As You Like It," *Scuitiz* 19 (1940).

Snider, Denton. *System of Shakespeare's Dramas.* St. Louis: G. I. Jones, 1877, vol. 2.

Sprague, Arthur Colby. "The Moments of Seriousness in Shakespearian Comedy." *Shakespeare Jahrbuch* (West), 1965.

Stauffer, Donald. *Shakespeare's World of Images: the Development of his Moral Ideas.* New York, 1949.

Stevenson, Juliet. in *Players of Shakespeare, 2* Eds. Russell Jackson and Robert Smallwood. Cambridge: Cambridge U Press, 1988.

Sunday Telegraph, 8 Oct. 1967.

Sunday Times, 9 July 1961.

Terry, Ellen. *The Story of My Life.* London: Hutchinson, 1908.

Theatrical Journal and Musical Intelligencer, III (1842).

Thompson, Peter. "Shakespeare Straight and Crooked: A Review of the 1973 Season at Stratford." *Shakespeare Survey*, 27 (1974).

The Times, 7 February 1786, 23 September 1789, 21 November 1789, 3 October 1842, April 23, 1919.

Tomarken, Edward. *Samuel Johnson on Shakespeare: The Discipline of Criticism*, Athens: University of Georgia Press, 1991.

Trewin, John. *Shakespeare on the English Stage 1900–1965.* London: Random House, 1964.

Ulrici, Hermann. *Shakespeare's Dramatic Art.* Tr. from the 3rd ed. of the Ger. by L Dora Schmitz. 2 vols. OUP, 1916. 1: 311–45.

Wells, Stanley. "Happy Endings in Shakespeare." *Shakespeare Jahrbuch* (West). 1966.

Whiter, William. *A Specimen of a Commentary on Shakespeare.* London, 1794.

Wickham, Glynne. "Reflections Arising from Recent Productions of *Loves Labour's Lost* and *As You Like It*." in *Shakespeare and the Sense of Performance*. Eds. Marvin and Ruth Thomson. Newark: University of Delaware Press, 1989.

Williams, Harcourt. *Four Years at the Old Vic*. London: Putman, 1988.

Willis, Susan. *The BBC Shakespeare Plays*. Chapel Hill: University of North Carolina Press, 1991.

Wofford, Susanne. "'To You I Give Myself, For I Am Yours': Erotic Performance and Theatrical Performatives in *As You Like It*." in *Shakespeare Reread: The Texts in New Contexts* Ed. Russ McDonald. Ithaca: Cornell U Press, 1994, pp. 146–69.

Young, B. A. *Financial Times*. 8 September 1977.

Young, David. *The Heart's Forest: A Study of Shakespeare's Pastoral Plays*. New Haven: Yale U Press, 1972.

THE SEVEN AGES OF MAN
DESCRIBED BY WILLIAM SHAKESPEARE

From a Collection of Prints from Pictures painted for the purpose of illustrating the dramatic works of Shakspeare by the Artists of Great-Britain. Published by John and Josiah Boydell. (London, 1803) Vol. 1: Plates 50–57.

THE INFANT.

THE SCHOOL-BOY.

THE LOVER.

THE SOLDIER.

THE JUSTICE.

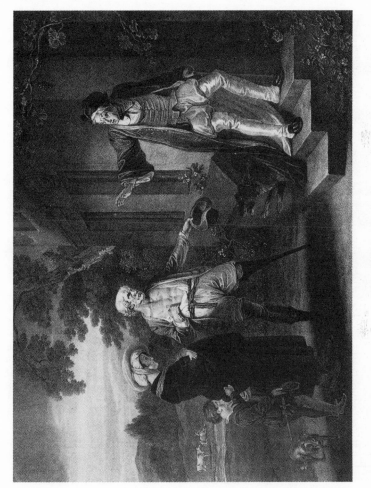

THE PANTALOON.

SECOND CHILDHOOD.

II   CRITICAL ESSAYS

REMARKS ON THE PLAYS OF SHAKESPEAR
Charles Gildon
1710

The Argument of *As you like it.*

Frederick the Duke of some part of *France* is Depos'd, and Banish'd by his younger Brother, and retir'd to the Forrest of *Arden*; many People of Fashion following him thither out of Love to him and Hatred of the Usurper; who retains *Rosalinda* his Brother's Daughter to gratify his own Daughter *Celia*, who Doated on her with a very peculiar Love and Affection. But being, afterwards Jealous of her Popularity banishes her likewise. But his own Daughter flies with her, *Rosalinda* being in Mens Cloaths under the Name of *Ganymede*, and *Celia* in Womans under the Name of *Aliena*. Hither likewise comes *Orlando* the youngest Son of Sir. Rowland *Du-Bois*, fled from his elder Brother's Cruelty and the Usurper's Hate. He wrestling before the Duke kills his Wrestler *Charles*, and wounds the Heart of *Rosalinda* as she did his. But meeting in the Forest he makes Love to her as *Rosalinda*, tho' in appearance a Lad, which Habit betray'd *Phebe*, a Shepherdess to fall likewise in Love with her as a Man, whom she uses scurvily to make her pity Silvius the Swain, that is in Love with her. *Orlando*'s Brother *Oliver* being forc'd to flie from the Rage of the Usurper, because his Brother had made his Escape, is deliver'd from a Lioness by the Valour of *Orlando* whose Life he had before so basely fought, but being thus reconcil'd falls in Love with *Celia* and she with him, so the Marriage being resolv'd on *Rosalinda* or rather then *Ganymede* promises *Orlando* that he shall have his true *Rosalinda* the next Day, and *Phebe*, that she will have her, on condition that if she refuse him she shall marry *Silvius*. Having perform'd all this, and the banish'd Duke having given her to *Orlando*, *Jaques Orlandos* and *Oliver*'s Brother brings News that the Usurper coming with Forces against them, was on the Way converted and gone into a Monastry leaving the Dukedom again to his Brother.

This Story has nothing Dramatic in it, yet *Shakespear* has made as good use of it as possible.

The Scene betwixt *Orlando* and his Brother *Oliver* in the opening of the

Play is well manag'd discovering something, that goes before in the Quarel between them; and *Oliver's* Management of the provoking *Charles* the Wrestler against *Orlando* is artful and natural.

Martial has this Distic–

Quem recitas meus est O! Fidentine! Libellus
Sed male dum recitas incipite esse tuus.

I will not say that *Shakespear* took the following Thought from this, but it is plainly the same. *Orlando* says to *Jaques*—*I pray thee mar no more of my Verses by reading them ill favour'dly.* The old Dukes Speech preferring that Solitude to the World is full of moral Reflections. *Now my Co-mates, and Brothers in Exile,* &c. The third Scene of the Second Act betwixt *Orlando* and *Adam* moving by the Gratitude of the old Servant is that fine Speech of *Jaques* taken notice of by Mr. *Rowe* in *Shakespear's* Life. That Pleasantry of the different Motion of Time is worth remarking. And *Rosalinda's* Character of a Man in Love is very pretty.

On the several sorts of Melancholy.

Jaques. I have neither the *Scholars* Melancholy, which is Emulation; nor the *Musicians,* which is Fantastical; nor the *Courtiers,* which is Proud: nor the *Soldiers,* which is Ambitious: nor the *Lawyers* which is Political: nor the *Ladies,* which is Nice: nor the *Lovers,* which is all these, &c.

Love.

Ros. No, that same wicked Bastard of *Venus,* that was begot of Thought, conceiv'd of Spleen, and born of Madness, that blind rascally Boy, that abuses every ones Eyes, because his own are out—&c. is shown what it is to be in Love,—*Good Shepherd (says* Phebe) *tell this youth what 'tis to Love,* &c.

A Courtier.

—He swears he has been a Courtier.
Clown. If any Man doubt that let him put me to the Purgation,—I have trod a Measure; I have flater'd a Lady; I have been Politic with my Friend, Smooth with my Enemy; I have undone three Taylors; I have had four Quarrels, and had like to have fought one.

Nicholas Rowe, ed. *The Works of Shakespeare,* Vol. 7.
(London: 1710): 325–27.

LOVE IN A FOREST
Charles Johnson
1723

TO THE
Worshipful Society
Of
FREE-MASONS.

Permit me, my Brethren, most humbly to beg your Protection for the following Scenes.

Since to flatter you, and not to speak Truth wou'd, on this Occasion, be equally impertinent; give me Leave only to say: If encouraging and being in useful Arts, if Humanity, Charity, Humility, in a Word, if all these Social virtues which raise and improve the Mind of Man are Praise-worthy, your Society have a Right to demand the Applause of Mankind.

You have taught all Nations one Idiom, which, at the same Time that it gives a mutual Understanding, inspires a mutual Benevolence, removes every Prejudice of a distant Sun and Soil, and no Man can be a Foreigner who is a Brother.

If it were not below the Dignity of the Brotherhood to boast what the Vulgar call Honours and Distinctions, you cou'd give a List of Royal Names, not only the first in Britain, *but in* Europe, *have been proud to wear the Badge of your Order, and who have held themselves distinguished even amidst the Glories that surrounded there, by having the Honour to call the Members of your Society* Brethren; *and it was owing only to the Unhappiness of her Sex that a most Illustrious Princess of our own cou'd not be admitted, and if her Curiosity was piqued at not knowing a Secret, perhaps it was the only Point in her whole Reign that ever the* Woman *got the better of the* Queen.

It must be own'd your Society hath Enemies, as the wisest, the greatest, and most virtuous Communities have ever had, and must have, for Ignorance is the Mother of Malice as well as of Devotion, and if malevolent and wrong-headed People will revile what they confess they do not understand, their Ill-nature recoils and hurts only their own Breasts: This, my Brethren, we have to say, and let us speak it boldly tho' not vainly, tho' there hath yet been no other Sanction invented by the Wit of Man, the Wisdom of Law-givers, or the Policy of Princes, but what bath been frequently and openly broke into, yet our very Enemies, who have the least Candor, confess the Secrets of the Masonary have been kept inviolable, and that too, during the Course of many Ages, among People of all Distinctions, Religions, and Nations in the known World.

> *I am, my Brethren,*
> *With the greatest Respect and Duty,*
> *Your most Obedient and devoted*
> *Brother and Servant,*
> Charles Johnson.

Dramatis Persona.

Men.

Frederick, the usurping Duke,	————————————		Mr. *Williams.*
Alberto, the banish'd Duke,	————————————		Mr. *Booth.*
Jaques,	}		} Mr. *Cibber.*
	}	two Friends to *Alberto,*	}
Amiens,	}		} Mr. *Cory.*
Oliver,	}		} Mr. *Thurmond.*
Orlando,	}	three Brothers,———	} Mr. *Wilks.*
Roberto,	}		} Mr. *Roberts.*
Le Beu, ——————————————————			Mr. Theo. *Cibber.*
Charles, Master of the Duke's Academy, ———			Mr. W. *Mills.*

Women.

Rosalind, —————————————————	Mrs. *Booth.*
Celia, ————————————————————	Mrs. *Thurmond.*
Hymen, ———————————————————	Miss *Linder.*

In the Mock-Play.

Pyramus, —————————————————	Mr. *Penkethman.*
Thisby, ————————————————————	Mrs. *Miller.*
Wall, —————————————————————	Mr. *Norris.*
Lion, —————————————————————	Mr. *Wilson.*
Moonshine, —————————————————	Mr. *Ray.*

Lords, Foresters, Gentlemen, Guards, Singers and Dancers.

S C E N E, Liege, *and the Forest of* Arden.

LOVE in a FOREST.
Act I. Scene I.

A Garden.

Orlando *and* Adam *entering.*

Orlando. You may remember, *Adam,* my Father bequeath'd me by Will but a poor 1000 Crowns, and, as thou say'st, charg'd my Brother on his Blessing to breed me well; and there begins my Sadness: My Brother *Robert* he keeps at School, and Report speaks goldenly of his Profit; for my Part, he keeps me rustically at Home, or to speak more properly, stays me here at Home unkept; for call you that Keeping for a gentleman of my Birth, that differs not from the Stalling of an Ox? His Horses are bred better, for besides that they are fair with their Feeding, they are taught their Menage, and to that End Riders dearly hir'd: But I, his Brother, gain nothing under him but Growth, for the which his Animals on his Dunghills are as much bound to him as I; besides this Nothing that he so plentifully gives me, the Something that Nature gave me, his Countenance seems to take from me, he lets me feed with his Hinds, bars me the Place of a Brother, and, as much as in him lies, mines my Gentility with my Education. This it is, *Adam,* that grieves me, and the Spirit of my Father, which I think is within me, begins to mutiny at this Servitude. I will no longer endure it tho' yet I know no wise Remedy how to avoid it.

Enter Oliver.

Adam. Yonder comes my Master, your Brother.

Orl. Go apart, *Adam,* and thou shalt hear how he will shake me up.

Oliver. Now, Sir, what make you here?

Orl. Nothing; I am not taught to make any thing.

Oliver. What, mar you then, Sir?

Orl. I am helping you to mar that which Heav'n made, a poor unworthy Brother of yours, with Idleness.

Oliver. Be better employ'd, Sir, and be Naught a-while.

Orl. Shall I keep your Hogs, and eat Husks with them? What prodigal Portion have I spent, that I should come to such Penury?

Oliver. Know you where you are, Sir?

Orl. Oh! Sir, very well, here in your Garden.

Oliver. Know you before whom, Sir?

Orl. Aye, better than him I am before knows me. I know you are my eldest Brother, and in the gentle Condition of Blood you shou'd so know me: The

Courtesy of Nations allows you my better, in that you are the First-born; but the same Tradition takes not away my Blood, were there twenty Brothers betwixt us, I have as much of my Father in me, as you; albeit, I confess your coming before me is something nearer to his Reverence.

Oliver. What, Boy!

Orl. Come, come, elder Brother, you are too young in this.

[*Laying his Hand on his Collar.*

Oliver. Wilt thou lay Hands on me, Villain?

Orl. I am no Villain: I am the younger Son of Sir *Rowland du Bois,* he was my Father, and he is thrice a Villain, [*shaking him*] that says such a Father begot Villains. Wert thou not my Brother, I wou'd not take this Hand from thy throat, till this other had pull'd out thy Tongue for saying so; thou hast rail'd on thy self.

Adam. Sweet Master be patient, for your Father's Remembrance be at accord.

Oliver. Let me go, I say.

Orl. I will not till I please; You shall hear me. My Father charg'd you in his Will to give me good Education: You have train'd me up like a Peasant, obscuring and hiding from me all Gentleman-like Qualities; the Spirit of my Father grows strong in me, and I will no longer endure it; therefore allow me such Exercises as may become a Gentleman, or give me the poor Allotment my Father left me by Testament; with that I will buy my Fortunes.

Oliver. And what wilt thou do, beg when that is spent? Well, Sir, get you in, I will not long be troubled with you; you shall have some Part of your Will, I pray you leave me.

Orl. I will no further offend you than becomes me for my Good.

Oliver to *Adam.* Get you with him, you Old Dog.

Adam. Is Old Dog my Reward? Most true I have lost my Teeth in your service: Heav'n be with my Old Master, he wou'd not have spoke such a Word.   [*Exeunt* Orlando *and* Adam.

Oliver. Is it even so? Begin you to grow upon me? I will Physick your Rankness, and yet give no 1000 Crowns neither. Holla! *Dennis!*

Enter *Dennis.*

Den. Calls your Worship?

Oliver. Was not *Charles,* the Duke's Fencer and Master of his Academy here to speak with me?

Den. So please you, he is here at the Door, and desires Access to you.

Oliver. Call him in; 'twill be a good Way;—to Morrow!—No, to Day if it may be.

Enter Charles.

Char. Good Morrow, Sir.

Oliver. Good Mons. *Charles,* what's the News at the new Court?

Char. There's no News at the Court, Sir, but the old News; that is the old Duke is banished by his younger Brother the new Duke, and three or four loving Lords have put themselves into a voluntary Exile with him, whose Lands and Revenues inrich the new Duke, therefore he gives them Leave to wander.

Oliver. Can you tell if *Rosalind,* the Duke's Daughter, be banish'd with her Father.

Char. Oh no, for the Duke's Daughter, her Cousin, so loves her, being ever from their Cradles bred together, that she wou'd have follow'd her Exile, or have died to stay behind her; She is at the Court, and no less belov'd of her Uncle than his own Daughter, and never two Ladies lov'd as they do.

Oliver. Where will the old Duke live?

Char. He is already in the Forrest of *Arden,* and many merry Men with him; and there they live like the old *Robin Hood* of *England*; then say many young Gentlemen have follow'd his Exile, and fleet the Time carelesly as they did in the Golden World; Nay, the very Mechanicks, and Labourers in Handicraft leave every Day their Occupations, and this populous city of *Liege,* and flock to visit their exiled Sovereign, as they call him.

Oliver. I am sorry for it, but I find the Factions against our Duke increase daily; and I must tell thee, *Charles,* for I have Set thee down my Friend, my domestic concerns are mingled with my Cares for the publick; for my Brother, my younger Brother *Orlando*——But art thou my Friend?—

Char. If you have set me down your Friend, I must tell you, I have set down the many Obligations that made me so.

Oliver. But art thou the Duke's Friend?

Char. He is my Royal Master, and my Life is his.

Oliver. Why then, *Charles,* I will prove thee no farther; my Brother *Orlando,* as I was saying, has long had a Design to practice against me, by Poison, but this, unnatural as it is, is the least of his Accusations: He is likewise enrolled with and attached to a very dangerous Knot of the Family and Friends of the banish'd Duke.

Char. How, Sir!

Oliver. This I am beyond Doubt assured of, this I know; now if thou wilt upon my Honour, which, with a Gentleman is equal at least to the Sanctity of an Oath, appeal him instantly of this Treason to the Duke, for the Plot is too ripe, too near Execution to admit the least delay; as I will unfold it to thee hereafter: I say, if thou wilt appeal him instantly of this Treason before the Duke, and answer it in Single Duel with thy Rapier, of which Skill, as of all other Gentlemanly Exercises, he is mainly ignorant, thou may'st happily win an undangerous Victory, and not only I, but the whole State be deliver'd from a very dangerous and hated Enemy.

Char. But if I undertake this and miscarry, as the most skilful may, ought my Family, which will be by this Means out of the Protection of the Duke, wholly to have their Reliance on your future Gratitude.

Oliver. Here is my Purse, use it, thou shalt have more, and often; doubt not thy Success, public Preferment will await thee; when, besides the Atchievement of conquering an avow'd Traitor, thou shalt be proclaim'd the Patron and Protector of *Frederick* Duke of *Burgundy.*

Char. And yet, methinks, it goes somewhat against me, this Gentleman, *Orlando,* has such a generally approv'd and unfoil'd Name.

Oliver. I know the Vulgar doat on him, he is one of their Errors, a staunch Hypocrite: Thou must think how much against my Heart it runs, thus to accuse my own Blood: But I assure thee, and almost with Tears I speak it, there is not One so young and so villainous this Day living: I speak but Brotherly of him, but should I Anatomise him to thee as he is, I must blush, and weep, and thou must look pale and tremble.

Char. You have warm'd me; I will accuse him instantly to the Duke, and call him to the Combat; if I do not give him the Reward both of his Parricide and his Treason, may my good Heart, and my good Sword both fail me: Farewel.   [*Exit* Charles.

Oliver. Farewel good *Charles,* and Heav'n prosper thee—Well, very well; now surely I shall see an End of this *Orlando*; for my Soul, yet I know not why, hates nothing more than him, yet he is gentle; and tho' never School'd, yet learn'd, and full of noble device; of all Sorts inchantingly belov'd, and indeed so much the Heart of the World; and especially of my own people, who best know him, that I am altogether misprised, but this Fencer shall clear all, and that without delay: I will immediately give another Lift to put this Wheel in Motion.   *Exit* Oliver.

A Chamber in the Duke's Palace.

Rosalind *and* Celia.

Celia. I prithee *Rosalind,* sweet my Cosin be merry.

Ros. Dear *Celia,* I show more Mirth than I am Mistress of; and wou'd you yet I were merrier? Unless you cou'd teach me to forget the Duke my Father, the banish'd Duke, you must not learn me how to remember any extraordinary pleasure.

Ca. Herein I see thou lovest not with the full Weight that I love thee.

Ros. Well, I will forget the Condition of my Estate, to rejoice in thine.

Ca. You know my Father hath no Child but me, nor none is like to have, and truly when he dies thou shall be his Heir; for what he hath taken away from thy Father by Force, I will render thee again in Affection; by my Honour I will, and when I break that Oath let me turn Monster: Therefore my sweet *Rose,* my dear *Rose,* be merry.

Ros. From henceforth I will, Cosin, and devise Sports; let me see, What think you of falling in Love?

Ca. Marry, I prithee do to make Sport withal; but love no Man in good earnest, nor no farther in Sport neither, than with Safety of a pure Blush thou may'st in Honour come off again.

Ros. What shall be the Sport then?

Ca. Let us sit and mock the good Housewife *Fortune* from her Wheel, that her Gifts may henceforth be bestow'd equally.

Ros. I wou'd we cou'd do so, for her Benefits are mightily misplac'd, and the bountiful blind Woman does most mistake in her Gifts to Women.

Ca. 'Tis true, for those that she makes fair, she scarce makes honest, and those that she makes honest, she makes very Ill-favoured.

Ros. Nay, now thou goest from Fortune's Office, to Nature's: Fortune reigns in Gifts of the World, not in the Lineaments of Nature—

Ca. No, when Nature hath made a fair Creature may she not by Fortune fall into the Fire: But soft a while, here comes Monsieur *Le-Beu.*

Enter Le-Beu.

Ros. With his Mouth full of News.

Ca. Which he will put upon us as Pigeons feed their young.

Ros. Then shall we be News cram'd.

Ca. All the better, we shall be the more Marketable.

Le-Beu. Fair Princesses, if you stay here you are like to lose much Sport.

Ca. Sport! of what Colour?

Le-Beu. What Colour, Madam! how shall I answer you?

Ros. As Wit and Fortune will.

Ca. Or as the Destinies decree.

Le-Beu. I was sent to inform you of the single Combat that is to be perform'd before the whole Court this Morning, indeed instantly; the Lists are prepar'd, the Combatants arm'd, the Duke and his Nobles present, the Heralds ready to sound, and nothing wanting but the Grace of your Noble Personages, most sweet Ladies, to make the Sport most gracious.

Ros. It is the first Time I ever heard Cutting of Throats was Sport for Ladies.

Le-Beu. Thus ev'rything being appointed, the Warriors impatient, and the Circumstances of Affairs—

Ros. Not to make your Words stumble in the Middle of their Career, pray, Monsieur, between whom and upon what Cause is this Blood to be shed on one Side, or both.

Le-Beu. Why thus, Ladies: *Charles* the Master of the Duke's Academy hath impeach'd of Treason *Orlando,* a younger Son of old Sir *Rowland du Bois.*

Ros. I have heard much of that old Gentleman, his eminent Worth was approv'd by general Voice, albeit he was thy Father's profess'd Enemy, *Celia.*

Ca. Well, Cousin, shall we see this Combat?

Ros. Custom sanctifies every Thing, or else how odd wou'd appear this judicial Trial by the Rapier of what is Right, or Wrong.

Ca. If a Man of Courage cou'd not be a Knave, nor a Coward Virtuous, a Fencing-Master wou'd make an excellent Chancellor.

Ros. And a Prize-Fighter a very good Chief Justice.

Ca. Yet to it is, and our Laws hold Decrees of this Sort to be as sacred and inviolable, as if Heaven were oblig'd to declare for the more Sinewy Arm.

Le-Beu. Ladies, shall I have the Honour to attend you?

Ca. You shall Sir, we will see this State Duel in all its Forms.   [*Exeunt.*

S C E N E *the Lists.*

Trumpets, Kettle-Drums, Musick, a Throne &c. Frederick *the Usurper, Lords on each Side the Throne,* Celia, Rosalind, *and Ladies in their Seats,* &c.

Duke. Marshall, have you demanded of the Champions
The Cause of their Arrival here, in Arms?

Marsh. My Liege, I have, each hath accused the other,
As a false Traitor to his King and Country,
They are appointed equal, search'd and sworn,
Each to defend the Justice of his Cause.

Duke. Then let them enter——

Marsh. Trumpets, sound a Call,—
And summon both the Champions to the Lists.

Trumpets sound, Enter at opposite Doors Orlando *and* Charles.

Char. Grant me the Combat, my most gracious Liege.

Orl. And me, my Lord, grant me the Combat too.

Duke. Say, Gentlemen, what makes you thus exclaim?
And wherefore claim you Combat, and with whom?

Char. First Heaven be the Record to my Speech,
In the Devotion of a Subject's Love,
And free from other misbegotten Hate,
Come I, appellant to my Royal Master.
Now young *Orlando* do I turn to thee,
And mark my Greeting well, for what I speak
My Body shall make good upon this Earth,
Or my divine Soul answer it in Heaven.

  Thou art a Traitor and a Miscreant,
And wish (so please my Sovereign) e're I move,
What my Tongue speaks, my right drawn sword may prove.

  Orl. Let not my cooler Words accuse my Zeal,
'Tis not the Trial of a Woman's War,
The bitter Clamour of two eager Tongues,
Can arbitrate this Cause between us two,
The Blood is hot that must be shed for this.

  First, the fair Reverence of this Presence curbs me
From giving Reins and Freedom to my Speech,
Else would I doubly thus in Virtue bold,
Return the Traitor, and the Miscreant;
And add a slanderous Coward, and a Villain:
Which to maintain, I wou'd allow him Odds;
And meet him, tho' oblig'd to run on Foot
Ev'n to the frozen Ridges of the *Alps,*
Or any other Ground inhabitable,
Where ever honest Man durst set a Foot.

  Ca. aside to Ros. How gracefully he deliver'd his Words, with an honest
Warmth and Modesty.

  Ros. And yet with a Spirit right and brave as *Hercules*.

  Ca. If he acquits himself as well with his Sword.

  Ros. Doubt it not, doubt it not.

  Marsh. On Pain of Death no Person be so bold,
Or daring hardy as to touch the Lists,
Except the *Marshall,* and such Officers,
Appointed to direct these fair Designs.

  Ros. to Ca. Ah *Celia*! I am not concern'd in this Quarrel, am I? No, no, and
yet my Heart says otherwise, wou'd I were invisible, to hold that Fencer's Arm
but a Moment.

  Ca. If I had a Thunder-bolt in my Hand I cou'd tell who should fall.

  Marsh. Sound Trumpets, and set forward Combatants.   [*Trumpets sound.*

  Charl. Come, Sir, I'll whip you from your foining Fence,

Spight of your *May* of Youth and Bloom of Blood.

    Orl. You promise well, come on, Sir, this to try
How well your Acts and Words agree.   [*they fight,*

[Charles *is wounded by* Orlando, *and falls.*

    Duke. Part 'em——No more of this;
He bleeds, he faints, how doest thou, *Charles.*

    Le-Beu. He can not speak, my Liege,

    Duke. Bear him away; What is thy Name young Man?

    Orl. Orlando, Sir, a younger Son of Sir *Rowland du Bois.*

    Duke. I wou'd thou hadst been Son to some Man else,
The World esteem'd thy Father honourable.
But I did find him still mine Enemy;
Thou shouldst have better pleas'd me with this Deed,
Hadst thou descended from another House;
But fare thee well, thou art a gallant Youth:
I wou'd thou hadst told me of another Father.
Now break we up the Lists; *Marshal,* Record
The Appeal, and the Success.   [*Exit Duke and Attendants.*

Orlando, Celia, Rosalind, Le-Beu.

    Orl. Yes, I am proud to be Sir *Rowland*'s Son,
His younger Son, nor wou'd I change that Name,
To be adopted Heir to *Frederick*.

    Ros. to *Ca.* My Father lov'd Sir *Rowland* as his Soul,
And all the World was of my Father's Mind;
Had I before known this young Man, his Son,
I should have added Tears unto my Wishes
For his Success.

    Ca. ——Gentle Cousin,
Let us go thank him, and encourage him,
My Father's rough and envious Disposition
Sticks me at Heart: [*to Orl.*] Sir, you have well deserv'd,
If you do keep your Promises in Love,
But justly, as you have exceeded all in Prowess,
Your Mistress will be happy.

    Ros. Sir, you will wear this for me: [*giving him a Favour.*
One out of Fortune's Favour that wou'd give more, but that her Hand lack
Means. Shall we go, Cousin?

Ca. Aye!—Fare you well, Sir.

Orl. Can I not say, I thank you? My better Parts
Are all thrown down, and that which here stands up
Is but a Statue, a meer Lifeless Block.

Ros. returning. He calls us back: My Pride fell with my Fortunes,
I'll ask him what he wou'd—Did you call, sir?
Sir, you have fought it well, and overthrown
More than your Enemies.

Ca. Will you go, Cousin?

Ros. Have with you—Fare you well.   [*Exeunt* Celia *and* Rosalind.

Orlando, Le-Beu.

Orl. What Passion hangs these Weights upon my Tongue,
I cannot speak to her, yet she urged Conference,
Oh! poor *Orlando,* thou art overthrown
And something, weaker than *Charles,* masters thee.
I pray ye tell me, Sir, which of these Ladies
Is Daughter to the Duke?

Le-Beu. Neither his Daughter, if we judge by Manners;
But yet, indeed, the taller is his Daughter,
The other is Daughter to the banish'd Duke,
And here detain'd by her usurping Uncle
To keep his Daughter Company, whose Loves
Are dearer than the natural Bond of Sisters:
But I can tell you, that of late this Duke
Hath ta'en Displeasure against his gentle Niece,
Grounded upon no other Argument
But that the People praise her for her Virtues,
And pity her for her good Father's Sake;
And, on my Life, his Malice 'gainst the Lady
Will suddenly break forth: Sir, fare you well
Hereafter in a better World than this,
I can desire more Love and Knowledge of you.

S C E N E *a Chamber.*

Celia *and* Rosalind.

Ca. Why, Cousin! why, *Rosalind*! Cupid have Mercy! Not a Word?

Ros. Not one to throw at a Dog.

Ca. No; thy Words are too precious to be thrown away upon Curs, throw some of them at me; come, lame me with Reasons! But is all this Melancholly for your Father?

Ros. No, some of it is for my Child's Father: Oh! how full of Briers is this Working-day World.

Ca. They are but Burrs, Cousin, thrown upon thee in Holy-day Foolery; if we walk in the trodden Paths our very Petticoats will catch 'em.

Ros. I cou'd shake them off my Coat ; these Burrs are in my Heart.

Ca. Hem them away.

Ros. I wou'd try, if I cou'd cry Hem, and have him.

Ca. Come, come, you must, like a good Christian, War with your Affections.

Ros. Alas! they take the Part of a better Warrior than myself.

Ca. Is it then possible, that so suddenly you should fall into so strange a liking of old Sir *Rowland*'s younger Son?

Ros. The Duke my Father loved his Father dearly.

Ca. Does it therefore ensue that you should love his Son dearly? By this Kind of Chase, I should hate him, for my Father hated his Father dearly; yet I hate not *Orlando*.

Ros. No faith! hate him not for my Sake.

Ca. Why should I not? Does he not deserve it?

Enter Duke Frederick, *with Lords*.

Ros. Let me love him for that, and do you love him because I do; look ye, here comes the Duke, your Father,

Ca. With his Eyes full of Anger.

Duke to Ros. Mistress, dispatch you with your safest Haste
And get you from our Court.

Ros. Me! Uncle?

Duke. You, Cousin; if thou art found within ten Days, so near our publick Court as twenty Miles, thou diest for it.

Ros. ——I do beseech your Grace,
Let me the Knowledge of my Fault bear with me,
If with myself I hold Intelligence,
Or have acquaintance with my own Desires,
If that I do not dream, or be not frantick,
Never so much as in a Thought unborn
Did I offend your Highness.

Duke. ——Thus do all Traitors,
If their Purgation did consist in Words,

They are as innocent as Grace itself;
Let it suffice thee that I trust thee not.

 Ros. Yet your Mistrust can not make me a Traitor,
Tell me, whereon the likelyhood depends?

 Duke. Thou art thy Father's Daughter, that's enough.

 Ros. So was I when your Highness took his Dukedom,
So was I when your Highness banish'd him,
Treason is not inherited, my Lord.

 Ca. Dear Sovereign, hear me speak.

 Duke. Aye, *Celia,* we stay'd her for your Sake,
Else had she with her Father rang'd along,
I will not be intreated, not a Word,
Firm and irrevocable is the Doom
Which I have pass'd upon her, she is banish'd.

 Ca. Pronounce that Sentence then on me, my Liege,
I can not live out of her Company.

 Duke. You are a Fool——You, Niece, provide yourself;
If you out stay the Time, upon my Honour,
And in the Greatness of my Word, you die.   *Exit Duke and Lord.*

Celia *and* Rosalind.

 Ca. Oh my poor Rosalind! whither wou't thou go,
I charge thee be not thou more griev'd than I am.

 Ros. I have more Cause.

 Ca. ——Thou hast not, Cousin,
Prithee be chearful, knowest thou not the Duke
Hath banish'd me his Daughter?

 Ros. That he hath not.

 Ca. No! Hath not? *Rosalind* lacks then the Love
Which should teach her that she and I are one,
Shall we be sundred? Shall we part sweet Girl?
No, let my Father seek another Heir:
Therefore devise with me how we may fly,
Whither to go, and what to bear with us,
And do not seek to take the Charge upon you,
To bear your Griefs yourself, and leave me out;
For by this Heaven, now as our Sorrows pale,
Say what thou can'st I'll go along with thee.

 Ros. ——Why whither shall we go?

 Ca. To seek my Uncle, in the Forrest of *Arden.*

Ros. Alass! what Danger will it be to us,
(Maids as we are) to travel forth so far?
Beauty provoketh Thieves sooner than Gold.

Ca. I'll put myself in poor and mean Attire,
And with a Kind of Umber smut my Face,
The like do you, so shall we pass along
And never stir Assailants.

Ros. ——Were it not better,
That I did suit me in all Points like a Man,
A gallant Cutlass by my Side,
A Boar-Spear in my Hand, and in my Heart,
Lie there what hidden Woman's Fear there will,
We'll have a Swaggering and Martial Outside,
As many other Mannish Cowards have
That do out-face it with their Semblances.

Ca. What shall I call thee, when thou art a Man?

Ros. I'll have no worse a Name than *Jove*'s own Page,
And therefore, look you, call me, *Ganymede:*
But what will you be call'd?

Ca. Something that has a Reference to my State,
No longer *Celia,* but *Aliena*.

Ros. ——Let's away,
And get our Jewels and our Wealth together,
Devise the fittest, and the safest Way
To hide us from Pursuit that will be made
After my Flight; Now go we in Content
To Liberty, and not to Banishment.   [*Exeunt.*

The End of the First A C T.

ACT II. SCENE 1.

OLIVER'S *House.*

Orlando *and* Adam.

Orl. Who's there?

Adam. What, my young Master; Oh my gentle Master,
Oh my sweet Master! Oh you Memory
Of old Sir *Rowland!*—Why, what make you here?
Why are you virtuous? Why do People love you?
And wherefore are you gentle, strong, and valiant?
Why wou'd you be so fond to overcome
The bonny Prizer of the humourous Duke?
Your Praise came too swiftly Home before you;
Know you not, Master, to some kind of Men
Their Graces serve them but as Enemies,
No more do yours; your Virtues, gentle Master,
Are sanctify'd, and holy Traitors to you:
Oh, what a World is this! when what is comely
Envenoms him that bears it.

Orl. Why, what's the Matter?

Adam. ——Oh, unhappy Youth,
Come not within these doors, beneath this Roof
The Enemy of all your Graces lives;
Your Brother, no, no Brother, yet the Son
(Yet not the Son, I will not call him Son)
Of him I was about to call his Father,
Hath heard your Praises, and this Night he means
To burn the Lodging where you us'd to lie,
And you within it; if he fail of that,
He will have other Means to cut you off;
I over-heard him and his Practices;
This is no Place, this House is but a Butchery;
Abhor it, fear it, do not enter it.

Orl. Why whither, *Adam*, wou'dst thou have me go?

Adam. No matter whither, so you come not here.

Orl. What, wou'dst thou have me go and beg my Food;
Or with a base and boisterous Hand inforce
A Thievish Living on the Common Road?
This I must do, or know not what to do:
Yet this I will not do, do how I can;

I rather will subject me to the Malice
Of a diverted Blood, and bloody Brother.

   Adam. But do not so; I have five hundred Crowns,
The thrifty Hire I saved under your Father,
Which I did Store to be my Foster Nurse
When Service shou'd in my old Limbs lie lame,
And unregarded Age in Corners thrown:
Take that——And He that doth the Ravens feed,
Yea providently caters for the Sparrow,
Be Comfort to my Age; here is the Gold,
All this I give you, let me be your Servant,
Tho' I look old, yet I am strong and lusty
For in my Youth I never did apply
Hot and Rebellious Liquors to my Blood,
Nor did I with unbashful Forehead woe
The Means of Weakness and Debility;
Therefore my Age is as a lusty Winter,
Frosty, but kindly; let me go with you,
I'll do the Service of a younger Man,
In all your Business, and Necessities.

   Orl. Oh good Old Man! how well in thee appears
The constant Service of the Antique World,
When Service sweat for Duty, not for Need;
Thou art not for the Fashion of these Times,
Where none will Sweat but for Promotion,
And having that, do choak their Service up
Even with the having; it is not so with thee;
But poor Old Man, thou prunest a rotten Tree,
That cannot so much as a Blossom yield
In lieu of all thy Pains and Husbandry.

Enter Le-Beu.

So, Sir, what News from Court?
   Le-Beu. Bad News towards you, *Orlando.*
   Orl. Say it then, good *Le-Beu*,
I have been hackney'd, worn in evil Fortune,
And shall receive it with a constant Mind.
   Le-Beu. The Duke, too jealous of his sickly State,
Perhaps of your Desert, commands you go
Within three Days after the Sight of this   *[giving him an Order.*
Into perpetual Banishment, or else

To Suffer as a Traitor convict.

    Orl. The jealous Duke prevents my Brother's Malice;
Behold, good *Adam*, that eternal Guard
That watches and provides for all its Creatures,
Warns us away to save us from Destruction;
Thus as what the Vulgar think Infliction, Pain,
Is often a Reward, and Virtue's Merit:
But come thy ways, we'll both along together,
And e'er we have the youthful Wages spent,
We'll light upon some settled low Content.

    Adam. Master, go on, and I will follow thee
To the last Gasp, with Truth and Loyalty,
From seventeen Years, till now almost fourscore,
Here liv'd I, but now live here no more:
At seventeen Years many their Fortunes seek,
But at fourscore, it is too late a Week;
Yet Fortune cannot recompence me better,
Than to die well, and not my Master's Debtor.   [*Exeunt.*

F R E D E R I C K's *Palace.*

Duke Frederick, *with Lords.*

    Duke. Can it be possible that no Man saw 'em?
It can not be, some Villains of my Court
Are of Consent and Sufferance in this.

    Lord. I cannot hear of any that did see her:
Hisperia the Princess's Gentlewoman
Confesses that she secretly o're heard
Your Daughter and her cousin much commend
The Parts and Graces of the young *Orlando,*
That did but lately foil the sinewy *Charles,*
And she believes wherever they are gone
That Youth is surely in their Company.

    Duke. Send to his Brother, fetch that Gallant hither,
If he be absent, bring his Brother to me;
I'll make him find him; do this suddenly,
And let no Search, no Inquisition quail;
Bring me again this foolish Runaway,   [*Exeunt.*

The Forest of Arden, *before the Duke's Cave.*

Duke Alberto, Amiens, Jaques, *and two or three Lords like Foresters.*

Duke. Now my Comates and Brothers in Exile,
Hath not old Custom made this Life more sweet
Than that of painted Pomp? Are not these Woods
More free from Peril, than the envious Court?
Here we do feel the Penalty of *Adam*,
The Season's Difference, the Icy Phang,
And churlish chiding of the Winter's Wind:
Which, when it bites and blows upon my Body
Even till I shrink with Cold, I smile and say,
This is no Flattery: These are Councellours
Who feelingly persuade me what I am.

Amiens. ——Happy is your Grace
That can translate the Stubborness of Fortune
Into so quiet and so sweet a Stile:
But, Sir, this Forest will become a City,
Your People quit the Tyrant's Court, and hither
Resort in Crouds; Mechanics of all Sorts
Petition to delight and serve your Grace;
They will obey you as their King and Father:
A double Tye of Duty.

Duke. ——My Heart bleeds
When I reflect, good *Amiens*, that my Power
Is weaker than my Love; No more of this:
Come, shall we go and kill us Venison?
And yet it irks me, the poor dapple Fools,
Being native Burghers of this Desart City,
Shou'd, in their own Confines, with forked Heads,
Have their round Haunches goar'd.

Jaques. Indeed, my Lord, it grieves me very much,
And in that Kind, I swear you more usurp,
Than does your Brother, who hath banish'd you;
Mark well my Story and you'll find it so:
To Day, my Lord of *Amiens*, and myself,
Lay in the Shade of an old Druid Oak,
Whose antique venerable Root peeps out
Upon the Brook that brawls along this Wood,
To which Place, a poor sequestred Stag,
That from the Hunter's Aim had ta'en a Hurt,
Did come to languish; and indeed, my Lord,
The wretched Animal heav'd forth such Groans,
That their Discharge did stretch his leathern Coat

Almost to bursting, while the big round Drops
Cours'd one another down his innocent Nose
In piteous Chace; and thus the hairy Fool
Stood on the extreamest Verge of the swift Brook,
Augmenting it with Tears.

    Duke. ——Didst thou not *Jaques*?
Didst thou not moralize this Spectacle?

    Jaques. Who cou'd behold it, Sir, and not reflect?
First for his Weeping in the unwanting Stream;
Is it not plain he made a Testament
As Worldlings do, giving his Sum of more
To that which had too much: Anon a careless Herd,
Full of the Pasture, jumps along the Verdure,
And never stays to greet him; there you see
A Crowd of fat and greasy Citizens
Looking with Scorn on a poor ruin'd Bankrupt.
Are we not all Usurpers, Tyrants, worse,
To fright these Animals and kill them thus
In their assign'd and native Dwelling-Place.

    Duke. Shew me this Place,
There will we sweetly moralize together,
And make our Contemplations give at once
Delight, and Use.

                                    [*Exeunt.*

SCENE *another Part of the Forest.*

Rosalind, *in Boys Cloaths, as* Ganymede; Celia, *dress'd like a Shepherdess, as*
Aliena.

    Ros. Oh, *Jupiter,* how weary are my Spirits?

    Ca. I care not for my Spirits, if my Legs were not tir'd.

    Ros. I cou'd find in my Heart to disgrace my Mans Apparel, and to cry like
a Woman; but I must comfort the weaker Vessel, as Hat and Breeches ought to
shew itself couragious to a Petticoat; therefore, Courage, good *Aliena.*

    Ca. I pray you bear with me, I can go no farther.

    Ros. Come, bear a Heart, Girl; there is a Creature [*Enter* Sylvius] looks like
a Man, I'll question him if he for Gold will give us any Food—Holla, Friend.

    Syl. Who calls?

    Ros. Good, even to you, Friend.

    Syl. And to you, gentle Sir, and to you both.

    Ros. I prithee, Shepherd, if that Love, or Gold,
Can in this Place buy any Entertainment,

Bring us where we may rest ourselves, and feed,
Here's a young Maid with Travel much oppress'd,
And faints for Succour.

Syl. ——Fair Sir, I pity her,
And wish for her Sake, more than for my own,
My Fortunes were more able to relieve her;
But I am Shepherd to another Man,
And do not sheer the Fleeces that I graze:
My Master is of Churlish Disposition,
And little cares to find the Way to Heaven
By doing Deeds of Hospitality:
Besides, his Coat, his Flocks, and Bounds of Feed,
Are now on Sale; and at our Sheepcoat, yonder,
By Reason of his Absence, there is nothing
That you will feed on; if there is, you'll see,
And in my Voice most Welcome shall you be.

Ros. I prithee, if it stand with Honesty,
Buy thou the Cottage, Pasture, and the Flock,
And thou shalt have to pay for it of us.

Ca. ——And we will mend thy Wages,
I like this Place, and willingly wou'd spend
My Time in it.

Syl. Assuredly the Thing is to be sold,
Go with me, if you like, upon Report,
The Soil, the Profit, and this kind of Life,
I will your very faithful Feeder be,
And buy it with your Gold.   [*Exeunt.*

Orlando *and* Adam.

Adam. Dear Master, I can go no farther:
Oh I die for Food: Here lie I down,
And Measure out my Grave; Farewel kind Master.

Orl. Why how now, *Adam*! No greater Heart in thee?
Live a little, Comfort a little, Chear thyself a little.
Thy Conceit is nearer Death, than thy Powers.
For my Sake be comfortable, hold Death a while
At Arms End: I will be here with you presently,
And if I bring thee not something to eat,
I will give thee Leave to die, but if thou diest
Before I come, thou art a Mocker of my Labour.
Well said, thou look'st chearly,

And I'll be with thee quickly; yet thou liest
In the bleak Air. Come I will bear thee to some Shelter,
And thou shalt not die for Lack of a Dinner, if
there live anything in this Desert: Chearly good
Adam.
                                        [*Exit* Orlando, *leading* Adam.

                Duke Alberto, Amiens, *and Nobles at a Banquet.*

    Duke. I think he is transform'd into a Beast,
For I can no where find him like a Man.
    Amiens. My Lord, he is but even now gone hence.
    Duke. Pray seek him, tell him I wou'd Speak with him.
    Amiens. He saves my Labour, by his own Approach.   [*Enter* Jaques.
    Duke. Why how now, Monsieur, What a Life is this?
That your poor Friends must woo your Company?
What, you look merrily!
    Jaques. A Fool, a Fool, I met a Fool i'the Forest,
A motly Fool, a miserable World!
As I do live by Food; I met a Fool;
Good Morrow, Fool, quoth I, no, Sir, quoth he,
Call me not Fool, till Heaven hath sent me Fortune;
And then he drew a Dial from his Poak,
And looking on it with lack-lustre Eye,
Says, very wisely, It is ten a Clock:
Thus we may see, quoth he, how the World wags;
'Tis but an Hour ago since it was nine,
And after one Hour more, 'twill be eleven,
And so from Hour to Hour we ripe, and ripe,
And then from Hour to Hour we rot, and rot,
And thereby hangs a Tale, Oh Noble Fool!
A worthy Fool, Motley's your only wear.
    Duke. What Fool is this?
    Jaques. A worthy Fool! One that has been a Courtier,
And says, if Ladies be but young and fair,
They have the Gift to know it: And in his Brain,
Which is as dry as the Remainder Biscuit
After a Voyage, he hath strange Places cram'd
With Observation, the which he vents
In mangled Forms. Oh that I were a Fool!
I am ambitious of a Motley Coat.
    Duke. Thou Shalt have one.
    Jaques. ——It is my only Suit.

Enter Orlando, *has Sword drawn.*

Orl. Forbear to eat no more.

Jaques. Why, I have eat none yet.

Orl. Nor shall not till Necessity be serv'd.

Jaques. Of what Kind shou'd this Cock come?

Duke. Art thou thus 'bolden'd, Man, by thy Distress?
Or else a rude Despiser of Good Manners,
That in civility thou seem'st so empty?

    Orl. You touch'd my Vein at first; the Thorny Point
Of bare Distress hath ta'en from me the Shew
Of smooth Civility; yet am I Inland bred,
And know some Nurture: But forbear, I say
He dies that touches any of this Fruit
Till I and my Affairs are answer'd.

    Jaques. And you will not be answer'd with Reason, I must die.

    Duke. ——What would you have?

    Orl. I almost die for Food, and let me have it.

    Duke. Sit down and feed, and welcome to our Table.

    Orl. Speak you so gently? Pardon me, I pray you,
I thought that all Things had been Savage here,
And therefore put I on the Countenance
Of stern Commandment. But whate'er you are
That in this Desart, inaccessible,
Under the Shade of melancholly Boughs,
Lose, and neglect the creeping Hours of Time,
If ever you have look'd on better Days;
If ever been where Bells have knowl'd to Church;
If ever sat at any Good Man's Feast;
If ever from your Eyelids wiped a Tear;
And know what 'tis to pity, and be pity'd,
Let Gentleness my strong Enforcement be,
In the which Hope, I blush, and hide my Sword

    Duke. True it is, that we have seen better Days,
And have with holy Bell been knowl'd to Church
And sat at Good Men's Feasts, and wip'd our Eyes
Of Drops that sacred Pity hath engender'd:
And therefore sit you down in Gentleness,
And take upon Command what help we have,
That to your Wanting may be ministred.

    Orl. Then but forbear your Food a little Time,

Whiles, like a Doe, I go to find my Fawn,
And give it Food. There is an Old poor Man
That after me hath many a weary Step
Limp'd in pure Love; till he be first sufficed,
Oppress'd with two weak Evils, Age and Hunger,
I will not touch a Bit.

    Duke. ——Go find him out,
And we will nothing waste till you return.

    Orl. I thank you, and be bless'd for your good Comfort.   [*Exit* Orlando.

    Duke. Thou see'st we are not all alone unhappy,
This wide and universal Theatre
Presents more woeful Pageants, than the Scene
Wherein we play.

    Amiens. Some Citizens from *Liege,* some of the many
Fled hither, Sir, for your Protection, beg by me
They may have Leave to entertain your Grace.

    Duke. How is it they propose to entertain?

    Amiens. A Play it shou'd be, Sir, what 'twill appear, I know not,
They have rehears'd it in the Wood this Morning.

    Duke. And what the Subject?

    Amiens. They call it, *A tedious brief Scene of young* Pyramus *and his Love*
Thisby; very tragical Mirth.

    Duke. Merry and Tragical, tedious and brief,
How Shall we find the Concord of this Discord?——
Well, let them be ready before our Cave in the Evening; there they shall
represent it; this Theatrical Performance will Stir thy Gall, *Jaques.*

    Jaques. ——Not at all;
He that can reflect wants not these Mirrours:
All the World's a Stage,
And all the Men and Women meerly Players;
They have their Exits and their Entrances,
And one Man in his Time plays many Parts;
His Life being Seven Ages: At first the Infant
Mewling and Puking in the Nurse's Arms:
And then the whining School-boy with his Satchel
And shining Morning Face, creeping like Snail
Unwillingly to School: And then the Lover
Sighing like Furnace, with a woeful Ballad
Made to his Mistres's Eyebrow: Then a Soldier
Full of strange Oaths, and bearded like the Pard,
Jealous in Honour, sudden and quick in Quarrel,

Seeking the Bubble Reputation——
Even in the Cannon's Mouth, And then the Justice
In fair round Belly, with good Capon lined,
With Eyes severe, and Beard of formal Cut,
Full of wise Saws, and modern Instances,
And so he plays his Part: The sixth Age shifts
Into the lean and slipper'd Pantaloon
With Spetacles on Nose and Pouch on Side;
His youthful Hose well sav'd a World too wide
For his shrunk Shank, and his big manly Voice
Turning again toward Childish treble Pipes,
And whistles in his Sound: Last Scene of all
That ends this strange eventful History
Appears in Nerves unbrac'd, Reflection lost,
A second Childishness, and meer Oblivion.

Enter Orlando, *leading* Adam.

Duke. Welcome, here rest your venerable Burthen,
And let him feed——
    Orl. I thank you most for him.
    Adam. ——So had you Need,
I scarce can speak to thank you for myself.
    Duke. Welcome, fall too, I will not trouble you
As yet, to question you about your Fortunes.
Give us some Musick——

S O N G.

Blow, blow, thou Winter Wind,
Thou art not so unkind, as Man's Ingratitude;
Thy Tooth is not so keen, because thou art not seen,
    Altho' thy Breath be rude.
    Freeze, Freeze, thou bitter Sky, that does not bite so nigh
        As Benefit's forgot:
    Tho' thou the Waters warp, thy Sting is not so sharp,
        As Friend remember'd not.

    Duke. If that you are the good Sir *Rowland*'s Son,
As you have whisper'd faithfully you are,
And as mine Eye doth his Effigies witness
Most truly limn'd, and living in your Face,
Be truly welcome hither: I am the Duke
That lov'd your Father, the Residue of your Fortune,

Go to my Cave and tell me.———Good old Man
Thou art right welcome, as thy Master is;
Support him by the Arm; give me your Hand,
And let me all your Fortunes understand.

The End of the second A C T.

The Third A C T.

S C E N E *the Forest.*

Orlando, *a Paper of Verses in his Hand.*

Orl. fixing the Paper on a Tree. Hang there my Verse, in Witness of Love;
And thou thrice crowned Queen of Night survey
With thy chast Eye, from thy pale Sphere above,
Thy Huntress Name that my full Life doth sway.
Oh, *Rosalind,* these Trees shall be my Books,
And in their Barks my Thoughts I'll Character,
That every Eye which in this Forest looks
Shall see thy Virtue witness'd every where;
Run, run, *Orlando,* carve on every Tree
The fair, the chaste, and unexpressive she.   [*Exit* Orlando.

S C E N E *continues.* Rosalind *and* Celia.

Ca. What have you there? [*Ros. takes the Paper* Orlando *had hung on the
Tree.*
Ros. More Rhymes, Cosin.
Ca. Aye! read them, read them.
Ros. reads. From the East to Western Inde
    No Jewel is like *Rosalind,*
    Her Worth being mounted on the Wind,
    Thro' all the World bears *Rosalind;*
    All the Pictures fairest lin'd,
    Are but black to *Rosalind;*
    Let no Face be kept in Mind
    But the Face of *Rosalind.*
Ca. Heyday; I'll Rhyme you so eight Years together, Dinners and Suppers,
and Sleeping Times excepted: For a Taste,
    If a Hart does lack a Hind,
    Let him Seek out *Rosalind;*
    If the Cat will after Kind,
    So be sure will *Rosalind;*
    Winter Garments must be lin'd,
    So must slender *Rosalind;*
    They that reap must sheaf and bind,
    Then to Cart with *Rosalind;*
    Sweetest Meat hath sowrest Rind,
    Such a Nut is *Rosalind.*

Ros. This is the very false Gallop of Verse; why do you infect yourself with them?

Ca. But doest thou not wonder, Cosin, how thy Name shou'd be hang'd and carved upon these Trees?

Ros. Look ye here, what I found on a Palm-Tree, I was never So Berhym'd since *Pythagoras's* Time, which I can hardly remember!

Ca. Tro you who hath done this?

Ros. It is a Man.

Ca. With a Ribond, you once wore, about his Arm;
Change you Colour?

Ros. I prithee who?

Ca. O Lord, Lord, it is a hard Matter for Friends to meet; but Mountains may be remov'd with Earthquakes, and so encounter.

Ros. Nay, but who is it?

Ca. Is it possible?

Ros. Nay, I prithee now, with most petitionary Vehemence, tell me who it is?

Ca. Oh wonderful! and most wonderfully wonderful! and yet again wonderful! and after that out of all hooping.

Ros. One Inch of Delay more, and I die before this Discovery. I prithee tell me, who is it? Quickly and speak apace, is he of Heavens making? What Manner of Man? Is his Head worth a Hat? Or his Chin worth a Beard?

Ca. Nay, he hath but a little Beard.

Ros. Why then I'll stay the Growth of his Beard, if thou delay me not the Knowledge of his Name.

Ca. It is then young *Orlando,* he who wounded yours and the Fencer's Heart, both in an Instant.

Ros. Nay, but the Devil take mocking? Speak, speak.

Ca. I'faith, Cousin, 'tis he.

Ros. Orlando!

Ca. Orlando.

Ros. Alas the Day, what shall I do with these Breeches? What did he when thou sawest him? What said he? How looked he? Where went he? What makes he here? Did he ask for me? Where remains he? How parted he with thee? And when shalt thou see him again? Answer me in one Word.

Ca. You must borrow me *Garagantua's* Mouth first; 'tis a Work too great for any Mouth of this Age's Size; to say at once aye and no together, to be general and particular at once, is beyond my Catechism.

Ros. But does he know that I am in this Forest, and in Mans Apparel? Looks he freshly as he did the Day he fought with *Charles* the Fencer?

Ca. It is as easy to count Atoms, as to resolve the Propositions of a Lover;

but take a Taste of my finding him, and relish it with good Observance:—I found him under an Oak, like a drop'd Acorn.

Ros. It may well be called JOVE's Tree, when it drops such Fruit.

Ca. Give me Audience, good Madam.

Ros. Proceed.

Ca. There lay he, stretch'd along, like a wounded Knight.

Ros. Tho' it be pity to see such a Sight, it well becomes the Ground.

Ca. Cry Holla to thy Tongue, I prithee, it curvets unreasonably. He was furnish'd like a Hunter.

Ros. Oh ominous! he comes to kill my Heart.

Ca. I would sing my Song without a Burthen, you put me out of time.

Ros. Do you not know I am a Woman? What I think I must speak: Sweet, say on.

Enter Orlando and Jaques.

Ca. You put me out;——Soft; Comes he not here?

Ros. 'Tis he, let us steal by and note him.

Jaques. I thank you for your Company, though, good Faith, I had as lieve been alone.

Orl. And so had I, but yet for Fashion sake, I thank you too for your Society.

Jaques. Good b'w'you, let's meet as little as we can.

Orl. I do desire we may be better Strangers.

Jaques. I pray ye mar no more Trees with writing Love-Songs in their Barks.

Orl. I pray you mar no more of my Verses with reading 'em ill-favour'dly.

Jaques. Rosalind is your Love's Name.

Orl. Yes, just.

Jaques. I do not like her Name.

Orl. There was no Thought of pleasing you, when she was christen'd.

Jaques. What stature is she of?

Orl. Just as high as my Heart: But why are you thus curious? You who are an obstinate Heretick in the Despight of Beauty, and the whole Female World.

Jaques. That a Woman conciev'd me I thank her: That she brought me up I likewise give her my most hearty Thanks; but that I will have a Recheate winded in my Forehead all Women shall pardon me: Because I will not do them the wrong to mistrust any, I will trust none.

Orl. I shall see thee e're I die look pale with Love.

Jaques. With Anger, with Sickness, or with Hunger, not with Love; prove that ever I loose more Blood with Love than I shall get again with a Bottle, pick out my Eyes with a Ballad-maker's Pen, and hang me up at the Door of a Brothel-house for the Sign of blind *Cupid*.

Orl. If thou shoud'st fall from this Faith.

Jaques. If I do, hang me in a Bottle like a Cat, and shoot at me, and he that hits me let him be clap'd on the Shoulder and call'd *Adam*.

Orl. In time the Savage Bull did bear the Yoak.

Jaques. The Savage Bull may, but if ever the sensible *Jaques* does, pluck off the Bull's Horns and set them in my Forehead, and let me be vilely painted, and in such great Letters as they write, Here are Horses to be let; let them signify under any Sign, Here liveth *Jaques* the marry'd Man.

Orl. If *Cupid* hath not spent all his Quiver, thou won't quake for this shortly.

Jaques. Hah! what have we here, a Wood Nymph and a Shepherd, these Animals are not of our Growth sure?

Orl. By their Habits and Mien you need not blush to own them; Are you sure they are human?

Jaques. Let us try and accost them, however, in human Terms.

Ros. to Ca. I will speak to him like a fancy Lacquey, and under that Habit play the Knave with him: Do you hear, Forester?

[Jaques *talks with* Celia, *they walk in another Glade of the Forest, while the Scene continues between* Rosalind *and* Orlando.

Orl. Very well——What wou'd you?

Ros. I pray you, what is it a Clock?

Orl. You shou'd ask me what Time o'the Day, there is no Clock in the Forest.

Ros. Then there is no true Lover in the Forest, Sighing else every Minute, and Groaning every Hour, wou'd detect the lazy Foot of Time as well as a Clock.

Orl. Where dwell you, pretty Youth?

Ros. With the Shepherdess you saw with me, my Sister, here in the Skirts of the Forest, like Fringe upon a Petticoat.

Orl. Are you Native of this Place?

Ros. As the Rabit, which thou see dwells where she is kindled.

Orl. Your Accent seems to be something finer than you cou'd purchase in so remoted a Dwelling.

Ros. I have been told so of many, but indeed an old religious Uncle of mine taught me to speak, who was in his Youth an Inland Man, one that knew Courtship too well, for there he fell in Love. I have heard him read many Lectures against it: I thank Heaven I am not a Woman to be touch'd with so many giddy Offences as he hath generally tax'd the whole Sex withal.

Orl. Can you remember any of the principal Evils that he laid to the Charge of Women?

Ros. There were none principal, they were all like one another as Half-pence are; every Fault seeming monstrous, till the Fellow Fault appear'd to match it.

Orl. I prithee, recount some of them.

Ros. No, I will not cast away any Physick but on those that are sick. There is a Man haunts this Foreft that abuses our young Plants with carving *Rosalind* on their Barks; hangs Odes upon Hawthorns; and Elegies on Brambles; all, forsooth, Deifying the Name of *Rosalind.* If I cou'd meet that Fancy-Monger, I wou'd give him good Counsel, for he Seems to have the Quotidian of Love upon him.

Orl. I am he so Love shaken; I pray you tell me your Remedy.

Ros. There are none of my Uncle's Marks upon you, he taught me how to know a Man in Love; in which Cage of Rushes I am sure you are no Prisoner.

Orl. What where his Marks?

Ros. A lean Cheeck, which you have not; a blue Eye, and sunk, which you have not; a Beard neglected, which you have not; but I pardon you for that, for simply your having no Beard is a younger Brother's Revenue: Then your Hose shou'd be ungarter'd, your Bonnet unbanded, your Sleeve unbutton'd, your Shoe unbuckled, and every Thing about you demonstrating a careless Desolation: But you are no such Man, you are rather Point Device in your Accoutrements, as loving yourself, than seeming the Lover of any other.

Orl. Fair Youth, I wou'd I cou'd make thee believe I love.

Ros. Me believe it? You may as soon make her that you love believe it, which I warrant she is apter to do, than to confess she does; that is one of the Points in which Women still give the Lie to their Consciences. But in good sooth, are you he that hangs the Verses on the Trees, wherein *Rosalind* is so much admired?

Orl. I Swear to thee, Youth, by the white Hand of *Rosalind,* I am he, that unfortunate he.

Ros. But are you so much in Love, as your Rhymes speak.

Orl. Neither Rhyme, nor Reason can express how much.

Ros. Love is meerly a Madness, and I tell you, deserves as well a dark House, and a Whip, as mad Men do: And the Reason why they are not so punished and cured is, that the Lunacy is so general, that the Whippers are in love too: Yet I profess curing it by Counsel.

Orl. Did you ever cure any so?

Ros. Yes, one, and in this Manner: He was to imagine me his Love, his Mistress; and I set him every Day to woo me. At which Time wou'd I; being but a Moonish Youth, grieve, be Effeminate changeable, longing and liking, proud, fantastical, apish, shallow, inconstant, full of Tears, full of Smiles, for every Passion something, and for no Passion truly any thing, as Boys and Women are for the most Part Birds of this Colour: Wou'd now like him, now loath him, then entertain him, then forswear him; now weep for him, then spit at him; till I drove this Suitor from his mad Humour of Love to a living Humour of Madness; which was to forswear the full Stream of the World, and to live in a Nook meerly Monastical: And thus I cured him, and this Way will I take upon me to wash your Liver as clear as a sound Sheep's Heart; that there shall not be one Spot of Love in it.

Orl. I wou'd not be cured, Youth.

Ros. I wou'd cure you if you wou'd but call me *Rosalind,* and come every Day to my Cave and woo me.

Orl. Now by the Faith of my Love I will, tell me where it is.

Ros. Go with me, and I will show it you; and by the Way you shall tell me where in the Forest you live.—Will you go?

Orl. With all my Heart, good Youth.

Ros. Nay, nay, you must call me *Rosalind.*   [*Exeunt* Orlando *and* Rosalind.

Jaques *and* Celia *coming forward.*

Ca. A Philosopher! what Sort of a Play-thing is that?

Jaques. A Thing that very oft sets up for Probity and Wisdom without one Ounce of either; it is generally Self-sufficient, seldom just, and always sower, more abounding in Ill-nature than knowledge.

Ca. Oh, Knowledge ill inhabited, worse than *Jove* in a thatch'd House.

Jaques. Are you honest?

Ca. If I had any Neighbours you might ask them.

Jaques. I hope you are not.

Ca. Why so, wou'd you not have me honest?

Jaques. No truly, unless thou wer't hard favour'd, for Honestly coupled with Beauty is to make Honey Sauce for Sugar.

Ca. Then you allow me handsome?

Jaques. Destructively handsome! I fancy too you have Understanding; but peradventure my Head takes Instructions from my Heart, for that, I feel by its Palpitation, gallops away in your Praise most dangerously.

Ca. You'll be in Love if you do not take good Heed, Signior Philosopher,— You have some Symptoms, have you not?

Jaques. I doubt so——Yet I hope not——When I lean'd my Shoulder against yours to read *Orlando*'s Verses, I caught a Tingling; aye,— here it is still; and creeps every Moment more and more into my Blood.——

Ca. Well, ——be a faithful Servant, and I will use you kindly.

Jaques. What a Bound has that given my Spirits! Heark ye, will you,——

tell Nobody of it tho'——Will you marry me?

Ca. Oh, you begin where you shou'd end, my true Knight; two Years hence, after many Services and various Adventures, it will be Time enough, sure, to ask that solemn Question.

Jaques. Two Years! What? How? Must I then, must I work in the Galleys two whole Years?

Ca. In the Galleys, heyday——You wicked Thing; you're a Suitor indeed, Ha, ha,—

Jaques. Well, then I will flatter thee like thy Glass.

Ca. Truth, good found Truth, is Food substantial enough for my Pride.

Jaques. Thou shalt be as humourous as thy sick Dog, thy Passions shall have no other Masters than thy Desires; thy——

Ca. Hold, hold, you are Railing on me, while you intend to praise me; indeed you do not make Love, but suffer it, it seems, to be in Spight of your Will.

Jaques. Wou'd it were in spight of my Heart too; but that is a Renegade, and has left its Master.

Ca. Well said, sigh a little; you'll soon trot easy in your Hands.

Jaques. But as I said before—Will you——'tis a hard Word, but will you marry me?

Ca. Two Years hence, if my Brother *Ganymede* consents, for without his Consent I am sworn not to convey myself away; if your Inclinations are the same, and mine alter,—why then we will talk this Matter over once again.

Jaques. I will ask your Brother's Consent.

Ca. That you may, and have an Answer, depend upon it; but now you have put me in Mind that I have miss'd him too long, that Way I think he went—— Adieu.   [*Exit* Celia, Jaques.

Jaques. Fare you well, Lady——I am a Turk an errant Miscreant, if I am not in Love, horribly strangely in Love! what! to have my Spirits caught at last by a Pair of bugle Eyeballs, and a Cheek of Cream——I Shall be the Jest of the World, I shall have Quirk and Witticisms broke on me innumerable,—Because I have railed on Marriage:—Why——Appetites alter, and one may love in his Age, I hope, what he cou'd not endure in his Youth. And yet if a Man were of a fearful Heart, he might stagger a little in this Attempt; and wou'd my Mistress marry me, which bears a Question likewise, we have here no Temple but the Wood, no Assembly but horned Beasts,—Horns,—Aye, they may be a Wife's Dowry, 'tis plain they can not be a Man's own getting;—And yet the nobler married Man hath them as huge as the Rascal;—Is a Batchelor, therefore, more honourable than a Husband?—No, as a walled Town is worthier than a Village, by so much is the armed Forehead of a married Man more honourable than the bare Brow of a Batchelor.——Surely this Wound is not very dangerous that I can tickle myself thus with scratching it:——I do not know how it is,——I am in silly Way,——Well——Well——We are all Babies, and cry ourselves sick for Play-things that we throw away the Moment after we have them.

[*Exit* Jaques.

Re-enter Celia *and* Rosalind.

Ros. I met the Duke Yesterday, and had much Question with him, he asked me of what Parentage I was, I told him of as good as he, so he laugh'd and let me go: But what talk we of Fathers when there is such a Man as *Orlando*.

Ca. But as I was saying, Coz, this Bluntness of *Jaques* becomes him, it is so unaffected; I think my Heart does incline a little to the Philosopher.

Ros. Then *Orlando*'s Hair; aye, his Hair is of the dissembling Colour.

Ca. Then *Jaques*'s Love looks a little awkward; it does not sit so easy on him; but his Words are full of Sincerity.

Ros. No faith, his Hair is of a good Colour.

Ca. I think he has got an Inch or two into my Heart,

Ros. Ah me! I am fifty Fathom deep in Love, I shall never recover it.

Ca. Lord, you can think of nothing but *Orlando*; but now I beg, I petition for a Word or two in Behalf of my Servant Senior *Jaques*.

Ros. Orlando swore he wou'd come again presently, is he not a true Lover, think you?

Ca. As hollow as a cover'd Goblet, or a Worm-eaten Nut.

Ros. Yet he Swore he was true.

Ca. Aye, so they do all, but they tell us, Cousin, and I tremble to think of it, that the Oath of a Lover is not to be depended on; but our Lovers are Courtiers too, and attend here on the Duke your Father, in this Forest: Now as Courtiers they have a certain Right to Promise-breaking.

Ros. No Matter, *Orlando* is not, can not, will not, shall not be false.

Ca. Oh he is a brave Man, writes brave Verses, speaks brave Words, swears brave Oaths, and notwithstanding your Resolution, Madamoiselle, he may break them as bravely. But what say you to Senior *Jaques,* once again? Will he make a good Husband?

Ros. Aye, a good Workyday Husband; you must have another for Sundays, but indeed your wise Fools make the best Lovers, 'tis your ——impenetrable Block only, that is ungovernable; thro' the Head of a wise Man there is a beaten Path to his Heart, that every Woman knows.

Ca. But year Advice, your Advice.

Ros. Alas, thou knowest I am sick of thy Distemper, and I must find a Cure for my own Malady before I presume to prescribe to thine.   [*Exeunt.*

The End of the Third A C T.

The Fourth ACT.

Jaques *and* Rosalind.

Jaques. I Come, young Shepherd, in the Name of that wimpled, whining, purblind, wayward Boy; Regent of Rhiming, Lord of folded Arms, anointed Soveriegn of Sighs and Groans, Don *Cupid*—!——

Ros. Say you so! Sir, Monsieur *Jaques* himself! is he inlisted in this blind Prince's Regiment of sighing Ideots.

Jaques. Aye—I wear his Colours, I love, I sue, I ask a Wife; prithee do not laugh at me, aye, I wou'd have a Woman—A Thing that is like a German Clock, always repairing——Ever out of Tune——Yes I am shot—Thumpt with the Boy's Bird-bolt under the Left Pap—'Faith.——Will you grant my Petition?

Ros. What! do all the Fools in Love's Hospital take me for their Physitian?

Jaques. I, that have been Love's Whip;—a very Beadle to a humourous Sigh.

Ros. But who are you in Love with?

Jaques. A Woman, I tell you—A whitely Wanton with a Velvet Brow, with two Pitch Balls stuck in her Face for Eyes.——I pray, I wish, I interceed, I petition, will you give me your Consent, aye, or no.——

Ros. Who is she?

Jaques. Don't you see her in my Face? Is not her Name in my Forehead already?

Ros. No really, as yet I think you have a smooth Brow,—her Name, her Name!

Jaques. The Lady, your Sister, *Aliena* I think you call her, the Gentlewoman your Companion and Friend.

Ros. With her! why you are utterly undone, she is as wild as a Feather, with an Understanding as perverse as a Fool's Jest, or a Child's Wish, Ha, ha,—how awkwardly it sits upon thee—Is it then possible that thy solemn Gravity shou'd relax into Wantonness at last?

Jaques. Aye! So it is, I do worship, yes I fall down, I am touch'd in the Liver Vein it seems, and have learn'd the Trick to turn a Green-Goose into a Deity—flat Idolatry!—Heaven mend me, I am much out o'the Way.

Ros. Aye, go thy Ways, and scourge thy self with thy own Discipline till thy Shoulders bleed, it is not my Business to injoin thee a Penance.

Jaques. Why then give me your Consent to be reveng'd on me for my Impertinence——Can you punish me more?

Ros. Why, Man, thy Sins, tho' they may be many and great, have hardly merited this Castigation; if you die of this Folly, you shall have a Stake thrust thro' you, and be bury'd in the Highway.

Jaques. I have a Stake thro' me—Here it is—Shall I have your Consent?

Ros. Never, St. *Cupid* be my Witness, never.

Jaques. Your Reason?

Ros. You are so rough, it will be impossible to polish you into a modern Husband.

Jaques. Why so?

Ros. Can that inflexible proud Heart of thine bend and be nealed into a commode, passive, obedient, necessary, blind, credulous Convenience call'd a Husband ? Why you rattle your Chains already like a raving Lunatic; what will you do, grave Sir, when you are shut up and shaved?

Jaques. Do, thrust thy Wit thro' and thro' me, cut me to Pieces with Satyr, I am an Ass to set up for a Lover, I confess my self a very Ass in Harness——I have not one Taffety Phrase, not a Silken Syllable——Well, Sir, you mean me well, I thank you, I will try to recover my Liberty, I will endeavour——If I am cured, and ever catch the Plague in my Eyes again—Fare you well. [*Exit* Jaques.

Ros. This Fellow's Reason has brought an Action against his Love; but it will go for the Defendent I see——Heigh ho, so it must be.

Enter Orlando *and* Celia.

Orl. My fair *Rosalind,* I come with all the Speed I cou'd, and within an Hour of my Promise, as your fair Sister here will witness.

Ros. Break an Hour's Promise in Love? He that will divide a Minute into a thousand parts, and break but one Part of the thousandth Part of a Minute in the Affairs of Love, it may be said of him, that *Cupid* hath clap'd him o'the Shoulder; but I will warrant him Heart whole.

Orl. Pardon me, dear *Rosalind.*

Ros. Nay, an you be so tardy, come no more in my Sight, I had as lieve be woo'd of a Snail.

Orl. Of a Snail!

Ros. Aye, of a Snail; for tho' he comes slowly, he carries his House on his Head; a better Jointure I think than you can make a Woman; besides, he brings his Destiny with him.

Orl. What's that?

Ros. Why Horns; which such as you are fain to be beholden to your Wives for; but he comes armed in his Forehead, and prevents the Slander of his Wife.

Orl. My *Rosalind* is virtuous.

Ros. And I am your *Rosalind*.

Ca. It pleases him to call you so, but he hath a *Rosalind* of a better Leer than you.

Ros. Come woo me, woo me, for now I am in a Holyday Humour, and like enough to consent; Am not I your *Rosalind*?

Orl. I take some Joy to say you are, because I wou'd be talking of her.

Ros. Well, in her Person, I say I will not have you.

Orl. I would not have my right *Rosalind* of this Mind, for I protest, her Frown might kill me.

Ros. By this Hand it will not kill a Flie; but come, now I will be your *Rosalind* in a more coming Disposition, and ask what you will, I will grant it.

Orl. Then love me, *Rosalind*.

Ros. Yes, faith will I, *Fridays,* and *Saturdays,* and all.

Orl. And wilt thou have me?

Ros. Aye, and twenty such. Come then, Sister, you shall be the Priest and marry us. Give me your Hand, *Orlando*; What do you say, Sister?

Orl. Prithee marry us.

Ca. I cannot say the Words.

Ros. You must begin, Will you *Orlando*——

Ca. Well then, Will you *Orlando* have to Wife this *Rosalind*?

Orl. I will.

Ros. Aye, but how long?

Orl. For ever and a Day.

Ros. Say a Day, without the ever; No, no, *Orlando,* Men are *April* when they woo, *December* when they are married; Maids are *May* when they are Maids, but the Sky changes when they are Wives; I will be more jealous of thee than a *Barbary* Cock-Pidgeon over his Hen, more clamorous than a Parrot against Rain, more new fangled than an Ape, more giddy in my Desires than a Monkey; when you are disposed to be merry, I will weep for nothing, weep like *Diana* in the Fountain; and when you are sad, I will laugh like the *Hyena,* and that too when You are inclined to Sleep

Orl. But will my *Rosalind* do so?

Ros. By my Life she will do as I do.

Orl. Oh but she is wise.

Ros. Or else she cou'd not have the Wit to do this, the wiser the waywarder, make the Doors fast upon a Woman's Wit and it will out at the Casement; shut that, and 'twill away through the Key-hole; stop that too, and it will fly with the Smoak up the Chimney.

Orl. But will you, when you shall see my sweet, my dear *Rosalind,* will you be my Voucher that she ought to give Credit to my Oaths, will you tell her you know, and are a Witness to the Sincerity and Ardour of my Love.

Ros. Oh no——I will tell her no such Thing, too well I know what Sort of Faith we Men to Women owe, my Father had a Daughter lov'd a Man; as it might be, perhaps, were I a Woman, I might love you.

Orl. And what is her History?

Ros. A Blank, she never told her Love, but let Concealment, since a Worm i'th Bud, feed on her Damask Cheek; she pined in Thought; and with a green and yellow Melancholly, she sat like Patience on a Monument, smiling at Grief——

Orl. Alass, poor Maid——Well, my dear *Rosalind,* for these two Hours I will leave thee.

Ros. Alass, dear Love, I cannot be without thee two Hours.

Orl. I must attend the Duke at Dinner; by two a Clock I will be with thee again.

Ros. Aye, go your Ways, go your Ways. I knew what you wou'd prove, my Friends told me as much, and I thought no less, that flattering Tongue of yours won me; 'tis but one cast away, and so come Death: Two o'the Clock is your Hour.

Orl. Aye, my sweet *Rosalind.*

Ros. By my Troth, and in good earnest, and so Heav'n mend me; and by all pretty Oaths that are not dangerous, if you break one Jot of your Promise, or come one Minute behind your Hour, I will think you the most pathetical Break-Promise, and the most hollow Lover, and the most unworthy of her you call *Rosalind,* that may be chosen out of the gross Band of the unfaithful; therefore beware my Censure and keep your Promise.

Orl. With no less Religion, than if thou wer't indeed my *Rosalind*—so Adieu.

Ros. Well—Time is the old Justice that examines all such Offenders, and let Time try Adieu.   [*Exit* Orlando.

Celia *and* Rosalind.

Ca. You have misus'd our Sex in your Love-Prate.

Ros. Oh Coz, Coz, Coz—my pretty little Coz—How many Fathom deep are we two in Love? Our Affections have an unknown Bottom, like the Bay of *Portugal.*

Ca. I wish they are not rather Bottomless——that as fast as we pour Affections in they run out again.

Ros. No, that same wicked Bastard of *Venus,* that was begot of Thought, conceiv'd of Spleen, and born of Madness; that blind Rascally Boy that abuses every Body's Eyes because his own are out, let him be Judge how deep I am in Love—I will tell thee, *Aliena,* I cannot live out of the Sight of *Orlando;* I'll go find a Shadow, and Sigh till he returns.

Ca. And I will go sleep, sleep peaceably if *Jaques,* alass, does not break in upon my Slumbers.   [*Exeunt.*

Amiens, *Lords, and Foresters.*

Amiens. Which is he that killed the Deer?

Lord. Sir. it was I.

Amiens. We will present him to the Duke like a Roman Conqueror, and it wou'd do well to set the Deer's Horns upon his Head for a Branch of Victory: Have you no Song, Forester, for this Purpose?

Forester. Yes, Sir.

Amiens. Sing it, 'tis no Matter how it is in Tune, so it makes Noise enough.

Forester sings.

What shall he have that kill'd the Deer?
His leathern Skin, and Horns to wear:
    Then sing him Home,
        Sing him Home.   [the Burthen by all.]

Take thou no scorn, to wear the Horn,
It was a Crest e'er thou wer't born;
    Thy Father's Father wore it,
    And thy Father bore it,
    The Horn, the Horn, the lusty Horn,
    Is not a Thing to laugh to Scorn:
Then sing him Home, sing him Home.   [*Exeunt.*

Rosalind *and* Celia.

Ros. And yet we hear nothing of *Orlando*——
How say you, is it not past two a Clock?

Ca. I warrant thee he will come with a pure
Heart and a troubled Brain.

Enter Robert du Bois.

Rob. Good Sir, one Word! I pray you, do you know
Where in the Purlieus of this Forest stands
A Sheepcote fenced about with Olive Trees?

Ca. West of this Place down in the Neighbour Bottom,
The Rank of Osiers by the murmuring Stream,
Left on the Right Hand, brings you to the Place;
But at this Hour the House doth keep itself,
There's none within.

Rob. I think I know you both by your Description,
Such Garments, and such Years; the Boy is fair,
Of Female Favour, and bestows himself
Like a ripe Sister: But the Woman
Browner than her Brother. Are not you

The Owners of the House I did inquire for?

    Ca. We are.

    Rob. Orlando doth commend him to you both,
And to that Youth he calls his *Rosalind*
He sends this bloody Handkerchief: Are you he?

    Ros. I am! What must we understand by this?

    Rob. When last the young *Orlando* parted from you,
He left a Promise to return again
Within an Hour; and pacing thro' the Forest,
Chewing the Food of sweet and bitter Fancy,
Lo what befel! he threw his Eye aside,
And mark what Object did present itself,
Under an old Oak, whose Boughs were moss'd with Age,
And high Top bald with dry Antiquity:
A wretched Man, o'erpower'd with Sleep and Travel,
Lay on his Back, around his naked Neck
A green and gilded Snake had wreath'd itself,
And with indented Glides did slip away
Into a Bush, under whose gloomy Shade
A Lioness, with Udders all drawn dry,
Lay couching Head on Ground, with Cat-like watch
When that the sleeping Man shou'd stir; for 'tis
The Royal Disposition of that Beast
To prey on nothing that does seem as dead;
This seen, *Orlando* did approach the Man,
And found it was his Brother, his youngest Brother.

    Ca. Oh! I have heard him speak of that same Brother
With much Concern, and natural Tenderness,
As left behind under the cruel Guardianship
Of his most cruel eldest Brother *Oliver.*

    Ros. But to *Orlando,* did he leave him there
Food to the suck'd and hungry Lioness?

    Rob. No, he gave Battle to the furious Beast,
Who quickly fell before him: In the Hurley,
From miserable Slumber I awoke.

    Ca. Are you his Brother?

    Ros. Was it you he rescued?

    Ca. We give you Joy, your Brother's Noble Spirit
Appears in every Action of his Life.

    Ros. Oh! my Heart beats;——but, Sir, the bloody Handkerchief?

    Rob. By and by——

When from the first to last between us two
Tears our Recountments had most kindly bathed,
As how I came into that Desart Place,
He led me instantly unto his Cave,
There stripped himself, and here upon his Arm
The Lioness had torn some Flesh away,
Which all this while had bled; and now he fainted,
And cry'd in fainting upon *Rosalind.*
Brief, I recover'd him, bound up his Wound,
When after some small Space being strong at Heart,
He sent me hither, Stranger as I am,
To tell this Story, that you might excuse
His broken Promise, and to give this Handkerchief,
Dy'd in his Blood, unto the Shepherd-Youth
That he in Sport doth call his *Rosalind.*   [Ros. *swoons into* Celia's *Arms.*

Ca. Why how now, *Ganymede,* sweet *Ganymede?*

Rob. Many will swoon when they but look on Blood.

Ca. There is no more in it: Brother *Ganymede!*

Rob. Look, he recovers.

Ca. I pray you take him by the Arm.

Rob. Be of good Cheer, Youth;—You a Man!
You lack a Man's Heart.

Ros. I do so, I confess it;—Ah!—A Body wou'd think this was well counterfeited: I pray you tell your Brother how well I counterfeited: Heigh-ho——

Ca. Came you, Sir, from the Court of *Frederick* directly.

Rob. From thence expresly to the banish'd Duke,
And partly, too, to bring *Orlando* News
Of our unnatural elder Brother's Death,
And of his Lands and antient Patrimony
Descended to him by this Accident.

Ros. What Accident, I pray you?

Rob. He died convicted of most foul Designs,
And *Charles* confess'd, with his last dying Breath,
The Fencer, *Charles,* whom he in single Combat
Subdued, confess'd, that *Oliver* practis'd with him;
He was suborn'd by *Oliver* to impeach
Orlando as a Traitor——*Frederick*
Resolv'd to punish him; but he prevented,
With a despairing Hand, the Sword of Justice;
And fell a Martyr to his own Misdoings.

Ca. We hide our Deeds from Heav'n, as Children do
Their Eyes from Daylight, and because we see not.
Believe we walk unseen.

Ros. Come, sir, this Story feeds your Melancholly,
You shall retire and take within our Cottage
What small Refreshment there you'll find.

Rob. I pray you first inform me, gentle sir,
Where in the Confines of this Forest dwells
Our good *Alberto,* with his banish'd Nobles,
I have some Business there, of such Import,
No Minutes shou'd be lost.

Ros. ——Then but a Minute,
And we'll conduct you to the good Duke's Cave.

Rob. I thank you, and will follow.

Ros. This Way, Sir,—Wee will attend you.   [*Exeunt.*

Enter Orlando *and* Jaques.

Orl. As yet your Fever does not intermit, but what will become of you in the cold Fit.

Jaques. I shall take the Jesuit's Bark of Matrimony.

Orl. A Specifick.

Jaques. I have had much Bustle with my Heart to little purpose; prithee ask him, this *Ganymede,* thou hast an Interest there, ask his consent, the Woman has agreed——We want his Approbation only.

Orl. And you persist——

Jaques. I will die a Martyr to my Folly.

Orl. Enough, I will engage your Brother *Ganymede,* and your Wedding shall be to Morrow; thither will I invite the Duke and all his contented Followers, go you and prepare *Aliena,* for look you here comes my *Rosalind.*

          [*Exit* Jaques.

Enter Rosalind.

Ros. Oh my dear *Orlando,* how it grieves me to see thee wear thy Arm in a Scarfe. Did your Brother tell you how I counterfeited Fainting, when he shewed me the Handkerchief.

Orl. Aye, and greater Wonders than that: But I have engaged you to consent that your Sister, and Senior *Jaques* may have Leave legally to go to Bed together.

Ros. Aliena has my Approbation; in a Word, the good People are in the very Wrath of Love and they will together whether I will or no, Clubs cannot part 'em——

Orl. They shall be marry'd to Morrow, and I will bid the Duke to their Nuptials. But oh how bitter a Thing it is to look into Happiness through another Man's Eyes; by so much more shall I to Morrow be the heavier in my Heart, by how much I shall think my Friend *Jaques* happy in having what he wishes for.

Ros. Why then, to Morrow, I cannot serve your Turn for *Rosalind.*

Orl. I can live no longer by thinking.

Ros. Know then that since I was seven Years old I have conversed with a Magitian, most profound in his Art and yet not damnable. If you do love *Rosalind,* and so near the Heart as you say, when *Jaques* marries *Aliena,* you shall marry her; I know into what Streights of Fortune she is driven, and it is not impossible to me, if it is not inconvenient to you, to set her before your Eyes to Morrow; human as she is and without any Danger.

Orl. Speakest thou in sober Meaning?

Ros. By my Life I do, which I tender dearly, tho' I say I am a Magitian; therefore put on your best Looks, for if you will be married to Morrow you shall, and to *Rosalind* if you will. Look ye, here comes another Pair of Lovers, even the captivated *Jaques,* and his Conquerour.

Enter Jaques *and* Celia.

Ca. Good Shepherd, tell us what it is to Love?

Ros. It is to be made all of Sighs and Tears.
It is to be all made of Fantasy,
All made of Passion, and all made of Wishes.
All Adoration, Duty, and Observance.

Jaques. And so am I for *Aliena.*

Ca. And I for *Jaques.*

Orl. And I for *Rosalind.*

Ros. And I for no Woman. Pray you no more of this, 'tis like the howling of Wolves against the Moon, to Morrow you agree to meet me, all together, before the Duke; if he will give his Approbation, you shall be marry'd to Morrow; I will content you, *Orlando,* if what pleases you contents you, and you shall be marry'd to Morrow; as you love *Rosalind,* meet, as you love Celia, meet, as you love *Jaques,* meet, and as I love no Woman I will meet. So fare you well, I have left you my Commands.

Ca. I will not fail, if I live.

Jaques. Nor I.

Orl. Nor I.

The End of the Fourth A C T.

The Fifth A C T.

Duke Alberto, Amiens, Jaques, Orlando, Celia.

Duke. Doest thou believe, *Orlando,* that the Boy,
This little, prating, buisy *Ganymede,*
Can do all this that he hath promised.

    Orl. I sometimes do believe, and sometimes do not.

Enter Rosalind.

    Ros. Patience once more while our Compact is urged,
You say, if l bring in your *Rosalind*   [*to the Duke.*
You will bestow her on *Orlando* here.

    Duke. That would I, had I Kingdoms to give with her.

    Ros. And you say, you will have her when I bring her.

    Orl. That wou'd I, were I of all Kingdoms King;
Tho' to have her and Death were equal both.

    Ros. Well! I engage to make these Masters even,
Keep you your Word, O Duke, to give your Daughter;
You yours, *Orlando,* to recieve his Daughter;
Keep you your Word that you will marry *Jaques,*
And you that you, with Transport, will recieve her;
And hence I go to make these Doubts all even
In half the Circle but of sixty Minutes.   [*Exit* Ros. *and* Celia.

    Duke. I do remember in this Sheepherd Boy,
Some lively Touches of my Daughter's Favour.

    Orl. My Liege, the first Time that I ever saw him,
Methought he was a Brother to your Daughter;
But, my good Lord, this Boy is Forest born
And hath been tutor'd in the Rudiments
Of many desperate Studies, by his Uncle,
Whom he reports to be a great Magitian
Obscured within the Circle of this Forest.

    Duke. Come, now what Entertainment shall we have
To waste this half an Age, this long half Hour,
When *Ganymede* has promis'd to perform
These Miracles of Love.

    Jaques. A Play there is, my Liege, some ten Words long,
Which is as brief as I have known a Play;
But by ten Words, my Lord, it is too long,
Which makes it tedious: For in all the Play
There is not one Word apt, one Player fitted,

And tragical, my noble Lord, it is:
For *Pyramus* therein doth kill himself;
Which when I saw rehears'd, I must confess,
Made mine Eyes Water; but more merry Tears
The Passion of loud Laughter never shed.

 Duke. What are they that do play it?

 Jaques. Some Citizens of *Liege,* who from pure Hearts
And loyal Love have follow'd your bad Fortune,
Who never labour'd in their Minds till now,
And they design at least to entertain.

 Duke. I'll hear this Play, nothing can be amiss:
Simplicity and Duty make it grateful.
Where I have come, great Clerks have purposed
To greet me with premeditated Welcomes;
And I have seen them shiver and look pale,
Make Periods in the midst of Sentences,
Throttle their practis'd Accents in their Fears,
And in Conclusion, dumbly have broke off,
Not paying me a Welcome. Trust me, Friends,
Out of this Silence, yet I pick'd a Welcome,
And in the Modesty of fearful Duty
I read much more than from the rattling Tongues
Of fancy and audacious Eloquence.

 Jaques. So please your Grace, the Prologue is address'd.

 Duke. Let him approach.

  Enter Quince *as Prologue, speaking very fast and without Stops.*

 Quince. If we offend it is with our Good Will
That you shou'd think we come not to offend
But with Good Will to shew our Simple Skill
That is the true Beginning of our End
Consider then we come but in Despight
We do not come as minding to content you
Our true Intent is all for your Delight
We are not here that you shou'd here repent you
The Actors are at Hand and by their Show
You shall know all that you are like to know.

 Duke. This Fellow doth not stand upon Points.

 Jaques. He hath rid his Prologue like a rough Colt: He knows not to stop; a Good Moral, Sir; it is not enough to speak, but to speak true.

Duke. He hath play'd on his Prologue, like a Child on the Recorder, a Sound, but not in Government.

Jaques. His Speech was like a tangled Chain; no thing impaired, but all disordered. Who is the next?

Enter Wall.

Wall. In this same Interlude it doth befall,
That I, one *Snowt* (by Name) present a Wall;
And such a Wall, as I wou'd have you think,
That had in it a crannied Hole, or Chink;
Thro' which the Lovers *Pyramus* and *Thisby*
Did whisper often very secretly.
This Loam, this Rough-cast, and this Stone doth show
That I am that same Wall; the Truth is so.
And this the Cranny is, righ, and sinister,
Thro' which the fearful Lovers are to whisper.

Duke. Wou'd you desire Lime and Hair to speak better?
Orl. This is the wittiest Partition that ever I heard Discourse.
Duke. See *Pyramus,* I suppose; he draws near. Silence.

Enter Pyramus

Pyr. O grim look'd Night! O Night with hue so black!
O Night which ever art, when Day is not!
O Night, O Night, alack, alack, alack,
I fear thy *Thisby*'s Promise is forgot:
And thou, O *Wall,* thou sweet and lovely *Wall,*
Shew me thy Chink to blink thro' with mine Ey'n.
Thanks, courteous *Wall; Jove* shield thee well for this.
But what see I?—No *Thisby* do I see.
O Wicked Wall, thro' whom I see no Bliss,
Curss'd be thy Stones for thus deceiving me.

Duke. The Wall methinks, being sensible, shou'd curse again.
Pyr. No, in Truth Sir, but he shou'd not, deceiving me, aye that is *Thisby*'s Cue; she is to enter, and I am to spy her thro' the Wall: You shall see it will happen just as I tell you: Yonder she comes.

Enter Thisby.

Thisby. O *Wall*! full often hast thou heard my Moans
For parting my fair *Pyramus* and me;
My Cherry Lips hath often kiss'd thy Stones,

Thy Stones with Lime and Hair knit up in thee.

Pyr. I see a Voice; now will I to the Chink,
To spy an I can hear my *Thisby*'s Face—*Thisby*—

Thisby. My Love thou art, my Love I think.

Pyr. Think what thou wilt, I am thy Lover's Grace,
And like *Limandar* am I trusty still.

Thisby. And I like *Helen* till the Fates me kill.

Pyr. Not *Shafalus* to *Procrus* was so true.

Thisby. As *Shafalus* to *Procrus* I to you.

Pyr. O kiss me thro' the Hole of this vile *Wall*.

Thisby. I kiss the *Wall*'s Hole, not your Lips at all.

Pyr. Wilt thou at *Ninny*'s Tomb meet me strait way?

Thisby. Tide Life, Tide Death, I come without Delay.

[*Exeunt* Pyr. *and* Thisby.

Wall. Thus have I, *Wall,* my Part discharged so,
And being done, thus *Wall* away doth go.   [*Exit* Wall.

Orl. This is the silliest Stuff that ever I heard.

Duke. The best in this Kind are but Shadows, and the worst are no worse, if Imagination amend them.

Orl. And yet if we imagine no worse of them than they of themselves, they may pass for excellent Men. Here come two noble Beasts in a Man and a Lion.

Enter Lion *and* Moonshine.

Lion. You, Ladies, you (whose gentle Hearts do fear
The smallest monstrous Mouse that creeps on Floor)
May now, perchance, both quake and tremble here,
When *Lion* rough in wildest Rage doth roar.
Then know that I one *Snug* the Joiner am,
No *Lion* fell, nor yet no *Lion*'s Dam:
For if I shou'd as *Lion* come in Strife
Into this Place, 'twere Pity of my Life.

Duke. A very good Beast, and of a good Conscience.

Jaques. The very best at a Beast that ever I saw.

Orl. This Lion is a very Fox for his Valour.

Jaques. And a Goose for his Discretion.

Moon. This Lanthorn does the horned Moon present.

Jaques. He shou'd have worn the Horns on his Head.

Moon. This Lanthorn does the horned Moon present,

Myself the Man i'th' Moon doth seem to be.

Duke. I am weary of this *Moon* already, wou'd he wou'd change; however, proceed, *Moon.*

Moon. Why all that I have to say is to tell you, that the Lanthorn is the Moon, I the Man in the Moon, this Thorn-bush, and this Dog my Dog.

Duke. Why all these shou'd be in the Lanthorn; for they are in the Moon; But Silence; here comes *Thisby.*

Enter Thisby.

Thisby. This is old *Ninny*'s Tomb, where is my Love?
Lion. (*Roars.*) Oh
    [Lion *roars, and* Thisby *runs off and leaves her Mantle behind.*

Orl. Well roar'd, *Lion.*
Duke. Well run, *Thisby.*
Jaques. Well shone, *Moon.*

Enter Pyramus.

Pyr. Sweet *Moon,* I thank thee for thy Sunny Beams,
I thank thee, *Moon,* for shining now so bright,
For by thy gracious, golden, glittering Streams,
I trust to taste of truest *Thisby*'s Sight.
But stay: O Spight! but mark poor Knight,
What dreadful Dole is here?
Eyes do you see! How can it be!
O dainty Duck: O Deer!
Thy Mantle good, What I stain'd with Blood!
Approach you Furies fell:
O Fates! Come, come; cut Thread and Thrum,
Quail, Crush, Conclude and Quell.

Duke. This Passion, and the Death of a dear Friend wou'd go near to make a Man look sad.

Pyr. O wherefore Nature didst thou Lions frame!
Since *Lion* wild hath here deflowr'd my Dear,
Which is: No, no, which was the fairest Dame
That liv'd, that lov'd, that lik'd, that look'd with Cheer;
Come Tears confound: Out Sword, and wonnd
The Pap of *Py—ramus:*
I, that left Pap, where Heart doth hop:

Thus die I, thus, thus, thus.
Now am I dead, now am I fled, my Soul is in the Sky;
Tongue lose thy Light, Moon take thy Flight,
Now die, die, die, die, die.

Duke. With the Help of a Surgeon he might yet recover and prove an Ass.

Orl. How chance the *Moonshine* is gone before *Thisby* comes back and finds her Lover.

Duke. She will find him by Star-Light; and her Passion and Speech end the Play.

Orl. Methinks she shou'd not use a long one for such a *Pyramus,* I hope she will be brief.

Enter Thisby.

Thisby. A sleep, my Love? What dead my Dove!
    O *Pyramus,* arise:
Speak: Speak! Quite dumb? Dead, dead? A Tomb must cover my sweet Eyes.
These Lilly Lips, this Cherry Nose, these yellow Cowslip Cheeks,
Are gone; are gone: Lovers make moan, his Eyes were green as Leaks,
O Sisters three, Come, come to me, with Hands as pale as Milk;
Lay him in Gore, since you have shore, with Sheers, this Thread of Silk.
Tongue not a Word, come trusty Sword, come Blade my Breast imbrue;
And farewel Friends, thus *Thisby* ends; Adieu, Adieu, Adieu.

Duke. Moonshine and *Lion* are left to bury the Dead.

Orl. Aye, and *Wall* too.

Pyr. (*rising*) No, I assure you, the Wall is down that parted their Fathers. Will it please you to see the Epilogue?

Duke. No Epilogue, I pray you, for your Play needs no Excuse, when the Players are all dead there need none to be blamed. Marry, if he that wrote it had play'd *Pyramus* and hung himself in *Thisby'*s Garter, it wou'd have been a fine Tragedy: And so it is truly, and very notably discharged—No more scraping, but vanish. Look yonder, *Orlando,* your young Magitian is performing his Promise in Form, I see, here they come, Music too. Let us attend them.

Soft Music; Enter Hymen *with his Torch,* &c. *introducing* Rosalind in
Woman's Cloaths and Celia

Hymen. *Then is there Mirth in Heaven,*
    When Earthly Things made even;
        Accord together.
    Good Duke, recieve thy Daughter,

Hymen *from Heaven brought her,*
    Tea, brought her hither,
That thou might'st join her Hand with his,
Whose Heart within his Bosom is.

Ros. (*to the Duke*) To you I give myself, for I am yours.
(*to Orlando*) To you I give myself, for I am yours.
    Duke. If there be Truth in Sight, you are my Daughter.
    Orl. If there be Truth in Sight, you are my *Rosalind.*
    Ros. I'll have no Father if thou be not he.
I'll have no Husband if thou be not he.
    Hymen. Peace ho! I bar Confusion:
        'Tis I must make conclusion
        Of these most strange Events.
        Here are four that must take Hands,
        To joyn in *Hymen*'s Bands,
        If Truth holds true contents,
        You and you no Cross shall part;
        You and you are Heart in Heart:
        While our Dancers tread a Ring,
        Feed yourselves with questioning:
        That Reason Wonder may diminish
        How we met, and these Things finish.
    Duke to Celia. Oh my dear Niece, welcome thou art to me;
Even, Daughter, welcome in no less Degree.

Enter Robert du Bois.

    Rob. Let me have Audience for a Word or two,
I am the youngest Son of old Sir *Rowland,*
That bring good Tidings to this fair Assembly:
Duke *Frederick,* hearing how from Day to Day
Men of great worth resorted to this Forest,
Address'd a mighty Power, which were on Foot
In his own Conduct, purposely to take
His Brother here, and put him to the Sword:
And to the Skirts of this wild Wood he came,
Where meeting with an old Religious Man,
After some Question with him, was converted
Both from his Enterprize, and from the World;
His Crown bequeathing to his banish'd Brother;
And all their Lands restor'd to them again

That were with him exiled. This to be true
I do engage my Life.

    Duke. ——Welcome young Man,
Thou offer'd fairly to thy Brother's Wedding;
To one his Lands withheld, and to the other
A Land itself at large, a potent Dukedom.
First in this Forest let us do those Ends
That here were well begun and well begot:
And after, all of this most happy Number
Shall share the good of our returned Fortune
According to the Measure of their States;
Mean Time forget this new fall'n Dignity,
And fall into our rustick Revelry.

A DANCE.

    Duke. Now let us solemnly compleat those Rites,
Which we do trust will end in true Delights.

FINIS.

PROLOGUE.

Spoken by Mr. *Wilks*.

In Honour to his name, and this learn'd Age,
Once more your much lov'd SHAKESPEAR *treads the Stage.*
Another Work from that great Hand appears,
His Ore's refin'd, but not impar'd by Years.
Those sacred Truths our Sages coldly tell
In languid Prose; as He *describes—we feel.*
He looks all Nature thro'; strikes at a Heat
Her various Forms, irregularly Great.

   See the Dictator *by the* Patriot *slain,*
And the World's mighty Victor bleed again;
His ROMANS, *Speak and Act like* ROMANS *all,*
We hear them Thunder in the Capitol:
Quick Cassius *raves, and* Brutus, *sternly good,*
Pierces the Father's in the Tyrant's Blood.

   In Timon Wordly Friendships we despise,
And View their Flattery with distrusting Eyes.
When Brave Othello's *generous Soul is mov'd*
By jealous Fraud to murder all he lov'd,

   Tell us, ye Fair, are Fields, and Trees, and Daws,
A Sight to be prefer'd to Bells and Beaus?
Behold there Country *Spouse, and Rural 'Squire,*
In a long Winter's Night by Log-wood Fire,
Dirty and dull;——to every Pleasure lost,
The Fair wou'd fain forget she was a Toast:
In her white Arms now snores a hunting Warrior
Till wak'd by Horns to follow Fox with Terrier:
They eat, they sleep, they like their Trees decay,
Grow old, and bald, and Vegetate *away.*

   Give us, who wake, Joys to dull Souls unknown,
The circulating Pleasures of the Town;
I mean those Pleasures that befit a Mind,
By regular and virtuous Laws refind;
Such may the S T A G E *continue still to give,*
May such alone your just Applause receive;
Pass then the Failures of our Writer's Pen,
And pardon what you find a guiltless Scene.
As here by reasonable J O Y s *you're mov'd,*
Be this, your noblest Pleasure, best aapprov'd.

(London: W. Chetwood, 1723)

THE PLAYS OF WILLIAM SHAKESPEARE
Samuel Johnson, Ed.
1765

AS YOU LIKE IT
A
C O M E D Y.

Dramatis Personæ*.

D U K E.

Frederick, *brother to the Duke, and usurper.*

Amiens, Jaques,}*Lords attending upon the Duke in his banishment.*

Le Beu, *a courtier attending upon* Frederick.

Oliver, *eldest Son to* Sir Rowland de Boys.

Jaques, Orlando,} *Younger brothers to* Oliver.

Adam, *an old servant of* Sir Rowland de Boys.

Touchstone, a clown.

Corin, Sylvia,} *Shepherds.*

William, *in love with* Audrey.

Sir Oliver Mar-text, *a country curate.*

Charles, *wrestler to the usurping Duke* Frederick.

Dennis, *servant to* Oliver.

Rosalind, *daughter to* Frederick.

Celia, *daughter to* Frederick.

Phebe, *a shepherdess.*

Audrey, *a country wench.*

Lords belonging to the two Dukes: with pages, foresters, and other attendants.

The SCENE lies, first near Oliver's *house; and afterwards, partly in the Duke's Court, and partly in the Forest of* Arden.

The first Edition of this play is in the Folio of 1623.

*The list of the persons, being omitted in the old Editions, was added by Mr. *Rowe.*

AS YOU LIKE IT.

ACT I. SCENE I.

O L I VE R's *Orchard.*

Enter Orlando *and* Adam.

ORLANDO.

AS I remember, *Adam,* it was upon this fashion bequeath'd me. By will, but a poor thousand crowns[1]; and, as thou say'st, charged my brother on his

---

[1] *As I remember,* Adam, *it was upon this* FASHION *bequeathed me by Will, but a poor thousand crowns,* &c.] The Grammar, as well as sense, suffers cruelly by this reading. There are two nominatives to the verb *bequeathed,* and not so much as one to the verb *charged*: and yet, to the nominative there wanted, [*his blessing*] refers. So that the whole sentence is confused and obscure. A very small alteration in the reading and pointing sets all right.———

As I remember, Adam, *it was upon this* MY FATHER *beqeathed me,* &c.] The Grammar is now rectified, and the sense also; which is this, *Orlando* and *Adam* were discoursing together on the cause why the younger brother had but a thousand crowns left him. They agree upon it; and *Orlando* opens the scene in this manner, *As I remember, it was upon this,* i.e. for the reason we have been talking of, that my Father left me but a thousand crowns; however, to make amends for this scanty provision, he charged my brother on his blessing to breed me well.   WARBURTON.

There is, in my opinion, nothing but a point misplaced, and an omission of a word which every hearer can supply, and which therefore an abrupt and eager dialogue naturally excludes.

I read thus: *As I remember,* Adam, *it was on this fashion bequeathed me. By*

Blessing to breed me well. And there begins my sadness. My brother Jaques he keeps at school, and report speaks goldenly of his profit.

For my part, he keeps me rustically at home; or to speak more properly, stays me here at home, unkept[2]; for call you that keeping for a gentleman of my birth, that differs not from the stalling of an ox? His horses are bred better; for besides that they are fair with their feeding, they are taught their manage, and to that end riders dearly hired; but I, his brother, gain nothing under him but growth; for the which his animals on his dunghills are as much bound to him as I. Besides this nothing that he so plentifully gives me, the Something that nature gave me[3], his countenance seems to take from me. He lets me feed with his hinds, bars me the place of a brother, and, as much as in him lies, mines my gentility with my education. This is it, Adam, that grieves me; and the Spirit of my father, which I think is within me, begins to mutiny against this servitude. I will no longer endure it, tho' yet I know no wise remedy how to avoid it.

SCENE II.

Enter Oliver.

Adam. Yonder comes my master, your brother.

Orla. Go apart, *Adam,* and thou shalt hear how he will shake me up.

Oli. Now, Sir, what make ye here?

Orla. Nothing: I am not taught to make any thing.

Oli. What mar ye then, Sir?

Orla. Marry, Sir, I am helping you to mar That which God made; a poor unworthy brother of yours, with idleness.

Oli. Marry, Sir, be better employ'd, and be nought a while[4].

---

will but a poor thousand crowns; and, as thou sayst, charged my brother on his blessing to breed me well. What is there in this difficult or obscure? the nominative *my father* is certainly left out, but so left out that the auditor inserts it, in spite of himself.

[2] STAYS *me here at home, unkept*.] We should read STYS, i.e. keeps me like a brute. The following words——*for call you that keeping——that differs not from the stalling of an ox,* confirms this emendation. So *Caliban* says,

    And here you STY *me in this hard rock*.   WARB.

Sties is better than *stays,* and more likely to be *Shakespear's*.

[3] *His* COUNTENANCE *seems to take from me*.] We should certainly read his DISCOUNTENANCE.   WARBURTON.

There is no need of change, a countenance is either good or bad.

[4] *Be better employed and* be nought a while.] Mr. *Theobald* has here a very

Orla. Shall I keep your hogs, and eat husks with them? what Prodigal's portion have I spent, that I should come to such penury?

Oli. Know you where you are, sir?

Orla. O. sir, very well; here in your Orchard.

Oli. Know you before whom, sir?

Orla. Ay, better than he, I am before, knows me. I know; you are my eldest brother; and in the gentle condition of blood, you should so know me. The courtesy of nations allows you my better, in that you are the first born: but the same tradition takes not away my blood, were there twentybrothers betwixt us. I have as much of my father in me, as you; albeit, I confess, your coming before me is nearer to his reverence[5].

Oli. What, boy!   [*menacing with his hand.*

Orla. Come, come, elder brother, you are too young in this.

---

critical note; which, though his modesty suffered him to withdraw it from his second edition, deserves to be perpetuated, *i.e. (says he) be better employed, in my opinion, in being and doing nothing. Your idleness as you call it may be an exercise, by which you may make a figure, and endear yourself to the world: and I had rather you were a contemptible Cypher. The poet seems to me to have that trite proverbial sentiment in his eye quoted, from* Attilius, *by the younger* Pliny *and others*; satius est otiosum esse quam nihil agere. *But* Oliver *in the perverseness of his disposition would reverse the doctrine of the proverb.* Does the Reader know what all this means? But 'tis no matter. I will assure him—— *be nought a while* is only a north-country proverbial curse, equivalent to a *mischief on you.* So the old poet *Skelton,*

> *Correct first thyselfe, walke and* BE NOUGHT.
> *Deeme what thou list, thou knowest not my thought.*

But what the *Oxford* Editor could not explain, he would amend, and reads,

> *——and do aught awhile*.   WARBURTON.

If be nought a while has the signification here given it, the reading may certainly stand; but till I learned its meaning from this note, I read,

> *be better employed, and be* naught *a while*.

In the same sense as we say *it is better to do mischief than to do nothing*.

[5] *Albeit, I confess your coming before me is nearer to his* REVERENCE.] This is sense indeed, and may be thus understood,—The reverence due to my father is, in some degree, derived to you, as the first born—But I am persuaded that *Orlando* did not here mean to compliment his brother, or condemn himself, something of both which there is in that sense. I rather think he intended a satirical reflection on his brother, who, by *letting him feed with his hinds,* treated him as one not so nearly related to *old* Sir *Rowland* as himself was. I imagine therefore *Shakespeare* might write,——*albeit your coming before me is nearer to his* REVENUE, *i.e.* though you are no nearer in blood, yet it must be owned, indeed, you are nearer in estate.   WARBURTON.

Oli. Wilt thou lay hands on me, villain?

Orla. I am no villain[6]: I am the youngest son of Sir *Rowland de Boys,* he was my father, and he is thrice a villain, that says, such a father begot villains. Wert thou not my brother, I would not take this hand; from thy throat, 'till this other had pulled out thy 'tongue for saying so; thou hast rail'd on thyself.

Adam. Sweet masters, be patient; for your father's remembrance, be at accord.

Oli. Let me go, I say.

Orla. I will not, 'till I please. You shall hear me.——My father charged you in his Will to give me good education; you have trained me up like a peasant, obscuring and hiding from me all gentleman-like qualities. The spirit of my father grows strong in me, and I will no longer endure it: therefore allow me such exercises as may become a gentleman, or give me the poor allottery my father left me by testament; with that I will go buy my fortunes.

Oli. And what wilt thou do? beg, when that is spent?——Well, Sir, get you in.——I will not long be troubled with you: you shall have some part of your will. I pray you, leave me.

Orla. I will no further offend you, than becomes me for my good.

Oli. Get you with him, you old dog.

Adam. Is old dog my reward? most true, I have lost my teeth in your service. God be with my old master, he would not have spoke such a word.

[*Exe.* Orlando *and* Adam.

SCENE III.

Oli. Is it even so?—Begin you to grow upon me?—I will physick your rankness, and yet give no thousand crowns neither. Holla, *Dennis*!

Enter Dennis.

Den. Calls your Worship?

Oli. Was not *Charles,* the Duke's Wrestler, here to speak with me?

Den. So please you, he is here at the door, and importunes access to you.

Oli. Call him in—[*Exit* Dennis.] 'Twill be a good way; and to-morrow the wrestling is.

---

[6] *I am no villain.*] The word *villain* is used by the elder brother in its present meaning, for a *wicked or bloody man*; by Orlando, in its original signification, for a *fellow of base extraction*.

Cha. Good-morrow to your Worship.

Oli. Good monsieur *Charles,* what's the new news at the new Court?

Cha. There's no news at the Court, Sir, but the old news; that is, the old Duke is banish'd by his younger brother the new Duke, and three or four loving lords have put themselves into voluntary exile with him; whose lands and revenues enrich the new Duke, therefore he gives them good leave to wander.

Oli. Can you tell, if *Rosalind,* the old Duke's daughter[7], be banish'd with her father?

Cha. O. no; for the new Duke's daughter her cousin so loves her, being ever from their cradles bred together, that she would have followed her exile, or have died to stay behind her. She is at the Court, and no less beloved of her uncle than his own daughter; and never two ladies loved, as they do.

Oli. Where will the old Duke live?

Cha. They say he is already in the forest of *Arden,* and a many merry men with him; and there they live like the old *Robin Hood of England.* They say, many young gentlemen flock to him every day, and fleet the time carelessly as they did in the golden world.

Oli. What, you wrestle to-morrow before the new duke?

Cha. Marry, do I, Sir; and I came to acquaint you with a matter. I am given, Sir, secretly to understand, that your younger brother *Orlando* hath a disposition to come in disguis'd against me to try a Fall. To-morrow, Sir, I wrestle for my credit; and he, that escapes me without some broken limb, shall acquit him well. Your brother is but young and tender, and for your love I would be loth to foil him; as I must for mine own honour, if he come in. Therefore, out of my love to you, I came hither to acquaint you withal; that either you might stay him from his intendment, or brook such disgrace well as he shall run into; in that it is a thing of his own search, and altogether against my will.

Oli. Charles, I thank thee for thy love to me, which thou shalt find I will most kindly requite. I had myfelf notice of my brother's purpose herein, and have by under-hand means laboured to dissuade him from it; but he is resolute. I tell thee, *Charles,* he is the stubbornest young fellow of *France*; full of ambition, an envious emulator of every man's good parts, a secret and villanous contriver against me his natural brother. Therefore use thy discretion; I had as lief thou didst break his neck, as his finger. And thou wert best look to't; for if thou dost him any slight disgrace, or if he do not mightily grace himself on

---

[7] *The old Duke's daughter*.] The words *old* and *new,* which seem necessary to the perspicuity of the dialogue, are inserted from Sir *T. Hanmer's* Edition.

thee, he will practise against thee by poison; entrap thee by some treacherous device, and never leave thee, 'till he hath ta'en thy life by some indirect means or other; for I asure thee (and almost with tears I speak it) there is not one so young and so villanous this day living. I speak but brotherly of him; but should I anatomize him to thee as he is, I must blush and weep, and thou must look pale and wonder.

Cha. I am heartily glad I came hither to you. If he come to-morrow, I'll give him his payment; if ever he go alone again, I'll never wrestle for prize more. And so, God keep your Worship.   [*Exit.*

Oli. Farewel, good *Charles.* Now will I stir this gamester: I hope I shall see an end of him; for my soul, yet I know not why, hates nothing more than him. Yet he's gentle; never school'd, and yet learned; full of noble device; of all Sorts enchantingly beloved; and, indeed, so much in the heart of the world, and especially of my own people who best know him, that I am altogether misprised. But it shall not be so long—this wrestler shall clear all. Nothing remains, but that I kindle the boy thither, which now I'll go about.   [*Exit.*

SCENE IV.

Changes to an Open Walk, before the Duke's Palace.

Enter Rosalind *and* Celia.

Cel. I Pray thee, *Rosalind,* sweet my coz, be merry.

Ros. Dear *Celia,* I show more mirth than I am mistress of; and would you yet I were merrier? Unless you could teach me to forget a banish'd father, you must not learn me how to remember any extraordinary pleasure.

Cel. Herein, I see, thou lov'st me not with the full weight that I love thee. If my Uncle, thy banished father, had banished thy uncle, the Duke my father, so thou hadst been still with me, I could have taught my love to take thy father for mine; so wouldst thou, if the truth of thy love to me were so righteously temper'd, as mine is to thee.

Ros. Well, I will forget the condition of my estate, to rejoice in yours.

Cel. You know, my father hath no child but I, nor none is like to have; and, truly, when he dies, thou shalt be his heir; for what he hath taken away from thy father perforce, I will render thee again in affection; by mine Honour, I will—

and when I break that oath, let me turn monster. Therefore, my sweet *Rose,* my dear *Rose,* be merry.

Ros. From henceforth I will, Coz, and devise Sports. Let me see—What think you of falling in love?

Cel. Marry, I pr'ythee, do, to make sport withal; but love no man in good earnest; nor no further in sport neither, than with safety of a pure blush thou may'st in honour come off again.

Ros. What shall be our sport then?

Cel. Let us sit and mock the good housewife Fortune from her wheel[8], that her gifts may henceforth be bestowed equally.

Ros. I would, we could do so; for her benefits are mightily misplaced, and the bountiful blind woman doth most mistake in her gifts to women.

Cel. 'Tis true; for those that she makes fair, she scarce makes honest; and those that she makes honest, she makes very ill-favoured.

Ros. Nay, now thou goest from fortune's office to nature's: fortune reigns in gifts of the world, not in the lineaments of nature.

Enter Touchstone, *a Clown.*

Cel. No! when nature hath made a fair creature, may she not by fortune fall into the fire? Though nature hath given us wit to flout at fortune, hath not fortune sent in this Fool to cut off this argument?

Ros. Indeed, there is fortune too hard for nature; when fortune makes nature's Natural the cutter off of nature's Wit.

Cel. Peradventure, this is not fortune's work, neither, but nature's; who, perceiving our natural wits too dull to reason of such Goddesses, hath sent this Natural for our whetstone: for always the dulness of the fool is the whetstone of the wits. How now, Wit, whither wander you?

Clo. Mistress, you must come away to your father.

Cel. Were you made the messenger?

Clo. No, by mine honour; but I was bid to come for you.

Ros. Where learned you that oath, fool?

Clo. Of a certain Knight, that swore by his honour they were good pancakes, and swore by his honour the mustard was naught. Now I'll stand to it, the pancakes were naught, and the mustard was good, and yet was not the Knight forsworn.

---

8 ——*mock the good housewife Fortune from her wheel.*] The wheel of fortune is not the *wheel* of a *housewife. Shakespeare* has confounded fortune, whose wheel only figures uncertainty and vicissitude, with the destiny that spins the thread of life, though indeed not with a wheel.

Cel. How prove you that in the great heap of your knowledge?

Ros. Ay, marry; now unmuzzle your wisdom.

Clo. Stand you both forth now; stroke your chins, and swear by your beards that I am a knave.

Cel. By our beards, if we had them, thou art.

Clo. By my knavery, if I had it, then I were; but if you swear by That that is not, you are not forsworn; no more was this Knight swearing by his honour, for he never had any: or if he had, he had sworn it away, before ever he saw those pancakes or that mustard.

Cel. Pr'ythee, who is that thou mean'st?

Clo. [9]One that old *Frederick* your father loves.

Cel. My father's love is enough to honour him:—enough! speak no more of him, you'll be whipt for taxation one of these days.

Clo. The more pity, that fools may not speak wisely what wise men do foolishly.

Cel. By my troth, thou say'st true; for since the little wit that fools have was silenced[1], the little foolery that wise men have makes a great show: here comes Monsieur *Le Beu.*

SCENE V.

Enter Le Beu.

Ros. With his mouth full of news.

Cel. Which he will put on us, as pigeons feed their young.

Ros. Then shall we be news-cram'd.

---

[9] Clo. *One, that old* Frederick *your father loves.*

Ros. *My Father's Love is enough to honour him enough*;] This Reply to the *Clown,* is in all the Books placed to *Rosalind*; but *Frederick* was not her Father, but *Celia's*: I have therefore ventur'd to prefix the Name of *Celia.* There is no Countenance from any Passage in the Play, or from the *Dramatis Persona,* to imagine, that Both the Brother-Dukes were Namesakes; and One call'd the Old, and the Other the Younger *Frederick*; and, without some such Authority, it would make Confusion to suppose it. **THEOBALD.**

Mr. *Theobald* seems not to know that the *Dramatis Personæ* were first enumerated by *Rowe.*

[1] ——*since the little Wit that fools have was silenc'd.*] *Shakespeare* probably alludes to the use of *fools* or *jesters,* who for some ages had been allowed in all courts an unbridled liberty of censure and mockery, and about this time began to be less tolerated.

Cel. All the better, we shall be the more marketable. *Bon jour, Monsieur le Beu*; what news?

LeBeu. Fair Princess, you have lost much good Sport.

Cel. Sport; of what colour?

Le Beu. What colour, Madam? How shall I answer you?

Ros. As wit and fortune will.

Clo. Or as the destinies decree.

Cel. Well said; that was laid on with a trowel[2].

Clo. Nay if I keep not my rank,—

Ros. Thou losest thy old smell.

Le Beu. You amaze me, ladies[3]. I would have told you of good wrestling, which you have lost the sight of.

Ros. Yet tell us the manner of the wrestling.

Le Beu. I will tell you the beginning, and, if it please your Ladyships, you may see the end, for the best is yet to do; and here where you are, they are coming to perform it.

Cel. Well—the beginning that is dead and buried.

Le Beu. There comes an old man and his three sons,——

Cel. I could match this beginning with an old tale.

Le Beu. Three proper young men, of excellent growth and presence;——

Ros. With bills on their necks: *Be it known unto all men by these presents*[4],——

Le Beu. The eldest of the three wrestled with *Charles* the Duke's Wrestler;

---

[2] ——*Laid on with a trowel.*] I suppose the meaning is, that there is too heavy a mass of big words laid upon a slight subject.

[3] *You amaze me, ladies.*] To amaze, here, is not to astonish or strike with wonder, but to perplex; to confuse; as, to put out of the intended narrative.

[4] *With* BILLS *on their necks: Be it known unto all men by these presents*;— —] The *ladies* and the *fool,* according to the mode of wit at that time, are at a kind *cross purpose*s. Where the words of one speaker are wrestled by another, in a repartee, to a different meaning. As where the *Clown* says just before—— *Nay, if I keep not my rank*. Rosalind replies—*thou losest thy old smell*. So here when *Rosalind* had said, *With bills on their necks,* the *Clown,* to be quits with her, puts in, *Know all men by these presents*. She spoke of an instrument of war, and he turns it to an instrument of law of the same name, beginning with these words: so that they must be given to him.　　　　　WARBURTON.

This conjecture is ingenious. Where meaning is so very thin, as in this vein of jocularity, it is hard to catch, and therefore I know not well what to determine; but I cannot see why *Rosalind* should suppose, that the competitors in a wrestling match carried *bills* on their shoulders, and I believe the whole conceit is in the poor resemblance of *presence* and *presents*.

which *Charles* in a moment threw him, and broke three of his ribs, and there is little hope of life in him: so he served the Second, and so the Third. Yonder they lie, the poor old man their father making such pitiful Dole over them, that all the beholders take his part with weeping.

Ros. Alas!

Clo. But what is the Sport, Monsieur, that the ladies have lost?

Le Beu. Why this, that I speak of.

Clo. Thus men may grow wiser every day! It is the first time that ever I heard breaking of ribs was sport for ladies.

Cel. Or I, I promise thee.

Ros. But[5] is there any else longs to see this broken musick in his sides? is there yet another doats upon rib-breaking? Shall we see this wrestling, cousin?

Le Beu. You must if you stay here: for here is the place appointed for the wrestling, and they are ready to perform it.

Cel. Yonder, sure, they are coming. Let us now stay and see it.

SCENE VI.

Flourish. Enter Duke Frederick, *Lords,* Orlando, Charles, *and Attendants.*

Duke. Come on. Since the Youth will not be entreated, his own peril on his forwardness.

Ros. Is yonder the man?

Le Beu. Even he, Madam.

Cel. Alas, he is too young; yet he looks successfully.

---

[5] *—is there any else longs to* SEE *this broken music in his sides*?] A stupid error in the copies. They are talking here of some who had their ribs broke in wrestling: and the pleasantry of *Rosalind's* repartee must consist in the allusion she makes to *composing* in *musick*. It necessarily follows therefore, that the poet wrote—SET *this* broken musick *in his sides*.

WARBURTON.

If any change were necessary I should write, *feel this broken musick,* for *see.* But *see* is the colloquial term for perception or experiment. So we say every day, *see* if the water be hot; I will *see* which is the best time; she has tried, and *sees* that she cannot lift it. In this sense *see* may be here used. The sufferer can, with no propriety, be said to *set* the musick; neither is the allusion to the act of tuning an instrument, or pricking a tune, one of which must be meant by *setting* musick. *Rosalind* hints at a whimsical similitude between the series of ribs gradually shortening, and some musical instruments, and therefore calls *broken ribs, broken musick.*

Duke. How now, Daughter and Cousin, are you crept hither to see the wrestling?

Ros. Ay, my liege, so please you give us leave.

Duke. You will take little delight in it, I can tell you, there is such odds in the* men: in pity of the challenger's youth, I would fain dissuade him, but he will not be entreated. Speak to him, ladies, see if you can move him.

Cel. Call him hither, good Monsieur Le Beu.

Duke. Do so, I'll not be by.   [Duke *goes apart.*

Le Beu. Monsieur the Challenger, the Princesses call for you.

Orl. I attend them with all respect and duty.

Ros. Young man, have you challenged *Charles* the wrestler?

Orla. No, fair Princess; he is the general challenger: I come but in, as others do, to try with him the strength of my youth.

Cel. Young Gentleman, your spirits are too bold for your years. You have seen cruel proof of this man's strength. If you saw yourself with your own eyes[6]; or knew yourself with your judgment, the fear of your adventure would counsel you to a more equal enterprize. We pray you, for your own sake, to embrace your own safety, and give over this attempt.

Ros. Do, young Sir; your reputation shall not therefore be misprised. We will make it our suit to the Duke, that the wrestling might not go forward.

Orla.[7] I beseech you, punish me not with your hard thoughts, wherein I confess me much guilty, to deny so fair and excellent ladies any thing. But let your fair eyes and gentle wishes go with me to my trial, wherein if I be foil'd, there is but one asham'd that was never gracious; if kill'd, but one dead that is willing to be so. I shall do my friends no wrong, for I have none to lament me; the world no injury, for in it I have nothing; only in the world I fill up a place, which may be better supplied when I have made it empty.

Ros. The little strength that I have, I would it were with you.

---

* Sir *T. Hanmer.* In the old Editions, the *man.*

[6] ——*If you saw yourself with* YOUR *eyes, or knew yourself with* YOUR *judgment.*] Absurd! The sense requires that we should read, OUR *eyes,* and OUR *judgment.* The argument is, *Your spirits are too bold, and therefore your judgment deceives you; but did you see and know yourself with our more impartial judgment, you would forbear.*   WARBURTON.

I cannot find the absurdity of the present reading. *If you were not blinded and intoxicated,* says the princess, *with the spirit of enterprise, if you could use* your own eyes to *see,* or your own judgment to know *yourself, the fear of your adventure would counsel you.*

[7] *I beseech you, punish me not,* &c.] I should wish to read, I *beseech you punish me not with your hard thoughts.* Therein *I confess myself much guilty to deny so fair and excellent ladies any thing.*

Cel. And mine to eke out hers.

Ros. Fare you well. Pray heav'n, I be deceiv'd in you.

Cel. Your heart's desire be with you!

Cha. Come, where is this young Gallant, that is so desirous to lie with his mother earth?

Orla. Ready, Sir. But his will hath in it a more modest working.

Duke. You shall try but one Fall.

Cha. No—I warrant your Grace; you shall not entreat him to a second, that have so mightily persuaded him from a first.

Orl. You mean to mock me after; you should not have mocked me before; but come your ways.

Ros. Now *Hercules* be thy speed, young man!

Cel. I would I were invisible, to catch the strong fellow by the leg!

[*they wrestle.*

Ros. O excellent young man!

Cel. If I had a thunderbolt in mine eye, I can tell who should down. [*shout.*

Duke. No more, no more.   [Charles *is thrown.*

Orla. Yes, I beseech your Grace. I am not yet well breathed.

Duke. How dost thou, *Charles?*

Le Beu. He cannot speak, my Lord.

Duke. Bear him away.—What is thy name, young man?

Orla. Orlando, my liege, the youngest Son of Sir *Rowland de Boys.*

Duke. I would, thou hadst been son to some man else!
The world esteem'd thy Father honourable,
But I did find him still mine enemy:
Thou shouldst have better pleas'd me with this deed,
Hadst thou descended from another House.
But fare thee well, thou art a gallant youth;
—I would thou hadst told me of another father.   [*Exit* Duke, *with his train.*

SCENE VII.

Manent Celia, Rosalind, Orlando.

Cel. Were I my father, coz, would I do this?

Orla. I am more proud to be Sir *Rowland*'s son,
His youngest Son, and would not change that calling
To be adopted heir to *Frederick.*

Ros. My father lov'd Sir *Rowland* as his soul,
And all the world was of my father's mind:

Had I before known this young man his son,
I should have given him tears unto entreaties,
Ere he should thus have ventur'd.

   Cel. Gentle Cousin,
Let us go thank him and encourage him;
My father's rough and envious disposition
Sticks me at heart. Sir, you have well deserv'd:
If you do keep your promises in love,
But justly as you have exceeded all promise,
Your mistress shall be happy.

   Ros. Gentleman,
Wear this for me; one out of suits with fortune[8],
That would give more, but that her hand lacks means.
—Shall we go, coz?   [*Giving him a Chain from her Neck.*

   Cel. Ay—Fare you well, fair gentleman.

   Orla. Can I not say, I thank you?——my better parts
Are all thrown down; and that which here stands up,
Is but a quintaine[9], a meer lifeless block.

   Ros. He calls us back—my pride fell with my fortunes.
I'll ask him what he would——Did you call, Sir?—
Sir, you have wrestled well, and overthrown
More than your enemies.

   Cel. Will you go, coz?

   Ros. Have with you—Fare you well.   [*Exeunt* Rosalind and Celia.

   Orla. What passion hangs these weights upon my tongue?
I cannot speak to her; yet she urg'd conference.

---

  8 ——*one out of suits with fortune,*] This seems an allusion to cards, where
he that has no more cards to play of any particular sort is *out of suit.*

  9 *Is but a quintaine, a meer lifeless block.*] A *Quintaine* was a *Post* or *Butt* set
up for several kinds of martial exercises, against which they threw their darts
and exercised their arms. The allusion is beautiful, *I am,* says *Orlando,* only a
quintaine, *a lifeless block on which love only exercises his arms in jest; the
great disparity of condition between* Rosalind *and me, not suffering to hope
that love will ever make a serious matter of it.* The famous satirist *Regnier,* who
lived about the time of our author, uses the same metaphor, on the same
subject, tho' the thought be different.

     Et qui depuis dix ans, jusquen ses derniers jours,
     A souteny le prix to l' esrime d'amours;
     Losse en fin de servir au peuple de QUINTAINE,
     Elle, &c.   WARBURTON.

Enter Le Beu.

O poor *Orlando*! thou art overthrown;
Or *Charles,* or something weaker, masters thee.
    Le Beu. Good Sir, I do in friendship counsel you
To leave this place. Albeit you have deserv'd
High commendation, true applause, and love;
Yet such is now the Duke's condition[1],
That he misconstrues all that you have done.
The Duke is humorous; what he is, indeed,
More suits you to conceive, than me to speak of.
    Orla. I thank you, Sir. And, pray you, tell me this,
Which of the two was daughter of the Duke
That here was at the wrestling?
    Le Beu. Neither his Daughter, if we judge by manners;
But yet, indeed, the shorter is his daughter.
The other's daughter to the banish'd Duke,
And here detain'd by her usurping Uncle
To keep his daughter company; whose loves
Are dearer than the natural bond of sisters.
But I can tell you, that of late this Duke
Hath ta'en displeasure 'gainst his gentle Niece;
Grounded upon no other argument,
But that the people praise her for her virtues,
And pity her for her good father's sake;
And, on my life, his malice 'gainst the lady
Will suddenly break forth.—Sir, fare ye well;
Hereafter, in a better world than this,
I shall desire more love and knowledge of you.   [*Exit.*
    Orla. I rest much bounden to you: fare ye well!
Thus must I from the smoke into the smother;
From tyrant Duke unto a tyrant brother:
But, heav'nly *Rosalind*!   [*Exit.*

---

[1] ——*the Duke's condition.*] The word *condition* means character, temper,
disposition. So *Antonio,* the *Merchant* of *Venice,* is called by his friend the *best
conditioned man.*

SCENE VIII.

Changes to an Apartment in the Palace.

Re-enter Celia *and* Rosalind.

Cel. WHY, Cousin; why, *Rosalind—Cupid* have mercy—not a word!

Ros. Not one to throw at a dog.

Cel. No, thy words are too precious to be cast away upon curs, throw some of them at me; come, lame me with reasons.

Ros. Then there were two cousins laid up; when the one should be lamed with Reasons, and the other mad without any.

Cel. But is all this for your father?

Ros. No, some of it is for my father's child[2], Oh, how full of briars is this working-day world!

Cel. They are but burs, cousin, thrown upon thee in holiday foolery; if we walk not in the trodden paths, our very petticoats will catch them.

Ros. I could shake them off my coat; these burs are in my heart.

Cel. Hem them away.

Ros. I would try, if I could cry hem, and have him.

Cel. Come, come, wrestle with thy affections.

Ros. O, they take the part of a better Wrestler than myself.

Cel. O, good wish upon you! you will try in time, in despight of a Fall.— But turning these jests out of Service, let us talk in good earnest. Is it possible on such a sudden you should fall into so strong a liking with old Sir *Rowland's* youngest son?

Ros. The Duke my father lov'd his father dearly.

Cel. Doth it therefore ensue, that you should love his son dearly? by this kind of chase[3], I should hate him; for my father hated his father dearly; yet I hate not *Orlando*.

Ros. No, faith, hate him not, for my sake.

Cel. Why Should I? doth he not deserve well?

---

[2] *—for my father's child*.] The old Editions have it, for *my child's father*, that is, as it is explained by Mr. *Theobald, for my future husband*.

[3] *——by this kind of chase*.] That is, by this way of *following* the argument. *Dear* is used by *Shakespeare* in a double sense, for *beloved*, and for *hurtful*, *hated*, *baleful*. Both senses are authorised, and both drawn from etymology, but properly *beloved* is *dear*, and *hateful* is *dere*. *Rosalind* uses *dearly* in the good,

Enter Duke, *with Lords.*

Ros. Let me love him for that; and do you love him, because I do. Look, here comes the Duke.

Cel. With his eyes full of anger.

Duke. Mistress, dispatch you with your safest haste,
And get you from our Court.

Ros. Me, Uncle!

Duke. You, cousin.
Within these ten days if that thou be'st found
So near our publick Court as twenty miles,
Thou diest for it.

Ros. I do beseech your Grace,
Let me the knowledge of my fault bear with me:
If with myself I hold intelligence,
Or have acquaintance with my own desires;
If that I do not dream, or be not frantick,
As I do trust, I am not; then, dear Uncle,
Never so much as in a thought unborn
Did I offend your Highness.

Duke. Thus do all traitors;
If their purgation did consist in words,
They are as innocent as grace itself.
Let it suffice thee that I trust thee not.

Ros. Yet your mistrust cannot make me a traitor;
Tell me whereon the likelihood depends.

Duke. Thou art thy father's daughter, there's enough.

Ros. So was I, when your Highness took his Dukedom ;
So was I, when your Highness banish'd him.
Treason is not inherited, my lord;
Or if we did derive it from our friends,
What's that to me? my father was no traitor.
Then, good my liege, mistake me not so much,
To think my poverty is treacherous.

Cel. Dear Sovereign, hear me speak.

Duke. Ay, *Celia,* we but staid her for your sake;
Else had she with her father rang'd along.

---

and *Celia* in the bad sense.

Cel. I did not then entreat to have her stay;
It was your pleasure, and your own remorse;
I was too young that time to value her,
But now I know her; if she be a traitor,
Why so am I; we still have slept together,
Rose at an instant, learn'd, play'd, eat together;
And wheresoe'er we went, like *Juno's* Swans,
Still we went coupled, and inseparable.
  Duke. She is too subtle for thee; and her smoothness,
Her very silence and her patience,
Speak to the people, and they pity her.
Thou art a fool; she robs thee of thy name,
And thou wilt show more bright, and seem more virtuous[4],
When she is gone. Then open not thy lips:
Firm and irrevocable is my doom,
Which I have past upon her. She is banished.
  Cel. Pronounce that sentence then on me, my Liege;
I cannot live out of her company.
  Duke. You are a fool—you, Niece, provide yourself;
If you outlay the time, upon mine Honour,
And in the Greatness of my word, you die.   [*Exeunt* Duke, *&c.*

SCENE X.

  Cel. O my poor *Rosalind*; where wilt thou go?
Wilt thou change fathers? I will give thee mine:
I charge thee, be not thou more griev'd than I am.
  Ros. I have more cause.
  Cel. Thou hast not, cousin;
Pr'ythee, be cheerful: knowest thou not, the Duke
Has banish'd me, his daughter?

---

[4] *And thou wilt shew more bright, and* SEEM *more virtuous.*] This implies
her to be somehow remarkably defective in virtue; which was not the speaker's
thought. The poet doubtless wrote,
        ——*and* SHINE *more virtuous.*
i.e. her virtues would appear more splendid when the lustre of her cousin's was
away.   WARBURTON.
  The plain meaning of the old and true reading is, that when she was seen
alone, she would be more noted.

Ros. That he hath not.

Cel. No? hath not? *Rosalind* lacks then the love[5],
Which teacheth thee that thou and I are one.
Shall we be sundred? shall we part, sweet Girl?
No, let my father seek another heir.
Therefore devise with me, how we may fly;
Whither to go, and what to bear with us;
And do not seek to take your change[6] upon you,
To bear your griefs yourself, and leave me out:
For by this heav'n, now at our sorrow's pale,
Say what thou canst, I'll go along with thee.

Ros. Why, whither shall we go?

Cel. To seek my uncle in the forest of *Arden.*

Ros. Alas, what danger will it be to us,
Maids as we are, to travel forth so far!
Beauty provoketh thieves sooner than gold.

Cel. I'll put myself in poor and mean attire,
And with a kind of umber smirch my face;
The like do you; so shall we pass along,
And never stir assailants.

Ros. Wer't not better,
Because that I am more than common tall,
That I did suit me all points like a man?
A gallant Curtle-ax[7] upon my thigh,
A boar-spear in my hand, and (in my heart
Lie there what hidden woman's fear there will)
I'll have a swashing and a martial outside,
As many other mannish Cowards have,
That do outface it with their semblances.

Cel. What shall I call thee, when thou art a man?

---

[5] ——Rosalind *lacks then the love,*
Which teacheth thee that thou and I are one.] The poet certainly wrote—
which teacheth ME. For if *Rosalind* had learnt to think *Celia* one part of
herself, she could not *lack* that love which *Celia* complains she does.

WARBURTON.

Either reading may stand. The sense of the established text is not remote or
obscure. Where could be the absurdity of saying, *You know not the law which
teaches you to do right.*

[6] —— *take your change upon you.*] In all the later editions from Mr. *Rowe's*
to Dr. *Warburton's, change* is altered to *charge,* without any reason.

[7] —*curtle-ax,* or *cutlace,* a broad-sword.

Ros. I'll have[8] no worse a name than *Jove's* own Page;
And therefore, look, you call me *Ganimed*.
But what will you be call'd?

 Cel. Something that hath a reference to my state:
No longer *Celia*, but *Aliena*.

 Ros. But, Cousin, what if we assaid to steal
The clownish fool out of your father's Court?
Would he not be a comfort to our travel?

 Cel. He'll go along o'er the wide world with me,
Leave me alone to woo him. Let's away,
And get our jewels and our wealth together;
Devise the fittest time, and safest way
To hide us from pursuit that will be made
After my flight: now go we in content,
To liberty, and not to banishment.   [*Exeunt.*

---

[8] *I'll have*] Sir T. *Hanmer,* for *we'll have.*

ACT II. SCENE I.

Arden *F O R E S T.*

Enter Duke Senior, Amiens, *and two or three Lords like Foresters.*

D u k e *Senior.*

NOW, my co-mates, and brothers in exile,
Hath not old custom made this life more sweet
Than That of painted Pomp? are not these woods
More free from peril, than the envious Court?
Here feel we but the penalty[9] of *Adam*,
The Seasons' difference; ask the icy fang,
And churlish chiding of the winter's wind;
Which, when it bites and blows upon my body,
Even till I shrink with cold, I smile, and say,
This is no Flattery: these are Counsellors,
That feelingly persuade me what I am.
Sweet are the uses of Adversity,
Which, like the toad, ugly and venomous,
Wears yet a precious jewel in his head[1]:
And this our life, exempt from publick haunt,
Finds tongues in trees, books in the running brooks,
Sermons in stones, and good in every thing.
    Ami. I would not change it.[*] Happy is your Grace,

---

[9] In former editions, *Here feel we* not *the Penalty*.] What was the Penalty of *Adam,* hinted at by our Poet? The being sensible of the Difference of the Seasons. The *Duke* says, the Cold and Effects of the Winter feelingly persuade him what he is. How does he *not* then feel the Penalty? Doubtless the Text must be restor'd as I have corrected it: and 'tis obvious in the Course of these Notes, how often *not* and *but* by Mistake have changed Place in Author's former Editions.   **THEOBALD**

[1] *Which, like the toad, ugly and venomous,*
Wears yet a precious jewel in his head.] It was the current opinion in *Shakespeare's* time, that in the head of an old toad was to be found a stone, or pearl, to which great virtues were ascribed. This stone has been often sought, but nothing has been found more than accidental or perhaps morbid indurations of the skull.

[*]*I would not change it.*] Mr. *Upton,* not without probability gives these words to the duke, and makes *Amiens* begin, *Happy is your Grace*.

THE PLAYS OF WILLIAM SHAKESPEARE   153

That can translate the stubbornness of fortune
Into so quiet and so sweet a style.
    Duke Sen. Come, shall we go and kill us venison?
And yet it irks me, the poor dappled fools,
Being native burghers of this desert city,
Should, in their own Confines, with forked heads
Have their round haunches gor'd.
    1 *Lord.* Indeed, my Lord,
The melancholy *Jaques* grieves at that;
And in that kind swears you no more usurp
Than doth your brother, that hath banish'd you.
To-day my Lord of *Amiens,* and myself,
Did steal behind him, as he lay along
Under an oak, whose antique root peeps out
Upon the brook that brawls along this wood;
To the which place a poor sequestred stag,
That from the hunters' aim had ta'en a hurt,
Did come to languish; and, indeed, my lord,
The wretched Animal heav'd forth such groans,
That their discharge did stretch his leathern coat
Almost to bursting; and the big round tears
Cours'd one another down his innocent nose
In piteous chase: and thus the hairy fool,
Much marked of the melancholy *Jaques,*
Stood on th' extremest verge of the swift brook,
Augmenting it with tears.
    Duke Sen. But what said *Jaques*?
Did he not moralize this spectacle?
    1 *Lord.* O yes, into a thousand similies.
First, for his weeping in the needless stream;
Poor Deer, quoth he, thou mak'st a testament
As worldlings do, giving thy sum of more
To that which had too much. Then being alone,
Left and abandon'd of his velvet friends:
'Tis right, quoth he, thus misery doth part,
The flux of company. Anon a careless herd,
Full of the pasture, jumps along by him,
And never stays to greet him: Ay, quoth *Jaques,*
Sweep on, you fat and greasy citizens,
'Tis just the fashion: wherefore do you look
Upon that poor and broken bankrupt there?

Thus most invectively he pierceth through
The body of the Country, City, Court,
Yea and of this our life; swearing, that we
Are meer usurpers, tyrants, and what's worse,
To fright the animals, and to kill them up
In their assign'd and native dwelling place.

 Duke Sen. And did you leave him in this contemplation?

 2 Lord. We did, my lord, weeping and commenting
Upon the sobbing deer.

 Duke Sen. Show me the place;
I love to cope him² too in these sullen fits
For then he's full of matter.

 2 Lord. I'll bring you to him straight.   [*Exeunt.*

SCENE II.

Changes to the PALACE *again.*

Enter Duke Frederick *with Lords.*

 Duke. CAN it be possible, that no man saw them?
It cannot be. Some villains of my Court
Are of consent and sufferance in this.

 1 Lord. I cannot hear of any that did see her
The ladies, her attendants of her chamber,
Saw her a-bed, and in the morning early
They found the bed untreasur'd of their mistress.

 2 Lord. My lord, the roynish Clown, at whom so oft
Your Grace was wont to laugh, is also missing.
Hesperia, the Princess' Gentlewoman,
Confesses, that she secretly o'er-heard
Your Daughter and her Cousin much commend
The parts and graces of the Wrestler,
That did but lately foil the sinewy *Charles*;
And she believes, where ever they are gone,
That youth is surely in their company.

 Duke. Send to his brother: Fetch that Gallant hither.
If he be absent, bring his brother to me,

———————————————————

² ——*to cope him,*] To encounter him; to engage with him.

I'll make him find him. Do this suddenly;
And let not Search and Inquisition quail
To bring again these foolish runaways.   [*Exeunt.*

SCENE III.

Changes to OLIVER'S *House.*

Enter Orlando *and* Adam.

Orla. WHO's there?
Adam. What! my young master? oh, my gentle master,
Oh, my sweet master, oh, you memory
Of old Sir *Rowland*! why, what make you here?
Why are you virtuous? why do people love you?
And wherefore are you gentle, strong, and valiant?
Why would you be so fond to overcome
The bony[3] Priser of the humorous Duke?
Your Praise is come too swiftly home before you.
Know you not, matter, to some kind of men
Their Graces serve them but as enemies?
No more do yours; your virtues, gentle master,
Are sanctified and holy traitors to you.
Oh, what a world is this, when what is comely
Envenoms him that bears it!
Orla. Why, what's the matter?
Adam. O unhappy youth,
Come not within these doors; within this roof
The enemy of all your graces lives:
Your brother—no; no brother—yet the son,—
Yet not the son—I will not call him son
Of him I was about to call his father,
Hath heard your praises, and this night he means
To burn the lodging where you use to lie
And you within it. If he fail of that,

---

[3] In the former editions, *The* BONNY *Priser*—] We should read BONEY
Priser. For this wrestler is characterised for his strength and bulk, not for his
gayety or good-humour.   WARBURTON
   So *Milton, Giants of mighty* bone.

He will have other means to cut you off;
I overheard him and his practices:
This is no place, this house is but a butchery;
Abhor it, fear it, do not enter it.

    Orla. Why, whither, *Adam,* wouldst thou have me go?

    Adam. No matter whither, so you come not here.

    Orla. What, wouldst thou have me go and beg my food?
Or with a base, and boisterous sword enforce
A thievish living on the common road?
This I must do, or know not what to do:
Yet this I will not do, do how I can;
I rather will subject me to the malice
Of a diverted blood[4], and bloody brother.

    Adam. But do not so. I have five hundred crowns,
The thrifty hire I sav'd under your father,
Which I did store, to be my softer nurse
When service should in my old limbs lie lame,
And unregarded age in corners thrown.
Take That: and he that doth the ravens feed,
Yea, providentially caters for the sparrow,
Be comfort to my age! Here is the gold,
All this I give you, let me be your servant;
Tho' I look old, yet I am strong and lusty;
For in my youth I never did apply
Hot and rebellious liquors in my blood;
Nor did I with unbashful forehead woo
The means of weakness and debility;
Therefore my age is as a lusty winter,
Frosty, but kindly. Let me go with you;
I'll do the service of a younger man
In all your business and necesities.

    Orla. Oh! good old man, how well in thee appears
The constant service of the antique world;
When service sweat for duty, not for meed!
Thou art not for the fashion of these times,
Where none will sweat, but for promotion;
And, having That, do cloak their service up
Even with the Having.[5] It is not so with thee.

---

[4] —*diverted blood.*] Blood turned out of the course of nature.

[5] *Even with the having.*] Even with the *promotion* gained by service, is

But, poor old man, thou prun'st a rotten tree,
That cannot so much as a blossom yield,
In lieu of all thy pains and husbandry.
But come thy ways, we'll go along together;
And ere we have thy youthful wages spent,
We'll light upon some settled low content.

    Adam. Master, go on; and I will follow thee
To the last gasp with truth and loyalty.
From seventeen years 'till now almost fourscore
Here lived I, but now live here no more.
At seventeen years many their fortunes seek;
But at fourscore, it is too late a week;
Yet fortune cannot recompence me better
Than to die well, and not my master's debtor.   [*Exeunt.*

SCENE IV.

Changes to the FOREST *of* Arden.

Enter Rosalind *in Boy's cloaths for* Ganimed, Celia *drest like a Shepherdess for* Aliena, *and* Touchstone *the* Clown.

    Ros. O *Jupiter*! how weary are my spirits[6]?

    Clo. I care not for my spirits, if my legs were not weary.

    Ros. I could find in my heart to disgrace my man's apparel, and cry like a woman; but I must comfort the weaker vessel, as doublet and hose ought to show itself courageous to petticoat; therefore, courage, good *Aliena.*

    Cel. I pray you bear with me; I can go no further.

    Clo. For my part, I had rather bear with you, than bear you; yet I should bear no cross, if I did bear you; for I think you have no money in your purse.

    Ros. Well, this is the forest of *Arden.*

---

service extinguished.

    [6] O Jupiter! *how merry are my spirits*?] And yet, within the Space of one intervening Line, She says, She could find in her Heart to disgrace her Man's Apparel, and *cry* like a Woman. Sure, this is but a very bad Symptom of the *Briskness of Spirits*: rather a direct Proof of the contrary Disposition. Mr. *Warburton* and I concurred in conjecturing it should be, as I have reformed in the Text:—*how weary are my Spirits*? And the Clown's Reply makes this Reading certain.   THEOBALD.

Clo. Ay; now I am in *Arden,* the more fool I; when I was at home, I was in a better place; but travellers must be content.

Ros. Ay, be so, good *Touchstone.* Look you, who comes here; a young man and an old in solemn talk.

Enter Corin and Silvius.

Cor. That is the way to make her scorn you still.

Sil. O *Corin,* that thou knew'st how I do love her!

Cor. I partly guess; for I have lov'd ere now.

Sil. No, *Corin,* being old, thou canst not guess,
Tho' in thy youth thou wast as true a lover,
As ever sigh'd upon a midnight pillow;
But if thy love were ever like to mine,
As, sure, I think, did never man love so,
How many Actions most ridiculous
Hast thou been drawn to by thy fantasy?

Cor. Into a thousand that I have forgotten.

Sil. O, thou didst then ne'er love so heartily.
If thou remember'st not the slightest folly[7],
That ever love did make thee run into;
Thou hast not lov'd.——
Or if thou hast not sate as I do now,
Wearying the hearer in thy mistress' praise,
Thou hast not lov'd.——
Or if thou hast not broke from company,
Abruptly as my passion now makes me;
Thou hast not lov'd.——   [*Exit* Sil.
O Phebe! Phebe! Phebe!

Ros. Alas, poor Shepherd! searching of thy wound,
I have by hard adventure found my own.

---

[7] I am inclined to believe that from this passage *Suckling* took the hint of his song.

> *Honest lover, whosoever,*
> *If in all thy love there ever*
> *Were one wavring thought, thy flame*
> *Were not even, still the same.*
> > *Know this*
> > *Thou lov'st amiss,*
> > *And to love true*
> *Thou must begin again and love anew, &c.*

Clo. And I mine. I remember, when I was in love, I broke my sword upon a stone, and bid him take that, for coming a-nights to *Jane Smile*; and I remember the kissing of her batlet[8], and cow's dugs that her pretty chopt hands had milk'd; and I remember the wooing of a peascod instead of her, from whom I took two*cods, and giving her them again, said with weeping tears, Wear these for my sake. We, that are true lovers, run into strange capers; but as all is mortal in nature, so is all nature in love mortal in folly.[9]

Ros. Thou speak'st wiser, than thou art 'ware of.

Clo. Nay, I shall ne'er be aware of mine own wit, 'till I break my shins against it.

Ros. Jove! Jove! this Shepherd's passion is much upon my fashion.

Clo. And mine; but it grows something stale with me.

Cel. I pray you, one of you question yond man,
If he for gold will give us any food;
I faint almost to death.

Clo. Holla; you, Clown!

Ros. Peace, fool; he's not thy kinsman.

Cor. Who calls?

Clo. Your Betters, Sir.

Cor. Else they are very wretched.

Ros. Peace, I say—Good Even to you, friend

Cor. And to you, gentle Sir, and to you all.

Ros. I pr'ythee, shepherd, if that love or gold
Can in this desert place buy entertainment,
Bring us where we may rest ourselves, and feed;
Here's a young maid with travel much oppress'd,
And faints for succour.

Cor. Fair Sir, I pity her,
And wish for her sake, more than for mine own,
My fortunes were more able to relieve her;
But I am Shepherd to another man,
And do not share the fleeces that I graze;

---

[8] *—batlet,—*] The instrument with which was hers beat their coarse cloaths.

* For *cods* it would be more like sense to read *peas,* which, having the shape of pearls, resembled the common presents of lovers.

[9] *——so is all nature in love mortal in folly.*] This expression I do not well understand. In the middle counties, *mortal,* from *mort* a great quantity, is used as a particle of amplification, as, *mortal tall, mortal little.* Of this sense I believe *Shakespeare* takes advantage to produce one of his darling equivocations. Thus the meaning will be, *so is all nature in love,* abounding *in folly.*

My Master is of churlish disposition,
And little recks to find the way to heav'n
By doing deeds of hospitality:
Besides, his Cote, his flocks, and bounds of feed
Are now on sale, and at our sheep-cote now,
By reason of his absence, there is nothing
That ye will feed on; but what is, come see;
And in my voice most welcome shall ye be. [1]

   Ros. What is he, that shall buy his flock and pasture?

   Cor. That young swain, that ye saw here but erewhile,
That little cares for buying any thing.

   Ros. I pray thee, if it stand with honesty,
Buy thou the cottage, pasture, and the flock,
And thou shalt have to pay for it of us.

   Cel. And we will mend thy wages.
——I like this place, and willingly could waste
My time in it.

   Cor. Assuredly, the thing is to be sold;
Go with me. If you like, upon report,
The soil, the profit, and this kind of life,
I will your very faithful feeder be;
And buy it with your gold right suddenly.   [*Exeunt.*

SCENE V.

Enter Amiens, Jaques, *and others.*

SONG.

Under the green-wood tree,
Who loves to lie with me,
And tune his merry note
Unto the sweet bird's throat,
Come hither, come hither, come hither.
   Here shall be see
   No enemy,
But winter and rough weather.

---

[1] *And in my voice right welcome shall ye be.*] *In my voice,* as far as I have a voice or vote, as far as I have power to bid you welcome.

Jaq. More, more, I pr'ythee, more.

Ami. It will make you melancholy, Monsieur *Jaques*.

Jaq. I thank it—more, I pr'ythee, more—I can suck melancholy out of a Song, as a weazel sucks eggs: more, I pr'ythee, more.

Ami. My voice is rugged *; I know I cannot please you.

Jaq. I do not desire you to please me, I do desire you to sing; come, come, another stanzo; call you 'em stanzo's?

Ami. What you will, Monsieur *Jaques*.

Jaq. Nay, I care not for their names, they owe me nothing—Will you sing?

Ami. More at your request, than to please myself.

Jaq. Well then, if ever I thank any man, I'll thank you; but That, they call Compliments, is like the encounter of two dog-apes. And when a man thanks me heartily, methinks, I have given him a penny, and he renders me the beggarly thanks.—Come, sing; and you that will not, hold your tongues.——

Ami. Well, I'll end the song. Sirs, cover the while;—the Duke will dine under this tree; he hath been all this day to look you.

Jaq. And I have been all this day to avoid him. He is too disputable for my company: I think of as many matters as he, but I give heav'n thanks, and make no boast of them.——Come, warble, come,

SONG.

Who doth ambition shun,
And loves to lie † *i'th' Sun.*
Seeking the food he eats,
And pleas'd with what he gets;
Come hither, come hither, come hither;
    Here shall he see
    No enemy,
But winter and rough weather.

Jaq. I'll give thee a verse to this note, that I made yesterday in despight of my invention.

Ami. And I'll sing it.

Jaq. Thus it goes.

If it do come to pass
That any man turn ass;

---

* In old editions, *ragged.*

† Old Edition, *to live.*

Leaving his wealth and ease
A stubborn will to please,
Ducdame, ducdame, ducdame*;
   Here shall he see
   Gross fools as he
An' if he will come to me.

Ami. What's that *ducdame*?
Jaq. 'Tis a *Greek* invocation, to call fools into a circle.—I'll go to sleep if I can; if I cannot, I'll rail against all the first-born of *Egypt*.
Ami. And I'll go seek the Duke: his banquet is prepar'd.

[*Exeunt, severally.*

SCENE VI.

Enter Orlando *and* Adam.

Adam. Dear master, I can go no further. O, I die for food! here lie I down, and measure out my grave.——Farewel, kind master.
Orla. Why, how now, *Adam*! no greater heart in thee?—live a little; comfort a little; cheer thyself a little. If this uncouth Forest yield any thing savage, I will either be food for it, or bring it for food to thee. Thy conceit is nearer death, than thy powers. For my sake be comfortable, hold death a while at the arm's end: I will be here with thee presently, and if I bring thee not something to eat, I'll give thee leave to die; but if thou diest before I come, thou art a mocker of my labour.—Well said—thou look'st cheerly, and I'll be with you quickly, Yet thou liest in the bleak air; come, I will bear thee to some shelter, and thou shalt not die for lack of a dinner, if there live any thing in this Desert. Cheerly, good Adam. [*Exeunt.*

---

* For *ducdame* Sir *T. Hanmer,* very acutely and judiciously, reads, *duc ad me.* That is, *bring him to me.*

SCENE VII.

Another part of the FOREST.

Enter Duke Sen. *and* Lord.   [*A table set out.*

Duke Sen. I think, he is transformed into a beast,
For I can no where find him like a man.
    1 *Lord.* My Lord, he is but even now gone hence;
Here was he merry, hearing of a Song.
    Duke Sen. If he, compact of jars, grow musical,
We shall have shortly discord in the spheres.
Go seek him. Tell him, I would speak with him.

Enter Jaques.

    1 *Lord.* He saves my labour by his own approach.
    Duke Sen. Why, how now, Monsieur, what a lift is this,
That your poor friends must woo your company?
What! you look merrily.
    Jaq. A fool, a fool;——I met a fool i' th' forest,
A motley fool—a miserable world[2]—
As I do live by food, I met a fool,
Who laid him down and bask'd him in the sun,
And rail'd on Lady Fortune in good terms,
In good set terms—and yet a motley fool.
Good-morrow, fool, quoth I—No, sir, quoth he,
Call me not fool, 'till heav'n hath sent me fortune;
And then he drew a dial from his poke,

---

[2] *A motley fool; a miserable* WORLD.] What! because he met a *motley fool,*
was it therefore *a miserable world*? This is sadly blundered; we should read,
        a *miserable* varlet.
His head is altogether running on this fool, both before and after these words,
and here he calls him *a miserable varlet,* notwithstanding he *railed on lady
fortune in good terms,* &c. Nor is the change we make so great as appears at
first sight.   WARBURTON.
    I see no need of changing *world* to *varlet,* nor, if a change were necessary,
can I guess how it should be certainly known that *varlet* is the true word. *A
miserable world* is a parenthetical exclamation, frequently among melancholy
men, and natural to *Jaques* at the sight of a fool, or at the hearing of reflections
on the fragility of life.

And looking on it with lack-lustre eye,
Says, very wisely, it is ten a-clock;
Thus may we see, quoth he, how the world wags:
'Tis but an hour ago since it was nine,
And after one hour more 'twill be eleven;
And so from hour to hour we ripe and ripe,
And then from hour to hour we rot and rot.
And thereby hangs a tale; when I did hear
The motley fool thus moral on the time,
My lungs began to crow like chanticleer,
That fools should be so deep contemplative:
And I did laugh, sans intermission,
An hour by his dial. O noble fool,
A worthy fool—motley's the only wear.
 Duke Sen. What fool is this?
 Jaq. O worthy fool! one that hath been a Courtier,
And says, if ladies be but young and fair,
They have the gift to know it: and in his brain,
Which is as dry as the remainder bisket
After a voyage, he hath strange places cramm'd
With observation, the which he vents
In mangled forms. O that I were a fool!
I am ambitious for a motley coat.
 Duke Sen. Thou shalt have one.
 Jaq. It is my only suit[3];
Provided, that you weed your better judgments
Of all opinion, that grows rank in them,
That I am wise. I must have liberty
Withal; as large a charter as the wind,
To blow on whom I please; for so fools have;
And they that are most gauled with my folly,
They most must laugh; and why, sir, must they so?
The why is plain, as way to parish church;
He[4], whom a fool doth very wisely hit,

---

[3] *Only suit*.] *Suit* means *petition,* I believe, not *dress*.

[4] *He, whom a Fool doth very wisely hit,*
Doth very foolishly, although he smart,
—Seem senseless of the bob. If not, &c.] Besides that the third Verse is defective one whole *Foot* in Measure the Tenour of what *Jaques* continues to say, and the reasoning of the Passage, shew it is no less defective in the Sense.

Doth very foolishly, although he smart,
Not to seem senseless of the bob. If not*,
The wise man's folly is anatomiz'd
Even by the squandring glances of a fool.
Invest me in my motley, give me leave
To speak my mind, and I will through and through
Cleanse the foul body of th' infected world,
If they will patiently receive my medicine.

  Duke Sen. Fie on thee! I can tell what thou wouldst do.

  Jaq. What, for a counter, would I do but good?

  Duke Sen. Most mischievous soul sin, in chiding sin:
For thou thyself hast been a libertine.
As sensual as the brutish sting itself[5];
And all the embossed sores and headed evils,
That thou with licence of free foot hast caught,
Would'st thou disgorge into the general world.

  Jaq. Why, who cries out on pride,
That can therein tax any private party?
Doth it not flow as hugely as the Sea,
'Till that the very very means do ebb?
What woman in the city do I name,
When that I say the city-woman bears
The cost of Princes on unworthy shoulders?
Who can come in, and say, that I mean her;
When such a one as she, such is her neighbour?
Or what is he of basest function,
That says, his bravery is not on my cost;
Thinking, that I mean him; but therein sutes
His folly to the metal of my speech?
There then; how then? what then? let me see wherein
My tongue hath wronged; if it do him right,

There is no doubt, but the two little Monosyllables, which I have supplyed, were either by Accident wanting in the *Manuscript* Copy, or by Inadvertence were left out.   THEOBALD.

 * *If not,* &c.] Unless men have the prudence not to appear touched with the sarcasms of a Jester, they subject themselves to his power, and the wise man will have his *folly* anatomized, that is, *dissected* and *laid open* by the *squandring glances* or *random shots* of a fool.

 [5] *As sensual as the brutish sting.*] Though the *brutish sting* is capable of a sense not inconvenient in this passage, yet as it is a harsh and unusual mode of speech, I should read the *brutish sty*.

Then he hath wrong'd himself; if he be free,
Why, then my taxing, like a wild goose, flies
Unclaim'd of any man—But who comes here?

S C E N E VIII.

Enter Orlando, *with Sword drawn.*

Orla. Forbear, and eat no more.——
Jaq. Why, I have eat none yet.
Orla. Nor shalt thou, 'till necessity be serv'd.
Jaq. What kind should this Cock come of?
Duke Sen. Art thou thus bolden'd, man, by thy distress;
Or else a rude despiser of good manners,
That in civility thou seem'st so empty?
Orla. You touch'd my vein at first. The thorny point[6]
Of bare distress hath ta'en from me the shew
Of smooth civility; yet am I inland bred,
And know some nurture. But forbear, I say:
He dies, that touches any of this fruit,
'Till I and my affairs are answered.
Jaq. If you will not
Be answered with reason, I must die.
Duke Sen. What would you have? your gentleness shall force,
More than your force move us to gentleness.
Orla. I almost die for food, and let me have it.
Duke Sen. Sit down and feed; and welcome to our table.
Orla. Speak you so gently?—Pardon me, I pray you;
I thought, that all things had been savage here;
And therefore put I on the countenance
Of stern commandment. But whate'er you are,
That in this desert inaccessible,
Under the shade of melancholy boughs,
Lose and neglect the creeping hours of time;
If ever you have look'd on better days;

---

[6] ——*The thorny point*
Of sharp distress has ta'en f*rom me the shew*
Of smooth civility.] We might read *torn* with more elegance, but elegance
alone will not justify alteration.

If ever been where bells have knoll'd to church;
If ever sate at any good man's feast;
If ever from your eyelids wip'd a tear,
And know that 'tis to pity and be pitied;
Let gentleness my strong enforcement be.
In the which hope I blush, and hide my sword.   [*Sheathing his sword.*

    Duke Sen. True is it, that we have seen better days;
And have with holy bell been knoll'd to church;
And sate at good men's feasts, and wip'd our eyes
Of drops, that sacred pity hath engender'd:
And therefore sit you down in gentleness,
And take upon command what help we have[7],
That to your wanting may be ministred.

    Orla. Then but forbear your food a little while,
Whiles, like a doe, I go to find my fawn,
And give it food. There is an old poor man,
Who after me hath many a weary step
Limp'd in pure love; 'till he be first suffic'd,
Oppress'd with two weak evils, age and hunger,
I will not touch a bit.

    Duke Sen. Go find him out,
And we will nothing waste till your return.

    Orl. I thank ye; and be bless'd for your good comfort!   [*Exit.*

SCENE IX.

    Duke Sen. Thou seest, we are not all alone unhappy:
This wide and universal Theatare
Presents more woful pageants, than the scene
Wherein we play.

    Jaq. All the world's a Stage,
And all the men and women meerly Players;
They have their *Exits* and their entrances,
And one man in his time plays many parts:
His acts being seven ages. At first the infant,
Mewling and puking in the nurse's arms.

---

    7 *Then take upon command what help we have.*] It seems necessary to read, *then take upon* demand *what help,* &c. that is, *ask* for what we can supply, and have it.

And then, the whining school-boy with his satchel,
And shining morning face, creeping like snail
Unwillingly to school. And then, the lover;
Sighing like furnace, with a woful ballad
Made to his mistress' eye-brow. Then a soldier:
Full of strange oaths, and bearded like the pard,
Jealous in honour, sudden, and quick in quarrel;
Seeking the bubble reputation
Even in the cannon's mouth. And then, the justice
In fair round belly, with good capon lin'd,
With eyes severe, and beard of formal cut,
Full of wise saws and modern instances[8],
And so he plays his part. The sixth age shifts[9]
Into the lean and slippered pantaloon,
With spectacles on nose, and pouch on side;
His youthful hose well sav'd, a world too wide
For his shrunk shank; and his big manly voice,
Turning again towards childish tremble, pipes
And whistles in his sound. Last Scene of all,
That ends this strange eventful History,
Is second childishness, and meer oblivion,
Sans teeth, sans eyes, sans taste, sans every thing.

---

[8] *Full of wise laws and* modern *instances*.] It is remarkable that *Shakespeare* uses *modern* in the double sense that the *Greeks* used ηαινοξ, both for *recens* and *absurdus*.

I am in doubt whether *modern* is in this place used for *absurd*: the meaning seems to be, that the justice is full of old sayings and *late* examples.

[9] *—The sixth age shifts*

Into the lean and slipper'd pantaloon.] There is a greater beauty than appears at first sight in this image. He is here comparing human life to *a stage play* of seven acts (which was no unusual division before our author's time). The sixth he calls the *lean and slipper'd pantaloon,* alluding to that general character in the *Italian* comedy called *Il Pantalone*; who is a thin emaciated old man in *slippers*; and well designed, in that epithet, because *Pantalone* is the only character that acts in slippers.   WARBURTON.

SCENE X.

Enter Orlando, *with* Adam.

Duke Sen. Welcome. Set down your venerable burden[1];
And let him feed.

Orla. I thank you most for him.

Adam. So had you need.
I scarce can speak to thank you for myself.

Duke Sen. Welcome, fall to: I will not trouble you,
As yet to question you about your fortunes.
Give us some musick; and, good cousin, sing.

Amiens sings.

SONG.

Blow, blow, the winter wind,
That art not so unkind
   As man's ingratitude;
Thy tooth is not so keen[2],

---

[1] —*Set down your venerable burthen.*] Is it not likely that Shakespeare had in his mind this line of the *Metamorphoses*?
——*Patremque*
Fert humerus, venerabile onus
   Cythercius heros.

[2] *Thy tooth is not so keen,*
   Because thou art not seen,]
This song is designed to suit the Duke's exiled condition, who had been ruined by *ungrateful flatterers*. Now the *winter wind,* the song says, is to be preferr'd to *man's ingratitude*. But why? *Because it is not* SEEN. But this was not only an aggravation of the injury, as it was done in secret, *not seen,* but was the very circumstance that made the keenness of the ingratitude of his faithless courtiers. Without doubt, Shakspeare wrote the line thus,
   Because thou art not SHEEN,
i.e. smiling, shining, like an ungrateful court-servant, who flatters while he wounds, which was a very good reason for giving the *winter wind* the preference. So in the *Midsummer's Night's Dream,*
   Spangled star light SHEEN;
and several other places. *Chaucer* uses it in this sense,

Because thou art not seen,
Altho' thy breath be rude.
Heigh ho! sing, heigh ho! unto the green holly;
Most friendship is feigning; most loving meer folly:
Then heigh ho, the holly!
This life is most jolly.

Freeze, freeze, thou bitter sky,
That dost not bite so nigh,
As benefits forgot :
Tho' thou the waters warp,
Thy sting is not so sharp
As friend remembred not.
Heigh ho! sing, &c.

Duke Sen. If that you were the good Sir *Rowland's* Son,
As you have whisper'd faithfully you were,
And as mine eyes doth his effigies witness,
Most truly limn'd, and living in your face,
Be truly welcome hither. I'm the Duke,
That lov'd your Father. The residue of your fortune

You blissful suster Lucina *the* SHENE.
And *Fairfax,*
The sacred Angel took his Target SHENE,
And by the Christian Champion stood unseen.
The *Oxford* editor, who had this emendation communicated to him, takes occasion from thence to alter the whole line thus,
Thou causest not that teen.
But, in his rage of correction, he forgot to leave the reason, which is now wanting, why the *winter wind* was to be preferred to *man's ingratitude.*
WARBURTON.
I am afraid that no reader is satisfied with Dr. *Warburton's* emendation, however vigorously enforced; and it is indeed enforced with more art than truth. *Sheen,* i.e. *smiling, shining.* That *sheen* signifies *shining* is easily proved, but when or where did it signify *smiling?* yet *smiling* gives the sense necessary in this place. Sir *T. Hanmer's* change is less uncouth, but too remote from the present text. For my part, I question whether the original line is not lost, and this substituted merely to fill up the measures and the rhyme. Yet even out of this line, by strong agitation, may sense be elicited, and sense not unsuitable to the occasion. *Thou winter wind,* says the Duke, *thy rudeness gives the less pain,* as thou art not seen, *as thou art an enemy that dost not brave us with thy presence, and whose unkindness is therefore not aggravated by insult.*

Go to my cave and tell me. Good old Man,
Thou art right welcome, as thy master is.
—Support him by the arm; give me your hand,
And let me all your fortunes understand.   [*Exeunt.*

ACT III. SCENE I.

The *P A L A C E.*

Enter Duke, *Lords, and* Oliver.

D U K E.

NOT see him since?—Sir, Sir, that cannot be—
But were I not the better part made mercy,
I should not seek an absent argument[3]
Of my revenge, the present: but look to it;
Find out thy brother, wheresoe'er he is;
Seek him with candle: bring him dead or living,
Within this twelvemonth; or turn thou no more
To seek a living; in our territory
Thy lands and all things that thou dost call thine,
Worth seizure, do we seize into our hands;
'Till thou canst quit thee by thy brother's mouth,
Of what we think against thee.
   Oli. Oh, that your highness knew my heart in this:
I never lov'd my brother in my life.
   Duke. More villain thou. Well—Push him out of doors;
And let my officers of such a nature
Make an Extent upon his house and lands:
Do this expediently[4], and turn him going.   [*Exeunt.*

---

[3] *An absent argument.*] An *argument* is used for the *contents* of a book,
thence *Shakespeare* considered it as meaning the *subject,* and then used it for
subject in yet another sense.

[4] *Expediently.*] This is, *expeditiously.*

SCENE II.

Changes to the F O R E S T.

Enter Orlando.

Orla. Hang there, my verse, in witness of my love;
    And thou, thrice-crowned Queen of night, survey[5],
With thy chaste eye, from thy pale sphere above,
    Thy huntress' name that my full life doth sway.
O Rosalind ! these trees shall be my books,
    And in their barks my thoughts I'll character;
That every eye, which in this Forest looks,
    Shall see thy virtue witness'd every where.
Run, run, *Orlando,* carve, on every tree,
The fair, the chaste, and unexpressive She[6].   [*Exit.*

SCENE III.

Enter Corin *and* Clown.

Cor. And how like you this shepherd's life, Mr. *Touchstone*?

Clo. Truly, shepherd, in respect of itself, it is a good life; but in respect that it is a shepherd's life, it is naught. In respect that it is solitary, I like it very well; but in respect that it is private, it is a very vile life. Now in respect it is in the fields, it pleaseth me well; but in respect it is not in the Court, it is tedious. As it is a spare life, look you, it fits my humour well; but as there is no more plenty in it, it goes much against my Stomach. Hast any philosophy in thee, shepherd?

Cor. No more, but that I know, the more one sickens, the worse at ease he is! and that he, that wants money, means, and content, is without three good friends. That the property of rain is to wet, and fire to burn: that good pasture makes fat sheep; and that a great cause of the night is lack of the Sun: that he,

---

[5] *Thrice-crowned Queen of night*.] Alluding to the triple character of *Proserpine, Cynthia,* and *Diana,* given by some Mythologists to the same Goddess, and comprised in these memorial lines:

   Terret, lustrat, agit, Proserpina, Luna, Diana,
   Ima, superna, feras, sceptro, fulgore, sagittis.

[6] *Unexpressive,* for *inexpressible.*

that hath learned no wit by nature nor art[7], may complain of good breeding, or comes of a very dull kindred.

Clo. Such a one is a natural philosopher[8]. Wast ever in Court, shepherd?

Cor. No, truly.

Clo. Then thou art damn'd.

Cor. Nay, I hope——

Clo. Truly, thou art damn'd, like an ill-roasted egg[9], all on one side.

Cor. For not being at Court? your reason.

Clo.[1] Why, if thou never wast at Court, thou never saw'st good manners; if thou never saw'st good manners, then thy manners must be wicked; andwickedness is sin, and sin is damnation: thou art in a parlous state, shepherd.

Cor. Not a whit, *Touchstone:* those, that are good manners at the Court, are as ridiculous in the Country; as the behaviour of the Country is most mockable at the Court. You told me, you salute not at the Court, but you kiss your hands; that courtesy would be uncleanly, if Courtiers were shepherds.

Clo. Instance, briefly; come, instance.

---

[7] *He that hath learned not wit by nature or art, may complain of* GOOD *breeding, or comes of a very dull kindred*.] Common sense requires us to read,
    may complain of GROSS *breeding*.
The *Oxford* Editor has greatly improved this emendation reading,——*bad breeding*.   WARBURTON.

I am in doubt whether the custom of the language in *Shakespeare's* time did not authorise this mode of speech, and make *complain of good breeding* the same with *complain* of the want of *good* breeding. In the last line of the *Merchant of Venice* we find that to *fear the keeping* is to *fear the* not *keeping*.

[8] *Such a one is a natural philosopher*.] The Shepherd had said, all the Philosophy he knew was the property of things, that *rain wetted, fire burnt*, &c. And the *Clown's* reply, in a satire on *Physicks* or *Natural Philosophy*, though introduced with a quibble, is extremely just. For the Natural Philosopher is indeed as ignorant (notwithstanding all his parade of knowledge) of the *efficient* cause of things as the Rustic. It appears, from a thousand instances that our poet was well acquainted with the Physics of his time: and his great penetration enabled him to see this remediless defect of it.   WARBURTON.

[9] *Like an ill roasted egg*.] Of this jest I do not fully comprehend the meaning.

[1] *Why; if thou never wast at Court, thou never saw'st good manners; if thou never*, &c.] This reasoning is drawn up in imitation of *Friar John's* to *Panurge* in *Rabelais*. *Si tu Coqun, ergo ta femme sera belle; ergo tu seras bien traité d'elle; ergo tu auras des Amis beaucoup; ergo tu seras sauvé*. The last inference is pleasantly drawn from the popish doctrine of the intercession of Saints. And, I suppose, our jocular *English* proverb, concerning this matter, was founded in Friar *John's* logic.   WARBURTON.

Cor. Why, we are still handling our ewes; and their fels, you know, are greasy.

Clo. Why, do not your Courtiers' hands sweat? and is not the grease of a mutton as wholsome as the sweat of man? shallow, shallow!—a better instance, I say: come.

Cor. Besides, our hands are hard.

Clo. Your lips will feel them the Sooner. Shallow again:—a more sound instance, come.

Cor. And they are often tarr'd over with the surgery of our sheep; and would you have us kiss tarr? the Courtier's hands are perfumed with civet.

Clo. Most shallow man!—thou worms-meat, in respect of a good piece of flesh—indeed!—learn of the wise, and perpend. Civet is of a baser birth than tarr; the very uncleanly flux of a cat. Mend the instance, shepherd.

Cor. You have too courtly a wit for me; I'll rest.

Clo. Wilt thou rest damn'd? God help thee, shallow man; God make incision in thee[2], thou art raw.

Cor. Sir, I am a true labourer, I earn that I eat; get that I wear; owe no man hate, envy no man's happiness; glad of other men's good, content with my harm; and the greatest of my pride is, to see my ewes graze, and my lambs suck.

Clo. That is another simple sin in you, to bring the ewes and the rams together; and to offer to get your living by the copulation of cattle; to be a bawd to a bell-wether[3]; and to betray a she-lamb of a twelve-month to a crooked-pated old cuckoldry ram, out of all reasonable match. If thou be'st not damn'd for this, the devil himself will have no shepherds; I cannot see else how thou shouldst 'scape.

Cor. Here comes young Mr. *Ganimed,* my new mistress's brother.

---

[2] Make incision *in thee*.] *To make incision* was a proverbial expression then in vogue, for to make to understand. So in *Beaumont* and *Fletcher's Humourous Lieutenant.*

——*O excellent King,*
Thus he begins, thou life and light of creatures.
Angel-ey'd King, vouchsafe at length thy favour;
And so proceeds to incision.——

i.e. to make him understand what he would be at.   WARBURTON.

[3] *Bawd to a Belwether.*] *Wether* and *Ram* had anciently the same meaning.

SCENE IV.

Enter Rosalind, *with a paper.*

Ros. From the east to western Inde,
   No jewel is like Rosalind,
   Her worth, being mounted on the wind,
   Through all the world bears Rosalind.
   All the pictures, fairest limn'd,
   Are but black to Rosalind.
   Let no face be kept in mind,
   But the face of Rosalind.

Clo. I'll rhime you so, eight years together; dinners, and suppers, and sleeping hours excepted: it is the right butter-woman's rate to market[4].
Ros. Out, fool!
Clo. For a taste——

   If a hart doth lack a hind,
   Let him seek out Rosalind.
   If the cat will after kind,
   So, be sure, will Rosalind.
   Winter-garments must be lin'd,
   So must slender Rosalind.
   They, that reap, must sheaf and bind;
   Then to Cart with Rosalind.
   Sweetest nut hath sowrest rind,
   Such a nut is Rosalind.
   He that sweetest rose will find,
   Must find love's prick, and Rosalind.

This is the very false gallop of verses; why do you infect yourself with them?
Ros. Peace, you dull fool, I found them on a tree.
Clo. Truly, the tree yields bad fruit.
Ros. I'll graff it with you, and then I shall graff it with a medler; then it will be the earliest fruit i'th' country; for you will be rotten ere you be half ripe, and that's the right virtue of the medler.
Clo. You have said; but whether wisely or no, let the Forest judge.

---

[4] *Rate to market*. So Sir *T. Hanmer*. In the former Editions *rank* to market.

SCENE V.

Enter Celia, *with a writing.*

Ros. Peace, here comes my Sister reading; stand aside.

Cel. Why should this a Desert be,
For it is unpeopled? No;
Tongues I'll hang on every tree,
That shall civil sayings show[5].
Some, how brief the life of man
Runs his erring pilgrimage;
That the stretching of a span
Buckles in his sum of age;
Some of violated vows,
'Twixt the souls of friend and friend;
But upon the fairest boughs,
Or at every sentence' end,
Will I Rosalinda write;
Teaching all that read, to know,
This Quintessence of every Sprite
Heaven would in little show.

Therefore heaven nature charg'd[6],
That one body should be fill'd
With all graces wide enlarg'd,
Nature presently distill'd
Helen's *cheeks, but not her heart,*
Cleopatra's *majesty;*

---

[5] *That shall civil sayings show.*] *Civil* is here used in the same sense as when we say *civil* wisdom or *civil* life, in opposition to a solitary state, or to the state of nature. This desert shall not appear *unpeopled,* for every tree shall teach the maxims or incidents of social life.

[6] *Therefore heaven nature charg'd.*] From the picture of *Apelles* or the accompishments of *Pandora.*

　　So before,
　　———But thou
　　So perfect, and so peerless art counted
　　Of ev'ry creature's best.　　　　　　　　　　　Tempest.
Perhaps from this passage *Swift* had his hint of *Biddy Floyd.*

Atalanta's *better part*[7];
   [8]*Sad* Lucretia's *modesty.*
Thus Rosalind, *of many parts*
   By heav'nly synod was devis'd;
Of many faces, eyes, and hearts,
   To have the Touches[9] *dearest priz'd.*
Heav'n would that she these gifts should have,
   And I should live and die her slave.

Ros. O most gentle *Jupiter*[1]!—what tedious homily of love have you wearied your Parishioners withall, and never cry'd, Have patience, good people!

Cel. How now? back-friends!—shepherd, go off a little—go with him, sirrah.

Clo. Come, shepherd, let us make an honourable retreat; tho' not with bag and baggage, yet with scrip and scrippage.   [*Exeunt* Corin *and* Clown.

SCENE VI.

Cel. Didst thou hear these verses?

Ros. O yes, I heard them all, and more too; for some of them had in them more feet than the verses would bear.

Cel. That's no matter; the feet might bear the verses.

Ros. Ay, but the feet were lame, and could not bear themselves without the verse, and therefore stood lamely in the verse.

---

[7] *Atalanta's better part.*] I know not well what could be the better part of *Atalanta* here ascribed to *Rosalind.* Of the *Atalanta* most celebrated, and who therefore must be intended here where she has no epithet of discrimination, the *better part* seems to have been her heels, and the worse part was so bad that *Rosalind* would not thank her lover for the comparison. There is a more obscure *Atalanta,* a huntress and a Heroine; but of her nothing bad is recorded, and therefore I know not which was the better part. *Shakespeare* was no despicable Mythologist; yet he seems here to have mistaken some other character for that of *Atalanta.*

[8] *Sad,* is *grave, sober,* not *light.*

[9] *The Touches.*] The features; *les traits.*

[1] *O most gentle* JUPITER!] We should read JUNIPER, as the following words shew, alluding to the proverbial term of a *Juniper lecture*: A sharp or unpleasing one! *Juniper* being a rough prickly plant.   WARBURTON.

Surely *Jupiter* may stand.

Cel. But didst thou hear, without wondring, how thy name should be hang'd and carv'd upon these trees?

Ros. I was seven of the nine days out of wonder, before you came; for, look here, what I found on a palm-tree;[2] I was never so be-rhimed since *Pythagoras's* time, that I was an *Irish* rat, which I can hardly remember.

Cel. Trow you, who hath done this?

Ros. Is it a man?

Cel. And a chain, that you once wore, about his neck: Change you colour?

Ros. I pr'ythee, who?

Cel. O Lord, Lord, it is a hard matter for friends to meet; but mountains may be remov'd with earthquakes, and so encounter.

Ros. Nay, but who is it?

Cel. Is it possible?

Ros. Nay, I pr'ythee now, with most petitionary vehemence, tell me who it is.

Cel. O wonderful, wonderful, and most wonderful wonderful, and yet again wonderful, and after that out of all whooping——

Ros. [3]Good my complexion! dost thou think, though I am caparison'd like a man, I have a doublet and hose in my disposition?[4] One inch of delay more is a

---

[2] *I was never so be-rhymed since* Pythagoras's *time, that I was an* Irish *rat.*] *Rosalind* is a very learned Lady. She alludes to the *Pythagorean* doctrine, which teaches that souls transmigrate from one animal to another, and relates that in his time she was an *Irish* rat, and by some metrical charm was rhymed to death. The power of killing rats with rhymes *Donne* mentions in his satires, and *Temple* in his treatises. Dr. Gray has produced a similar passage from *Randolph.*

　——*My Poets*
　Shall with a saytire steeped in vinegar
　Rhyme them to death, as they do rates in Ireland.

[3] *Good my complexion!*] *This is a mode of expression,* Mr. *Theobald says, which he cannot reconcile to common sense.* Like enough; and so too the *Oxford Editor.* But the meaning is, *Hold good my complexion,* i.e. let me not blush.　　　　　　　　　　　　　　　　　　　　　　　WARBURTON.

[4] *One inch of delay more is a South Sea of discovery.*] This is stark nonsense; we must read—*off* discovery, *i.e.* from discovery. "If you delay me one inch of time longer, I shall think this secret as far from discovery as the *South sea* is.　　　　　　　　　　　　　　　　　　　　　　　WARBURTON.

This sentence is rightly noted by the Commentator as nonsense, but not so happily restored to sense. I read thus:

One inch of delay more is a South sea. Discover, *I pr'ythee: tell me who is it quickly!*—When the transcriber had once made *discovery* from *discover, I*, he easily put an article after *South-sea.* But it may be read with still less change,

South-sea of discovery. I pr'ythee, tell me, who is it; quickly, and speak apace; I would thou couldst stammer, that thou might'st pour this concealed man out of thy mouth, as wine comes out of a narrow-mouth'd bottle; either too much at once, or none at all. I pr'ythee take the cork out of thy mouth, that I may drink thy tidings.

Cel. So you may put a man in your belly.

Ros. Is he of God's making? what manner of man? is his head worth a hat? or his chin worth a beard?

Cel. Nay, he hath but a little beard.

Ros. Why, God will send more, if the man will be thankful; let me stay the growth of his beard, if thou delay me not the knowledge of his chin.

Cel. It is young *Orlando* that tripp'd up the wrestler's heels and your heart both in an instant.

Ros. Nay, but the devil take mockings; speak, sad brow, and true maid.

Cel. I'faith, coz, 'tis he.

Ros. Orlando!

Cel. Orlando!

Ros. Alas the day! what shall I do with my doublet and hose? what did he, when thou saw'st him? what said he? how look'd he? wherein went he? what makes he here? did he ask for me? where remains he? how parted he with thee? and when shalt thou see him again? answer me in one word.

Cel. You must borrow me *Garagantua's*[5] mouth first; 'tis a word too great for any mouth of this age's size. To say, ay, and no, to these particulars, is more than to answer in a catechism.

Ros. But doth he know that I am in this Forest, and in man's apparel? looks he as freshly as he did the day he wrestled?

Cel. It is as easy to count atoms, as to resolve the propositions of a lover: but take a taste of my finding him, and relish it with good observance. I found him under a tree like a dropp'd acorn[6].

---

and with equal probability. *Every Inch of delay more is a* South sea discovery: *Every delay,* however short, is to me tedious and irksome as the longest voyages, as a voyage of *discovery* on the *South-sea.* How much voyages to the South-sea, on which the *English* had then first ventured, engaged the conversation of that time, may be easily imagined.

[5] —Garagantua's *mouth.*] *Rosalind* requires nine questions to be answered in *one word*; *Celia* tells her that a word of such magnitude is too big for any mouth but that of *Garagantua,* the giant of *Rabelais.*

[6] —*I found him under a tree like a dropp'd acorn.*] We should read,
    Under AN OAK *tree.*
This appears from what follows—*like a dropp'd acorn.* For how did he look like a *dropp'd acorn* unless he was found under an oak-tree? And from

Ros. It may well be call'd *Jove's* tree, when it drops forth such fruit.

Cel. Give me audience, good Madam.

Ros. Proceed.

Cel. There lay he stretch'd along like a wounded Knight.

Ros. Tho' it be pity to see such a sight, it well becomes the ground.

Cel. Cry, holla! to thy tongue, I pr'ythee; it curvets unseasonably. He was furnish'd like a hunter.

Ros. Oh, ominous! he comes to kill my heart.

Cel. I would sing my song without a burden; thou brings't me out of tune.

Ros. Do you not know I am a woman? when I think, I must speak—Sweet, say on.

SCENE VII.

Enter Orlando *and* Jaques.

Cel. You bring me out. Soft, comes he not here?

Ros. 'Tis he; slink by, and note him.   [Celia *and* Rosalind *retire.*

Jaq. I thank you for your company; but, good faith, I had as lief have been myself alone.

Orla. And so had I; but yet, for fashion sake, I thank you too for your society.

Jaq. God b'w' you, let's meet as little as we can.

Orla. I do desire we may be better strangers.

Jaq. I pray you marr no more trees with writing love-songs in their barks.

Orla. I pray you, marr no more of my Verses with reading them ill-favouredly.

Jaq. Rosalind, is your love's name?

Orla. Yes, just.

Jaq. I do not like her name.

Orla. There was no thought of pleasing you, when she was christen'd.

Jaq. What stature is she of?

Orla. Just as high as my heart.

Jaq. You are full of pretty answers; have you not been acquainted with goldsmiths wives, and conn'd them out of rings?

Rosalind's reply, *that it might well be called* Jove's *tree*: For the *Oak* was sacred to *Jove*.   WARBURTON.

Orla. Not so:[7] but I answer you right painted cloth, from whence you have studied your questions.

Jaq. You have a nimble wit; I think, it was made of *Atalanta's* heels. Will you sit down with me, and we two will rail against our mistress, the world, and all our misery.

Orla. I will chide no breather in the world but my self, against whom I know most faults.

Jaq. The worst fault you have, is to be in love.

Orla. 'Tis a fault I will not change for your best virtue. I am weary of you.

Jaq. By my troth, I was seeking for a fool, when you shall see him.

Orla. He is drown'd in the brook; look but in, and you shall see him.

Jaq. There I shall see mine own figure.

Orla. Which I take to be either a fool, or a cypher.

Jaq. I'll stay no longer with you; farewel, good Signior love!   [*Exit.*

SCENE VIII.

Orla. I am glad of your departure; adieu, good Monsieur melancholy!
[*Cel. and* Ros. *come forward.*

Ros. I will speak to him like a sawcy lacquey, and under that habit play the knave with him—Do you hear, forester?

Orla. Very well; what would you?

Ros. I pray you, what is't a clock?

Orla. You should ask me, what time o'day; there's no clock in the Forest.

Ros. Then there is no true lover in the Forest; else, sighing every minute, and groaning every hour, would detest the lazy foot of time, as well as a clock

Orla. And why not the swift foot of time? had not that been as proper?

Ros. By no means, Sir: time travels in divers paces, with divers persons; I'll tell you whom time ambles withal, whom time trots withal, whom time gallops withal, and whom he stands still withal.

Orla. I pr'ythee, whom doth he trot withal?

---

[7] ——*but I answer you right painted cloth.*] This alludes to the Fashion, in old Tapestry Hangings, of Motto's and mortal Sentences from the Mouths of the Figures work'd or painted in them. The Poet again hints at this Custom in his Poem, call'd *Tarquin* and *Lucrece*:

> *Who fears a Sentence, or an old Man's Saw,*
> *Shall by a* painted Cloth *he kept in Awe*.   THEOBALD.

Sir *T. Hammer* reads, *I answer you right,* in the stile of the *painted cloth.* Something seems wanting, and I know not what can be proposed better.

Ros. Marry, he trots hard with a young maid, between the contract of her marriage, and the day it is solemnized: if the interim be but a sennight, timed pace is so hard that it seems the length of seven years

Orla. Who ambles time withal?

Ros. With a priest that lacks *Latin,* and a rich man that hath not the gout; for the one sleeps easily because he cannot study; and the other lives merrily, because he feels no pain: the one lacking the burden of lean and wasteful learning; the other knowing no burden of heavy tedious penury. These time ambles withal.

Orla. Whom doth he gallop withal?

Ros. With a thief to the gallows: for though he go as softly as foot can fall, he thinks himself too soon there.

Orla. Whom stays it still withal?

Ros. With lawyers in the vacation; for they sleep between term and term, and then they perceive not how time moves.

Orla. Where dwell you, pretty youth?

Ros. With this shepherdess, my sister; here in the skirts of the forest, like fringe upon a petticoat.

Orla. Are you native of this place?

Ros. As the cony, that you see dwell where she is kindled.

Orla. You accent is something finer, than you could purchase in so removed a dwelling.

Ros. I have been told so of many; but, indeed, an old religious Uncle of mine taught me to speak, who was in his youth an[*] inland man, who knew courtship too well: for there he fell in love. I have heard him read many lectures against it; I thank God, I am not a woman, to be touch'd with so many giddy offences as he hath generally tax'd their whole sex withal.

Orla. Can you remember any of the principal evils, that he laid to the charge of women?

Ros. There were none principal, they were all like one another, as half-pence are; every one fault seeming monstrous, 'till his fellow fault came to match it.

Orla. I pr'ythee, recount some of them.

Ros. No; I will not cast away my physick, but on those that are sick. There is a man haunts the Forest, that abuses our young Plants with carving *Rosalind* on their barks; hang Odes upon hawthorns, and Elegies on brambles; all, forsooth, deifying the name of *Rosalind.* If I could meet that fancy-monger, I

---

[*] *—inland man,*] Is used in this play for one *civilised,* in opposition to the *rustick* of the priest. So Orlando before— *Yet am I* inland *bred, and know some nurture* .

would give him that good counsel, for he seems to have the Quotidian of love upon him.

Orla. I am he, that is so love-shak'd; I pray ye tell me your remedy.

Ros. There is none of my Uncle's marks upon you, he taught me how to know a man in love; in which cage of rushes, I am sure, you are not prisoner.

Orla. What were his marks?

Ros. A lean cheek, which you have not; a blue eye and sunken, which you have not; an unquestionable spirit[8], which you have not; a beard neglected, which you have not;—but I pardon you for that, for simply your Having in beard is a younger Brother's revenue;——then your hose should be ungarter'd, your bonnet unbanded, your sleeve unbutton'd, your shoe untied, and every thing about you demonstrating a careless desolation. But you are no such man, you are rather point-de-vice in your accoutrements, as loving yourself, then seeming the lover of any other.

Orla. Fair youth, I would I could make thee believe I love.

Ros. Me believe it? you may as soon make her, that you love, believe it; which, I warrant, she is apter to do, than to confess she does; that is one of the points, in the which women still give the lye to their consciences. But, in good sooth, are you he that hangs the Verses on the trees, wherein *Rosalind* is so admired?

Orla. I swear to thee, youth, by the white hand of *Rosalind,* I am That he, that unfortunate he.

Ros. But are you so much in love, as your rhimes speak?

Orla. Neither rhime nor reason can express how much.

Ros. Love is merely a madness, and, I tell you deserves as well a dark house and a whip, as mad men do: and the reason why they are not so punished and cured, is, that the lunacy is so ordinary, that the whippers are in love too: yet I profess curing it by counsel.

Orla. Did you ever cure any so?

Ros. Yes, one, and in this manner. He was to imagine me his love, his mistress: and I set him every day to wooe me. At which time would I, being but a moonish youth, grieve, be effeminate, changeable, longing, and liking; proud, fantastical, apish, shallow, inconstant, full of tears, full of smiles; for every passion something, and for no passion truly any thing, as boys and women are for the most part cattle of this colour; would now like him, now loath him; then entertain him, then forswear him; now weep for him, then spit at him; that I

---

[8] —*an unquestionable spirit.*] That is, a spirit not *inquisitive,* a mind indifferent to common objects and negligent of common occurrences. Here *Shakespeare* has used a passive for an active mode of speech: so in a former scene, *The Duke is too* disputable *for me,* that is too *disputatious.*

drave my suitor from his mad humour of love, to a living humour of madness[9];
which was, to forswear the full stream of the world, and to live in a nook
merely monastick; and thus I cur'd him, and this way will I take upon me to
wash your liver as clear as a found sheep's heart, that there shall not be one
spot of love in't.

Orla. I would not be cur'd, youth.

Ros. I would cure you, if you would but call me *Rosalind,* and come every
day to my cote, and wooe me.

Orla. Now, by the faith of my love, I will. Tell me where it is.

Ros. Go with me to it, and I will shew it you ; and, by the way, you shall tell
me where in the Forest you live. Will you go?

Orla. With all my heart, good youth.

Ros. Nay, nay, you must call me *Rosalind*—Come, sister, will you go?

[*Exeunt.*

SCENE IX.

Enter Clown, Audrey, *and* Jaques *watching them.*

Clo. Come apace, good *Audrey,* I will fetch up your goats, *Audrey;* and
now, *Audrey,* am I the man yet? doth my simple feature content you?

Aud. Your features, Lord warrant us! what features?

Clo. I am here with thee and thy goats, as the most capricious poet honest
Ovid was among the *Goths.*

Jaq. [*aside*] O' knowledge ill-inhabited, worse than *Jove* in a thatch'd
house!

Clo. When a man's verses cannot be understood nor a man's good Wit
seconded with the forward child, Understanding; it strikes a man more dead

---

9 ——*to a living humour of madness*;] If this be the true reading, we must by
living understand *lasting,* or *permanent,* but I cannot forbear to think that some
antithesis was intended, which is now lost; perhaps the passage stood thus, *I
drove my suitor from a* dying *humour of love to a living humour of madness.* Or
rather thus, *from a mad humour of love to a* loving *humour of madness,* that is,
from a *madness* that was *love,* to a *love* that was *madness.* That seems
somewhat harsh and strained, but such modes of speech are not unusual in our
poet: and this harshness was probably the cause of the corruption.

than a great reckoning in a little room[1]; truly, I would the Gods had made thee poetical.

Aud. I do not know what poetical is; is it honest in deed and word? is it a true thing?

Clo. No, truly; for the truest poetry is the most feigning; and lovers are given to poetry; and what they swear in poetry[*], may be said, as lovers, they do feign.

Aud. Do you wish then, that the Gods had made me poetical?

Clo. I do, truly; for thou swear'st to me, thou art honest now if thou wert a poet, I might have some hope thou didst feign.

Aud. Would you not have me honest?

Clo. No, truly, unless thou wert hard-favour'd; for honesty coupled to beauty, is, to have honey a sawce to sugar.

Jaq. [*aside.*][2] A material fool!

Aud. Well, I am not fair; and therefore I pray the Gods makes me honest!

Clo. Truly, and to cast away honesty upon a foul slut, were to put good meat into an unclean dish.

Aud. I am not a slut, though I thank the Gods I am foul[†].

Clo. Well, praised be the Gods for thy foulness! sluttishness may come hereafter: but be it as it may be, I will marry thee; and to that end I have been

---

[1] ——*it strikes a man more dead than a great reckoning in a little room*;] Nothing was ever wrote in higher humour than this simile. A great reckoning, in a little room, implies that the entertainment was mean, and the bill extravagant. The poet here alluded to the *French* proverbial phrase *of the quarter of hour of Rabelais*: who said, there was only one quarter of an hour in human life passes ill, and that was between the calling for the reckoning and paying it. Yet the delicacy of our *Oxford Editor* would correct this into, *It strikes a man more dead than a great* reeking *in a little room*. This is amending with a vengeance. When men are joking together in a merry humour, all are disposed to laugh. One of the company says a good thing; the jest is not taken; all are silent, and he who said it, quite confounded. This is compared to a tavern jollity interrupted by the coming in of a *great reckoning*. Had not *Shakespeare* reason now in this case to apply his simile, to his own case, against his critical editor? who, 'tis plain, taking the phrase to *strike dead* in a literal sense, concluded, from his knowledge in philosophy, that it could not be so effectually done if by a *reckoning* as by a *reeking*.   WARBURTON.

[*] ——*and what they swear in poetry,* &c] This sentence seems perplexed and inconsequent; perhaps it were better read thus, *What they swear as lovers they may be said to feign as poets*.

[2] *A material fool*!] A fool with *matter* in him; a fool stocked, with notions.

[†] *By foul* is meant *coy* or *frowning*.   HANMER.

with Sir *Oliver Mar-text,* the vicar of the next village, who hath promis'd to meet me in this place of the forest, and to couple us.

Jaq. [*aside.*] I would fain see this meeting.

Aud. Well, the Gods give us joy!

Clo. Amen. A man may, if he were of a fearful heart, stagger in this attempt; for here we have no temple but the wood, no assembly but horn-beasts. But what tho'[3]? courage. As horns are odious, they are necessary. It is said, many a man knows no end of his goods: right: many a man has good horns, and knows no end of them. Well, that is the dowry of his wife, 'tis none of his own getting; horns? even so—poor men alone?—no, no, the noblest deer hath them as huge as the rascal: is the single man therefore blessed? no. As a wall'd town is more worthier than a village, so is the forehead of a married man more honourable than the bare brow of a bachelor; and by how much defence is better than no skill, so much is a horn more precious than to want.

Enter Sir Oliver Mar-text.

Here comes Sir *Oliver*—Sir *Oliver Mar-text*[4], you are well met. Will you dispatch us here under this tree, or shall we go with you to your Chapel?

Sir Oli. Is there none here to give the woman?

Clo. I will not take her on gift of any man.

Sir Oli. Truly, she must he given, or the marriage is not lawful.

Jaq. [*discovering himself*] Proceed, proceed; I'll give her.

Clo. Good even, good master *what ye call*: how do you, Sir? you are very well met: God'ild you for your last company! I am very glad to see you—even a toy in hand here, Sir—nay; pray be covered.

Jaq. Will you be married, *Motley*?

Col. As the ox hath his bow, Sir, the horse his curb, and the faulcon his bells, so man hath his desire; and as pigeons bill, so wedlock would be nibling.

Jaq. And will you; being a man of your breeding, be married under a bush like a beggar? get you to church, and have a good priest that can tell you what marriage is; this fellow will but join you together as they join wainscot; then one of you will prove a shrunk pannel, and, like green timber, warp, warp.

Clo. I am not in the mind, but I were better to be married of him than of

---

[3] —what tho'?] What then.

[4] *Sir* Oliver.] He that has taken his first degree at the University, is in the academical style called *Dominus,* and in common language was heretofore termed *Sir.* This was not always a word of contempt; the graduates assumed it in their own writings; so *Trevisa* the historian writes himself *Syr* John de Trevisa.

another; for he is not like to marry me well; and not being well married, it will be a good excuse for me hereafter to leave my wife.

Jaq. Go thou with me, and let me counsel thee.

Clo. Come, sweet *Audrey,* we must be married, or we must live in bawdry. Farewel, good Sir *Oliver;* not[5] *O sweet* Oliver, *O brave* Oliver, *leave me not behind thee,* but wind away, begone, I say, I will not to wedding with thee.

Sir *Oli.* 'Tis no matter; ne'er a fantastical knave of them all shall flout me out of my Calling.   [*Exeunt.*

SCENE X.

Changes to a Cottage in the Forest.

Enter Rosalind *and* Celia.

Ros. NEVER talk to me—I will weep.

Cel. Do, I pr'ythee; but yet have the grace to consider, that tears do not become a man.

Ros. But have I not cause to weep?

Cel. As good cause as one would desire; therefore weep.

---

[5] *Not* O sweet *Oliver,* O brave, &c.] Some words of an old ballad.
WARBURTON.

Of this speech, as it now appears, I can make nothing, and think nothing can be made. In the same breath he calls his mistress to be married, and sends away the man that should marry them. Dr. *Warburton* has very happily observed, that *O sweet* Oliver is a quotation from an old song; I believe there are two quotations put in opposition to each other. For *wind* I read *wend*, the old word for *go.* Perhaps the whole passage may be regulated thus,

Clo. *I am not in the mind, but it were better for me to be married of him than of another, for he is not like to marry me well, and not being well married it will be a good excuse for me hereafter to leave my wife*——*Come, sweet* Audrey, *we must be married, or we must live in bawdry.*

Jac. *Go thou with me, and let me counsel thee.*   [they whisper.

Clo. *Farewel, good Sir* Oliver, *not* O sweet *Oliver,* O brave *Oliver,* leave me not behind thee,——*but*

    Wend away.

    Begone, I say,

    I will not to wedding with thee to day.

Of this conjecture the reader may take as much as shall appear necessary to the sense, or conducive to the humour.

Ros. His very hair is of the dissembling colour.

Cel. Something browner than *Judas's*: marry his kisses are *Judas's* own children.

Ros. I'faith, his hair is of a good colour[6].

Cel. An excellent colour: your chestnut was ever the only colour.

Ros. And his kissing is as full of sanctity, as the touch of holy Beard[7].

Cel. He hath bought a pair of cast lips of *Diana;* a nun of Winter's sisterhood[8] kisses not more religiously; the very ice of chastity is in them.

Ros. But why did he swear he would come this morning, and comes not?

Cel. Nay, certainly, there is no truth in him.

Ros. Do you think so?

Cel. Yes. I think he is not a pick-purse nor a horse-stealer; but for his verity in love, I do think him as concave as a cover'd goblet[9], or a worm eaten nut.

Ros. Not true in love?

---

[6] There is much of nature in this petty perverseness of *Rosalind*; she finds faults in her lover, in hope to be contradicted; and when *Celia* in sportive malice too readily seconds her accusations, she contradicts herself, rather than suffer her favourite to want a vindication.

[7] —*as the touch of holy* beard.] We should read *beard,* that is, as the kiss of an holy saint or hermit, called the *kiss of charity*: This makes the comparison just and decent; the other impious and absurd. WARBURTON.

[8] —*a nun of Winter's sisterhood*] This is finely expressed. But Mr. *Theobald* says, *the words give him no idea.* And 'tis certain, that words will never give men what nature has denied them. However, to mend the matter, he substitutes *Winifred's sisterhood*. And, after so happy a thought, it was to no purpose to tell him there was no religious order of that denomination. The plain truth is, *Shakespare* meant *an unfruitful sisterhood,* which had devoted itself to charity. For as those who were of the sisterhood of the spring were the votaries of *Venus*; those of summer, the votaries of *Ceres*; those of autumn, of *Pomona*; so these of the *sisterhood of winter,* were the votaries of *Diana*: Called, *of winter,* because that quarter is not, like the other three, productive of fruit or increase. On this account, it is, that, when the poet speaks, of what is most *poor,* he instances in *winter,* in these fine lines of *Othello,*

> *But riches endless is* as poor as winter
> *To him that ever fears he shall be poor.*

The other property of winter that made him term them of its sisterhood is its *coldness*. So in *Midsummer's Night's Dream,*

> *To be a* barren sister *all your life,*
> *Chanting saint hymns to the* cold fruitless *moon*. WARBURTON.

[9] —*as concave as a cover'd goblet,*] Why a *cover'd*? Because a goblet is never kept *cover'd* but when *empty. Shakespeare* never throws out his expressions at random. WARBURTON.

Cel. Yes, when he is in; but, I think, he is not in.

Ros. You have heard him swear downright, he was.

Cel. Was, is not *is;* besides, the oath of a lover is no stronger than the word of a tapster; they are both the confirmers of false reckonings. He attends here in the Forest on the Duke your Father.

Ros. I met the Duke yesterday, and had much question with him: he asked me, of what parentage I was; I told him of as good as he; so he laugh'd, and let me go. But what talk we of fathers, when there is such a man as *Orlando*?

Cel. O, that's a brave man! he writes brave verses, speaks brave words, swears brave oaths, and breaks them bravely, quite travers, athwart[1] the heart of his lover; as a puisny tilter, that spurs his horse but on one side, breaks his staff like a noble goose; but all's brave that youth mounts, and folly guides; who comes here?

Enter Corin.

Cor. Mistress and master, you have oft enquired
After the shepherd that complain'd of love;
Whom you saw sitting by me on the turf,
Praising the proud disdainful shepherdess
That was his mistress.

---

[1] —*quite travers, athwart,* &c.] An unexperienced lover is here compared to a *puisny Tilter,* to whom it was a disgrace to have his Lance broken across, as it was a mark either of want of Courage or Address. This happen'd when the horse flew on one side, in the career: And hence, I suppose, arose the jocular proverbial phrase *of spurring the horse only on one side*. Now as breaking the Lance against his Adversary's breast, in a direct line, was honourable, so the breaking it *across* against his breast was, for the reason above, dishonourable: Hence it is, that *Sidney,* in his *Arcadia,* speaking of the mock-combat of *Clinias* and *Dametas* says, *The wind took such hold of his staff that it* crost quite over his breast, &c.——And to *break across* was the usual phrase, as appears from some wretched verses of the same author, speaking of an unskilful Tilter.

 Me bought some Staves be mist, if so, not much amiss:
 For when he most did hit, he ever yet did miss.
 One said he brake across, *full well it so might be,* &c.

This is the allusion. So that *Orlando,* a young Gallant, affecting the fashion (for *brave* is here used, as in other places, for fashionable) is represented either *unskilful* in courtship, or *timbrous*. The Lover's meeting or appointment corresponds to the Tilter's Career; And as the one breaks Staves, the other breaks Oaths. The business is only meeting fairly, and doing both with Address: And 'tis for the want of this, that *Orlando* is blamed.   WARBURTON.

Cel. Well, and what of him?

Cor. If you will see a pageant truly play'd,
Between the pale complexion of true love,
And the red glow of scorn and proud disdain;
Go hence a little, and I shall conduct you,
If you will mark it.

Ros. Come, let us remove;
The sight of lovers feedeth those in love:
Bring us but to this sight, and you shall say
I'll prove a busy Actor in their Play.   [*Exeunt.*

SCENE XI.

Changes to another part of the Forest.

Enter Silvius *and* Phebe.

Sil. Sweet *Phebe,* do not scorn me—do not, *Phebe*—
Say, that you love me not; but say not so
In bitterness; the common executioner,
Whose heart th' accustom'd sight of death makes hard,
Falls not the ax upon the humbled neck,
But first begs pardon: will you sterner be [2]
Than he that dies and lives by bloody drops?

---

[2] —*Will you sterner be,*
Than he that dies and lives by blooody drops?] This is spoken of the
executioner. He lives indeed, by bloody Drops, if you will: but how does he *die*
by bloody Drops? The poet must certainly have wrote—*that* deals *and lives,*
&c. i.e. that gets his bread by, and makes a trade of cutting off heads: But the
Oxford Editor makes it plainer. He reads,
     Than he that lives and thrives by bloody drops.   WARBURTON.
Either Dr. *Warburton's* emendation, except that the word *deals* wants its
proper construction, or that of Sir *T. Hanmer* may serve the purpose; but I
believe they have fixed corruption upon the wrong word, and should rather
read,
     Than he that dies his lips by *bloody drops*?
Will you speak with more sternness than the executioner, whose *lips* are used
to be *sprinkled* with blood? The mention of *drops* implies some part that must
be sprinkled rather than dipped.

Enter Rosalind, Celia *and* Corin.

Phe. I would not be thy executioner;
I fly thee, for I would not injure thee.
Thou tell'st me, there is murder in mine eyes;
'Tis pretty, sure, and very probable,
That eyes, that are the frail'st and softest things,
Who shut their coward gates on atomies,
Should be call'd tyrants, butchers, murderers!—
Now do I frown on thee with all my heart,
And if mine eyes can wound, now let them kill thee
Now counterfeit to swoon; why, now fall down;
Or if thou can'st not, oh, for shame, for shame,
Lye not to say mine eyes are murderers,
Now shew the wound mine eyes have made in thee;
Scratch thee but with a pin, and there remains
Some scar of it; lean but upon a rush,
The cicatrice and capable impressure[3]
Thy Palm some moments keeps: but now mine eyes
Which I have darted at thee, hurt thee not;
Nor, I am sure, there is no force in eyes
That can do hurt
    Sil. O. dear *Phebe,*
If ever (as that ever may be near)
You meet in some fresh cheek the power of fancy[4],
Then shall you know the wounds invisible
That love's keen arrows make.
    Phe. But 'till that time,
Come not thou near me; and when that time comes
Afflict me with thy mocks, pity me not;
As, 'till that time, I shall not pity thee.
    Ros. And why, I pray you?—Who might be your mother[5]

---

[3] *The cicatrice and capable impressure*] *Cicatrice* is here not very properly
used; it is the scar of a wound. *Capable impressure arrows mark.*

[4] *—power of fancy,*] *Fancy* is here used for *love,* as before in *Midsummer
Night's Dream.*

[5] *——Who might be your mother,*] It is common for the poets to express
cruelty by saying, of those who commit it, that they were born of rocks, or
suckled by tigresses.

That you insult, exult, and all at once[6]
Over the wretched? what though you have beauty[7],
(As, by my faith, I see no more in you
Than without candle may go dark to bed)
Must you be therefore proud and pitiless?
Why, what means this? why do you look on me?
I see no more in you than in the ordinary
Of nature's sale-work[8]: odds, my little life!
I think she means to angle mine eyes too:
No, faith, proud mistress, hope not after it;
'Tis not your inky brows, your black silk hair,
Your bugle eye-balls, nor your cheek of cream,
That can entame my spirits to your worship[9].
You foolish shepherd, wherefore do you follow her
Like foggy South, puffing with wind and rain?
You are a thousand times a properer man,
Than she a woman. 'Tis such fools as you,
That make the world full of ill-favour'd children;
'Tis not her glass, but you, that flatter her;
And out of you she sees herself more proper,
Than any of her lineaments can show her.
But, mistress, know yourself; down on your knees,

---

[6] *That you insult, exult, and* ALL *at once*] If the Speaker intended to accuse the person spoken to only for *insulting* and exulting; then, instead of——*all at once*, it ought to have been, *both at once*. But by examining the crime or the person accused; we shall discover that the line is to be read thus,

    That you insult, exult, and RAIL *at once*.

For these three things *Phebe* was guilty of. But the *Oxford Editor* improves it, and, for *rail at once,* reads *domineer*.   WARB.

[7] —*what though you have no beauty,*] Tho' all the printed Copies agree in this Reading, it is very accurately observed to me by an ingenious unknown Correspondent, who signs himself L. H. (and to whom I can only here make my Acknowledgements) that the *Negative* ought to be left out.   THEOBALD.

[8] *Of nature's* sale-work:] *i.e.* those works that nature makes up carelessly and without exactness. The allusion is to the practice of Mechanicks, whose *work* bespoke is more elaborate, than that which is made up for chance-customers, or to sell in quantities to retailers, which is called *sale-work*.

                                      WARBURTON.

[9] *That can* ENTAME *my spirits to your worship*.] I should rather think that *Shakespeare* wrote ENTRAINE, draw, allure.   WARB.

    The common reading seems unexceptionable.

And thank heav'n fasting, for a good man's love;
For I must tell you friendly in your ear,
Sell when you can; you are not for all markets.
Cry the man mercy, love him, take his offer;
Foul is most foul, being foul to be a scoffer[1]:
So take her to thee, shepherd—fare you well.

 Phe. Sweet youth, I pray you chide a year together
I had rather hear you chide, than this man woo.

 Ros. [*aside*] He's fallen in love with her foulness[2]; and she'll fall in love with my anger. If it be so, as fast as she answers thee with frowning looks, I'll sauce her with bitter words—Why look you so upon me?

 Phe. For no ill-will I bear you.

 Ros. I pray you, do not fall in love with me;
For I am falser than vows made in wine;
Besides, I like you not. If you will know my house,
'Tis at the tuft of Olives here hard by.
Will you go, Sister?—Shepherd, ply her hard—
Come, sister—shepherdess, look on him better.
And be not proud. Though all the world could see[3].
None could be so abus'd in fight as he.
Come, to our flock.   [*Exeunt* Ros. Cel. *and* Corin.

 Phe. Dead shepherd, now I find thy Saw of might
Who ever lov'd, that lov'd not at first sight?

 Sil. Sweet *Phebe*!

 Phe. Hah! what say'st thou, *Silvius*!

 Sil. Sweet *Phebe,* pity me.

 Phe. Why, I am sorry for thee, gentle *Silvius.*

---

[1] *Foul is most foul, being* FOUL *to be a scoffer*:] The only sense of this is, *An ill-favour'd person is most ill-favoured, when, if he be ill-favoured, he is a scoffer*. Which is a deal too absurd to come from *Shakespeare*; who, without question, wrote,

 Foul is most foul, being FOUND *to be a scoffer.*
i.e. where an ill-favour'd person ridicules the defects of others, it makes his own appear excessive.   WARBURTON.

 The sense of the received reading is not fairly represented; it is, *The ugly seem most ugly when,* though *ugly, they are scoffers.*

[2] ——*with her foulness,*] So Sir *T. Hanmer*; the other editions, *your* foulness.

[3] —*Though all the world could see,*

 None could be so abus'd in fight as he.] Though all mankind could look on you, none could be so *deceived* as to think you beautiful but he.

Sil. Where-ever sorrow is, relief would be;
If you do sorrow at my grief in love,
By giving love, your Sorrow and my grief
Were both extermin'd.

    Phe. Thou hast my love; is not that neighbourly?

    Sil. I would have you.

    Phe. Why, that were Covetousness.
Silvius, the time was, that I hated thee;
And yet it is not, that I bear thee love;
But since thou canst talk of love so well,
Thy company, which erst was irksome to me,
I will endure; and I'll employ thee too:
But do not look for further recompence,
Than thine own gladness that thou art employ'd.

    Sil. So holy and so perfect is my love,
And I in such a poverty of grace,
That I shall think it a most plenteous crop
To glean the broken ears after the man
That the main harvest reaps: loose now and then
A scatter'd smile, and that I'll live upon.

    Phe. Know'st thou the youth, that spoke to me ere-while?

    Sil. Not very well, but I have met him oft;
And he bath bought the cottage and the bounds,
That the old *Carlot* once was maker of.

    Phe. Think not, I love him, tho' I ask for him;
'Tis but a peevish boy—yet he talks well.
But what care I for words? yet words do well,
When he that speaks them, pleases those that hear:
It is a pretty youth—not very pretty——
But, sure, he's proud; and yet his pride becomes him;
He'll make a proper man; the best thing in him
Is his Complexion; and faster than his tongue
Did make offence, his eye did heal it up:
He is not very tall, yet for his years he's tall;
His leg is but so, and yet 'tis well;
There was a pretty redness in his lip,
A little riper and more lusty red
Than that mix'd in his cheek; 'was just the difference
Betwixt the constant red and mingled damask.
There be some women, *Silvius,* had they mark'd him
In parcels as I did, would have gone near

To fall in love with him; but, for my part,
I love him not, nor hate him not; and yet
I have more cause to hate him than to love him;
For what had he to do to chide at me;
He said, mine eyes were black, and my hair black:
And, now I am remembred, scorn'd at me;
I marvel, why I answer'd not again;
But that's all one; omittance is no quittance.
I'll write to him a very taunting letter,
And thou shalt bear it; will thou, *Silvius*?

    Sil. Phebe, with all my heart.

    Phe. I'll write it straight;
The matter's in my head, and in my heart,
I will be bitter with him, and passing short:
Go with me, *Silvius*.   [*Exeunt.*

ACT IV. SCENE I.

Continues in the F O R E S T.

Enter Rosalind, Celia, *and* Jaques.

JAQUES

I Pr'ythee, pretty youth, let me be better acquainted with thee.

Ros. They say you are a melancholy fellow.

Jaq. I am so; I do love it better than laughing.

Ros. Those that are in extremity of either, are abominable fellows; and betray themselves to ever modern censure, worse than drunkards.

Jaq. Why, 'tis good to be sad, and say nothing.

Ros. Why, then, 'tis good to be a post.

Jaq. I have neither the scholar's melancholy, which is emulation; nor the musician's, which is fantastical; nor the courtier's, which is proud; nor the soldier's, which is ambitious, nor the lawyer's, which is politick; nor the lady's, which is nice; nor the lover's, which is all these; but it is a melancholy of mine own, compounded of many simples, extracted from many objects, and, indeed, the sundry contemplation of my travels, on which my often rumination wraps me in a most humorous sadness.

Ros. A traveller! By my faith, you have great reason to be sad: I fear, you have sold your own lands, to see other mens; then, to have seen much, and to have nothing, is to have rich eyes and poor hands.

Jaq. Yes; I have gained me experience.

Enter Orlando.

Ros. And your experience makes you sad: I had rather have a fool to make me merry, than experience to make me sad, and to travel for it too.

Orla. Good-day, and happiness, dear *Rosalind*!

Jaq. Nay then—God b'w'y you, an you talk in blank verse.   [*Exit.*

Ros. Farewel, monsieur traveller; look, you lisp, and wear strange suits; disable all the benefits of your own Country; be out of love with your nativity, and almost chide God for making you that countenance you are; or I will scarce think you have swam in a Gondola[4].—Why, how now, *Orlando,* where have

---

[4] —*swam in a Gondola.*] That is, *been at* Venice, the seat at that time of all licentiousness, where the young *English* gentlemen wasted their fortunes, debased their morals, and sometimes lost their religion.

you been all this while? You a lover?—an you serve me such another trick, never come in my sight more.

Orla. My fair *Rosalind,* I come within an hour of my promise.

Ros. Break an hour's promise in love! he that will divide a minute into a thousand parts, and break but a part of the thousandth part of a minute in the affairs of love, it may be said of him, that *Cupid* hath clapt him o' th' shoulder, but I'll warrant him heart whole.

Orla. Pardon me, dear *Rosalind.*

Ros. Nay, an you be so tardy, come no more in my sight. I had as lief be woo'd of a snail.

Orla. Of a snail?

Ros. Ay, of a snail; for tho' he comes slowly, he carries his house on his head: a better jointure, I think, than you can make a woman. Besides, he brings his destiny with him.

Orla. What's that?

Ros. Why, horns; which such as you are fain to be beholden to your wives for; but he comes armed in his fortune, and prevents the slander of his wife.

Orla. Venue is no horn-maker, and my *Rosalind* is virtuous.

Ros. And I am your *Rosalind.*

Cel. It pleases him to call you so; but he hath a *Rosalind* of a better leer than you.

Ros. Come, woo me, woo me; for now I am in a holyday humour, and like enough to consent. What would you say to me now, an I were your very, very *Rosalind?*

Orla. I would kiss, before I spoke.

Ros. Nay, you were better speak first, and when you were gravell'd for lack of matter, you might take occasion to kiss. Very good orators, when they are out, they will spit; and for lovers lacking, God warns us, matter, the cleanliest shift is to kiss.

Orla. How if the kiss be denied?

Ros. Then she puts you to entreaty, and there begins new matter.

Orla. Who could be out, being before his beloved mistress?

Ros. Marry, that should you, if I were your mistress; or I should think my honesty ranker than my wit.

Orla. What, of my suit?

The fashion of travelling, which prevailed very much in our author's time, was considered by the wiser men as one of the principal causes of corrupt manners. It was therefore gravely censured by *Ascham* in his *Schoolmaster,* and by Bishop *Hall* in his *Quo Vadis,* and is here, and in other passages ridiculed by *Shakespeare.*

Ros. Not out of your apparel, and yet out of your suit. Am not I your Rosalind?

Orla. I take some joy to say, you are; because I would be talking of her.

Ros. Well, in her person, I say, I will not have you.

Orla. Then in mine own person I die.

Ros. No, faith, die by attorney; the poor world is almost six thousand years old, and in all this time there was not any man died in his own person, *videlicet,* in a love cause. *Troilus* had his brains dash'd out with a *Grecian* club, yet he did what he could to die before, and he is one of the patterns of love. *Leander,* he would have lived many a fair year, tho' *Hero* had turn'd nun, if it had not been for a hot midsummer night; for, good youth, he went but forth to wash in the *Hellespont,* and, being taken with the cramp, was drown'd; and the foolish chroniclers of that age[5] found it was,—*Hero* of *Sestos.* But these are all lyes; men have died from time to time, and worms have eaten them, but not for love.

Orla. I would not have my right *Rosalind* of this mind; for, I protest, her frown might kill me.

Ros. By this hand, it will not kill a fly—but come; now I will be your *Rosalind* in a more coming-on disposition; and ask me what you will, I will grant it.

Orla. Then love me, *Rosalind.*

Ros. Yes, faith, will I, *Fridays* and *Saturdays,* and all.

Orla. And wilt thou have me?

Ros. Ay, and twenty such.

Orla. What say'st thou?

Ros. Are you not good?

Orla. I hope so.

Ros. Why then, can one desire too much of a good thing? come, sister, you shall be the priest, and marry us. Give me your hand, *Orlando:* what do you say Sister?

Orla. Pray thee; marry us.

Cel. I cannot say the words.

Ros. You must begin—Will you, *Orlando—*

Cel. Go to—Will you, *Orlando,* have to wife this *Rosalind*?

Orla. I will.

Ros. Ay, but when?

Orla. Why now, as fast as she can marry us.

Ros. Then you must say, I take thee *Rosalind* for wife.

Orla. I take thee *Rosalind* for wife.

---

5 *—chroniclers of that age*.] Sir *T. Hanmer* reads, *coroners,* by the advice, as Dr. *Warburton* hints, of some anonymous critick.

Ros. I might ask you for your commission, but I do take, thee *Orlando* for my husband: there's a girl goes before the priest, and certainly a woman's thought runs before her actions.

Orla. So do all thoughts; they are wing'd.

Ros. Now tell me, how long would you have her, after you have possest her?

Orla. For ever and a day.

Ros. Say a day, without the ever. No, no, *Orlando,* men are *April* when they woo, *December* when they wed: maids are *May* when they are maids, but the sky changes when they are wives. I will be more jealous of thee than a *Barbary* cock-pigeon over his hen; more clamorous than a parrot against rain; more new-fangled than an ape; more giddy in my desires than a monkey; I will weep for nothing, like *Diana* in the fountain; and I will do that, when you are dispos'd to be merry; I will laugh like a hyena, and that when you are inclin'd to sleep[6].

Orla. But will my *Rosalind* do so?

Ros. By my life, she will do as I do.

Orla. O, but she is wife.

Ros. Or else she could not have the wit to do this; the wiser, the waywarder: make the doors fast upon a woman's wit, and it will out at the casement; shut that, and 'twill out at the key-hole; stop that, it will fly with the smoak out at the chimney.

Orla. A man that had a wife with such a wit, he might say, *Wit, whither wilt*[7]?

Ros. Nay, you might keep that check for it, 'till you meet your wife's wit going to your neighbour's bed.

Orla. And what wit could wit have to excuse that?

Ros. Marry, to say she came to seek you there. You shall never take her without her answer, unless you take her without her tongue. O that woman, that cannot make her fault her husband's occasion[8], let her never nurse her child herself, for she will breed it like a fool!

Orla. For these two hours, *Rosalind,* I will leave thee.

---

[6] ——*and when you are inclin'd to SLEEP*.] We should read, *to* WEEP.
WARBURTON.
I know not why we should read *to weep*. I believe most men would be more angry to have their *sleep* hindered than their grief interrupted.

[7] —*Wit, whither wilt?*] This must be some allusion to a story well known at that time, though now perhaps irretrievable.

[8] *make her fault her husband's occasion,*] That is, represent her fault as occasioned by her husband. Sir *T. Hanmer* reads, *her husband's* accusation.

Ros. Alas, dear love, I cannot lack thee two hours.

Orla. I must attend the Duke at dinner. By two o'clock I will be with thee again.

Ros. Ay, go your ways, go your ways—I knew what you would prove, my friends told me as much, and I thought no less—that flattering tongue of yours won me—'tis but one cast away, and so come death—two o'th' clock is your hour!

Orla. Ay, sweet *Rosalind.*

Ros. By my troth, and in good earnest, and so God mend me, and by all pretty oaths that are not dangerous, if you break one jot of your promise, or come one minute behind your hour, I will think you the most pathetical break-promise[9], and the most hollow lover, and the most unworthy of her you call *Rosalind,* that may be chosen out of the gross band of the unfaithful; therefore beware my censure, and keep your promise.

Orla. With no less religion, than if thou wert indeed my *Rosalind*; so adieu.

Ros. Well, time is the old Justice that examines all such offenders, and let time try. Adieu! [*Exit* Orla.

Cel. You have simply misus'd our sex in your love-prate: we must have your doublet and hose pluck'd over your head, and shew the world what the bird hath done to her own nest.

Ros. O coz, coz, coz, my pretty little coz, that thou didst know how many fathom deep I am in love; but it cannot be founded: my affection hath an unknown bottom, like the Bay of *Portugal.*

Cel. Or rather, bottomless; that as fast as you pour affection in, it runs out.

Ros. No, that same wicked bastard of *Venus,* that was begot of thought, conceiv'd of spleen, and born of madness, that blind rascally boy, that abuses every one's eyes, because his own are out, let him be judge, how deep I am in love; I'll tell thee, *Aliena,* I cannot be out of the sight of *Orlando;* I'll go find a shadow, and sigh 'till he come.

Cel. And I'll sleep. [*Exeunt.*

---

[9] —*I will think you be the most* PATHETICAL *break promise,*] There is neither sense nor humour in this expression. We should certainly read,— ATHEISTICAL *break promise.* His answer confirms it, that he would keep his promise *with no less Religion, than*——. WARBURTON.

I do not see but that *pathetical* may stand, which seems to afford as much sense and as much humour as atheistical.

SCENE IV.

Enter Jaques, Lords, *and Foresters.*

Jaq. Which is he that kill'd the deer?

Lord. Sir, it was I.

Jaq. Let's present him to the Duke, like a *Roman* Conqueror; and it would do well to set the deer's horns upon his head, for a branch of Victory; have you no Song, Forester, for this purpose?

For. Yes, Sir.

Jaq. Sing it; 'tis no matter how it be in tune, so it make noise enough.

Musick Song.

What shall he have that kill'd the deer?
His leather skin and horns to wear;
Then sing him home:—take thou no Scorn³ }
To wear the horn, the horn, the horn: } The rest shall bear this Burden.
It was a crest, ere thou wast born. }
Thy father's father wore it,
And thy father bore it,
The horn, the horn, the lusty horn,
It is not a thing to laugh to scorn.

[Exeunt.

[Please note that the scene and footnote numbers are not sequential in this act.]

---

³ In former Editions:

Then sing him home, the rest shall bear this burden.] This is no admirable Instance of the sagacity of our preceding Editors, to say nothing worse. One should expect, when they were *Poets,* they would at least have taken care of the *Rhimes,* and not foisted in what has nothing to answer it. Now, where is the Rhime to, *the rest shall bear this Burden*? Or, to ask another Question, where is the Sense of it? Does the poet mean, that He, that kill'd the Deer, shall be sung home, and the rest shall bear the Deer on their Backs! This is laying a Burden on the Poet, that We must help him to throw off. In short, the Mystery of the Whole is, that a Marginal Note is wisely thrust into the Text: the Song being design'd to be sung by a single Voice, and the Stanza's to close with a Burden to be sung by the whole company.   THEOBALD.

This note I have given as a specimen of Mr. *Theobald's* jocularity, and of the eloquence with which he recommends his emendation.

Enter Rosalind *and* Celia.

Ros. How say you now, is it not past two o'clock? I wonder much, *Orlando* is not here.

Cel. I warrant you, with pure love and troubled brain, he hath ta'en his bow and arrows, and is gone forth to sleep: look, who comes here.

Enter Silvius.

Sil. My errand is to you fair youth,
My gentle *Phebe* bid me give you this: [*Giving a letter.*]
I know not the contents; but, as I guess,
By the stern brow and waspish action
Which she did use as she was writing of it,
It bears an angry tenour. Pardon me,
I am but as a guiltless messenger.
　　Ros. [*reading.*] Patience herself would startle at this letter,
And play the swaggerer—bear this, bear all—
She says, I am not fair; that I lack manners;
She calls me proud, and that she could not love me
Were man as rare as phoenix. 'Odds my will!
Her love is not the hare that I do hunt.
Why writes she so to me? Well, shepherd, well,
This is a letter of your own device.
　　Sil. No, I protest, I know not the contents;
Phebe did write it.
　　Ros. Come, come, you're a fool,
And turn'd into th' extremity of love.
I saw her hand, she has a leathern hand,
A free-stone-colour'd hand; I verily did think,
That her old gloves were on, but 'twas her hand;
She has a huswife's hand, but that's no matter—

---

4 The foregoing noisy scene was introduced only to fill up an interval, which is to represent two hours. This contraction of the time we might impute to poor *Rosalind's* impatience, but that a few minutes after we find *Orlando* sending his excuse. I do not see that by any probable division of the acts this absurdity can be obviated.

I say, she never did invent this letter—
This is a man's invention, and his hand.
    Sil. Sure, it is hers.
    Ros. Why, 'tis a boisterous and a cruel stile,
A stile for challengers; why, she defies me,
Like *Turk* to Christian; woman's gentle brain
Could not drop forth such giant rude invention;
Such *Ethiop* words, blacker in their effect
Than in their countenance, Will you hear the letter?
    Sil. So please you, for I never heard it yet;
Yet heard too much of *Phebe's* cruelty.
    Ros. She *Phebe's* me—mark, how the tyrant writes.
[Reads] *Art thou God to shepherd turn'd,*
       That a maiden's heart hath burn'd,

Can a woman rail thus?

    Sil. Call you this railing?

    Ros. [Reads.]   *Why, thy Godhead laid apart,*
             Warr'st thou with a woman's heart?
Did you ever hear such railing?
    Whiles the eye of man did woo me,
    *That could do no vengeance** to me.*

Meaning me a beast.

    If the scorn of your bright eyne
    Have power to raise such love in mine,
    Alack, in me, what strange effect
    Would they work in mild aspect?
    Whiles you chid me, I did love;
    How then might your prayers move?

    He, that brings this love to thee,
    Little knows this love in me;
    And by him seal up thy mind,
    Whether that thy Youth and Kind[5]

---

* *Vengeance* is used for a *mischief.*
[5] *Youth and Kind.*] *Kind* is the old word for *nature.*

Will the faithful offer take
Of, me, and all that I can make;
Or else by him my love deny.
And then I'll study how to die.

Sil. Call you this chiding?

Cel. Alas, poor shepherd!

Ros. Do you pity him? no, he deserves no pity—Wilt thou love such a woman—what, to make thee an instrument, and play false strains upon thee? not to be endured!—Well, go your way to her; for I see love hath made thee a tame snake, and say this to her; "that if she love me, I charge her to love thee"; "If she will not, I will never have her", unless thou "intreat for her." If you be a true lover, hence, and not a word, for here comes more company. [*Exit* Silvius.

SCENE VI.

Enter Oliver.

Oli. Good-morrow, fair ones: pray you, if you know
Where, in the purlew's of this forest, stands
A sheep-cote fenc'd about with Olive-trees?

Cel. West of this place, down in the neighbour bottom,
The rank of osiers, by the murmuring stream,
Left on your right-hand, brings you to the place;
But at this hour the house doth keep itself,
There's none within.

Oli. If that an eye may profit by a tongue,
Then should I know you by description,
Such garments, and such years: "the boy is fair,
"Of female favour, and bestows himself
"Like a ripe Sister: but the woman low,
"And browner than her brother." Are not you
The owner of the house, I did enquire for?

Cel. It is no boast, being ask'd, to say, we are.

Oli. *Orlando* doth commend him to you both,
And to that youth, he calls his *Rosalind,*
He sends this bloody napkin. Are you he?

Ros. I am; what must we understand by this?

Oli. Some of my Shame, if you will know of me
What man I am, and how, and why, and where,
This handkerchief was stain'd.

Cel. I pray you, tell it.

Oli. When last the young *Orlando* parted from you,
He left a promise to return again
*Within an hour; and pacing through the forest,
Chewing the food of sweet and bitter fancy,
Lo, what befel! he threw his eye aside,
And mark what object did present itself.
Under an oak, whose boughs were moss'd with age,
And high top bald with dry antiquity;
A wretched ragged man, o'er-grown with hair,
Lay sleeping on his back; about his neck
A green and gilded snake had wreath'd itself,
Who with her head, nimble in threats, approach'd
The opening of his mouth, but suddenly
Seeing *Orlando,* it unlink'd itself,
And with indented glides did slip away
Into a bush; under which bush's shade
A Lioness, with udders all drawn dry,
Lay couching head on ground, with cat-like watch
When that the sleeping man should stir, for 'tis
The royal disposition of that beast
To prey on nothing that doth seem as dead:
This seen, *Orlando* did approach the man,
And found it was his brother, his eldest brother.

Cel. I have heard him speak of that same brother,
And he did render him the most unnatural
That liv'd 'mongst men.

Oli. And well he might so do;
For, well I know, he was unnatural.

Ros. But, to *Orlando*—did he leave him there,
Food to the suck'd and hungry lioness?

Oli. Twice did he turn his back, and purpos'd so:
But kindness, nobler ever than revenge;
And nature stronger than his just occasion,
Made him give battle to the lioness,
Who quickly fell before him; in which hurtling
From miserable slumber I awak'd.

Cel. Are you his brother?

Ros. Was it you he rescu'd?

---

* We must read, *within two hours.*

Cel. Was't you that did so oft contrive to kill him?

Oli. 'Twas I, but 'tis not I; I do not shame
To tell you what I was, since my conversion
So sweetly tastes, being the thing I am.

    Ros. But, for the bloody napkin?——

    Oli. By, and by.
When from the first to last, betwixt us two,
Tears our recountments had most kindly bath'd,
As how I came into that desert place;
In brief, he led me to the gentle Duke,
Who gave me fresh array and entertainment,
Committing me unto my brother's love;
Who led me instantly unto his cave,
There stripp'd himself, and here upon his arm
The lioness had torn some flesh away,
Which all this while had bled; and now he fainted,
And cry'd, in fainting, upon *Rosalind.*——
Brief I recover'd him; bound up his wound;
And, after some small space; being strong at heart,
He sent me hither, stranger as I am,
To tell this story, that you might excuse
His broken promise; and to give this napkin,
Dy'd in his blood, unto the shepherd youth,
That he in sport doth call his *Rosalind.*

    Cel. Why, how now? *Ganymed*!——Sweet!——*Ganymed*!

                        [Rosalind *faints.*

    Oli. Many will swoon, when they do look on blood.

    Cel. There is more in it:—cousin—*Ganymed**!

    Oli. Look, he recovers.

    Ros. Would I were at home!

    Cel. We'll lead you thither.

—I pray you, will you take him by the arm?

    Oli. Be of good cheer, youth—you a man?—you lack a man's heart.

    Ros. I do so, I confess it. Ah, Sir, a body would think, this was well counterfeited. I pray you, tell your brother how well I counterfeited: heigh ho!

    Oli. This was not counterfeit: there is too great testimony in your complexion, that it was a passion of earnest.

    Ros. Counterfeit, I asure you.

---

   * *Cousin, Ganymed.*] *Celia* in her fright forgets *Rosalind's* character and disguise, and calls out *Cousin,* then recollects herself and says *Ganymed.*

Oli. Well then, take a good heart, and counterfeit to be a man.

Ros. So I do; but i'faith, I should have been a woman by right.

Cel. Come, you look paler and paler; pray you, draw homewards—good Sir, go with us.

Oli. That will I; for I must bear answer back,
How you excuse my brother, *Rosalind.*

Ros. I shall devise something. But, I pray you commend my counterfeiting to him—Will you go!   [*Exeunt.*

ACT V. SCENE I.

The FOREST.

Enter Clown *and* Audrey.

CLOWN.

WE shall find a time, *Audrey*—patience, gentle *Audrey*.

Aud. Faith, the Priest was good enough, for all the old gentleman's saying.

Clo. A most wicked *Sir Oliver, Audrey;* a most vile *Mar-text.*—But *Audrey,* there is a youth here in the Forest lays claim to you

Aud. Ay, I know who 'tis, he hath no interest in me in the world; here comes the man you mean.

Enter William.

Clo. It is meat and drink to me to see a Clown. By my troth, we that have good wits, have much to answer for: we shall be flouting; we cannot hold.

Will. Good ev'n, *Audrey.*

Aud. God give ye good ev'n, *William.*

Will. And good ev'n to you, Sir.

Clo. Good even, gentle friend—Cover thy head, cover thy head; nay, pr'ythee, be cover'd.—How old are you, friend?

Will. Five and twenty, Sir.

Clo. A ripe age: is thy name *William*?

Will. William, Sir.

Clo. A fair name. Wast born i'th' forest here?

Will. Ay, Sir, I thank God.

Clo. Thank God—a good answer: art rich?

Will. 'Faith, Sir, so, so.

Clo. So, so, is good, very good, very excellent good; and yet it is not; it is but so so. Art thou wise?

Will. Ay, Sir, I have a pretty wit.

Clo. Why, thou say'st well: I do now remember a Saying; *the fool doth think he is wise, but the wise man knows himself to be a fool.*[6] The heathen

---

[6] *The heathen philosopher, when he desired to eat a grape,* &c.] This was designed as a sneer on the several trifling and insignificant sayings and actions, recorded of the ancient philosophers, by the writers of their lives, such as *Diogenes Laertius, Philostratus, Eunapius,* &c. as appears from its being

philosopher, when he had a desire to eat a grape, would open his lips when he put it into his mouth; meaning thereby, that grapes were made to eat, and lips to open. You do love this maid?

Will. I do, Sir.

Clo. Give me your hand: art thou learned?

Will. No, Sir.

Clo. Then learn this of me; to have, is to have. For it is a figure in rhetorick, that drink being poured out of a cup into a glass, by filling the one doth empty the other. For all your writers do consent, that *ipse* is he: now you are not *ipse;* for I am he.

Will. Which he, Sir?

Clo. He, Sir, that must marry this woman; therefore you, Clown, abandon—which is in the vulgar, leave—the society—which in the boorish, is company—of this female—which in the common, is—woman; which together is, abandon the society of this female; or Clown, thou perishest; or, to thy better understanding, diest; or, to wit, I kill thee, make thee away, translate thy life into death, thy liberty into bondage;[7] I will deal in poison with thee, or in bastinado, or in steel I will bandy with thee in faction; I will over-run thee with policy; I will kill thee a hundred and fifty ways; therefore tremble and depart.

Aud. Do, good *William.*

Will. God rest you merry, Sir.   [*Exit.*

Enter Corin.

Cor. Our master and mistress seek you; come away, away.

Clo. Trip, *Audrey;* trip, Audrey; I attend, I attend.   [*Exeunt.*

SCENE II.

Enter Orlando *and* Oliver.

Orla. Is't possible, that on so little acquaintance you should like her? that, but seeing, you should love her? and loving, woo? and wooing, she should grant? and you persevere to enjoy her?

Oli. Neither call the giddiness of it in question; the poverty of her, the small

---

introduced by one of their *wise sayings.*   WARBURTON.

[7] *I will deal in poison with thee, or in bastinado, or in steel; I will bandy with thee in faction,* &c.] All this seems to be an allusion to Sir *Thomas Overbury's* affair.   WARBURTON.

acquaintance, my sudden wooing, nor her sudden consenting; but say with me, I love *Aliena;* say with her, that she loves me; consent with both, that we may enjoy each other; it shall be to your good; for my father's house, and all the revenue that was old Sir *Rowland's,* will I estate upon you, and here live and die a shepherd.

Enter Rosalind.

Orla. You have my consent. Let your wedding be to-morrow; thither will I invite the Duke, and all his contented followers: go you, and prepare *Aliena;* for look you, here comes my *Rosalind.*

Ros. God save you, brother.

Oli. And you, fair sister[8].

Ros. Oh, my dear *Orlando,* how it grieves me to see thee wear thy heart in a scarf.

Orla. It is my arm.

Ros. I thought thy heart had been wounded with the claws of a lion.

Orla. Wounded it is, but with the eyes of a lady.

Ros. Did your brother tell you how I counterfeited to swoon, when he shewed me your handkerchief?

Orla. Ay, and greater wonders than that.

Ros. O, I know where you are—Nay, 'tis true—There was never any thing so sudden, but the sight of two rams, and *Caesar's* thrasonical brag of I *came, saw,* and *overcame*; for your brother and my sister no sooner met, but they look'd; no sooner look'd, but they lov'd; no sooner lov'd, but they sigh'd; no sooner sigh'd, but they ask'd one another the reason; no sooner knew the reason but they sought the remedy; and in these degrees have they made a pair of stairs to marriage, which they will climb incontinent, or else be incontinent before marriage; they are in the very wrath of love, and they will together. Clubs cannot part them[9].

Orla. They shall be married to-morrow; and I will bid the Duke to the Nuptial. But, O how bitter a thing it is to look into happiness through another man's eyes! by so much the more shall I to-morrow be at the height of heart-heaviness, by how much I shall think my brother happy, in having what he wishes for.

Ros. Why then to-morrow I cannot serve your turn for *Rosalind.*

---

[8] *And you, fair sister*.] I know not why *Oliver* should call *Rosalind* sister. He takes her yet to be a man. I suppose we should read, *and you*, and your *fair sister.*

[9] *Clubs cannot part them*.] Alluding to the way of parting dogs in wrath.

Orla. I can live no longer by thinking.

Ros. I will weary you then no longer with idle talking. Know of me then, for now I speak to some purpose, that I know you are a gentleman of good conceit. I speak not this, that you should bear a good opinion of my knowledge; insomuch, I say, I know what you are; neither do I labour for a greater esteem than may in some measure draw a belief from you to do yourself good, and not to grace me. Believe then, if you please, that I can do strange things; I have, since I was three years old, converst with a magician, most profound in his Art, and yet not damnable. If you do love *Rosalind* so near the heart, as your gesture cries it out, when your brother marries *Aliena,* you shall marry her. I know into what streights of fortune she is driven; and it is not impossible to me, if it appear not inconvenient to you, to set her before your eyes to-morrow; human as she is[1], and without any danger.

Orla. Speak'st thou in sober meaning?

Ros. By my life, I do; which I tender dearly, tho' I say, I am a magician[2]: therefore put you on your best array; bid your friends; for if you will be married to-morrow, you shall; and to *Rosalind,* if you will.

SCENE III.

Enter Silvius *and* Phebe.

Look, here comes a lover of mine, and a lover of hers.

Phe. Youth, you have done me much ungentleness,
To shew the letter that I writ to you.

Ros. I care not, if I have: it is my study
To seem despiteful and ungentle to you.
You are there follow'd by a faithful shepherd;
Look upon him, love him; he worships you.

Phe. Good Shepherd, tell this youth what 'tis to love.

Sil. It is to be made all of sighs and tears,
And so am I for *Phebe.*

Phe. And I for *Ganymed.*

Orla. And I for *Rosalind.*

---

[1] *Human as she is.*] This is not a phantom, but the real *Rosalind,* without any of the danger generally conceived to attend the rites of incantation.

[2] *Which I tender dearly, tho' I say I am a magician:*] Hence it appears this was written in *James's* time, when there was a severe inquisition after witches and magicians.

Ros. And I for no woman.

Sil. It is to be made all faith and service;
And so am I for *Phebe.*

Phe. And I for *Ganymed.*

Orla. And I for *Rosalind.*

Ros. And I for no woman.

Sil. It is to be all made of fantasy,
All made of passion, and all made of wishes,
All adoration, duty, and observance,
All humbleness, all patience, and impatience,
All purity, all trial, all observance;
And so am I for *Phebe.*

Phe. And so am I for *Ganymed.*

Orla. And So am I for *Rosalind.*

Ros. And so am I for no woman.

Phe. If this be so, why blame you me to love you?   [*To* Ros.

Sil. If this be so, why blame you me to love you?   [*To* Phe.

Orla. If this be so, why blame you me to love you?

Ros. Who do you speak to, *why blame you me to love you?*

Orla. To her that is not here, nor doth not hear.

Ros. Pray you, no more of this; 'tis like the howling of *Irish* wolves against the moon—I will help you if I can; [*To* Orlando.] I would love you, if I could; [*To* Phebe]—to-morrow meet me all together—I will marry you, [*To* Phebe.] if ever I marry woman, and I'll be married to-morrow—I will satisfy you, [*To* Orlando] if ever I satisfy'd man, and you shall be married to-morrow—I will content you, [*To* Silvius.] if, what pleases you, contents you; and you shall be married to-morrow——As you love *Rosalind,* meet [*To* Orlando.]—as you love *Phebe,* meet [*To* Silvius]—and as I love no woman, I'll meet——So fare you well; I have left your commands.

Sil. I'll not fail, if I live.

Phe. Nor I.

Orla. Nor I.   [*Exeunt.*

SCENE IV.

Enter Clown *and* Audrey.

Clo. To-morrow is the joyful day, *Audrey*—to-morrow will we be married.

Aud. I do desire it with all my heart; and, I hope, it is no dishonest desire, to desire to be a woman of the world. Here come two of the banish'd Duke's pages.

Enter two Pages.

1 *Page.* Well met, honest gentleman.

Clo. By my troth, well met: come, sit, sit, and a Song.

2 *Page.* We are for you. Sit i'th' middle.

1 *Page.* Shall we clap into't roundly, without hawking or spitting, or saying we are hoarse, which are the only prologues to a bad voice?

2 *Page.* I'faith, i'faith, and both in a tune, like Gypsies on a horse.

SONG[3].

It was a lover and his lass,
    With a hey, and a ho, and a hey nonino,
That o'er the green corn field did pass,
    In the spring time; the pretty spring time,
When birds did sing, hey ding a ding, ding,
    Sweet lovers love the spring.

Between the acres of the rye,
    With a hey, and a ho, and a hey nonino,
These pretty country-folks would lie,
    In the spring time, &c.

The Carrol they began that hour,
    With a hey, and a ho, and a nonino,
How that a life was but a flower,
    In the spring time, &c.

And therefore take the present time,
    With a hey, and a ho, and a nonino,
For love is crowned with the prime,
    In the spring time, &c.

Clo. Truly, young gentleman, though there was no great matter in the ditty,

---

[3] The stanzas of this song are in all the editions evidently transposed: as I have regulated them, that which in the former copies was the 2d stanza is now the last.

yet the note was very untunable[4].

    1 *Page.* You are deceiv'd, Sir, we kept time, we lost not our time.

    Clo. By my troth, yes: I count it but time lost to hear such a foolish Song. God b'w'you, and Go mend your voices. Come, *Audrey.*   [*Exeunt.*

SCENE V.

Changes to another Part of the Forest.

Enter Duke Senior, Amiens, Jaques, Orlando, Oliver, *and* Celia.

    Duke Sen. DOST thou believe, *Orlando,* that the boy
Can do all this that he hath promised?

    Orla. I sometimes do believe, ard sometimes do not;
As those that fear, they hope, and know they fear[5].

Enter Rosalind, Silvius, *and* Phebe.

    Ros. Patience once more, whiles our compact is urg'd:
You say, if I bring in your *Rosalind,*   [*To the* Duke.
You will bestow her on *Orlando* here?

    Duke Sen. That would I, had I Kingdoms to give with her.

    Ros. And you say, you will have her when I bring her.   [*To* Orlando.

    Orla. That would I, were I of all Kingdoms King.

---

    [4] *Truly, young Gentleman, tho' there was no great Matter in the Ditty, yet the note was very untunable.*] Tho' it is thus in all the printed Copies, it is evident, from the Sequel of the Dialogue, that the Poet wrote as I have reform'd in the Text, *untimeable*—*Time and Tune,* are frequently misprinted for one another in the old editions of *Shakespeare.*   THEOBALD.

    This emendation is received, I think very undeservedly, by Dr. *Warburton.*

    [5] *As those that fear* THEY HOPE, *and know* THEY *fear.*] This strange nonsense should be read thus,

    As those that fear THEIR HAP, *and know* THEIR *fear.*

i.e. As those who fear the issue of a thing when they know their fear to be well grounded.   WARBURTON.

    The depravation of this line is evident, but I do not think the learned Commentator's emendation very happy. I read thus,

    As those that fear with *hope, and hope* with *fear.*

Or thus, with less alteration,

    As those that fear, they *hope, and* now *they fear.*

Ros. You say, you'll marry me, if I be willing.   [*To* Phebe.

Phe. That will I, should I die the hour after.

Ros. But if you do refuse to marry me,

You'll give yourself to this most faithful shepherd.

Phe. So is the bargain.

Ros. You say that you will have *Phebe* if she will?   [*To* Silvius.

Sil. Tho' to have her and death were both one thing.

Ros. I've promis'd to make all this matter even.

Keep you your word, O Duke, to give your daughter:

You yours, *Orlando,* to receive his daughter:

Keep your word, *Phebe,* that you'll marry me,

Or else, refusing me, to wed this shepherd:

Keep your word, *Silvius,* that you'll marry her,

If she refuse me; and from hence I go

To make these doubts all even.   [*Exeunt* Ros. *and* Celia.

Duke Sen. I do remember in this shepherd-boy

Some lively touches of my daughter's favour.

Orla. My lord, the first time that I ever faw him,

Methought he was a brother to your daughter;

But, my good Lord, this boy is forest-born,

And hath been tutor'd in the rudiments

Of many desperate studies by his uncle;

Whom he reports to be a great magician,

Obscured in the circle of this forest.

SCENE VI.

Enter Clown *and* Audrey.

Jaq. There is, sure, another flood toward, and these couples are coming to the Ark.[6] Here come a pair of very strange beasts, which in all tongues are call'd fools.

---

[6] *Here come a pair of* VERY STRANGE *beasts,* &tc.] What! *strange beasts*? and yet such as have a name in all languages? *Noah's* Ark is here alluded to; into which the *clean* beasts entered by *sevens,* and the unclean by two, male and female. It is plain then that *Shakespeare* wrote, *here come a pair of* UNCLEAN *beasts,* which is highly humourous.   WARBURTON.

Strange beasts are only what we call *odd* animals. There is no need of any alteration.

Clo. Salutation, and greeting, to you all!

Jaq. Good, my Lord, bid him welcome. This the motley-minded gentleman, that I have so often met in the forest: he hath been a Courtier, he swears.

Clo. If any man doubt that, let him put me to my purgation. I have trod a measure; I have flatter'd a lady; I have been politick with my friend, smooth with mine enemy; I have undone three taylors; I have had four quarrels, and like to have fought one.

Jaq. And how was that ta'en up.

Clo. 'Faith, we met; and found, the quarrel was upon the seventh cause[7].

Jaq. How the seventh cause ?—Good my lord, like this fellow.

Duke Sen. I like him very well.

Clo. God'ild you, Sir, I desire you of the like[8]. I press in here, Sir, among the rest of the country copulatives, to swear and to forswear, according as marriage binds, and blood breaks[9]——a poor virgin, Sir, an ill-favour'd thing, Sir, but mine own—a poor humour of mine, Sir, to take That that no man else will. Rich honesty dwells like a miser, Sir, in a poor house; as your pearl, in your foul oyster.

Duke Sen. By my faith, he is very swift and sententious.

Clo. According to the fool's bolt, Sir, and such dulcet diseases[*].

Jaq. But, for the seventh cause; how did you find the quarrel on the seventh cause?

Clo. Upon a lye seven times removed; (bear your body more seeming, *Audrey*) as thus, Sir; I did dislike the cut of a certain Courtier's beard[1]; he sent

---

[7] *We found the quarrel was upon the seventh cause.*] So all the copies; but it is apparent from the sequel that we must read; *the quarrel was not upon the seventh cause*.

[8] *—I desire you of the like:*] We should read, *I desire of you the like*. On the Duke's saying, *I like him very well,* he replies, I desire you will give me cause that I may like you too.   WARBURTON.

[9] *According as marriage binds, and blood breaks.*] The construction is, *to swear as marriage binds*. Which I think is not *English*. I suspect *Shakespeare* wrote it thus, *to swear and to forswear, according as marriage* BIDS, *and blood* BIDS *break*.   WARBURTON.

I cannot discover what has here puzzled the Commentator: *to swear according as marriage binds,* is to take the oath enjoin'd the ceremonial of marriage.

[*] *Dulcet diseases.*] This I do not understand. For *diseases* it is easy to read *discourses*: but, perhaps the fault may lie deeper.

[1] *As thus, Sir; I did dislike the cut of a courtier's beard;*] This folly is touched upon with high humour by *Fletcher* in his *Queen* of *Corinth*.

    —Has he familiarly

me word, if I said his beard was not cut well, he was in mind it was. This is call'd the *Retort courteous.* If I sent him word again it was not well cut, he would send me word he cut it to please himself. This is call'd the *Quip modest.* If again, it was not well cut, he disabled my judgment. This is call'd the *Reply churlish.* If again, it was not well cut, he would answer, I spake not true. This is call'd the *Reproof valiant.* If again, it was not well cut, he would say, I lye. This is call'd the *Countercheck quarrelsome;* and so, the *Lye circumstantial,* and the *Lye direct.*

Jaq. And how oft did you say that his beard was not well cut?

Clo. I durst go no further than the *Lye circumstantial;* nor he durst not give me the *Lye direct,* and so we measur'd swords and parted.

Jaq. Can you nominate in order now the degrees of the Lye?

Clo. [2]O Sir, we quarrel in print, by the book; as you have books for good

---

> *Dislik'd your yellow starch, or said your doublet*
> *Was not exactly frenchified?——or drawn your sword,*
> *Cry'd 'twas ill mounted? Has he given the* lye
> *In* circle *or* oblique *or* semi-circle
Or direct parallel; *you must challenge him.* WARBURTON.

[2] *O Sir, we quarrel in print, by the book;*] The Poet has, in this scene, rallied the mode of formal dueling, then so prevalent, with the highest humour and address; nor could he have treated it with a happier contempt, than by making his *Clown* so knowing in the forms and preliminaries of it. The particular book here alluded to is a very ridiculous treatise of one *Vincentio Saviolo,* intitled, Of *honour and honourable quarrels,* in Quarto, printed by *Wolf,* 1594. The first part of this tract he intitles, *A discourse most necessary for all gentlemen that have in regard their honours, touching the giving and receiving the lye, whereupon the* Duello *and the* Combat *in divers forms doth ensue; and many other inconveniences, for lack only of true knowledge of honor, and the* RIGHT UNDERSTANDING OF WORDS, *which here is set down*. The contents of the several chapters are as follow. I. *What the reason is that the party unto whom the lye is given ought to become challenger, and of the nature of lies*. II. *Of the manner and diversity of lies*. III. *Of the lye certain,* or direct. IV. *Of conditional lies,* or the lye circumstantial. V. *Of the lye in general.* VI. *Of the lye in particular.* VII. *Of foolish lies.* VIII. *A conclusion touching the wrestling or returning back of the lye,* or the countercheck quarrelsome. In the chapter of *conditional lies,* speaking of the particle IF, he says—*Conditional lies be such as are given conditionally thus*—IF *thou hast said so or so, then thou liest. Of these kind of lies, given in this rnanner, often arise much contention, whereof no sure conclusion can arise.* By which he means, they cannot proceed to cut one another's throats, while there is an IF between. Which is the reason of *Shakespeare's* making the *Clown* say, *I knew when seven justices could not make up a quarrel: but when the parties were met themselves, one of them*

manners. I will name you the degrees. The first, the Retort courteous; the second, the Quip modest; the third, the Reply churlish; the fourth, the Reproof valiant; the fifth, the Contercheck quarrelsome; the sixth, the Lye with circumstance; the seventh, the Lye direct. All these you may avoid, but the Lye direct; and you may avoid that too, with an *If.* I knew, when seven Justices could not make up a quarrel; but when the parties were met themselves, one of them thought but of an *If;* as, if you said so; then I said so; and they shook hands, and swore brothers. Your *If* is the only peace-maker; much virtue in *If.*

Jaq. Is not this a rare fellow, my Lord? he's good at any thing, and yet a fool.

Duke Sen. He uses his folly like a stalking horse, and under the presentation of that he shoots his wit.

SCENE VII.

[3] *Enter* Hymen, Rosalind *in woman's cloaths, and* Celia

STILL MUSICK.

Hym. Then is there mirth in heav'n,
 When earthly things made even
  Atone togetber.
 Good Duke, receive thy daughter,
 Hymen *from heaven brought her,*
  Yea, brought her hither:
 That thou might'st join her hand with his,
 Whose heart within his bosom is.

Ros. To you I give myself; for I am yours.   [*To the* Duke.
To you I give myself; for I am yours.   [*To* Orlando.
 Duke Sen. If there be truth in sight, you are my daughter.
 Orla. If there be truth in sight*, you are my *Rosalind*!

---

thought but of an IF, *as if you laid so, then I said so, and they shook hands, and swore brothers. Your* IF *is the only peace-maker; much virtue in* IF. *Caranza* was another of these authentick Authors upon the *Duello. Fletcher* in his last Act of *Love's Pilgrimage* ridicules him with much humour. WARBURTON.

[3] *Enter* Hymen.] *Rosalind* is imagined by the rest of the company to be brought by enchantment, and is therefore introduced by a supposed aerial being in the character of *Hymen*.

* *If there be truth in sight.*] The answer of *Phebe* makes it probable that *Orlando* says; *if there be truth in* shape: that is, *if a form may be trusted*; if one

Phe. If sight and shape be true,
Why, then my love adieu!

    Ros. I'll have no father if you be not he.   [*To the* Duke.
I'll have no husband; if you be not he.   [*To* Orlando.
Nor ne'er wed woman, if you be not she.   [*To* Phebe.

    Hym. Peace, hoa! I bar confusion:
'Tis I must make conclusion
    Of these most strange events:
Here's eight that must take hands
To join in *Hymen's* bands,
    If truth holds true contents[4].
You and you no cross shall part;   [*To* Orlando *and* Rosalind.
You and you are heart in heart;   [*To* Oliver *and* Celia.
You to his love must accord,
Or have a woman to your lord.   [*To* Phebe.
You and you are sure together,
As the winter to foul weather: [*To the* Clown *and* Audrey.
Whiles a wedlock-hymn we sing,
Feed yourselves with questioning:
That reason wonder may diminish,
How thus we meet, and these things finish.

SONG.

Wedding is great Juno's *Crown,*
    O blessed bond of board and bed!
'Tis Hymen *peoples every town,*
    High wedlock then be honoured:
Honour, high honour and renown
To Hymen, *God of every town!*

    Duke Sen. O my dear niece, welcome thou art to me,
Ev'n daughter-welcome, in no less degree.

    Phe. I will not eat my word—now thou art mine,
Thy faith my fancy to thee doth combine.

---

cannot usurp the form of another.

    [4] *If truth holds true contents.*] That is, if there be *truth in truth,* unless truth fails of veracity.

SCENE VIII.

Enter Jaques de Boys.

Jaq. de B. Let me have audience for a word or two——
I am the second son of old Sir *Rowland,*
That bring these tidings to this fair assembly.
Duke *Frederick,* hearing how that every day
Men of great worth resorted to this forest,
Address'd a mighty power, which were on foot
In his own conduct purposely to take
His brother here, and put him to the sword:
And to the skirts of this wild wood he came,
Where meeting with an old religious man,
After some question with him, was converted
Both from his enterprize, and from the world;
His crown bequeathing to his banish'd brother,
And all their lands restor'd to them again,
That were with him exil'd. This to be true,
I do engage my life.
    Duke Sen. Welcome, young man:
Thou offer'st fairly to thy brothers' wedding;
To one, his lands with-held, and to the other,
A land itself at large, a potent Dukedom
First, in this forest, let us do those ends
That here were well begun, and well begot:
And, after, every of this happy number,
That have endur'd shrewd days and nights with us,
Shall share the good of our returned fortune,
According to the measure of their states.

Mean time, forget this new fall'n dignity
And fall into our rustick revelry:
Play, musick; and you brides and bridegrooms all
With measure heap'd in joy, to th' measures fall.
    Jaq. Sir, by your patience: if I heard you rightly
The Duke hath put on a religious life,
And thrown into neglect the pompous Court.
    Jaq. de B. He hath.
    Jaq. To him will I: out of these convertites
There is much matter to be heard and learn'd.

You to your former Honour I bequeath. [*To the* Duke.
Your patience and your virtue well deserve it.
You to a love, that your true faith doth merit; [*To* Orla.
You to your land, and love, and great allies; [*To* Oli.
You to a long and well-deserv'd bed; [*To* Sil.
And you to wrangling; for thy loving voyage [*To the* Clown.
Is but for two months victual'd—So to your pleasures:
I am for other than for dancing measures.
    Duke Sen. Stay, *Jaques,* stay.
    Jaq. To see no pastime, I—what you would have!
I'll stay to know at your abandon'd Cave. [*Exit.*
    Duke Sen. Proceed, proceed; we will begin these rites;
As, we do trust, they'll end, in true delights.

EPILOGUE.

    Ros. It is not the fashion to see the lady the Epilogue; but it is no more unhandsome, than to see the lord the Prologue. If it be true, that *good wine needs no bush,* 'tis true, that a good play needs no Epilogue. Yet to good wine they do use good bushes; and good Plays prove the better by the help of good Epilogues. What a case am I in then[5], that am neither a good Epilogue, nor can insinuate with you in the behalf of a good Play? I am not furnish'd like a beggar[6]; therefore to beg will not become me. My way is to conjure you, and I'll begin with the women. I charge you, O women[7], for the love you bear to

---

    [5] —*What a case am I in then,* &c.] Here seems to be a chasm, or some other depravation, which destroys the sentiment here intended. The reasoning probably stood thus, *Good wine needs no bush, good plays need no epilogue, but bad wine requires a good bush,* and a bad play a good Epilogue. *What case am I in then?* To restore the words is impossible; all that can be done without copies is, to note the fault.

    [6] —*furnish'd like a beggar;*] That is, *dressed:* so before, he was *furnished* like a huntsman.

    [7] —*I charge you, O women, for the love you bear to men, to like as much of this play as pleases you: and I charge you, O men, for the love you bear to women,—that between you and the women,* &c.] This passage should be read thus, *I charge you, O women, for the love you bear to men, to like as much of this play as pleases* THEM: *and I charge you, O men, for the love you bear to women,*— TO LIKE AS MUCH AS PLEASES THEM, *that between you and the women,* &c. Without the alteration of *You* into *Them,* the invocation is nonsense; and without the addition of the words, *to like as much as pleases them,* the inference of, *that between you and the women the play may pass,*

men, to like as much of this Play as pleases you: and I charge you, O men, for the love you bear to women (as I perceive by your simpring, none of you hate them) that between you and the women, the Play may please. If I were a woman[8], I would kiss as many of you as had beards that pleas'd me, complexions that lik'd me, and breaths that I defy'd not: and, I am sure, as many as have good beards, or good faces, or sweet breaths, will for my kind offer, when I make curt'sy bid me farewel.   [*Exeunt omnes*[9].

Samuel Johnson, ed. *The Plays of William Shakespeare.*
(London, 1765) Vol. II: 1–108.

---

would be unsupported by any precedent premises. The words seem to have been struck out by some senseless Player, as a vicious redundancy.
                                                                            WARBURTON.
The words *you* and *ym* written as was the custom in that time, were in manuscript scarcely distinguishable. The emendation is very judicious and probable.

[8] ——*If I were a woman,*] Note that in this author's time the parts of women were always performed by men or boys.   HANMER.

[9] Of this play the fable is wild and pleasing. I know not how the ladies will approve the facility with which both *Rosalind* and *Celia* give away their hearts. To *Celia* much may be forgiven for the heroism of her friendship. The character of *Jaques* is natural and well preserved. The comick dialogue is very sprightly, with less mixture of low buffoonery than in some other plays; and the graver part is elegant and harmonious. By hastening to the end of his work *Shakespeare* suppressed the dialogue between the usurper and the hermit, and lost an opportunity of exhibiting a moral lesson in which he might have found matter worthy of his highest powers.

THE DRAMATIC CENSOR; OR, CRITICAL COMPANION
Francis Gentleman
1770

THIS pastoral comedy, for such it may properly be stiled, opens with Orlando and Adam, the former a young gentleman, recounting to the latter, steward of the family, the scanty provision made for him by the will of his father, and the cruelty of his elder brother, who treats him with much contempt, not only neglecting his education, but putting him under the severe necessity of associating with menial servants; this, he confesses, rankles in his mind, and he expresses a commendable determination to bear it no longer. Here his elder brother, Oliver appears, and accosts him in a churlish manner, to which he replies at first with complacence, but, upon irritation, makes spirited retorts, and their conference rises to a quarrel, which the old man endeavours to soften; Orlando claims his small patrimony, or more respectful usage; the former seems most agreeable to Oliver, who partly promises it, and then not only dismisses his brother with much malevolence, but forbids Adam his house also.

From an interview between Oliver and Charles, the wrestler, we find that Duke Senior is banished by his brother, but that Rosalind, on account of the affection Celia, Duke Frederic's daughter bears her, does not go into exile with him; upon Charles's mention that he hears Orlando has a private intention of wrestling with him, suggests to Oliver a most brutal idea, no less than the destruction of his innocent brother, and this he cultivates by bribing the wrestler to exert all his superior strength against him, with the utmost malevolence; and after this ready agent of his malice disappears, gives a most extraordinary reason for his hatred of Orlando, no other than the many amiable qualities of that youth, which he is either unable or unwilling to imitate.

Rosalind and Celia succeed this worthy blade, the former expressing a dejection of spirits, on account of her father's exile, the latter offering cordial consolation, which prevails, and produces sportive mention of love, which Celia rather seems to think dangerous to play with; some speeches, when fortune is proposed as a subject of their mockery, we cannot help transcribing, on account of the truth and pleasantry of those ideas they create. "Benefits, says

Rosalind, are mightily misplaced, and the bountiful, blind lady doth most mistake in her gifts to women:" to which Celia prettily replies, "'Tis true, for those that she makes fair, she scarce makes honest, and those that she makes honest she makes very ill-favoured:" however, we think, according to a custom of SHAKESPEARE'S, they play too long upon words, and wear imagination threadbare; the clown appears as a messenger, and desires Celia to go to her father, in that familiar stile adopted by such gentry; his assuring the truth of what he has said upon his honour, occasions an egregious but laughable quibble of terms.

When Le Beu enters, he acquaints the ladies that they have lost much sport; upon enquiry into the nature of the amusement they have missed, it appears to be a wrestling match, wherein three young fellows have had many bones broke, are in danger of their lives, while their aged father is distracted with grief at their misfortune, which, as the clown sensibly observes, must be notable sport for ladies.

Duke Frederic, with Orlando, Charles, &c. enter, the duke humanely pitying Orlando's inequality of person for an athletic contention, has endeavoured to dissuade him from the trial, but in vain; wherefore Frederic desires the young ladies to try their persuasion; this kind task they readily undertake, and delicately enter upon the subject; however, the young man appears to be under a gloominess of mind, which makes life or death a matter of indifference to him; the ladies seeing him so hazardously bent afford him all they can, good wishes for success.

The wrestler vaunts his superiority with great apparent confidence, while Orlando shews engaging contrast modesty; this contention, though an odd incident for the stage, occasions an agreeable anxiety, and the effect of it, Orlando's victory, very pleasing sensations; making Rosalind and her cousin extend favour to the weaker party, is a just, and genteel compliment to female generosity.

Upon enquiry who Orlando is, and finding him the son of Sir Rowland de Boys, Duke Frederic seems to entertain strong prejudice against his father, and goes off abruptly. Rosalind here mentions the affectionate regard *her* father had for Sir Rowland, which prejudices her in favour of Orlando, to whom she and her cousin offer congratulation for his escape and unexpected success; upon their going off he drops a hint in two lines of a particular effect Rosalind has had on him. Here Le Beu enters, and acquaints Orlando, that whatever fair appearance Duke Frederic might wear, his temper is of a dangerous, uncertain nature, and cannot safely be trusted, therefore advises his departure.

Orlando's enquiry which was the duke's daughter, is answered by information, that Rosalind, the taller, is daughter of the banished, and Celia of the reigning duke; who, by Le Beu's intimation, entertains a dislike of his niece, which is soon likely to appear; Orlando thanks his friendly adviser, and they go off severally.

Celia and Rosalind re-enter, from what occurs between them we perceive, that Rosalind has suddenly conceived more than a friendly regard for Orlando. The duke now makes his appearance in great wrath, though from what immediate provocation we know not, and dooms his niece to sudden banishment; Rosalind modestly pleads her innocence, and Celia urges her friendship as motives for remission of so harsh a sentence, but the duke seems immoveable in his whimsical severity, and even limits the extent of means inadequate, and their goings off stamps a regard which must render them both acceptable to the audience whenever they appear.

Rosalind, in her masculine habit, with Celia and the Clown now present themselves, much wearied with their journey; however, the Clown indulges his quaint witticisms. Corin, an old shepherd, and Sylvius, a young one, come forward, the latter mentioning his love for Phœbe, the former advising him to a moderation of his passion; Rosalind sympathizes with Sylvius; they ask Corin for his assistance in respect of some refreshment, and receive an hospitable answer; upon his telling them that the farm and flocks he belongs to are to be sold, Rosalind and Celia express a desire of becoming purchasers, and constitute the old shepherd their agent for that purpose.

A very insignificant scene between Jaques, Amiens; &c. ensues, indeed, there is a song which, by the help of Dr. ARNE'S very agreeable music, renders it tolerable.

We next perceive Orlando sustaining Adam, who faints for want of food, with very tender care; and promising to procure something, he desires the good old man to rest under some shelter till he comes back.

Duke Senior and his lords appear next, to whom Jaques comes with mirthful aspect, occasioned, as he says, by a conference he has had with a motley fool, of which he gives a beautiful and instructive account; upon their sitting down to a rural entertainment, they are accosted by Orlando, whose sudden, unreserved attack, occasions the duke to enquire what the cause of such an abrupt intrusion may be, which he explains by a plea of necessity; on receiving a cordial invitation to sit at the table, he softens into grateful gentleness, and expresses himself in the following truly poetical lines.

> I thought that all things had been savage here.
> And therefore put I on the contenance
> Of stern commandment—But whate'er ye are
> That in this *desart inaccessible,*
> Under the shade of melancholy boughs,
> *Lose* and *neglect* the creeping hours of time.

> If ever you have look'd on better days,
> If ever been where bells have knolled to church,
> If ever sat at any good man's feast,
> If ever from you eye-lids wiped a tear,
> And know what 'tis to pity and be pitied,
> Let gentleness my strong enforcement be,
> In the which thought I blush and hide my sword.

Notwithstanding the evident beauties in this speech, we conceive two objections, one is to the word *inaccessible*, which puts us in mind of what an Irish judge once said to the high sheriff of a county: "Really, Mr. Sheriff, the roads to this town are *impassable*;" to which the sheriff very properly replied, "Pray then, how did your lordship get hither:" so might the duke ask Orlando how he got into the inaccessible place—The word *desart* also seems very much misapplied when speaking of a forest, for, as we apprehend, the term properly implies a waste tract of country, with scarce any trace of vegetation; our second objection to the manner of placing the words lose and neglect, they should certainly be transposed.

The duke's replying to Orlando upon those ideas he has suggested, is prettily imagined, and the young man's attention to his old friend extremely amiable. This unexpected guest, and the account he has given, draws from the duke a most useful, consolatory and philosophical remark: That however unhappy we may be, there are others as much or more so. Jaques here delivers that masterly picture of human life, commonly called the Seven Ages, which we should think it our duty to transcribe, but that it has been so often quoted and parodied, that scarce any person can be unacquainted with it.

Orlando entering with Adam, they receive a kind welcome, and partake of the entertainment, while Amiens sings that agreeable and sensible song, "Blow, blow, thou winter's wind." The duke learns who Orlando is, and mentions in the conclusive speech of this act, the regard he had for that young man's father.

Duke Frederic appears at the beginning of the third act, demanding Orlando of his brother Oliver in angry terms, and upon not receiving a satisfactory answer, he orders a sequestration of Oliver's effects, with banishment of his person; this short scene is often omitted in representation, but we think it should always be retained.

Orlando now constituted one of Duke Senior's followers, as a tribute to his love, hangs up a copy of verses, addressed to Rosalind, in a tree, expressing his passion in an agreeable soliloquy.

Corin and Touchstone entertain us with a conversation which exhibits several strokes of sensible, tho' whimsical satire, but delicacy is much offended by several passages; however, the following speech of Corin makes amends for many slips: "Sir, I am a true labourer, I earn that I eat, get that I wear, owe no man hate, envy no man's happiness, glad of other men's good, content with my harm, and the greatest of my pride is to see my ewes graze and my lambs suck."

Rosalind comes in reading Orlando's verses on herself, which the Clown very humorously burlesques. Celia enters reading another poem of amorous tendency; after sending off the Clown and Corin, she enters into a conference with her cousin Rosalind, upon the verses and the writer of them, and after teizing her with suspense, informs her that Orlando is the man, which throws Rosalind into a pretty, natural palpitation of heart. Seeing Orlando and Jaques approach, they draw back, while a short discourse passes between those gentlemen, the latter of whom cynically rails at the former's soft amorous tendency, which brings on retorts from each side not of the civilest nature; when Jaques goes off, Rosalind approaches with confidence, under favour of her disguise, and rallies Orlando with very pleasing vivacity; her distinctions respecting the paces of time are peculiarly pleasant.

The picture drawn of a lover, and the method of cure for amorous feelings, shew a just idea of nature. Rosalind's mode of drawing in Orlando to woo her, as his mistress, is an agreeable device, for this purpose she takes him off to shew him her cot, that he may call every day.

A scene of some little laugh succeeds between the Clown and Audry, which is generally concluded in representation by a most pitiful and fulsome rhime to the woman's name. Rosalind and Celia succeed, expressing some doubts concerning Orlando's constancy; the old shepherd comes on, and aquaints them, that the love-sick swain, Silvius, whom they have often enquired after, is at hand, with his hardhearted mistress; when the Sylvan pair enter, they listen; on finding Phœbe obstinately bent against Silvius's solicitation, Rosalind steps in to his assistance, and catechises the scornful shepherdess with great humour; checking him also for prostituting his praise to encrease that vanity which damps his suit. Phœbe throws out a few hints of tender regard for Rosalind, which are treated with disdain, and Silvius is ordered to pursue her. After Rosalind and Celia go off, we find Phœbe lavish in praise of the former, as a captivating youth; however, she softens so far in favour of Silvius, that she admits of his wooing; then expresses some resentment at the freedom with which Rosalind treated her, determines on writing a sharp letter in return, which Silvius promises to deliver, and thus the act concludes.

In the first scene of the fourth act, we are entertained with a good deal of spirited quibble and wordcatching, between Rosalind and Orlando; one passage is so peculiarly beautiful, that its merit will sufficiently apologize for its appearing here. When Orlando says he will love for ever and a day, she replies,

"Say a day without the ever: no, no, Orlando, men are April when they woo,

December when they wed; maids are May when they are maids, but the sky changes when they are wives. I will be more jealous of thee than a Barbary cock pigeon over his hen; more clamorous than a parrot against rain; more new fangled than an ape; more giddy in my desires than a monkey; I will weep for nothing, like Diana in the fountain; and I will do that when you are disposed to be merry. I will laugh like a hyena, and that when you are asleep."

When Orlando goes off to attend the duke at dinner, Rosalind professes regard for him even to a romantic degree of warmth, and she gives a whimsical account of Cupid. Here a short scene between Jaques and some other forresters intervene, but is omitted, in representation, so that Silvius comes on directly to Rosalind with Phœbe's letter, which is no sooner perused but Rosalind stiles it rank abuse; however, on communicating the contents, it appears, the enamoured shepherdess has strung together several jingling couplets of compliment; Silvius is confounded by his message and the strange interpretation of it, which causes Rosalind to send him with a charge to Phœbe, that she must love him.

Here Oliver approaches the ladies, enquiring for their cottage. Celia points out its situation; however, from appearance, he judges them to be the persons he seeks for; upon being confirmed in his opinion, he presents a bloody napkin to Rosalind, and Orlando's excuse for not coming according to appointment. The description of his own perilous situation, and the generous interposition of Orlando to save his life, are set forth with much poetical beauty; but absurdity, in point of circumstances, strikes our perception plainly; for how could all he mentions have happened during the short interval of Orlando's abscence; particularly, how has he had time to change from the wretched state of being ragged and overgrown with hair, in which he lay under the oak, to his present appearance; indeed, he talks of being led to the duke, who ordered him array and entertainment; but, upon the whole, we think matters are oddly huddled together, merely to savour a flight of fancy.

The hurt Orlando has received in his skirmish with the lioness, overpowers the spirit of Rosalind, that she faints under the depression, and is led home by Celia and Oliver.

At the beginning of the fifth act, Touchstone and Audry offer themselves to view, and are joined by William, a simpleton, upon whose weakness, Touchstone indulges his own supposed wit very liberally; an account of Audry, at last he breaths out most terrible threats if William should entertain any thoughts of that amiable creature; this is a scene which makes us laugh without our knowing why, and consists more of mere whim than good sense or useful satire; upon a summons by the old shepherd they go off.

Orlando and Oliver next appear, the Former, as well he may, expressing some surprize that Celia, as Aliena should have so sudden and forceable an effect upon the latter; it is indeed an affair of much haste, however Oliver not only acquaints us with his own passion, but also informs us, that Aliena has exchanged love with him; when Duke Frederic banished Oliver, order was given to sequester all his possession, and from the condition in which Orlando found him, it is reasonable to think those orders had been amply fulfilled; yet here he proposes giving his estate to Orlando, and turning shepherd himself for the sake of Aliena.

When Rosalind comes on, after expressing concern for Orlando's accident, she confirms Oliver's account of the love affair between him and Celia; we wish a hint, with which her observation upon the proposed marriage concludes, was made delicate. On Orlando's expressing concern that his happiness is not so near as his brother's she comes to the point, and promises, if he is so inclined, that when his brother is married, he shall marry Rosalind; Silvius and Phœbe joining company, the several parties express themselves prettily as their dispositions lead; their conversation is a sort of cross purposes, which Rosalind ends by satisfying all parties with a string of enigmatical promises.

In representation Duke Senior with his followers come next; to them enter Rosalind, Silvius and Phœbe; the heroine under favour of disguise urges a previous compact on all sides; from her father she extracts a promise, that upon restoring his daughter he will give her to Orlando, from Orlando that he will receive her, from Phœbe that she will marry her, or declining that, Silvius; then goes off as she says to make all doubts even.

Touchstone and Audry coming forward, the company are entertained with some free, significant remarks, by the former: his proofs of being a courtier, and his dissertation upon quarrelling, are admirable; we have not met a severer reproof of the false fire and romantic honour of formal duellists, than this affair of Touchstone's, upon a cause seven times removed.

Rosalind, restored to the customary appearance of her sex, enters, is recognized by her father and lover, rejected as a woman by Phœbe, and thus her compact with all parties becomes fulfilled. Matters being brought to this agreeable conclusion, Jaques de Boys comes on, and acquaints the duke of his restoration; Duke Frederic having been checked in the career of his wickedness, and persuaded to resign the dukedom by a religious hermit, with this favourable account, and a prose epilogue, which never fails of working a very pleasing effect, the comedy of AS YOU LIKE IT concludes.

This piece considered at large has a very romantic air, the unities suffer severe invasion, several scenes are very trifling, and the plot is hurried on to an imperfect catastrophe: we hear something of Oliver's being punished as an unnatural, abominable brother, but have a strong objection to crowning such a monster with fortune and love. An interview between the dukes would have afforded an opportunity for genius and judgment to exert themselves commendably; however, with all its faults, there is not a more agreeable piece on the stage; the characters are various, and all well supported; the incidents if not striking, are certainly pleasing; the sentiments, with very few exceptions, are pregnant with useful meaning; and the language, though quaint in some places, shews in general strength and spirit worthy of SHAKESPEARE'S pen.

Duke Senior is an amiable character, sustained with philosophical dignity, turning the frowns of fortune, as every man should do, into the means and motives of instruction: what he says is not of sufficient length to constitute a very conspicuous part in action, but if a performer has any declamatory merit, he may shew it to advantage here. We have no objection to Mr. BURTON in this noble exile, but with Mr. ACKMAN may never think of him, except as a feast upon his own benefit night, that happy season when annuals vegetate into characters of consequence in the drama, and large capital letters in the bills.

Duke Frederic is a notorious villain, of whom no performer can possibly make any thing, wherefore we shall not mention any body. Jaques, a cynical speculatist, possessing much good sense with great oddity: Mr. QUIN was an object of much admiration in this part, but from the opinion we have already delivered of that gentleman's declamatory abilities, it is impossible to admit that praise the partial, misled public allowed him. Mr. SHERIDAN wants nothing criticism can demand, he looks the part well enough, and speaks it with the same degree of emphatic, descriptive feeling with which the author wrote. Mr. DIGGES did it considerable justice; Mr. SPARKS and Mr. BERRY both had merit, but were too laborious and heavy; Mr. LOVE'S utterance of Jaques's fine, flowing periods, puts us in mind of liquor gurgling through the dissonant passage of a narrow-necked bottle.

Orlando, without any striking qualifications, is an agreeable personage, and never can appear to more advantage than through the late Mr. PALMER'S representation of him; there was a degree of spirited ease manifested by him not easily met with, and his personal appearance was most happily adapted: Mr DEXTER, a performer of merit, in several parts, rendered this young man very pleasing; and Mr. Ross, gave as much satisfaction upon the whole as any audience could reasonably expect; as to Mr. REDDISH, he does not look at all like the character, and speaks it too sententiously, wherefore we cannot allow him that approbation he mostly deserves, and we are glad to give him.

Adam is a most interesting old man, and though little seen, must always remain in the recollection of a distinguishing spectator; we don't recollect to have received greater pleasure from any body than Mr. MOODY, in this faithful steward: whose tender sensibility must sit well also upon the feelings and expression of Mr. HULL.

Touchstone, in sentiment and expression, is made up of whim, a character quite outré; therefore in action cannot be tied down to any exact line of nature. Mr. MACKLIN marked the meaning of this character very strongly, but wanted volubility; Mr. WOODWARD is extremely pleasant, and indulges an extravagance not censurable; however, in respect of pointedness and spirit properly mixed, a forceable yet free articulation, Mr. KING stands foremost in our estimation.

We remember to have had the singular pleasure of seeing no less than five ladies perform Rosalind with great merit, whose names we shall set down in the succession allotted them by our judgment; Mrs. BARRY, Mrs. PRITCHARD, Mrs. WOFFINGTON, Miss MACKLIN, and Mrs. HAMILTON; the three former had a very evident superiority over the two latter, and the two first we deem so equal in merit, that we only prefer Mrs. BARRY as having a more agreeable, characteristic appearance; Mrs. WOFFINGTON'S figure was unexceptionable, but her utterance and deportment were too strongly tinctured with affectation, especially for the rural Swain; there is a peculiarity and embarrassment of expression in this part which requires good natural parts or able instruction, to hit it off happily.

Celia has a good deal of pretty, unimpassioned speaking as well calculated for Mrs. BADDELY and Mrs. W. BARRY as possible, nothing is wanted in the part which those ladies cannot agreeably furnish; and Audry in Mrs. BRADSHAW'S hands, deserves the tribute of laughter, for being well figured, and as well spoke.

It is almost needless to remark, that as not one of SHAKESPEARE'S pieces is without abundant beauties, so not one can claim the praise of being free from egregious faults; however, in AS YOU LIKE IT, the latter fall very short of the former; and we make no scruple to affirm, that this piece will afford considerable instruction from attentive perusal, with great addition of pleasure from adequate representation.

We are now come to the end of our first volume, with the very singular satisfaction of not having one material objection, either public or private, offered against our humble endeavours, notwithstanding that living authors and performers have been treated with undisguised, and we hope liberal freedom; if any person mentioned in the foregoing sheets can prove a trace of partial, interested friendship, unbecoming timidity, or determined malevolence; if the praise and censure alternately bestowed on the same persons do not appear founded upon reason and nature, or at least the offsprings of involuntary error, the authors of this work will then give up all claim to the unbiassed veracity they originally professed; and they once again declare, that no connection or view whatever, shall, in the continuation of this work, warp opinion: several attempts have been made for that purpose, but without effect; which they hope will prevent any future ones; critics, like the Roman, should exercise justice, even upon a son.

It was intended to add an investigation of each performer's particular requisites and defects, but by respectable advice, which we shall always follow, that part of our design is deferred to the last number of the second volume; to which also we shall add a dissertation upon public elocution in general, and lay down rules by which most of our criticisms on performance may be tried.

We have nothing further to add at present, but cordial gratitude for the very candid reception we have met; and hope that our slips, as several there must be in such a variety of considerations, may be pointed out with the same spirit of kind censure, we have used to others; in the fulness of heart we declare that praise in every instance has given us considerable pleasure, and the irksome necessity of finding fault, has furnished an equal degree of pain.

The list of theatrical mushrooms is also by desire postponed to the end of the next volume, when it will no doubt be considerably enriched.

(London: 1770): Vol. 1, 460–79.

NOTES TO *AS YOU LIKE IT*
Edward Capell
1779

As I remember, Adam, &c.] There was never a more certain emendation
than this of the Oxford editor in the sentence the play begins with; it is pointed
out and confirm'd by the context, in so plain a manner as to need no enforcing:
The words *"upon this,"* relate (probably) to some over-spirited action of
Orlando's first youth, that displeas'd his father, and occasion'd the bequest that
is spoken of, and the injunction concerning his breeding: a hint of it, was
proper; more than a hint had been injudicious, as being foreign to the business
in hand. ~ The last sentence of the page affords another example of that
singulast usage of the common verb—*seem,* which is so conspicuous in two
passages of the Poet's "Macbeth," (5, 23 & 15, 6.) in both which, it
comprehends the idea of desire or intention: so here,—*"seems to take from me,"*
means—seems as if it wish'd to take from me: and *"his countenance,"* is—his
countenance towards me, his evil countenance; and so a better word than—
discountenance, which the two latter editors have put into the text in its room.

4, 18.

and be nought a while.] If this be, as an editor has told us, a provincial
mode of expressing—"a mischief on you!" (or, rather,—be hang'd to you! for
that is now the phrase with the vulgar) we need look no further; otherwise, we
must (I think) conclude a corruption, and seek for amendment: that of the
Oxford editor,—"do aught a while," will hardly be relish'd by the judges of
ease and English. ~ His alteration of *"reverence"* into *"revenue"* is of a better
kind: the only sense that the sentence can have, with the former word in it, has
been express'd by the speaker before, (l. 29.) and in apter terms, which must be
allow'd a just exception to *reverence*; and the reader need not be told—how
easy a transition it is from thence to *revenue*, nor how perfectly that word suits
the occasion of speaking it: Add to this—that Oliver's taking fire as he does,
which gives occasion to his brother to collast him, was caus'd by something in

the tail of this speech that gave him offence; and this he could not find in the submissive word—*reverence.*

9, 30.

ill-favour'dly.] Alter'd by the four latter moderns into—*ill-favoured*; in order, as may be suppos'd, to make the antithesis the rounder: But how if that roundness was dislik'd by the Poet, as thinking it destructive of the ease of his dialogue? yet this he might think, and with great reason: And for the same reason, might admit of some little inaccuracies; such as—"*than he*" (8, 15.) instead of—*than him*; and "but *I*" (9, 8.) instead of—*but me*; and yet he is not suffer'd to do it in either, by the Oxford editor. ~ Another speech of the Poet's (6, 16.) is stiffen'd by all these gentlemen; who put a comma at "*Charles,*" instead of the colon that is seen in the folio's; but the true point is, a note of admiration; and then the force of that speech, duly pronounc'd, will be,—"Ah, *good monsieur Charles!* are you here?—Well, *what's the new news at the new court?*'

11, 7.

ROS. My father's &c.] Two of the Poet's editors, the third and the fourth, have given this speech to Celia; assigning for reasons, first—that she is the questionist; that the answer therefore ought naturally to be address'd to her, and reply'd to by her: and in the next place,—that "*Frederick*" is the name of *her* father; and this indeed appears beyond controversy from two subsequent passages, one in p. 15, l. 29, the other in p. 92, l. 21: To the first of these reasons, it may be reply'd,—that Celia is effectually answer'd; but the matter of his answer concerning Rosalind most, the Clown turns himself in speaking to her: to the second,—that "*Frederick*" is a mistake,—either of the Poet's through haste, or of his compositor's,—as we shall endeavour to shew by and by; first observing—that the speech cannot be Celia's, for two very good reasons: we have no cause to think, that she would have been so alert in taking up the Clown for reflecting upon her father; who (besides) is not the person reflected upon, that person being call'd—"*old* Frederick." Throughout all this play, Shakespeare calls his two dukes—"*Duke senior,*" and "*Duke junior;*" giving no proper name to either of them, except in this place, and the two that are refer'd to above: his original makes them both kings, and kings of France; calling the elder—Gerismond; the younger, and the usurping king,—Torismond: these names the Poet chose to discard, (perhaps, for that he thought them too antiquated) putting "*Frederick*" instead of the latter; but not instantly hitting upon another that pleas'd him, when he had occasion to mention the former, he put down "*Frederick*" there too, with intention to alter it afterwards: There is a name in the Novel, which might (possibly) be that intended for

Gerismond; and this the reason why it was taken away from it's owner, Orlando's second brother; and "*Jaques*" bestow'd upon him for "Fernandine," his name in the novelist: however that be, it can be no very great licence,—to put "Fernandine" into l. 6, or *Ferdinand* rather; and get rid of a name by that means, which will be for ever a stumbling-block to all those who read with attention.

12, 11.

With bills on their necks, &c.] A banter upon le Beu, for his formal exordium; which Rosalind thinks would be mended by adding to it the words of her speech: The humour of it, such as it is, took it's rise from le Beu's word—"*presence*." "*Bills*" are—labels.

D°. 28.

to set this broken musick] If it be allowable, to call "*rib-breaking*" "*broken musick in the sides*," (expressions that we can no way get rid of) there can surely be no reasonable exception to calling the action of breaking by so proper a term as—*setting* that musick; especially, as no one can possibly contend for the old reading—"*see*;" which yet has a place in all copies, down to the third modern. "*Men*," in the next page, l. 16, is a correction of the fourth modern's; those in l. 22, of the third; and those in l. 32, of the fourth again: all of them palpably necessary, even the last; notwithstanding the arraignment of it by the author of the "*Revisal*," who has deceiv'd himself by an imaginary reading—"your own eyes," that exists in no copy whatever.

14, 9.

wherein I confess me much guilty,] This does not seem express'd with that neatness which is so conspicuous in this play above any of the others; For with what propriety can Orlando be said to be guilty in the ladies' *hard* thoughts? or why *confess* himself guilty in those thoughts? He might indeed confess himself guilty, in denying their request; and this leads to what (perhaps) is the true reading,—*herein*: "*wherein*" stands at the head of another period, only two lines below; which might be the occasion of it's getting in here. ~ Celia's speech (l. 23.) is tacitly transfer'd to Orlando, by the three latter moderns; in which, they make him no "*quintaine*" there, whatever he be in another place.

16, 7.

If you do keep &c.] The comma at the end of this line is misplac'd, inadvertently; it should be taken from thence, and put after "*justly*:" No one can be at a loss to comprehend the speaker's whole meaning in the passage before us, though her terms are less full than they might be, and a little inaccurate besides: but such things have their beauty in free dialogue; and this may also be said of that unperfected sentence in the page before this, l. 27, that is put into the mouth of Orlando. ~ The correction in this page, and those in the opposite, belong to other editors; and the last of them merits attending to: as it shews— that alterations must sometimes be ventur'd upon, where there is no trace of similitude between the old and new words; nor any other reason to justify, but that of making the Poet consistent with himself. v. 21, 26.

18, 10.

for my child's father:] Meaning one that she hop'd to have children by,— Orlando; But this,—though worded obliquely, and spoken to a sister alone,— was probably thought an indelicacy by three of the moderns; who have chosen to read, without notice,—*for my father's child*: let the reader too choose as he pleases.

21, 6.

Which teacheth me, &c.] The inexpressible sweetness of the sentiment contain'd in this line, and that before it, is lost by the old reading—*"thee;"* which were alone sufficient to justify the corrector, and those who have follow'd him in his change, the two latter moderns. ~ But are there not some other corruptions behind, in the line that is quoted? The freedom us'd with grammar in—*"am,"* has (perhaps) a reason for't; the diction, it will be said, is more forcible in that than in—are: But is either diction or pathos improv'd, by the transition from Rosalind in the third person in one line to Rosalind in the second in this? if they are not, *"thou"* should give place to—*she,* as *"thee"* has to—me. ~ *"Charge,"* in l. 11, means—burden: and *"virtuous,"* in the opposite page, l. 19, means—gifted, not with *virtue* but *virtues,* virtuous and good qualities of all sorts.

22, 29.

Here feel we but *the* &c.] A self-evident correction; started by the third modern editor, and embrac'd by those who came after him. ~ It has been propos'd, to join the words—*"I would not change it,"* (l. 10, in the opposite page) to the duke's speech; assigning for reason,—that 'tis more in character for him to speak them, than Amiens: But the reverse of this is true: Amiens, as a courtier, might make the declaration, being only a mode of assenting to the truth of what his master had spoken; but the duke could not, without impeachment of dignity, of being wanting to himself and his subjects; accordingly, when occasion of *change* presents itself at the end of the play, we see it embrac'd with great readiness: Add to this,—that the following reflection of Amiens, *"Happy is your grace,"* &c. would come in too abruptly, were the other words taken away. ~ The last speech of this scene is prefac'd in the modern editions by the words—2. *Lord*, without any authority from the two elder folio's; who do, indeed, put those same words to the speech next but one before that: but the present editor has dar'd to displace them; both because he thinks it a folly to multiply speakers unnecessarily, and is clearly of opinion—that "*Amiens*" was the person intended. ~ He has also made another amendment in p. 25, (l. 21.) but has no title to the three that precede it; nor to any that follow it, as low down as to p. 32, inclusive.

30, 4.

weeping tears,] Here the Poet is wag enough to raise a smile at the experience of his friend the novelist; who employs these words seriously in a something that he calls—a sonnet, without once seeing the ridicule of them.

32, 29.

the duke will drink &c.] The moderns have made a change in this sentence, and another in the opposite page, l. 5,—and both without notice,—that are not barely unnecessary, they are even injurious: They have—*dine*, in this place, instead of "drink:" but bidding the attendants, "*cover*," was telling them—the duke intended to *dine* there; *drink* tells them something more,—that he meant too to pass his afternoon there, under the shade of that tree: ~ *To lye i'the sun*,—their other change in the line above-mention'd,—is a phrase importing absolute idleness, the idleness of a motley. (v. 35, 4.) but "*live i' the sun*," which is Shakespeare's phrase, imports only—a living in freedom; a flying from courts' and cities, the haunts of "*ambition*," to enjoy the free blessings of heaven in such a place as the finger himself was retir'd to; whose panegyrick upon this sort of life is converted into a satire by Jaques, in a very excellent parody that follows a few lines after. ~ In that parody, the words—"*Come hither, come hither, come hither*," are latiniz'd by the composer; but not strictly, for then his word had been,—*Ducdame*; and the Latin words crouded together into a strange single word, of three syllables, purely to let his hearer a staring; whom he bambouzles still further, by telling him—"'*Tis a Greek invocation*:" The humour is destroy'd, in great measure, by the two latter editors; by decompounding and setting them right, and giving us—*duc ad me*, separately.

35, 2.

a miserable world!] "What," says an editor, "because he met a motley fool, was it therefore a miserable world?" yes; in the estimation of Jaques, and others equally cynical: who disrelish the world; arraigning the dispensations of Providence in a number of articles, and in this chiefly—that it has created such beings as fools. ~ This scene is evidently the very same spot with that which the present speaker appear'd upon last; and the intermediate scene, VI, is as evidently one at a distance: it was necessary to make this remark, that the reader might not be misled by the words at the head of that scene, which imply only the place general,—the forest: In representing this play, a second forest will be requisite; which may serve for that sixth scene, and the fifth of the next act.

36, 13.

Not to seem &c.] One would think it requir'd no great cunning to supply the accidental omission of the words in black letter, and that the sense might have pointed them out even to a compositor: yet so it is,—that they never appear'd in this place, 'till the time of the third modern; and another, a page or two back, (v. 34, l. *ult*.) has been suffer'd to stand unsupply'd 'till the present edition: "*Company*" (the word preceding that line) has the same point after it in the folio's that it has in this copy, which circumstance alone indicates an omission; but it further appears from the sense, if a little attended to; For what great crime is it, that Jaques must be *woo'd* for his company? but that he makes his friends *woo* it, and won't let them *have* it after all, is an accusation of some weight; The words now inserted, carry this charge; but not the certainty of being the Poet's own words, that is visible in the passage above.

39, 6. *

Wherein we play in.] As a friend to correctness and Shakespeare, the editor could wish to see this sentence amended; not by throwing out "*in*," (as some others have done) but by reading—*Which we* do *play in.* ~ From the same motives, he recommends too the dismission of "*Of*" from the head of the eighteenth line in page 37: and for this further reason besides,—that the line becoming thus an hemistich, the whole scene will then proceed (as it should do) in metre; for what the speaker says next, (l. 28, of that page) is made metre also, by dividing it as the four latter moderns have done,—"*An you will not* | *Be answered with reason, I must die*:" which division seems eligible upon another account,—that the speaker's hemistich, l. 18, is perfected in what he says now.

D°. 24.

modern instances,] Well interpreted by the author of the "*Revisal*," to signify—"stories of whatever had happened within the Justice's own observation and remembrance;" in which sense, they are properly oppos'd to "*wise saws*," which mean mostly—the saws of antiquity.

D°. 26.

Into the lean &c.] Into a being, thin, shrivel'd, and squeaking; the very figure, in person and habit too, of that character in the Italian comedy that is call'd—*il Pantalone*: this being, the Poet makes a performer in his drama's sixth act; which he lengthens with one act more, after the example of a few elder writters, Bale being one. ~ Pantaloon and his mates, seem to have found their way into England about the year 1607; the conjecture is founded upon a large and remarkable extract from a play of that date, intitl'd—"*Travels of three* English *Brothers,*" that may be seen in the "*School*:" Should the Poet's acquaintance with the character he has just been describing have arisen from this visit, his play (it is likely) was much of the same date with the play above-mention'd.

40, 4.

Set down your venerable burthen,] A traditional story was current some years ago about Stratford,—that a very old man of that place,—of weak intellects, but yet related to Shakespeare,—being ask'd by some of his neighbours, what he remember'd about him; answer'd,—that he saw him once brought on the stage upon another man's back; which answer was apply'd by the hearers, to his having seen him perform in this scene the part of Adam: That he should have done so, is made not unlikely by another constant tradition,— that he was no extra ordinary actor, and therefore took no parts upon him but such as this: for which he might also be peculiarly fitted by an accidental lameness, which,—as he himself tells us twice in his "*Sonnets*," v. 37, and 89,—befell him in some part of life; without saying how, or when, of what sort, or in what degree; but his expressions seem to indicate—latterly.

D°. 26.

because thou art not seen,] The many disputes about the sense of this line, which happen'd at the time of the Oxford publication, (whose reading of it is— *Thou causest not that teen,*) put the editor upon considering it then: and the sense he at last understood it in, co-incided with what he had the pleasure to see some years after in the "*Revisal*," deliver'd in these words: "The impressions thou [the wind] makest on us are not so cutting [as man's ingratitude] because thou art an unseen agent, with whom we have not the least acquaintance or converse, and therefore have the less reason to repine at thy treatment of us:" the Poet has not express'd himself well; but this is not the only place of his works, in which he has been drawn by his rhime into faults of the same nature. The thought is not very remote from one the reader may see in "*k. L.*" p. 58, l. 9, &c. ~ "*Remember'd*" (l. 31.) is chang'd to—*remembring*, in the Oxford edition; which is certainly a clearer expression, but of more unmusical found than the other, and therefore not chosen: though *"remember'd"* is subject to great ambiguity in this place; as signifying—who is not remember'd by his friend, as well as—who has no remembrance of his friend; which was sometimes its signification of old, and is so here.

43, 5.

may complain of good breeding,] May complain of it being no better, or, for having taught them no better; a complaint that may often be brought against it by those who have been taken most pains with: The two latter editors read, one of them—*bad* breeding, the other—*gross*. ~ The clown's remark on this speech is a meer piece of wit, without any such deep satire in it as the last gentleman has discover'd. ~ Neither is there any great likelihood, that the Poet was indebted to Rabelais for that admirable stories which he puts into the Clown's mouth, beginning at l. 15: he might have pick'd up many similitudes of it in conversations or writings at home; and have his knowledge from them too of Garagantua, (or *"Gargantua,"* as he calls him; 49, 8.) and of his swallowing windmills; the only expression we find in him, that intimates an acquaintance with Rabelais.

44, 13.

God make incision in thee!] Meaning, as the *"Revisal"* observes,—"God give thee a better understanding, thou art very raw and simple as yet:" In allusion "to the common proverbial saying, concerning a very silly fellow, that he ought to be cut for the simples." ~ *"Rank,"* in p. 45, (l. 9.) means—the *order* observ'd by such women; travelling all in one road, with exact intervals between horse and horse; which makes it a very apposite simile to Rosalind's verses. The second chance in that page, has a place in four latter moderns; but *"limn'd,"* l. 3, is spelt in all of them—*lin'd*.

47, 22.

I was seven &c.] It is still a common saying amoungst us,—that a wonder lasts nine days; seven of which (says Rosalind) are over with me, for I have been wondering a long time at some verses that I have found. But why is she said to have been the subject of more rimes, when *"an* Irish *rat, in Pythagoras' time?"* this can only have reference to the great antiquity of poetry among that people, and it's universality.

48, 10.

Od's my complexion!] An emendation of the third modern's; which he has abundantly justify'd, by quoting two similar expressions of the very same speaker, at 62, 5, and 73, 10: the peculiarity of her phrase in this place, springs from consciousness of the change that is wrought in her face by her cousin's news; and the meaning of it (if such phrases as these can be said to have meaning)—so God save my complexion. ~ The same editor alter'd "*of*" into "*off,*" l. 13: but he should have gone a step farther, and join'd it to—"*South-sea;*" for the English language admits of such compounds, but not of interpreting "*off*" by—from. ~ Another singular phrase in this page, (l. 29.) is of the proverbial kind; but has not been met with elsewhere, in any of the editor's walks: the force of it is,—answer me soberly, and as an honest maid should do.

49, 19.

drops such fruit.] No such phrase is acknowledg'd by Englishmen, as that in the old reading; "*forth*" therefore should have been dismiss'd by the editors, for an accidental intruder: The "*Revisal*" thinks "*in*" should be serv'd so, a few lines above, (l. 11.) and with some shew of reason; both for that the sense is then clearer, and the period better rounded. ~ The metaphor in l. 26, is taken from colour'd needle-work; whose figures are more or less beautiful, according to the ground they are lay'd upon.

50, 25.

right painted cloth,] In the painted cloth style, *i. e.* briefly and pithily. Tapestries are improperly call'd—painted cloths: therefore, the cloths here alluded to, seem rather those occasional paintings, that were indeed done upon cloth, *i. e.* linnen or canvas; and hung out by the citizens upon different publick occasions, but chiefly—entries: the figures on these cloths were sometimes made to converse and ask questions, by labels coming out of their mouths; and these are the speeches that Jaques is accus'd of studying. There was also a furniture of painted cloth: the devices and legends of one of them, the possessors of sir Thomas More's works may see among his poems.

55, 26.

worse than Jove &c.]This "*thatch'd house*" is the same that don Pedro speaks of, in "*m. a. a. n.*" 19, 28. But does not this reflection of Jaques upon Touchstone's speech, imply a sort of consciousness in the Poet,—that he had made his Clown a little too learned? for,—besides that he has made him acquainted with Ovid's situation in Pontus, and his complaints upon that subject in his poems "*de Tristibus,*"—he has put into his mouth a conundrum that certainly proves him a latinist;" "*capricious*" (l. 25.) not having it's usual signification in that place, but a constrain'd one—goatish; as if it sprung directly from—*caper*, without the medium either of the French—*caprice*, or the Italian—*capriccio*: The Poet has indeed qualify'd his learning a little, by giving him "*Goths*" for—*Getes*.

57, 27.

As the ox hath his bough, sir,] The wooden collar or yoke, that lyes across the neck of draft oxen, and to which their traces are fasten'd, is call'd their *bow*; and this being the spelling of the word in former editions, it has probably been the sense it was taken in: but a little attention to the true meaning of the other two similies, and to the matter they are meant to illustrate, will shew that we must seek for another interpretation of *"bow:"* The faulcon is thought to take delight in her *"bells,"* and to bear her captivity the better for them; "curbs," and their jingling appendages, add a spirit to horses; and if we interpret *"bow"* to signify—*"bough"* of a tree, the ox becomes a proper similitude too, who, thus adorn'd, moves with greater legerity: and the same effect that these things have upon the several animals, *"desires,"* and their gratifications, have upon men; making them bear their burthens the better, and jog on to the end of life's road.

58, 13.

Not, o Sweet Oliver, &c.] These words have no appearance of ballad, as an editor has fancy'd; but rather of a line in some play, that perhaps might run thus,—*O my Sweet Oliver, leave me not behind thee*; which this wag of a Clown puts into another sort of metre, to make sport with sir Oliver: telling him,—I'll not say to you, as the play has it, *"O sweet Oliver, | O brave Oliver, | Leave me not behind thee;"* but I say to you, *"wind away,"* &c, continuing his speech in the same metre: In this light, the passage is truly humorous; but may be much heighten'd, by a certain droleness in speaking the words, and by dancing about sir Oliver with a harlequin gesture and action.

59, 7.

He hath bought &c.] The emendation in the line before this, is certainly right; and as rightly interpreted by the maker of it, the third modern, to signify—the kiss of a hermit or holy man call'd also—the kiss of charity: ~ His preferring *"cast,"* in this line,—the reading of the first folio,—to *"chast,"*—the reading of the second, and of the editors before him,—is equally right: ~ and his propos'd alteration of a word in the next line, will be relish'd by many readers: *"Winter's sisterhood"* has, indeed, meaning; but some will be apt to say of it,—that 'tis as poor and *cold* as the season itself: such persons therefore will incline to think *"winter's"* a corruption, and that—*Winifred's* may be the word: the objection to it is,—that there was no order of nuns so denominated; but this is of no weight; *"a nun of* Winifred's *sisterhood"* means only—a nun as chaste as saint Winifred, and therefore not improperly call'd—of her sisterhood. The legend of saint Winifred need not be retail'd to the reader, he may pick it up any where: Neither is there much occasion for telling him,—that *"a pair of cast lips of Diana's,"* mean—a pair that Diana had left off.

60, 28.

Than he that eyes, &c.] *i. e.* that is accustom'd to look upon blood, and gets his livelihood by it: That this is the sense of the line, and "*eyes*" the true correction of the printer's word "*dies*," will want no proving to him that but considers it's nearness, and gives another perusal to the third line before it: ~ What the editor has ventur'd to add too, to l. 18. in the opposite page, will appear (upon a little reflection) to be neither forc'd nor unnecessary.

61, 31.

What though you have no beauty,] The gentlemen who have thrown out the negative, and the other who has chang'd it to—*some*, make the Poet a very bad reasoner in the line that comes next to this sentence; and guilty of self-contradiction in several others, if "*no*" be either alter'd or parted with: besides the injury done to him in robbing him of a lively expression, and a pleasantry truly comick; for as the sentence now stands, the consequence that should have been from her *beauty*, he draws from her "*no beauty*," and extorts a smile by defeating your expectation. ~ This "*no beauty*" of Phebe's is the burthen of all Rosalind's speeches, from hence to her exit: In the second, the Oxford editor has made a very proper amendment, by substituting "*her*" for "*your*;" but his interpretation of "*Foul*," in l. 24,—to wit, *frowning*, *lowring*,—is extravagant enough; and had never been thought of by himself, had he not previously alter'd the sentence that is the subject of this note: "*Foul*" has there it's ordinary meaning,—foul in favour or beauty, but is put substantively; and the sense of this jingling line is as follows;—We may now say of thy *Foul*—that 'tis *most foul*, for 'tis *foul to be a scoffer*; and such art thou, and foul-favour'd besides.

63, 10.

Dead shepherd, &c.] This "*saw*," as the Poet calls it, will be found in the "*School* " in two places; and in them is seen the title of the poem 'tis taken from, and the name of the "*dead shepherd*" it's author.

68, 15.

the foolish chroniclers &c.] If to make his author more witty than there is reason to think he design'd to be, was an editor's business, he of Oxford may *seem* to have demean'd himself rightly, by reading (as he does) in his text—*and the foolish coroners of that age found it* Hero *of* Sestos: but the judicious will hardly allow of this; nor reject an establish'd old reading that appears upon very good grounds to have come from the author himself, which is the case of the reading in question: "*Chroniclers*" could never be a mistake, nor "*was*" a meer insertion of printers; *coroners*, and the phrase recommended, being too well known to them to suspect an alteration of either for what was certainly not so

NOTES TO *AS YOU LIKE IT*   245

familiar: It follows then, if the above observation be just, that they were true to their copy in this place: and the Poet will stand acquitted for writing so, if it be consider'd—that too much wit, or wit too much pointed, is not a beauty in comedy; especially in such comedy as this, which is simple and of the pastoral kind.

70, 17.

that cannot make her fault her husband's occasion,] *i. e.* that cannot make her husband the cause of it: but this does not satisfy the last-mention'd editor, who is for improving again, by reading—*her husband's accusation*; that is—convert her own fault into an accusation or charge on her husband: and it must be confess'd,—that this too is plausible like his other amendment; for the way the wife takes to excuse herself or bring herself off, is indeed as accusing her husband.

71, 31.

Entry and Song.] Minute changes of many sorts having been made in this short scene by the editor, and only one of them notic'd, it becomes his duty—to do that by the rest in a note, which he could not do in the ordinary way. The entry in old editions is thus,—"*Enter Jaques and Lords, Foresters*;" and both the replies made to Jaques are prefac'd by—"*Lor.*" The *Song* is in nine lines, without other division, or assignment to any person; it's third and fourth are as follows:—"*Then sing him home, the rest shall beare this burthen*; | *Take thou no scorne, to weare the horne*, | *It was*" &c. The entry of the moderns is—*Jaques, Lords, and Foresters*; and their second reply has—*For.* before it: the three last ease the Song of it's "*burthen*;" and give us instead of it,—*Then sing him home*:—*take thou no Scorn* | *To wear the horn, the horn, the horn*: | *It was* &c. putting the words omitted in margin, and this is all their reform: except, that the Oxford editor,—to make a correspondence of measure between ls. 17 & 18,—has lengthen'd the last of them, by reading—*And thy own father bore it.* Other changes, whether in the song or the dialogue, belong to the present editor; who does not mean to defend them, or set forth their fitness: the trouble of making that out, he leaves to his readers; but thinks, it will not cost them much of it. If the last- mention'd line should be perfected,—for which the editor sees no necessity,—he should choose to do it, by reading—*Ay, and thy father*, &c. or (if improvement may be suffer'd in him too) by—*Ay, and his father bore it*, meaning— his father's father's father; which makes the satire the keener, by extending the blot to another generation; and avoids the apparent indelicacy, of taxing a person present with bastardy. Note,—that " I *V* & 2 *V*," mean, first and second Voice; "*both*," the two Voices conjointly; and "*cho*." the whole band of foresters, Jaques and all. ~ The emendations in l. 26, must be plac'd to this editor's account; that in the opposite is the reading of all the moderns.

73, 17.

And turn'd into &c.] Had Silvius been at first a cool lover, as now a hot one, the word "*turn'd*" had been proper: but as this was never the case, we must either put a sense upon *turn'd* that is not common,—to wit, got or fall'n; or else suspect a corruption, and look out for amendment: the "*Various Readings*" have two; both within the bounds of probability, but the first of them seems the most eligible: for "*turned*" will signify—head-turned; and then Rosalind's meaning will be,—Come, come, you're a simpleton, and the violence of your love has turn'd your head.

75, 9.

West of this place, &c.] "*Bottom*" should have a fuller stop after it, a semi-colon; for the meaning of these lines,—whose construction is a little perplex'd,—is as follows:—It stands to the *west of this place*, and *down in the neighbour bottom*; if you leave *the rank of osiers*, that grows by the brook side, *on your right hand*, it will bring *you to the place*.

D°, 32.

Within an hour ;] Orlando's promise was—"*two hours*," and therefore the Oxford editor puts them in here; not considering—that this exceeding punctiliousness is destructive of ease and nature. ~ The epithets given to "*Fancy,*" in the line after this, look'd so like a translation of the Greek—γλυηπιηρον, that the editor thought for some time,—the Poet must, somehow or other, have been fishing in those waters: but turning again to his novelist, he found a passage he had not reflected upon, and that is not in the "*School*;" and thus it runs,—"*Wherein I have noted the variable disposition of fancy, * * *, being as it should seeme a combat* [f. comfort] *mixt with disquiet, and a bitter pleasure wrapt in a sweet prejudice*;" the words are address'd to Rosalind by this identical speaker, but the novelist calls him—Saladine.

77, 11. *

When from the first to last, &c.] No heedful peruser of this line, and the three it is follow'd by, can think we have the passage entire; other heads of these brothers' *recountments* are apparently necessary, to make the Poet's "*In brief,*" right and sensible: What the accident was, or whose the negligence, that has depriv'd us of these heads, the editor does not take upon him to say; this only he is bold to assert,—that there is a *lacuna*, and (perhaps) of two lines: if the publick thinks well to admit of them, here are two that may serve to fill up with;—*How in that habit; what my state, what his;* | *And whose the service he was now engag'd in; — |In brief,* &c.

78, 1.

There is more in it;—] A reading of the two elder folio's, and of the third and last moderns; the others have,—*There is no more in it*; which, if they saw the true reading, (as two of them might) shews them blind to the beauty of it: Celia's fright makes her almost forget herself; begin, with telling more than she should do; and end, with calling Ganimed—*"cousin,"* whom her hearer has call'd—*"brother,"* and believes him to be so. The incident that gives birth to this fright, the *"bloody napkin,"* has no existence in the Novel that furnish'd most of the others.

79, 30.

The beaten philosopher, &c.] The humour of this scene consists in the Clown's taking state upon him, and giving himself great airs, talking one while very wisely, another while very big: William's answer to the question he put to him,—*"Art thou wise?"* helps him to lug in a saw; and that saw, the present *"heathen philosopher:"* what he says of him, is occasion'd by seeing his hearer stand gaping, (as well he might) sometimes looking at him, some times the maid; who, says he,—is not a grape for your lips; concluding with—*"You do love this maid?"* and upon William's replying affirmatively, proceeds first to bambouzle, and then to bully him. When the Poet was writing this speech, his remembrance was certainly visited by some other expressions in "Euphues;" where Phebe is made to say to her lover,—*"Phebe is no lettice for your lips, and her grapes hang so hie, that gaze at them you may, but touch them you cannot."*

83, 5.

By my life, I do; &c.] This is made an argument by the last modern editor,—that the play was writ in the time of king James; a persecutor of witches and conjurers, and the maker of a fresh act against them in the year 1604. ~ The word *"observance"* in l. 32, coming so immediately after another *"observance"* in l. 30, gives room to imagine—that it may have crept in there by mistake of the printer in the room of some other word, which the *"Revisal"* thinks might be—*perseverance*: a word that is better fitted to the place, that the recommender of it seems to have known; for it's primitive was—*persever*, at that time of day, and itself the derivative accented upon the antipenultima. *v.* "M." 63, 14. ~ The corrections in the next page, are met with in all the moderns.

86, 4. *

And therefore &c.] There can be no need of arguing, to satisfy any one—that this is the song's concluding stanza; reading it, is sufficient: but the negligence of it's first printer made it the second stanza; and there it has been suffer'd to stand in all succeeding editions, old and new. The reader of Sidney's poems in any oldish impression, will find—that "*hey, nonino,*" and "*ding a ding, ding,*" strange as they are, were songs of great fame before Shakespeare,—at least, the musick of them,—which (probably) was that of this burthen. ~ The third editor's correction of a word in l. 9, is certainly right, and ought to have been adopted: "*untimeable*" was easily convertible at the press into—*untuneable*; is a fitter word for the speaker; and a manifest trap of his laying, to abuse the Pages by.

D°, 23.

fear their hope,] That is—"fear a disappointment of it;" as the, "Revisal" rightly interprets, when proposing this very amendment that had been made by the present editor some years before ~ The words "*dulcet diseases*" in p. 88, (l. 24.) mean—wits, or witty people; so call'd, because the times were infected with them; they, and fools,—that is, such fools as the speaker,—being all their delight.

89, 17.

O, sir, we quarrel in print, by the book; &c.] Whoso pleases to turn to the "*School,*" will find a book of the year 95, which is there intitl'd—"*Practice of the Duello,*" but it's true title is this;—"*Vincentio Saviolo his Practice. In two Bookes. The first intreating of the use of the Rapier and Dagger. The second of Honor and honorable Quarrels.*" Passages are extracted from both of them, and chiefly the last; which being thrown all together at the end of the others, and intermix'd with a few observations, are recommended to the reader's perusal as a note upon this place. The gentleman who has made a like extract, (the last editor) pronounces in peremptory manner,—that this *is* the book meant by the Poet, and these the passages that his divisions are grounded on: but this is being too positive; considering,—that there were many other books on the subject, as Saviolo himself witnesses in one of his prefaces; some or other of which may possibly be discover'd hereafter, and found to be more in point than Saviolo, and perhaps of a later date. In a note of the third modern editor's, upon this same passage, you have the titles of two other books, and their authors' names; to wit,—"Lewis di Caranza *on Fencing*, and Giacomo di Grassi's *Art of Defence*;" but this is all you are told of them, and was probably all that he knew.

NOTES TO *AS YOU LIKE IT*   249

Re-enter &c.] The following masque-like eclarcissement, which is wholly of the Poet's invention, may pass for another small mark of the time of this play's writing: for precisely in those years that have been mention'd in former notes, (*v*. 39, 26 & 83, 5.) the foolery of masques was predominant; and the torrent of fashion bore down Shakespeare, in this play and the "*Tempest*," and a little in "Timon" and "Cymbeline." But he is not answerable for one absurdity in the conduct of this masque, that must lye at his editors' doors; who, by bringing in Hymen in *propria persona*, make Rosalind a magician indeed; whereas all her conjuration consisted—in sitting up one of the foresters to personate that deity, and in putting proper words in his mouth. If, in representing this masque, Hymen had some Loves in his train, the performance would seem the more rational: they are certainly wanted for what is intitl'd— the "*Song*;" and the other musical business, beginning—"*Then is there mirth in heaven*," would come with greater propriety from them, though editions bestow it on Hymen.

92, 16.

Sir, by your patience:—] To the duke; putting himself, without ceremony, between him and de Boys, and then addressing the latter: and the subject of this address is the most admirable expedient for Jaques to make his exit in character, that ever human wit could have hit upon; nor can the drama afford an example, in which Horace's—*servetur ad imum* has been better observ'd than in this instance.

93, 14.

I charge you, O women, &c.] The subsequent passage appear'd first in the form it now bears in the Oxford edition; and was taken up by the next in succession, the publisher of which has this proper remark on it: that—"without the alteration of *You* into *Them* the invocation is nonsense; and without the addition of the words, *to like as much as pleases them*, the inference of, *that between you and the women the play may please*, would be unsupported by any precedent premises." To which reasoning, the present editor subscribes very heartily; and, of consequence, to the justness of both emendations: only observing,—that omissions of words nearly similar, or words repeated are the most common of all accidents both in writing and printing.

From *Notes and Various Readings*.
(London, 1779): 54–69.

A SPECIMEN OF A COMMENTARY ON SHAKESPEARE
Walter Whiter
1794

AS YOU LIKE IT

119 [I. i. I]. "As I remember, Adam, it was upon this fashion. He bequeathed me by will but a poor thousand crowns; and, as thou say'st, charged my brother, on his blessing, to breed me well" &c.] This is the reading of Sir William Blackstone. Dr. Johnson reads, "As I remember, Adam, it was on this fashion bequeathed me. By will but a poor thousand crowns; and, as thou sayest, &c." "The nominative *my father*" (says Dr. Johnson) "is certainly left out, but so left out that the auditor inserts it, in spite of himself." *Dr. Warburton* reads, and *Mr. Capell is* of opinion, that "there was never a more certain emendation," "*As I remember, Adam, it was upon this* MY FATHER *bequeathed me, &c.*" Amidst these various emendations, the reading and pointing of the old Copy are certainly right, "As I remember *Adam,* it was upon this fashion bequeathed me by will, . . . and as thou saist, charged my brother on his blessing." *Father* is not the nominative case to *charged,* but the construction must be supplied by *it was charged.* His by the artifice of the poet relates to something understood, that the audience may be impressed with the idea of a previous conversation; and as if he had not sufficiently explained himself in this place, he afterwards adds (122 [I .i. 70]) "My *father* charged you in his will." It may be further observed on this passage, that the old Copy reads *but poore a thousand Crownes,* which I believe to be right.

120 [I. i. 38]. "Marry, sir, be better employ'd, and be naught a while."] The sense of this passage may be collected from the several notes of the Commentators, though it is extremely singular that the *true* sense of the phrase, *Be naught awhile,* should be gathered from the passages which have been produced by our Critics to support *three* different interpretations. Dr. Warburton thinks that the expression, *Be nought a while,* is only a North country proverbial curse equivalent to *a mischief on you.* So the old poet Skelton,

> "Correct first thyselfe, walke and *be nought,*
> Deeme what thou list, thou knowest not my thought."

Mr. Steevens thinks that this explanation *is farfetched,* and believes "that the words *be nought a while* mean no more than this: *Be content to be a cypher, till I shall think fit to elevate you into consequence.*["] "This was certainly" (says he) "a proverbial saying. I find it in *The Storie of King Darius,* an interlude, 1565."

> Come away, *and be nought a whyle,*
> Or surely I will you both defyle.

Again in K. Henry IV. p. 2. Falstaff says to Pistol, "Nay, if he do nothing but speak nothing, *he shall be nothing here.*"

Though Mr. Malone allows that the words *naught* and *nought* are frequently confounded in old English books (which in the edition of 1785 he has shewn, by producing some passages where *nought is* spelt *naught;*) and though he once coincided with the interpretation of Mr. Steevens, yet he is now induced by a passage in *Sweetnam,* a comedy, 1620, to concur with the explanation given by Dr. Johnson, who thinks, that *"Be better employ'd, and he naught a while,"* is used in the same sense as we say, *It is better to do mischief than to do nothing.* The passage from *Sweetnam* is,

> "Get you both in and be *naught a while.*"

This is spoken by a chambermaid to her mistress with a lover.

Now is it not manifest, that in all these passages (from which our Commentators have extracted such opposite interpretations) the phrase in question has invariably the same meaning? *Be naught or nought a while* certainly means—*Retire—begone,* or as we now say in a kind of quaint, colloquial language, *make yourself* SCARCE—*vanish—vote yourself an* EVANESCENT QUANTITY. In the same style we say, to express the absence of a person whom we had good reason to expect,—*There's* NONE *of William—Here's* NO *Thomas;* and in this very play we find a similar expression applied in the same sense, though with an ironical meaning (208 [IV. iii. I]). "Is it not past two o'clock? and *here* MUCH *Orlando.*"—Mr. Malone was misled in his interpretation of the passage from *Sweetnam* by the equivoque contained in it, which in its secondary sense certainly refers to what Mr. Malone supposes. A double meaning was likewise intended by Shakspeare in the sentence before us, and there is an allusion to the proverb, which *Dr. Johnson* imagines. This explanation agrees with the succeeding speech of

Orlando, "Shall I keep your hogs, and eat husks with them?" That is, *"Shall I be driven from your house, and herd with your swine?"*

121 [I. i. 52]. "I have as much of my father in me, as you; albeit I confess your coming before me is nearer to his *reverence*.["]] The note, which Mr. Malone has added to this passage, is calculated to mislead the reader, by annexing the name of *Warburton* to the following explanation: "The reverence due to my father is, in some degree, derived to you, as the first-born." We might from hence imagine that such a sense was adopted by Warburton; but this he only gives as a possible interpretation, and is *firmly persuaded* that the poet had a different meaning. He proposes therefore to read *revenue* for *reverence;* and this emendation appears to have been generally admitted into the text. Mr. Capell has observed, that in the original reading no reason can be given for the sudden anger of Oliver, which is certainly occasioned by something offensive at the conclusion of Orlando's speech. The reading however of the old Copy is unquestionably the true one. *Reverence* appears to have been the appropriate term for the *"reverential* condition or character of an old man." So in *Much Ado about Nothing,* Benedick says, "I should think this a gull, but that the white-bearded fellow speaks it: knavery cannot, sure, hide himself in such *reverence."* (Act II. S. iii. p. 242 [II. iii. 223]). Again Leonato says,

> "Thou hast so wrong'd my innocent child, and me,
> That I am forc'd to lay my *reverence* by;
> And, with grey hairs, and bruise of many days,
> Do challenge thee to tryal of a man."
> (Act v. S. i. p. 286 [v. i. 63]).

Cordelia says, in *Lear,*

> "O my dear father! Restoration, hang
> Thy medicine on my lips; and let this kiss
> Repair those violent harms, that my two sisters
> Have in thy *reverence* made!"
> (Act IV. S. vii. p. 655 [IV. vii. 26])

Again Gloster reading the letter supposed to be written by Edgar, "This policy, and *reverence* of age, makes the world bitter to the best of our times; keeps our fortunes from us, till our oldness cannot relish them." (Act I. S. ii. p. 508 [I. ii. 48]). In the Second Part of Henry VI, we have the following lines, where Mr. Malone refers us to this passage in *As You Like It.*

"Wast thou ordain'd, dear father,
To lose thy youth in peace, and to atchieve
The silver livery of advised *age;*
And, in thy *reverence,* and thy chair-days, thus
To die in ruffian battle?"

(Act v. S. ii. p. 251 [v. ii. 45]).

[In the Tragedy of *Thierry & Theodoret* we have "Now in my hours of age & REVERENCE (B. & Fl., vol. 10, 129.)]

In the present instance *Orlando* uses the word in an ironical sense, and means to say that his "brother by coming before him is nearer to a respectable and venerable elder of a family." The phrase, *His reverence,* is still thus ironically applied, though with somewhat of a different meaning; and we frequently use the expression of *your worship* both with a grave and ludicrous signification nearly in the same manner.—The sense, which I have here given, is certainly right; and will account for the *anger* of Oliver; and for the *words* which they mutually retort upon each other respecting their *ages.*

"*Orlando.* Albeit, I confess your coming before me is nearer to his *reverence.*
Oliver. What, *boy*!
Orlando. Come, come, *elder* brother, you are too *young* in this.["]

It is extremely curious, that our Poet has caught many words and even turns of expression belonging to the novel, from which the play is taken; though he has applied them in a mode generally different, and often very remote from the original. This has certainly taken place in the present instance, and the passage which contains it will likewise supply us with another example. *Rosader,* or *Orlando,* is introduced making, for the first time, his reflections on the indignities which he had suffered from his brother *Saladine,* or *Oliver.* —"As thus (says the Novelist) he was ruminating of his melancholie passions, in came Saladyne with his men, and seeing his brother in a browne studie, and to forget his wonted *reuerence,* thought to *shake* him out of his dumps thus."] (*Euphues' Golden Legacy.*) *Orlando* says in Shakspeare, "Go apart, Adam, and thou shalt hear how he will *shake* me up." (120 [I. i. 29]). Our Poet, in his character of the good *Adam,* has omitted a compliment which he might have paid to his country. In the novel he is called "*Adam Spencer an Englishman.*" He has likewise omitted (as our Commentators have remarked) to reward him in the catastrophe for his fidelity.

125 [I. ii. 27]. *"Rosalind.* What think you of falling in love?

"*Celia.* Marry, I pr'ythee, do, to make sport withal: but love no man in good earnest; nor no further in sport neither, than with safety of a pure blush thou may'st in honour come off again."] It is in this dangerous diversion, that Rosalind indulges herself in the original novel. "She accounted loue a toye, and fancie a momentarie passion, that as it was taken in with a gaze, might be shaken off with a winck."

130 [I. ii. 175]. "The princesses call for you."] The old Copy reads "*the princesse calls,*" which is right. It is Celia only who calls for him; and the answer of Orlando, "I will attend *them,*" as Celia is accompanied by Rosalind, does not invalidate the ancient reading.

133 [l. ii. 261].   "My better parts
               Are all thrown down; and that which here stands up,
               Is but a *quintaine,* a mere lifeless block."]

The propriety of this comparison is yet undiscovered. The explanation given by Mr. Guthrie is neither just in itself, nor is it applicable to the case in question; he appears to have been misled, by supposing that the first part of the speech must necessarily be included in the simile, and relate to the Quintaine. Mr. Malone's interpretation is extremely vapid and defective. I have not the least doubt but that the shape of the Quintaine among the rustics of our Poet's time, was sometimes in the figure *of a* MAN. This gives sense and spirit to the image. "*My better parts are all thrown down—the powers of my reason are overthrown; and I stand here senseless as the Quintaine, a* MAN ONLY IN MY FORM." Among the French and Italians, the Quintaine was commonly in a human shape. *Menestrier,* in his treatise on Tournaments, has the following curious account of this diversion: "La Quintaine n'est autre chose qu'un tronc d'arbre, ou un pilier contre lequel on va rompre la lance, pour s'accoutumer a atteindre l'ennemi par des coups mesurez. Nous l'appelons *la course au Faquin,* Parcequ'on se sert souvant d'un faquin, ou d'un portefaix, armé de toutes pieces, contre lequel on court. Les Italiens la nomment *la course a l'homme arme: & le Sarrasin;* parce qu'ils transfigurent ce faquin en Turc, en More, ou en Sarrasin, pour rendre ces courses plus mysterieuses. On se sert ordinairement d'une figure de bois en forme d'homme, plantée sur un pivot, afin qu'elle soit mobile. Elle demeure ferme quand on la frappe au front, entre les yeux, & sur le nez; qui font les meilleurs coups: & quand on la frappe ailleurs, elle tourne si rudement, que si le Cavalier n'est adroit pour esquiver le coup, elle le frappe d'un sabre de bois ou d'un *sac plein de terre;* ce qui donne a rire aux spectateurs." For this passage I am indebted to *Menage* in his

Origines de la Langue Francoise. The Italian proverb, *Esser Saracino di Piazza* (*To be the Butt of every body*) refers to the figure of the Saracen in this exercise. (See *Torriano* in his *Proverbial Phrases* sub voce *Saracino*).

Most nations appear to have had a martial or mock exercise of this kind, which would certainly be extremely various according to the genius of the age and the manners of the people; but we may observe, that under every circumstance the most obvious form for this object of attack would be the *human shape,* of which, as it is not difficult to make rude and ridiculous representations, we may well conceive, that among the simplest rustics it would often be assumed for the form of the Quintaine. In the figure of it, which is given by *Stowe,* I have not the least doubt but that the transverse moveable piece of wood, with the mode of its acting, was derived from the idea of the human shape, and was intended to represent that arms.—I have before hinted, that "my better parts are all thrown down," is not connected with the succeeding comparison, and our Commentators were deceived probably by the metaphorical expression *thrown down.* This however is not taken from the exercise of the Quintaine, as may be evident from the expression *stands up,* which is put in opposition to it. Nothing is more certain, than that these terms are derived from WRESTLING. In the next speech of Rosalind, and the succeeding one of Orlando, *overthrown* is used with the same allusion; and I am surprised that our critics were not aware of this coincidence.—If the reader should enquire why a simile, apparently so remote as the Quintaine, should on this occasion be presented to the mind of our Poet, I will inform him, that the association was derived from *the feats of activity* in which Orlando had been just engaged; and the *love adventure* with which they were connected. The diversion of the *Quintaine* (we know) was common at *marriages,* "When Jac and Tom, Dic, Hob and Will strove for the gay garland;" and their exertions, we may suppose, were not a little roused by the hopes of succeeding with their *mistresses.* So *Randolph,* in the same poem which Mr. Malone has quoted,

> "A jolly swain was he
> Whom Peg and Susan after Victory
> Crown'd with a Garland they had made, beset
> With Daisies, Pinks and many a Violet,
> Couslip and Gilliflower."

The reader will not perfectly understand what is intended by this *Association of Ideas,* till he has perused the observations which form the latter part of the volume.

142 [II. i. 5]. "Here feel we *but* the penalty of Adam,
   The season's difference; as, the icy fang,
   And churlish chiding of the winter's wind;
   Which when it bites and blows upon my body,
   Even till I shrink with cold, I smile, and say,—
   This is no flattery: these are counsellors

   That feelingly persuade me what I am."
  ["Sweet are the uses of adversity;
   Which, like the toad, ugly and venemous,
   Wears yet a precious jewel in his head:
   And this our life, exempt from publick haunt,
   Finds tongues in trees, books in the running brooks,
   Sermons in stones, and good in everything."]]

The old Copy reads *not,* which Mr. Theobald changed into *but.* Though all our critics appear to have coincided in this emendation, yet I still persuade myself that the original reading is right. Mr. Theobald is of opinion, that the penalty of Adam expressed by the Poet was "the being sensible of the difference of the seasons." I do not think that this is the allusion intended. I read the whole passage thus,

   "Here feel we *not* the penalty of Adam:
   The seasons' difference, as the icy fang
   And churlish chiding of the winter's wind—
   (Which when it bites and blows upon my body
   Even till I shrink with cold, I smile and say
   This is no flattery;)—these are counsellors,
   That feelingly persuade me what I am."

The penalty of Adam, to which our Poet has here alluded, may be gathered from the following passages in Scripture. "Cursed is the *ground* for thy sake; in *sorrow* shalt thou *eat* of it all the days of thy life." (Gen. iii. 17.)—"In the *sweat* of thy face shalt thou *eat* bread." (v. 19.)—"Therefore the Lord God sent him forth from the garden of Eden, *to till the ground* from whence he was taken." (v. 23.)—We here plainly see, that the only curse or penalty imposed on Adam, which can have any reference to the condition of a country life, is the toil of cultivating the ground, and acquiring by that labour the means of sustenance. The Duke therefore justly consoles himself and his companions with the reflection, that *their* banishment into those woods from the *paradise of* a *Court* (if we may be still permitted to continue the allusion) was not attended with the penalty pronounced on Adam—a life of pain and of labour; but that on the contrary it ought to be considered as a philosophical retirement of ease and independence.—With respect to the minute inconvenience which they might suffer from the difference of the seasons—the biting frost and the winter's wind—*these* (he observes) should not be regarded in any other view than as sharp but salutary counsellors, which made them *feel* only for the promotion of their good, and the improvement of their virtue.

144 [II. i. 50]. "Left and abandon'd of his velvet *friends.*"] The old Copy has *friend,* which is right. The singular is often used for the plural with a sense more *abstracted,* and therefore in many instances more poetical.

149 [II. iv. 1]. "*Ros.* O Jupiter! how *weary* are my spirits!
Touch. I care not for my spirits, if my legs were not weary.
Ros. I could find in my heart to disgrace my man's apparel, and to cry like a woman: but I must comfort the weaker vessel, as doublet and hose ought to show itself courageous to petticoat; therefore, courage, good Aliena."] On this passage Mr. Malone has the following remark: "She invokes Jupiter, because he was supposed to be always in good spirits. So afterwards: 'O most gentle *Jupiter!*'—A *jovial* man was a common phrase in our author's time. One of Randolph's plays is called ARISTIPPUS, *or the* JOVIAL *Philosopher;* and a comedy of Broome's, *The* JOVIAL *Crew, or The* MERRY *Beggars.* The old Copy reads, *How* MERRY. The emendation, which the context and the clown's reply render certain, was made by Mr. Theobald." The context however, and the Clown's reply, added to the comment of Mr. Malone, establish the *original* reading, and render the emendation of Mr. Theobald *certainly wrong.* Does not the reader perceive, that the whole humour of the passage consists in the word MERRY, and that Rosalind speaks thus ironically in order to comfort Celia? "O Jupiter!" (says she) 'what MERRY spirits I am in!' To which the clown replies, 'I care not whether my spirits were good or bad, if my legs were not weary.'— 'Indeed,' adds Rosalind, 'to speak the truth, tho' I pretend in my *mannish* character to be in *good* spirits, and *not* to be weary, yet "I could find in my heart to disgrace my man's apparel and to cry like a woman["]: as it becomes me however to comfort the weaker vessel, I must assume a quality which I have not:—therefore, *courage,* good Aliena,—bear fatigue as I do, good Aliena.' Nothing is more certain than this explanation.

151 [II. iv. 38]. "Wearying thy hearer in thy mistress' praise."] The old Copy has *wearing,* which is right. *Weary* is derived from *wear.* "Quoniam" (says *Junius*) "quotidiano usu conteri solent ea, quæ assidue gerimus, hinc Anglis etiamnum, *to wear or waste away,* est Tabescere; atq. adèo quoq. ab hac

postremá verbi acceptione, *to weary,* cæpit accipi pro Fatigare; quod lassitudo corpora nostra maxime frangat atq. ipsos quoq; spiritus vitales valde imminuat." (Etymol. Anglican. sub voce *Wear.*) But the following quotation from Jonson's Masque of *The Gypsies* puts the matter out of dispute:

"Only time, and Ears out-*wearing.*"

(Page 625. Edit. 1672.)

151 [II. iv. 52]. "And I remember the wooing a *Peascod* instead of her."] Why should our Poet fix upon a *Peascod* to be courted by Touchstone for a *woman?* It might be supposed that some ludicrous resemblance was intended; and however remote the likeness may appear, the following proverb will shew that such a notion prevailed:

Se la *donna* fosse cosi picciola come è buona,
Il minimo *bacello* le farebbe una veste & una corona.
If women were as little as they are good,
A *Peascod* would make them a gowne and a hood.

(John Florio's second Frutes, p. 174. 159I.)

153 [II. v. 4].   "And *tune* his merry note
Unto the sweet bird's throat."]

The old Copy has *turne,* which is certainly right. To *turn a tune,* in the counties of York and Durham, is the appropriate and familiar phrase for modulating the voice properly according to the *turns* or air of the tune. This I learnt in a journey which I have lately made into the North, where a Commentator on Shakspeare will find many peculiar expressions still used in the same sense which our author has annexed to them.—He who travels into the North may likewise learn that which is most precious in the intercourse of social life. He may there see the polish of cultivated manners united with the cordial feelings of hospitality.

155 [II. v. 56].   *"Duc ad me, duc ad me, duc ad me;*
Here shall he see
Gross fools as he,
An if he will come to me."]

This is Sir T. Hanmer's reading for *Ducdame;* and an anonymous critic has proposed *Duc ad me.* Dr. Farmer reads *Ducdame* with an accent on the last syllable, and thinks it is a "word coined for the nonce." Mr. Steevens informs us, as a confirmation of the old reading, that Dr. Farmer being at a house not far from Cambridge, when news was brought of the hen-roost being robbed, a facetious old Squire who was present, sung the following "Stanza, which" (says he) "has an odd coincidence with the ditty of Jaques."

> "*Dame,* what makes your Ducks to die?
> *duck, duck, duck,*
> *Dame,* what makes your chicks to cry?
> *chuck, chuck, chuck.*["]

I have been favoured with a couple of Stanzas, which are common in the counties of Cambridge and Norfolk, and which certainly belong to the same song, that was sung by the facetious Squire:

> Dame, what makes your Ducks to die?
> What the pize ails 'em, what the pize ails 'em,
> They kick up their heels and there they lie,
> What the pize ails 'em now?
> Heigh, Ho! Heigh, Ho!
> Dame, what ails your Ducks to die?
> What a pize ails 'em, what a pize ails 'em?
> Heigh, Ho! Heigh, Ho!
> Dame, what ails your Ducks to die?
> Eating o' Pollywigs, eating o' Pollywigs. (*i.e. Tadpoles.*)
> Heigh, Ho! Heigh, Ho!

In the foregoing Stanzas it is of no consequence either as to the sense or the metre, whether Dame be read in its usual way, or whether we pronounce it Dame with the accent on the last syllable. They are all however manifestly addressed to the *Dame,* the good housewife of the family, under whose care we may suppose the poultry to be placed; and it may be observed, that the *Ducks* are particularly specified on account of the alliteration with *Dame.* This beauty is mightily cultivated in effusions of this sort; and indeed it is often the only reason for the existence of the composition.—I therefore see no difficulty in the derivation of the word *Ducdame,* which has so much embarrassed our Commentators. What is more natural, or obvious, than to suppose *Duc Dame* or *Duc Dame* to be the usual cry of the Dame to gather her Ducks about her; as if she should say, *Ducks come to your Dame,* or *Ducks come to your Dame*? The rhyme requires that we should read it with Dr. Farmer *Ducdame,* placing the accent on the last syllable. It is common for persons in their addresses to young and helpless animals, either to make diminutives of themselves, or of the animals which they are addressing. The explication here given of this passage is the only one, which at all properly corresponds with the context. 1st, According to this sense, *Ducdame, Ducdame, Ducdame,* becomes (what Jaques certainly intended it to be) a ridiculous parody on the burden of the former song, *Come hither, Come hither, Come hither.* This effect, I think, will hardly be produced by an indirect and insipid translation of *Come hither* into Latin. 2dly, This sense likewise accounts for the ignorance of Amiens, and the explanation of Jaques. It is no wonder that a courtier should not understand a term derived from the occupation of rustics; and the answer of Jaques plainly points out that the expression was intended for a certain cry to collect together some silly species of animals, "'Tis a Greek invocation," says he, "to call fools into a circle."—If Shakspeare is to be explained, neither the writer nor the reader should become fastidious at the serious discussion of such trifling topics.

155 [II. v. 60]. "An if he will come *to me.*"] Dr. Farmer reads *to Ami,* that is, to Amiens, and gives a reason for the rejection of the common reading, which of all others it will not admit:—"Jaques," he says, "did not mean to ridicule himself." It is however, on the contrary, peculiarly in character for such a humourist as Jaques thus to ridicule himself; and he produces this very song as a parody on the former one, intending by it to expose the folly both of himself and his companions. *Amy* however is the reading of the old Copy; and is certainly right. It surely was incumbent on the Doctor, or some of his fellow critics, to have given us this information; especially as their attention must naturally be awake in the discussion of so disputed a passage. I have seldom found the interests of learning much promoted by literary fellowships.

159 [II. vii. 53]. "He, that a fool doth very wisely hit,
  Doth very foolishly, although he smart,
  Not to seem senseless of the bob: if not,
  The wise man's folly is anatomiz'd
  Even by the squand'ring glances of the fool."]

"The words *Not to*" (says Mr. Malone), "which are wanting in the old copy to complete both the metre and sense, were added by Mr. Theobald." It is strange, that our Commentators should be desirous of *making* a text for the Poet, when it is their business to explain that which he has given us. Neither Mr. Theobald nor Mr. Malone need be solicitous about the metre; and the sense is full as good in the original text as with the emendation of Mr. Theobald.

I read and point the passage thus:

"He, that a fool doth very *wisely* hit,
Doth, *very foolishly* although he smart,
Seem senseless of the bob; if not etc."

That is, a wise man, whose failings should chance to be well rallied by a simple unmeaning jester, even though he should be weak enough really to be hurt by so foolish an attack, appears always insensible of the stroke. Nothing is more certain than this explication.

With regard to the metre of our Poet, we may observe in general, that whenever the rythm of a disputed verse is defective to our ear, we have good reason to suspect it is corrupted; so, on the contrary, when the line is smooth and easy, it will not be necessary for us to disturb the text on the authority of our fingers. As the poet did not write with such a process, so he ought not to be tried by such a test. In short, the controversy about the metre of Shakspeare is merely a dispute of *words*. When it is said on the one side, that the metre is defective, it is replied on the other, that Shakspeare only differs from other poets as to the number of syllables which the same word is supposed to contain. (See Mr. Capell's Essay on Verse, App. 227, and Mr. Malone's Pref. 35.) If the verse in question be repeated, nothing unpleasant or defective will be discovered by the ear; and if the reader should be farther desirous of reforming it to the touchstone of his fingers, he may suppose, if he pleases, that *seem* and *bob* are used as dissyllables. Nothing however can be more inharmonious than the verse as it is supplied by Mr. Theobald, and the repetition of *not* at the extremities of the line is particularly rough and inelegant.

159 [II. vii. 74]. "Till that the *very very* means do ebb."] The old Copy reads "The wearie verie," which is certainly right. The sense is, 'till that the very means being weary do ebb.' *Very-very* is an extremely lame emendation indeed!

165 [II. vii. 184].   "Freeze, freeze, thou bitter sky,
That dost not bite so nigh
As benefits forgot:
Though thou the waters *warp,*
Thy sting is not so sharp
As friend remember'd not."]

The strange propensity in Commentators to reject what is obvious, and to seek what is remote, has been perpetually observed. Yet I know not, whether in the whole history of criticism we can find so signal an example of this propensity as the present instance will afford us. Mr. Kenrick remarks, that "the surface of *waters,* so long as they remain unfrozen, is apparently a perfect plane; whereas, when they are frozen, this surface deviates from its exact flatness, or warps." Dr. Johnson observes, with more good sense than usually belongs to his remarks, that "to *warp* was probably in Shakspeare's time, a colloquial word, which conveyed no distant allusion to any thing else, physical or medicinal;" and yet he adds, as if it were impossible for him to continue long in the same vein of good sense, "To *warp* is to *turn,* and to *turn* is to *change*: when milk is *changed* by curdling, we now say, it is *turned:* when water is *changed* or *turned* by frost, Shakspeare says, it is *curdled.* To be *warp'd* is only to be changed from its natural state." Mr. Steevens thinks that Dr. Johnson is right: and Dr. Farmer is of opinion, that *warp'd* signifies to be *curdled.* Mr. Malone seems desirous of leaving his fellow Commentators behind him in this contest of critical perversion, and accordingly he doubts whether there be any allusion at all to the operation of frost. "The influence of the winter's sky or season" (says he) "may, with sufficient propriety, be said to *warp* the surface of the *ocean,* by agitation of its waves alone." Did our Commentators never learn, that *warp* signifies to *contract,* and that it is so used without any allusion to the precise physical process which takes place in that contraction? Cold and winter have been always described as *contracting*—heat and summer as *dissolving* or *softening.* The cold is said to *warp the waters,* when it *contracts* them into the solid substance of ice, and suffers them no longer to continue in *a liquid* or *flowing* state. Hence water is said to *stop*—to be *bound*—to *come together,* and one of the words to express *ice* among the Greeks is derived from a verb which signifies to *compress* or *contract.* Every school-boy will immediately call to mind the common-place descriptions of Spring and Winter; in which expressions of this sort perpetually occur—the *solvitur* acris hiems—Gelu flumina *constiterint* acuto, &c. &c. He may perhaps likewise recollect the following passages:

> *Adstringit* Scythico glacialem frigore pontum.
> (Lucan. Pharsal. I. 18. See too 5. 434.)

> Pigrior *adstrictis* torpuit Hebrus aquis.
> (Claudian. Præfat. ad Rapt. Proserp.)

> Et *coit adstrictis* barbarus Ister aquis.
> (Ovid. Epist. ex Pont. lib. 3. ep. 3. 26.)

It would be an idle task to accumulate the trite examples which relate to this subject; nor should we have thought it necessary to detail what is so obvious, had it not been so strangely overlooked or rejected in the preceding interpretations. There is however one passage in *Horace,* which has much divided his Commentators, and which the reader of taste will be pleased to see illustrated by two authorities from an English Classic.

> Quod si bruma nives Albanis illinet agris,
> Ad mare descendet vases tuus, & sibi parcet,
> *Contractusq*; leget. (Hor. Epist. lib. i. 7. v. 10, 11, 12.)

A man *throng'd up with cold.* (Pericles, 520 [II. i. 77.])

The *shrinking* slaves of *Winter.* (Cymbeline, 437 [IV. iv. 30.])

These passages are completely parallel; and will determine the opinion of the reader respecting the disputed sense of *Contractus.*

165 [II. vii. 190]. "As friend remember'd not."] *Remember'd* for *remembering,* says Mr. Malone. Certainly not. If ingratitude consists in one friend not *remembering* another, it surely must consist likewise in one friend not *being* remem*ber'd* by another. So in the former line, "*benefits forgot*"—by our friend, or our friend for*getting* benefits, will prove him equally ungrateful.

168 [III. ii. 30]. "He, that hath learned no wit by nature nor art, may *complain of good breeding,* or comes of a very dull kindred."] By one Commentator it is read *gross,* and by another *bad* breeding. Mr. Malone thinks it means—"may complain of a good education, for being so inefficient, of so little use to him." Dr. Johnson is in doubt "whether the custom of the language in Shakspeare's time did not authorise this mode of speech, and make *complain of good breeding* the same with *complain* of the WANT of *good breeding.*" This is a mode of speech common, I believe, to all languages; and the most ignorant might have taught Dr. Johnson, that such a mode of expression occurred even before the time of Shakspeare:

Εἶτ' αρ ' ὄγ' Εὐχωλη s Ἐπιμέμφεται Εἶθ Ἑκατόμβη s

(II. i. 65.)

Whether he *complains* of the WANT *of prayers* or *of sacrifices.*

170 [III. ii. 97]. "All the pictures, fairest limn'd,
                    Are but black to Rosalind."]

The old Copy has *fairest linde,* which is the true reading. The Poet means, that the most beautiful *lines* or touches exhibited by art are inferior to the natural traits of beauty which belong to Rosalind.

170 [III. ii. 103]. "It is the right butter-women's *rate* to market."] This is the emendation of Sir T. Hanmer, which Mr. Malone thinks is right. Dr. Grey proposes *rant:* the old reading is *rank,* which Mr. Capell imagines to be "the *order* observed by such women; travelling all in one road with exact intervals between horse and horse." The explanation of Mr. Capell will appear more forcible, if we consider that on account of the badness of the roads in our Author's time the women must travel from their villages in the manner which is here described. Something of this sort may be observed at present. Mr. Malone, as an addition to his note on this passage, thus remarks in the Appendix: "The following line in King Richard the Third may be urged to shew that the familiar image of the butter-woman's *horse* going to market was in our author's thoughts:

But yet I run before my horse to market."

May not the same line be urged in confirmation of Mr. Capell's sense, to shew that the image of travellers to market *succeeding* each other was likewise familiar to the thoughts of our Author? In short, if *rate* conveys a sense suitable to the occasion, *rank* will certainly be preferable; as it expresses the same thing with an additional idea; and perhaps the very idea in which the chief force of the comparison is placed. "The right Butter-women's *rank to* market" means the *jog-trot rate* (as it is vulgarly called) with which Butter-women *uniformly* travel *one after another* in their road to market: in its application to Orlando's poetry, it means a *set* or *string* of verses in the *same coarse cadence* and *vulgar uniformity of rythm.*

172 [III. ii. 133].   "Why should this desert *silent* be?
For it is unpeopled? No;
Tongues I'll hang on every tree,
That shall civil sayings show."]

Silent is the emendation of Mr. Twyrwhitt, and it has received the approbation both of Mr. Steevens and Mr. Malone. The old Copy reads "Why should this *desert be?*" And Mr. Pope corrects it, "Why should this *a* desert be." "But although" (says Mr. Tyrwhite) "the metre may be assisted by this correction, the sense is still defective; for how will the *hanging of tongues on every tree* make it less a desert?" The old reading however, I believe, is genuine. Mr.

Tyrwhitt is sometimes lost in the mazes of his own subtlety. Surely the same *metaphor* has power to *people* woods, which is able to afford them *speech.* — Even Dr. Johnson is on this point correct and perspicuous. "This desert" (says he) "shall not apper *unpeopled,* for every tree shall teach the maxims or incidents of social life."—If the metre should be thought defective; *why* may be taken for one of our Poet's dissyllables, as he has used *fire—sire.* (See Mr. Malone's Pref. 35.) Let the reader of taste, who is used to the rhythm of Shakespeare, repeat the line in question with a gentle pause upon *why;* and he will find no reason to reject it for deficiency of metre.

> 173 [III. ii. 154]. "Helen's cheek, but not her heart;
>   Cleopatra's majesty;
>   *Atalanta's better part;*
>   Sad Lucretia's modesty."]

There is no passage in Shakspeare which has more embarrassed his Commentators than this celebrated line, which enumerates among the perfections of a beauty *the better part of Atalanta.* Dr. Johnson observes, that the *better part of Atalanta* "seems to have been her heels;" yet he is inclined to think that our Poet, though no despicable mythologist, has mistaken some other character for that of Atalanta.—Dr. Farmer is of opinion, that her *better part* is her *wit,* that is, the *swiftness of her mind;* and Mr. Malone observes, that a passage in Marston's *Insatiate Countesse* might lead us to suppose that the *better part* of Atalanta was her *lips.* Mr. Tollet remarks, that "perhaps the poet means her beauty and graceful elegance of shape, which he would prefer to her swiftness;" but he afterwards asks, whether *Atalanta's better part* may not mean "her virtue or virgin chastity."

The explication of Mr. Tollet is the only one, which affords any suitable sense to this disputed expression; yet I am persuaded that the genuine spirit of the image is yet perfectly unknown. The reader of taste, who is ardent in the study of our Poet, will, I hope, be considerably gratified when I shall have placed before him the whole passage with a new vein of illustration; nor will he, I trust, be of opinion that I have been too laboured or minute in the discussion of a principle refers not only to the present instance, but may be frequently applied with singular success in the elucidation of Shakspeare. It is well known and acknowledged, that our old Poets derived many of their allusions and descriptions from *pictures and representations in Tapestry,* which were then equally familiar to themselves and to their readers.

We must not therefore be astonished if their imagery should sometimes be deficient in that *abstraction of sentiment,* which we have been so accustomed to admire in the delineations of other Poets; nor is it difficult to imagine, that their colourings would be often marked by some peculiar allusions, which can now only be understood by conceiving, that the works of the Artist were still present to the mind of the Poet, and that the operations of the fancy were controuled by the impressions of the eye. This observation, which is rigorously applicable to our ancient bards, *Chaucer, Gower,* and *Lydgate,* may be extended likewise with considerable truth to the Poets of succeeding times, and will afford the intelligent critic a very important principle in illustrating the writers of the sixteenth century. It has been remarked by our Commentators, that Shakspeare has himself borrowed many of his images from *prints—statues—paintings—* and *exhibitions in tapestry;* and we may observe, that some allusions of this sort are to be found in the play before us, and especially in those places which describe the beauties of Rosalind. There was however another reason why this peculiar vein of allusion should naturally abound in *dramatic* compositions, as the stage was not only covered with *arras* or *tapestry hangings,* but when that arras was faded or decayed, they were accustomed to adorn it (according to the expression of Jonson) with "fresh *pictures.*" I have not the smallest doubt that but this practice suggested to Shakspeare the idea in Hamlet of presenting before the Queen the portraits of her two husbands:

> Look here upon this picture and on this,
> The counterfeit presentment of two brothers.

It is evident (as the Commentators have remarked) from the following words, "A station like the herald Mercury;" that these pictures, which are now produced on the stage as miniatures, were meant as full lengths, "being part of the furniture of the Queen's closet;" and that the introduction of these miniatures is a modern innovation. Mr. Malone is of opinion, that when tragedies were acted, the stage was hung with black; and I am inclined to think in general that the stage was often furnished with those pictures, which were somewhat suitable to the genius of the performance. Let me venture likewise to conjecture, that possibly the subject of these pictures, and the representations on these hangings, might be of such a nature as to supply the place of that *dumb shew* which Mr. Warton is surprised to find discontinued in the plays of Shakspeare, and for the absence of which he professes himself unable to account. Let us now examine whether the present passage may not be illustrated by a principle which has been allowed universally to operate on our ancient Poets; and which has been proved in various instances to have acted on the imagination of Shakspeare. I have always been firmly persuaded, that the *imagery,* which our Poet has selected to discriminate the more prominent perfections of *Helen, Cleopatra, Atalanta,* and *Lucretia,* was not derived from the abstract consideration of their general qualities; but was caught from those *peculiar traits* of beauty and character, which are impressed on the mind of him who contemplates their portraits. It is well known, that these celebrated heroines of romance were in the days of our Poet the favourite subjects of popular representation, and were alike visible in the coarse hangings of the poor and the magnificent arras of the rich.—In the portraits of *Helen,* whether they were produced by the skilful artist, or his ruder imitator, though her face would certainly be delineated as eminently beautiful, yet she appears not to have been adorned with any of those charms which are allied to *modesty;* and we accordingly find that she was generally depicted with a loose and insidious countenance, which but too manifestly betrayed the inward wantonness and perfidy of her heart. The following quotation from Don Quixote is singularly in point, as it will serve to shew us how *universally* the same expressions of faithless beauty were considered as characteristic of the portraits of Helen— "He was lodged in a low chamber, to which certaine olde worne curtaines of painted serge served in lieu of tapistry hangings, as commonly they use in country villages. In one of the pieces might be seene painted by a bungling and unskilful hand, the rape of Helen, at what time her fond-hardy ghest stole her from Menelaus. In another was the history of Dido and Æneas; shee on an high turret, with a sheet making signe unto her fugitive ghest, who on the sea, carried in a ship, was running away from her. Don Quixote observed in these two stories, that Helen seemed not to be discontented with her rape; for so much as she *leered and smiled underhand;* whereas beauteous Dido seemed to trickle down teares from her eyes as big as walnuts." (Shelton's Don Quixote, Part II. p. 480.)

With respect to the *Majesty of Cleopatra,* it may be observed, that this notion is not derived from Classical authority, but from the more popular storehouse of legend and romance: for though indeed many instances of her *Majestic* appearance and conduct might be collected from the former source, yet I think that we should not from thence be led to speak familiarly of that quality, as the most prominent and distinguished part of her character. When our Poet had afterwards occasion in his *Antony and Cleopatra* to delineate her portrait at full length from a Classical original, we do not find that the idea of her *Majesty is* particularly inculcated. I infer therefore that the *familiarity* of this image was impressed both on the Poet and his reader from pictures and representations in tapestry, which were the lively and faithful mirrors of popular romances.— *Atalanta,* we know, was considered likewise by our antient Poets as a celebrated beauty; and we may be assured therefore that her portraits were every where to be found. From the passage in Pliny quoted by Mr. Tollet, we learn that there were two pictures at Lanuvium placed by each other of Helen and Atalanta, which were both painted by the same artist, and represented as eminently beautiful; though the charms of the latter were distinguished from those of the former by the appearance of a *virgin* modesty. Whether among the painters of after ages, it was customary thus to contrast the dissimilar beauties of Helen and Atalanta, I cannot determine: we know however that such contrasts are familiar to the artists of every period, and the quotation which I have above produced from Don Quixote, may shew us, that in the most rude and imperfect pieces it was not unusual to imitate the refinements of more exquisite performances. Since the story of *Atalanta* represents that heroine as possessed of singular beauty, zealous to preserve her virginity even with the death of her lovers, and accomplishing her purposes by extraordinary swiftness in running, we may be assured that the skill of the artist would be employed in displaying the most perfect expressions of *virgin purity,* and in delineating the *fine proportions and elegant symmetry of her person.—* "*Lucretia*" (we know) "was the grand example of conjugal fidelity throughout the Gothic ages;" and it is this spirit of unshaken chastity, which is here celebrated under the title of *modesty.* The epithet *sad* is but ill calculated to represent the abstract notion of *conjugal virtue,* and we may be assured therefore that it was forced upon the mind of our Poet from a very different impression. I am aware however that *sad* may signify in certain cases (as Dr. Johnson supposes it in the present) *grave* or *solemn;* yet even in this sense the idea of something *gloomy* or *unengaging* is, I believe, generally understood; and it is *certain* that the epithet cannot with any propriety be applied to the abstract notion of that species of beauty, in which the charms of nature are rendered still more attractive by the cheerful though composed graces of a genuine modesty. I am persuaded that the meaning of *sad* in this passage is *sorrowful* or *lamenting,* and that it was impressed on the imagination of our bard by the melancholy appearance which *Lucretia* commonly bore in her portraits and representations. Sir Philip Sidney in his *Defence of Poesie* talks of "the constant *though* LAMENTING *looke of Lucretia,"* as she is exhibited in *paintings;* and in our Author's *Rape of Lucrece* the epithet *sad* frequently occurs in the same sense, and is often applied to LUCRETIA herself in the several mournful occasions of her affecting story. In the following lines, which are taken from the above poem, we find the *sadness* of her countenance combined with the graces of her *modesty:*

> "Her pity-pleading eyes are *sadly* fix'd
> In the remorseless wrinkles of his face;
> Her *modest* eloquence with sighs is mix'd,
> Which to her oratory adds more *grace.*"

> (Page 119 [561–4].)

—Let us suppose therefore that the portraits of these celebrated beauties, *Helen—Cleopatra—Atalanta—*and *Lucretia,* were delineated as I have above described—that in the days of Shakspeare they continued to be the favourite subjects of popular representation, and that consequently they were familiarly impressed on the mind of the Poet and on the memory of his audience. Let us now investigate what the bard, or the lover, under the influence of this impression, would select as the *better parts* of these celebrated heroines, which he might wish to be transferred to his own mistress as the perfect model of female excellence. In contemplating the portrait of *Helen,* he is attracted only by those charms which are at once the most distinguished, and at the same time are the least employed in expressing the feelings of the heart. He wishes therefore for that rich bloom of beauty, which glowed upon her *cheek,* but he rejects those lineaments of her countenance which betrayed the loose inconstancy of her mind—the insidious smile and the wanton brilliancy of her eye. Impressed with the effect, he passes instantly to the cause. He is enamoured with the *better part* of the beauty of *Helen;* but he is shocked at the depravity of that *heart,* which was too manifestly exhibited by the worse. To convince the intelligent reader, that *cheek is* not applied *to beauty in general;* but that it is here used in its appropriate and original sense, we shall produce a very curious passage from one of our Author's Sonnets, by which it will appear that the portraits of Helen were distinguished by the consummate beauty which was displayed upon *her cheek.*

> Describe Adonis, and the ** counterfeit* (*i.e. *picture*)
> Is poorly imitated after you;
> On Helen's *cheek* all art of beauty set,
> And you in Grecian tires are *painted* new.
>
> (Sonnet 53.)

—In viewing the *portrait* of Cleopatra, we should all naturally agree in admiring the stately air and majestic appearance of her person; though in the bare contemplation of her *character,* we should not have equally concurred in speaking familiarly of her majesty as the most eminent and distinguished of her qualities.—In surveying the portrait of *Atalanta,* and in reflecting on the character which it displayed, the lover would not find it difficult to select the *better part* both of her mind and of her form, which he might wish to be transfused into the composition of his mistress. He would not be desirous of that perfection in her person, which contributed nothing to the gratification of his passion, and he would reject that principle of her soul which was adverse to the object of his wishes. He would be enamoured with the fine proportions and elegant symmetry of her limbs; though his passion would find but little reason to be delighted with the quality of *swiftness,* with which that symmetry was connected.—He would be captivated with the blushing charms of unsullied virginity; but he would abhor that unfeeling coldness, which resisted the impulse of love; and that unnatural cruelty which rejoiced in the murder of her lovers.—The Poet lastly wishes for the Modesty of the *sad Lucretia*—that firm and deep-rooted principle of female chastity, which is so visibly depicted in the *sadness* of her countenance lamenting for its involuntary loss; and which has rendered her through all ages the pride and pattern of conjugal fidelity.—Such then are the wishes of the lover in the formation of his mistress, that the *ripe* and *brilliant beauties* of *Helen* should be united to the *elegant symmetry* and *virgin graces* of *Atalanta;* and that this union of charms should be still dignified and ennobled by the *majestic mien* of *Cleopatra* and the *matron modesty* of *Lucretia.*

Finally; it is extremely observable, and will indeed considerably confirm the diligent reader of our Poet in the truth of this new interpretation, that *allusions to Pictures,* or at least *terms,* which are on all hands acknowledged to be *derived from Painting,* are found to accompany the passage which is the subject of our present commentary:

> But upon the fairest boughs,
> Or at every sentence' end,
> Will I Rosalinda write;
> Teaching all that read, to know
> The quintessence of every sprite
> Heaven would in *little* show.
> Therefore Heaven nature charg'd
>   That one body should be fill'd
> With all graces wide enlarg'd:
>   Nature presently distill'd
> Helen's cheek, but not her heart;
>   Cleopatra's Majesty;
> Atalanta's better part;
>   Sad Lucretia's Modesty.
> Thus Rosalind of many parts
>   By heavenly synod was devis'd;
> Of many faces, eyes, and hearts,
>   To have the *touches* dearest priz'd.

I will conclude this note by observing likewise what our Commentators appear not to have considered, that our Poet, in forming this model of female excellence, has not shewn himself forgetful of that description which he had before given us of Rosalind. She is represented as *more than common tall,* and on that account best qualified to assume the dress and appearance of a man.

> Were it not better,
> Because that I am more than common tall,
> That I did suit me all points like a man?
> A gallant curtle-ax upon my thigh,
> A boar-spear in my hand. (141 [I. iii. 116].)

The Poet therefore might very properly invest her with the majestic air of Cleopatra; and that figure, which was so well adapted to become the curtle-ax and the boar-spear, would naturally suggest to his recollection the manly though elegant appearance of Atalanta attired for the exercise of the course, or furnished with the dress and implements of the chase: We may observe, that in our ancient poets the huntress, and the *swift-footed Atalanta,* seem to have been confounded. As I consider the subject of this note to be intimately connected with a theory, which I propose afterwards to unfold, I have not hesitated to be thus minute and circumstantial in the explanation of this passage, that the reader might be at once possessed with a general notion of a species of *indirect* allusion, which occurs perpetually in our ancient poets, and which, when duly understood, will afford us a new and uniform light in discovering the peculiar spirit of their descriptions, and the *associating* principle of their imagery. In the *present* instance it will not, I trust, be objected, that I have imposed a meaning on the passage, which is too ample both for the words which convey it, and the occasion which I have imagined to suggest it. The reader of taste will not fail to remember, that the vigorous language of the poet will express concisely what he at once conceives richly; while the humble critic must be contented to *illustrate* by a long, a laboured, and a feeble commentary.

179 [III. ii. 290]. "Not so; but *I answer you right painted cloth.*"] This phraseology, which Mr. Malone calls *singular,* is very common in Shakspeare. I am astonished that our commentators did not recollect a very pointed example in the preceding scene, "Nay but the devil take mocking; *speak sad brow and true* maid." So in Othello (523 [II. iii. 281]) "Drunk? and *speak parrot?* and squabble?" In the *Lover's Complaint* we have

> "When he most burn'd in heart-wish'd luxury,
> He *preach'd pure maid,* and prais'd cold chastity."
>
> Vol. x. p. 370 [314–15]

184 [III. ii. 439]. "I drave my suitor from his mad humour of love, to a *living* humour of madness."] "Dr. Johnson" (says Mr. Malone) "proposes to read—from his mad humour of love, to a *loving* humour of madness; that is, from a *madness* that was *love,* to a love that was *madness.* Dr. Farmer would

read—to a humour of *loving* madness." Mr. Malone himself imagines that a LIVING *humour of madness* is, "in our author's licentious language, a humour of *living madness,* a mad humour that operates on *the mode of living; or,* in other words, and more accurately, a *mad humour of life.*" Perhaps the following line from Othello may throw light on this passage.

> *Oth.* Give me a *living* reason that she's disloyal.
>
> (Act 3. S. iii. p. 560 [III. iii. 409].)

That is, give me a *direct, absolute,* and *unequivocal* proof. Why then may not the *living* humour of madness mean a *confirmed, absolute,* and *direct* state of madness? This signification is easily deduced from the sense which the original word bears in the phrases of "Done or expressed to the *life*"—ad *vivum* expressum.

185 [Ill. iii. 3]. "Doth my simple *feature* content you?"] *Feature* appears to have three senses. "1st. The cast and make of the face. 2d. Beauty in general. 3d. The whole turn of the body." Out of innumerable instances take the following, which I have chosen as the most unequivocal:

John says to Hubert, referring to what he before called his "abhorr'd *aspect.*"

> 1. "Forgive the comment that my passion made
>   Upon thy *feature.*" (King John, 539 [IV. ii. 63].)

> 2. "Her grace, gesture, and beautie liked them all extremely, and made them account Don Fernando to be a man of little understanding, seeing he contemned such *feature.*" (Shelton's Don Quixote, part I. 300.) (See too 405.) "Puestanta *belleza* desechava." Tom. ii. p. 277. Ed. Bowles.

> 3. "I that am curtail'd of this fair proportion,
>   Cheated of *feature* by dissembling nature,
>   Deform'd, unfinish'd." (Rich. III. 455 [I. i. 18].)

[In this passage Feature signifies *the full & compleat* form. From the same sense however of *figure* or *shape* in general, it is applied in a signification apparently opposite, to denote the *bare outlines* or the *skeleton* of the figure. *Milton,* referring to the "meager *Shadow*",—DEATH, says;

"So sensed the grim FEATURE and upturn'd
His nostrils wide into the murky air."

(Paradise Lost. 10. v. 279.)

The following lines from Burton's *Anatomy of Melancholy* will illustrate the passage from Milton—*Burton,* explaining the Catts belonging to the frontispiece of his book, begins thus.

"Old Democritus under a tree,
Sittes on a stone with booke on knee,
About him hang there many FEATURES,
Of Cattes, Dogges and such like creatures,
Of which he makes *Anatomy* etc. etc."]

I cannot help observing, that in two instances quoted by Mr. Malone, as well as in the passage of Shakspeare, feature is joined with *content.*

"I see then, artless *feature* can *content.*"

(Daniel's Cleopatra, 1594.)

"My *feature* is not to *content* her sight."

(*Spanish Tragedy*)

This is *not* merely accidental. *Content* has a peculiar and appropriate sense, and it marks the *gratification* which is derived from the attractions of *person* or of *sex. Rosalind,* as it appears, alludes to this sense in her address to *Silvius.* "I will *content* you, if what pleases you *contents* you, and you shall be married to-morrow." (page 221 [V. ii. 126].) That is, I will *content* you by marrying you to a woman whose *beauty contents* you. In *Lodge's Euphues,* from which this play is derived, we have "able to *content* the eye with *beauty.*"—*Horatio* says to *Belimperia* in the *Spanish Tragedy,* Act ii. (p. 145.)

"Now, madam, since by favour of your love,
Our hidden smoak is turn'd to open flame,
And that with looks *and words we* feed our thoughts,
(Two chief *contents*) where more cannot be had."

We have the following passage likewise in *Romeo and Juliet.* (Act I. S. 3 [I-iii. 82–5].)

"Read o'er the volume of young Paris' face,
And find delight writ there with beauty's pen;
Examine every married lineament,
And see how one another lends *content.*"

In the *Widow's Tears,* Eudora deliberating about taking a *husband,* says,

"What might a wise widow resolve upon this point now?
Contentment is the end of all worldly beings."

(Old Plays, 6. p. 163.)

In the same play, *Tharsalio* (about whom she is deliberating) requests of her "some measure of favour from" her "sweet tongue," or her "sweeter lips," "or what else" (says he) "your good ladyship shall esteem more conducible to your divine *contentment.*" (Id. p. 175.)

"Let the best joys of Hymen compass her,
And her young husband, my Eugenio,
With full *content.*"

(Albumazar, Old Plays, v. 7. p. 250.)

Annabella.   "Oh, how these stol'n *contents*
        Would print a modest crimson on my cheeks,
        Had any but my heart's delight prevail'd."

('Tis pity she's a whore. Old Plays, vol. 8. p. 25.)

Bellanima.   "Why would Physander
        Cut wedlock's gordian, and, with looser eyes,
        Doat on a common wanton? What is pleasure,
        More than a lustful motion in the sense?
        The prosecution full of anxious fears,
        The end repentance. Though *content* be call'd
        The soul of action, and licentious man
        Propounds it as the reason of his life."

(Microcosmus. Old Plays, 9. p. 148.)

[Sylvia.   What is't? a noble husband: In that word,
        'A noble husband', all *content* of women
        Is wholly comprehended. He will rouse her,
        As you say, with the sun; and so pipe to her,
        As she will dance, ne'er doubt it; and hunt with her,

Upon occasion, until both be weary;
              ... A loving,
And but add to it, a gamesome bedfellow
Being the sure physician."

> (Beaumont & Fletcher. *Elder Brother.* A. I.
> S. 1. vol. 2 pag. 112. last Edit.)

"She studies to undo the court, to plant here
The enemy to our age, Chastity.
She is the first that e'er balk'd a close arbour,
And the sweet *contents* within."

> (*The Humorous Lieutenant.* A. 4. S. I. Last
> Ed. of Beaumont & F. v.3. p. 66.)

Calis, in the address *to Venus* at her oracle in Paphos, says,

"Oh, fair sweet goddess, queen of loves,
Soft and gentle as thy doves,
Humble ey'd, and ever ruling
Those poor hearts, their loves pursuing!
Oh, thou mother of delights,
Crowner of all happy nights,
Star of dear *content* and pleasure,
Of mutual loves the endless treasure!"

> (The *Mad Lover.* A. 5. S. I. Last Edit. of Beaumont &
> F. v. 3. pag. 288. See too pag. 299.)

Estifania. "The most kind man, and the ablest also
To give a wife *content*! He's sound as old wine,
And to his soundness rises on the palate;
And there's the man!"

> (*Rule a Wife & have a Wife*—Act 2. See last Ed.
> Of Beaumont & F. vol. 3. pag. 444.)

Some of these passages are expressed with great delicacy, while others border upon grossness. The term *Content is* sometimes applied in a very coarse manner indeed, as may be seen by the use of it in John Florio under *Carnafau,* and the reader will wonder, that the term should ever have been applied, as we have seen it under so decorous a form, when it had been once stained with an application of this sort. In Torriano it is printed *Carna-fan,* which is right, who omits the part relating to *Content.* In Florio we hardly know, whether the *foramen* "of CONTENT," about which he speaks, in quo infantes vel liberi gignuntur means the Foramen delectationis or the Foramen *Continens.*]

To "live in sweet *contentment* with a wife," occurs in the play of *Grim, the Collier of Croydon.* (Old Plays, II. p. 196.) and in the *Parson's Wedding* (1664) by *Killigrew,* we have, "I would do as little to give mine *content* as any she in town." The traces of this sense appear in the *Paradise Lost*; and there is one very singular passage, which derives all its grace and delicacy from the latent allusion to this *peculiar* signification. It is from hence that the heavenly vision becomes, as it were, brighten'd with a smile by anticipating the object to which the thoughts of Adam were directed, and by rejoicing at the capacity of happiness, which was destined for the nature of man. Adam thus bewails his condition before the creation of Eve.

> "In solitude
> What happiness, who can enjoy alone,
> Or all enjoying, what CONTENTMENT find?
> Thus I presumptuous; and the vision bright,
> As with a *smile more brighten'd,* thus reply'd."
> (B. 8. v. 364. &c. See B. 10. v. 973.)

187 [III. iii. 39]. "*Aud.* I am not a slut, tho' I thank the Gods I am *foul.*"] Sir Thomas Hanmer understands by *foul, coy* or *frowning.* Mr. Tyrwhitt thinks that *foul* is the rustic pronunciation for *full;* and adds (as it appears) with great gravity, that Audrey "was more likely to *thank the Gods* for a belly-full, than for her being *coy* or *frowning.*" Mr. Malone confirms Mr. Tyrwhitt's conjecture. What can be more manifest than that the humour of the passage (such as it is) consists in the equivocal sense of *foul,* which in our poet's time not only signified what it does at present, but meant likewise *plain* or *homely*? It is frequently used in the latter signification in this play: "*Foul* is most *foul,* being *foul* to be a scoffer." (197 [III. v. 62].) That is, says Dr. Johnson, "the ugly seem most ugly, when, though ugly, they are scoffers."

193 [III. iv. 55]. "*Clor.* If you will see a *pageant* truly play'd,
> Between the pale complexion of true love
> And the red glow of scorn and proud disdain,
> Go hence a little, and I shall conduct you,
> If you will mark it."]

This *pageant* of *love* seems to have been impressed on the mind of our poet. So in the *Midsummer Night's Dream, Puck* says to *Oberon*:

> "Captain of our fairy band,
> Helena is here at hand;
> And the youth mistook by me,
> Pleading for a *lover's* fee;
> Shall we their fond *pageant* see?
> Lord, what fools these mortals be!
>
> (Act 3. S. 2. p. 494. [III. ii. 110].)

[*Pageant* appears to have been a familiar term, when applied to *courtship*. *Barnet* in The *Old Couple* after hearing the *courting* dialogue between *Lady Lovet* and *Sr. Argent,* says, "What a strange kind of *Pageant* have we seen." (Old Plays 10. 488.)]

Will the speech of *Touchstone* receive any illustration from [the above lines in the *Midsummer Night's Dream*?] "We, that are true lovers, run into strange capers; but as all is mortal in nature, so is all nature in love *mortal* in folly." (152 [II. iv. 55].) Perhaps it means, *all nature*—even we, the superior intelligences of nature, when in *love,* are equal in folly to the ordinary race of *mortals.*

195 [III. v. 37]. "What though you have *mo* beauty,
(As, by my faith, I see no more in you
Than without candle may go dark to bed,)
Must you be therefore proud and pitiless?"]

The old copy reads *no,* which Mr. Malone has changed into *mo.* This emendation is extremely inelegant, and totally opposite to our author's meaning. The spirit of the passage is well explained by *Mr. Capell.* The rejection of the negative makes "the poet" (says he) "a very bad reasoner in the line that comes next to this sentence, and guilty of self-contradiction in several others"—by "robbing him of a lively expression, and a pleasantry truly comick; for, as the sentence stands in the old copy, the consequence that should have been from her *beauty,* he draws from her *no beauty,* and extorts a smile by defeating your expectation. This *no beauty* of Phoebe's is the burden of all Rosalind's speeches from hence to her exit." Mr. Tollet likewise considers the old reading "as a humourous way of expressing her little share of beauty," though the instance which he produces is foreign to the purpose. Take an example in point from this very play. "Truly, young gentlemen, *though* there was *no* great matter in the ditty, yet the note was very *un*tuneable." (223 [v. iii. 36].) So the nurse in *Romeo and Juliet,* p. 86 [II. v. 40]. "Romeo! no, not he; though his face be better than any man's, yet his leg excels all men's; and for a hand, and a foot, and a body,—*though* they be not to be talk'd on, yet they are past compare."

206 [IV. i. 194]. "*Ros.* If you break one jot of your promise, or come one minute behind your hour, I will think you the most *pathetical* break-promise, and the most hollow lover."] Mr. Steevens observes, that the epithet occurs again in *Love's Labour lost,* and with as little apparent meaning;—"most *pathetical* nit." By *pathetical* break-promise, Mr. Malone thinks is meant a lover whose falsehood would most *deeply affect* his mistress. *Pathetical,* in its first sense, means *full of* PASSION and SENTIMENT. In a ludicrous sense, *a pathetical break-promise* is a *whining, canting, promise-breaking swain.* Our poet, perhaps, caught this word from the novel, to which he is indebted for his play. The novelist is speaking of *Phoebe,* and *Silvius,* or *Montanus.* "But she measuring all his passions with a coye disdaine, and triumphing in the poore Shepheardes *patheticall* humours, &c." (*Lodge's Euphues.*) *Pathetical nit,* in *Love's Labour lost,* is spoken by *Costard* of *Armado's* page, and means *a little creature full of life, spirit,* and *wit.*

> "And his page o't'other side, that handful of wit!
> Ah! heavens, it is a most *pathetical nit!*"
>
> (Act 4. S. I [IV. i. 149].)

Armado himself applies this word to the *lively* sayings of his page, "Sweet invocation of a child! most pretty, and *pathetical*" (Act I. S. 2 [I. ii. 102].)

In the *Widows Tears* we have, "These are strange occurrents, brother; but pretty and *pathetical.*" (Old Plays, v. 6. p. 181.)

In a quotation produced by Mr. Malone on another occasion, we have the title of Nashe's celebrated pamphlet, as it appeared in the first edition. "Pierce Pennilesse his supplication to the Divell, describing the over-spreading of vice and suppression of vertue. Pleasantly interlaced with variable delights, and *pathetically* intermix 'with conceipted reproofes.'" (Malone's Hist. of the Stage, p. 133.)

[In Burton (sic) *Anatomy of Melancholy* we have "At *Abdera* in *Thrace* (*Andromeda* one of *Euripides* Tragedies being played) the spectators were so much moued with the object, and those PATHETICALL loue speeches of *Perseus* amongst the rest, O, *Cupido, prince of God and men,* etc["]—Again "Still . . . they were so possessed all with that rapture, and thought of that PATHETICALL loue speech." (Pag. 490. 4th Edit. 1632.) In another place we have "Lucian in that PATHETICAL Loue passage or pleasant description of Jupiter's stealing of Europa." (Pag. 540.)]

219 [V. ii. 58]. "*Ros.* Know of me then (for now I speak to some purpose), that I know you are a gentleman of good conceit: I speak not this, that you should bear a good opinion of my knowledge, insomuch I say, I know you are."] This thought we find in Hamlet.

"*Osrick. You* are not ignorant of what excellence Laertes is.—

Hamlet. I dare not confess that, lest I should compare with him in excellence; but, to know a man well, were to know himself."

221–2 [V. iii. 4]. "I hope it is no dishonest desire, to desire to be a *woman of the world.*"] "To *go to the world* (says Mr. Steevens) is to be married." So, in *Much ado about nothing:* "Thus (says Beatrice) every one *goes to the world,* but I." The phrase again occurs in *All's well that ends well* (372 [I. iii. 19].) "But, if I may have your ladyship's good-will *to go to the world.*" To these instances, which our commentators have noticed, add the following from John Florio's *Second Frutes,* p. 29.

> P. Why? is it so great a sinne?
> A. Yea Sir, to visite women.
> P. Yea, *worldly women.* Si le donne del mondo.
> A. Be not all *women of the world*? Tutte le donne, non sono del mondo.
> P. Yes, Sir, but yet not all *worldly.* Signor si, ma non tutte mondane.

222 [V. iii. 17]. "It was a lover, and his lass,
> With a hey, and a ho, and a hey nonino,
> That o'er the green corn-field did pass
> In the spring time, the only pretty *rank* time,
> When birds do sing, hey ding a ding, ding;
> Sweet lovers love the spring.

> II
> "Between the acres of the rye,
> With a hey, &c.
> These pretty country folks would lie,
> In spring time, &c."

The old copy reads *rang* time. Dr. Johnson "frolicks in conjecture," and reads *rank*. Mr. Pope reads *spring,* and Mr. Steevens proposes *ring* time, that is, the aptest time for *marriage.* I fear that the latter reading does not perfectly coincide with the spirit of the context. Mr. Malone imagines that the passage does not deserve much consideration; though I cannot discover what "exquisite reason" he can have for thus devoting it to neglect and obscurity.—Why may not *rang* time be written for *range* time, and the *only pretty range time* will then signify the only *pleasant* time for *straying* or *ranging* about?

There is little reason to doubt the truth of this explanation. The spelling of the words is not to be regarded in our ancient writers. The term *ranging* is particularly applied to *archery*; and from thence it is transferred to the present signification. (See *Evans' Old Ballads*, vol. I. *passim*).

(London, 1794): 9–54.

THE WORKS OF WILLIAM SHAKESPEARE
J. Payne Collier
1842

INTRODUCTION

"As You like It" is not only founded upon, but in some points very closely copied from, a novel by Thomas Lodge, under the title of "Rosalynde: Euphues Golden Legacie," which was originally printed in 4to, 1590, a second time in 1592, and a third edition came out in 1598. We have no intelligence of any re-impression of it between 1592 and 1598. This third edition perhaps appeared early in 1598; and we are disposed to think, that the re-publication of so popular a work directed Shakespeare's attention to it. If so, "As You Like It" may have been written in the summer of 1598, and first acted in the winter of the same, or in the spring of the following year.

The only entry in the registers of the Stationers' Company relating to "As You Like It," is confirmatory of this supposition. It has been already referred to in the "Introduction" to "Much Ado about Nothing" (vol. ii. p. 183); and it will be well to insert it here, precisely in the manner in which it stands in the original record:—

"4 August.
"As you like yt, a book. Henry the ffift, a book. Every man in his humor, a book. The Commedie of Much adoo about nothinge, a book."

Opposite this memorandum are added the words "to be staied." It will be remarked, that there is an important deficiency in the entry, as regards the purpose to which we wish to apply it:—the date of the year is not given; but Malone conjectured, and in that conjecture I have expressed concurrence, that the clerk who wrote the titles of the four plays, with the date of "4 August," did not think it necessary there to repeat the year 1600, as it was found in the memorandum immediately preceding that we have above quoted. Shakespeare's "Henry the Fifth," and "Much Ado about Nothing," were both printed in 1600, and Ben Jonson's "Every Man in his Humour" in the year following; though Gifford, in his edition of that poet's works (vol. i. p. 2), by a strange error, states, that the first impression was in 1603. The "stay," as regards "Henry the Fifth," "Every Man in his Humour," and "Much Ado about Nothing," was doubtless soon removed; for "Henry the Fifth" was entered again for publication on the 14th August; and, as has been already shown (vol. ii. p. 183), Wise and Aspley took the same course with "Much Ado about Nothing" on the 23rd August. There is no known edition of "As You Like It" prior to its appearance in the folio of 1623, (where it is divided into Scenes, as well as Acts) and we may possibly assume that the "stay" was not, for some unexplained and uncertain reason, removed as to that comedy.

Malone relied upon a piece of internal evidence, which, if examined, seems to be of no value in settling the question when "As You Like It" was first written. The following words are put into the mouth of Rosalind:—"I weep for nothing, like Diana in the fountain" (A. iv. sc. 1), which Malone supposed to refer to an alabaster figure of Diana on the east of Cheapside, which, according to Stowe's "Survey of London," was set up in 1598, and was in decay in 1603. This figure of Diana did not "weep;" for Stowe expressly states that the water came "prilling from her naked breast." Therefore, this passage proves nothing as far as respects the date of "As You Like It." Shakespeare probably intended to make no allusion to any particular fountain.

It is not to be forgotten, in deciding upon the probable date of "As You Like It," that Meres makes no mention of it in his *Palladis Tamia,* 1598; and as it was entered at Stationers' Hall on the 4th August [1600], we may conclude that it was written and acted in that interval. In A. iii. sc. 5. a line from the first Sestiad of Marlowe's "Hero and Leander" is quoted; and as that poem was first printed in 1598, "As You Like It" may not have been written until after it appeared.

There is no doubt that Lodge, when composing his "Rosalynde: Euphues Golden Legacie," which he did, as he informs us, while on a voyage with Captain Clarke "to the islands of Terceras and the Canaries," had either "The Coke's Tale of Gamelyn" (falsely attributed to Chaucer, as Tyrwhitt contends in his Introd. to the Cant. Tales, I. clxxxiii. Edit. 1830.) strongly in his recollection, or, which does not seem very probable in such a situation, with a manuscript of it actually before him. It was not printed until more than a century afterwards. According to Farmer, Shakespeare looked no farther than Lodge's novel, which he followed in "As You Like It" quite as closely as he did Greene's "Pandosto" in the "Winter's Tale." There are one or two coincidences of expression between "As You Like It" and "The Coke's Tale of Gamelyn," but not perhaps more than might be accidental, and the opinion of Farmer appears to be sufficiently borne out. Lodge's "Rosalynde" has been recently printed as part of "Shakespeare's Library," and it will be easy, therefore, for the reader to trace the particular resemblances between it and "As You Like It."

In his Lectures in 1818, Coleridge eloquently and justly praised the pastoral beauty and simplicity of "As You Like It;" but he did not attempt to compare it with Lodge's "Rosalynde," where the descriptions of persons and of scenery are comparatively forced and artificial: —"Shakespeare," said Coleridge, "never gives a description of rustic scenery merely for its own sake, or to show how well he can paint natural objects: he is never tedious or elaborate, but while he now and then displays marvellous accuracy and minuteness of knowledge, he usually only touches upon the larger features and broader characteristics, leaving the fillings up to the imagination. Thus in 'As You Like It' he describes an oak of many centuries growth in a single line:—

'Under an oak whose antique root peeps out.'

Other and inferior writers would have dwelt on this description, and worked it out with all the pettiness and impertinence of detail. In Shakespeare the 'antique root' furnishes the whole picture."

These expressions are copied from notes made at the time; and they partially, though imperfectly, supply an obvious deficiency of general criticism in vol. ii. p. 115. of Coleridge's "Literary Remains."

Adam Spencer is a character in "The Coke's Tale of Gamelyn," and in Lodge's "Rosalynde;" and a great additional interest attaches to it, because it is supposed, with some appearance of truth, that the part was originally sustained by Shakespeare himself. We have this statement on the authority of Oldys's MSS.: he is said to have derived it, intermediately of course, from Gilbert Shakespeare, who survived the Restoration, and who had a faint recollection of having seen his brother William "in one of his own comedies, wherein, being to personate a decrepit old man, he wore a long beard, and appeared so weak and drooping, and unable to walk, that he was forced to be supported and carried by another person to a table, at which he was seated among some company, who were eating, and one of them sung a song." This description very exactly tallies with "As You Like It," A. ii. sc. 7.

Shakespeare found no prototypes in Lodge, nor in any other work yet discovered, for the characters of Jaques, Touchstone, and Audrey. On the admirable manner in which he has made them part of the staple of his story, and on the importance of these additions, it is needless to enlarge. It is rather singular, that Shakespeare should have introduced two characters of the name of Jaques into the same play; but in the old impressions, Jaques de Bois, in the prefixes to his speeches, is merely called the "Second Brother."

(London: 1842) Vol. 3: 3–5.

SHAKESPEARE COMMENTARIES
Dr. G. G. Gervinus
1863

The Pastoral comedy *As You Like It* has always extraordinarily pleased all German interpreters; it is only a pity that their interpretations have not had a similar fate. Tieck who called it Shakespeare's most playful comedy, maintained that the poet had in this play trifled most capriciously with time and place, that in the development and combination he had ridiculed and frivolously avoided rules which he had usually observed, and that he had even sacrificed, as in parody of himself, the truth of motive and the fundamental basis of composition, that he might write a truly free and merry comedy. According to this view, it would seem that Tieck found in playfulness, in irregularity, and in capriciousness as to composition and ground of action, the qualification of a "true" comedy! This Ulrici took up, and carried it out with respect to the impulses both of characters and actions. In the whole piece, he says, each acts or not, as he pleases; every character according to his humour indulges his inclinations to good and evil, as it occurs to him; the contingencies are not so much outward and objective, as inward and subjective, the humour and caprice of persons in their influence one upon another is that from which the whole action proceeds, and in which at the same time the fantastical character of the piece consists. But in truth this capriciousness and neglect of rules on the part of the poet or his characters, does not exist at all in this piece. According, to the designs of character in Frederick, Oliver, and the rest, neither the dethronement of the banished Duke is to be called whimsically capricious, as is here maintained, nor is the pursuit of Orlando groundless, nor his design to wrestle with Charles accidental, nor the turning, and winding up of the whole plot to be considered fantastical. What further rules the poet should have frivolously avoided, or disregarded, Delius has already asked with wonder and surprise, without being able to reply. And that time and place are here more capriciously shifted, than in other pieces, in which Shakespeare gave access to the marvelous, is so little the case, that far rather among all dramas of this kind, this piece evidently makes the most timid use of the fanciful.

All that may have furnished a cause for these views and for these observations on our present comedy is limited to the following. We may regard this piece as probably intended for a masque, a style of drama in which the poet, whether by the introduction of wonderful machinery or by the display of all kinds of pageantry, permitted himself somewhat more license than elsewhere, but in no wise a license which interfered with the truth of his grounds for action or the just unravelling of his plot. Thus we are here transported to a romantic Arcadia, into which the forest of Arden is metamorphosed. Shakespeare met with this in the tale which furnished him with the material for his play; lions were from thence brought to France, and our poet added serpents and palm-trees. If here with respect to the locality a slightly fanciful feature is introduced, this is also the case with respect to the human circumstances in Rosalind's pretence (and this Shakespeare likewise found in the source from which he drew), of having learned witchcraft from an uncle. But this feature also touches so skilfully on the limits of ordinary reality, that clever management in the performance might completely efface it; nothing prevents the piece from being thus understood, that Orlando, reminded of Oliver, recognized the beautiful Ganymede after his swoon, and let him only carry on his play that he might not mar his mirth; the subtleness of the play will be extraordinarily increased, if this is so taken in the performance. In this manner, our comedy only borders on the limits of the fantastical. And the justification of this lies in the style itself; whether it be that the poet composed the work as a masque, or as a pastoral drama, or as a piece uniting the two. Shakespeare borrowed the whole plan of the piece from a pastoral romance by Thomas Lodge, (Rosalynde; Euphues golden Legacy, 1590 and later) and he has evidently wished to form from it a pastoral play. The fanciful and ideal belonged to this species of poem, which here nevertheless lies rather in the general colouring than in single lines; the operatic style was peculiar to plays of this kind; many songs are therefore introduced, which in the performance very essentially contribute to produce the frame of mind in which this comedy should be received. A play like that which Rosalind makes Hymen perform, belongs to the characteristic style either of the pastoral or the masque. The truly pastoral scene between Silvius and Phœbe is called a pageant; rightly performed, it would stand out in the general description of rural and forest life in our drama, as a play within the play, composed in a still more idealistic style than the real pastoral piece; acted by the best players, in all the unadorned simplicity of representation, it ought to be exhibited with such an odour of refinement as to show these children of nature raised above and withdrawn from the rude and agitated world. All these peculiarities of this species of poem, place our piece certainly somewhat out of the sphere of ordinary dramas; but we shall find the composition in its own way so profound, that even in this case the fact will be confirmed, that Shakespeare involuntarily improved and elevated every new material and style which he touched with his hand. It is true that in other more realistic pieces of Shakespeare's it does not occur that scenes, as here is twice the case, (Act IV. sc. 2. and Act V. sc. 3.) are inserted merely as stop-gaps without any action, but this is characteristic of idle rural life, where nothing of more importance happens than a slaughtered deer and a song about it. It is true that here more than in Shakespeare's other pieces, there are small subordinate parts, which signify little or nothing, but even in this respect more license is necessarily avowed to comedy than to tragedy. It is true that the characters are only here and there sketched in general outline, and even in those more worked out, it is rather by words than action. But this also is justified by the kind of poem; the subject for representation settled the characters, whose general social position and qualities were here more in question than their moral characteristics; and even in the principal figures, the mental character, the intellectuality, as in *Love's Labour's Lost,* was almost more to be displayed than the power of the will and the motive for important actions. For this reason the actor will have some trouble in finding out these characters; but this done, he will be just as delighted and surprised at their inner congruity and truth, as in any other of our poet's themes. He will there perceive, that Shakespeare has not acted here otherwise than formerly, that he has in no wise parodied himself, that it may rather be considered a parody of all criticism, when our Romanticists, as in this case, would prove to us the poet's virtues by his faults.

Shakespeare met with the design of the story of this comedy in Lodge's pastoral romance; he only added the characters of the clown and of the melancholy Jaques, of William and Audrey; the remaining persons, under other names, work the threads of the action, as in Shakespeare. The style of the romance is prolix, affected, and bombastic, like all works of the kind; an exaggerated loquaciousness is the most striking characteristic of the extravagant mannerism of this narrator, as it is of all conceit-writers; Adam in the forest near starvation, and Orlando seeing the lion watching for its prey, hold long conversations. Many of the Ovid-like reminiscences and much of the mythological learning, with which the romance abounds, still adheres to Shakespeare's play, but on the whole he has completely eradicated the pastoral mannerism, and as ever, he simplifies the motives of the actions, and ennobles the actions themselves. The rude emnity between Oliver and Orlando, degenerating into acts of violence according to the romance, is properly moderated by our poet. He has set aside the unnaturalness of Celia's banishment by her father on her protest against the banishment of Rosalind. The war, by which the exiled prince regains his throne, the rescue of the ladies from robbers, with which in the romance Celia's love for Oliver is introduced, these the dramatist has omitted, that he might not disturb the peace and merry sports of his rural life by any discords. The play between Orlando and Rosalind is in the romance only a pastoral song, but to this Shakespeare has precisely joined on the continuation of the action in the last act. In all the rest, the poet follows very truly the course of the story in the novel, without much addition and omission. Even the moral of the narrative he preserved closely before him, which in the romance is declared by perpetual repetitions, and is well adapted to the nature and position of the characters. The "sweetest salve for misery," this is the drift of the "golden legacy" of the tale, "is patience, and the only medicine for want that pretious implaister of content." We must brave misfortune with equanimity and meet our destiny with resignation. Thus the two ladies, and thus Orlando, laugh at Fortune and disregard her power. All the three, or counting Oliver four, principal figures have this in common in their lot, that love is added as a new evil (it is thus viewed) to their outward misfortunes, to banishment and poverty. This also they strive to meet with the same weapon, with control and moderation, not too much evading it, nor too much desiring it, with more regard to virtue and nature, than to riches and rank, like Rosalind, when she chooses the posthumous Orlando, and Oliver the shepherdess Celia. The loving pastoral couple forms a contrast in this respect, that Silvius loves too ardently, whilst Phœbe despises love too coldly. If we concentrate this moral reflection into one idea, we shall find that it is self-mastery, equanimity, self-command in outward suffering and inward passion, whose praise is to be proclaimed. That this idea lies at the root of Shakespeare's comedy also, we should scarcely imagine at the first glance. So completely is every reflection avoided, so entirely in the lightest and freest play of action and conversation is a mere picture sketched for our contemplation.

The author of the romance of Rosalind contrasts town- and court-life with rural and pastoral life, the one as a natural source of evil and misery, which finds its natural remedy in the other. "The greatest seas," he says, "have the sorest storms, small currents are ever calm. Cares wait upon a crown. Joyfulness dwells in cottages. The highest birth has more honour, but is subject to the most bale. Griefs are incident to dignity, and sorrows haunt royal palaces." On the contrary contentment lives in the country, and we "drink there without suspicion and sleep without care, unstirred by envy. Desires mount not there above our degrees, nor our thoughts above our fortunes." Just so Shakespeare makes his Corydon sensible of the dignity of his pastoral condition, in which he lives upon his honest gains, envying no man's happiness, glad of other men's good, content with his toil. Just so he appears to let the sorrows, which arise at the court in the first and second acts, find their cure in the pastoral life of the three last acts. Just so he has imputed the cause of the disasters created there, to the vices which belong to courts and to worldly life, to the envy and hatred, which arise from covetousness and ambition, and in the same manner he has sought the remedy for the wounds there struck, in that moderation and simple contentment, to which a life of solitude invites or even compels. The first acts begin therefore like a tragedy; they exhibit the actors in a state of war, from which they subsequently escape or are driven away to the merry sports of pleasure and peace, which await them in the forest of Arden with its hunting-life and in the Shepherds' cottages on its border. Duke Frederick is called even by his daughter a man of harsh and envious mind; he appears to be perpetually actuated by gloomy fancies, by suspicion and mistrust, and to be urged on by covetousness. He has banished his brother and usurped the throne, he has robbed all the lords who have gone with him, of their property, he has regarded with hostile suspicion all honourable men, the old Rowland de Bois as well as his brave Orlando, he has surrounded himself with the dishonourable, who nevertheless, like Le Beau, are not devoted to him. Orlando's victory over the wrestler is enough to kindle his suspicion against him; once awakened it lights upon the hitherto spared Rosalind with no other ground, than because she throws his daughter into the shade, at which the father's vein of envy is roused, a passion, which he wishes the inoffensive Celia to share also. When both the friends upon this disappear at the same time with Orlando, Frederick's suspicion and covetousness now fall upon Oliver, whom he had hitherto favoured. In this eldest son of the brave Rowland de Bois, there flows the same vein of avarice and envy as in the Duke. He strives to plunder his brother of his poor inheritance, he undermines his education and gentility, he first seeks to stifle his son, and then he lays snares for his life: all from an undefined hatred of the youth, whom he is obliged to confess is full of noble device, but who for this very quality draws away the love of all his people from Oliver to himself, and on this account excites his envious jealousy. Both, the Duke and Oliver, equally forfeit the happiness which they seek, the one, the heir of his usurped dukedom, the other his lawful and unlawful possessions. And in this lies the first impulse and the material motive for their subsequent renunciation of the world; a more moral incentive to this change of mind is given to Oliver in the preservation of his life by Orlando, and to the Duke in the warning voice of a religious man, who speaks to his conscience and his fear. These are only sketches of characters, not intended to play conspicuous parts; but we see, that they are drawn by the same sure hand, which we have seen at work throughout Shakespeare's works.

The misery, which proceeds from these two covetous and ambitious men, who were not even contented in and with their prosperity, first of all affected the deposed Duke. He took flight with "a many merry men" to the forest of Arden, where they live "like the old Robin Hood of England, and fleet the time carelessly, as they did in the golden world." They spend their days in hunting, singing, and meditation. Their songs call their thoughts from ambition to nature and simple life, where no ingratitude of man, no forgotten kindness and friendship torments, but at the most the rough air and storms of winter, which they praise in smiling consideration, that they are no flatterers, but counsellors, that feelingly warn them what they are. Thus withdrawn from the dangers of the "envious court", they have learned to love exile beyond the painted pomp of the palace; endowed with patience and contentment, they have translated "the stubbornness of fortune into so quiet and so sweet a style"; and sweet, appear to them

> "the uses of adversity,
> Which, like the toad, ugly and venomous,
> Wears yet a precious jewel in his head".

In this life, they find

> "Tongues in trees, books in the running brooks,
> Sermons in stones, and good in every thing".

The fragrance of the country, the scent of the wood, the tone of solitude, in this part of the piece, have been always justly admired; colouring and scenery gently and tenderly attune the imagination of the reader; they make us understand, how hermits in such a region feel impelled to fill up the leisure and void with meditation and reflection, and to open the heart to every soft emotion; the noise of the world falls only from afar on the ear of the happy escaped ones, and the poet has carefully avoided, in any way inharmoniously to disturb this profound peace . When the starved Orlando casts in the first and last discord, by frightening the Duke and his companions at their meal, how wonderfully is this discord resolved at once by the loving gentleness, with which they meet and help the needy one!

Only the one danger does this life possess, that by its monotony it awakes in one and another, ennui, melancholy, and ill-humour. In the hunting circle round the duke, Jaques is in this condition. He shares with the Duke and his companions the propensity for drawing wisdom and philosophy from the smallest observation and consideration; he has the gift to excess, of linking reflections to the least event, and in this seclusion from the world they have assumed a touch of despondency. The melancholy which this man sucks out of every occasion, always appeared to most readers and especially to most actors, mild, human, and attractive, and it is thus represented: but it is rooted rather in a bitterness and ill-humour, which render the witty and sententious worldling far more a rude fault-finder than a contented sufferer like the rest. He is of that class of men to whom Bacon addresses this sentence: —"He who is prudent, may seek to have a desire; for he who does not strive after something with eagerness, finds everything burdensome and tedious." In his hypochondriacal mood, in his spirit of contradiction, while the remembrance of his travels and his former worldly life have left a sting behind, Jaques finds this forest-life just as foolish as that of the court which they have quitted; he carries the state of nature and peace too far, he considers the chase of the animals of the forest to be greater usurpation than that of the unlawful duke; he flees from the solitary company into still greater solitude, and likes to hide his thoughts, the fruit of his former experience and of his present leisure; then again with great eagerness he goes in quest of society and cheerful company. Wholly "compact of jars", he is blunted to all friendly habits, he is discontented with all, and even with the efforts of others to satisfy him; angry at his own birth and at his fortune, he rails against "all the first-born of Egypt", he blames the whole world, finds matter for censure in the great system of the world, and stumbles over every grain of dust in his path. Long experienced in sin, he has learned to find out the shadow-side of every age of man; he has satiated himself with the world and has not entered upon this life of retirement, furnished with the patience and contentment of the others, but from a natural passion for the contrary. If his satire is directed more to things in general and is free from bitterness towards stated individuals, this is only a result of his inactive nature, which is rather calculated for observation and reflection, than for work and action, and of his isolated position in this idyllic life so free from jars, in which moreover the poet will suffer no discord to arise. This character is entirely Shakespeare's property and addition. It furnishes a fresh instance to us of the two-sidedness of the poet's mind, with which so many proofs have made us familiar. Shakespeare does not imitate the trivial tradition of the pastoral poets, who praise the quiet life of nature in itself as a school for wisdom and contentment. He shows in the contrast between Jaques and the duke, that those who would desire enjoyment and advantage from this life, must in themselves have a natural disposition for moderation and self-mastery, they must be able to disarm misfortune, and to do without outward happiness. But this Jaques, according to the Duke, has been himself a libertine, leading a sensual and dissolute life, and he has now leaped from one extreme to another, a blásé man, an exhausted epicurean, an outcast from life. The sensible Orlando with true instinct perceives his censoriousness, regarding him as a fool or cipher; Rosalind discovers it, who quite in the poet's own meaning with regard to those who are in extremity of either joy or sorrow, calls the fools who are ever laughing and those who carry melancholy to excess, "abominable fellows who betray themselves to every modern censure, worse than drunkards". Thus carrying to excess his gloomy love of calumny, Jaques rebounds in another extreme, when he wishes to be invested in the fool's motley, to have "as large a charter as the wind," to blow on whom he pleases, and to cleanse "the foul body of the infected world". Quite mistaking the inoffensive vocation of the fool, he wishes to "disgorge" into the general world the poison he has caught from his bad experience. As no opportunity for this is offered, he turns at last, retaining his former part, to the hermit Frederick, because "out of these convertites there is much matter to be heard and learned".

We have seen how the banished duke has converted his misery into smiling happiness. He is joined subsequently by the two ladies, Rosalind and Celia, and by Orlando. In them the poet has shewn us, what qualities caused them to spend the time in the "golden world" of Arden more pleasurably than the melancholy Jaques. A more than sisterly bond inseparably chains the two cousins; in the romance they are compared with Orestes and Pylades; and in their fervent friendship alone we see the gift of self-renunciation, which renders them strangers to all egotism. Innocent and just, Celia solemnly promises at a future time to restore to Rosalind her withdrawn inheritance; she demands of her in return to be as merry as she is herself; she would, she says to her, had their positions been different, have been happier, and she proves this subsequently, when, more friend than daughter, she follows the banished cousin into exile. Rosalind has for a long time disarmed her uncle's envy and suspicion by her innocent nature, which even in thought wishes no evil to an enemy; he was overcome by the universal impression of her character, which won for her the praise and pity of the people. She bore her sorrow in smoothness, silence, and patience; her friendship for Celia lightened it; she constrained herself from love to her, to be more cheerful than became her position. We recognize plainly the nature, with which Lodge also invested Rosalind in his novel, that disposition to command herself and to deprive misfortune of its sting. But for this we must not consider her cold and heartless. She feels deeply, that fortune has punished her with disfavour; and when in the person of Orlando she meets one equally struck by fate, her heart, taken unawares, betrays how accessible she is to the most lively feelings. The similarly hapless circumstances which Orlando announces to her, his combat with the wrestler, his descent from an old friend of her father's, —all this added to his attractive manner helps to conquer *her,* who has already vanquished *him.* Her pride fell with her fortunes; she gives the victor a chain, which seals at once her fate and her almost hereditary love; she rashly and involuntarily reveals her feelings, because she has only moments in which to see him, she turns back to him, once again she even says to him, that he has overthrown more than his enemies; and immediately afterwards we find her fallen fathom-deep in love. We see indeed that here is a violent passion to be mastered; *how* she may master it, is afterwards the problem, which she has to solve in her subsequent meeting with Orlando. In this Orlando on his side we perceive just as readily the same naturally excitable temperament, and at the same time the power of self-command, which knows how to restrain it. He has been trained like a peasant by his brother and treated like a slave; he feels the disadvantage of his deficient education more than the crushed nobility of his birth; the spirit of his father grows strong in him; he will no longer endure the unworthy treatment, and when Oliver insults in him the honour of his father, he attacks his elder brother, not so far, however, as according, to the romance to forget himself in violence against him or to lay snares for revenge, but even in anger he is master of himself. The feeling of his nothingness struggles in his mind with an ambitious striving. He seeks the combat with the feared wrestler Charles, contented to meet death, since he has no honour to lose and no friends to wrong, but still hoping to recommend himself by victory and to secure himself from his brother. Instead of this he provokes the duke to suspicion and excites Oliver to designs against his life, and although he has just tested his power, he prefers to wander away, than to meet the malice of his brother. So in the wood afterwards, with the anxiety of childlike fidelity and the strength of an irritated wild beast, he is quickly resolved to maintain with sword and violence the life of his fainting old servent, but he is gentle as a lamb again, when he meets with friendly courteousness. Still later, when he sees his brother sleeping in the arms of danger, he is not untempted to revenge, but fraternal love prevails. Throughout we see the healthful, self-contained, calm nature of a youth, which promises a perfect man. All in him bespeaks a child of nature, who has remained pure and injured in the midst of a corrupt world. What a shaming contrast to the calumniator Jaques, to whom he thus replies, when he invites him to rail with him against the deceitful world, "I will chide no brother in the world, but myself; against whom I know most faults"! How innocent does the young Hercules appear in his laconic bashfulness, when love has "overthrown" him, when Rosalind makes him her valuable gift and her more valuable confession, and he finds no words to thank her for the one and to reply to the other!

In all these characteristics, with all the three, we shall not mistake the predisposition to a natural power of resistance against the overwhelming force of outward evil, as well as of the inward emotions of the mind. Endowed with this gift, they bear about with them a spring, of happiness, as the ladies prove by their merry league, in the very scene of hatred and persecution. But this spring will surely flow more richly as soon as it is set free from hindrances, as soon as it is freed from the intricate and manifold passions of a rude and intriguing society, left to itself; and thrown on its own affections and feelings. Hardly, therefore, is Rosalind's forced uneasy connection with her uncle broken up, than she feels herself freer in the unhappiness of exile, than in the happiness of a court-life; the true friendship of Celia gives loose to her innate good humour, which had hitherto been fettered; the prospect of seeing her father again makes her enterprising and bold; she conquers her womanly fear, and takes upon herself to play the part of a man, and that a martial one. The fair Ganymede in his hunter's dress exhibits forthwith a certain power of self-command when compared to the enervated Celia; the weariness of the journey, the meeting with Silvius, whose tears open his love-wounds afresh, cannot destroy his good humour. Rosalind endures her love silently; not so the wandering Orlando, who tells his to the deaf woods, while he carves the name of Rosalind on the barks, and hangs odes to her praise, the essays of an untutored talent, upon the trees. Celia finds the poet; amid the convulsions of their fate, the two, so suddenly united and separated, meet again strangely and unexpectedly; when Rosalind surmises it by the hints of Celia, we see again the intensely agitated being, who appears unable to conceal her feelings. How her blood rises to her cheeks! What haste is there in her questions! With what sweet impatience does her anticipation burst forth! One inch of delay seems to her more than "a South-sea-off discovery"! When she now hears of his presence, and ventures to hope to retain him, to possess him, pursued by no envious eye, entirely and undisturbed in this pastoral solitude and retirement, here where (according to the words of the romance) opportunity, (the sweetest friend to Venus), harbours in the cottages, we now see her who was before at the court so gentle, so silent, and so patient, suddenly seized with a wanton love of teazing, with the most excited joy, with breathless talkativeness; her happiness overflows like a springtide, from which we are inclined to fear everything. But in love as she was, says the novel, she "shrouded her pains in the cinders of honourable modesty". To love, says Rosalind in Shakespeare, is a woman's way, but also, not to confess that she does. At the time when, under the impulse of the moment she discovered herself to Orlando, she gave the lie to this her own rule, and all that she now does in the delight of perfect idleness, is as if she would make amends for her fault. The characters are changed; once he was bashful and flattering, and she was candid, now she is reserved with her love, when he is confessing it to the winds and to men, to all who will listen to it. Once she had betrayed her feelings to him, now she delights on their first meeting in drawing *his* confession from him, and she goes through all the variations of it with secret delight, with feigned jest and derision. It is not difficult, to bring one so proud of his love to an avowal, that he is the poetical panegyrist of Rosalind; then she discovers, that he does not look like a lover, that he has nothing of the "careless desolation" of the lover about him: she would fain hear his protest. She tries to set him against his love that she may test its constancy; it is a tonic to her, when with calm certainty he says that he would not be cured of his love. With her ingenious acuteness, she knows how to place herself in a position to be herself, and yet not to appear so, to enjoy the presence and affection of her lover, and yet not to surrender herself immodestly to one untested,—to love, as she said, yet not to confess, and thus to fulfil the desires of her impatient patience, of her eloquent silence. Whilst Shakespeare, following the romance, thus prepares the ground, so that Rosalind without violating her morality can give free scope to her love, he has avoided all the express moralizing, of the romance, both here and in Oliver's connection with Celia. There also Celia warns herself to love with patience, not to be too timid nor too bold; she first yields, when Oliver speaks of marriage; modesty is here also the guide of action. Shakespeare has treated this connection of Celia's very shortly; from an expression while at the court, we may conclude, that she regards love-affairs altogether more coldly and more practically than Rosalind; her rapid engagement to Oliver is therefore not without its design; but that Shakespeare also regarded the speedy marriage as a preventive against unchastity, may be gathered from a single word. It would have weakened the power of the comedy, had the poet entered in any way further into the meaning, of the moral lectures of the romance. Moreover he has so maintained Rosalind's character, that the truth of the delineation itself exempted him from this prosaic interruption. In herself she is little qualified for reflection; not from minute deliberation, but from a natural instinct, which adroitly seizes an offered opportunity, she hits upon the expedient for curbing her passion by forcing it into a play of fancy, and for mastering heart and feeling by giving employment to mind and soul. In this way she preserves her morality and wards off melancholy and sadness from herself and her lover, and thus the poet in quite another manner to Lodge in his romance, obtains the unusual esthetic advantage of introducing into the barrenness of retired life this spring of wit, which gushes forth in its unhindered course, in free nature, far from all conventionality. Formerly in her paternal home the dark Celia was the more merry of the two friends, but now her more quiet reserve constitutes a foil to the playfulness of Rosalind, which in her unexpected prosperity knows no bounds.

Orlando enters into Rosalind's sport rather passively than actively. In their similar circumstances in the town, he was the active one, as the man ought to be, and she the enduring one; in this little love-intrigue the woman is rightly the instigator and leader. He allows himself, neither willingly nor unwillingly, to be drawn into the strange plan of wooing Ganymede as his Rosalind. He discovered the resemblance between the two, he regards her at first as the brother of his beloved one, he is at ease and pleased when near her, he has an object for his sighs, and what lover lamented and did not gladly evidence his love! But with all this he is not so ardent in his service, because his healthful nature does not possess the melancholic and sentimental vein of amorousness. Rosalind thinks, when he keeps not his title, that it might well be said of him that "Cupid had clapped him o' the shoulder, but had left him heart-whole. In this tone she torments the poor man, who naturally cannot satisfy her, and this inflicted pain is only made amends for by that which she suffers herself, as soon as she is alone. Then we see by her impatient humour, by her upbraidings, by her fears, by her fear of losing him again, that her teazing frolicsomeness really demanded self-mastery, that she in fact needed self-command to sustain her part, that tenderness and feeling went ever hand in hand with her playfulness. This we might readily forget in those passages, where she tortures him with assumed cruelty, where she almost heartlessly endeavours to make him fearful and anxious respecting his marriage and his mistress, where she seems to exhibit the characteristics of a cold ironical nature. There also, when she depicts to him a woman's wit (Act IV. sc. 1.) never to be checked, never to be put out of countenance, one might argue indeed sadly for poor Orlando. But in her nature throughout there is in rare union the most just balance of the powers of feeling and intelligence; the sensibility of Viola and the wit of Beatrice are blended in her; the poet has invested her with a remarkably free tongue, in order that we may not be misled into the error of believing that in her discretion even a trace of conventional reserve or of asceticism might have been at work; Phœbe designates exactly this two-sidedness of her nature, when she says, that her soft eye is at variance with her sharp words, and heals the wounds which her tongue makes. In the midst of her merriment therefore, when Orlando goes away, how suddenly the softness of heart breaks forth in the words: "Alas, dear love, I cannot lack thee two hours"! How she makes every effort to have him back quickly! How she sighs away the while the short time of separation! And then when, instead of him, Oliver comes and tells the story of Orlando's hurt, she faints away; the complete woman comes to light in the disguised man, and her perfect love breaks forth from its covering. The riddle is now solved. Oliver sees through her; "You a man!" he says; "you lack a man's heart." Then she betrays herself further, by expecting him to believe that her swoon was counterfeited. He believes her not. The conviction strikes him; he leaves her, jestingly calling her Rosalind. We must assume that Oliver imparted his discovery to Orlando. Now it is Orlando's turn to carry on the sport, that he may not spoil her pleasure, and this is no small trial of his patience. She asks him, if his brother told him that she had counterfeited a swoon. He answers ambiguously, "Ay, and greater wonders than that". It is as if she feared his discovery, when she refers this reply at once to Celia's betrothal. Every following word of Orlando's increases in delicacy, if the part is thus understood, that he knows from this time forth, with whom he has to do. And thus it becomes also explicable, when at last the disclosure scarcely excites any surprise.

The contrast, which the pastoral episode between Phœbe and Silvius affords, will now become clear; or should it not, we must gather the explanation of it likewise from Lodge's romance, where it is perspicuous even to dulness. In contrast to the active excitement of the court and town, peace and quiet rule in this pastoral life; while in the one, envy and hatred carry on their intrigues, in the other love at most plays its innocent tricks. Love is, according to the romance, as precious in a shepherd's eye as in the looks of a king; the opportunity for love and its fidelity belongs especially to this class, because solitude increases the disposition to sociability. Thus we find Silvius possessed of a violent and importunate love, full of all those thousand follies, in which lovers magnify the smallest thing that affects their passion, into the most sacred and important matter. The tale, always true to its one moral, upbraids him with the immoderateness of his love, because he knows not how to conceal it with patience. We here see plainly the contrast to the love of Rosalind, although in Shakespeare she says, that her passion was much upon the fashion of Silvius'. But this indeed as little, as Rosalind approaches the fashion of Phœbe, in whose tone indeed, and wholly in like manner, she shews herself averse to all hyperbolical protestations of love. But this in her is a healthful nature, which dislikes every exaggeration; in Phœbe, whom the poet depicts as a regular beauty (black-haired, with bugle eye-balls and cheeks of cream), it is coyness, hatred of love, and the presumptuous pride of wishing to conquer it. The wise medium, which the two friends seek between timidity and craving for love, is missed by Phœbe and Silvius in an opposite manner. That Rosalind has a certain share of the fashion of both of them, places her upon a middle ground, upon which she shows herself at once capable and ready to humble the pride of Phœbe with greater pride, and on the other hand to strengthen the humility of the poor worm Silvius. Between them both, the town-lady and her Orlando appear as the really ingenuous children of true nature, contrasted with the overstrained creations of a conventional fiction.

Another contrast is formed by the relation of the clown to Audrey, which is wholly Shakespeare's addition. Touchstone, in his verses to the rough country-girl, in intercourse with whom he imagines himself like Ovid among the Goths, parodies the languishing poetry of Orlando, in his false marriage by Sir Oliver he parodies that of Rosalind and Orlando by Celia, and in his submissive humour in marrying the ugly Audrey, he parodies the unequal unions of the rest. His marriage, however, is only pretended; he contracts it not like Celia, to avoid immorality, but to indulge in it. He does the contrary to Rosalind and Orlando; he misuses this natural life of retirement, in the intention of again casting off Audrey at a convenient season. He uses the opportunity which here presents itself, without possessing the fidelity, which according to Lodge's romance should belong to the place. He seems equally devoid of the morality of either town or country. His language reminds us of the time when he belonged to this rural life and its habits, but now he would fain act the courtier. As Jaques went with the Duke into retirement, so he followed Celia from attachment to her, but not from personal inclination; he behaves like a courtier, when he speaks of his condescending affection, when he repulses the poor William, when he displays his knowledge of the catechism of honour to the courtly bully, when he depreciates the shepherd's life to Corin, and in jesting exaggeration perceives the same sin in the propagation of sheep, as Jaques seriously does in the chase. And in the same manner he displays his loose courtly morals with respect to the honourable Audrey.

In Touchstone, Shakespeare has for the first time produced a fool of a somewhat more elevated nature. In all the earlier comedies clowns only have played, natural fools whose wit is more studied or mechanically prepared or is given out in droll unconsciousness. The fool alone in *All's Well that Ends Well* has somewhat of the "prophetic" vein in him, which he ascribes to himself according to the general notion of the age, that fools, in virtue of their capacity for speaking "the truth the next way", possessed something of a divine and foretelling character. Shakespeare rendered complete homage to this notion of the age respecting the higher significance of fools, at least in his artistic efforts. The over-wisdom, which from learned haughtiness and pedantry, or from self-love, or corrupt taste, looks down contemptuously or censuringly on these characters of comedy, he left to the Ben Jonsons and the Malvolios, without regarding them. He has, as we have now often seen, invested even the simple clowns with a deeper significance, in the relations which he always gave them to the action of the piece, without fearing to place constraint on nature and truth; for who has not often witnessed in living, examples, how mother-wit solves unconsciously and without trouble problems over which the wise labour, and a childlike mind executes in simplicity, that which no understanding of the intelligent perceives? But a higher value than this is attributed by Shakespeare to the men of wit, to the real fools, who play their part with knowledge, to whom full power is given to speak the truth, to rend asunder, as often as they will, the veil of mere propriety and hypocrisy, and wittily to unmask the folly of others under cover of their own folly. This appeared to Shakespeare "a practice, as full of labour as a wise man's art", and as useful as a chaplain's discourse. For it appeared to him to belong to the most expert knowledge of the world and of men, of the "quality of persons and the time", to use appropriately and wisely the sting of seeming folly; marvelous appeared to him the watchful and acute mind, which was quick enough to discover the veiled weaknesses of men and understood how like "the haggard to check at every feather, that comes before his eye". But for men in general he considered the presence of a fool as a useful test of head and heart. To Parolles, Malvolio, and such-like knaves or angular pedants, the witticisms of fools are like inopportune "cannon-bullets", while to the generous and the guiltless, who have a free conscience, they pass for "slight bird-bolts". The wit of fools shoots vainly past these innocent ones; those who shrink at the whizzing of its arrows, discover their folly, though perhaps the motley man did not even aim them. When life approached not this play of fancy, this privileged folly was a profession, a vocation. Just at Shakespeare's time it passed from life to the stage, and with this it began to disappear from society itself. This was perhaps a further challenge to Shakespeare, to dignify it, and to rescue it for his art. But from the coarseness of the actors, and the inclination of the people to laugh alone at the clumsy ludicrous jokes of the clown, this was very difficult. We have before mentioned, what misuse of the privileges of the fool, Tarlton and Kempe made upon the stage; as long as this continued, as long as the principal art of these actors and the principal pleasure of the public was, that they should stretch out the chin, let their hands hang, and twirl their wooden swords, Shakespeare could hardly venture to bring a more refined character of this sort upon the stage. Kempe twice withdrew from the company at the Blackfriars' theatre. Only when he and his like were removed, could Shakespeare write that more refined programme in Hamlet for the actor of the fool, only then could he bring upon the stage the fools of *As You Like It, What You Will,* and *Lear.* Touchstone in our present piece is not quite so expert nor so sensible of his wit as the fools in *What You Will* and *Lear*; but he is also not on the same ground with Costard, Launce, and Launcelot. He stands on the doubtful limit between instinct and consciousness, where this character is the most acceptable. Jaques regards him as a clown, who has "crammed" the strange places of his dry brain with observation, which "he vents in mangled forms"; he considers him as one of those "natural philosophers" (by whom Warburton ought to have understood nothing more than a natural fool), of whom Touchstone himself says, that they have learned no wit by nature nor art. The two ladies call him by turns a natural and a fool; Celia, in his face, ascribes to him the dulness of the fool, which is the whetstone of the witty, while to the true fool the folly of others is the whetstone of his wit. And Touchstone himself assumes the appearance of being wiser, than he himself knew; he shall, he says, ne'er be 'ware of his own wit, till he breaks his shins against it. On the other hand from his expressions in other passages he regards himself as far superior to the clown and the natural philosopher, and the Duke readily perceives his design behind his interposing folly; "he uses his folly," he says, "like a stalking-horse, and under the presentation of that, he shoots his wit."

Entirely corresponding with this two-sided capacity are his actions and language throughout the piece. He performs his tricks in the manner of the clowns with whom roguish acts pass for wit. On the other hand the poet has consigned to him the part of the comic chorus in the comedy, in which the fool should be always employed. We have shewn above, in what contrast the connection between Touchstone and Audrey is brought to that of the other couples; the idealized pastoral love is parodied in it by one of a more real nature. These contrasts were peculiar to the pastoral drama. Thomas Heywood, in characterizing the pastoral plays of Shakespeare's time, uses these words: "If we present a pastoral, we shew the harmless love of shepherds, diversely moralized, distinguishing between the craft of the city and the innocency of the sheepcote." We see indeed, according to this definition that Shakespeare's play is nothing else than a pastoral; the habits of town and country are brought into manifold contrasts; the moral, which the poet draws, may indeed be essentially diverse from that, which, in the pastoral romances and dramas of the age, would be usually inferred from that distinction of town and country. Shakespeare has employed the mouth of his fool as his stalking-horse, to express his opinion of the customary idealizing of shepherd-life in pastoral poetry, in the same sense, as it is manifested in his play and in the scenes it contains. On Corin's question, as to how he likes this shepherd's life, Touchstone answers him: "Truly, shepherd, in respect of itself, it is a good life; but in respect, that it is a shepherd's life, it is naught. In respect, that it is solitary, I like it very well; but in respect, that it is private, it is a very vile life. Now in respect it is in the fields, it pleaseth me well; but in respect it is not in the court, it is tedious. As it is a spare life, look you, it fits my humour well; but as there is no more plenty in it, it goes much against my stomach. Hast any philosophy in thee, shepherd?" It seems to me, that perhaps all pastoral poetry put together scarcely contains so much real wisdom, as this philosophy of the fool. He finds nothing to say against the shepherd's life, but nothing also against the contrary manner of living, and the homely simplicity of Corin himself is on his side in this, that he leaves courtly manners to the court, and country ones to the country. Shakespeare knew nothing of the one-sidedness, which condemned or rejected either life in the world or life in retirement, the one for the sake of the other. Rather does the fool's wit consider him who merely knows the one, or as the meaning, is, merely esteems the one, as "damned, like an ill-roasted egg, all on one side". In Shakespeare's play, no expression of preference rests on either of the two kinds of life. In neither of the two circles does he find the condition of happiness or virtue in itself, but he sees happiness most surely dwelling, not in this or that place, but in the beings, who have a capacity and a natural share of qualification for either or for every other kind of existence; in those beings, who, exiled from the world, do not feel themselves miserable, just as little so, as when they are recalled to the world from their solitude. The poet knows nothing of a certain situation, condition, or age, which would be a sure source of happiness, but he knows that there are men in all classes and generations, like his Duke, his Rosalind, his old Adam Spencer, who bear in their bosoms that equanimity and contentment, which is the only fruitful soil of all true inner happiness, and who carry with them wherever they go, a smiling Eden and a golden age.

Translated by F. E. Bunnet, Vol. I
(London, 1863): 539–566.

SHAKSPEARE'S DRAMATIC ART
Hermann P. Ulrici
1876

CHAPTER II.

1. AS YOU LIKE IT.

THIS charming comedy is also one of the mixed species, but with a decided preponderance of the fanciful element. Even a summary estimate of the contents of the piece will, I think, prove this most clearly.

We have two royal dukes, one of whom has unlawfully (we are not told how) driven the other from the throne; the exiled Duke has thereupon fled into the Forest of Arden where, with his followers, he leads a free and fantastic sort of life; two other aristocratic brothers, the elder of whom so persecutes the younger that he seeks refuge with the exiled Duke in the Forest of Arden; two princesses, the daughters of the two dukes, deeply attached to one another, one of whom is exiled and is accompanied by the other, likewise wend their way to the Forest; two fools, a merry one and a melancholy one; and lastly shepherds and shepherdesses described according to an idealised view of nature—such are the principal characters of the play. Their graceful groupings and the contrast in which they stand to one another enliven the romantic wildernesses of the Forest, and their various situations, relations and characters determine all that takes place in the play. Taken singly nothing that happens is actually contrary to nature, there are no extraordinary or unusual beings or phenomena; taken singly every character, every situation and action might belong to ordinary reality. It is only the introduction of lions and serpents into the mountainous scenery of Europe which gives us a gentle intimation that we are standing upon the ideal soil of poetic fancy. And still more emphatically is this expressed in the development and the composition—the style and the tone, the spirit and the character of the piece in general, and in the position and relation of the individual parts in particular—in short, in the totality of the circumstances and situations, actions and events. We are clearly given to understand that the drama is not a picture of common experience, but that it conceives life from a peculiarly poetical point of view, and that it is intended to exhibit a fantastic reflex of life in the mirror of caprice and humour. For if we consider the whole somewhat more closely, we shall at once have to admit that such things as the play presents, do not and could not happen in actual experience; that such a romantic mode of life in the loneliness of a forest is but a poetical dream; that, in fact, real life cannot be carried on or treated in the manner in which it is by almost all the persons represented; that the good Duke, Orlando, Rosalinde, Celia, Jacques and Touchstone, are figures which the realistic mind would call oddities, enthusiasts, romancists; that, in reality, a character like the unrighteous Duke would not readily be converted by a recluse hermit, or a man like Oliver de Bois be wholly changed by a single magnanimous action on the part of his persecuted brother.

It may, therefore, be asked wherein, amid this apparent unreality, lies the poetical truth of the piece? And which is the internal bond that gathers together all the confused and strangely involved threads, forming them into one harmonious whole? We must bear in mind that it is the comic view of life which here forms the basis of the drama, and accordingly that the truth of human life is not represented directly, but by means of contrast, that is, by accident, caprice and waywardness paralysing one another, and by the true agent of human life—the eternal order of things—being brought vividly into view. This becomes clearly evident when we consider how the unrighteous caprice (whatever may have been its motive), which suddenly drove the good old Duke into exile, as suddenly reverts against itself, destroying its work and restoring what it had wrongfully appropriated; how, in like manner, by a similar change of sentiment, the right relation between the two brothers de Bois is also brought about; how the love between Orlando and Rosalinde, between Celia and Oliver—which arose suddenly by the concurrence of circumstances— attains its object by an equally sudden change of circumstances and relations; and lastly, how the coyness of the shepherdess Phœbe is overcome much in the same way, and she is in the end united to her faithful, good-natured simpleton of a lover.

Thus the general comic view of life is reflected throughout the whole play, and forms the foundation and platform upon which the action moves. If, however, it be now asked what is the *special* standpoint from which the poet has here taken his view of life, or—what is the same thing—where is the central point of unity which gives the play its peculiar stamp, we shall again find that the title furnishes us with some clue. For the title is so striking, so original, so completely without any reference to the action represented, as such, that we have to declare it to be, either utterly senseless and meaningless, or assign to it a concealed reference to the internal significance and to the ideal meaning of the whole. Like the similar title of 'What You Will,' it has been referred to the relation between the play and the public (A. W. von Schlegel), and has been so interpreted as to convey the meaning that the piece was intended to present itself to the spectators in any form they pleased. But this, in fact, as already pointed out, is *not* and *cannot* be the case. On the other hand, it is perhaps possible (as Tieck thinks) that the title alludes to a passage in Ben Jonson's 'Cinthia's Revels,' and to the interspersed sallies it contains against the easy and apparently irregular and arbitrary compositions of Shakspeare and the earlier School. But the allusion does not exactly hold good, for the only words in B. Jonson's comedy that can be meant are 'If you like it,' whereas the heading to Shakspeare's play is 'As you like it,' and thus even Tieck's Interpretation: 'If you like it, then it is a comedy, that is, a comedy *par excellence,*' is rendered meaningless. The same applies to the equally far-fetched reference to the words: 'If you like it, so, and yet I will be yours in dutie, if you be mine in favours,' in the Preface to Lodge's pastoral and chivalrous romance, from which Shakspeare drew the subject of this play? Shakspeare perhaps intended by means of the title to smile at the vain endeavours of his opponents to bring his fanciful comedies (which certainly differed very widely from Ben Jonson's) into discredit; but even the circumstance of his changing the *If* into *As* proves that he would not have chosen the title, had it not borne within itself some independent significance, some reference to the meaning and spirit of the play itself. Such a reference, I think, it is not difficult to find upon a more careful examination. In the first place it is evident that 'As You Like It,' both in style and character, stands in close affinity to 'What You Will.' The difference in reality is only that in the latter case the element of intrigue plays a prominent part while it is wholly wanting in the first case. The motives which in the present case set the whole in motion are merely chance, the unintentional encounter of persons and incidents, and the freaks, caprices and humours, the sentiments, feelings and emotions to which the various personages recklessly give way in what they do and leave undone. Nowhere does the representation treat of conscious plans, definite resolves, decided aims and objects; nowhere do we find preconsidered, or, in fact, deeper motives proceeding from the inmost nature of the characters. The characters themselves—even though clearly and correctly delineated—are generally drawn in light, hurried outlines—but are full of life, gay and bold in action, and quick in decision; they appear, as already said, either inconstant, variable, going from one extreme to the other, or possess such a vast amount of imagination, sensitiveness and love for what is romantic and adventurous, that their conduct to a prosaic mind can only appear thoughtless, capricious and arbitrary, and such a mind would be inclined to declare them all fools, oddities and fantastic creatures (in the same way as Sir Oliver Martext in the play itself, iii. 3, calls the whole company in the forest 'fantastical knaves'). And, in fact, all do exactly what and as they please; each gives him or herself up, in unbridled wilfulness, to good or evil, according to his or her own whims, moods or impulses whatever the consequences may prove to be. Each looks upon, and turns and shapes life as it pleases him or herself. The Forest of Arden is their stage, and with its fresh and free atmosphere, its mysterious chiaroscuro, its idyllic scenery for huntsmen and shepherds, is, at the same time, the fitting scene for the realisation of a mode and conception of life such as is here described. It is a life such as not only must please the dramatic personages themselves, but would please every one, were such a life only possible; it is the poetical reflex of a life *as you like it,* light and smooth in its flow, unencumbered by serious tasks, free from the fetters of definite objects, and from intentions difficult to realize; an amusing play of caprice, of imagination, and of wavering sensations and feelings. A life like this, however, is possible only in the Forest of Arden, in the midst of similar scenery, under similar circumstances and conditions, and with similar companions and surroundings. At court, in more complicated relations, in a state of impure feelings and selfish endeavours, it would lose its poetical halo, its innocence and gaiety, and become untruth, hypocrisy, injustice and violence, as is proved by the reigning Duke, his courtiers and Oliver de Bois. The point of the piece seems to me to lie in this contrast; but care had to be taken not to make the point too pointed, not to make it a serious moral conflict. If Shakspeare wished to give the play a humorous character, the gay appearance of 'as you like it,' he could not solve the contrast except by allowing selfish injustice and violent arbitrariness to become untrue to themselves, and to turn into their opposites—of course, in perfect accordance with the plan, the meaning and spirit of the whole, but nevertheless entirely without motives. This, at the same time, unravels the other complications into which the play of accident and caprice and their own 'as we like it,' have involved the dramatic personages and the piece closes in perfect harmony inasmuch as what is right and rational is everywhere happily brought about. Thus the dominion, and the very ground hitherto held by accident and caprice, excessive imagination and adventurous romance, is entirely withdrawn from them.

Shakspeare's intention—that is, the sense in which he conceived Lodge's narrative and transformed it into a drama—which, as I think, is clearly enough manifested in the spirit and character of the whole, as well as reflected in the several parts, is concentrated, and, so to say, condensed in the second and more personal contrast in which the two fools of the piece stand to one another. They and the unimportant figure of the shepherdess whom Touchstone chooses as his sweetheart, are the only persons whom Shakspeare did not find in Lodge's narrative, but freely invented. This addition, however, is in so far of great importance as it alone gives the original subject-matter a different character and colouring, and, so to say, forms the ideal norm, which determines the other alterations introduced by Shakspeare. The two fools, by virtue of the contrast in which they stand to each other, mutually complete each other. The melancholy Jacques is not the fool by profession, he appears rather to be simply a comic character *par excellence;* but his meditative superficiality, his witty sentimentality, his merry sadness have taken so complete a hold of his nature, that it seems to contradict itself, and therefore upon a closer examination distinctly bears the impress of folly, although it certainly is an original kind of folly. The contradiction into which he has fallen, he involuntarily and unconsciously carries about with him, for it is rooted in his very life and character. Of good birth and education, and not without the taste for what is good and noble, but easily led, weak, wanting in independence, and a slave to his easily-excited feelings, he had in his day been a profligate, who in indulging his caprices, desires and passion, had drained the enjoyments of life to the very dregs. And because he found no lasting satisfaction in them, he has withdrawn himself from the world—not having strength or inclination to conceive life from its other and right side—but continues to cherish and foster his inclinations, caprices and humours; these, however, have now taken the form of sentimental melancholy and express themselves more in speeches full of black views of life, than in actions. This melancholy, this contempt of life and men, this sentimental slander and slanderous sentimentality not only please and amuse himself, but he carries them ostentatiously about, and has found a fitting soil for them in the company around the good Duke. In reality he only acts the melancholy misanthrope, the world-despising hermit, he is himself unconscious of the part he is playing, is not conscious that he is wearing a mere mask behind which lie concealed his old love of life, his old caprices, inclinations and sympathies. His observations therefore are in most cases certainly meditative and profound, and he fancies that on their wings he will be able to rise far above the sphere of ordinary mortals; but he is not aware that this meditation when carefully examined is after all very superficial in its contradictory one-sidedness. His effeminate sentimentality he considers to be genuine, deep feeling, and yet it is not only full of witty points, but, so to say, the bow from which he shoots forth the arrows of his scorn and slander. His melancholy does not call forth tears of sorrow but of joy, and these cause more merriment than the most exuberant frolic, not only to others but in reality to himself also. While the other characters in the foreground look upon life more or less in the light of a gay and festive game of humour and of frolic, he apparently regards it as a sombre funeral procession, where every mourner, in tears and lamentations, is advancing towards his own grave. However, while in the case of the other personages, the merriment of the play bears within itself a hidden seriousness, in his case, on the contrary, the solemn funeral procession changes insensibly into a merry procession of fools. Thus he is always his own counterpart, and at the same time always the very thing which he attacks and combats. In a word, he is exactly like the fool by profession, the personification of capriciousness, as well as of the love of wit and ridicule, except that he unconsciously and involuntarily wears a cloak of melancholy and sentimentality. Hence his honest admiration of the real, acknowledged fool, and his wish to be able himself to play the part of the privileged fool.

The fool whom Jacques so envies, who is his counterpart and mental kinsman, is the merry clown Touchstone. He is a genuine old English clown— in the Shakspearian form—such as we have already met with in 'What You Will'; a fool with the jingling cap and bells, one who is and wishes to be a fool; the same personification of caprice and ridicule, and with the same keen perception of the faults and failings of mankind as Jacques, but a fool with his own knowledge and consent, and not merely passive but active also. He speaks, acts and directs his whole life in accordance with the capricious folly and foolish capriciousness which he considers to be the principles of human existence. While therefore the other lovers are in pursuit of their high ideals of beauty, amiability and virtue, and yet do not in reality attain anything beyond the common human standard, he takes to himself quite an ordinary, silly, ugly, peasant girl; he loves her, in fact, just because she pleases him, and she pleases him just because he loves her. This is the obstinacy of love in its full force, as conceived by Shakspeare in his comedies. And yet this capriciousness which apparently ridicules itself, at the same time, contains a significant trait in which he exhibits his inmost nature, a trait of what is simple, natural, and common to all men, in contrast to what is exaggerated and unnatural, and to all that which is sentimental, eccentric and fantastic—a genuine human trait which, however, he had hitherto been unable to show. While, further, all the other characters have chosen the secluded free life of the Forest of Arden on account of their outward circumstances or inward impulse, in short, with good reason or free will, he alone has gone there without any occasion or reason whatever; he has even done so against his own inclination as the good cheer at court suited him far better; in other words he has done so deliberately in the actual sense of the word. And yet it is just in this that he again, under the mask of folly, shows a trait of genuine human nature, noble unselfishness and fidelity. Lastly, while all the other characters appear more or less like the unconscious play-balls of their own caprices and whims, feelings and impulses, he proves himself to be the one that makes game both of himself and of all the others; by this very means, however, he shows his true independence and freedom. And inasmuch as he consciously and intentionally makes himself a fool and gives free reins to his caprices, freaks and humours, he, at least, shows that he possesses the first necessary elements of true freedom, the consciousness of, and sovereignty over himself. He the professed Fool may frankly be declared the most rational person of the whole curious company, for he alone invariably knows his own mind; in regarding everything as sheer folly, he, at the same time takes it up in the humour in which it is meant to be understood. Accordingly, in Touchstone (who, as it were, personifies the humour which pervades the whole), we find all the perversities and contradictions of a life and mode of life *as you like it* reflected in a concave mirror; but this exterior, at the same time, conceals the poetic truth of the reverse side of the whole. Therefore we find a striking contrast to him in Sir Oliver Martext, the very embodiment of common prose, who will not suffer anything to lead him from his own text, but in doing this thoroughly perverts the text of true living reality, the ideal, poetical substance of the book of life.

The other characters also are conceived, arranged and grouped in as significant a manner, in as pure a harmony, and in as vivid a contrast. In 'Twelfth Night' Viola was the heroine, here we have Rosalinde. In comedies Shakspeare is especially fond of assigning the principal parts to the female sex. Thus in 'The Winter's Tale,' 'Love's Labour's Lost,' 'All's Well That Ends Well,' 'The Merchant of Venice,' and in 'Much Ado About Nothing,' etc. Woman with her natural tendency to intrigue and equally great capriciousness, thoughtlessness, and inconsistency is, in fact, particularly suited to be the bearer of the comic action according to his idea of comedy. In the case of Rosalinde, Shakspeare has made the dangerous attempt of embodying humour—the comic in its capriciousness or fancifulness—in the form of a *woman,* or rather, which is still more venturesome, in that of a *girl.* Rosalinde possesses all the qualities with which we became acquainted in Viola, except that her nature is freer, gayer, and more frank. It is only at times that mischievous ideas come into Viola's head, otherwise she is absorbed in dreamy, serious and melancholy thoughts. Rosalinde, on the other hand, is absolute mischief, absolute caprice, and exuberance of spirits; she even makes fantastic game of her serious love for Orlando. Her playfulness, however, not like that of a well-bred princess, but the innate grace and *naivete* of a free child of nature, whose very freedom gives her noble and beautiful nature all the charms of genuine good-breeding. She possesses as little practical cleverness as Viola, and in this respect is inferior to Portia, because described more as a girl than the latter, who, although unmarried, and presented to us in the full bloom of youth, can be imagined only as a mature and complete woman in contrast to the budding girl Rosalinde. However, she is less in need of such cleverness, because, owing to her bold frankness, her gaiety and *naivete,* she is not easily embarrassed and would not readily enter into any complicated business where cleverness and practical intelligence were required. For in spite of her brilliant, inexhaustible wit, she nevertheless does not possess a spark of that knowledge of the world which is able to grapple with the affairs of common life. Her wit and her judgment are rooted wholly in the poetical soil of a rich imagination, and in a delicate, pure state of feeling out of which her whole being has, so to say, sprung forth. When severed from this soil, her nature becomes withered and stunted like a tender flower that has been taken from its native earth and transplanted into a foreign land. At her uncle's court, Rosalinde appears inclined to be melancholy; for her nature, in spite of the fulness of the natural truth of her womanly heart, is, in regard to mind, so ethereal, so romantically poetic, so genially eccentric that the rude breath of prosaic reality could not but destroy its loveliest blossoms. On this very account it would be useless to endeavour, in a detailed delineation, to point out the several delicate outlines with which Shakspeare's masterly skill and genial hand has sketched the charming picture. I fear that even the few gentle allusions I have already given may have rather damaged than benefited the picture which the reader's own imagination had formed.

The same may be said of the other characters; their fundamental traits—the noble frankness and candour, and the imperishable force of a good disposition as exhibited in Orlando—the pure feeling for humanity, the greatness of mind and goodness of heart, in the amiable, jovial old Duke, whom misfortune has made but the nobler, the happier, and the more cheerful—the simple, touching fidelity of Adam—the self-sacrificing, heartfelt friendship of Celia—in short, all, in spite of their strangeness, thoughtlessness, and perversity, reflect so much of what is beautiful in humanity and are so clearly brought forward, that a closer analysis would only destroy the delicate, poetical fragrance with which the whole is imbued. It must, however, be obvious to every reader that the characters are all conceived and worked out entirely in keeping with the meaning of *as you like it,* which, indeed is the fundamental theme of the whole. The fantastic capriciousness which shows itself either as the inner motive or the outward impulse to their resolves and actions, rules the best and noblest, as well as the worst and lowest characters in the most manifold modifications. This is clearly evident from the course of the *action.* The arbitrary, unlawful dethronement of the good Duke forms the basis of the plot, the unreasonable persecution of Orlando by his brother—which is founded on a completely indefinite and undefinable cause of hate—his whim to fight the king's wrestler, likewise, the equally unreasonable banishment of Rosalinde—whom her uncle had long tolerated at his court, and suddenly drives into exile without any cause—are the first and chief motives of its advance. In the Forest of Arden all then abandon themselves to the most unrestrained and most diversified play of caprice and fancy. The play proceeds in this way till the wicked-brother and the unlawful Duke are brought to see their transgressions and are converted, and Rosalinde throws aside her disguise. Thus even the mainsprings of the action are in perfect accordance with the meaning and spirit of the play. All the various parts form one perfect harmony, round which play the most graceful melodies; all is so delicate and ingenious, so free, so fresh and gay, so full of bantering humour and genial exuberance of spirits, that everyone who possesses the sense and understanding for the poetical chord here struck, must acknowledge this comedy as deserving the first prize; those who do not possess these requisites for its appreciation will pass it by with indifference or wholly misunderstand it.

Most critics assign the play to the year 1600. That it did not appear till after 1598 is certain, not only from the fact that Meres does not mention it in the often-quoted passage in his *Palladis Tamia,* but also from a line occurring in the play itself (act iii. s. 5.) taken from Marlowe's 'Hero and Leander,' which did not appear in print till 1598. Edm. Capell's supposition that 'As You Like It' belongs to the year 1605, is an arbitrary one, and is proved untenable by the fact that the play is entered at Stationers' Hall as early as August 4th, 1600. The edition which he supposes to have existed, may have actually appeared, but it has been wholly lost. Probably, however, obstacles were placed in the way of its being printed—perhaps by Shakspeare's own theatrical company, which would testify to the unusually great popularity of the piece. It presumably did not appear in print till in the folio of 1623.

Originally published in English.
(Oxford: Oxford University Press, 1876) Vol. 2: 253–70.

SYSTEM OF SHAKESPEARE'S DRAMAS
Denton J. Snider
1877

In this drama we see placed in striking contrast the actual and the idyllic world. The former contains society, state, business, and their manifold interests and complications; the latter is the simple pastoral existence, without care, struggle, or occupation—almost without want. The former is the world of Reason, and exhibits man in his rational development, and for this very cause has within it the deepest and most terrific contradictions. The loftier the summit the greater the fall; the more highly organized a society the mightier are the collisions slumbering or struggling in its bosom. But an idyllic existence is almost without contradiction, and, hence, it happens that men sometimes flee from a more concrete social life, in order to get rid of its difficulties, and betake themselves to a simple state of the shepherd.

More commonly, however, they remain in society, but construct, with the aid of imagination, a world of their own, suited exactly to their notion of things, whither they can flee out of the rugged and disagreeable reality surrounding them. Such a realm may be called the ideal, as distinguished from the idyllic, though both have the same fundamental principle, since they are abstractions from actual existence. An imaginary world of this kind has always been a favorite theme with a certain class of minds, particularly with the poets and theologians. But in some social conditions, especially in periods of revolution and disintegration, it is the resort to which all intelligence flees, and the construction of ideal societies becomes a phase of national consciousness. Such a state is generally thrown back into the distant past, long antecedent to history, when man was absolutely innocent, and even the lower animals shared in his condition—that is, the negative side of man and nature is wholly eliminated—thought away. Of this character was the Paradise of the ancient Hebrews and the Golden Age of the ancient Greeks. It will be noticed that there is a great advantage in placing this world in the past, since we are thus continually receding from it, while, according to the well-known law of distance, it is increasing in enchantment to the spectator. But more hardy spirits have dared to project this world into the future, where it is in danger of being overtaken. Still, the Millennium has thus far always kept a thousand years ahead, and it is likely to do so for an indefinite time to come.

But, now, this consciousness—so general, so deeply grounded in human nature—the Poet proposes to make the subject of a comedy. That it is capable of a comic treatment is manifest when we reflect that the very realization of the ideal world must be its annihilation, for then it is real and no longer ideal. Thus the pursuit of such an end, as absolute and final, is contradictory and null in itself, since it must terminate in just the opposite of that which is sought. Now, Comedy exhibits the individual pursuing ends which are nugatory, and, therefore, destroy themselves in their realization. That the Poet had this consciousness in mind is clear from his allusions to Robin Hood, the English ideal hero of the forest; and still more plainly does the same fact appear when he speaks of "those who fleet the time carelessly as they did in the golden world," an obvious reference to the Greek ideal realm. To this latter he likens the Forest of Arden, a comparison by which he lets us know what he meant by that forest.

But it is through beholding the organization of the drama that the purpose of the Poet will be most clearly revealed. There are three movements, which, however, are merely the essential phases of one and the same general process. The first movement depicts the Real World of Wrong, in which institutions have fallen into conflict, and in which the individual is assailed in his personal lights. Here there are two threads, of which the central figures are, respectively, a man and a woman—Orlando and Rosalind. Both are the victims of wrong in this unsealed society; both have to flee from domestic and political oppression; they also become enamored of one another—the common bond of misfortune easily changes to the common bond of love. The second movement portrays the Idyllic Realm to which the individual has fled in order to get rid of the institutional world and its injustice; it is the simple pastoral and sylvan life before society. Here also there are essentially two threads; the first is the banished Duke and lords, who have been driven off by the existing wrongs of the civilized State and have gone to the woods, there to dwell in the primitive peace of nature; the second thread is made up of three groups, which must be considered together—that of Orlando and his servant, and his brother; that of Rosalind and Celia, and the clown; and, finally, that of the native shepherds. The third movement is the restoration of the Real World of Right—the idyllic realm dissolves of its own inherent necessity, and there is a complete return of the banished members to society, which is healed of its wrong by the departure and repentance of the usurping Duke.

I. 1. We shall now glance at the incident of the play, and trace the first movement through its various parts. The first thread of it brings before us at once the Real World of Wrong. Orlando has been deprived of his share in the paternal estate by his brother Oliver, and, what is much worse, his education has been utterly neglected, in violation of the will of his father. Here is shown the wrong in the Family; but this is not all. The rightful Duke has been expelled from his government by his brother, and thus we see that the wrong extends into the State. The play does not unfold, but rather presupposes, these two great acts of injustice, and, hence, society is portrayed as in condition of strife and contradiction. But Orlando has developed his physical nature, though his intellect may have been neglected; he exhibits his prowess first against his brother, and then at court he overcomes the Duke's wrestler. A curious result of this adventure is the love which springs up between himself and Rosalind, which, however, has received the most ample and beautiful motive from the Poet. Nowhere has he more successfully shown the budding, blooming, and ripening of the tender passion.

But soon this world of injustice comes into full activity and manifests its inherent character. The Duke, as the violator of all individual right, must naturally become jealous of all individuals; hence he has banished a number of lords who seemed dangerous to his power. And so this process must continue as long as anybody is left in the country, since the existence of one man must be a continual source of fear to such a tyrant. Hence Orlando, as the son of an old enemy, excites his suspicion, and has to leave the court with precipitation. The innocent youth has simply thrown the Duke's wrestler in a fair match; but this, together with his name, is sufficient to cause his speedy flight.

But the wrongs of Orlando do not end with his departure from court. He returns to his brother's estate only to find his life conspired against there, and his condition more hopeless than ever. Accompanied by his trusty servant, Adam, a second time he betakes himself to flight. It is impossible to mistake the meaning of these scenes. The Poet has here portrayed society in contradiction with its fundamental object; it has driven off those whom, by every tie of blood and of right, it was bound to protect; both State and Family have become the instruments of the direst injustice; on all sides we behold the *world of wrong*.

2. Such is the first thread of this movement; the second thread has as its central figure, Rosalind, daughter of the former Duke, who has been driven off by his brother, the present usurper. She is not disposed to be merry under the circumstances; her cousin, Celia, tries to enliven her spirits; Touchstone, the devoted clown, also seeks to drive away the heavy hours with pleasantry. Then Orlando appears for the wrestling match. The modest, sad-visaged youth seems unequal to his enterprise, and at once excites the warm sympathy of Rosalind, who feels her own sorrowful lot in his sorrowful words and looks. But when she finds that he is the son of an old friend of her banished father, her sympathy rapidly ripens into love. Rosalind now meets with the same treatment from the suspicious Duke that Orlando has received. She is driven out of his dominions

in the most wanton manner, but is accompanied by the daughter of the usurper—a just retribution upon his own family for the wrong done his brother's. The two young ladies now disguise themselves for their journey. Rosalind assumes the garb of a man, which she retains through all her adventures in the idyllic land. Here we have the chief instrumentality of comic situation—Disguise—which furnishes the intrigue of the play, though this is by no means its sole, or even its leading, element.

Both Orlando and Rosalind have, therefore, to flee; each is the victim of wrong in the Family and in the State. Moreover, we see in the background the general condition of society. There is no rightful authority; the true Duke has been expelled by an usurper; many lords have been compelled to leave their country. Such is the first movement. We are now prepared to make the transition to the second movement, in which will be portrayed the Idyllic World—the sphere of mediation.

II. But whither must these people go? Society has banished them, has wronged them, and, hence their object is to find a place where the injustice of society does not exist, where there is no civil order. Such is the Forest of Arden, into which we are ushered in the beginning of the Second Act. Its nature has already been sufficiently indicated by the Poet when he compared it with the Golden Age. Its logical character is determined by the fact that it is the negation of all social organization—that simple primitive state before society.

1. Moreover, we find already here the banished Duke and lords, those for whom the social contradictions were too strong, and, hence, have betoken themselves to a less complex existence. The Duke rejoices in the new situation; he makes a glowing contrast between their present life and that which they have abandoned. Here is no flattery, no ambition, no crime; he can find quite all the advantages of society in the trees, the stones, and the brooks. Nature, were she only looked into, can furnish all the content of reason. Nothing can surpass the freshness and the idyllic beauty with which he describes their life in the forest; the aroma of the country is in every line. Then comes Amiens, the lyrist of the company, who embodies these sentiments in the most ethereal song. The poetic representation of their abode is thus complete.

But hold! a disagreeable contrast arises. The Duke feels that even in this new life he has not wholly avoided the old difficulty, for there still remains the struggle with the animal world—the burghers of the wood—for physical maintenance. Nay, there is one of these lords who cannot find here any solution of the trouble—who declares that injustice is as rife in the Forest of Arden as in society. Witness the slaughter of the innocent beasts of the field, and that same usurpation of their domains by the banished Duke and lords of which they themselves were the victims in society. This is Jaques whose negative character can find repose nowhere; he even sees in Nature herself only discord and evil;

the deer is as bad as man—it leaves its wounded neighbor to perish, while it passes haughtily on. Thus is our Idyllic World, from which we had thought to shut out all negation, disturbed by its reappearance, like a ghost among children. Indeed, man can hardly get rid of the negative in this way; though he flee to the woods, he will find it there. In fact, his very existence depends upon destruction—upon swallowing a certain amount of vegetable and animal existence. Hence, in order to get rid of the negative, he must first get rid of life. Such is the logical result of abandoning State and society with the design of seeking a solution of their contradictions, namely, suicide—a result which men seldom insist upon practically realizing, though it is not unknown in the history of the human species that this result has been carried out to the bitter end.

2. These persons the play presupposes to have already gone to the Idyllic Realm, but now behold the new arrivals. First, Rosalind and Celia, in their disguise, appear at its entrance. Their difficulties, weariness, and hunger are specially noticed; they find the transition from the Real to the Ideal—from the luxury of the court and conveniences of society to the meager life of the shepherd—by no means easy. Though they are in an Ideal World, the Real makes itself very unpleasantly felt. But the nature of the place is soon made manifest. Two beings, called Corin and Silvius, suddenly rise upon their view, natives of the land, whose appearance shows them to be shepherds. Moreover, their language assumes a poetical form, and has for its theme the wail of unrequited love. Also, their names sound quite familiar—are, in fact, some old familiar names of pastoral poetry. With one of them Rosalind enters into conversation, and the result is that the new-comers buy a shepherd's hut, and are firmly planted in the idyllic land. Strange to say, Orlando and his old, devoted servant, Adam, have arrived in another part of the same territory, a proceeding which seems at first somewhat arbitrary on the part of the Poet. Yet, whither else had they to go? They have fled society, and, hence, must proceed to a place where social order is unknown, which place has been identified as the Forest of Arden. We also find that they have the same difficulty, on entering this realm, which was experienced by the last party; Orlando even thinks of violence in order to obtain food, but he is soon changed by the gentle manner of the Duke, who, of course, could not do harm to any human being. With the end of the Second Act we find everybody fairly established in the new country.

The next question which arises is: What are they to do here? What is to be the content of their lives? We are not long left in ignorance, for soon we find Orlando wholly occupied with love, carving the name of his fair one upon the bark of trees, making love-ditties and hanging them upon the bushes—in fine, consumed with the most intense passion. Nor is Rosalind much better off, though she preserves her disguise in his presence. Touchstone—the clown— too, becomes infected with the prevailing frenzy, and the native shepherd

Silvius, who is also heart-stricken, is again introduced, together with the disdainful shepherdess, Phebe, who, in her turn, falls in love with the disguised Rosalind. The result of the Third Act is that we have three pairs of lovers, native and foreign, to whom one pair is added in the following Acts. Thus our Ideal Realm is, for the new-comers, transformed into a sort of love-land, where the young people seem wholly occupied with their passion though the old-comers are not so affected.

That such a state of existence should take this form is in the natural order of things. Let us analyze this remarkable transition. Man without society is without content to his life. Here society exists not, business is impossible, ambition in the State is cut off, the physical wants are reduced to the smallest compass and are satisfied with the smallest amount of exertion. Without occupation, without incentive—in general, without content to his life—man is reduced to the *natural individual.* Thus left alone to himself, his finitude begins to show itself in every direction; for man, single, is one-sided—a half—as is manifest by reflecting a moment on the sexual diremption. He is thus the half, yet would be the whole, and his entire nature drives him to overcome the contradiction; for, in truth, he is not himself; his existence is in and through another, namely, one of the opposite sex. Such is the feeling of love, for it is here not conscious, not in reflection, but the impulse of the individual to cancel his own finitude. Now, we have just seen that this natural individuality was quite the sum of pastoral life, and, hence, its chief content is love. Thus the Poet is true to the character of this realm, when he makes those who dwell in it totally occupied with the tender passion.

But there is another consequence of this life, which the Poet has not neglected. We see here the origin and the purport of the idyl. Pastoral poetry, in its native simplicity, is mainly amatory, and allows but little reflection—which belongs to a more cultivated period. Moreover, it is here that poetry begins, as the simplest expression of the primitive human passion. The Imagination gains absolute control and paints the loved one in the fairest colors; the stricken shepherd sees in the bush, in the flower, in the clouds, her fleeting form; all nature is turned into the image of her shape—love is his whole being. When man thus transmutes his existence into forms of the Imagination and gives them expression, the result is poetry. It does not seem a forced interpretation when it is said that Shakespeare meant to indicate the nature and the presence of the poetic element by the introduction of the native shepherds, Corin, Silvius, and Phebe. Their language falls at once into verse, their theme is some collision of love, and their names are taken from the pastoral poets. Moreover, Shakespeare has introduced perhaps the most common theme of this species of poetry—the neglected lover and the disdainful shepherdess; in fact, it occurs twice—Phebe disdains Silvius, and is herself disdained by Ganymede.

Certainly the greatest charm of pastoral poetry is this simple idyllic love, springing from nature direct, with the faintest shadow of social forms and conventionalities. Description of rural scenery and of pastoral manners is quite subordinate to the amatory element; but, when reflection enters, or allusions to a more complex social organization are brought in, the pastoral loses its native relish, without attaining the higher forms of poetry. This play is not, therefore, a pastoral drama in the sense of *Aminta* or *The Faithful Shepherdess,* both of which do not get beyond the shepherd's life, while here the pastoral element is merely a transitory phase of both poetic and social development. Such is the second movement of the play.

III. 1. But what is the outcome of the drama? The complication, which rests wholly in the disguise of Rosalind, is solved by her appearance in woman's clothes, and the four pairs are united in the presence of the Duke. Hymen is thus the magician who reconciles these collisions of love-land, and the result of the pastoral world is Marriage—the family, which again results directly in society. So, viewed on this side, the Ideal World cancels itself—passes over into a system of social order. The four pairs, who quite represent the various classes of people, make already a little State.

2. But the banished Duke and lords cannot thus return out of their idyllic existence, for it is supposed that they are too old for passion, or have previously entered the family relation. It is the State which has driven them off, and through the State they must be brought back. So the Poet introduces a new— and, of course, the true—motive for their return. The world of wrong, of which the usurping Duke is the representative, must continue its assaults upon the individual, since it is based upon the destruction of personal right. The result must be that soon a majority—or, if injustice be carried to its extreme logical end, all—of the people will be driven off to the Forest of Arden, where the rightful Duke resides. In such case the Idyllic Realm is at once converted into the same State from which they have fled, lacking only the soil and the usurping Duke. But the return must be complete—must be to the old territory. Hence the usurper is made to repent when he sees that he is deserted, and the old ruler and his attendant lords are restored *peacefully*—an important point, for it would ill comport with their peaceful character, and their simple, unoffending life in the woods, to come back by violence. Thus the reconciliation is complete; harmony is restored; the world of wrong dissolves of its own accord, the world of right returns with the rightful Duke. The diremption with which the play begins is now healed over, the Ideal World being the means whereby the regeneration takes place.

(St. Louis: 1877) Vol. I: 41–52.

MISS GRACE LATHAM ON ROSALIND, CELIA, AND HELEN
Grace Latham
1887–92

ROSALIND, CELIA, AND HELEN.

(Read at the 151st Meeting of the Society, Friday, April 11, 1890.)

> "The reason firm, the temperate will,
> Endurance, foresight, strength, and skill;
> A perfect woman, nobly planned,
> To warn, to comfort, to command;
> And yet a spirit still, and bright
> With something of an angel light."
>
> WILLIAM WORDSWORTH.

FRIENDSHIP is one of Shakspere's favourite early themes, and he shows it to us under one of its most beautiful forms in Rosalind and Celia. This is the more remarkable, as when *As You Like It* was written, he was probably passing through an experience which gave him cause to cry out with Amiens: "Most friendship is feigning, most loving mere folly," and yet as though to contradict it in the strongest possible way, he shows us, in the same play, the faithful loves of Orlando and Rosalind, and her equally true friendship with her cousin.

Shakspere was at a turning-point in his life's history; while rapidly gaining fame, wealth, and worldly consideration, he had to endure the treachery of a friend, whom he had idealized as only a very loving and imaginative nature could do, and having loved and won a too frail beauty of the court of Elizabeth, found himself deserted by her for the very man on whom he had fixed his supreme belief and affection.

As You Like It shows traces of the stress under which it was written. It has the fancy and imagination, the luxuriant ornament of his early period, its brilliant wit, and buoyant young life, with its delight in the beauty of nature, but underlying all we find, perhaps for the first time, a sense of disenchantment with the world, and a tendency to look below the surface of life to the sins and virtues whose combat he later never wearied of depicting.

This it is which gives the character of Rosalind its peculiar interest, and special difficulty from a dramatic point of view. When read the play is so beautiful, and furnishes so much food for thought and amusement, that this difficulty is hardly apparent, but when it is represented, most people must have felt disappointed; as soon as Orlando and she meet in Arden, the romantic hero of the first two Acts sinks into a puppet, on whom the heroine spends her witticisms; the conclusion is obvious, and except for her love of tormenting her swain, there seems no reason why the comedy should not be brought to a conclusion at once.

Shakspere however does not thus aimlessly spin out his creations, and the apparent defect is due to inadequate study of the text. The comedy side of Rosalind is so obvious and so brilliant, that it absorbs the attention of her exponents, to the neglect of the graver part of her nature.

She is one of those mirthful ladies with a sharp tongue, and a quick eye for the humorous and absurd, which delighted the young Shakspere, and are so well adapted for dramatic uses; Rosaline in *Love's Labour's Lost* is an attempt at such a one. Rosalind is however more than this; she belongs to a group of four highly finished and subtly conceived female characters—Beatrice, Viola, Helen and herself—written at a time when Shakspere was evidently giving special study to the psychology of woman, for they are the chief figures in the plays in which they appear, and each is grouped with another woman, less prominent, but as carefully and thoroughly thought out.

In a different sphere of life Rosalind might possibly have become a wider-minded, more lovable Maria. She has the same ready tact, instinctive knowledge of character, an equal love of mischief and fun; but the daughter of Duke Senior has been trained in the school of adversity, amid the refinements and corruptions of a court, and has been moulded into something stronger, nobler, and far more charming. Shakspere impresses these facts upon us with steady persistence; by scattered hints, and by the events of the first two scenes in which she appears. Their import is often overlooked but they contain the key to the characters of Rosalind and Celia.

While both were children Duke Frederick banished his brother, and usurped the Dukedom; but remorse for his own deed, in which we see the foreshadowing and possibility of his later repentance, and perhaps pity for his lonely little girl, who had neither brother nor sister, led him to keep his niece at court. The children were brought up in the closest intimacy. Celia says:

> "We still have slept together,
> Rose at an instant, learn'd, play'd, eat together;

And wheresoe'er we went, like Juno's swans
Still we went coupled, and inseparable."

Thus the foundation of their love was laid in nursery days, and bonds then formed are the most lasting of all. Rosalind, the child of the elder brother, may have been a year or two older than her cousin, over whose softer nature she won absolute empire.

Girls pass from passive childhood to early womanhood in a surprisingly short time. Before the country had done talking of the new duke and the old—news was news far longer in Shakspere's day—Rosalind and Celia had become two charming young women, with independent wills and judgments, whose steady, tender friendship gave rise to much comment. Both were lonely and in need of tenderness at the age when it is most wanted; surrounded by courtiers, a self-seeking, time-serving race, they were driven to cling all the more closely together.

Celia is one of the most perfect characters Shakspere ever depicted. Absolutely unselfish, her love finds its expression and its reward in tender, devoted service. She is ever ready to cheer her friend with playful wiles and loving words, or to avert possible dangers and complications from her with timely hints, checks, and counsels. Of a very clinging nature, she has a store of loving epithets: "my sweet Rose, my dear Rose," "sweet my coz," "thy precious words"; but her love is preserved from weakness by its strength and selflessness, and she has a fund of common-sense, and a power of acting promptly and advisedly in an emergency, which make her a very tower of strength to her impulsive cousin, who leans on her more than she is aware, and turns to her in every trouble and difficulty. Gentle and unsuspicious, Celia is full of kindness for all who approach her; for the poor jester, who is ready to "go along o'er the wide world" with her, or for the young Orlando unjustly and roughly chidden by the Duke.

Rosalind is far cleverer and more intellectual. Without being cold-hearted, she is not given to manifestations of affection, and has no sentiment whatever. There is a proverb that in every friendship one of the parties gives, while the other accepts, affection, and it is somewhat the case here: Rosalind receives and submits to Celia's loving care, without realizing the strength and constancy of the devotion lavished on her. Keen-witted and keen-sighted, she sees through the people with whom she comes in contact at a glance; has a rooted hatred of all that is mean or false, and a love of truth and uprightness which is one of her best features, but the very clearness of her vision makes her less trustful, more prone to suspect evil than her friend.

This character has been fostered by circumstances. In Shakspere's time the position of a possible claimant to the throne was full of peril; Rosalind felt she was living on dangerous ground, and behaved accordingly. Naturally gay and talkative; inclined to court, rather than avoid, observation; she is believed to be gentle and patient, silent, smooth and subtle. The necessity for caution sharpened her inherent power of observation, and her unimportant position, together with the increasing enmity of the Duke, must have made those around her comparatively careless how much of their real natures they betrayed before her. The court was evidently most corrupt; its women were pure only when it was impossible for them to be otherwise, for even kind Celia is obliged to say: "'Tis true; for those that she (Fortune) makes fair she scarce makes honest, and those that she makes honest she makes very ill-favouredly." Thus Rosalind gained a wider knowledge of life than is usual with a girl of her age and station. Too full of common-sense, and too healthy-minded to become morbid, her spirits droop; she broods over her father's wrongs, and the condition of her own estate, contrasting it almost bitterly with that of Celia.

When we first see the cousins, Celia is striving to drive away one of Rosalind's dark moods, almost to her annoyance: "Dear Celia, she says, I show more mirth than I am mistress of, and would you yet I were merrier?" Celia knows well that she does not receive the measure of love she gives, but she answers rather with a view to rouse Rosalind from her depression, than to reproach her in good earnest: "Herein I see thou lovest me not with the full weight that I love thee"; and to avoid paining the loving girl by seeming to envy the better fortune, which she so eagerly and seriously promises to resign, Rosalind tries to cast away her sadness and devise sports. But her mirth is forced; her wit is full of strained conceits, and turns involuntarily on the injustice of Fortune, the dominant thought in her mind. Celia too dislikes the proposal to fall in love, made for want of something better to say; she has no desire to give up her school-mate, and she dreads to see her entangled with some one, who might not allow her, "with the safety of a pure blush," to come off in honour. A factious lord would have found Rosalind's hand an excellent lever to forward his intrigues. The allusion seems obscure to us, but it was not so when Elizabeth jealously watched the marriages of her connections.

The cousins' attempt at merriment is not a success, and on Touchstone's entrance, Rosalind gradually drops out of the conversation.

Into this shadowed life the young Orlando came like a burst of sunlight. His fresh simplicity attracted her inexpressibly; his hot-headed bravery woke the pity and admiration of both girls; but while gentle Celia implores him not to fight with one so evidently stronger them he is, the quicker Rosalind supplies a pretext for his not doing so, without risking the imputation of cowardice: "We will make it our suit to the Duke that the wrestling might not go forward." His confession that, like hers, his life was sad and lonely, would have created a link between them, even without the fame of his victory over Charles, the discovery of his relationship to her father's friend, or the consequent rough treatment of him by the Duke.

Sweet Celia, burning with shame at her father's injustice, wishes to "go thank him and encourage him"; she makes him a courtly, well-turned compliment, as gracious as it is pretty. In Rosalind's speech we already feel the vibration of passion, combined with intense regret that her poverty prevents her from giving him the help he seems to need; then, overcome by her own boldness, she ejaculates: "Shall we go, coz?" but still she lingers. In the fallen fortunes, never absent from her mind, she finds an excuse for courting speech from him; and then yielding to a sudden impulse, she hints the declaration of love, which her superior rank almost obliged her to speak the first. No wonder Celia, alarmed by such suddenness, cries peremptorily: "Will you go, coz?" and Rosalind flies, leaving Orlando hardly realizing her meaning, but wholly in love with her.

Now she must mourn over an absent lover, but there is pleasure in the very pain, and assurance that life may hold another fate for her, beside that of a State prisoner, and her words flow more lightly and quickly. She is sadly cross with poor, patient Celia, who puts her temper aside with sweet playful words. There is perhaps a faint touch of jealousy at this sudden diversion of Rosalind's love. Celia is not greatly inclined to like Orlando: "Why should I not hate him!" she asks, half in earnest, but her chief wish is to save her friend from the troubles of a misplaced affection; caught, as she warningly hints, beyond "the trodden paths" of their life; she cannot as yet quite believe in it, or understand its suddenness, but we see that she will end by dutifully obeying Rosalind, and loving him because she does,

Then the storm, which has long been gathering, breaks; unexpected by the princesses, but foreseen by the courtiers, whose trade it is to note their sovereign's humours.

With only ten days' notice, for no fault of her own, Rosalind is banished, to satisfy the misgivings of a tyrant, who sees a plot against his crown even in her attempt to shrink out of sight. He calls her a traitor, whom he mistrusts by reason of her parentage; and then her fiery, untamed nature, which has remained covered up and hidden for so long, flashes into sight; she returns him scorn for suspicion, and her warm justification of her father and herself is too defiant to allay the Duke's fears. The speech is worth noting, as it is the only time the full strength and fire of her character shows itself; even the address to Phœbe is in a softer key, but the spirit is there, and we feel its presence in the vivacity of her talk, in the decision and energy of her actions.

Where she loves Celia is submissive; had she not, as it were, borne both her own and her cousin's part in their connection, she would probably have been more responsive to her affection. Let however some one dear to Celia be in trouble, then she rises to the occasion, to defend or act for them. Now she braves her father's "eyes full of anger," to plead courageously, earnestly, and yet with modest self-possession, for her cousin and their friendship. His attempts to disturb it are useless. Without vanity or small jealousy, to "show more bright and seem more glorious" has no attraction for her: "Banish me too," she says, "I cannot live out of her company." Essentially faithful and dutiful, Celia has been a loyal daughter to a father whom she could not respect. She checked Touchstone for speaking discourteously of him, but she privately condemned his usurpation of the crown, noted his tyranny, and now his last injustice has snapped the slight bond which held her to him. In a burst of pain and regret, she cries: "Oh, my poor Rosalind, whither wilt thou go? Wilt thou change fathers? I will give thee mine"; and then in terror at her silence: "I charge thee be not thou more grieved than I am." A flood of bitterness at past and present wrongs is seen in Rosalind's short sentence: "I have more cause." She does not realize, what is self-evident to Celia, that the Duke has practically banished her too.

> "Rosalind lacks then the love
> Which teacheth thee that thou and I am one:
> Shall we be sunder'd? shall we part, sweet girl?
> No; let my father seek another heir.
> Therefore devise with me how we may fly,
> Whither to go, and what to bear with us:
> And do not seek to take your charge upon you,
> To bear your griefs yourself, and leave me out;
> For, by this heaven, now at our sorrows pale,
> Say what thou canst, I'll go along with thee."

She at once takes the lead in planning their escape. Her sheltered existence prevents her from guessing what perils will meet them on the way, and she combats Rosalind's fears with sensible, practical suggestions. They are to go, disguised as poor women, to their natural protector, "my uncle in the forest of Arden," when her cousin's spirits suddenly rise: she sees a way of escape from a life she hates; Celia is going with her; and in the description of the disguise she means to assume, we get our first glimpse of the joyous, daring Rosalind of Arden, who comes to our minds every time the play of *As You Like It* is mentioned. As soon as she recovers herself, Celia drops contentedly back into the second place, without claiming or receiving a word of thanks for her marvellous self-devotion. Now that the burden of leadership is off her shoulders, there is a touch of sadness at her lonely future: "No longer Celia, but Aliena," and Rosalind, half to comfort her with the presence of an old and faithful servant, half because out of her rougher experiences she sees the need of some male companion, if not defender, proposes that Touchstone shall be persuaded to go with them, and the girls set forth with happy hearts "to liberty, and not to banishment." Shakspere accounts for the diversion of pursuit into a wrong track, by the eaves-dropping of "Hesperia, the princess' gentlewoman," and while the Duke's emissaries are searching for Orlando, the fool and the princesses get clear away.

Once free Rosalind's real character asserts itself. She delights in the independence her boy's dress gives her, in the successful way in which she wears it, and never alludes to it without some humorous touch. She leads the little party with a capability which shows her born to rule, encourages Celia, checks poor Touchstone's sighs after the comforts he has left, with an unselfishness she is already better able to appreciate. Sweeter far in happiness than in adversity, she prevents him from treating Corin with contempt, and hears the complaints of Silvius with fellow-feeling. The self-centered, almost egotistic Rosalind of the court is gone, and in her place we have a delightful, sympathetic woman, bearing hardship with endurance, and lightening her own and others' burdens with a genial sense of humour, which sees the absurd side of the most unpleasant situations.

Eager to establish some settled home for her party, when she hears of a flock and pastures for sale, she tries to buy it over the heads of other purchasers: "so that it stand with honesty"; there is no touch of the usurper in her. Celia follows her lead, and in fine ladylike ignorance of all farm life involves, of its profits and losses, which appear so clearly to the old shepherd, she adds: "and we will mend thy wages: I like this place, and willingly could waste my time in it."

Till now Rosalind has known nothing of Orlando's love for her, and when she finds the forest besprinkled with elegies and odes, though she hopes they come from him, she fears he may be merely using her name as a vehicle for poetic display, in the fashion of the courtly gallants of the time. Then follows a pretty bit of feminine fencing; Celia wishes to break the news of Orlando's arrival to Rosalind, to discover what her feelings now are towards him, and begins with a meaningless question, to be set aside or not as she wishes: "Didst thou hear these verses?" and Rosalind, desiring above all things to talk about them, answers with lengthy criticisms. Celia goes on with quiet amusement: "Trow you who hath done this?" Rosalind feigns ignorance: "Is it a man? *Celia:* And a chain, that you once wore, about his neck: Change you colour?" Still Rosalind will not be forced to speak the name she longs to hear; she would be too much ashamed if her hopes were unfounded, and she has her share of that natural coyness, which at first prompts a young girl to shrink away from her lover; then she in her turn becomes the questioner, while Celia holds back the desired information, with a mischievous enjoyment of her anxiety; but when it is given Rosalind cries, with a charming mixture of humour and womanly shame: "Alas the day! what shall I do with my doublet and hose?" The little scene preserves for us the softness and womanly feeling of the heroine, who might have been forgotten in the gay sauciness with which she plays the page's part. Rosalind's object in speaking to Orlando is to discover the authorship of the verses, and his real feelings towards her; but she is unexpectedly thwarted. She supports her assumed character so well, that though he perceives her likeness to his lady, he sees in her only a quick-witted stripling, with a clever tongue. Thus when she speaks of true lovers, instead of crying out, as she hoped, "Such a one am I," he replies with good-humoured criticism of the epithet "lazy," and disappoints her again and again. He patronizes the bright boy, takes pains to draw him out; she, determined to lengthen the interview, and longing to shine in his presence, puts out all her brilliancy, and succeeds at last in interesting him: "Where dwell you, pretty youth?" he asks, and at this first step forward she makes her only mistake: "With this shepherdess, my sister; here in the skirts of the forest, like fringe upon a petticoat." So feminine an image was enough to betray her, but Orlando asked his question too carelessly to notice the slip, farther than to feel that her answer does not ring quite true, and rouses himself to inquire farther, and to notice her refined accent. Then she tries, by calumniating women in general, to tempt him to defend himself in particular. Alas for her wishes! he asks for details of their faults, hoping to elicit another series of humorous sketches such as he had already heard. She will not however allow him to stray from the point to which she is leading him. Having forced him to talk of women, she uses the opportunity in the most masterly manner, to bring forward her own name, and by affecting disbelief in his love, extracts the longed-for protestation: "Fair youth, I would I could make thee believe I love." She has self-command not to betray herself, and in the riddling speech: "Me believe it! you may as soon make her that you love believe it; which I warrant she is apter to do than to confess she does: that is one of the points in which women still give the lie to their consciences," she expresses her delight, and preserves her presence of mind with a timely touch of self-ridicule. Another curious point in this speech is that though almost unnerved by strong feeling, she seems at the same time to survey the drama passing in her soul from without, as though it were happening in that of some other person. This is a position peculiar to artists, whose instinct it is to study their own feelings and experiences for future use, even when they are most overpowering. It shows the turn of mind of the writer, for it is a fact not easily understood by any but artistic persons, and it stamps Rosalind as a born actress. Shakspere shows us many women in a disguise, but none support it with less effort, none enter into it so fully, so enjoyingly, as this bright Amazon, and the part formerly imposed on her at her uncle's court was carried out as perfectly, though with less satisfaction to herself.

Then she craftily questions Orlando, desiring greater assurance of his truth, and again comes a burst of joy, veiled in sarcasm, in which, by reckoning herself among the whippers who are in love too, she seems to give herself up as hopelessly, irrecoverably in love. With the utmost tact she leads up to a proposal, which, under the guise of curing him of his folly, will secure constant meetings with him.

There is no bitterness in this scene, all Rosalind's words are full of joy and lightheartedness, and we hardly know which to admire most—her intellectual or womanly qualities; the keen insight into human nature, the finished, epigrammatic brilliancy of her perfectly turned speeches, the ready tact with which she governs the whole interview, leading the unconscious Orlando to say and do exactly what she desires; or her warm affection, genuine modesty, and perfect self-control. The path of true love had its roughnesses for Rosalind; soon she and Celia begin to doubt Orlando's truth. They, knowing the real state of affairs, did not realize that he could not be expected to keep his appointments with "young master Ganymede," even when made to talk of his beloved, as punctually and eagerly as he would have done with the beloved herself; nor that the coldness in his kisses, the hollow ring in his love-making, which made his oaths sound "no stronger than the word of a tapster . . . the confirmer of false reckonings," came from the same cause.

Rosalind is weeping-ripe, ready to accuse and defend him in the same breath. Celia once more shows herself a wise and faithful friend. Full of sympathy, and indignant with the false lover, who is deceiving and torturing her cousin, she will not encourage her in what seems a hopeless passion; strives to divert her from it by playful sarcasm; and by the tonic of timely rebukes, helps her to avoid the break-down which must have betrayed her sex.

While in this state of excited feeling they are called to witness the unhappy wooing of Silvius.

It is noticeable that Rosalind usually speaks prose, except when deeply moved. Although her romantic adventures, her beauty, her dancing wit and happy nature make her one of the most poetic figures in the play, her mind is not in any sense that of a poet. Hans Andersen says in his *Goloshes of Fortune,* that many people are by nature poets, possessing their feelings, perceptions, and experiences, but that the so-called poet is he who has a memory for these impressions and can translate them into words. Neither case suits Rosalind. Endowed with infinite humour and excellent sense, she sees everything and everybody by their light, and as a rule it is people's weaknesses and peculiarities which arrest her attention. When she bought her sheepcote, she saw the practical side of the affair; to her Arden was a "desert place" in which food and shelter had to be found. Shakspere does not place one reference to its loveliness in her mouth; it is Celia who feels its charm, who directs Oliver so poetically to her cot. The beauty of Rosalind's speech consists in its terseness, in the fitness of her words to her thoughts: ornament it has none. To such a mind as hers prose is the natural and suitable mode of expression; but when the fire slumbering within her is stirred by anger, indignation, or love, her speech changes; her emotion carries her out of herself; she lives poetry, without perceiving it, and when deeply moved, she uses metre.

One of these moments has now come. Unobserved she has seen the gratuitous torture of Silvius; the affectation and cruelty of his mistress jar on the mood of the disguised princess, and she interrupts the astonished pair with words winged by scorn and indignation. Why should this village beauty plume herself upon her rustic graces, so as to "insult and exult over the wretched"? Why should she disdain the full measure of a perfect love, when Rosalind must spend hers on a possibly faithless object? "Down on your knees and thank Heaven fasting for a good man's love," she cries, and again she lashes the vanity and false pretension which alone prevent Phœbe's heart from being touched.

Phœbe's beauty was of a class quite unlike Rosalind's finished ideals, who therefore was not likely to admire her, but it is her hatred of humbug and love of truth that revolt from the falseness and cruelty of the woman.

Jacques she contemplates as she might some strange bit of natural history; his pretence of wisdom, his causeless melancholy, which he seeks her acquaintance to display, his conceit and self-absorption are patent to her at once, and rouse only laughter and contempt; life is as real and interesting to her as it is vague and objectless to him. No one would guess that less than half an hour had passed since her stormy interview with Phœbe, or that she is even now grieving over Orlando's absence, so lightly does she speak; but she is accustomed, from her courtly training to present a surface view of herself; the strength and fluctuations of her real feelings can often only be guessed or inferred; this makes her seem colder then she really is.

As soon as she is alone with Orlando the scolding which has been burning in her heart and on her tongue begins. She is not the woman to bear wrong with meek submission, or to control anger with cool reason. She reproaches him not only with insincerity, but with his poverty, and with jealousy, which, if it existed, was on her side rather than on his.

Orlando's attraction for her is his straightforward, genuine nature, and that he should be unpunctual is a grief, not only because she wanted him earlier, but because her ideal has failed her. He promised and did not fulfil; hence she argues he cannot love her truly, and she would have been right had he known she was indeed his Rosalind.

It is in this scene that we find the chief traces of her former experiences; the remembrance of which has been stirred up by these cruel doubts of her lover. She harps on the unreality of love, on the sins and weaknesses of men and women; nearly always in jest, and without personal bitterness, for his calm assertion of his belief in her virtue drives all clouds away. She passes, with that suddenness which is one of her great charms, into a joyous, mischievous mood; first in holiday humour making him woo her, as she delights to do, until he answers somewhat indifferently to a pretended refusal: "Then in mine own person I die"; when she changes once more to a sarcastic, teasing vein, finding it more profitable than a tender one which he cannot fully appreciate, and rails on his sex and hers.

Our conversation, even when merriest, is the outcome of our lives in one form or another, especially with women, and though Rosalind is pure and good, she must have seen the corruptions of the world at her uncle's court, or she would never have so insisted on them; they would not have occurred to her; she would have teased Orlando in some other fashion.

The description of the men who "have died from time to time, and worms have eaten them but not for love," was not learnt from books only; it must have been inspired by something that touched her own life, if only from the outside. True as steel herself, she has been brought into contact with the Cressidas and Cleopatras of the world, for there is the same line of thought in—"Men are April when they woo, December when they wed: maids are May when they are maids, but the sky changes when they are wives. I will be more jealous of thee than a Barbary cock-pigeon over his hen; more clamorous than a parrot against rain; more newfangled than an ape; more giddy in my desires than a monkey: I will weep for nothing, like Diana in the fountain, and I will do that when you are disposed to be merry; I will laugh like a hyen, and that when thou art inclined to sleep. . . . The wiser, the waywarder."—(Act IV. Sc. i.); and—

> "Yet hold I off. Women are angels, wooing:
> Things won are done, joy's soul lies in the doing:
> That she belov'd knows nought that knows not this,—
> Men prize the thing ungain'd more than it is:
> That she was never yet that ever knew
> Love got so sweet, as when desire did sue:
> Therefore this maxim out of love I teach,—
> Achievement is command; ungain'd, beseech:
> Then though my heart's content firm love doth bear,
> Nothing of that shall from mine eyes appear."
>
> *Troilus and Cressida*, Act I. Sc. ii.

Charmian advises Cleopatra in dealing with Antony:

> "In each thing give him way, cross him in nothing.
> *Cleopatra.* Thou teachest like a fool: the way to lose him."

The only difference is that Rosalind applies the lesson to the keeping of a husband; the two others, to the securing of a lover. When the talk of a pure woman turns on the corruption of the world, it often means, as it does here, that she has seen or heard things which have shocked and pained her, which she longs and strives not to believe, and yet that she has for a time accepted an exaggerated view of evil, without allowing for the counterbalancing good, which seems to her to be blotted out.

The underlying thought in the play is this struggle between good and evil; going on in different forms, according to the natures of the *dramatis persona,* Rosalind being its central figure; Jacques is the hero of evil; Orlando, that of goodness. It is never allowed to be very apparent; *As You Like It* is intended to be a true comedy, therefore the world-bitterness is only its undercurrent or ground swell. We trace it in the regularity with which a morbid thought is contradicted by a wholesome one, an ugly fact opposed to a beautiful; but it forms the key-note to the character of Rosalind, and its significance is increased when we remember that it has been introduced by Shakspere himself, there being no trace of it in the novel of Thomas Lodge, *Euphus Golden Legacie,* from which the plot is taken. The morbid philosopher Jacques, the worldly philosopher Touchstone, and Amiens, the singer of "all friendship is feigning," being also Shakspere's own creations, while he has given Duke Senior the counterbalancing part of the philosopher of good. While keeping the character of an exquisite pastoral comedy, the play is also its author's protest against the falseness and evil of the world, which the bitter sorrow that was pressing on him when it was written had brought home to his mind, and as its name implies it may be taken from either point of view: *As You Like It.*

Rosalind receives assurance of the existence of good in Orlando's astonished reception of her words, in his steady defence of herself, and learns how fully he comes up to the ideal she has formed of him. For once Shakspere intended to draw a perfect hero in Orlando; brave, honest, generous, and forgiving, he will resist injustice, but it cannot embitter him. With steady common-sense, which refuses to accept either the morbid philosophy of Jacques, or an undue estimate of the sins and follies of life, decked out with lusty youth, and with just a spice of conceit in his verses, and fantasy in his love, he is the very man to fascinate a girl who has seen too early and too much of the crooked ways of the world. We find him perhaps a little tedious, but to Rosalind he was not merely an ideal, but a revelation. No wonder she was many fathoms deep in love with him.

Silvius puzzles Rosalind; she does not understand his perfect unselfish love, which even at its own cost would give the object of his affection her heart's desire, and can suffer wrong without a thought of retaliation. At first, with her usual suspicion, she jumps to the conclusion that he has forged the letter he bears, to discover if Ganymede be inclined to requite Phœbe's love; and to find out if he is acquainted with the contents, she gives a perfectly false account of them, adding with much emphasis: "Her love is not the hare that I do hunt . . . Well, shepherd, well, this is a letter of your own device." Not content with his earnest denial, she reads it aloud, perverting its sense with her comments, until the extreme sadness of his words, "Call you this chiding," leaves her no choice but to believe him innocent. His sorrow moves Celia with a great pity; Rosalind in her youthful energy almost despises him for being such "a tame snake"; she would not have endured such treatment so meekly; but she is too kind-hearted not to pity him too, and as her nature is, she expresses it in action, sending a message to the shepherdess: "If she love me, I charge her to love thee; if she will not, I will never have her, unless thou entreat for her." Rosalind cannot, and will not, like Phœbe; her cruelty, her forwardness, her affectation of fine-ladyism disgust the princess, and provoke the one touch of haughty disdain we see in her:

> "I saw her hand: she has a leathern hand,
> A freestone-coloured hand; I verily did think
> That her old gloves were on, but 'twas her hands:
> She has a huswife's hand."

Such an outburst is not usual with Rosalind, who is kind and courteous to every one, and thinks but little of the rank which she has always been accustomed to possess.

It is when we are thrown into new and strange contact with people of a higher or lower level than ourselves, of a class to which we are not accustomed, that our difference to them strikes us. This scene is chiefly in metre; partly because it is generally used by Silvius, and also because Rosalind is moved and excited. As soon as she finds he has not tried to impose upon her, she calms down and returns to prose.

We pass again to metre for the account of Oliver's repentance and Orlando's wound. It shows the force of Rosalind's love, that though she has borne up while hearing the story, and knows he is safe and "strong at heart," she should faint at the sight of his blood; though she covers it with her usual quick-wittedness, and all white and trembling as she is, cries: "Ah, sirrah, a body would think this was well counterfeited."

In the moment of need Celia again comes forward with ready help; though frightened and astonished by the sudden weakness of her to whom she has lately looked for support and guidance, she cries, "Cousin," and nearly betrays them.

Sweet Celia is now provided with a lover of her own in Oliver, and we feel that her gentle nature will suit his, which will always seek to predominate, far better than that of the quieter, less self-asserting Orlando. There is no need to question the suddenness of the affair, as has been done by some critics. Love at first sight is not uncommon in Shakspere's plays, and Celia has no doubts to lead her to prolong the wooing. It was necessary to the happy conclusion of the comedy that she should not be left desolate, when her own unselfishness had helped to take the partner of her girlhood from her, and it would be impossible to make her and her suitor more prominent without interfering with the two central figures, especially at this moment when their love story is coming to its climax, as Celia stands upon the same plane as they do. Silvius and Phœbe, Touchstone and Audrey are sedulously kept on other levels, sustaining one the pastoral, the other the low comedy interest, and therefore their histories admit of fuller treatment, without injury to the chief interest of the play.

Celia's future is decided before Rosalind is at all sure of Orlando's feelings. When she alludes to her counterfeiting he hardly responds, his mind is too full of envy at his brother's happiness, to take much heed of Ganymede's simulated coquetry; but when he breaks out into genuine, unsolicited regret at his own lonely condition, she receives the assurance she has so long waited for. She does not discover herself to him at once, as a less cautious and a less modest nature would have done; she waits till she can give herself away in her own proper dress, with her father's full consent; neither does she now or later bow down before him as her lord and king, like Portia and Juliet. She is not given to such outpourings of love and sentiment. They would hardly be in accordance with her independent nature, which, as has been already indicated, having won Orlando, will bend all its energies to keep him her own for ever. But what she does say is far more characteristic of her: "I know you to be a gentleman of a good conceit." And therefore, knowing him to be in every way the fulfilment of her ideal, if indeed he love Rosalind, she will give her to him.

It is not uninteresting to compare Rosalind with Beatrice, the character which comes nearest to her in all Shakspere's plays. The first draws the material for her wit from her experience of men and things, the second from passing events and words, which give opportunity to her ready tongue and active fancy. Both are clear-sighted, but Rosalind has had far more need and scope for using this power; Beatrice has lived sheltered in her uncle's home, and her world is the limited one of a happy girl, in a good social position, with a fairly large acquaintance. Beatrice flouts her suitors, but she is of a more trusting nature, and has none of Rosalind's doubts as to their sincerity and love-worthiness. Again in the keener mind of Rosalind impressions take a more exact and definite shape, and she is far less given to "the lusty hyperbole" in which Beatrice delights. Each is active, practical, and filled with common-sense. Again, each has a friend of a quieter, more retiring disposition than herself, but Beatrice is perhaps less passionate, and certainly is of a more affectionate nature. In Rosalind passion swamps affection, and though equally kind and true, she would never be as devoted or tender a friend to one of her own sex; when she has seen Orlando, her love for her father is annihilated, as it was only fed by imaginations and much brooding, over his and her own wrongs. Beatrice loves Benedick entirely, but her affection for Hero is to the last as intense and active as ever, who indeed is throughout the play the passive partner in that friendship.

HELEN. *ALL'S WELL THAT ENDS WELL.*

THERE is perhaps no character which shows how closely Shakspere had studied women's natures than that of Helen in *All's Well that Ends Well.* She has repelled some of her commentators by the means she adopts to gain her ends, and has aroused the extravagant admiration of others; to nearly all she is more or less a riddle. Pure, humble, loving, and faithful, she becomes possessed of Bertram by stratagem and against his will, establishes her empire over him by apparently furthering an impure intrigue, and yet never forfeits the respect and affection of her friends.

Her character is not a very common one, but it is sufficiently usual for us to consider her as the type of a class; that of the determined, tactful woman, who will use any means, and submit to almost any degradation or hardship, to gain her ends, hut who, preferring the substance of power to its shadow, never forces those whom she governs, quite unconsciously to themselves, to recognize the extent of her intellect and strength.

Where evil tendencies are combined with such a nature, the woman becomes a consummate schemer; when she is poor also, a successful adventuress; when, as with Helen, good qualities are in the ascendant, she dominates in every connection or undertaking in which she is concerned, all the more surely as her power and its sources are never fully known. She governs her home and its inmates, ruling despotically over willing subjects, or she is the successful leader in far-reaching social or charitable enterprises; but whether she be good or bad, woe to those who oppose her, for she is a dangerous enemy.

Helen does not start with the ball at her foot. She is the ward and gentlewoman of the Countess of Rousillon, the daughter of her late physician, who left his child to her protection. Poor, of small account to all but her protectress, Helen compels people and circumstances to serve her as she wills; and this, as far as she is concerned, who, after all, is the hero of the play, and would, as his manner is, have hinted it to us long before. There is, however, no trace of it and even before Helen's first appearance at Court, Bertram was eager to leave it; we can only took upon all he says of Lafeu's daughter as being among the falsehoods in which he indulges so freely throughout the scene. The lines, "She whom all men praised, and whom myself since I have lost have loved," bear a greater colour of truths; they are intended to increase the probability of the subsequent reconciliations; we know that the news of her death was a great shock to him, and regret for a hitherto unvalued good when it has passed out of our keeping is only too common.

Bertram's newly-learnt regard for appearances leads him to invent another romantic story to account for the possession of Helen's ring; he is but young in deceit, and does not know that the best cover for a secret is not a series of inventions which are always liable to be disproved. He is at once involved in the darkest suspicions; his careless eyes had never noticed the jewel on Helen's hand, and witnesses start up on every side to prove it hers. Thus at Diana's entrance he is already discredited; he lies, contradicts himself, and blunders deeper and deeper into the mire. She bravely holds to the story she has been taught, and says, all unconscious of the question there has already been about it: "Send for your ring again." Parolles is only too glad to revenge himself upon his late master by giving evidence against him; and then as Bertram stands shamed, convicted of double wrong-doing, with the shadow of a terrible suspicion upon him, Helen enters to his deliverance, and with a sudden revulsion of feeling he takes his better self to his heart, while his evil genius, Parolles, passes out of their lives into the service of the Lord Lafeu.

When we compare the characters treated of in this paper, we find that passion, intellect, and will are the chief forces in Rosalind and Helen, but that the first *guides* her life through them, the second *shapes* hers. Keen-witted and clear-sighted, Rosalind can read hearts and characters, and will use a passing opportunity to attain her desire, but she does not think out an elaborate plan, requiring the co-operation of others to bring it to perfection; she rules through the affection she inspires. Helen on the contrary is slow-brained, rather observant than clear-sighted, only seeing the surface of life, unless compelled to do otherwise; but what she does perceive, her tact and intellect enable her to use with wonderful effect; and the tremendous force of her will, the motive power with her, which is always concentrated on the one object, enables her to control circumstances. Rosalind is, as it were, a spectator at the comedy of human life, and the possession of so brilliant and humorous a tongue inspires her with a desire to shine. Helen is not brilliant, and has but a girlish sense of fun; she never thinks of the personal effect she produces, and her mind is thus left free to occupy itself with carrying out her will. Rosalind loathes all that is false, and has an innate delicacy and modesty, notwithstanding her boy's dress and free talk, while Helen considers only the legitimacy of the end she has in view, and to gain it will stoop to the most repellent trickery, hardly realizing its baseness. Thus she has an enormous advantage over Rosalind, whose very superiority ties her hands. Change their places, and Rosalind would have fretted her heart out for Bertram, just as she did when she was a poor dependent at her uncle's court, and while she was separated from Orlando; Helen would have made uncle, father, and lover bow to her will. Poverty and a dependent position could not affect her, except by teaching her to understand those in a like case; not only was she kindly treated at Rousillon, but she is too strong to be embittered by petty annoyances.

Thus far the comparison is rather to Rosalind's advantage; but she wants Helen's infinite tenderness and sweetness, her deep humility and unconsciousness of self, and her need to serve the beloved, all which remind us of Celia; and if Helen is egoistic in gaining the object of her love, she is at least nobly unselfish in its exercise. Rosalind is raised and redeemed from world-bitterness by her lover; Helen, on the contrary, believes devoutly in the better nature of hers, and will in the end, we feel assured, raise him to her own higher level. Touched with "the passion poesy," she translates her feelings into fair images drawn from the most beautiful natural objects, and her vehicle of expression is metre; while Rosalind, who sees life without glamour but such as is derived from her own good spirits, generally uses prose. In her infectious light heartedness she lifts the weight of care from our souls; and her glancing wit, her constant change from one charming mood to another, make us think of the sunlight gleaming through the trees of the forest of Arden. Helen is like the steady sun of early summer, whose temperate heat warms without scorching. She teaches us to endure with calm self-possession, to cut our way from among the sorrows that besiege us.

We are sorry *for* Rosalind, we grieve with Helen, but we feel that the most womanly if least powerful of the three, is the gentle, loving, unselfish Celia.

(London: *New Shakespeare Society's Translation*, 1887–92): 285–318.

"THE GRAPHIC" GALLERY OF SHAKESPEARE'S HEROINES
W. E. Henley
1888

SHAKESPEARE was commonly no respecter of persons: impartial as Nature, he finished his Iago as carefully as his Juliet, his Antony as dispassionately as his Macbeth. But he seems to have had a very human weakness for his Rosalind. She is even more the heroine of *As You Like It* than Orlando—though for him the Master wrote what is perhaps his most exquisite prose—is the hero. She is heard of in the very first scene; she appears in the next; she possesses act after act with peculiar magic; she cuts the knot of the intrigue, and gives out happiness with both hands; and when the most enchanting of all sylvan romances is wound out, she re-appears before the curtain—"though it is not the fashion to see the lady the epilogue"—to speak the poet's valediction, and ask his hearers' favour for herself and for the play.

As You Like It is the story of two Dukes, who were brothers, and of their respective daughters, Rosalind and Celia, the two fair cousins. Rosalind's father, the Banished Duke, has been discrowned by Celia's father, Duke Frederick, and has sought refuge in Arden forest, where he and his train of broken lords "fleet the time carelessly as in the golden world;" and Rosalind herself, having seen the dispossessed Orlando throw her uncle's champion, and fallen in love with him upon the instant, is no sooner exiled by the usurper than she too resolves to repair to Arden. Being, as she puts it, "more than common tall," she elects to suit her "all points like a man;" she calls herself Ganymede, for she will "have no worse a name than Jove's own page;" and, taking with her her little cousin (who "cannot live out of her company") disguised as a rustic maid, and their common friend Touchstone, her uncle's jester, she proceeds upon her journey early in the second act. The party arrive in Arden, whither, by a pleasing coincidence, Orlando has preceded them; and there, having carried their jewels with them, they buy a farm—the "cote" and "flocks" and "bounds of feed" of a certain churlish shepherd—and sit down to fleet the time carelessly as the Banished Duke himself.

It is not long ere Ganymede falls in with Orlando. That youth, indeed, is deep in love with Rosalind, as she, though he knows it not, is with him; and, having none to whom he may tell his passion, he has fallen into the trick of making verses, and hanging them here and everywhere about the forest. Ganymede finds and reads one set; and Celia not only finds and reads another, but recognises the poet, and reveals him to her cousin. "I will speak to him like a saucy lackey," says the masquing lady, when he comes along," and under that habit play the knave with him." As Rosalind has said, so Ganymede proceeds to do; and in the course of their first encounter he makes the lovelorn gentleman declare himself, and volunteers, by way of relief, to play his mistress to him whenever he is minded so far to make-believe. He will do it with such spirit and authority that his fellow actor shall soon, he pledges himself, be healed of his malady. He has done it before; and he undertakes, "if you would but call me Rosalind, and come every day to my cote and woo me," to do it again. Orlando accepts the challenge, and Ganymede plays Rosalind to the life. "That thou did'st know," he cries to his cousin after one such experience, "how many fathom deep I am in love!" Soon he is within an ace of discovering his secret to the world; for when it is told him, that Orlando has been hurt by a lion, he swoons away. He tries to put it off upon the messenger, that it is "well counterfeited;" but he is assured in return, "there is too great testimony in your complexion that it was a passion of earnest."

Rosalind's affairs, indeed, are by now in something of a tangle; for Ganymede, by the mere charm of insolence and disdain, has made the haughty shepherdess Phœbe so instant in his pursuit that he is fain to promise her his faith, if ever he bestows it upon woman, while to Orlando he must profess himself a magician, and therewithal both able and willing to give him the white hand of his Rosalind, and that no later than the very next day. These engagements he ratifies before the Banished Duke; and to that potentate and his lords, awaiting the event, there enters, under no less an escort than Hymen's, Rosalind in her true shape, and with her the faithful Celia. Thus does Ganymede keep his word. He restores his daughter to the Duke, and his mistress to Orlando, while he takes from Phœbe all hope of her new desire. Celia, meanwhile, has paired off with Orlando's brother Oliver, a penitent at last and, like Orlando, an exile in Arden; and as on the instant of the great discovery it is announced that Duke Frederick has made amends for his past, and "put on a religious life," the play ends, as it ought, in a dance and universal happiness.

(London, 1888): 26–27.

SOME OF SHAKESPEARE'S FEMALE CHARACTERS
Helena Faucit, Lady Martin
1891

ROSALIND.

Bryntysilio, *September* 1884.

"But heavenly Rosalind!"

"That gaze
Kept, and shall keep me to the end her own!
She was above it—but so would not sink
My gaze to earth."

—*Colombe's Birthday,* Act ii. sc, 1.

MY DEAR MR BROWNING,—

THE note in which you thanked me with so many kind words for sending you my letter upon Imogen, ended with the following suggestion, "And now you must give us Rosalind." I would fain think you were moved to write these stimulating words by some not unpleasing remembrance of the way in which, to use Rosalind's own phrase, "I set her before your eyes, human as she is," in the days when our kindred studies,—yours as a dramatist, mine as an interpreter of the drama,—first drew us into the communion which has ripened into a lifelong friendship. For whom would I try with more alacrity to execute a task so difficult, yet so congenial, than for the poet whose Lucy Carlisle, whose Mildred Tresham, and, last not least, whose exquisite Colombe are associated with the earliest recollections of my artist life?

With what sweet regret I look back to the time when with other gifted men,—Talfourd, Bulwer, Marston, Troughton, and the rest,—you made common cause with Mr Macready in raising the drama of our time to a level not unworthy of the country of Shakespeare! How generously you all wrought towards this end! How warmly were your efforts seconded by the public! And yet I use the word "regret," because of the sudden end which came to all our strivings, when Mr Macready threw up the enterprise just when it seemed surest of success. It was an evil hour for my own art, and not less evil, I venture to think, for the literature of the drama. But for this mischance, we might have looked to you for that fuller development of your dramatic genius, which I can well believe you did not care to put forth, when you were no longer sure of a combination of trained actors and actresses to understand, and to make others understand, the characters you had drawn. Grateful as I am for what you have given to the world in many ways, I have always felt how great a loss the stage has suffered from the diversion into other channels of that creative dramatic power which you, of all our contemporaries, seem to me pre-eminently to possess. You may remember saying at a casual meeting in Hyde Park, when I was expressing my love and admiration for Pompilia,—"Ah, if I could have had you for Pompilia, I would have made the story into a drama." Your words made me very happy. How gladly would I have done my best to illustrate a character so finely conceived !

"And now you must give us Rosalind." Your words lie before me as I take up your letter again, after a long interval of suffering, which, for nearly two years, has made writing, and even continuous thought, impossible. They are my encouragement to throw myself again into that world, so ideal yet so real, in which, with Rosalind, it was my delight to sojourn, and endeavour to put before you what was in my heart and my imagination when I essayed to clothe her with life. Ah me! what it will be to me to enter again into that delicious dreamland out of the life in death in which, for so long, I have been "doomed to go in company with pain"!

I need not tell you that, when you first saw my Rosalind, "I was too young that time to value her," and could not enter so fully into her rich complex nature as to do justice to it. This is no more possible than it would have been for Shakespeare to have written, before the maturity of manhood, a play so full of gentle wisdom, so Catholic in its humanity, so subtle in the delineation, so abounding in nicely balanced contrasts, of character, so full of happy heart, so sweetly rounded into a harmonious close, as *As You Like It.* His mind had assuredly worked its way through the conflicts and perplexities of life, within as well as without, and had settled into harmony with itself, before this play was written.

In my first girlhood's studies of Shakespeare this play had no share. Pathos, heroism, trial, suffering—in these my imagination revelled, and my favourites were the heroines who were put most sorely to the proof. Juliet, Desdemona, Cordelia, Imogen, I had brooded over until they had become, as it were, part of my life; and, as you may remember, in the more modern plays, in which I performed the heroines, the pathetic or tragic element almost invariably predominated. When, therefore, I was told by Mr Macready that he wished me to act Rosalind for my benefit at the end of a season, I was terrified. I did not know the words, nor had I ever seen the play performed, but I had heard enough of what Mrs Jordan and others had done with the character, to add fresh alarm to my misgivings. Mr Macready, however, was not to be gainsaid; so I took up my Shakespeare, determined to make the best of what had to me then all the aspect of a difficult and somewhat irksome task. Of course I had not time to give to the entire play the study it requires, if Rosalind is to be rightly understood.

The night of trial came. Partly because the audience were indulgent to me in everything I did, partly, I suppose, because it was my benefit night, the performance was received with enthusiasm. I went home happy, and thinking how much less difficult my task had been than I had imagined. But there a rude awakening met me. I was told that I had been merely playing, not acting, not impersonating a great character. I had not, it seemed to my friends, made out what were generally considered the great points in the character. True, I had gained the applause of the audience, but this was to be deemed as nothing. Taken in the mass, they were as ignorant as I was, perhaps more so, as probably, even in my hasty study, I had become better acquainted with the play than most of them. It was very necessary, I have no doubt, and wholesome for me, to receive this lesson. But oh, what a pained and wounded heart I took with me that night to my pillow! I had thought that upon the whole I had not been so very bad,—that I had been true at least to Shakespeare in my general conception, though, even as I acted, I felt I had not grasped anything like the full significance of the words I was uttering. Glimpses of the poet's purpose I had, no doubt, for I do not think I ever altered the main outlines of my first conception; but of the infinite development of which it is capable I had no idea. It was only when I came to study the character minutely, and to act it frequently, that its depths were revealed to me.

As I recall the incidents of this first performance, I am reminded how little the public knew of the disadvantages under which, in those days, one used sometimes to be called upon to play important parts. To an artist with a conscience, and a reputation to lose, this was a serious affair. In much the same hurried way I was originally required to act Lady Macbeth, and this before the Dublin audience, which, I had been told, was then in many respects more critical than that of London. After the close of the Drury Lane season, in June, I acted a short engagement in Dublin with Mr Macready. Macbeth was one of his favourite parts, and to oblige the manager, Mr Calcraft, I had promised to attempt Lady Macbeth; but in the busy work of each day, up to the close of the London season, I had had no time to give the character any real thought or preparation. Indeed the alarm I felt at the idea of presuming to go upon the stage in such a character, made me put off grappling with it to the last possible moment. The mere learning of the words took no time. Shakespeare's words seem to fasten, without an effort, upon the minds and to live there for ever. Mr Macready at our one rehearsal taught me the business of the scene, and I confided to him the absolute terror I was in as the time of performance drew near. He kindly encouraged me, and said, from what he had seen during the rehearsal, he was sure I should get on very well. At night, when it was all over, he sent to my dressing room to invite me to take the call of the audience along with him. But by this time the poor frightened "Lady" had changed her sleep-walking dress with the extremest haste, and driven away home. I was rather scolded the next day by Mr Macready, who reminded me that he had asked me to remain, feeling assured the audience would wish to see me. This I had quite forgotten, thinking only of the joy of having got over my fearful task, and desirous of running away and forgetting it as quickly as possible.

I have no remembrance of what the critics said. But Mr Macready told me that my banquet and sleep-walking scenes were the best. In the latter, he said, I gave the idea of sleep, disturbed by fearful dreams, but still it was sleep. It was to be seen even in my walk, which was heavy and unelastic, marking the distinction—too often overlooked—between the muffled voice and seeming-mechanical motion of the somnambulist, and the wandering mind and quick fitful gestures of a maniac, whose very violence would wake her from the deepest sleep,—a criticism I never forgot, always endeavouring afterwards to work upon the same principle, which had come to me then by instinct. Another remark of his about the sleep-walking scene I remember. He said: "Oh, my child, where did you get that long-drawn sigh? What can you know of such misery as that sigh speaks of?" He also said that my first scene was very promising, especially the soliloquy, also my reception of Duncan, but that my after scenes with him were very tame. I had altogether failed in "chastising with the valour of my tongue."

The only criticism I remember on this my first attempt in Dublin, besides Mr Macready's, was that of a most highly cultivated and dear lady friend, who said to me a day or two afterwards: "My dear, I will never see you again in that terrible character. I felt horror-stricken. Lear says of Cordelia, 'So young and so untrue!' I should say of your Lady Macbeth, 'So young and yet so wicked!'"

Her antipathy was equalled by my own. To the last time of my performing the character I retained my dread of it, and to such a degree, that when I was obliged to act it in the course of my engagements (as others did not seem to dislike seeing me in the character so much as I disliked acting it), I invariably took this play first, so as not to have it hanging over my head, and thus cleared my mind for my greater favourites. Not that, in the end, I disliked the character as a whole. I had no misgivings after reaching the third act, but the first two always filled me with a shrinking horror. I could not but admire the stern grandeur of the indomitable will which could unite itself with "fate and metaphysical aid" to place the crown upon her husband's brow. Something, it seemed to me, was also to be said in extenuation of the eagerness with which Lady Macbeth falls into his design, and urges him on to catch that crown "the nearest way." If we throw our minds into the circumstances of the time, we can understand the wife who would adventure so much for so great a prize, though we may not sympathise with her. Deeds of violence were common; succession in the direct line was often disturbed by the doctrine that "might was right"; the moral sense was not over-nice, when a great stake was to be played for. Retribution might come, or it might not; the triumph for the moment was everything, and what we should call, and rightly call, murder, often passed in common estimation for an act of valour. Lady Macbeth had been brought up amid such scenes, and one murder more seemed little to her. But she did not know what it was to be personally implicated in murder, nor foresee the Nemesis that would pursue her waking, and fill her dreams with visions of the old man's blood slowly trickling down before her eyes. Think, too, of her agony of anxiety, on the early morning just after the murder, lest her husband in his wild ravings should betray himself; and of the torture she endured while, no less to her amazement than her horror, he recites to Malcolm and Donalbain, with fearful minuteness of detail, how he found Duncan lying gashed and gory in his chamber! She had faced that sight without blenching, when it was essential to replace the daggers, and even to "smear the sleepy grooms with blood;" but to have the whole scene thus vividly brought again before her was too great a strain upon her nerves. So wonder that she faints. It was not Macbeth alone, as we soon see, whose sleep was haunted by the affliction of terrible dreams. She says nothing of them, for hers was the braver, more self-sustained nature of the two; but I always felt an involuntary shudder creep over me when, in the scene before the banquet scene, he mentions them as afflicting himself. He has no thought of what she, too, is suffering; but that a change has come over her by this time is very clearly indicated by her words at the beginning of the same scene (Act iii. sc. 2):—

> "Nought's had, all's spent,
> Where our desire is got without content:
> 'Tis safer to be that which we destroy,
> Than by destruction dwell in doubtful joy,"—

words which must never be lost sight of, pointing, as they do, to the beginning of that mental unrest brought on by the recurrence of images and thoughts which will not "die with them they think on," and which culminates in the "slumbery agitation" of the troubled nights that were quickly followed by her death, of which, in the sleep-walking scene, we have a glimpse.

I acted Lady Macbeth, for the second time, during Mr Macready's management at Drury Lane; it was then also upon an emergency, caused by the sudden illness of Mrs Warner, the Lady Macbeth of the theatre. Not long afterwards I had to take this character, among others selected for a series of performances in Paris. This and Ophelia and Virginia I had consented to play, to oblige Mr Mitchell of Bond Street, whose enterprise it was, upon the understanding that I was to act in other plays more identified with my name, which I selected. When I made my engagement with Mr Mitchell, Mr Macready was in America. On his return my plays were put aside by him, and others of his own substituted. Mr Mitchell came to me in great distress, and represented that, did I not feel for him, and give in to his necessity, the whole scheme would collapse, and all his labour and his expense would be thrown away.

Juliet I had only the opportunity of acting once, and that was on the last night of the twelve performances. *Romeo and Juliet* had been, with other plays, cut out of the list by Mr Macready; but Mr Mitchell took it for his benefit, telling me that I should at least have the chance of acting one character of my own selecting. That was a happy night to me, for the audience went with me enthusiastically throughout the performance. The success, indeed, was so great, that Mr Mitchell was most anxious I should renew my engagement without Mr Macready; but he could not get the use of the theatre for a longer period. I was told at the time that his disappointment was attributable to the intervention of the Parisian actors, who appealed to the authorities to prevent the prolongation of the English performances—a piece of jealousy so unworthy, that I found it hard to believe it.

Upon the whole, as things turned out, I had no great reason to regret having yielded to Mr Mitchell's necessities. It was a delight to play to audiences so refined and sympathetic, and to learn, from the criticisms of such men as Victor Hugo, Alexandre Dumas, Edouard Thierry, and Jules Janin, that I had carried them along with me in my treatment of characters so varied. I remember well how strange they seemed to think it, that the same actress should play Juliet, Ophelia, Desdemona, and Lady Macbeth—impressing each, as they were indulgent enough to say, with characteristics so distinct and so marked, as to make them forget the actress in the woman she represented.

In what they said and wrote I had some compensation for the chagrin I naturally felt at being deprived by Mr Macready of the opportunity of personating before a Parisian audience the characters which were considered more peculiarly my own. Mr Macready was a great actor, and a distinguished man in many ways; but you will, I daresay, remember that he would never, if he could help it, allow any one to stand upon the same level with himself. I read once in *Punch,* that they supposed Mr Macready thought Miss Helen Faucit had a very handsome back, for, when on the stage with her, he always managed that the audience should see it and little else. But I must say that I was never so conscious of this unfairness with him, as with his, in my opinion, very inadequate successor Mr Phelps, who always took his stand about two feet behind you, so that no face should be seen, and no voice be distinctly heard, by the audience, but his own. I remember finding this particularly unpleasant on the night I played Lady Macbeth at the first performance given in honour of the Princess Royal's marriage. These performances took place at Her Majesty's Theatre in the Haymarket, soon afterwards burned down. The stage was the largest in London, and fully one-third of it was occupied by the proscenium. I was then, as was my choice after my marriage, acting very rarely, and at long intervals. From want of continuous practice, therefore, I was not so sure of the penetrating power of my voice, especially in a theatre of such unusual size. At one of the rehearsals, kind Sir Julius Benedict warned me against speaking further back than the proscenium. He said no voice, however powerful, could be heard behind it, and that the singers invariably planted themselves well in front. I mentioned this to Mr Phelps, who was the Macbeth, and he seemed to agree to act upon the suggestion. But at night, from his first entry to Lady Macbeth, he took up a position far behind me, and kept it, wherever possible, throughout all my scenes with him. In my subsequent experience with him, I found this to be his invariable practice. Tricks of this sort are as foolish as they are ungenerous, and could never enter the minds of those who desire to be truly artists. When actors have told me, as they often have, that I was always so fair to act with, I could only express my surprise; for how can you hope to represent characters faithfully unless mind is acting upon mind and face meeting face, so that the words flow naturally in answer to the thoughts you see depicted there?

Forgive these details, which have thrust themselves in by the way, and return with me to *As You Like It*. When I resolved to make a thorough study of the play, I little thought how long, yet how fascinating, a task I had imposed upon myself. With every fresh perusal new points of interest and new charms revealed themselves to me; while, as for Rosalind, "she drew me on to love her" with a warmth of feeling which can only be understood by the artist who has found in the heroine she impersonates that "something never to be wholly known," those suggestions of high qualities answerable to all the contingencies or trials of circumstance by which we are captivated in real life, and which it is her aim and her triumph to bring home to the hearts and imaginations of her audience as they have come home to her own. Often as I have played Rosalind since, I have never done so without giving fresh thought to the character, nor without finding in it something that had escaped me before. It was ever, therefore, a fresh delight to bring out as best I could in action what had thus flashed upon me in my hours of meditation, and to try to make this exquisite creature as dear and fascinating to my audience as she had become to myself. In the very acting I learned much; for if on the stage you leave your mind open to what is going on around you, even an unskilful actor by your side—and I need not say how much more a gifted one—may, by a gesture or an intonation, open up something fresh to your imagination. So it was I came to love Rosalind with my whole heart; and well did she repay me, for I have often thought, "and have been told so of many," that in impersonating her I was able to give full expression to what was best in myself as well as in my art.

It was surely a strange perversion which, we read, assigned Rosalind, as at one time it had assigned Portia, to actresses whose strength lay only in comedy. Even the joyous, buoyant side of her nature could hardly have justice done to it in their hands; for that is so inextricably mingled with deep womanly tenderness, with an active intellect disciplined by fine culture, as well as tempered by a certain native distinction, that a mere comedian could not give the true tone and colouring even to her playfulness and her wit. Those forest scenes between Orlando and herself are not, as a comedy actress would be apt to make them, merely pleasant fooling. At the core of all that Rosalind says and does, lies a passionate love as pure and all-absorbing as ever swayed a woman's heart. Surely it was the finest and boldest of all devices, one on which only a Shakespeare could have ventured, to put his heroine into such a position that she could, without revealing her own secret, probe the heart of her lover to the very core, and thus assure herself that the love which possessed her being was as completely the master of his. Neither could any but Shakespeare have so carried out this daring design, that the woman thus rarely placed for gratifying the impulses of her own heart, and testing the sincerity of her lover's, should come triumphantly out of the ordeal, charming us, during the time of probation, by her wit, her fancy, by her pretty womanly waywardnesses playing like summer lightning over her throbbing tenderness of heart, and never in the gayest sallies of her happiest moods losing one grain of our respect. No one can study this play without seeing that, through the guise of the brilliant-witted boy, Shakespeare meant the charm of the high-hearted woman, strong, tender, delicate, to make itself felt. Hence it is that Orlando finds the spell which "heavenly Rosalind" had thrown around him, drawn hourly closer and closer, he knows not how, while at the same time he has himself been winning his way more and more into his mistress's heart. Thus, when at last Rosalind doffs her doublet and hose, and appears arrayed for her bridal, there seems nothing strange or unmeet in this somewhat sudden consummation of what has been in truth a lengthened wooing. The actress will, in my opinion, fail signally in her task, who shall not suggest all this, who shall not leave upon her audience the impression that, when Rosalind resumes her state at her father's court, she will bring into it as much grace and dignity, as by her bright spirits she had brought of sunshine and cheerfulness into the shades of the forest of Arden.

To me, *As You Like It* seems to be essentially as much a love-poem as *Romeo and Juliet,* with this difference—that it deals with happy love, while the Veronese story deals with love crossed by misadventure and crowned with death. It is as full of imagination, of the glad rapture of the tender passion, of its impulsiveness, its generosity, its pathos. No "hearse-like airs," indeed, come wailing by, as in the tale of those "star-crossed lovers," to warn us of their too early tragic "overthrow." All is blended into a rich harmonious music, which makes the heart throb, but never makes it ache. Still the love is not less deep, less capable of proving itself strong as death; neither are the natures of Orlando and Rosalind less touched to all the fine issues of that passion than those of "Juliet and her Romeo."

Is not love, indeed, the pivot on which the action of the play turns—love, too, at first sight? Does it not seem that the text the poet meant to illustrate was that which he puts into Phebe's mouth—

> "Dead shepherd, now I find thy saw of might,—
> 'Who ever loved, that loved not at first sight?'"

And this, too, the Phebe who but a few minutes before had smiled with scorn at her suitors warning—

> "If ever (as that ever may be near),
> You meet in some fresh cheek the power of fancy,
> Then shall you know the wounds invisible
> That love's keen arrows make."

Love at first sight, like that of Juliet and Romeo, is the love of Rosalind and Orlando, of Celia and Oliver, and of Phebe herself for Ganymede. The two latter pairs of lovers are perhaps but of little account; but is not the might of Marlowe's saw as fully exemplified in Rosalind and Orlando as in the lovers of Verona?

Happily for them, and for us, there were no ancestral feuds, no unsympathetic parents to step in and place a bar upon their affections. Whether or not Shakespeare believed his own words (*A Midsummer Night's Dream,* Act i. sc. 1)—"The course of true love never did run smooth," who may tell? I venture to think he no more held this creed than he did many of what are called his opinions, which, although most apt in the mouths of his characters, were never meant to be taken as universally true. What, for example, can be more absurd than the too common habit of quoting, as if it expressed Shakespeare's personal conviction, the phrase, "What's in a name?" No man, we may be sure, better understood how *very much* there may be in a name. As Juliet uses it, the phrase is apt and true. In the rapture of her love it was nothing to her that Romeo bore the name of the enemy of her house. What were ancestral feuds to her, who saw in him "the god of her idolatry"? "His gracious self" was her all in all. What, then, was in his name? But the phrase is not only meaningless, but false, when cited, as it too often is, without regard to person, place, or circumstance. In any case, Shakespeare has given us in this play a supreme instance in disproof of Lysander's sad axiom. The love in it does run smooth all through, with no more check or difficulty than serves to prove how genuine it is, and to bring two "true minds" into, that perfect unison which is the only right prelude to marriage. Circumstances, sad enough in themselves, have left both the lovers untrammelled by the ties of kindred. Orlando's father is dead. His elder brother defrauds him of his fortune, stints him of the training due to his rank, and hates him. Rosalind's father has been deposed from his dukedom while she was yet in early girlhood, and she has not seen him for years. She owes no allegiance to her uncle, at whose court she has been detained. The wills of both lovers are thus entirely free, and, by the time that each has found out what is in the other's heart, the turn of events makes everything smooth for their marriage, after the intermediate period of probation, which is in itself happiness as nearly perfect as heart could desire.

With what skill does Shakespeare at the outset of the play engage our interest for Orlando! In vain his elder brother has tried to crush in him, by neglect, and by "keeping him rustically at home" without the liberal culture of a gentleman, the inherent nobility of his nature. His father had left him "but a poor thousand crowns." Good old Sir Rowland was no doubt fettered by the usage that makes eldest sons rich at the cost of the younger; but he had charged Oliver "on his blessing" to breed Orlando well, feeling confident that this training only was wanted to enable him to carve out fortune for himself. How had Oliver obeyed the charge? "You have trained me," Orlando tells him, "like a peasant, obscuring and hiding from me all gentlemanlike qualities." But as he has grown into manhood, this state of things has become intolerable:—

"The Spirit of my father grows strong in me, and I will no longer endure it: therefore, allow me such exercises as may become a gentleman, or give me the poor allottery my father left me by testament; with that I will go buy my fortunes."

Why did Oliver treat him thus? Why was it that, as he says, "he hates nothing more than he, and yet he knows not why"? Was it that Orlando had been his father's favourite, as indeed he seems to have inherited the virtues of that good man? "O my sweet master!" says old Adam (Act ii. sc. 3)—

"O you memory
Of old Sir Rowland!
Why are you virtuous? Why do people love you?
And wherefore are you gentle, strong, and valiant?
. . . Your virtues, gentle master,
Are sanctified and holy traitors to you."

No lack of "inland nurture" was able to spoil a nature so manly, in which the best instincts of "race" were paramount. We picture him handsome, courteous, modest, gallant, with the fresh cheek and the frank cordial eyes that speak of health, of active habits, and a genial nature such as wins men's hearts. Even Oliver is forced to admit that his efforts to spoil him have completely failed. "He's gentle; never schooled, and yet learned; full of noble device; of all sorts enchantingly beloved; and, indeed, so much in the heart of the world, and especially of my own people, who best know him that I am altogether misprised."

But of what avail is all this? Orlando has no career before him; all his powers are lying unused. He is in the saddest of all plights—that of a poor gentleman, full of noble aspirations, and without a chance of proving that he is not of the common herd. What wonder, then, that we see him dejected and out of heart, or that his words should vibrate with feeling, when he entreats Celia and Rosalind to forgive him for not yielding to their entreaty that he will not risk his life by wrestling with Charles, "the bony prizer of the humorous Duke"?—

"I beseech you, punish me not with your hard thoughts; wherein I confess me much guilty, to deny so fair and excellent ladies anything. But let your fair eyes and gentle wishes go with me to my trial: wherein if I be foiled, there is but one shamed that was never gracious; if killed, but one dead that is willing to be so! I shall do my friends no wrong, for I have none to lament me; the world no injury, for in it I have nothing; only in the world I fill up a place, which may be better supplied when I have made it empty."

Such words in the mouth of one so young, so obviously at all points a gentleman, could not fail to touch a gentlewoman's heart; and in Rosalind's case they were all the more likely to do so, because in her own fortunes and her own mood at the time there was much to beget in her a sympathetic feeling. The world had not gone well with her, either. When her father was deposed she was yet a child, little likely, perhaps, to appreciate the change from a princess of the reigning to a princess of the dethroned house. She and her cousin Celia, the daughter of the man who dispossessed her father of his throne, had been "ever from their cradles bred together," and her superior charm and force of character had so won upon the affections of her cousin, that, as Shakespeare is at pains to tell us, through the mouth of Charles the Wrestler (Act i. sc. 1), when Rosalind's father was banished—"Celia would have followed her exile, or have died to stay behind her." The usurping Duke, whose only child Celia was, would not let Rosalind go into banishment with her father, for fear of the effect upon his daughter. "We stay'd her," as he says to Celia, "for your sake; else had she with her father ranged along." But the beauty and gentle bearing of Rosalind, as the years went on, made her dear to the people, who had probably found out by this time that they had made a bad exchange in the "humorous Duke" for the amiable and accomplished ruler whom he had supplanted,—just as the retainers of Oliver had found that not in him, but in his youngest brother, "the memory of old Sir Rowland" was perpetuated. Celia's father holding his place by an uncertain tenure, and therefore jealous of one who must be ever painfully reminding him of his usurpation, did not fail to observe this feeling among his subjects. It was dangerous to let it grow to a head; and so we see that, before the play opens, the thought had been present to his mind that Rosalind must stay no longer at his court. As he tells his daughter—

> "Her very silence, and her patience,
> Speak to the people, and they pity her."

To a mind like his, full of misgiving as to his own position, the observation of this fact must have been an hourly torment. But the old difficulty, the affection between Rosalind and his child, was by this time increased rather than diminished. "Never two ladies loved as they do," says Charles; "Their loves," says Le Beau, "are dearer than the natural love of sisters,"—both speaking the common voice of the people. And how united were their lives, we learn from Celia herself—

> "We still have slept together,
> Rose at an instant, learn'd, play'd, ate together;
> And wheresoe'er we went, like Juno's swans,
> Still we went coupled and inseparable."

But her father's feeling of distrust had of late been growing into one antipathy. Le Beau, a shrewd observer in spite of all his courtierly manner, and with a good heart, which the selfish habits of a court life have not wholly spoiled, sees pretty clearly the fate that is hanging over Rosalind:—

> "Of late this duke
> Hath ta'en displeasure 'gainst his gentle niece,
> Grounded upon no other argument
> But that people praise her for her virtues,
> And pity her for her good father's sake;
> And, on my life, his malice 'gainst the lady
> Will suddenly break forth."

What the courtly Le Beau had so plainly seen to be the state of the Duke's mind was not likely to have escaped Rosalind's quick sensitive nature. She feels the cloud of her uncle's displeasure hanging over her, and ready to burst at any moment. She will not pain Celia with her forebodings, who is so far from surmising the truth, that the first lines she speaks are a gentle reproach to Rosalind for her want of gaiety; to which Rosalind replies, "I show more mirth than I am mistress of; and would you yet I were merrier?" Then, throwing the blame of her present table upon an old sorrow, she adds: "Unless you could teach me to forget a banished father, you must not learn me how to remember any extraordinary pleasure." From Celia's reply, it is obvious she has no idea that Rosalind has fallen out of favour with the usurping Duke. "If my uncle, thy banished father, had banished thy uncle, the Duke my father, so thou hadst been still with me, I could have taught my love to take thy father for mine." Too well Rosalind knows that the obstacle to this pretty proposal lies not with herself, but with Celia's father. Still she will hide from Celia the trouble she sees looming for herself in the not far distance. She will not show her "the darks undream'd of" into which their pleasant sisterly life is running. Why "forestall her date of grief"? Why throw a shade over her cousin's happy spirit, or refuse anything to one so generous in her assurance, that she will atone for the wrong done by her father to Rosalind, given in such words as these?—

> "You know my father hath no child but I, nor none is like to have: and, truly, when he dies, thou shalt be his heir; for what he hath taken away from thy father perforce, I will render thee again in affection; by mine honour I will; and when I break that oath, let me turn monster: therefore, my sweet Rose, my dear Rose, be merry."

A sad smile breaks over Rosalind's face as she replies,—"From henceforth I will, coz, and devise sports." "Let me see," she adds,—little dreaming how near was the reality,—"what think you of falling in love?" To which Celia rejoins,— "Marry, pry'thee, do, to make sport withal: but love no man in good earnest; nor no farther in sport neither, than with safety of a pure blush thou mayst in honour come off again." And so these loving cousins prattle on brightly upon the lawn before the ducal palace, where presently an incident occurs which is to change the current of their lives. They have just heard from Le Beau of the murderous triumphs of the wrestler Charles, and would fain have escaped from seeing a repetition of his "rib-breaking." But before they can get away, the Duke arrives with his suite upon the ground to see the contest to which Orlando has challenged Charles, with a determination, very clearly shown, to lower the tone of the professional braggart, if skill and good heart can do it.

At once the attention of the ladies is riveted by Orlando's appearance. "Is yonder the man?" are the words that break from Rosalind. "Alas," exclaims her cousin, "he is too young! yet he looks successfully." The Duke, judging from his looks that the odds are all against the young fellow, tells the ladies they will take delight in the wrestling, and urges them to try to dissuade him from persevering in his challenge. Celia, as the reigning Duke's daughter, and also because she is probably not so much moved as her cousin, does most of the talking; but not a word, either of her entreaties or of Orlando's refusal, escapes Rosalind. She could not but respect a resolution so manly, yet so modestly expressed, however she may fear the issue. Orlando's heart must have leapt within him when she says, "The little strength that I have, I would it were with you. Fare you well. Pray heaven, I be deceived in you!" Deceived she shall be, he is determined, for her words have given to his sinews the strength of steel.

No thought now of leaving the ground. The ladies will see the fate of the young hero, and "rain influence" on him with their bright eyes. The wrestling begins—

"*Ros.* O excellent young man!
Cel. If I had a thunderbolt in mine eye, I can tell who should down."

Charles is thrown by Orlando, and carried off insensible. And now they are to learn who the young hero is. In answer to the Duke, he tells his name, adding that he is the youngest son of Sir Rowland de Bois. Here is the link between Rosalind and Orlando. Sir Rowland has been loyal to the banished Duke—a sin the usurper cannot pardon in the son.

"The world esteemed thy father honourable.
But I did find him still mine enemy.
. . . . Thou art a gallant youth
I would thou hadst told me of another father.'

Celia's heart revolts at this injustice. Turning to Rosalind, she says—

"Were I my father, coz, would I do this?"

And what says Rosalind?—

> "My father loved Sir Rowland as his soul,
> And all the world was of my father's mind:
> Had I before known this young man his son,
> I should have given him tears unto entreaties,
> Ere he should thus have ventured."

She needs not the prompting of her cousin to "go thank him and encourage him"; but while Celia finds ready words, Rosalind's deeper emotion suggests to her a stronger token of the admiration he has roused. She has taken a chain from her neck, and stealthily kissing it—at least I always used to do so—she gives it to Orlando, saying:—

> "Gentleman,
> Wear this for me, one out of suits with fortune,
> That could give more, but that her hand lacks means."

Here she pauses, naturally expecting some acknowledgment from Orlando; but finding none come, and not knowing how to break off an interview which has kindled a strange emotion within her, she adds, "'Shall we go, coz?" Celia, heart-whole as she is, has no such difficulty. "Ay. Fare you well, fair gentleman," she says, and turns away. Rosalind is going with her. Meanwhile Orlando, overcome by a new feeling, finds himself spell-bound.

> "*Orl.* Can I not say I thank you? My better parts
> Are all thrown down; and that which here stands up
> Is but a quintain, a mere lifeless block."

It cannot be that he should let them go thus without a word of thanks! Rosalind at least will not think so. What he mutters faintly to himself must surely have been meant for them.

> "*Ros.* He calls us back: my pride fell with my fortunes;
> I'll ask him what he would.—Did you call, sir?'"

But his heart is too full, his tongue too heavily weighted by passion, to find vent in words. His action is constrained. He bows but makes no answering sign, and with trembling lips she continues:—

> "Sir, you have wrestled well, and overthrown
> More than your enemies."

This "more than your enemies" is very significant, and speaks plainly enough, though spoken as it would be with great reserve of manner, of the favourable impression which the young wrestler has made upon her. We may be sure that, but for his modest demeanour, Rosalind would not have allowed herself to confess so much.

Celia aroused, and disposed to rally her cousin about what looks to her rather more than "falling in love in sport," accosts Rosalind mockingly in the phrase she has used but a few moments before, "Will you go, coz?" "Have with you," Rosalind rejoins, quite understanding the roguish sparkle in her cousin's eyes, but not deterred by it from giving to Orlando as she goes an earnest "Fare you well!" But she is still slow to leave, hoping and longing for some words from his lips addressed to herself. When Celia takes her hand and is leading her away, Celia bows slightly to Orlando; but Rosalind in a royal and gentle manner curtseys to him, wishing to show her respect for the memory of his father, the dear friend of her father, and also her sympathy with his fortunes. These she can give him, if nothing else.

This scene, you will agree, needs most delicate touching in the actress. Rosalind has not much to say, but she has to make her audience feel by subtle indications the revolution that is going on in her heart from the moment her eyes fall upon her future lover, down to the parting glance with which her lingering farewell is accompanied. It is Juliet in the ball-room, but under conditions that demand a far greater variety of expression. There is no avowal of love; but when she leaves the stage, the audience must have been made to feel that in her case, as in Juliet's, her heart has made its choice, and that a change has come over her akin to that which has come over Orlando. Only when she is gone can he find words to tell it.

> "What passion hangs these weights upon my tongue?
> I cannot speak to her, yet she urg'd conference.
> O poor Orlando, thou art overthrown;
> Or Charles, or something weaker, masters thee."

He is in this state of strange bewildered delight when Le Beau, whom I like very much, and who, I am sure, was a favourite with Rosalind, returns, and warns him not to linger near the court. The sympathy of the bystanders for the brave young fellow has alarmed the Duke, and Le Beau's keen eyes have seen

> "Such is now the Duke's condition,"

he tells Orlando,

> "That he misconstrues all that you have done;"

adding, with a nice sense that a certain reticence is becoming in himself as a member of the ducal court,—

> "The Duke is humorous: what he is, indeed,
> More suits you to conceive than me to speak of.

Orlando is in no mood to think much about his own safety. Besides, what is the court to him? The all-important thing in his eyes is to know which of the two gracious ladies "that here were at the wrestling" is daughter of the Duke? He has lived near the court, and must have often heard the names of the two princesses. When, therefore, Le Beau replies, "The shorter is his daughter," he knows that the name of the daughter of the banished Duke, who left her chain with him, is Rosalind. Only after he is satisfied of this does he bethink him of what danger may await him.

> "Thus must I from the smoke into the smother;
> From tyrant duke unto a tyrant brother."

But come what may, one image, we see, will be ever present with him,—that of "heavenly Rosalind." When soon after we see her with her cousin, it is no secret between them that the sweet poison of love is working no less strongly in her. She is surprised at herself, she tells us, because she finds herself unable to resist it. How charmingly is this brought before us!—

> "*Cel.* Why, cousin; why, Rosalind; Cupid have mercy!—Not a word?
> *Ros.* Not one to throw at a dog.
>
> . . . .
>
> *Cel.* But is all this, for your father?
> *Ros.* No; some of it is for my father's child.
>
> . . . .
>
> *Cel.* Come, come, wrestle with thy affections.
> *Ros.* Oh, they take the part of a better wrestler than myself!
> *Cel.* Oh, a good wish upon you! . . . Is it possible, on such a sudden, you should fall into so strong a liking with old Sir Rowland's youngest son?
> *Ros.* The duke my father lov'd his father dearly.
> *Cel.* Doth it therefore ensue that you should love his son dearly? By this kind of chase, I should hate him, for my father hated his father dearly; yet I hate not Orlando.
> *Ros.* No, 'faith, hate him not, for my sake.
> *Cel.* Why should I not? Doth he not deserve well?
> *Ros.* Let me love him for that; and do you love him because I do."

But now the storm bursts, of which Rosalind had lived for some time in apprehension. The Duke enters, his "eyes full of anger," and his "rough and envious disposition" vents its long-pent-up jealousy upon her in the cruel words—

> "Within these ten days, if that thou be'st found
> So near our public court as twenty miles,
> Thou diest for it."

At this sentence the spirit of the princess must have grown warm within her. She knows her uncle too well to think of remonstrance. But what has she done to justify or to provoke this sudden outburst of his wrath? Still she controls herself, and asks in a tone of entreaty—

> "I do beseech your grace,
> Let me the knowledge of my fault bear with me;
> If with myself I hold intelligence,
> Or have acquaintance with mine own desires;
> If that I do not dream, or be not frantic
> (As I do trust I am not), then, dear uncle,
> Never so much as in a thought unborn
> Did I offend your highness."

His reply, "Thus do all traitors," &c., rouses the royal blood within her; gentleness gives place to righteous remonstrance:—

> "Your mistrust cannot make me a traitor:
> Tell me whereon the likelihood depends?"

His reply—

> "Thou art thy father's daughter; there's enough"—

brings the instant answer, in which years of silent endurance find a voice. She can bear any reproach to herself, but her loyalty to her father gives pungency to her answer:—

> "So was I when your highness took his dukedom;
> So was I when your highness banish'd him.
> Treason is not inherited, my lord;
> Or, if we did derive it from our friends,
> What's that to me? My father was no traitor."

In speaking this I could never help laying a slight emphasis on the last words. For what but a traitor had the Duke himself been? The sarcasm strikes home; but, recovering herself a little for Celia's sake, she adds more gently—

> "Then, good my liege, mistake me not so much,
> To think my poverty is treacherous."

In vain Celia tries to shake her father's resolution, telling him that, when first he had kept back her cousin to be her companion—

> "I was too young that time to value her;
> But now I know her: if she be a traitor,
> Why so am I."

Celia heeds not her father when he replies that she suffers in general estimation by the presence of Rosalind:—

> "She robs thee of thy name;
> And thou wilt show more bright and seem more virtuous
> When she is gone!"

And when he renews his doom of banishment, she proves, by her reply, that the yearning of the child had become the fixed resolution of the woman:—

> "Pronounce that sentence, then, on me, my liege;
> I cannot live out of her company."

The angry tyrant, thinking these to be but idle words, and unable to conceive a friendship of this exalted strain, breaks away, saying—

> "You are a fool. You, niece, provide yourself:
> If you outstay the time, upon my honour,
> And in the greatness of my word, you die."

Then comes a passage, than which what prettier picture of more than sisterly devotion was ever painted?—

> "*Cel.* O my poor Rosalind! whither wilt thou go?
> Wilt thou change fathers? I will give thee mine.

> I charge thee, be not thou more griev'd than I am.
>
> *Ros.* I have more cause.
>
> *Cel.*   Thou hast not, cousin:
> Pr'ythee, be cheerful. Know'st thou not, the Duke
> Hath banish'd me, his daughter?
>
> *Ros.*   That he hath not.
>
> *Cel.* No? hath not? Rosalind lacks, then, the love
> Which teacheth thee that thou and I am one.
> Shall we be sunder'd? Shall we part, sweet girl?
> No: let my father seek another heir.
> Therefore devise with me how we may fly,
> Whither to go, and what to bear with us:
> And do not seek to take your change upon you,
> To bear your grief yourself, and leave me out;
> For, by this heaven, now at our sorrows pale,
> Say what thou canst, I'll go along with thee."

Rosalind, touched to the heart, and feeling that she also could not live without Celia, accepts the generous offer without remonstrance. It told that Celia's love, never very deep for such a father, had been so completely alienated by his injustice to her cousin, as well as by his late ungenerous treatment of Orlando, that to have remained behind, subject to his "rough and envious disposition," would have been misery. When Rosalind, half despondingly, says—

> "Why, whither shall we go?"

her cousin's ready answer—

> "To seek my uncle in the forest of Arden,"

opens up, we may conceive, a delightful vision of freedom and independence. But then the danger to them—

> "Maids as we are, to travel forth so far!"

Celia is ready with her plan:—

> "I'll put myself in poor and mean attire,
> The like do you: so shall we pass along,
> And never stir assailants."

Rosalind was not likely to be behind her friend in courage. Besides, is not Celia sacrificing all for her, and has she not, therefore, a claim upon her for protection? So she betters Celia's suggestion:—

> "Were it not better,
> Because that I am more than common tall,"

(How glad I always felt that in this respect, at least, I was akin to the poet's Rosalind!)

> "That I did suit me all points like a man!"

Her fancy quickens at the thought, and with that fine buoyancy of spirit, and play of graceful humour, of which we are anon to see so much, she goes on to complete the picture:

> "A gallant curtle-axe upon my thigh,
> A boar-spear in my hand; and (in my heart
> Lie there what hidden woman's fear there will)
> We'll have a swashing and a martial outside;
> As many other mannish cowards have,
> That do outface it with their semblances."

Celia enters with delight into the idea:—

> "*Cel.* What shall I call thee, when thou art a man?
> *Ros.* I'll have no worse a name than Jove's own page;
> And therefore look you call me Ganymede.
> But what will you be call'd?"

Aliena, Celia says, shall be her name, as having "reference to her state"; and now they have grown so happy at the thought of escaping from the trouble which seemed so terrible at first, that they can jest and play with the anticipation of the life before them. Touchstone, the court fool, shall be their companion—

> "He'll go along o'er the wide world with me; "

says Celia. He will be both a comfort and a protection; and so with happy hearts they set about getting their "jewels and their wealth together" for the enterprise, which is to lead them

> "To liberty and not to banishment."

While things have thus come to an extremity with his "heavenly Rosalind," a similar fate is overtaking Orlando. His brother, foiled in the hope that he would be killed by Charles, is determined to get rid of him by more desperate means. This Orlando learns from Adam, that ideal pattern of an old retainer, made doubly dear to us by the tradition that this was one of the characters which Shakespeare himself delighted to impersonate. You remember, doubtless, Coleridge's words, as reported by Mr Payne Collier: "Great dramatists make great actors. But, looking at Shakespeare merely as a performer, I am certain that he was greater as Adam in *As You Like It,* than Burbage as Hamlet or Richard the Third. Think of the scene between him and Orlando, and think again that the actor of that part had to carry the author of it in his arms! Think of having had Shakespeare in one's arms! It is worth having died two hundred years ago to have heard Shakespeare deliver a single line. He must have been a great actor." I love to think so. Especially does my fancy gladly picture him in this scene, and find in doing so a richer music in the exquisite cadences of the lines in which the devotion and humble piety of that "good old man" are couched. Through his lips we learn how worthy in all ways to be loved is Orlando—a matter of first importance in one who is to be beloved by such a woman as Rosalind. The devotion of Celia to the heroine of the play also finds its counterpart in that of Adam to the hero—and the plot derives a fresh interest from the introduction of a character, not only charming in itself, but most skilfully used, both in this scene and the few others in which he appears, to heighten the favourable impression of Orlando's character created by his demeanour in the earlier scenes. The savings of Adam's life enable the old man and his young master to seek better fortunes elsewhere, in hopes to light "upon some settled low content." And so they, too, go forth, to reappear in that wondrous forest of Arden.

Of the little world there we are given a delightful glimpse, before either Celia and Rosalind, or Orlando and Adam, become its denizens. The second act opens in it, and shows us in Rosalind's father, the banished Duke, a character widely different from her own, with none of her vivacity or force, though with something of her sweetness of disposition. Like Prospero, a scholarly man, his retiring and unostentatious habits have, as in Prospero's case, given scope for an ambitious brother to rob him of his kingdom. Like Prospero, too, in this, "so dear the love his people bore him," they would not have endured any attempt upon his life, so that the worst his brother dared had been to banish him. To one who had,—again like Prospero,—"neglected worldly aids," dedicating the time, which ought more fitly to have been devoted to the duties of government, "to closeness, and the bettering of his mind," banishment has obviously been no great privation. Custom very soon has made the rough forest life "more sweet than that of painted pomp." Adversity has given him clearer views of men, and taught him more of his own heart, than he could have ever learned in "the envious court." His calm, meditative mind discovers in the scenes around him delightful incidents, reminding him by contrast of the turmoil and perils of his former state. He

> "Finds tongues in trees, books in the running brooks,
> Sermons in stones, and good in everything,"

and has in fact translated

> "The stubbornness of fortune
> Into so quiet and so sweet a style,"

that any regrets for his lost wealth and honours are to all appearance dead. Unlike Prospero, he shows no bitterness against his usurping brother, and has no yearnings for the power of which he has been despoiled. The easy dreamy life of the woods suits his languid temperament. He likes nothing better than an argument with Jacques, whose cynical views of life excite and amuse him, though he has no sympathy with them. Amiable, but weak, separation from his daughter does not seem to have cost him much regret. He believes she is happy where he has left her, in the position and with the surroundings that become her birth, and which, in his banishment, he could not give her. And she, on the other hand, is no doubt aware that her presence is by no means essential to his happiness. Thus she has no temptation to make herself known to him, when they meet casually in the forest, and when to have done so would have broken up the sweet masking intercourse with her lover, in which she was by that time involved.

When we first see Rosalind on the outskirts of the forest, wayworn and weary, we have scarce time to note how she tries to forget her own fatigue, and to comfort "the weaker vessel," her still more weary cousin, "as doublet and hose ought to show itself courageous to petticoat." Her thoughts, and ours, are soon carried off in another direction by the dialogue between the shepherd Corin and the young Silvius, in whose passion for the shepherdess Phebe Rosalind finds the counterpart to her own haunting dreams about Orlando. Something of what these have been her words show: "Alas, poor shepherd! searching of thy wound, I have by hard adventure found mine own." In this train of thought Rosalind for the moment forgets weariness and hunger; but Celia, "faint almost to death," has to be thought for. Corin comes to their help, and puts them in the way of buying that cottage "by the tuft of olives" on the skirts of the forest, to which lovers of this play will always in their day-dreams find their way, leaving to the right "the rank of osiers, by the murmuring stream," that mingled its music with the songs of the birds and the rustling of the forest-leaves.

In this delightful retreat one loves to picture these two charming women in the full enjoyment of their new-born liberty, made more piquant by their little secret and by Rosalind's masquerading attire. For all her mannish dress and airs, there was, of course, something of a feminine character about the youth. "The boy is fair, of female favour," we are told later on, and, by contrast with Celia, "bestows himself like a ripe sister"; while Celia is "low, and browner than her brother." Again, Rosalind's picture is drawn for us by Phebe, and what a picture it is!—

> "It is a pretty youth:—not very pretty:—
> But, sure, he's proud; and yet his pride becomes him:
> He'll make a proper man: the best thing in him
> Is his complexion; and faster than his tongue
> Did make offence, his eye did heal it up.
> He is not tall; yet for his years he's tall:
> His leg is but so-so; and yet 'tis well:
> There was a pretty redness in his lip;
> A little riper and more lusty red
> Than that mixed in his cheek; 'twas just the difference
> Betwixt the constant red and mingled damask."

This is as she appeared to the rustic Phebe. Orlando, however, has seen something finer and nobler in his "heavenly" Rosalind during their brief meeting at the court. And naturally so, for she is then a lovely woman, and in a woman's flowing dress her height and carriage would make her look fairer and more majestic. So he ascribes to her

> "Helen's cheek, but not her heart;
>   Cleopatra's majesty;
> Atalanta's better part;
>   Sad Lucretia's modesty."

Add to this fine health, fine spirits, a vivid fancy, the courage of a pure heart and a frank generous nature, together with a voice rich, melodious, resonant, clear, that filled the ear and left its tones lingering there, and the picture will be complete.

To a nature such as hers, the woodland life must have given exquisite pleasure. In her rambles a vision of the young Orlando would often mingle with her thoughts, and not unpleasantly. His forlorn position, so like her own, his bravery, his modesty, had made a deep impression on her, and yet this impression was one which she must have felt it would be foolish to cherish. They were now separated in such a way that their paths were not likely again to cross each other. Their worlds were different. Her heart's fancy must therefore be put aside, forgotten. How long this inward struggle has been going on, Shakespeare does not tell us—it could not have been very long, for Orlando must have reached the glades of Arden soon after she did,—when roaming through the forest, she comes across a copy of verses hung (delightful defiance of local truth!) upon a palm- tree. Think of the throb at her heart, as she reads her own name running through every couplet! Still there are many Rosalinds in the world; and how should he, of whom she has been dreaming, even know her name,—or how should he, of all men, be there in Arden? No, no, it must be mere coincidence; and yet the pulse is quickened, the heart-throb felt. Presently she sees Celia coming through the wood, and she, too, is reading verses in praise of this unknown Rosalind. Although she has listened to every word with panting eagerness, Rosalind affects indifference, taxing Celia with inflicting upon her hearers "a tedious homily of love." Before Celia answers, she sends Touchstone away, for she has just seen the author of this homily, and knows enough of her cousin's heart to be sure that her tone will alter the moment she learns who it is, and may thus betray her secret to the sharp eyes of "the roynish fool." Untouched by love herself, and so seeing only the humorous side of the passion, Celia begins by tantalising Rosalind with the question, "Trow you who hath done this?" With the same air of affected indifference Rosalind replies, "Is it a man?" and at first thinks Celia is only teasing her, when she rejoins, "And a chain, that you once wore, about his neck?" The tell-tale blood now rushes to Rosalind's cheek, as she exclaims, " I pr'ythee, who?" It may be Orlando then after all, and yet how should it be? Is Celia merely mocking her? "Nay, I pray thee now, with most petitionary vehemence, tell me who it is." Celia, unconscious of the torture of suspense in which she is keeping her cousin, parries all her questions. At last, after what seems to Rosalind an age, she owns that "It is young Orlando, that tripp'd up the wrestler's heels, and your heart, both in an instant." Rosalind will not believe her, but thinks her still mocking. "Nay," she says, "speak sad brow, and true maid." When Celia replies, " I' faith, coz, 'tis he!" not even yet can such happiness be believed. Again the question must be asked—"Orlando?" The name we see by this had been often spoken between them. "Orlando!" Celia answers, and this time gravely, for Rosalind's emotion shows her this is no jesting matter.

Oh happiness beyond belief, oh rapture irrepressible! The tears at this point always welled up to my eyes, and my whole body trembled. If before Rosalind had any doubt as to the state of her own heart, from this moment the doubt must have ended. Overwhelmed as she is at the bare idea of Orlando's being near, the thought flashes upon her—"Alas the day! what shall I do with my doublet and hose?" but Celia has seen him—he perhaps has seen Celia—and that perplexing thought is put aside in her eagerness to learn full particulars about her lover.

"What did he, when thou saw'st him? What said he? How look'd he? Wherein went he? What makes he here? Did he ask for me? Where remains he? How parted he with thee? and when shalt thou see him again?"

These questions, all different, all equally to the purpose, huddled with breathless eagerness one upon another, yet each with different meaning and urged with varying intonation, must all—so ravenous is her curiosity—be answered "in one word." Well may Celia reply that she must borrow for her Gargantua's mouth first, for "to say ay, and no, to these particulars, is more than to answer in a catechism." But Rosalind's questions are not even yet exhausted. She must learn whether Orlando knows that she is in the forest, and in man's apparel? And then comes, to sum up all, the sweet little womanly question, "Looks he as freshly as he did the day he wrestled?" After some further banter as to the general unreasonableness of lovers, Celia mentions that she saw him under a tree, where he lay "stretched along," evidently having no eyes for her or any one, "like a wounded knight. He was furnished like a hunter."

"*Ros.* O ominous! he comes to kill my heart.
Cel. I would sing my song without a burden: thou bring'st me out of tune.
Ros. Do you not know I am a woman? when I think, I must speak. Sweet, say on."

At this moment Orlando is seen approaching with Jaques through the trees. A glance assures Rosalind that it is indeed he; but now the woman's natural shyness at being discovered in so strange a dress comes over her. "Slink by and note him," she says; and withdrawing along with Celia to a point where she may see and not be seen, she listens,—with what delight we may conceive,—to the colloquy in which her lover more than holds his own, when the misanthrope Jaques rallies him on being in love, and marring the forest trees "with writing love-songs in their barks." On the assurance given by Orlando's answers that she is the very Rosalind of these songs, her heart leaps with delight. Not for the world would she have Orlando recognise her in her unmaidenly disguise; but now a sudden impulse determines her to risk all, and even to turn it to account as the means of testing his love. Boldness must be her friend, and to avert his suspicion, her only course is to put on a "swashing and a martial outside," and to speak to him "like a saucy lacquey, and under that habit play the knave with him." He must not be allowed for an instant to surmise the "hidden woman's fear" that lies in her heart. Besides, it is only by resort to a rough and saucy greeting and manner that she could mask and keep under the trembling of her voice, and the womanly tremor of her limbs. I always give the "Do you hear, forester?" with a defiant air, as much as to say, What are you doing here, you, a stranger, intruding in the forest on those who are "natives of the place?" With such a swagger, too, that Orlando feels inclined, at first, to turn round sharply upon the boy, as he had just done upon the cynical Jaques. But despite this swagger, verging almost upon insolence, Orlando at once feels something that interests him in the "pretty youth," for as he afterwards tells her father—

> "My lord, the first time that I ever saw him,
> Methought he was a brother to your daughter."

Once fairly launched on her delicate venture, Rosalind does not give Orlando time to examine her appearance too closely, or to question himself wherein this attraction lies. She engages him in brilliant talk of a kind such as he had never before heard, but which his natural aptitude and shrewdness enable him thoroughly to appreciate.

How witty it all is, and how directly bearing upon the topic of his love, of which she wishes to bring him to speak more!

"*Ros.* I pray you, what is't o'clock?

Orl. You should ask me what time o' day; there's no clock in the forest.

Ros. Then there is no true lover in the forest; else sighing every minute, and groaning every hour, would detect the lazy foot of Time as well as a clock.

Orl. And why not the swift foot of Time? Had not that been as proper?

Ros. By no means, sir. Time travels in divers paces with divers persons. I'll tell you who Time ambles withal, who Time trots withal, who Time gallops withal, and who he stand still withal.

Orl. I pr'ythee, who doth he trot withal?

Ros. Marry, he trots hard with a young maid, between the contract of her marriage and the day it is solemnised. If the interim be but a se'n-night, Time's pace is so hard that it seems the length of seven years.

Orl. Who ambles Time withal?

Ros. With a priest that lacks Latin, and a rich man that hath not the gout; for the one sleeps easily because he cannot study, and the other lives merrily because he feels no pain . . . These Time ambles withal.

Orl. Who doth he gallop withal?

Ros. With a thief to the gallows; for though he go as softly as foot can fall, he finds himself too soon there.

Orl. Who stays it still withal?

Ros. With lawyers in the vacation; for they sleep between term and term and then they perceive not how Time moves."

Strange that one who gives himself out as forest-born, "as the coney that you see dwell where she is kindled," should possess so much knowledge of the world, so much fluency and polish of expression. But when Orlando gives vent to his surprise, by telling Ganymede that his "accent is something finer" than was to be purchased in so "removed a dwelling," Rosalind, after scarcely an instant's pause, is ready with her answer: "I have been told so of many; but, indeed, an old religious uncle of mine taught me to speak." She cannot, however, keep off the theme that is uppermost in her heart, as it is in Orlando's, so she continues,—"one that knew courtship too well, for there he fell in love." And then, to throw Orlando off the scent of her being otherwise than the boy she seems, adds: "I have heard him read many lectures against it; and I thank Heaven I am not a woman to be touched with so many giddy offences as he hath generally taxed their whole sex withal." By this time Orlando's attention is thoroughly arrested. The note has been touched that is all music for him— Woman. For him at that moment there was but one in the world, and what "giddy offence" could be truly laid to her charge? He will learn, however, if he can, some of the "principal evils" imputed to her sex. When Rosalind replies with witty promptitude, "There were none principal; they were all alike one another as half-pence are: every one seeming monstrous, till its fellow fault came to match it," he entreats her to recount some of them. What an opening here for her to put her lover to the test, to hear him say all that woman most longs to hear from him she loves, while he is all the while ignorant that he is laying bare his heart before her!

"No," she rejoins, "I will not cast away my physic, but upon those that are sick. There is a man haunts the forest, that abuses our young plants with carving 'Rosalind' on their barks"—(she has just heard Jaques say he did so, but obviously says this merely upon his report),—"hangs odes upon hawthorns, and elegies on brambles: all, forsooth, deifying the name of Rosalind: if I could meet that fancy-monger, I would give him some good counsel, for he seems to have the quotidian of love upon him."

Poor Orlando, racked by what he believes to be a hopeless passion, would fain be helped to overcome the love-sickness that consumes him. With what secret joy Rosalind hears his avowal! "I am he that is so love-shaked; I pray you, tell me your remedy." But she is determined he shall say as much again and again—for what words are so sweet to her ear?—and so she affects to disbelieve him, telling him he has none of her uncle's marks upon him,—the lean cheek, the blue eye and sunken, the beard neglected, the hose ungartered, the bonnet unbanded, the sleeve unbuttoned, the general air of "careless desolation," which are supposed to denote the man in love. "But you are no such man; you are rather point-device in your accoutrements; as loving yourself rather than seeming the lover of any other." His earnest protest, "Fair youth, I would I could make thee believe I love," only provokes the further teasing remark, "Me believe it! you may as soon make her that you love believe it;" and then, incapable of resisting the humour of the situation, she adds, "which, I warrant, she is apter to do than to confess she does: that is one of the points in which women still give the lie to their consciences." She sees that Orlando is rather dashed by this sarcastic remarks; possibly pained, but she knows she holds the remedy for his pain in her own hands; and she puts him at his ease again by asking, with a softened voice—

"But, in good sooth, are you he that hangs the verses on the trees wherein Rosalind is so admired."

Orl. I swear to thee, youth, by the white hand of Rosalind, I am that he, that unfortunate he.

Ros. But are you so much in love as your rhymes speak?

Orl. Neither rhyme nor reason can express how much."

Oh, how intently has she watched for that answer! with what secret rapture heard it! But he must discern nothing of this. So, turning carelessly away, and smiling inwardly to think that she is herself an illustration of what she says, she exclaims—

"Love is merely a madness, and, I tell you, deserves as well a dark house and a whip as madmen do: and the reason why they are not so punished and cured is, that the lunacy is so ordinary that the whippers are in love too."

But now, coming back to the plan which has sprung up in her heart for riveting still closer Orlando's devotion, she adds—

"Yet I profess curing it by counsel.

Orl. Did you ever cure any so?

Ros. Yes, one, and in this manner. He was to imagine me his love, his mistress; and I set him every day to woo me: At which time would I, being but a moonish youth, grieve, be effeminate, changeable, longing, and liking, proud, fantastical, apish, shallow, inconstant, full of tears, full of smiles, for every passion something and for no passion truly anything, as boys and women are for the most part cattle of this colour; would now like him, now loath him; then entertain him, then forswear him; . . . that I drave my suitor from his mad humour of love to a living humour of madness; which was,—to forswear the full stream of the world and to live in a nook merely monastic. And thus I cured him; and this way will I take upon me to wash your liver as clean as a sound sheep's heart, that there shall not be one spot of love in't."

In the range of Shakespearian comedy there is probably no passage that demands more subtle treatment in the actress than this. Rosalind's every faculty is quickened by delight, and this delight breaks out into a witty picture of all the wayward coquettishness that has ever been imputed to her sex. She rushes into this vein of humorous detraction, in order to keep up the sham of curing Orlando of his passion by a picture of some of their "giddy offences." Note the aptness, the exquisite suggestiveness and variety of every epithet, which, woman as she is, she is irresistibly moved to illustrate and enforce by suitable changes of intonation and expression. But note also, so ready is her intelligence, that she does not forget to keep up the illusion about herself, by throwing in the phrase, that boys as well as women "are for the most part cattle of this colour." All the playfulness, the wit, the sarcasm bubble up, sparkle after sparkle, with bewildering rapidity. Can we wonder they should work a charm upon Orlando? What, he thinks, might a gifted creature like this not do? What if the boy were indeed able to accomplish what he has said he could? No, that would be to rob life of all that made life worth; so he replies, "I would not be cured, youth!" And yet there is a certain mysterious fascination which draws him on; and when this strangely imperious youth rejoins, with an air of unhesitating confidence, "I would cure you, if you would but call me Rosalind"—how she would linger on the name!—"and come every day to my cote, and woo me;" he can but answer—"Now, by the faith of my love, I will: tell me where it is." She will show it to him at once, and by the way he shall "tell her where in the forest he lives." And when to her invitation, "Will you go?" he replies, "With all my heart, good youth," she begins the remedial lesson by telling him archly, with a playful smile that goes to his heart—"Nay, you must call me Rosalind." And turning to Celia, who must have seen with no small amazement the unexpected development of her cousin's character in this dialogue, calls to her to go home with them.

I need scarcely say how necessary it is for the actress in this scene, while carrying it through with a vivacity and dash that shall avert from Orlando's mind every suspicion of her sex, to preserve a refinement of tone and manner suitable to a woman of Rosalind's high station and cultured intellect; and by occasional tenderness of accent and sweet persuasiveness of look to indicate how it is that, even at the outset, she establishes a hold upon Orlando's feelings, which in their future intercourse in the forest deepens, without his being sensibly conscious of it, his love for the Rosalind of his dreams. I never approached this scene without a sort of pleasing dread, so strongly did I feel the difficulty and the importance of striking the true note in it. Yet, when once engaged in the scene, I was borne along I knew not how. The situation, in its very strangeness, was so delightful to my imagination, that from the moment when I took the assurance from Orlando's words to Jaques, that his love was as absolute as woman could desire, I seemed to lose myself in a sense of exquisite enjoyment. A thrill passed through me; I felt my pulse beat quicker; my very feet seemed to dance under me. That Rosalind should forget her first woman's fears about her "doublet and hose" seemed the most natural thing in the world. Speak to Orlando she must at any hazard. But oh, the joy of getting him to pour out all his heart, without knowing that it was his "very Rosalind" to whom he talked,—of proving if he were indeed worthy of her love, and testing, at the same time, the depth and sincerity of her own devotion! The device to which she resorted seemed to suggest itself irresistibly; and, armed with Shakespeare's words, it was an intense pleasure to try to give expression to that archness, the wit, the quick ready intellect, the ebullient fancy, with the tenderness underlying all, which give to this scene its transcendent charm. Of all the scenes in this exquisite play, while this is the most wonderful, it is for the actress certainly the most difficult.

How mistaken, I think, is the opinion of those who maintain that Shakespeare was governed, in drawing his heroines, by the fact that they were acted by boys, and that this was one of his reasons for choosing stories in which they had to assume male attire! As if Imogen, Viola, and Rosalind severe not "pure women" to the very core; as if, indeed, this were not the secret of the way in which they win the hearts of those whom they meet. Their disguise is never surmised, not even by their own sex, for Olivia falls passionately in love with Viola, and Phebe with Rosalind; and how markedly is Shakespeare's genius shown by the difference of the way this circumstance is handled in the case of each! Viola, gentle, self-sacrificing, generous, but with no spark of the heroic in her nature, sees the humorous absurdity of being wooed by a lady; but she is more perplexed than amused by it. She neither struggles against her own unrequited love, nor makes an effort to win requital for it. But, if placed in Viola's situation, Rosalind's mother-wit and high spirit would, I fancy, have enabled her to extricate herself handsomely. At all events, if, like Viola, she had fallen in love with the Duke Orsino, the attractions of Olivia which fascinated that dreamy personage would have grown daily fainter before the address, and vivacity, and bright intelligence of such a woman as Rosalind. By the time the discovery of her sex was made, his heart would have gone clean out of him, for he was capable of loving a noble woman nobly. How fine is his phrase, "Heaven walks on earth" (Act v. sc. 1), as he sees Olivia approaching! It would have been to his lips, and not to Viola's, that words laden with passion would have risen on discovering her sex,—he would have clasped her to his breast with irrepressible eagerness, instead of coldly giving her his hand, with the chilling request—

> "Give me thy hand,
> And let me see thee in thy woman's weeds."

Rosalind was not one to care for being loved in this stately fashion, nor indeed for being taken up on any terms at second-hand. In her eyes, one of the chief attractions of Orlando was that his love was a first love, unsophisticated by any mixture of personal vanity or of selfish interest. His feeling, as he thinks of her, she sees, is the same as that of Helena in *All's Well that Ends Well*—

> "'Twere all one,
> That I should love a bright particular star
> And think to wed it, she is so above me."

And this feeling is made more precious to Rosalind by her own consciousness of the complete conquest he has made of her own heart. Very woman as she is, she cannot help showing this in the next scene in which we see her. Orlando has not kept a promise to be with her that morning and she is "in the very height of heart-heaviness" in consequence. In vain Celia tries to laugh her out of her depression. To Celia his absence is easily to be accounted for. She has learned he is in attendance on the banished Duke, and that, being so, he is not master of his own time. But not till she has teased Rosalind by maintaining that "there is no truth in him," that she does not think he is in love, and, "besides, the oath of a lover is no stronger than the word of a tapster: they are both the confirmer of false reckonings," does she suggest such an explanation. In this Rosalind manifestly finds some ease; she turns from the subject to tell Celia—

"I met the Duke yesterday, and had much question with him. He asked me of what parentage I was; I told him, of as good as he; so he laughed, and let me go. But what talk we of fathers, when there is such a man as Orlando?"

What a world of passionate emotion is concentrated in that last sentence, and how important it is to bear this in mind in the subsequent scenes with Orlando!

At this point Rosalind's thoughts are turned into a new channel by the arrival of old Corin, who comes to tell them that "the shepherd that complained of love," after whom they have often inquired, is now with "the proud disdainful shepherdess that was his mistress;" and that if they

>"Will see a pageant truly play'd,
>Between the pale complexion of true love
>And the red glow of scorn and proud disdain,"

he will take them to the place. Rosalind jumps at the suggestion, for

>"The sight of lovers feedeth those in love.
>Bring us to this sight, and you shall say,
>I'll prove a busy actor in their play."

Herself loving deeply, and prizing a good man's love as her best treasure, she is
in no mood to be tolerant of the scornful cruelty shown by Phebe to Silvius, of
which in the scene that ensues she is an unseen witness. At the same time, his
love-sickness, which has taken all the manhood out of him, inspires her with
something not very far from contempt. But the poor fellow pleads his cause
well. His passion is genuine, and his words are echoes of a feeling in her own
heart:—

>"O dear Phebe,
>If ever (as that ever may be near)
>You meet in some fresh cheek the power of fancy,
>Then shall you know the wounds invisible
>That love's keen arrows make."

They merited at least a gentle answer; and when Phebe heartlessly replies—

>"But till that time,
>Come thou not near me: and when that time comes,
>Afflict me with thy mocks, pity me not;
>As, till that time, I shall not pity thee"—

Rosalind can restrain herself no longer, and breaks in upon the speakers. In
what ensues she seems to me to show something of that quality, characteristic
of princely blood and training, which, without directly claiming deference,
somehow commands it, and which is frequently exemplified in the progress of
the play:—

>"*Ros.* And why, I pray you? Who might be your mother,
>That you insult, exult, and all at once,
>Over the wretched? What though you have some beauty,
>(As, by my faith, I see no more in you,

Than without candle may go dark to bed,)
Must you be therefore proud and pitiless?"

How great must have been the charm of the seeming boy, when the haughty
rustic beauty does not fire up at such a rebuke as this! Yet there she stands,
breathless, all eyes, all admiration. Rosalind continues:—

"Why, what means this? Why do you look on me?
I see no more in you than in the ordinary
Of nature's sale-work. 'Od's my little life,
I think she means to tangle my eyes too!
No, faith, proud mistress, hope not after it:
'Tis not your inky brows, your black silk hair,
Your bugle eyeballs, nor your cheek of cream,
That can entame my spirits to your worship."

With her wonted readiness of wit she follows up this vivid picture of
commonplace beauty by words that, while giving encouragement to Silvius, are
cleverly designed to take some of Phebe's conceit out of her:—

"You foolish shepherd, wherefore do you follow her . . .
You are a thousand times a properer man
Than she a woman: 'tis such fools as you
That make the world full of ill-favoured children:
'Tis not her glass, but you, that flatters her. . . .
But, mistress, know yourself: down on your knees,
And thank heaven, fasting, for a good man's love:
For I must tell you friendly in your ear,—
Sell when you can: you are not for all markets."

Then with a softer tone, almost entreatingly she adds—

"Cry the man mercy, love him, take his offer: . . .
So take her to thee, shepherd: fare you well."

But Phebe has by this time "felt the power of fancy" too strongly to let the
interview break off so soon. "Sweet youth," she exclaims, as she runs after to
detain him,

"I pray you, chide a year together; I had rather hear you chide than this man
woo."

The situation is becoming too absurd. The tables have indeed been turned upon Phebe. With all her sense of humour Rosalind, as a woman, could not but feel some pity for her, as Viola does for Olivia. She must be told at once, and in unmistakable terms, to put all thought of Ganymede out of her head:—

> "*Ros.* I pray you, do not fall in love with me,
> For I am falser than vows made in wine.
> Besides, I like you not.
>
> . . . .
>
> Will you go, sister? Shepherd [*aside to him*], ply her hard.
> Come, sister. Shepherdess [*aside to her*], look on him better,
> And be not proud: though all the world could see,
> None could be so abused in sight as he."

I have already called attention to the picture of the boy Ganymede drawn for us by Phebe, after he has left her. It is not merely the beauty of his person that strikes her; she feels the distinction of his bearing,—the unconscious imperiousness of Rosalind, the princess—"Sure, he's proud; and yet his pride becomes him"—and how this is blended with a strange tenderness, that tempers the severity of his rebuke to herself, for

> "Faster than his tongue
> Did make offence, his eye did heal it up."

In this scene, as elsewhere, the woman's heart modifies the keenness of Rosalind's wit, and the combination makes her ascendancy over all those she cares for more complete.

But when we see her next, at the opening of the fourth act, in colloquy with Jaques, her intellect alone is called into play, and the cynic comes off second-best in the encounter. He, too, feels the attraction of the young Ganymede, and would fain be intimate with him;—"I prithee, pretty youth, let me be better acquainted with thee." To Rosalind this patronising address would be far from agreeable. By a natural instinct she recoils, as we have previously seen Orlando recoil, from the society of a man who has exhausted the zest for life in years of sensual indulgence, and who sees only the dark side of human nature and of the world, because he has squandered his means and used up his finest sensations. She has heard of him and his morbid moralisings, and so replies—

> "They say you are a melancholy fellow."

Her healthy common-sense is roused by his answer, "that he is so, and that he loves it better than laughing," and she replies—

"Those that are in the extremity of either are abominable fellows; and betray themselves to every modern censure worse than drunkards.

Jaq. Why, 'tis good to be sad and say nothing.

Ros. Why, then, 'tis good to be a post."

Jaques then runs off into his famous definition of the varieties of melancholy, winding up—self-complacent egotist as he is, always referring everything to himself and his own perverted experiences—with the intimation, that "indeed the sundry contemplation of his travels, in which his often rumination wraps him, is a most humorous sadness." This answer in no way increases Rosalind's respect. "A traveller! " she exclaims—

"By my faith, you have great reason to be sad: I fear you have sold your own lands to see other men's; then, to have seen much and to have nothing, is to have rich eyes and poor hands.

Jaq. Yes, I have gained my experience.

Ros. And your experience makes you sad: I had rather have a fool to make me merry, than experience to make me sad; and to travel for it too!"

Jaques, unused to be picked to pieces in this way,—for the people about the banished Duke, though amused by this moping philosopher's churlish temper, seem to stand rather in awe of it,—is glad to take the opportunity afforded by Orlando's appearance to escape from the "pretty youth," whom he has found to be so unexpectedly formidable. But Rosalind cannot refrain from sending after him some further shafts from her quiver:—

"Farewell, Monsieur Traveller: look you lisp and wear strange suits, disable all the benefits of your own country, be out of love with your nativity, and almost chide Heaven for making you that countenance you are, or I will scarce think you have swum in a gondola."

Not till she has seen Jaques fairly out of hearing, does she turn to Orlando, who has by this time thoroughly learned the first lesson she had set him. He accosts her throughout the scene as "dear Rosalind," "fair Rosalind," and never trips into speaking to the boy otherwise than as the lady of his love. His visits to the sheepcote, we see, have been frequent, but the promised cure has clearly made no progress. The feminine waywardness with which the boy menaced him has served only to establish a sweet, and to him, mysterious control over his heart and will. Again he has failed in coming at the appointed hour. See how she punishes him for the little pang of disappointment he has caused her!—

"Why, how now, Orlando! where have you been all this while? You a lover! An you serve me such another trick, never come in my sight more.

Orl. My fair Rosalind, I come within an hour of my promise.

Ros. Break an hour's promise in love! He that will divide a minute into a thousand parts, and break but a part of the thousandth part of a minute in the affairs of love, it may be said of him that Cupid hath clapped him o' the shoulder, but I'll warrant him heart-whole.

Orl. Pardon me, dear Rosalind.

Ros. Nay, an you be so tardy, come no more in my sight: I had as lief be wooed of a snail.

Orl. Of a snail?

Ros. Ay, of a snail; for though he comes slowly, he carries his house on his head; a better jointure, I think, than you can make a woman."

And now we are to see how Rosalind carries out in practice her own suddenly devised fiction of the way she once cured a lover of his passion—by being effeminate, changeable, "full of tears, full of smiles, would now like him, now loathe him, now entertain, now forswear him." She throws aside her first mood of pouting and banter. Her own heart is brimful of happy love, and only by variety of mood and volubility of utterance can she keep down its emotion. "Come, woo me!" she exclaims. Seeing Orlando taken aback by the suddenness of this invitation, she repeats it: "Woo me; for now I am in a holiday humour, and like enough to consent." Still he hangs back; but she is not to be foiled in her determination to makes him play the lover, so she adds—"What would you say to me now, an I were your very very Rosalind?" This brings from him the laughing answer, "I would kiss before I spoke." "Nay," she rejoins, "you were better speak first, and when you were gravelled for lack of matter, you might take occasion to kiss." After some more *badinage* on this theme, Rosalind turns suddenly upon Orlando with the question—"Am not I your Rosalind?" and as she does so, her voice, I fancy, vibrates with feeling she finds it hard to conceal. But this vein is dangerous; and when Orlando answers, "I take some joy to say you are, because I would be talking of her," she dashes off again into her playful mocking mood, with the words, "Well, in her person I say I will not have you." This elicits from Orlando the very avowal for which she yearns— "Then in mine own person I die!" But the opening thus offered to her to profess a disbelief, which she does not feel, in the sincerity of all such protestations is not to be lost, and her fancy revels in throwing ridicule upon the model heroes of romantic love:—

"No, faith, die by attorney. The poor world is almost six thousand years old, and in all this time there was not any man died in his own person, *videlicet,* in a love-cause. Troilus had his brains dashed out with a Grecian club; yet he did what he could to die before; and he is one of the patterns of love. Leander, he would have lived many a fair year though Hero had turned nun, if it had not been for a hot midsummer night; for, good youth, he went but forth to wash him in the Hellespont, and being taken with the cramp was drowned: and the foolish chroniclers of that age found it was—Hero of Sestos. But these are all lies: men have died from time to time, and worms have eaten them, but not for love.

Orl. I would not have my right Rosalind of this mind; for, I protest, her frown might kill me."

Rosalind's rejoinder, "By this hand, it will not kill a fly," should, I think, be given with a marked change of intonation, sufficient to indicate that, notwithstanding all the wild raillery of her former speech, there is in herself a vein of tenderness which would make it impossible for her to inflict pain deliberately. We should be made to feel the woman just for the moment,—before she passes on to her next words, which, playful as they are, lead her on unawares to what I believe was regarded by her as a very real climax to this sportive wooing:—

"But come, now I will be your Rosalind in a more coming-on disposition; and ask me what you will, I will grant it.

Orl. Then love me, Rosalind.

Ros. Yes, faith, will I—Fridays and Saturdays, and all.

Orl. And wilt thou have me!

Ros. Ay, and twenty such.

Orl. What say'st thou?

Ros. Are you not good?

Orl. I hope so.

Ros. Why, then, can one desire too much of a good thing?"

Who does not feel through all this exuberance of sportive raillery the strong emotion which is palpitating at the speaker's heart? She has proved and is assured of Orlando's devotion, and now she will plight her troth to him—irrevocably, as she knows, but as he does not know. Turning, to Celia, she says—

"Come, sister, you shall be the priest, and marry us. Give me your hand, Orlando. What do you say, sister?

Orl. Pray thee, marry us. . . .

Ros. You must begin,—'Will you, Orlando—'

Cel. Go to. Will you, Orlando, have to wife this Rosalind?

Orl. I will.

Ros. Ay, but when?

Orl. Why now; as fast as she can marry us.

Ros. Then you must say,—'I take thee, Rosalind, for wife.'

Orl. I take thee, Rosalind, for wife.

Ros. I do take thee, Orlando, for my husband."

It is not merely in pastime, I feel assured, that Rosalind has been made by Shakespeare to put these words into Orlando's mouth. This is for her a marriage, though no priestly formality goes with it; and it seems to me that the actress should show this by a certain tender earnestness of look and voice, as she replies, "I do take thee, Orlando, for my husband." I could never speak these words without a trembling of the voice, and the involuntary rushing of happy tears to the eyes, which made it necessary for me to turn my head away from Orlando. But, for fear of discovery, this momentary emotion had to be overcome, and turned off by carrying his thoughts into a different channel. Still Rosalind's gravity of look and intonation will not have quite passed away—for has she not taken the most solemn step a woman can take?—as she continues—

"*Ros.* Now tell me how long you would love her, after you have possessed her?

Orl. For ever and a day.

Ros. Say a day, without the ever. No, no, Orlando; men are April when they woo, December when they wed: maids are May when they are maids, but the sky changes when they are wives."

Here, however, Rosalind finds herself running into a strain of serious earnest, with too much of the apprehensive woman in it; so she takes up her former cue of exaggerating the capriciousness of her own sex:—

"I will be more jealous of thee than a Barbary cock-pigeon lover his hen; more clamorous than a parrot against rain; more new-fangled than an ape; more giddy in my desires than a monkey: I will weep for nothing, like Diana in the fountain, and I will do that when you are disposed to be merry; I will laugh like a hyena, and that when thou art inclined to sleep.

Orl. But will my Rosalind do so?

Ros. By my life, she will do as I do.

Orl. O, but she is wise.

Ros. Or else she could not have the wit to do this: the wiser the waywarder: make the doors upon a woman's wit, and it will out at the casement; shut that, and 'twill out at the keyhole; stop that, 'twill fly with the smoke out at the chimney."

Rosalind through all this scene is like the bird "that cannot get out its song" for very joy. She dares not give direct vent to the happiness that fills her heart, and so she seeks relief by letting her fancy run riot in these playful exaggerations. We feel how these flashes of sprightly fancy, that amuse even while they bewilder him, all help to weave a spell of fascination around Orlando's heart. Rosalind sees this, and revelling in her triumph, pursues to the uttermost the course she had told him would cure him of his passion. Observe how this is carried out, when he tells her presently that he must leave her for two hours. Here is an opportunity for showing what Ganymede has formerly told Orlando a woman cannot choose, but must be. She is now to "grieve, be effeminate, changeable."

"*Ros.* Alas, dear love, I cannot lack thee two hours.

Orl. I must attend the Duke at dinner: by two o'clock I will be with thee again.

Ros. Ay, go your ways, go your ways; I knew what you would prove: my friends told me as much, and I thought no less: that flattering tongue of yours won me: 'tis but one cast away, and so,—Come, death! "

This is to be "full of tears"; and when she has put a pang into her lover's heart by this semblance of reproachful grief, she suddenly floods it with delight by turning to him, her face radiant with smiles, and saying, "Two o'clock's your hour!" This is to be "full of smiles," and the charm so works upon him, that we see he has lost the consciousness that it is the boy Ganymede, and not his own Rosalind, that is before him, as he answers, "Ay, sweet Rosalind." And she too, in her parting adjuration to him, comes nearer than she has ever done before to letting him see what is in her heart:—

"By my troth, and in good earnest, and so Heaven mend me, and by all pretty oaths that are not dangerous, if you break one jot of your promise, or come one minute behind your hour, I will think you the most pathetical break-promise, and the most hollow lover, and the most unworthy of her you call Rosalind, that may be chosen out of the gross band of the unfaithful. Therefore, beware my censure, and keep your promise.

Orl. With no less religion than if thou wert indeed my Rosalind: so adieu!"

Celia—who, admirable as she may be, is by no means of a highly imaginative nature—is no sooner alone with Rosalind than she takes her to task for what appears to her the unfavourable light in which her pictures of the waywardness of women in courtship and in marriage have placed her sex. "You have simply misused our sex in your love-prate," she says; but this is a matter Rosalind is too full of her own emotions to discuss. Her tongue has run wild in trying to conceal the pressure at her heart; and she has talked herself out of breath only to get deeper in love.

"O coz, coz, my pretty little coz," she replies, "that thou didst know how many fathoms deep I am in love! But it cannot be sounded. . . . That same wicked bastard of Venus, that was begot of thought, conceived of spleen, and born of madness, that blind rascally boy that abuses every one's eyes because his own are out, let him be judge how deep I am in love. I'll tell thee, Aliena, I cannot be out of the sight of Orlando: I'll go find a shadow, and sigh till he come."

We see from this confession how great has been the constraint he has been keeping upon her emotions through all her sparkling *badinage* in the interviews with Orlando. He was to be but two hours absent, and had protested he should be with her by two o'clock; but when we next see her, two o'clock has come, but not Orlando. "How say you now?" she says to Celia. "Is it not past two o'clock? and here much Orlando!" While she is in this state of disappointment and unrest, Silvius arrives with the love-letter of which Phebe has made him the bearer. Such is the rare elasticity of Rosalind's temperament, and the activity of her intelligence that she at once puts aside her own vexation—which could not have been small—and does what she can to give something of a manly spirit to this most forlorn of lovers. So far from thinking the letter he has brought to be one of love, he is under the impression, from "the stern brow and waspish action" of Phebe in writing it, that "it bears an angry tenor," and apologises for being the bearer of it. Rosalind at once follows out this idea, though she has of course seen, by a glance at its contents, how very far this is from the truth:—

> "Patience herself would startle at this letter
> And play the swaggerer; bear this, bear all:
> She says I am not fair, that I lack manners;
> She calls me proud; and that she could not love me,
> Were man as rare as phoenix. 'Od's my will!
> Her love is not the hare that I do hunt:
> Why writes she so to me? Well, shepherd, well,
> This is a letter of your own device."

In answer to his vehement protestations to the contrary, she goes on to depict its contents with her wonted fertility of fancy:—

> "Why, 'tis a boisterous and a cruel style,
> A style for challengers. . . . Women's gentle brain
> Could not drop forth such giaut-rude invention,
> Such Ethiop words, blacker in their effect
> Than in their countenance. Will you hear the letter?"

She then proceeds to read it, commenting on its evident avowals of admiration in the same ironical spirit. But when she comes to the lines—

> "He that brings this love to thee
> Little knows this love in me,"

followed by the request that Ganymede will use Silvius to bear his answer back, she is revolted by Phebe's treachery and scarcely less by the pusillanimous insensibility of her suitor to it. Celia, in her matter-of-fact way, exclaims, "Alas, poor shepherd!" But Rosalind, wiser and higher-hearted, takes a different view:—

"Do you pity him? no, he deserves no pity. Wilt thou love such a woman? What, to make thee an instrument and play false strains upon thee! not to be endured!"

But not even this can rouse him; so she dismisses him in a gentler strain:—

"Well, go your way to her, for I see love hath made thee a tame snake, and say this to her: That if she love me, I charge her to love thee; is she will not, I will never have her unless thou entreat for her."

Still Orlando comes not. The fond woman's heartache, into which some shade of anxiety at his failure to keep his promise would by this time be sure to steal, has not time to reassert itself, when her attention is arrested by a stranger inquiring the way to the "sheepcote fenced about with olive-trees," which is her home. Attention deepens into interest as she finds from his words that he is a messenger from Orlando:—

> "Orlando doth commend him to you both,
> And to that youth he calls his Rosalind
> He sends this bloody napkin. Are you he?"

Interest now becomes apprehension, and she answers, "I am: what must we understand by this?" With breathless eagerness she listens as the stranger tells how Orlando had found his elder brother asleep in the forest, doubly threatened with death by "a green and gilded snake" on the one hand, and on the other by "a lioness with udders all drawn dry." The different natures of Celia and Rosalind are well expressed by the ways, each so different, in which they are affected by this narrative. Celia exclaims:—

> "Oh, I have heard him speak of that same brother;
> And he did render him the most unnatural
> That lived 'mongst men."

Rosalind's first thought is not of this brother's cruelty, but whether her lover has forgot the past and interposed to save his life.

> "But, to Orlando: did he leave him there,
> Food to the suck'd and hungry lioness?"

How her heart leaps within her as she learns that, conquering the first impulse to leave his brother to his fate, Orlando has given "battle to the lioness, who quickly fell before him"! When the stranger goes on to tell them that he is that brother, Rosalind's first impulse naturally is to turn with undisguised aversion from the man who had for years done Orlando such grievous wrong. But his answer to her question, "Was't you he rescued?" disarms her.

> "*Oli.* 'Twas I, yet 'tis not I. I do not shame
> To tell you what I was, since my conversion
> So sweetly tastes, being the thing I am."

By the word "conversion," coupled with Oliver's downcast looks and contrite tone, Rosalind is touched. She feels that she has been ungenerous, and turning to him with a much gentler voice and manner, almost as though asking pardon for the resentment she had shown, she asks, "But for the bloody napkin?" And here arises one of the many opportunities which are afforded in this play for that silent suggestive acting which is required to give effect to the purpose of the poet. "The woman, naturally born to fears," has now to be indicated by the changing expression of Rosalind's look and manner, as she listens to Oliver's narrative Her lover,—her more than lover—her plighted husband ever since she gave him her hand when they last met,—has still further proved his worthiness by making it his first care to introduce his brother to the banished Duke. Still, what does the bloody napkin imply? And how much is there to rouse her alarm, when Oliver goes on to say that, on leaving the Duke, his brother led him to his own cave,

> "There stripp'd himself, and here upon his arm
> The lioness had torn some flesh away,
> Which all this while had bled; and now he fainted,
> And cried, in fainting, upon Rosalind"?

The sweet feeling of admiration for her lover's courageous endurance, and of delight that his foremost thought had been of his Rosalind, cannot keep her from thinking of his wound as something more serious than it proves to be. A sick feeling comes over her as Oliver proceeds:—

> "Brief, I recover'd him, bound up his wound;
> And, after some small space, being strong at heart,
> He sent me hither, stranger as I am,
> To tell this story, that you might excuse
> His broken promise, and to give this napkin
> Dyed in his blood unto the shepherd youth,
> That he in sport doth call his Rosalind."

As he speaks, Rosalind's vivid imagination brings before her the peril of the contest in which her lover had been engaged, and how near she has been to losing him. The strain upon her feelings is too much even for her powers of self-command, great as they are, and she falls fainting into her cousin's arms. She has borne up, however, so well, that Oliver has no suspicion of her sex, and ascribes her fainting to the not uncommon experience, that "Many will swoon when they do look on blood." When she recovers, and he says to her, "Be of good cheer, youth; you a man! You lack a man's heart," she admits the fact, but, ready and adroit as ever, tries to avert his suspicion by affecting to have merely feigned to swoon. The rest of the scene, with the struggle between actual physical faintness and the effort to make light of it, touched in by the poet with exquisite skill, calls for the most delicate and discriminating treatment in the actress. The audience, who are in her secret, must be made to feel the tender loving nature of the woman through the simulated gaiety by which it is veiled; and yet the character of the boy Ganymede must be sustained. This is another of the many passages, to which the actress of comedy only will never give adequate expression. How beautiful it is!—

"Ah, sirrah, a body would think this was well counterfeited! I pray you, tell your brother how well I counterfeited. Heigh-ho!

Oli. This was not counterfit: there is too great testimony in your complexion that it was a passion of earnest.

Ros. Counterfeit, I assure you.

Oli. Well, then, take a good heart, and counterfeit to be a man

Ros. So I do: but i'faith, I should have been a woman by right.

Cel. Come, you look paler and paler: pray you, draw homewards. Good sir, go with us.

Oli. That will I, for I must bear answer back, how you excuse my brother, Rosalind.

Ros. I shall devise something: but, I pray you, commend my counterfeiting to him. Will you go?"

And that her quick wit did devise something to the purpose, who can doubt? for it is clear that Orlando's suspicions were not aroused. But in the brief interval that elapses before she again sees him, events have occurred which turn his thoughts into another channel. In that charmed forest region, where everything is "as you like it," events move swiftly. Celia, who has hitherto mocked at love, becomes, as such mockers often do, its unresisting victim. She has met her fate in the repentant Oliver, and he his fate in her. Making all allowance for the necessity of bringing the action of the play to a speedy conclusion, the readiness with which Celia succumbs to Oliver's suit is somewhat startling. Shakespeare perhaps felt this himself, and so does his best to take the edge off its apparent improbability. How wittily has he made Rosalind discourse of it to Orlando!—

"There never was anything so sudden but the fight of two rams, and Cæsar's Thrasonical brag of 'I came, saw, and overcame:' for your brother and my sister no sooner met but they looked, no sooner looked but they loved, no sooner loved but they sighed, no sooner sighed but they asked one another the reason, no sooner knew the reason but they sought the remedy; and in these degrees have they made a pair of stairs to marriage. . . . They are in the very wrath of love, and they will together; clubs cannot part them."

This is very amusing, but Orlando can only think how enviable is his brother's case compared with his own. "They shall be married to-morrow," he says, "and I will bid the Duke to the nuptial. But, oh, how bitter a thing it is to look into happiness through another man's eyes!" The sad earnestness with which this is said finds an echo in Rosalind's own feelings, as she replies, "Why, then, to-morrow I cannot serve your turn for Rosalind?" Can we wonder at his answer, "I can live no longer by thinking"—worked up to a very fever-heat of yearning devotion as he has been to his ideal Rosalind by the hours and days he has spent in playing the lover to the pretty youth who has borne her name, and kept her image continually before him, fascinating him hour after hour by all the qualities which he had dreamed his ideal to possess? When Rosalind had herself got to the point, that she "could not live out of the sight" of her lover, and had learned, by what she suffered at the thought of his recent danger, how essential he had become to her happiness, she was not likely to be deaf to this outcry of Orlando's hungry heart. The time has come for her to yield. But she will keep up a little longer the illusion under which he labours, so she answers:—

"I will weary you no longer then with idle talking. Know of me then, for now I speak to some purpose . . . that I can do strange things. I have, since I was three years old, conversed with a magician, most profound in his art, and yet not damnable. If you do love Rosalind so near the heart as your gesture cries it out, when your brother marries Aliena, shall you marry her. I know into what straits of fortune she is driven; and it is not impossible for me, if it appear not inconvenient to you, to set her before your eyes, human as she is, and without any danger.

Orl. Speakest thou in sober meanings?

Ros. By my life, I do; which I tender dearly, though I say I am a magician. Therefore, put you in your best array, bid your friends; for, if you will be married to-morrow, you shall,—and to Rosalind, it you will."

Their colloquy is interrupted by the arrival of Phebe with Silvius. Phebe tasks Ganymede with "much ungentleness" for having shown Silvius her letter. With pretty imperiousness Rosalind replies:—

> "I care not if I have: it is my study
> To seem ungentle and despiteful to you:
> You are there followed by a faithful shepherd;
> Look upon him, love him: he worships you."

The humbled Phebe can only answer by asking Silvius to "tell this youth what 'tis to love." The charming scene which ensues, in which Silvius fulfils his task with a skill the most passionate lyrist might envy, gives Rosalind a further opportunity of assuring herself of her lover's devotion. All that Silvius protests he feels for Phebe, Orlando protests he feels for Rosalind; and when at last, addressing Rosalind, he says, "If this be so, why blame you me to love you?" he speaks as though it were his "very very Rosalind" he was addressing. On this she at once catches him up, saying—

Ros. Whom do you speak to? 'Why blame you me to love you?'
Orl. To her that is not here, nor doth not hear."

But Rosalind, finding the "homily of love," in which Orlando, Silvius, and Phebe echo each other, grow tedious, breaks in upon them with the words—

"Pray you no more at this; 'tis like the howling of Irish wolves against the moon. I will help you [to *Silvius*] if I can: I would love you [to *Phebe*] if I could. Tomorrow meet we all together. I will marry you [to *Phebe*] if ever I marry woman, and I'll be married to-morrow. I will satisfy you [to *Orlando*] if ever I satisfied man, and you shall be married to-morrow. I will content you [to *Silvius*], if what pleases you contents you, and you shall he married to-morrow. As you [to *Orlando*] love Rosalind, meet; as you [to *Silvius*] love Phebe, meet; and as I love no woman, I'll meet. So fare you well; I have left you commands."

The ascendancy which the boy Ganymede has established over all who come within his sphere is so complete, that Orlando, Phebe, and Silvius part from him with a complete belief that he will accomplish everything he has promised. Orlando reports to the Duke the hope that has been held out to him; and any misgiving he may have had would be dispelled, when presently he finds (Act v. sc. 4) that the boy Ganymede comes to ask the banished Duke if, when he shall bring in his daughter, he will give her to Orlando. His answer, "That would I, had I kingdoms to give with her," removes the only obstacle which as a dutiful daughter she would recognise. But not until she has obtained a fresh assurance from Orlando, that he would marry his Rosalind "were he of all kingdoms king," and from Phebe that if she refuses to marry Ganymede she will give herself to Silvius, does she go away "to make all doubts even" by appearing forthwith in her own true character, along with Celia, and led on by "Hymen."

It is Rosalind, of course, who has arranged the masque of Hymen, keeping up to the last the film of glamour which she has thrown around her lover and the other strangers to her secret. Mr Macready, in his revival of the play at Drury Lane, with Mrs Nesbitt as Rosalind, restored it to the stage; but beautiful as it is in itself, and bringing this charming love-romance most appropriately to a close, yet it delays the action too much for scenic purposes. Hymen's lines, as he leads in Rosalind and Celia in their wedding-robes, are like a strain of sweet music, solemn but not sad, as befits a bridal hymn:—

"Then is there mirth in heaven,
When earthly things made even

Atone together.

Good Duke, receive thy daughter:
Hymen from heaven brought her,
     Yea, brought her hither,
That thou might'st join her hand in his
Whose heart within her bosom is."

How beautiful is this last line, and how fully does it express that perfect union of the two lovers' hearts!

With her masking guise, Rosalind drops the witty volubility that has served her purpose so well. Her words are few, but they are pregnant with feeling. Turning to her father, she says, "To you I give myself, for I am yours;" and while still hanging on his breast, she holds out her hand to Orlando, repeating the same words. What others could so well express the surrender which a loving daughter here makes of herself to the lover "whose heart within her bosom is"? Her own heart is too full to say much; her soul too much enwrapped in the thoughts which the climax of marriage brings to a noble woman, for her to sport with the surprise which this sudden revelation produces:—

"*Duke.* If there be truth in sight, you are my daughter.

Orl. If there be truth in sight, you are my Rosalind.

Phebe. If sight and shape be true,
Why, then, my love, adieu!

Ros. I'll have no father, if you be not he;
I'll have no husband if you be not he;
Nor ne'er wed woman, if you [to *Phebe*] be not she."

But the "conclusion of these most strange events" is not yet. Oliver, we have been told, had determined to settle upon Orlando "all the revenue that was old Sir Rowland's, and live and die a shepherd in the forest" with his Aliena. She, on the other hand, had, as we have seen, long since told Rosalind that, when Duke Frederick died, Rosalind should be his heir. But now Rosalind is to resume her state by means more direct. The usurping Duke, smitten with remorse, as we learn from Sir Rowland's second son, who at this point appears upon the scene, has taken to a religious life—

"His crown bequeathing to his banish'd brother,
And all their lands restored to them again
That were with him exiled."

Thus is the wrong made right: this alone was wanted to complete the story, *As You Like It*.

No word escapes from Rosalind's lips, as we watch her there, the woman in all her beauty and perfect grace, now calmly happy, beside a father restored to a "potent dukedom," and a lover whom she knows to be wholly worthy to wield that dukedom, when in due season she will endow him with it as her husband. Happiest of women ! for who else ever had such means of testing that love on which her own happiness depends? In the days that are before her, all the largeness of heart, the rich imagination, the bright commanding intellect, which made her the presiding genius of the forest of Arden, will work with no less beneficent sway in the wider sphere of princely duty. With what delight will she recur with her lover-husband to the strange accidents of fortune which "forced sweet love on pranks of saucy boyhood," and to the never-to-be-forgotten hours when he was a second time "o'erthrown" by the wit, the playful wiles, the inexplicable charm of the young Ganymede! How, too, in all the grave duties of the high position to which his alliance will raise him, will Orlando not only possess in her an honoured, beloved, and admired companion, but will also find wise guidance and support in her clear intelligence and courageous will! It is thus, at least, that I dream of my dear Rosalind and her Orlando.

> "O, they will walk this world,
> Yoked in all exercise of noble end,
> And so through those dark gates across the wild
> That no man knows."

Oliver's proposal to make over his estates to Orlando, and "to live and die a shepherd in the forest," naturally falls to the ground with the reinstatement of Rosalind's father in his duchy. Oliver will resume his former position—his "land and great allies," as Jaques says—and Rosalind and Celia will not be separated. Is it likely that Rosalind should be outdone in generosity? When the heavens were "at their sorrows pale," Celia insisted upon sharing her banishment. Could Rosalind's happiness be complete without the love and presence of that constant dearest friend? No! If they might not henceforward move, "like Juno's swans, still coupled and inseparable," yet they must pass their lives near to each other, and in ever sweet and loving communion.

Much as I have written, I feel how imperfectly I have brought out all that this delightful play has been and is to me. I can but hope that I have said enough to show why I gave my heart to Rosalind, and found an ever new delight in trying to impersonate her.

Never was that delight greater than the last time I did so. As it happened, it was the last time I appeared upon the stage. The occasion was a benefit, in October 1879, for the widow of Mr Charles Calvert, himself an excellent actor, who had spent many years in producing Shakespeare worthily to the Manchester public at the Prince's Theatre. In his revivals he had kept the scene-painter and the costume-maker under wise control, insisting that what they did should be subservient to the development of character and of plot. His death was justly felt by the Manchester public to be a great loss to the dramatic art, and it was a pleasure to me to join with them in doing honour to his memory. He told me once a pretty story of his wife. He had sent her to see me in Rosalind, at the Theatre Royal—for I never acted in his theatre. On returning home, he found her in tears. Upon inquiring the reason, she replied, "How could you ever allow me to go upon the stage for Rosalind? I am ashamed of myself, for I see I knew nothing about her." It reminded me of what had been my own case, until I had made the loving study of her which I have tried to describe.

I can never forget the warmth of my Manchester friends that night, when I left my retirement to join in helping the widow and children, whom their old manager had left behind him. I had expected, and thought I had nerved myself to meet, a cordial greeting, but this was so prolonged and so overwhelming, that it took away my breath and my courage; and even when at last it ceased, I could not recover myself enough to speak. My agitation quite alarmed the young lady by my side, who acted Celia, Miss Kate Pattison, and we stood like a pair of mutes for a moment or two, until the renewed plaudits of the audience roused us to a sense of what was expected from us. The old sensation of stage-fright, never completely lost, came back upon me as freshly then as upon the night of my first appearance. After a while, when this hall somewhat passed away in the interest of the scene, I was full of gratitude to find that I had not rusted in my privacy. I had found also in the rehearsal of the previous day, which, from the large number attending it, became almost a performance, that I had as much delight as ever in depicting the life of one so dear to my imagination, and that I could do so with as much freshness and elasticity as at the beginning of my career.

I was very much interested in seeing the careful study which the actors on this occasion, mostly amateurs, had given to all the characters, great and small, in the play. It was a pleasure to act beside so much intelligence and artistic talent. I felt quite a keen regret when this not-to-be-repeated performance was over.

How many good parts there are in this play, as indeed there must be in every fine play, and how great would be the delight of acting in it. With every character adequately represented! How little do those who usually act what are called the smaller parts in Shakespeare know the gems within their reach, and the splendid opportunities they throw away! I have tried in my rehearsals to bring those who acted with me up to the highest level I could, by calling their attention to these opportunities (though not always with success), and by showing them the value of the passages they had overlooked. Some were incapable of seeing the author's meaning, some indifferent to it; others have looked as though I were taking a liberty, and had no business to leave my own character and interfere with theirs; some few, I am glad to say, have thanked me when they found the audience recognise and appreciate the significance given to the text by following my suggestions.

Out of London I never saw the play of *As You Like It* more fully enjoyed or better acted than in Edinburgh. There, in the first years of my visits, a fine illustration was given of the way in which a minor part may be raised into importance by the actor's skill. Mr Murray, the manager, was the William. Night after night I used to go to the side scene to see the only occasion in which in the fifth act William appears with Touchstone. He was the very man, one felt, whom Shakespeare had in his mind,—dress, voice, look, manner, were all life-like;—just such a blunder-headed, good-natured, staring, grinning, frightened oaf as at once provokes and falls an easy victim to the waggishness of Touchstone. He had so little to say, and yet so much to suggest.

The Touchstone of the same theatre in those days, a Mr Lloyd, was almost the best I have ever seen; and though wanting in the courtly demeanour, which I think is one of Touchstone's characteristics, he brought out the dry, quaint, sententious humour of the man with the happiest effect.

One word about the Epilogue before I conclude. This, as it is written, was fit enough for the mouth of a boy-actor of women's parts in Shakespeare's time, but it is altogether out of tone with the Princess Rosalind. It is the stage tradition to speak it, and I, of course, had to follow the tradition—never, however, without a kind of shrinking distaste for my task. Some of the words I omitted, and some I altered, and I did my best, in speaking it, to make it serve to illustrate how the high-toned winning woman reasserted herself in Rosalind, when she laid aside her doublet and hose. I have been told that I succeeded in this. Still, speaking the Epilogue remained the one drawback to my pleasure. In it one addresses the audience neither as Ganymede nor as Rosalind, but as one's own very self. Anything of this kind was repugnant to me, my desire being always to lose myself in the character I was representing. When taken thus perforce out of my ideal, I felt stranded and altogether unhappy. Except when obliged, as in this instance, I never addressed an audience, having neither the wish nor the courage to do so. Therefore, as I advanced to speak the Epilogue, a painful shyness came over me, a kind of nervous fear, too, lest I should forget what I had to say,—a fear I never had at other times,—and thus the closing words always brought to me a sense of inexpressible relief.

And now, my dear Mr Browning, you must be glad that I have at last come to the end of what I have to say about my much-loved Rosalind. Let me, then, set you free; for which release I hope you will kindly, in the words of that Epilogue, "when I make curtsy, bid me farewell."—Ever most sincerely yours,

HELENA FAUCIT MARTIN.

(London: Blackwood, 1884–91): 227–85.

SHAKESPEARE'S HEROINES
Charles Wingate
1895

ROSALIND.
(As You Like It.)

The comedy quickly changed to tragedy. Joyful mimic life became on the instant sad real life.

It was natural Covent Garden Theatre should be crowded that night; for were not Anderson, Wigall, and Madame Gondeau enjoying their benefit performance? and was not glorious Peg Woffington, the pet of the town, appearing in that *role* which she so admirably acted,—sparkling Rosalind, the heroine of the Forest of Arden? Mistress Woffington, to be sure, though she had not reached her fortieth year, had shown signs of fading beauty and weakening strength; and the young blades of London had begun to look curiously at one another with suggestive glance, as if to intimate that some day—perhaps not to-morrow, or the next day, but yet before long—the gay, jovial, dashing Woffington would have to yield her leading place to a new star in the sky of popular favor. But who could have anticipated the outcome of that fatal night, the 3d of May, 1757?

Rosalind had changed her flowing gown for the doublet and hose, and with the devoted Celia, in whom the play-goers recognized Mrs. Vincent, had made Orlando swear eternal love in the old, old, captivating way by which the fair lady in actual life had drawn so many gallants, high and low. With delight the spectators fed their eyes on that still lingering charm of face, heightened now by the powders of the dressing-room, while the unpleasantly rasping voice was forgotten in the fascination of roguish action. But Peg, poor woman, had already felt a premonition of ill. Valiantly did she resist the distressing faintness; and none in the audience noticed aught was wrong until, clothed in her bridal gown, Rosalind entered for the last act of all in "As You Like It," and the last act of Woffington in her career upon the stage.

Through the text the actress struggled bravely until the epilogue was reached; and then, with something of her old fervor and coquetry, she began:—

"If it be true that good wine needs no bush, 'tis true that a good play needs no epilogue"—

And then she faltered. One last effort brought her strength to offer Rosalind's charge to the women and to the men; but as she uttered the succeeding lines,—

"If I were among you, I would kiss as many of you as has beards that pleased me"—

Her voice faded away, her eyes grew dim, her limbs trembled, and then, with the wild, despairing cry, "O God! O God!" Peg Woffington, glorious Peg Woffington, the idol of the stage, fell into a companion's arms, stricken with paralysis. Her last words upon the stage had been uttered, her last *role* had been acted. Life itself hung in the balance for days; and though partial recovery followed, yet the three remaining years of her life were the sad, hopeless declining years of a doomed woman.

Woffington, thus appearing for the last time as Rosalind in 1757, had first essayed the character in 1742, and but one actress is known to have preceded her in this part.

The handsome boy who, in the time of Shakespeare, first sustained the lagging form of Celia in the Forest of Arden, is not immortalized by recording history. Rosalind, Celia, Jaques, Orlando, Touchstone,—all the pretty lads in women's garb or masquerading doublet and hose, and the stalwart men who interpreted the goodly people of "As You Like It," in the initial performances of that ever-enduring comedy, before the applauding audience in the rude playhouse, are "out of the cast" to-day. We know the actors; we do not know the parts assigned them, save, indeed, the part assumed by the creator of all the characters, Shakespeare himself. From the lips of the brother of the master-poet has been handed down the tradition that, in one of his own comedies, Shakespeare appeared as a decrepit old man, with long beard, who, fainting and weak, was borne by another actor to the table around which men were eating, the while one sang for the pleasure of all. Who else could this be but faithful old Adam?

For a hundred years and more after Shakespeare's day the delightful comedy slept; though one reckless "adapter," at least, did venture to put forward an "improved" comedy founded on the lines of the masterpiece. He called it "Love in a Forest;" and summarily he swept Audrey, Phebe, Touchstone, William, and Corin off the stage, while, to fill the hiatus, he interpolated various scenes from other plays. But in 1740 the genuine version reappeared when, at Drury Lane Theatre, the "inimitably charming" Rosalind, Mrs. Pritchard, made love to Milward, then in the last year of his life. She was not handsome, this large-formed, hard-featured Mrs. Pritchard, nor with her coarse expressions and thoughts was she, by nature, gifted with the intellectual beauty of Rosalind, yet she was sincere and earnest, and she achieved success.

But a greater Rosalind followed, a Rosalind whose lovely face would have captured the world, even had it not been set off by a bewitching roguishness of manner and dashing vivacity of action—the Rosalind of Peg Woffington, whose solemn last impersonation has been described. Her parentage was humble, as we have seen; but as the sparkling impersonator of Sir Harry Wildair and of other "breeches parts," of which she was so fond, this Peg Woffington, of fragile virtue but wonderful histrionic skill, was long the favorite of the town.

And next comes the erstwhile belle of Bath, the unfortunate lady who, jilted by one lover, took up with another, and after his death with another, and after his death with still another. Mrs. Dancer, Mrs. Barry, Mrs. Crawford,—all the names belong to her, and under the first two in turn she played fair Rosalind; on the one occasion she was thirty-three years of age, on the other forty. "The most perfect representation of the character I ever witnessed," says old John Taylor. "It was tender, animated, and playful to the highest degree." She was a modest appearing lady, in spite of her amorous temperament, and was graceful and attractive.

It was Spranger Barry's second appearance as Jacques on that night when his wife, in a costume that defied archæology, first played the dashing, roguish sweetheart of Orlando in Covent Garden. Mrs. Mattocks was Celia, and from her lips the audience, with some curiosity, heard the words of the Cuckoo Song:

> "When daisies pied and violets blue
>   And lady-smocks all silver white
> And cuckoo-buds of yellow hue
>   Do paint the meadows with delight,
> The cuckoo then, on every tree,
>   Mocks married men; for thus sings he,
>   Cuckoo;
> Cuckoo, cuckoo: O word of fear,
> Unpleasing to a married ear!"

The listeners wondered why Mrs. Barry did not sing the song. They knew that the sprightly, even if coarse ditty, set to music by Dr. Arne, had been stolen from "Love's Labor's Lost" twenty-seven years before, by impetuous Kitty

Clive, and interpolated by her, as Celia, for the first time in "As You Like It;" but they also knew that Mrs. Dancer, in the Drury Lane production seven years before, had taken the song from Celia to herself. Now, why did she let it leave her lips? Did she realize its inaptness in following Rosalind's merry, yet innocent banter—for it was introduced after the lines, "Oh, that woman that cannot make her fault her husband's occasion, let her never nurse her child herself, for she will breed it like a fool"—or was she losing the music in her voice? We of a century later do not know. We do know, though, that other Rosalinds afterwards retained the song in their lines.

In Dublin, as well as in London, Mrs. Barry acted Rosalind; but the unpropitious gods of the theatre brought the Dublin essay to disaster, so that handsome, silver-tongued Spranger and his wife, departing the Irish shores, left behind, according to the catalogue of goods, such things as "battlements torn," "elephant very bad," and eighty-three thunderbolts, besides "a pair of shepherd's breeches" which, Boaden is sure, belong "to the dear woman's own Rosalind."

There were several minor Rosalinds now bounding on the stage—for one, that strangely prudish Miss Macklin, whose delight in masquerading as the boy upon the stage has been described, together with her strange modesty in refusing to allow a surgeon to remove a tumor from below her knee after tight-gartering had brought that affliction upon her; for another, Mrs. Bulkley, the original Miss Hardcastle in "She Stoops to Conquer" and of Julia in "The Rivals;" and yet another, Miss Younge, who ten years later, as Mrs. Pope, was to repeat the character. Then, too, there was vulgar "Tripe" Hamilton.

How this woman could assume the high-bred bearing of Rosalind would be difficult to surmise, when one recalls the way she won that title of "Tripe." Her admirers always filled the gallery, but never the boxes; and when a rival actress threw out innuendoes about the cheap character of her followers, Mrs. Hamilton took revenge by failing to appear for that rival's benefit. Of course, the disappointed audience hissed her when next she did come forward; but the Queen of Spain (for in that majestic character she appeared, with her gem-bedecked head, according to Colley Cibber, resembling a furze-bush stuck round with glow-worms) resented the disapprobation with a speech more befitting a scullion maid than a Queen, and well suited to win her kitchen title. "Gentlemen and ladies," declared the actress of women of quality, "I suppose as how you hiss me because I did not play Mrs. Bellamy's benefit. I would have performed; but she said as how my audience were all tripe people, and made the house smell." Up rose the pit to cry at once, "Well said, *Tripe!*" and "Tripe" Hamilton she became from that day.

There may have been applause in 1783, when a young actress of theatrical family, Miss Frodsham by name, made her first appearance in London, playing

Rosalind at the Haymarket; but it was as snapping crackers to cannons' roar compared with the plaudits showered upon her more famous father, the York Roscius so called, when in response to a call, after a certain performance, he dashed upon the stage bearing his wife upon his back. It was the custom in those days for a husband never to appear without his lady whenever the gallery rained down commands for a curtain call; and Frodsham, with eccentric ingenuity, brought his better half forward as a Queen upon a human chariot. The daughter of this pair made her metropolitan *debut* the 30th of April, 1783, and then—did little else worthy of record on the London stage.

While this same fair Miss Frodsham was endeavoring to make the town accept her impersonation as ideal, an actress destined to be greater than she ever was, greater than all who preceded her, was anxiously yet happily finishing her first successful season on the boards of Old Drury. A few years before, Mrs. Siddons had passed a preliminary season in London; and though it was her Rosalind that, in the provinces, had won over Garrick's ambassador, and so secured for her the London engagement, yet she was obliged to stand in the wings, idle and envious, while Miss Younge, whom she afterwards so gloriously to supplant, acted the part. We may imagine the feelings of the two—the older actress calmly indifferent of the insignificant young lady lately from the country; the younger actress confident of her powers, pleased with Mr. Garrick's kindness and attention, and wishing for a single chance to drive these unrecognizing rivals from the centre of the stage.

The desired chance came at last, and Mrs. Siddons reigned. Yet not with Rosalind did this magnificent actress, with her classic beauty and her brilliancy of action, exert her full influence. And little the wonder, considering that eccentric prudery she had regarding all *roles* where women must masquerade as boys. For Ganymede's doublet and hose she constructed a dress indicative neither of male nor of female, but designed, as she herself admitted, as a screen to curious eyes. This costume the critics ridiculed, nor did they find that Mrs. Siddons laid aside sufficiently her tragic air when essaying the playful Rosalind.

"For the first time," said Anne Seward, "I saw the justly celebrated Mrs. Siddons in comedy in Rosalind; but though her smile is as enchanting as her frown is majestic, as her tears are irresistible, yet the playful scintillations of colloquial wit which most strongly mark the character suit not the dignity of the Siddonian form and countenance. Then, her dress was injudicious. The scrupulous prudery of decency produced an ambiguous vestment that seemed neither male nor female."

Miss Seward, however, found some points to favor in the impersonation, declaring that when Mrs. Siddons first came on as the Princess, nothing could be more charming; and praising also the scene where the actress resumed her original character and exchanged comic spirit for dignified tenderness. So, too, others praise the beauty of the Siddon's elocution, pointing particularly to her delivery of the lines, "My pride fell with my fortunes," and, "Sir, you have wrestled well and overthrown more than your enemies." But, altogether, there was too much of the tragic in her constitution to meet the playful wit and sportive fancy of roguish Rosalind, while that prudery with the boy's dress was denounced even by Boaden, her biographer. It demonstrated, he thought, "the struggle of modesty to save all unnecessary exposure;" but yet it "more strongly reminded the spectators of the sex which she had laid down, than that which she had taken up." Mrs. Siddons had no idea of hiding her motive in designing her new costume. She wrote plainly to Hamilton, the artist, asking "if he would be so good as to make her a slight sketch for a boy's dress to conceal the person as much as possible."

Young affirmed, indeed, that "her Rosalind wanted neither playfulness nor feminine softness, but it was totally without archness—not because she could not properly conceive it, but how could such a countenance be arch?" It was a bitter disappointment, we may well believe, to be scolded by the critics in this *role;* for, as Mrs. Abington years afterwards remarked to Crabb Robinson, "Early in life Mrs. Siddons was anxious to succeed in comedy, and played Rosalind before I retired." To which quotation Mr. Robinson adds, "Mrs. Siddons she praised, though not with the warmth of a genuine admirer."

Very rarely did the great Siddons repeat her Rosalind. Perhaps from the stage she saw in the auditorium such strange scenes, during the comedy, as Croker pictures in his "Familiar Epistles on the Irish Stage" when a lady wept plentifully throughout the whole of "As You Like It," while Mrs. Siddons was playing Rosalind, from an unhappy impression that it was the character of Jane Shore in the tragedy of that name. "I am glad to relate the anecdote," he adds, with dry humor, "that so much good tears should not go for nothing."

Mrs. Siddons was twenty-nine when she first played Rosalind. Mrs. Jordan was twenty-five when she first frolicked in the Forest of Arden; and after Dora Jordan embraced the character, the Siddons shrank from its arms. Mrs. Jordan was not the most beautiful of Rosalinds, by any means; but her merry vivacity, her rollicking spirit, and her fine figure carried the town by storm. For many a year after that there was no Rosalind like Jordan's. "There never was, there never will be, there never can be" her equal in the part, declared one enthusiastic writer.

For this reason it was natural that expectations should run high when Mrs. Alsop first essayed the *role* of Rosalind, for Mrs. Alsop was the daughter of Dora Jordan. But, alas! neither a physical nor a mental resemblance to the noted mother was detected. "The truth is," said Hazlitt, speaking of her Rosalind, "Mrs. Alsop is a very nice little woman who acts her part very sensibly and cleverly, and with a certain degree of arch humor, but is no more like her mother than we are to Hercules. Her voice is clear and articulate, but not rich or flowing. In person she is small, and her face is not prepossessing. Her delivery of the speeches was correct and excellent as far as it went, but without much richness or power."

Mrs. Alsop had lived in Wales on an allowance from her mother before taking up the stage; and, as Mrs. Jordan lived for a year after the daughter's essay with Rosalind, the latter probably continued a pensioner even after she started upon a theatrical career. Her husband was a worthless fellow. He it was, who, dissolute and unscrupulous, had not hesitated to raise the blank checks generously given him by his mother-in-law to sums entirely unexpected by her, and then, overwhelmed by debts, to quit his wife and country. He had been a clerk in the Ordinance office before marrying Frances, the daughter of Dora Jordan and Magistrate Ford. Mrs. Alsop herself came to America as a "star," and died May 2, 1821, in Charleston, S.C.

Now comes Miss Duncan, a bright maid, an excellent actress, and a woman who spent her years from childhood till death in the service of her Muse, fair Comedy. It was Miss Duncan who created the *role* of Juliana when "The Honeymoon" was first brought out; and Elliston, her first Orlando, was the original Duke Aranza in Tobin's still surviving play. "The Little Wonder" was the title given our Rosalind by her predecessor in high comedy Miss Farren; and both as maiden and as wife Mrs. Duncan-Davison satisfied the eulogy.

There, too, were Miss Wallis; Mrs. Bartley, afterwards the first Hermione of "The Winter's Tale" that America ever saw; Miss Boyle; slender, elegant Mrs. Yates; Mrs. Henry Siddons, daughter-in-law of the great Siddons; Mrs. Sterling; and Miss Brunton. As to Mrs. Henry Siddons, she appears to have been superior to her husband on the stage, though he was the son of the great Siddons. The Stranger was the only *role* in which he achieved any degree of success; while she, as Miss Murray and as Mrs. Henry Siddons, had the grace and charming manner of a perfect lady, as well as histrionic ability.

Miss Taylor, whom Leigh Hunt so enthusiastically praised, and lovely Miss Foote, who afterwards became the Countess of Harrington, now followed; but let them pass, for the days of Nisbett and of Faucit are at hand.

The tall, supple, buoyant daughter of Captain Macnamara, the original of Miss Fotheringay in "Pendennis," was a beautiful woman; and though in the eyes of Macready she was unequal to the part of Rosalind when played to his Jaques, yet Samuel Phelps, a warm lover of Shakespeare's work, made of Nisbett's Rosalind an idol. Listen to the experienced manager of Sadler's Wells: "Not having seen her, you don't know what beauty is. Her voice was liquid music. Her laugh—there never was such a laugh! Her eyes, living crystals, lamps lit with light divine! Her gorgeous neck and shoulders—her superbly symmetrical limbs, her grace, her taste, her nameless but irresistible charm." It was as Rosalind that the handsome Mrs. Nisbett was last seen upon the stage, appearing then under Anderson's management at Drury Lane with the manager as Orlando, Vandenhoff as Jaques, and Cooper as Adam. Under the low forehead of this Rosalind shone brilliant eyes that lighted up the clear oval face, over which tossed a crown of wavy dark hair, making an ideal heroine in portraiture as well as in action. Little wonder she gained rank off the stage as well as on.

Mrs Louisa Nisbett became Lady Boothby; Miss Helen Faucit became Lady Theodore Martin. To Miss Faucit's Rosalind, Macready gave glowing commendation. Her noble figure, lovely face, gentle voice, and expressive action enabled her to enter into the soul of Orlando's tantalizing sweetheart. In 1845 Miss Faucit played the character; and again in 1879 she acted the part—a Rosalind at twenty-five, a Rosalind at fifty-nine. It was her final *role* upon the stage, as it had been the last of Mrs. Nisbett.

To Phelp's Jaques, when that actor-manager carried out his splendid revival of Shakespeare at Saddler's Wells, Mrs. Charles Young, afterwards Mrs. Hermann Vezin, was a sweet and vivacious, but rather monotonous Rosalind; while to Charles Kean's Jaques, in his noticeable revivals at the Princess's, Ellen Tree (Mrs. Charles Kean) was a splendidly successful heroine. Her sister, Maria Tree, also tried the part, but with only moderate success.

How they troop upon the stage, these Rosalinds of later days—Mme. Vestris, Fanny Cooper, and that noblest of Cleopatras, Isabel Glyn-Dallas; Millicent Palmer and Carlotta Leclerq, with whom Fechter in America was associated; the lovely Mrs. Rousby, the beautiful Mrs. Scott-Siddons, great granddaughter of Mrs. Siddons of old, Sarah J. Woolgar, and Mary Provost; Amy Sedgewick, who at the age of twenty-four tried the *role* without much success, and Margaret Robertson, whom the present generation admires as Mrs. Kendal; Alice Marriott, a Hamlet as well as a Rosalind and a Lady Macbeth of the stage; and Jean Davenport, to-day, as Mrs. Lander, claimed as an American; Mrs. Langtry, the elegant if not handsome Marie Litton, the second Miss Wallis, now better known as Mrs. Lancaster-Wallis, Marie De Grey, Ada Cavendish,—no, why mention the names? Of all the later Rosalinds one alone stands pre-eminent, Adelaide Neilson.

A lovely, fascinating Rosalind was Miss Neilson. Her arch smile, as she looked back at her friends in the mystic forest, said one admirer, describing the scene, made her face seem half divine, and the tones of her voice were as a suffusion of sweet sounds, ranging high and ranging low. Her utterance of the simple words, "woo me! woo me!" to Orlando, as her cheek was laid upon his shoulder and her arm stole coyly about his neck, was sweet as a blackbird's call to its mate. And again in saying to her lover, "Ay, go your ways! go your ways!

... 'Tis but one cast away, and so, come, death," the low, thrilling cadences filled the house with such mournful music, such despairing sweetness, as were never heard there. The effect upon the audience was almost miraculous; for a stillness fell upon it broken only by some sobbing women in the boxes, who, in the next moment, were startled from their delicious tears by the actress's sudden change to the most jubilant laughter evoked by her triumphant befooling of her lover.

Lilian Adelaide Neilson—or, if we were to use her little known real name, Elizabeth Ann (Brown) Lee—was in her twenty-third year when these praises were sung, shortly after her first appearance as Rosalind in America; but she had originally played the part four years before that (Sept. 25, 1868) at the Edinburgh Theatre Royal, and on the 18th of December, 1871, had acted Rosalind at Drury Lane, London. The beautiful girl, with romantic Spanish blood in her veins, at the age of fourteen had run away from home, and after sundry escapades as a bar-maid, had secured a place upon the stage where, at the age of seventeen, she was to make her *debut* in a part afterwards the most famous in her *repertoire,* though then giving her little success, that of Juliet. Shortly after her Edinburgh performance of Rosalind, an influential critic, Mr. Joseph Knight, of the London *Athenaeum,* saw her play a melodramatic *role,* and declared that "practice and care are alone required to secure for Miss Neilson a high and enduring reputation." It was that criticism, as the actress understood, which started her reputation upon the high road of popularity; and so much did she appreciate the effect that, in her will, she left to Mr. Knight five thousand dollars.

The romantic, poetic drama was essentially Miss Neilson's *forte,* while her splendid figure gave additional appropriateness to her selection of Rosalind as one of her chief characters. Though somewhat slight in form, she had a royal bearing; and her small, shapely head was set off by large, voluptuous eyes and ruddy-brown hair. That she studied Rosalind carefully is illustrated by an incident narrated some years ago by L. Clarke Davis: in a well thumbed pocket volume of "As You Like It," lying on her table, were found scraps of paper, torn note sheets, and fragments, all written over in her clear, bold hand with such conclusions as she had evolved from almost every passage in the part of Rosalind. It is of her first Rosalind in America that the same writer says: "From the rising of the curtain to the fall there was nothing more apparent than that the actress was in exquisite sympathy with the part. So much was this the case that when in the fourth act she was told of her lover's hurt, and she seemed to affect such counterfeit distress, her eyes were swimming in real tears, and her bosom heaved with sorrow that was not counterfeit. It was not alone the glamour of youth, beauty, and classic grace which filled the spectator's mind with pleasurable emotion, but, adding to the charm of the character and the completeness of the artist's triumph, were the intelligence to recognize the subtle wit, the delicate refinement, and the masterful power to portray them all. In the more tender and emotional passages of the play her quiet pathos appealed irresistibly to every heart; for, underlying all she did, there was a wondrous sweetness of womanly dignity and an adherence to nature which rendered the performance altogether worthy of her fame."

Neilson twice afterwards visited America, playing Beatrice, Isabella, Viola, and Imogen. In 1877 she was divorced from her husband, Philip Lee, an English clergyman's son; and on May 24, 1880, at Booth's Theatre, she gave her farewell performance. The following August she was dead in Paris. It is an interesting fact to notice,—a point which comes to mind as I hold the scattered memoranda of dates before me,—that while Neilson, the chief of later Rosalinds, first essayed the character in 1868 at Edinburgh, in the same city Helen Faucit, the chief of all Rosalinds back to the days of Macready, a year later made her last appearance at the Scottish capital (always very friendly to her) in that same character.

Westland Marston—the veteran English playwright who died but recently, and who had written for Miss Neilson that play of "Life for Life," in which she so happily attracted the critical attention of Mr. Knight—was wont to regard Miss Neilson's Rosalind as best in its humorous side. He thought she failed in the poetry of the character, but excelled in an almost wanton, hoidenish frolicsomeness that captured the audience.

Here in America Rosalind had originally sprung into existence the year after Mrs. Siddons had first shown her super-modest Ganymede to London town. Indeed, America's first Rosalind may have seen the great Siddons in the *role,* for three months before Mrs. Kenna delighted our forefathers with the picture of the frolicsome lady of Arden that actress was in England. She had been drawn to the New World as an addition to the little colony of playactors here settled; and on the 14th of July, 1786, in the rough, gaudy-colored John Street Theatre in New York, she impersonated the "heavenly Rosalind."

The Quaker City, some six years later, saw the second Rosalind in the chubby-faced, sprightly little Mrs. Marshall. She, too, had come from England, but her departure from the mother-land was under less honorable conditions than those of the preceding Rosalind; there she was known as Mrs. Webb, but, as one wit of the day said,—alluding to the actor, Mr. Marshall,—"A son of sock became entangled with a dramatic Webb," and hence the two emigrated across the water.

In Boston the first Rosalind (1794), but nineteen years of age, was a bride of only a few months. The obnoxious legislative act of 1760, prohibiting theatrical performances, had at last, in 1793, been repealed, and a theatre was quickly erected at the corner of Federal and Franklin Streets. It was opened Feb. 3,

1794, with Charles Stuart Powell as manager. The season was not very successful; but better results were anticipated when, on the 15th of December, 1794, the second season opened with "As You Like It," and Mrs. Brook's "Rosina."

In those days there came forward the first professional dramatic critic in America, Thomas Paine, the son of Robert Treat Paine, one of the signers of the Declaration of Independence. Thomas Paine—who afterwards changed his name to Robert Treat Paine, Jr., because he wanted "a Christian name," and who married Miss Baker, of the theatre, only afterwards to pay too much attention, for family harmony, to other ladies of the *corps dramatique*—was a young man finely educated and gifted with poetic tastes. He pronounced Mr. Taylor, as Orlando, a valuable acquisition to the company, declaring that he eclipsed every competitor. Celia and Rosalind were two sisters, the one, Miss Harrison, with "neither face, nor voice, nor form, nor action;" the other, Mrs. Snelling Powell, who displayed as the heroine "more than her usual excellence."

The tall, elegant, and beautiful Mrs. Johnson, whose life was a model of propriety, and whose grace and taste set the fashion for the fine ladies of New York a hundred years ago, soon took up the captivating *role,* and on one occasion to her there bowed, with foppish elaboration, a Le Beau whom the world of to-day must regard with as warm a favor as did the world of yesterday—for, has he not given to us, through his son, that most perfect of dramatic idealists, Joseph Jefferson? In the first month of the year 1798, "As You Like It," with Mrs. Johnson as Rosalind, opened the Park Theatre in New York.

A rather curious fact in the history of Mrs. Duff, the noted tragic actress of the early part of this century, lay in the fact that she acted Rosalind but once in her entire career. That was on the 1st of April, 1822, when she and her husband were members of the Boston Theatre Company. The sparkling eyes that lighted up her handsome face, the trim, well-formed figure, and the musical voice accredited to this actress in her youth, might well make her, at the age of twenty-eight, an excellent Rosalind in appearance; but her bent was toward tragedy, and "As You Like It" never more appeared in her *repertoire.*

As Rosalind, Ellen Tree made her American *debut,* Dec. 12, 1836. On Jan. 29, 1842, after playing in "The Honeymoon" at Dublin with Charles Kean, she was privately married to that capable son of a remarkable actor; and on April 4th of that year, the names of Mr. and Mrs. Charles Kean appeared for the first time together in London, at the Haymarket, in "As You Like It" and a few other standard plays. Three years later Mr. Kean for the third time visited America; and while the lady repeated her Rosalind here, with other parts (and impressed her spectators with having lost her earlier beauty and fascination), Mr. Kean then gave his first interpretation of Jaques in this country. From 1850 to 1859 Kean made the Princess's Theatre famous for its Shakespearian revivals, "As You Like It" being brought out there in 1851. But Kean's bronchial trouble turned his bard's own words against him. His performance of Jaques was summed up by a critic in this paraphrase of lines from "As You Like It." "How does this Charles?" "He cannot speak, my lord." "Take him away!"

When Charlotte Cushman returned from her successes in Europe, she gave "As You Like It" during her first engagement in New York. She had been tempted to England by the encouragement of Macready; and there in the spring of 1845, when she was in her twenty-ninth year, she won a recognition that naturally set her heart in a flutter. "Mrs. Nisbett's Rosalind," exclaimed one enthusiast, "was a sweet bit of acting, full of honey; Madame Vestris's Rosalind is all grace and coquetry; Miss Helen Faucit's (by far the best of them) is full of wit, mirth, and beauty; but Miss Cushman *is Rosalind.*" Yet other English critics—and American critics later—found the great tragedienne too heavy for the character, lacking the proper buoyancy and exuberance. When Miss Cushman first played the character after her return to America, in October, 1849, the Jaques of the cast was C. W. Couldock, then making his *debut* in this country, but now known from one end of the land to the other as the original Dunstan Kirke in "Hazel Kirke."

Many a fair Rosalind is to be recalled by those play-goers with whom the memory of former years still clings. In fact, then, as now, almost every leading actress sought the bright and captivating *role.* But from the long list may be selected a number whose performances are of special interest.

There was the beautiful Mrs. Barrett, wife of "Gentleman George," whose own sad habits were her worst enemies. There, too, was Charlotte Crampton, petite and fascinating actress of sad career, whose delight for robust *roles* led her to essay not only the spectacular Mazeppa, but also Hamlet, Shylock, and Richard. Laura Addison, one of the Sadler's Wells group of actresses, coming to America in 1851, played Rosalind here, but her death a year after her American *debut* limited the acquaintance Americans had with her acting. Mrs. Anderson, *nee* Ophelia Pelby, well known to Boston play-goers; Mrs. Cramer; Mrs. Thomas Barry, an actress of celebrity, and the wife of an actor-manager of note; the graceful Mrs. W. Humphrey Bland, sister of Helen Faucit of the English stage, and herself the first interpreter in America of Shakspere's Cleopatra; Mrs. W. H. Smith, long a favorite in Boston; and Mrs. J. W. Wallack, Jr., one of the famous family in the annals of America's stage—were all heroines of Arden.

Before undue weight brought listlessness to Josephine Clifton, her beauty of face and neatness of person made her an attractive Rosalind to look upon. She had not passed her fourth decade when death suddenly came. In 1831 she made her *debut;* four years later she played in London, having the distinction (so it is claimed) of being the first American-born actress to visit England as a star: two years after that she received from N. P. Willis the manuscript of the tragedy "Bianca Visconti," which he had written for her. A little more than a year before her death, which occurred in 1847, she married Robert Place, a New Orleans manager.

A more sterling, intellectual interpreter of Rosalind was found in Mrs. Jean Davenport Lander, who in "Medea," "Queen Elizabeth," and "Marie Stuart," courted rivalry with Ristori, and whose noble work for the soldiers in the Rebellion, after had she had become the wife of a Union officer, added to that personal fame she had won by her excellent acting. Mrs. Banister, another Rosalind, was the Cassy in the first production in New York (1853) of Aiken's version of "Uncle Tom's Cabin," the version which was afterwards to hold the stage for years. Mrs. Anna Cruise-Cowell, who played Juliet to Charlotte Cushman's Romeo, was a Ganymede in her younger days, making her Boston *debut* in that character at the old National Theatre in the season of 1847–1848.

An admirable Rosalind of a little later date was Mrs. E. L. Davenport, who has but recently passed away, and whose husband was a Jaques worthy of fame. Among the other Rosalinds to Davenport's Jaques was Miss Rose Evans. Mrs. Anna Cora Mowatt, author as well as player; Mrs. W. M. Fleming and Mrs. Thomas Flynn; Mrs John Drew, who began her stage career in America, sixty-eight years ago, as the Duke of York to the Richard III of Junius Brutus Booth, and who is still living, an unexcelled Mrs. Malaprop; and Eliza Logan, whose mobile face and attractive voice, so it is said, won a Georgia planter to such enthusiasm that, on the spur of the moment, he presented her with a negro slave, instead of the customary floral offering— these were Rosalinds well worth remembering.

Miss Kimberly, the lady who would play heavy tragedy, comedy, drama, and farce in the same engagement with her "As You Like It" production, and who would even essay the character of Hamlet, appeared in Rosalind before Laura Keene took up the *role.* The latter, whose experience was filled with so many ups and downs, played Rosalind during her first appearances on the American stage at Wallack's Lyceum, New York, with the elder Wallack as Jaques, and "J. Lester," the name that then disguised the afterwards famous Lester Wallack, as the sighing Orlando. This production marked the closing of the first season of Wallack's management of the theatre. Miss Keene opened her new theatre, Nov. 18, 1856, with "As You Like It," and then acted Rosalind "with great archness and vigor," making "a remarkable escape from the coarser temptations in which the character abounds."

The beautiful Mrs. Julia Bennett Barrow, who, though English born and the daughter of an English player, adopted the American stage after the honeymoon of her marriage had passed, became a favorite in this land, and delighted many with her brilliant Rosalind.

Mrs. Mary F. Scott-Siddons, the classic beauty and highly cultured lady of the English stage,—though never so successful behind the footlights as she was upon the reading platform, in spite of her histrionic name,—held Rosalind as a favorite in her *repertoire,* and on one occasion alternated with Clara Jennings the part of Rosalind with that of Celia. Her London *debut* was made as Rosalind, and her American *debut* was made as Rosalind. It was of Mrs. Scott-Siddons that Fanny Kemble said, "Her exquisite features present the most perfect living miniature of her great-grandmother's majestic beauty." Born a Siddons, and married to a gentleman by the name of Canter, she became a Scott-Siddons through her husband's adopting the maiden name of his mother, and uniting that with the patronymic of his wife, because his father had put forth most strenuous objections to having his honored name go upon the programs of the play-house. Mrs. Scott-Siddons was twenty-five when she first played Rosalind.

Other heroines of Arden crowd the scene,—it were impossible to mention every ambitious actress, or would-be actress, who has essayed this favorite *role*—and play-goers with more or less vividness recall as Rosalind, Fanny Davenport, who now apparently has deserted comedy for nerve-tingling tragedy; Louise Howard; Rose Coghlan, who had the distinction of acting Rosalind in the first open-air performance in America (at Manchester, Mass., Aug. 8, 1887); Mrs. Louise Pomeroy; Agnes Booth; Annie Clark, for so many years the favorite leading lady at the Boston Museum; and Mary Anderson, who appeared as Rosalind for the first time at the Shakespeare Memorial Theatre at Stratford-on-Avon, Aug. 29, 1885, six weeks or more before her appearance in the character on the American stage.

We all know how the later Rosalind of Miss Anderson was regarded. Let us see what an expert critic thought of the young American's first attempt with the character. This was what William Archer, the London writer, said at that time: "Her Rosalind was girlish rather than womanly; but it was so brightly, frankly, healthily girlish that to have quareled with it would have been sheer captiousness." Her reproving speech to the Duke in the first act, he held, was too loud and unpolished, "invective rather than self-restrained sarcasm;" but in the forest scene her success was assured. "A cleverly designed costume, modest without prudery, combined with her lithe, well-knit, and in no way redundant figure to make her a perfect embodiment of the saucy lackey. Her claret-colored mantle, exquisitely handled, gave her the means for much significant by-play through which she prevented the audience forgetting her sex, without in any way suggesting it to Orlando. Her tastefulness was, perhaps, the great charm of her Rosalind."

After Mary Anderson we saw Adele Belgarde, a young Mississippi lady, who made her experimental *debut* as Romeo in 1879, and her professional *debut* as Rosalind the same year in New York; Adelaide Moore, the comely, graceful actress drawn to the stage, as she claimed, through the fascination of the earlier Rosalind, Adelaide Neilson; Ada Rehan, Julia Marlowe, Margaret Mather, and Minna Gale, whose impersonations are so familiar.

Rehan's glorious regality of form and bearing has made audiences bow before the imperiousness of her proudly uplifted head, her dashing figure, and her purring voice. Marlowe's beautiful, deep eyes, modest demeanor, and winsome maidenliness have wound a web of equal fascination around admirers who can praise Minerva while they bend before Juno. Rehan has conquered in Rosalind; Marlowe has charmed. Against the ardent, exultant Ganymede of Mr. Daly's leading actress but one small criticism is expressed—and that a smile at the odd little shriek of the lady of the supposed "swashing outside" when she discovers Orlando, a nervous shriek for all the world like a school-girl discovering a mouse.

A lithe, supple Rosalind, with a merry sparkle in the eye and a jovial brightness in the tone, is Julia Marlowe's portrait of our heroine. Clad in brown from top to toe,—doublet and hose, hat and cloak, wallet and gloves all one color,—and with the proper, high-strapped boots to serve as protectors in the briery wood; this is the framing for the pretty mobile face of Mrs. Marlowe-Taber. She looks Orlando straight in the eye; she claps Sylvius sturdily on the shoulder; she manfully chides the amorous Phebe; and she describes, with true sense of humor, the chance meeting with her father when he knew not his daughter. In short, her Rosalind is a girl of spirit who enjoys the masquerade.

Miss Mather's costuming of the character (it is needless to say much of her acting, since by giving a sweet, lovable Rosalind, with nothing of the roguish and assumed martial air, she misses the key-note of the part) is a good illustration of the inaccuracy too often found upon the stage. Her Ganymede wanders through the brambles in low lace boots that must themselves suffer severely in the bush, and cause more suffering to the tender, unprotected flesh of Rosalind; while the meeting of the characters in the final act is emphasized in somewhat startling manner—unless we assume a Worth to have lived in the enchanted forest—by the display of fashionable, elaborate dresses suddenly brought to light.

Rose Coghlan, picturesque and accurate in costume, with her noble-toned voice, her crystal enunciation, and her dashing bearing, gives to Rosalind a robust style and an incessant animation that last in the memory.

Modjeska's Rosalind is chiefly to be criticized as being too dainty and over-refined; to which criticism, however, the actress answers that those who think Rosalind should be rough and boisterous should recall the words of the Duke in the first act: "Her smoothness, her very silence, and her patience speak to the people, and they pity her."

Ada Cavendish, the English actress already mentioned, first assumed the garb of Ganymede while on a tour of this country; and Carlotta Leclereq, pronounced too heavy, sensuous, and demonstrative in the *role,* Mrs. Rousby, Amy Sedgewick, who gave the part such a lugubrious tone as to rob it of its vivacity and archness, and Mrs. Langtry, are among the English actresses, other than those already mentioned, who have given in the United States their impersonations of Rosalind.

All our early actresses, naturally, were English born, and for many years the most noted stars on the American stage were visitors from the British theatre. But now reciprocity is recognized; and while the English players appear in this land, the American players carry their interpretations to the home of their cousins. Yet, it must be admitted, preponderance in number still favors the people of the tight little isle. It may be different in years to come. Let us hope so.

(New York, 1898): 129–64.

WILLIAM SHAKESPEARE: A CRITICAL STUDY
Georg Brandes
1898

XXVIII

*THE INTERVAL OF SERENITY—AS YOU LIKE IT—THE ROVING
SPIRIT—THE LONGING FOR NATURE—JAQUES AND SHAKESPEARE—
THE PLAY A FEAST OF WIT*

NEVER had Shakespeare produced with such rapidity and ease as in this
bright and happy interval of two or three years. It is positively astounding to
note all that he accomplished in the year 1600, when he stood, not exactly at the
height of his poetical power, for that steadily increased, but at the height of his
poetical serenity. Among the exquisite comedies he now writes, *As You Like It*
is one of the most exquisite.

The play was entered in the Stationers' Register, along with *Much Ado
About Nothing,* on the 4th of August 1600, and must in all probability have
been written in that year. Meres does not mention it, in 1598, in his list of
Shakespeare's plays; it contains a quotation from Marlowe's *Hero at Leander,*
published in 1598—

"Who ever lov'd, that lov'd not at first sight?"

a quotation, by the way, which sums up the matter of the comedy and we find
in Celia's words (i 2), " Since the little wit that fool have was silenced," an
allusion to the public and judicial burning of satirical publications which took
place on the 1st of June 1599. As there does not seem to be room in the year
1599 for many works than we have already assigned to it, *As You Like It* may
be taken as dating from the first half of the following year.

As usual, Shakespeare took from another poet the whole material of this
enchanting comedy. His contemporary, Thomas Lodge (who, after leaving
Oxford, became first a player and play-wright in London, then a lawyer, then a

doctor and writer of medical subjects, until he died of the plague in the year 1600), had in 1590 published a pastoral romance, with many poems interspersed, entitled *Euphues golden Legacie, found after his death in his Cell at Silexedra,* which he had written, as he sets forth in his Dedication to Lord Hunsdon, "to beguile the time" on a voyage to the Canary Islands. The style is laboured and exceedingly diffuse, a true pastoral style; but Lodge had that gift of mere external invention in which Shakespeare, with all his powers, was so deficient. All the different stories which the play contains or touches upon are found in Lodge, and likewise all the characters with the exception of Jaques, Touchstone, and Audrey. Very remarkable to the attentive reader is Shakespeare's uniform passivity with regard to what he found in his sources, and his unwillingness to reject or alter anything, combined as it is with the most intense intellectual activity at the points upon which he concentrates his strength.

We find in *As You Like It,* as in Lodge, a wicked Duke who has expelled his virtuous brother, the lawful ruler, from his domains. The banished Duke, with his adherents, has taken refuge in the Forest of Arden, where they live as free a life as Robin Hood and his merry men, and where they are presently sought out by the Duke's daughter Rosalind and her cousin Celia, the daughter of the usurper, who will not let her banished friend wander forth alone. In the circle of nobility subordinate to the princes, there is also a wicked brother, Oliver, who seeks the life of his virtuous younger brother, Orlando, a hero as modest and amiable as he is brave. He and Rosalind fall in love with each other the moment they meet, and she makes sport with him throughout the play, disguised as a boy. These scenes should probably be acted as though he half recognised her. At last all ends happily. The wicked Duke most conveniently repents; the wicked brother is all of a sudden converted (quite without rhyme or reason) when Orlando, whom he has persecuted, kills a lioness—a lioness in the Forest of Arden!—which is about to spring upon him as he lies asleep. And the caitiff is rewarded (no less unreasonably), either for his villainy or for his conversion, with the hand of the lovely Celia.

This whole story is perfectly unimportant; Shakespeare, that is to say, evidently cared very little about it. We have here no attempt at a reproduction of reality, but one long festival of gaiety and wit, a soulful wit that vibrates into feeling.

First and foremost, the play typifies Shakespeare's longing, the longing of this great spirit, to get away from the unnatural city life, away from the false and ungrateful city folk, intent on business and on gain, away from flattery and falsehood and deceit, out into the country, where simple manners still endure, where it is easier to realise the dream of full freedom, and where the scent of the woods is so sweet. There the babble of the brooks has a subtler eloquence than any that is heard in cities; there the trees and even the stones say more to the wanderer's heart than the houses and streets of the capital; there he finds "good in everything."

The roving spirit has reawakened in his breast—the spirit which in bygone days sent him wandering with his gun through Charlcote Park—and out yonder in the lap of Nature, but in a remoter, richer Nature than that which he has known, he dreams of a communion between the best and ablest men, the fairest and most delicate women, in ideal fantastic surroundings, far from the ugly clamours of a public career, and the oppression of everyday cares. A life of hunting and song, and simple repasts in the open air, accompanied with witty talk; and at the same time a life full to the brim with the dreamy happiness of love. And with this life, the creation of his roving spirit, his gaiety and his longing for Nature, he animates a fantastic Forest of Arden.

But with this he is not content. He dreams out the dream, and feels that even such an ideal and untrammelled life could not satisfy that strange and unaccountable spirit lurking in the inmost depths of his nature, which turns everything into food for melancholy and satire. From this rib, then, taken from his own side, he creates the figure of Jaques, unknown to the romance, and sets him wandering through his pastoral comedy, lonely, retiring, self-absorbed, a misanthrope from excess of tenderness, sensitiveness and imagination.

Jaques is like the first light and brilliant pencil-sketch for Hamlet. Taine, and others after him, have tried to draw a parallel between Jaques and Alceste—of all Molière's creations no doubt, the one who contains most of his own nature. But there is no real analogy between them. In Jaques everything wears the shimmering hues of wit and fantasy, in Alceste everything is bitter earnest. Indignation is the mainspring of Alceste's misanthropy. He is disgusted at the falsehood around him, and outraged to see that the scoundrel with whom he is at law, although despised by every one, is nevertheless everywhere received with open arms. He declines to remain in bad company, even in the hearts of his friends; therefore he withdraws from them. He loathes two classes of people:

> "Les uns parcequ'ils sont méchants et malfaisants,
> Et les autres pouretre aux méchants complaisants."

These are the accents of Timon of Athens, who hated the wicked for their wickedness, and other men for not hating the wicked.

It is, then, in Shakespeare's Timon, of many years later, that we can alone find an instructive parallel to Alceste. Alceste's nature is keenly logical, classically French; it consists of sheer uncompromising sincerity and pride, without sensibility and without melancholy.

The melancholy of Jaques is a poetic dreaminess. He is described to us (ii. 1) before we see him. The banished Duke has just been blessing the adversity which drove him out into the forest, where he is exempt from the dangers of the envious court. He is on the point of setting forth to hunt, when he learns that the melancholy Jaques repines at the cruelty of the chase, and calls him in that respect as great a usurper as the brother who drove him from his dukedom. The courtiers have found him stretched beneath an oak, and dissolved in pity for a poor wounded stag which stood beside the brook, and "heaved forth such groans. That their discharge did stretch his leathern coat Almost to bursting." Jaques, they continue, "moralised this spectacle into a thousand similes: "—

> "Then, being there alone,
> Left and abandon'd of his velvet friends;
> 'Tis right,' quoth he; 'thus misery doth part
> The flux of company.' Anon, a careless herd,
> Full of the pasture, jumps along by him,
> And never stays to greet him. 'Ay,' quoth Jaques,
> 'Sweep on, you fat and greasy citizens;
> 'Tis just the fashion: wherefore do you look
> Upon that poor and broken bankrupt there?"

His bitterness springs from a too tender sensibility, a sensibility like that of Sakya Mouni before him, who made tenderness to animals part of his religion, and like that of Shelley after him, who, in his pantheism, realised the kinship between his own soul and that of the brute creation.

Thus we are prepared for his entrance. He introduces himself into the Duke's circle (ii. 7) with a glorification of the fool's motley. He has encountered Touchstone in the forest, and is enraptured with him. The motley fool lay basking in the sun, and when Jaques said to him, "Good morrow, fool!" he answered, "Call me not fool till heaven have sent me fortune." Then this sapient fool drew a dial from his pocket, and said very wisely—

> "'It is ten o'clock:
> Thus may we see,' quoth he, 'how the world wags:
> 'Tis but an hour ago since it was nine,
> And after one hour more 'twill be eleven;
> And so from hour to hour we ripe and ripe.
> And then from hour to hour we rot and rot,
> And thereby hangs a tale.'"

"O noble fool!" Jaques exclaims with enthusiasm. "A worthy fool! Motley's the only wear."

In moods of humorous melancholy, it must have seemed to Shakespeare as though he himself were one of these jesters, who had the privilege of uttering truths to great people and on the stage, if only they did not blurt them out directly, but disguised them under a mask of folly. It was in a similar mood that Heinrich Heine, centuries later, addressed to the German people these words: "Ich bin dein Kunz von der Rosen, dein Narr."

Therefore it is that Shakespeare makes Jaques exclaim—

> "O, that I were a fool!
> I am ambitious for a motley coat."

When the Duke answers, "Thou shalt have one," he declares that it is the one thing he wants, and that the others must "weed their judgments" of the opinion that he is wise:—

> "I must have liberty
> Withal, as large a charter as the wind,
> [To blow on whom I please; for so fools have:
> And they that are most galled with my folly,
> They most must laugh.
>
> . . . .
>
> Invest me in my motley: give me leave
> To speak my mind, and I will through and through
> Cleanse the foul body of the infected world,
> If they will patiently receive my medicine."

It is Shakespeare's own mood that we hear in these words. The voice is his. The utterance is far too large for Jaques: he is only a mouthpiece for the poet. Or let us say that his figure dilates in such passages as this, and we see in him a Hamlet *avant la lettre*.

When the Duke, in answer to this outburst, denies Jaques' right to chide and satirise others, since he has himself been "a libertine, As sensual as the brutish sting itself," the poet evidently defends himself in the reply which he places in the mouth of the melancholy philosopher:—

> "Why, who cries out on pride,
> That can therein tax any private party?
> Doth it not flow as hugely as the sea,
> Till that the weary very means do ebb?
> What woman in the city do I name,
> When that I say, the city-woman bears

The cost of princes on unworthy shoulders?
Who can come in, and say that I mean her,
When such a one as she, such is her neighbour?"

This exactly anticipates Holberg's self-defence in the character of Philemon in *The Fortunate Shipwreck*. The poet is evidently rebutting a common prejudice against his art. And as he makes Jaques an advocate for the freedom which poetry must claim, so also he employs him as a champion of the actor's misjudged calling, in placing in his mouth the magnificent speech on the Seven Ages of Man. Alluding, no doubt, to the motto of *Totus Mundus Agit Histrionem,* inscribed under the Hercules as Atlas, which was the sign of the Globe Theatre, this speech opens with the words:

"All the world's a stage,
And all the men and women merely players;
They have their exits and their entrances;
And one man in his time plays many parts."

Ben Jonson is said to have inquired, in an epigram against the motto of the Globe Theatre, where the spectators were to be found if all the men and women were players? And an epigram attributed to Shakespeare gives the simple answer that all are players and audience at one and the same time. Jaques' survey of the life of man is admirably concise and impressive. The last line—

"Sans teeth, sans eyes, sans taste, sans everything"—

with its half French equivalent for "without," is imitated from the *Henriade* of the French poet Garnier, which was not translated, and which Shakespeare must consequently have read in the original.

This same Jaques, who gives evidence of so wide an outlook over human life, is in daily intercourse, as we have said, nervously misanthropic and formidably witty. He is sick of polite society, pines for solitude, takes leave of a pleasant companion with the words: "I thank you for your company; but, good faith, I had as lief have been myself alone." Yet we must not take his melancholy and his misanthropy too seriously. His melancholy is a comedy-melancholy, his misanthropy is only the humourist's craving to give free vent to his satirical inspirations.

And there is, as aforesaid, only a certain part of Shakespeare's inmost nature in this Jaques, a Shakespeare of the future, a Hamlet in germ, but not that Shakespeare who now bathes in the sunlight and lives in uninterrupted prosperity, in growing favour with the many, and borne aloft by the admiration and goodwill of the few. We must seek for this Shakespeare in the interspersed songs, in the drollery of the fool, in the lovers' rhapsodies, in the enchanting babble of the ladies. He is, like Providence, everywhere and nowhere.

When Celia says (i. 2), "Let us sit and mock the good house wife, Fortune, from her wheel, that her gifts may henceforth be bestowed equally," she strikes, as though with a tuning-fork, the keynote of the comedy. The sluice is opened for that torrent of jocund wit, shimmering with all the rainbows of fancy, which is now to rush seething and swirling along.

The Fool is essential to the scheme: for the Fool's stupidity is the grindstone of wit, and the Fool's wit is the touchstone of character. Hence his name.

The ways of the real world, however, are not forgotten. The good make enemies by their very goodness, and the words of the old servant Adam (Shakespeare's own part) to his young master Orlando (ii. 3), sound sadly enough:—

> "Your praise is come too swiftly home before you.
> Know you not, master, to some kind of men
> Their graces serve them but as enemies?
> No more do yours: your virtues, gentle master,
> Are sanctified, and holy traitors to you.
> O, what a world is this, when what is comely
> Envenoms him that bears it!"

But soon the poet's eye is opened to a more consolatory life philosophy, combined with an unequivocal contempt for school-philosophy. There seems to be a scoffing allusion to a book of the time, which was full of the platitudes of celebrated philosophers, in Touchstone's speech to William (v. 1), "The heathen philosopher, when he had desire to eat a grape, would open his lips when he put it into his mouth, meaning thereby that grapes were made to eat and lips to open;" but no doubt there also lurks in this speech a certain lack of respect for even the much-belauded wisdom of tradition. The relativity of all things, at that time a new idea, is expounded with lofty humour by the Fool in his answer to the question what he thinks of this pastoral life (iii. 2):—

> "Truly, shepherd, in respect of itself it is a good life, but in respect that it is a shepherd's life, it is naught. In respect that it is solitary, I like it very well; but in respect that it is private, it is a very vile life Now, in respect it is in the fields, it pleaseth me well; but in respect it is not in the court, it is tedious. As it is a spare life, look you, it fits my humour well; but as there is no more plenty in it, it goes much against my stomach. Hast any philosophy in thee, shepherd?"

The shepherd's answer makes direct sport of philosophy, in the style of Molière's gibe, when he accounts for the narcotic effect of opium by explaining that the drug possesses a certain *facultas dormitativa*:—

Corin. No more, but that I know, the more one sickens, the worse at ease he is; and that he that wants money, means, and content, is without three good friends; that the property of rain is to wet, and fire to burn; that good pasture makes fat sheep, and that a great cause of the night is lack of the sun. . . .
"*Touchstone.* Such a one is a natural philosopher."

This sort of philosophy leads up, as it were, to Rosalind's sweet gaiety and heavenly kindness.

The two cousins, Rosalind and Celia, seem at first glance like variations of the two cousins, Beatrice and Hero, in the play Shakespeare has just finished. Rosalind and Beatrice in particular are akin in their victorious wit. Yet the difference between them is very great; Shakespeare never repeats himself. The wit of Beatrice is aggressive and challenging; we see, as it were, the gleam of a rapier in it. Rosalind's wit is gaiety without a sting; the gleam in it is of "that sweet radiance" which Oehlenschläger attributed to Freia; her sportive nature masks the depth of her love. Beatrice can be brought to love because she is a woman, and stands in no respect apart from her sex; but she is not of an amatory nature. Rosalind is seized with a passion for Orlando the instant she sets eyes on him. From the moment of Beatrice's first appearance she is defiant and combative, in the highest of spirits. We are introduced to Rosalind as a poor bird with a drooping wing; her father is banished, she is bereft of her birthright, and is living on sufferance as companion to the usurper's daughter, being, indeed, half a prisoner in the palace, where till lately she reigned as princess. It is not until she has donned the doublet and hose, appears in the likeness of a page, and wanders at her own sweet will in the open air and the greenwood, that she recovers her radiant humour, and roguish merriment flows from her lips like the trilling of a bird.

Nor is the man she loves, like Benedick, an overweening gallant with a sharp tongue and an unabashed bearing. This youth, though brave as a hero and strong as an athlete, is a child in inexperience, and so bashful in the presence of the woman who instantly captivates him, that it is she who is the first to betray her sympathy for him, and has even to take the chain from her own neck and hang it around his before he can so much as muster up courage to hope for her love. So, too, we find him passing his time in hanging poems to her upon the trees, and carving the name of Rosalind in their bark. She amuses herself, in her page's attire, by making herself his confidant, and pretending, as it were in jest, to be his Rosalind. She cannot bring herself to confess her passion, although she can think and talk (to Celia) of no one but him, and although his delay of a few minutes in keeping tryst with her sets her beside herself with impatience. She is as sensitive as she is intelligent, in this differing from Portia, to whom, in other respects, she bears some resemblance, though she lacks her persuasive eloquence, and is, on the whole, more tender, more virginal. She faints when Oliver, to excuse Orlando's delay, brings her a handkerchief stained with his blood; yet has sufficient self-mastery to say with a smile the moment she recovers, "I pray you tell your brother how well I counterfeited." She is quite at her ease in her male attire, like Viola and Imogen after her. The fact that female parts were played by youths had, of course, something to do with the frequency of these disguises.

Here is a specimen of her wit (iii. 2). Orlando has evaded the page's question what o'clock it is, alleging that there are no clocks in the forest.

"*Rosalind.* Then, there is no true lover in the forest; else sighing every minute, and groaning every hour, would detect the lazy foot of Time as well as a clock.

"*Orlando.* And why not the swift foot of Time? had not that been as proper?

"*Ros.* By no means, sir. Time travels in divers paces with divers persons. I'll tell you, who Time ambles withal, who Time trots withal, who Time gallops withal, and who he stands still withal.

"*Orl.* I pr'ythee, who doth he trot withal?

"*Ros.* Marry, he trots hard with a young maid, between the contract of her marriage, and the day it is solemnised: if the interim be but a se'nnight, Time's pace is so hard that it seems the length of seven years.

"*Orl.* Who ambles Time withal?

"*Ros.* With a priest that lacks Latin, and a rich man that hath not the gout; for the one sleeps easily, because he cannot study; and the other lives merrily, because he feels no pain. . . .

"*Orl.* Who doth he gallop withal?

"*Ros.* With a thief to the gallows; for though he go as softly as foot can fall, he thinks himself too soon there.

"*Orl.* Who stays it still withal?

"*Ros.* With lawyers in the vacation; for they sleep between term and term, and then they perceive not how Time moves."

She is unrivalled in vivacity and inventiveness. In every answer she discovers gunpowder anew, and she knows how to use it to boot. She explains that she had an old uncle who warned her against love and women, and, from the vanity ground of her doublet and hose, she declares—

"I thank God, I am not a woman, to be touched with so many offences, as he hath generally taxed their whole sex withal.

"*Orl.* Can you remember any of the principal evils that he lay the charge of women?

"*Ros.* There were none principal: they were all like one another half-pence are; every one fault seeming monstrous, till its fellow came to match it.

"*Orl.* I pr'ythee, recount some of them.

"*Ros.* No; I will not cast away my physic but on those that are. There is a man haunts the forest, that abuses our young plants carving Rosalind on their barks; hangs odes upon hawthorns; elegies on brambles; all, forsooth, deifying the name of Rosalind: could meet that fancy-monger, I would give him some good counsel for he seems to have the quotidian of love upon him."

Orlando admits that he is the culprit, and they are to meet daily that she may exorcise his passion. She bids him address her in jest, as though she were indeed Rosalind, and answers (iv. I):—

"*Ros.* Well, in her person, I say—I will not have you.

"*Orl.* Then, in mine own person, I die.

"*Ros.* No, 'faith, die by attorney. The poor world is almost a thousand years old, and in all this time there was not any man died in his own person, *videlicet*, in a love-cause. Troilus had his brains dashed out with a Grecian club; yet he did what he could to before, and he is one of the patterns of love. Leander, he would have lived many a fair year, though Hero had turned nun, if it had not been for a hot midsummer night; for, good youth, he went but forth to wash him in the Hellespont, and, being taken with the cramp, was drowned and the foolish chroniclers of that age found it was—Hero of Sestos. But these are all lies: Men have died from time to time, and worms have eaten them, but not for love."

What Rosalind says of women in general applies to herself in particular: you will never find her without an answer until you find her without a tongue. And there is always a bright, merry fantasy in her answers. She is literally radiant with youth, imagination, and the joy of loving so passionately a being so passionately beloved. And it is marvellous how thoroughly feminine is her wit. Too many of the witty women in books written by men have a man's intelligence. Rosalind's wit is tempered by feeling.

She has no monopoly of wit in this Arcadia of Arden. Every one in the play is witty, even the so-called simpletons. It is a festival of wit. At some points Shakespeare seems to have followed no stricter principle than the simple one of making each interlocutor outbid the other in wit (see, for example, the conversation between Touchstone and the country wench whom he befools). The result is that the piece is bathed in a sunshiny humour. And amid all the gay and airy wit-skirmishes, amid the cooing love-duets of all the happy youths and maidens, the poet intersperses the melancholy solos of his Jaques:—

"I have neither the scholar's melancholy, which is emulation; nor the musician's, which is fantastical; nor the courtier's, which is proud; nor the soldier's, which is ambitious; nor the lawyer's, which is politic; nor the lady's, which is nice; nor the lover's, which is all these; but it is a melancholy of mine own, compounded of many simples, extracted from many objects."

This is the melancholy which haunts the thinker and the great creative artist; but in Shakespeare it as yet modulated with ease into the most engaging and delightful merriment.

Originally published in English.
(Copenhagen, 1898): Vol. 1, 258–68.

WILLIAM SHAKESPEARE
John Masefield
1911

THE PLAYS

The play treats of the gifts of Nature and the ways of Fortune. Orlando, given little, is brought to much. Rosalind and Celia, born to much, are brought to little. The Duke, born to all things, is brought to nothing. The usurping Duke, born to nothing, climbs to much, desires all, and at last renounces all. Oliver, born to much, aims at a little more, loses all, and at last regains all. Touchstone, the worldly wise, marries a fool. Audrey, born a clown, marries a courtier. Phebe, scorning a man, falls in love with a woman.

Jaques, the only wise one, is the only one not moved by Fortune. Life does not interest him; his interest is in his thoughts about life. His vision of life feasts him whatever life does. Passages in the second act, in the subtle seventh scene, corrupt in a most important line, show that in the character of Jaques Shakespeare was expounding a philosophy of art. The philosophy may not have been that by which he, himself, wrought; but it is one set down by him with an extreme subtlety of care, and opposed, as all opinions advanced in drama must be, by an extreme earnestness of opposition.

The wisest of Shakespeare's characters are often detached from the action of the play in which they appear. Jaques holds aloof from the action of this play, though he is perhaps the best-known character in the cast. His thought is the thought of all wise men, that wisdom, being always a little beyond the world, has no worldly machinery by which it can express itself. In this world the place of the chorus, interpreter or commentator is not given to the wise man, but to the fool who has degraded the office to a profession. Jaques, the wise man, finds the place occupied by one whose comment is platitude. Wisdom has no place in the social scheme. The fool, he finds, has both office and uniform.

Seeing this, Jaques wishes, as all wise men wish, not to be counted wise but to have as great liberty as the fool to express his thought—

> "weed your better judgments
> Of all opinion that grows rank in them
> That I am wise. I must have liberty
> Withal, as large a charter as the wind,
> To blow on whom I please; for so fools have
> ... give me leave
> To speak my mind, and I will through and through
> Cleanse the foul body of the infected world,
> If they will patiently receive my medicine."

He is answered that, having learned of the world's evil by libidinous living, he can only do evil by exposing his knowledge. He replies, finely expressing Shakespeare's invariable artistic practice, that his aim will be at sin, not at particular sinners.

In the middle of his speech Orlando enters, raging for food. It is interesting to see how closely Shakespeare follows Jaques' mind in the presence of the fierce animal want of hunger. He is too much interested to be of help. The Duke ministers to Orlando. Jaques wants to know "of what kind this cock should come of." He speaks banteringly, the Duke speaks kindly. The impression given is that Jaques is heartless. The Duke's thought is "here is one even more wretched than ourselves." Jaques thought, always more for humanity than for the individual, is a profound vision of the world.

The play is a little picture of the world. The contemplative man who is not of the world, is yet a part of the picture. We are shown a company of delightful people, just escaped from disaster, smilingly taking the biggest of hazards. The wise man, dismissing them to their fates with all the authority of wisdom, gives up his share in the game to listen to a man who has given up his share of the world. Renunciation of the world is attractive to all upon whom the world presses very heavily, or very lightly.

Rosalind and Phebe are of the two kinds of woman who come much into Shakespeare's early and middle plays. Rosalind, like Portia, is a golden woman, a daughter of the sun, smiling-natured, but limited. Phebe, like Rosalind, is black-haired, black-eyed, black-eyebrowed, with the dead-white face that so often goes with cruelty. Shortly after this play was written he began to create types less external and less limited.

(London: William & Norgate, 1911): 129–33.

THE CULMINATING COMEDIES
C. Herford
1912

As You Like It (c. 1600).—The woman and the wit are still more finely mated in the heroine of *As You Like It*. They are here indeed less competitors than allies, and the plot is little more than Rosalind's delightful make-believe in the service of her love. So unsubstantial is the story, so delicately spun the lines of action and the threads of interest, that the great public has never taken very kindly to the play. Too little happens, and the things that do happen belong too completely to a romantic and idyllic world which the great public does not recognise as at all like its own. This Arden forest is indeed an enchanted region like the world of the Golden Age, where villainy cannot enter, where the inmates "see no enemy but winter and rough weather," and where the kind of interest that hangs upon conspiracies against life or happiness accordingly has no place. Jaques and Frederick doubtless mean mischief, no less than Don John in *Much Ado;* but their plans miscarry, or turn to the good of their intended victims; while their own ill-nature itself magically dissolves as they approach the charmed precincts of Arden. They appear formidable only in the First Act, the whole purpose of which is to sift the well-natured people from the ill, and bring them all together in this woodland " remote from public haunt," leaving the others to plot and quarrel as they will in the outer world. A band of robbers, who in the original romance attacked Celia, are refused entrance into the Shakespearean Arden; the only harmful thing there is a lion, which exists only to be overcome by Orlando. But the forest is not wholly unreal. Its greenwood scenery, its brooks and troops of deer, and the ardours of the chase, are felt and seen. And legend and reality in the same way cross and mingle in the inmates. Phœbe and Silvius are shepherds such as rhymed and sighed for each other in the literary Pastoral romances of the day; but William and Audrey and Corin are homely herdsfolk of real life. The contrast of court with country, of the world with sylvan seclusion, runs all through the play; and the unworldly side of the contrast is touched with a sympathy hardly to be looked for in the poet who had so gaily satirised the woodland Academe of Navarre. Some of the finest and deepest things said, before Rousseau, about the life according to Nature are put into the mouth of the banished Duke, and some of its freshest and blithest poetry into that of Amiens; while the humour, variously flavoured, that springs so abundantly from these contrasts of Nature and Society, is conveyed through the lips of the two wonderful originals, Touchstone and Jaques. Touchstone is, with Lear's Fool, Shakespeare's finest study of the court jester. He is a rustic who has learnt the trick of court raillery without forgetting his native mother-wit, and can banter Rosalind and browbeat Corin with equal effect. Jaques is the disillusioned man of the world, bitter as Touchstone is dry. His sentimentality is rooted in cynicism, and when he bids the fresh and healthy-minded Orlando sit down and rail at the world, it is no lofty idealism but the jaded temper of the world itself which speaks through him. Neither of them contribute anything of moment to the action. Detached philosophic contemplation is the cue, or the pose, of both; but their burlesque or sardonic comments add a delightful tang to the romantic atmosphere of the play; and this critical or hostile element puts romance on its mettle, and gives it occasion to vindicate its own soundness, sweetness, and truth.

In Rosalind and Orlando, indeed, Shakespeare makes romance at once provocative and irresistible. He let them do all the absurd things which the impossible lovers of Pastoral were accustomed to do, and yet he compels us to feel that there is real blood in their veins and true passion in their hearts. Orlando carves verses on the barks of trees, which Rosalind reads with effusion; and her arch device of all is but a variation on the noted shift of the lovelorn heroines of Pastoral, who pursued their lover in doublet and hose. But she herself is no pastoral heroine, and when she encounters one, in Phœbe, she overwhelms her with the gayest and healthiest mockery; as, on the contrary, when she encounters Jaques, she brilliantly flouts his scorn of love. Cynicism and sentimentality are equally foreign to this tender-hearted madcap, in whom passion and humour lie equally deep, and whose deliberate love-strategy is a piece of hilarious fun.

(London, 1912): 54–59.

SHAKSPERE AS A PLAYWRIGHT
Brander Matthews
1913

IV

In 'As you Like it' the supporting underplot scarcely ever attains even the semi-tragic. It is only an induction, a framework for the episodes in the Forest of Arden. We have our attention called to it in the beginning of the play and again at the end, but in the middle of it Rosalind draws all eyes to her and to her lover. Shakspere finds his story not in an earlier play, but in a long-winded and pedantic pastoral romance. As usual he handles his material with full freedom; he omits and condenses, he rearranges incidents and he adds new characters— Jaques and Touchstone and Audrey. Above all, he heightens and he brightens the tale he borrows, bestowing a generous humanity upon the traditional figures of the pastoral play, which was an elaborately artificial form. Perhaps he recalled the rustic scenes of Greene's 'Friar Bacon and Friar Bungay,' and perhaps he was influenced by two Robin Hood pieces produced by rival companies only a few months earlier than 'As you Like it.'

He does not trouble himself to complicate the story into a really dramatic plot, relying rather upon the contrast of character than upon the sharpness of a struggle between contending desires. Yet his exposition is clear and swift. Orlando is posed before us at once, strong of body and direct of will, manly and resolute. The animosity of his elder brother is shown in action; and we are made to feel the sense of impending peril, not to be taken very seriously, but none the less plainly visible. Then in the episode of the wrestling we behold the actual danger from which the young hero escapes, and we are made spectators of the love at first sight of Rosalind and Orlando. After that the banishment follows immediately, first of Orlando, and then of Rosalind; and our longing has been awakened to behold their meeting later in the Forest of Arden, where the rest of the action is to take place. This is the necessary introduction, skilfully outlined to arouse sympathetic expectancy.

It is to the succession of episodes in the Forest of Arden that 'As you Like it' owes its abiding charm, to the lovely groves and glades as well as to the lovely beings who range through them. When we follow Orlando and Rosalind into that enchanted woodland we take a vacation from the workday world and we enter a domain of indisputable happiness, where no one grieves deeply whatever may befall, and where even the banished are reconciled to their exile and take life cheerily, letting their blithe hearts overflow in song. In this happiest of his comedies Shakspere invites us, so Andrew Lang declared, "into that ideal commonwealth for which all men in all times have sighed: the land of an easeful liberty; the life natural, which has never existed in nature, where there is neither war nor toil, but endless security and peace beneath the sky and the trees." It is a forest akin to the Sherwood of the old ballads, but inhabited by beings less boisterous. It is fragrant with the aroma of romance, an enchanted region of unattained and restful delight, the dream of lyric youth.

Here, outdoors, in the open air, under the cloudless sky, while the fresh breeze blows across the sylvan spaces and rustles the shimmering tree-tops, life fleets merrily, touched with tender sentiment, and never stirred by the depths of passion. The atmosphere may be that of Virgilian eclogue, but the attitude is rather that of Horatian revery. The tone of the comedy is that of the most delicate "familiar verse," blithe and buoyant. 'As you Like it' is in many ways the most fanciful and the most lyric of Shakspere's plays; it is the comedy of young love, as 'Romeo and Juliet' is the tragedy of young love. It is an eternal spring-poem, set in dialogue and action and singing itself to its own music. And yet, strangely enough, it has less verse than almost any other of Shakspere's plays. The exquisite colloquies of Rosalind and Orlando, instinct with poetry, are largely in prose, although the talk of Silvius and Phœbe is allowed to soar aloft into blank verse, which is often allotted also to Jaques. Perhaps nothing displays more certainly Shakspere's intuitive mastery over every chord of the lyre than the intangible art by which the wooings of Rosalind are etherealized into poetry, while the medium of expression is but prose.

It may be that Shakspere was led to utilize Lodge's history because it required the heroine to disguise herself as a lad. This was a common dramaturgic device under Elizabeth, deriving a part of its piquancy from the performance of the female characters by boys. Shakspere had already employed it in the 'Two Gentlemen of Verona' and the 'Merchant of Venice'; and he was to make use of it again in 'Twelfth Night.' In fact, in this group of romantic-comedies Beatrice is the only heroine who is not required to don the apparel of the opposite sex. In 'As you Like it' the piquancy is redoubled, since Rosalind, played by a youth, attires herself as a lad and then has to pretend to Orlando that she is a girl—a trick of surpassing theatrical effectiveness.

Amusing as the situation is in itself, its histrionic possibilities are increased by Rosalind's demure enjoyment of it. She feels the fun of it, for she has an eager sense of humor as well as a bubbling wit. She is unfailingly witty as she is unfailingly feminine; and her tongue has no tang to it. Her wit is not coruscating or aggressive in attack; it is lambent and illuminating. Here she is unlike Beatrice, who fences for sheer delight in the passage of arms itself, and who cares little if the button chances to drop from her foil. Petulant as Rosalind may be on occasion, and provoking, she is ever womanly, with a depth of sentiment not inferior to Viola's. She is at once sprightly and tender, frank and cheerful, the English ideal of a healthy girl, glad to be wooed.

In her wholesome happiness Rosalind stands in sharp contrast with the melancholy Jaques, in whom sentiment has turned sour. Jaques is one of the characters that Shakspere added to those he took from Lodge's tale. The playwright must have fitted all his plays, one after another, to the special company of actors for whom they were composed and by whom they were produced, it may not be fanciful to suggest that Jaques was possibly written into the play on purpose to supply a part for some important actor who was a good elocutionist, perhaps for Burbage himself. Certainly Jaques does nothing but stand and deliver speeches; he exists only to talk; he has no function to perform in the plot. He might be cut out without affecting the structure of the story, and yet what would the play be without him? He supplies the element of subacid humor, which contrasts so pleasantly with the happiness of all the rest; and he also is happy in his gift of speech. He finds delight in railing at the world, and he gets obvious pleasure out of the impression he produces upon his hearers, for it can hardly be denied that he is constantly playing to the gallery, improving the occasion for the sake of the effect he is making upon his fellow-exiles.

These associates of his under the greenwood tree understand his ways and they humor his humor. They take him for what he is, waiting to hear what he will say next. They are amused rather than grieved when he proceeds to gird at all mankind, in his speech on the seven ages. Perhaps this rhetorical excursus, this tenor-solo of a sweet nature which has fermented into cynicism, owes its origin to the necessity of filling the time while Orlando is bringing in Adam. In like manner, the learned disquisition of Touchstone upon a lie seven times removed, which seems hopelessly out of place in the final scene of a play, when everything ought to be hastening to a conclusion, had its origin also in a technical necessity—the need for bridging the gap while Rosalind was changing back into the habiliments of her own sex. The set speech for its own sake was common enough in the Elizabethan drama; but in these two instances Shakspere makes it useful as well as ornamental. Touchstone was also an addition of Shakspere's to the characters of the original story; and he may also have been introduced to supply a part for a special performer.

When Rosalind is made to marry Orlando, the play is over and the plot is promptly wound up in the most peremptory fashion, as though the story itself mattered little. The characters of the semi-tragic underplot whom we have seen at the beginning of the piece are now transformed in the twinkling of an eye in semi-comic fashion, so that the spectators in the yard need not be kept standing any longer. The usurping Duke suddenly sees a great light and experiences a change of heart. The wicked elder brother has his life saved by Orlando, so he also repents on the spot and immediately falls in love with Celia, his brother's bride's friend, and she with him, an even more startling case of love at first sight than Rosalind's and Orlando's. And so the happiest of Shakspere's comedies ends happily, as no one of the audience could ever have doubted from the beginning.

V

'Twelfth Night' differs from the three earlier romantic-comedies in that its love story is supported by a subplot which is comic rather than semi-tragic, although more than one character is for a moment in deadly danger. Perhaps the success of 'As you Like it' had shown Shakspere that he did not need to emphasize the serious elements as sharply as he had done in the 'Merchant of Venice' and in 'Much Ado.' And in 'Twelfth Night' he also illustrates his customary economy of invention; that is to say, his constant tendency to employ again devices already approved by experience. Julia in the 'Two Gentlemen of Verona' had anticipated Viola in her disguise as a boy and in then carrying a message from the man she loved to the woman he thought himself in love with Phœbe in 'As you Like it' had anticipated Olivia in her falling in love with a woman disguised as a man. The likeness of the twins of the 'Comedy of Errors,' a likeness extending even to costume, had already led the one to be taken for the other before a similar confusion befell Viola and Sebastian, sister and brother, who look alike and are dressed alike; and the father of the two Antipholi had adventured himself rashly in a hostile country before Antonio put himself into a similar peril. Even the trick which Maria plays upon Malvolio in making him believe that Olivia is in love with him is closely akin to that played upon Benedick and Beatrice. It is true that these devices are ingeniously varied in 'Twelfth Night,' but it is true also that they had been employed in the earlier plays.

Perhaps because the serious episodes are few and unimportant 'Twelfth Night' has a more obvious harmony of tone than the 'Merchant of Venice' and 'Much Ado.' It is a delicious compound of sentiment and humor shading into one another by exquisite gradations. The exposition is simple and clear. First of all, we learn that Orsino is almost hopelessly in love with Olivia; then we are told of Viola's shipwreck and of her intention to attach herself to Orsino; and immediately thereafter we are introduced to Olivia's strangely assorted household. A little later the appearance of Sebastian promptly arouses an interest of expectancy. All the threads of the action are then in the hands of the spectator, who can follow the story in security while Viola is falling in love with Orsino and Olivia with the disguised Viola. We can see for ourselves that Olivia is as plain-spoken in declaring her affection for Viola, and later for Viola's brother (who so resembles his sister), as Rosalind was in telling Orlando that he had overcome more than his enemy. Olivia's sending the ring after the disguised Viola is the equivalent of Rosalind's throwing her chain over Orlando's shoulders.

While Olivia is as undaunted in making up to the disguised Viola as Rosalind is in her maidenly avowal to Orlando, Viola's lack of hesitancy in telling Orsino that she has a tender sentiment for him (although she then knows that he thinks himself in love with another woman) is subtler, since he accepts her for a boy and is therefore unable to take her meaning. Viola can put on a bold front when she first meets Olivia, and she can brisk out a pert sentence or two on occasion; but she lacks the demure fun of Rosalind and also Rosalind's flashing wit. Her humor has a tender tinge as becomes her experience of life; it is a humor tinctured with melancholy and shot through with sentiment. She may very well have perceived, with a true woman's swiftness of perception, that Orsino's love for Olivia was lacking in the energy of real passion, contenting itself with longing and sighing. Orsino is not really unhappy in his paraded misery; he is in love with love rather than with Olivia, and he is ripe for a deeper affection for Viola when he shall discover her to be a woman.

His change of heart may be startlingly sudden; and startlingly sudden also is Sebastian's swift flame for Olivia. But neither of these fifth-act conversions is as improbable as the unforeseen marrying off of Celia and Oliver in 'As you Like it.' Viola is a lovely creature, and why should not Orsino become enamoured of her on the spot when he knows her at last for a woman and when he may recall her expressions of affection for him? Olivia is also a beauty; and why should not Sebastian welcome the prize which falls plump into his arms? All that is improbable in 'Twelfth Night' is the celerity of the mating, a celerity almost justified here by the pressure of the action to its conclusion. Besides, these two weddings are only what the spectators have dimly descried and vaguely desired; whereas, in 'As you Like it' the union of Celia and Oliver takes even the audience by surprise, since the playwright has in no wise prepared us for it. In 'Twelfth Night' the dramatist is only availing himself liberally of the privilege of condensing time and of letting us see on the stage in a fifth act what in real life would not have happened until a sixth or a seventh act.

Viola and Olivia were plainly written for the boy actors who had already played Rosalind and Celia, Beatrice and Hero, Portia and Nerissa; and Maria was as obviously composed for the boy actor who had impersonated Mrs. Ford. So the performer of Malvolio may already have appeared as Jaques, the performer of Sir Toby as Dogberry (and perhaps also as Falstaff), and the performer of Sir Andrew as Slender Feste fell naturally to the man who had acted Touchstone and who was later to undertake the Fool in 'King Lear.'

The more humorous creations are sturdily English in their robust fun, even if they pretend to live in Illyria, just as Dogberry and Verges had established a fictitious domicile in Messina. Nothing more clearly displays the easy mastery of stage-craft to which Shakspere has now attained than the skill with which he here conjoins the pensive melancholy of Viola's love story with the buxom merriment of Maria's trick upon Malvolio. Viola is the central female figure in the comedy as Malvolio is the central male figure, and they scarcely meet in the course of the play. It is Olivia who serves as the connecting-link between the episode of sentiment and the more robustious underplot; and she performs this artistic function without in any way derogating from her high estate as the second heroine. The author here artfully intertwines a delightful fantasy with the infectious laughter of honest mirth; and he so contrives his action that we are never made aware of any incongruity. He passes from the poetry of sentiment to the prose of riotous humor by imperceptible gradations that never interfere with the pervading unity of tone.

In no other comedy is the group of comic characters more exhilaratingly comic than in 'Twelfth Night.' Here are no longer the traditional figures of earlier English Comedy. Shakspere is now able to individualize every character, however unimportant. The jests of these humorous creations are no longer extraneous and casual witticisms; they are evoked by the situation itself or else they are the ripe expression of character revealing itself in dialogue. There is no straining for points, no overt effort, such as is only too evident in the earlier comedies. There is no display of cleverness for its own sake. What the several characters say is what they would say, and not what the author has chosen to put in their mouths; it is what they cannot help saying. The fun is no longer in the words, even if it is often in the words also; it is even more in the characters themselves than in the situations, amusing as these are. Of course, Shakspere has not ceased to be an Elizabethan; no man may step off his own shadow; and the belief in Malvolio's insanity is treated in accord with the Elizabethan acceptance of madness as comic in itself.

VI

These four plays do not fall into any of the ordinarily accepted classifications; they do not strictly belong to the comedy-of-manners or the comedy-of-sentiment, the comedy-of-humors or to the comedy-of-character; and they are equally remote from that type of high-comedy which Molière evolved and in which the action is caused by the clash of character on character. They do not conform to Stendhal's dictum that tragedy is the development of an action and comedy the development of a character which is to be shown by a succession of ideas; for this these four comedies are too full of fantasy, of romance, of poetry. They belong to the type of romantic-comedy, to which Shakspere alone had the clue—even if Musset was able to stray a little way into the path Shakspere had pointed out; and Musset was a lyric poet who was a playwright almost by accident. This romantic-comedy is compounded of capricious fancy and of exuberant humor; it is fundamentally joyous, although it may now and again wander almost to the verge of impending disaster. It bears us away from this workaday world across the gulf of time to a fabled shore where we may find measureless relief from sordid care. It commingles poetry and even pathos with wit and humor. Perhaps the deepest note is struck in 'Twelfth Night,' the latest of the four, and also the boldest note of skylarking fun. In fact, it needs to be noted that 'Twelfth Night,' which is one of the most pervadingly poetic of Shakspere's comedies, is the last of his plays in which the humor is broad and hearty, the last in which there is any true gaiety or any richly comic characters. For whatever reason, internal or external, his succeeding plays were to take on a more somber color; and when he had finished 'Twelfth Night' he was ready to begin 'Hamlet.'

(London: Longmans, 1913): 156–67.

DISGUISE PLOTS IN ELIZABETHAN DRAMA
Victor O. Freeburg
1915

A play differs essentially from a story, which is merely to be imagined. Consequently we have two kinds of probability. One is the probability of the plot as we see it in the mind's eye, and the other is the probability of the action as we actually see it represented physically with mechanical aids on a fixed spot and within a limited time. It is conceivable that a real Rosalind might deceive a real Orlando in a real forest of Arden. That is at least one aspect of the question of probability. But that a hundred and sixty pound, well-molded actress should deceive a hundred and thirty-five pound, slender, fifteen year younger actor into believing that she is a sentimental shepherd boy is preposterous. Yet such a *reductio ad absurdum* has been known even on our contemporary stage.

The vision of the mind's eye must not be obscured by the rough beams of the theater. All the art of the actor and the stage manager must unite to obviate jarring improbabilities, and to make a disguise situation seem at least poetically probable. It will be interesting in the succeeding paragraphs to note the development of the art of representing disguise situations on the English state. It is a record, not only of a development of skill in theatrical costuming and make-up, but also of an awakening consciousness of the rich theatricality in disguise situations.

II

The staging of disguise may be considered as advancing in three steps. First, there was only a change of name, but no change at all in appearance. Second, there was a partial change of appearance, or merely a symbol to represent a change. Third, there came a consistent attempt to make the disguised person really look his part in detail. Thus the acting of disguise parts developed from the mere pretending of children at play, to the art of the well-equipped and practiced mimic.

In Skelton's *Magnificence* the whole plot depends on the hero's mistaking

Fancy for Largess, Crafty Conveyance for Sure Surveyance, Courtly Abusion for Lusty Pleasure, Folly for Conceit, and Cloaked Collusion for Sober Sadness. Yet all except one of these characters have remained unchanged in appearance. They have confessedly merely changed their names. The disguise which these characters pretend is a disguise of abstract character, a spiritual metamorphosis, which is after all best indicated by a change of name. We may imagine such a disguise but cannot easily present it by physical garments.

(New York: Columbia University Press, 1915), 18–19.

SHAKESPEARE'S USE OF SONG
Richmond Noble
1923

AS YOU LIKE IT

SONGS.

Those by Amiens.

Act II, Scene 5.
Under the greenwood tree,
Who loves to lie with me,
And turn his merry note,
Unto the sweet bird's throat:
Come hither, come hither, come hither:
Here shall he see
No enemy,
But Winter and rough weather.
All together here.
Who doth ambition shun,
And loves to live in the sun:
Seeking the food he eats,
And please with what he gets:
Come hither, come hither, come hither:
Here shall he see
No enemy,
But Winter and rough weather.

Jaques.
If it do come to pass,
That any man turn ass;
Leaving his wealth and ease,
A stubborn will to please,
Ducdame, ducdame, ducdame:
Here shall he see
Gross fools as he.
An if he will come to me.

Act II, Scene 7.

Blow, blow, thou winter wind,
Thou art not so unkind,
    As man's ingratitude:
Thy tooth is not so keen,
Because thou art not seen,
    Although thy breath be rude.
Heigh-ho, sing heigh-ho, unto the green holly;
Most friendship is feigning; most loving, mere folly:
    Then heigh-ho, the holly,
    This life is most jolly.

Freeze, freeze, thou bitter sky,
That dost not bite so nigh
    As benefits forgot:
Though thou the waters warp,
Thy sting is not so sharp,
    As friend remembered not.
Heigh-ho, sing heigh-ho, &c.

Act IV, Scene 2. Sung by Lord, probably Amiens.
What shall he have that killed the deer?
His leather skin, and horns to wear:
    Then sing him home (*The rest shall bear this burden*):
Take thou no scorn to wear the horn,
It was a crest ere thou wast born,
    Thy father's father wore it,
    And thy father bore it,
The horn, the horn, the lusty horn,
Is not a thing to laugh to scorn.

Act V, Scene 3. Sung by two Pages.
It was a lover and his lass,
    With a hey, and a ho, and a hey nonino,
That o'er the green cornfield did pass,
    In the spring time,
    The only pretty ring time,
    When birds do sing,
    Hey ding a ding, ding,
    Sweet lovers love the spring.

Between the acres of the rye,
   With a hey, and a ho, and a hey nonino,
These pretty country folks would lie,
   In the spring time, &c.

This carol they began that hour,
   With a hey, and a ho, and a hey nonino,
How that a life was but a flower,
   In the spring time, &c.

And therefore take the present time,
   With a hey, and a ho, and a hey nonino,
For love is crowned with the prime,
   In the spring time, &c.

While it can hardly be maintained that *As You Like It* attains the high perfection of gay comedy of *Twelfth Night*, there can be no doubt that none of Shakespeare's comedies surpasses its appeal to the hearts of men. It is the comedy of romantic unreality, of the Arcadian existence of which we have a glimpse in the canvases of Watteau. To such a comedy the service of song is indispensable, for without the aid of music we should be unable to realize its ideality or its entire removal from any kind of life with which we are acquainted. The interest of the play lies in what its characters think and say and as to how they dispose of their leisure, of which, despite the hardness of their lot, they seem to have an ample supply. The plot is of minor consequence, in fact it appears to be merely an excuse for conveying to us a picture of the simple life in the forest far away from the more frequented haunts of men. All men delight to dream of an existence in picturesque surroundings as far removed from 'their wealth and ease' and the drab conditions of their everyday life as it is possible for the imagination to make it, and it is here that the secret of the charm of the comedy lies. Song heightens the effect.

Since the plot of *As You Like It* is lazy and only moves by violent fits and starts, it is not surprising that none of the songs helps to develop the action; there is not one that brings on the scene as does *O mistress mine* in *Twelfth Night*. Neither is there any song, if we except those by Hymen, which is part and parcel of the action as are the two opening songs by Ariel in *The Tempest*. In fact, in the case of all the songs except *Blow, blow, thou winter wind*, the scenes would appear to have been created in order that the songs might be sung—a feature that would suggest that songs had been inserted to counter the competition of the Children at Blackfriars. Nevertheless each song fulfils a very important dramatic function, that of conveying colour of scene and sense of atmosphere to make good the lack of the assistance of a scene painter in appealing to the imagination of an audience. In this play, therefore, song is employed definitely as scenery, and, for this reason alone, *As You Like It* constitutes a considerable advance in the dramatist's use of song.

Amiens, the principal singer, is a poet and gifted amateur, not like Feste a professional, nor like Ariel, one to whom it is nature to sing. His two songs are favours besought, not commanded. They are both extremely important in the history of English dramatic song, for they are the first wherein the temperament of the singer is reflected in the lyric. Both songs are charged with poetic emotion tinged with misanthropy—their object is to extol unsheltered solitude and thereby by contrast to make society appear unfavourably.

The first song, *Under the greenwood tree* (Act II, Sc. 5), serves to make us acquainted personally with Jaques, of whom we have heard previously. In this scene, Jaques is the champion of realism just as eventually his contrary spirit leads him to become a convert to romanticism on the restoration of his friends' fortunes. Amiens sings of the joy of the careless existence, where one lies under the tree and emulates the notes of the birds with nothing to annoy, except the inclemency of the season, and Jaques finds the singing so pleasing that he importunes Amiens for a second stanza, in which all are required to join. Then Jaques turns round and parodies the whole theme of the song—'I'll give you a verse to this note, that I made yesterday in spite of my intention'. Unfortunately, when this scene occurs on the stage, it is usual for Jaques to recite his parody, whereas it were more effective were he to make an effort in some sort to sing it.

No serious meaning ought to be attached to 'Ducdame', which occurs in the parody instead of 'Come hither'; it is just Jaques's jargon, improvised or imitated from some stray vagabond, and we may be content to take it from him that it is 'a Greek invocation to call fools into a circle', even although it be only pedlar's Greek. However, if any one would like to be informed of curious Gaelic and Welsh folk-lore, which may have a possible relation to it, he is referred to Mackay's '*Glossary of Obscure Words in Shakespeare*'.

The second song, *Blow, blow, thou winter wind* (Act II, Sc 7), is sung by Amiens in response to the Duke's 'Give us some music, and good Cousin sing'. The song affords an opportunity for the Duke to be informed of Orlando's circumstances without the spectators being wearied by the repetition of that which is already familiar to them. The theme of the song is a variant of *Under the greenwood tree*, only its misanthropic vein is more pronounced. Winter, with all its harshness, is more tolerable than the ingratitude and insincerity of man.

Some commentators have manufactured difficulties in regard to the meaning of the lines, 'Thy tooth is not so keen, Because thou art not seen'. No man with ordinary common sense is in the least puzzled by the line. As Dr. Johnson pointed out, it means 'Thy rudeness gives the less pain as thou art not seen, as thou art an enemy that dost not brave us with thy presence, and whose unkindnes is therefore not aggravated by insult'.

Arne's setting of the song omits the fine refrain, and it is to be regretted that his is the setting most frequently used on the stage. His *Blow, blow* is by no means one of his happiest ventures, but whatever merit it may possess certain it is that he failed to suggest the open air, and the melody would be as suitable for the summer as for the winter. Tradition lingers long on the stage, as may be gathered from the fact that Colley Cibber's version of *King Richard III* survived in the theatre down to the time of Irving, and consequently there is little hope of Arne's setting disappearing from the stage in our time.

It is important to note that neither Amiens's songs in this comedy nor Balthazar's in *Much Ado* ought to be addressed obviously to the audience. They are songs to the other characters on the stage, and therefore the singer is prohibited from advancing to the footlights as he is far too prone to do in modern practice.

In a side scene (Act IV, Sc. 2), usually omitted in modern representations, we have, at Jaques's request, a song, *What shall he have that killed the deer?* The scene is evidently intended to cover up the break of two hours agreed upon in the previous scene between Rosalind and Orlando—a device rendered superfluous by the modern drop curtain. I can see no sound reason why Scenes 1 to 3 should not proceed as one uninterrupted scene—playgoers are not exacting as to lapse of time, for they are never so absolutely bereft of their senses as not to be aware that they are witnessing a pretence. One is intolerant of the interruptions to which one is subjected in the modern theatre, and just when the spectators' interest has been aroused and piqued by the events in Scene I, it is folly to let it escape and to be compelled to make efforts to regain it. It would therefore be advisable to retain this episode without change of location and thus to keep the action continuous. If *As You Like It* were more generally regarded as a pictorial representation of sylvan life in its various phases, then the idea of making this hunting party a connecting link between two incidents would be better appreciated.

The scene ends very abruptly, after the conclusion of the song, in a manner quite unlike Shakespeare's usual practice. Perhaps if we had had a full description of the stage business, as in *The Merry Wives*, the deficiency might have been supplied. That Jaques should be dumb after the song had been rendered passes belief. Possibly some lines have been dropped by the printer. More probable it is that the party, which Jaques has encountered, is on its road home to the Duke, and it stops for a moment by the way, and that the last strains of the song are uttered as the singer and his companions are leaving the stage. It is desirable to occupy as little time as possible, for naturally the audience is all agog to know the sequel to Rosalind's appointment with Orlando.

Music was set to the song, as a round for four basses, by John Hilton, junior, organist of St. Margaret's, Westminster; he was born in 1599 and died in 1657.

Finally, in Act V, Scene 4, we have the ever delightful Spring Song, *It was a lover and his lass*, sung by two page boys sitting on either side of Touchstone, who presumably joined in the lines common to all the stanzas. From the context, it may be inferred that the boys sing in unison, 'both in a tune like two gipsies on a horse'. (One of these boys would afterwards take the part of Hymen.)

To the ditty there appears a setting in Thomas Morley's '*First Book of Airs or little short songs*', 1600. This setting is the ideal of what a Shakespearian setting ought to be, for it exactly fits not only the subject of the song but also the character of the fresh boys appointed to sing it. A dramatic song differs from any other song most of all in the fact that the singer, who attempts to sing it, must also impersonate the character for whom it was originally devised. This fact is far too frequently overlooked by composers in their settings for Shakespearian lyrics—they have only read the words and have not considered who the singer is. There is vitality, too, in the traditional setting, a ringing metal quality admirably suited to English singing.

The scene, wherein the song is contained, was evidently added—it has no bearing whatever on the development of the action, unless we assume that it was designed that, by means of the song, lapse of time should be indicated, that the season had now changed from the boisterous Winter of Amiens's songs to the bright and cheery Spring of the Pages. It is, however, more probable that the episode was specially devised to meet the growing taste for song and possibly to counter the attractions of the Children at Blackfriars, where there were the best trained choristers the metropolis possessed. But while the addition may have been made and for the motive named, yet it is no less clear that Shakespeare did not allow the feature to go to waste, but caused it to serve the same dramatic end, as did the other songs in the comedy, namely to act as scenery.

Originally Published in Richmond Noble, *Shakespeare's Use of Song* (Oxford: Oxford University Press, 1923): 69–78.

THE ENGLISH COMIC CHARACTERS
J. B. Priestley
1925

TOUCHSTONE

As the sunlight filters through the leaves of Arden, scattering gold along its
paths and deep into its glades, and the persons of the company there, who 'fleet
the time carelessly, as they did in the golden age,' pass and repass, hardly
distinguishable, in their travel-stained russet and green, from the background of
forest, we notice that two figures stand out in sharp relief. One is the sad-suited
Jaques and the other is Touchstone, bright in his motley. The eye sets these two
apart from the rest of the company, and so too does the mind of the spectator,
for indeed Jaques and Touchstone stand apart; they are *in* the forest, but, unlike
the others for the moment, they are not *of* the forest; they remain detached,
unconquered by any prevailing enthusiasms, critical. This fact has often been
noted by the commentators, and the matter has been put very shortly by Sir
Arthur Quiller-Couch: 'The comedy, then, is less a comedy of dramatic event
than a playful fantastic criticism of life: wherein a courtly society being
removed to the greenwood, to picnic there, the Duke Senior can gently moralise
on the artificiality he has left at home, and his courtiers—being courtiers still,
albeit loyal ones —must ape his humour. But this in turn, being less than
sincere, needs salutary mockery: wherefore Shakespeare invents Jaques and
Touchstone, critics so skilfully opposed, to supply it.' Jaques can be set aside
for the moment, left to his endless contemplation: our business is with the critic
in motley.

To many it will seem strange that a comic figure should have any claim to
the title of critic, whatever that title may happen to mean. But Touchstone is no
ordinary comic figure; he is the representative, and easily the best
representative (Falstaff stands by himself), of a special class of comic figures.
Unlike most other humorous characters, he has no unconscious absurdities, and
that is why he cannot be counted among those who wear the fine flower of the
ridiculous; he is not laughable in himself, he is only droll by vocation.

Although he is a Clown, a Fool, he is obviously a superior member of his order; he is no common buffoon making the most of some natural deformity and finding his fun in bladder play and monkey tricks, but the first of Shakespeare's great Fools, a professional wit and humorist, who publishes his jests and sarcasms daily at the dinnertable instead of bringing them out in octavo in the spring and autumn publishing seasons. Our laughter is his applause. It may be sometimes necessary for him to turn himself into a butt, a target for his witty superiors, for, as Celia remarks, 'the dulness of the fool is the whetstone of the wits'; but actually there is little of Celia's or anyone's wit that is whetted on the dullness of Touchstone. Certainly for us he is no mere butt, for we laugh with him and not at him. Even when he is gabbling nonsense, and that is not often, he is, of course, angling for a laugh and usually preparing to launch some shrewd home-truth. Nor must it be forgotten that the fashion in wit changes, and that the poor nonsense that Touchstone occasionally achieves once passed for wit. When Elizabeth's dramatists and poets were all scribbling and the playhouses were packed, language was like a new glittering toy that had only to be tossed rapidly from speaker to speaker to set the house in a roar. Those were the days when bearded gentlemen, resting between two epics of endurance and courage, could get drunk on metaphors and similes and dance with delight under a shower of puns: language was not yet locked up in dictionaries but grew apace, new words glimmering on the horizon like Eldorado. The verbal battledore and shuttlecock played by Rosalind, Celia, and Touchstone in the first act of *As You Like It* may seem a poor game to us now, but there was a time, before a ball had bounced at Lord's or Wimbledon, when it was as enthralling as good cricket or tennis. And even in these scenes there is a taste of the 'dull fool's' real quality. The Duke puts the matter in a nutshell when he says of Touchstone: 'He uses his folly like a stalking-horse, and, under the presentation of that, he shoots his wit.' Indeed, as Jaques surmised, motley is the only wear for a satirist, who will be allowed to utter the most unpleasant truths so long as he jangles his bells. After all, we murmur, as we see the shafts striking home, it is only the Fool: thus our superiority remains unassailed and vanity sits more firmly than ever on its throne.

Jaques too bears witness to the quality of Touchstone. In that famous speech, describing their meeting in the forest, he recognises a fellow philosopher, in his new acquaintance:

> One that hath been a courtier;
> And says, if ladies be but young and fair,
> They have the gift to know't: and in his brain—
> Which is as dry as the remainder biscuit
> After a voyage,—he hath strange places cramm'd

With observation, the which he vents
In mangled forms. . . .

And ever afterwards, he pursues Touchstone through the greenwood as the lovers pursue their ladies, and it is doubtful if some of Touchstone's escapades are not staged purely for his amusement; though Touchstone, with the detachment of the genuine humorist, is quite capable of acting foolishly merely for the satisfaction of enjoying his own folly. There is, of course, a strain of patronage, of easy contempt, in Jaques' attitude towards Touchstone; but then rank has not been forgotten even in Arden, where the courtiers are only playing at adversity, are only staging a pastoral. Moreover, this same strain is discovered in Jaques' attitude towards everything and everybody. This cynic-sentimentalist deserves a word to himself. Ever since the delighted commentators have made the discovery that Jaques is not merely the poet's mouthpiece but a distinct character like the rest of the personages in the comedy, they have pressed hard upon him and abused him without stint. He is almost regarded as the villain of the piece. One would suppose that critics are themselves men of thought rather than men of action, even though they are often more active than thoughtful, and yet, oddly enough, the very sight of a contemplative character, such as Jaques, always sends them into a rage. From their diatribes it would be easy to imagine that all the harm in the world is done by the few eccentric persons who stand on one side to watch the tragi-comedy of existence and are content to find entertainment in their own thoughts. That the melancholy of Jaques is not a very serious business, that it is a piece of whimsical self-indulgence, half play-acting, goes without saying; but there is room in Arden for his whims just as there is for the antics of the Duke, the courtiers, and the lovers. Though Duke Senior criticises Jaques somewhat roughly, actually there is as much to be said for the one as for the other. Indeed, Jaques is the more consistent, for at the very end, hearing that the usurping Duke has taken to religion, he decides to join him:

Out of these convertites
There is much matter to be heard and learned. . . .

Whereas Duke Senior, for all his comfortable talk after lunch, surrounded by his admiring courtiers, of 'sermons in stones, and good in everything,' shows no great reluctance to return to 'the envious court' when his time comes. But though we preach tolerance for Jaques, we need not be blind to his defects. His attitude of mind is sickly. And as he has the apparent softness, so too he has the real hardness of the chronic querulous invalid. Although he can weep over wounded deer, we feel, and rightly too, that there is really something hard, inelastic, griping about his mind. This is because he is that not unfamiliar type, the pure seeker after sensations: he does not identify himself with anything in the whole world, but uses experience as if it were merely a restaurant to dine in; he can enjoy, for he enjoys his cynicism, his tears, his exquisite disillusion, and not least, for it gives support to all the rest, his massive feeling of superiority, but it is impossible for him to be really happy because never for a single moment can he forget himself. Tasting life is not living any more than dabbling a hand in the water is swimming. Jaques has never waved farewell to pride and secure self-possession and dived into experience, there to discover real sorrow and joy, genuine bitterness, and, perhaps, lasting contentment. He has, like so many of his kind, travelled widely (he boasts of it, you remember, to Rosalind, and is neatly dismissed), but actually he has gained little by it. He imagined, as most of us have done at some time or other, that under the enchantment of distance the one drastic step could be taken, that in some far-off country, among alien faces and to the strange music of foreign tongues, he could somehow slip out of himself, throw off at last the burden of the peering, shivering self, and so do that which he had long affected to despise, namely, grapple with reality, plunge into the wash and roar of real emotions and risk all; but having imagined this, he found that distance had no magic so potent, and so slipped back into delicate untruth. Love is the enemy of such sentimentalism, whose pallid shoots are scorched by the sun of its joy or beaten down by the hail of its sorrow; and, it will be noticed, the lovers in the forest, Orlando, Rosalind, have little time to spare for Jaques, and dismiss him and his elaborate but flimsy humours with a shrug. He on his side is clearly uneasy in the presence of Love and its votaries and is significantly delighted with Touchstone's mockery of the passion. After all, what is love but the passionate awareness of other selves, and what has this— alas!—to do with Jaques and all his kind?

Now, as we have seen, Jaques and Touchstone stand in somewhat similar relation to the rest of the company. They are 'the critics,' detached from the main action, observing, mocking. Whatever departs from sincerity receives a flick of the whip from them; or, if you will, they supply the chorus to the piece; one, the sad-suited gentleman, this somewhat eighteenth-century figure with his exquisite sensibility and his lack of real warm human sympathy, plays the part of cynical-sentimental-moralistic chorus; the other, motleying for more than mere beef and ale, an embassy from the Spirit of Comedy, supplies the comic chorus. But while these two seem to run together most of the way, Touchstone parodying to Jaques' applause, there is a very real and very important difference in their respective attitudes. Motley is a better critic than Melancholy. He is a better critic because, unlike Jaques, he does not completely detach himself from his fellow mortals but identifies himself with them; he does not say, in effect, 'What beasts you are!' but 'What fools we are!'; and so, like a true comic genius, he is universal. He does not stand entirely apart, but plays the courtier and the pastoral lover like the rest, only taking care that everything he does shall be plunged into his own atmosphere of exaggeration and absurdity; he parodies humanity, which looked at from one angle is fundamentally ridiculous, in his own activities and in his own person; and he does this not simply because he is a Fool, a professional humorist, but also because he is by temperament and inclination a kind of comic philosopher. In this leafy republic of Arden, with its moralising gentlemen, rhyming lovers, passionate shepherds, where so many moods and whims are being dandled throughout the long golden days, the Comic Spirit, scenting profitable negotiations, has established its embassy, and Touchstone, full-dressed in his motley, is the ambassador.

The two persons who know him best and who are responsible for his being in the forest at all, Rosalind and Celia, rather miss his real character: they see the Fool but are blind to the comic philosopher. To them he is 'the clownish fool.' It is true that Rosalind has her suspicions. When the three of them, wandering in the forest, chance to overhear the passionate Silvius describe the effect of passion, Rosalind exclaims:

> Alas, poor shepherd! searching of thy wound,
> I have by hard adventure found mine own.

and Touchstone, very characteristically, makes the whole thing ridiculous by the use of a few grotesque images:

> And I mine. I remember, when I was in love I broke my sword upon a stone, and bid him take that for coming a-night to Jane Smile: and I remember the kissing of her batlet, and the cow's dugs that her pretty chapp'd hands had milk'd: and I remember the wooing of a peascod instead of her; from whom I took two cods, and, giving her them again, said with weeping tears, Wear these for my sake. We that are true lovers run into strange capers; but as all is mortal in nature, so is all nature in love mortal in folly.

At which Rosalind remarks:

> Thou speak'st wiser than thou art 'ware of;

and Touchstone replies, enigmatically:

> Nay, I shall ne'er be 'ware of mine own wit till I break my shins against it.

But then two romantic young ladies, grappling with the problem of lovers and fathers, are no audience for a humorist of Touchstone's metal. Though both have wit and humour of their own, one of them, Rosalind, being famous for her high spirits, much of Touchstone's humour is of that mysterious and faintly disquieting kind that they and all their sisters would now describe as either 'silly' or 'vulgar.' It has a trick of reducing everything to one grotesque level; there is nothing that it cannot twist into matter for a laugh or, at least, a sardonic grin; and against this kind of humour, a very mannish affair, the feminine mind, which has hallowed chambers that must be spared the jangle of motley's bells, has always vigorously protested. Rosalind's humour—and what would Arden be without her ripple of laughter!—is very different from Touchstone's; it does not try to lay bare the tangled twisted roots of the Tree of Life, but plays, like a wavering gleam of sunshine or a cluster of bright birds, in its high foliage; it is indeed playfulness, girlish high spirits, rather than humour, something April-hearted, for ever dancing on the very edge of tears. Rosalind, once in the forest and certain of her lover, is a happy woman who knows that now her greatest ship is snugly in port she can afford to frolic for an hour at the quayside. Secure in her knowledge of their love, she can torment and tease her bewildered Orlando now just as afterwards she will continue to torment and tease him and his children after him.

But if Rosalind and Celia hardly testify to Touchstone's quality as a humorist, they do show us, in one flash, something of his quality as a man. They pay him a magnificent compliment, for they single him out to be their companion in their flight to Arden. 'Should he not be a comfort to our travel?' whispers Rosalind, plotting. Celia replies: 'He'll go along o'er the wide world with me; leave me alone to woo him.' This shows us a new Touchstone. Companions for such a journey are not lightly chosen, even by a Rosalind: our comic philosopher is clearly a man to be depended on; Motley covers a stout heart. And if Rosalind's suggestion tells us much, Celia's reply tell us even more. 'He'll go along o'er the wide world with me'; this demure young lady knows her power; she has the Fool in thrall. He is not then altogether in the service of the Comic Spirit; his detachment is not complete, for now, it seems, he shows himself to be a romantic at heart, ready to exchange his comfortable berth at court, that dinner-table which is the field of glory for the humorist, for the discomforts and dangers of secret flight. Celia's father, Duke Frederick, may not appear an ideal master for a Touchstone, for he passes from crude villainy to equally crude conversion, and it is not of such unwholesome persons that a humorist's best audience is composed; but nevertheless he seems to have held Touchstone ('the roynish clown, at whom so oft your Grace was wont to laugh') in some esteem, and it says much for the Fool's devotion and courage that he should have quitted such a post to go with the 'foolish runaways.' When the three of them stagger into the forest, Rosalind crying, 'Well, this is the Forest of Arden,' and Touchstone replying, 'Ay, now am I in Arden; the more fool I; when I was at home, I was in a better place; but travellers must be content'; he speaks only the bare truth. He has flung away safety and comfort and applause for a lady's whim, and has thereby betrayed his genial cynicism. Remove the motley, the cap and the bells, the irreverent jests and sarcasms, the ripe disillusionment, and there remains Touchstone the romantic, set wandering by a glance from his lady's eye, a wave of her hand. Thus he arrives in Arden.

Romance, however, having enticed him into her own green Arcadia, has to be content with that and nothing more, for once there, Touchstone returns to his ancient loyalties and promptly goes about his own business of parody and mockery, of clowning illuminated by criticism. The chief targets for his wit are the pastoral life, which the Duke and his companions are busy praising with suspicious enthusiasm, and the passion of love, which is leading so many of the gentle foresters into delightful affectations and whimsies. Touchstone brings scepticism into the greenwood. Hear him with Corin, the old shepherd:

CORIN: And how like you this shepherd's life, Master Touchstone?

TOUCHSTONE: Truly, shepherd, in respect of itself, it is a good life; but in respect that it is a shepherd's life, it is naught. In respect that it is solitary, I like it very well; but in respect that it is private, it is a very vile life. Now, in respect it is in the fields, it pleaseth me well; but in respect it is not in the court, it is tedious. As it is a spare life, look you, it fits my humour well; but as there is no more plenty in it, it goes much against my stomach. . . .

'Zimmermann's celebrated work on Solitude,' Hazlitt remarks, 'discovers only *half* the sense of this passage.' Touchstone does indeed lay a finger, not merely upon the defects of a pastoral life, but upon those human limitations that prevent our declaring, with any sincerity, that any way of life is perfect; we cannot—more's the pity!—be in two places at once, cannot have our cake and eat it too; so every gain enumerated by Touchstone is quickly followed by its corresponding loss, every positive by its negative, and all cancels out. Well might he conclude by asking, 'Hast any philosophy in thee, shepherd?' He enjoys himself hugely in the company of this shepherd, to whom he is 'Master Touchstone,' the gentleman from the court, and not the 'dull Fool' or 'the roynish clown'; and it is good to hear him discussing the likeness between shepherds and courtiers, to see him trotting this simple companion from quip to quip, for he does it all with immense relish, and all somewhat condescendingly and with a hint of negligence, like a professional conjurer practising a few tricks in front of his landlady. When he concludes by rebuking Corin for playing Pander in Arcadia:

That is another simple sin in you; to bring the ewes and the ram together, and to offer to get your living by the copulation of cattle; to be bawd to a bell-wether; and to betray a she-lamb of a twelve-month to a crooked-pated, old, cuckoldy ram, out of all reasonable match. If thou be'st not damn'd for this, the Devil himself will have no shepherds; I cannot see how thou shouldst 'scape,

he appears to be unconsciously parodying the hyper-aesthesia of Jaques, who considered Duke Senior as much a usurper as his brother Frederick because he hunted the deer, the 'native burghers' of the place. Most of Touchstone's whimsicalities are of this kind, a distorted reflection of what passes elsewhere in the drama.

When Touchstone does at last meet the Duke, he is at pains to prove that he has been a courtier:

If any man doubt that, let him put me to my purgation. I have trod a measure; I have flatter'd a lady; I have been politic with my friend, smooth with mine enemy; I have undone three tailors; I have had four quarrels, and like to have fought one.

There is no habitual practice of the courtier's, from dancing to sending shopkeepers into bankruptcy, foreign to him, he tells us; and then there follows his famous thrust at those elaborate codes of Honour fashionable among gallants of the time. The quarrel that he almost fought was upon the Seventh Cause:

Upon a lie seven times removed;—bear your body more seeming, Audrey;—as thus, sir: I did dislike the cut of a certain courtier's beard: he sent me word, if I said his beard was not cut well, he was in the mind it was: this is call'd the Retort Courteous. If I sent him word again, it was not well cut, he would send me word, he cut it to please himself: this is call'd the Quip Modest. If again, it was not well cut, he disabled my judgment: this is call'd the Reply Churlish. If again, it was not well cut, he would answer, I spake not true: this is call'd the Reproof Valiant. If again, it was not well cut, he would say, I lied: this is call'd the Countercheck Quarrelsome: and so to the Lie Circumstantial and the Lie Direct.

JAQUES: And how oft did you say his beard was not well cut?

TOUCHSTONE: I durst go no further than the Lie Circumstantial, nor he durst not give me the Lie Direct; and so we measured swords, and parted.

JAQUES: Can you nominate in order now the degrees of the lie?

TOUCHSTONE: O sir, we quarrel in print, by the book; as you have books for your good manners: I will name you the degrees. The first, the Retort

Courteous; the second, the Quip Modest; the third, the Reply Churlish; the fourth, the Reproof Valiant; the fifth, the Countercheck Quarrelsome; the sixth, the Lie with Circumstance; the seventh, the Lie Direct. All these you may avoid, but the Lie Direct; and you may avoid that too with an *if.* I knew when seven justices could not take up a quarrel; but, when the parties were met themselves, one of them thought but of an *if,* as, *If you said so, then I said so;* and they shook hands, and swore brothers. Your *if* is the only peacemaker; much virtue in *if.*

All this was very much to the point at the time, for the book to which Touchstone refers, *Of Honour and Honourable Quarrels* (with chapters on the Lie and its circumstances), had appeared only a few years before the play, and was probably much in use. Now, the satire passes us by, for as individuals we have long ago let such nonsense go whistling down the wind; but sanity comes first to individuals and only leavens whole communities after long ages, and we can still observe empires and republics occupied with these questions of honour and honourable quarrels, and their foreign offices giving one another the Reproof Valiant and the Countercheck Quarrelsome, and so going forward to the Lie Direct before they set twenty thousand cannon roaring for honour's sake. Perhaps the Fool still titters in Arden.

So Touchstone goes wandering about the greenwood, lounging from one group to another, now mimicking Orlando's bad verse, now dismissing a yokel, now joining the tuneful pages in a catch:

> This carol they began that hour,
> With a hey, and a ho, and a hey nonino,
> How that a life was but a flower
> In spring-time, the only pretty ring-time . . .

their voices coming down the years to us and their lovely idle words outlasting so many treatises and grave proclamations; and so he wanders, fleeting the time between duke and shepherd, courtier and lover. And as it is both his business and his pleasure to mock the fashion of the hour, he does not fail to play the pastoral lover himself. If Orlando must have his Rosalind, Oliver his Celia, Silvius his Phebe, so Touchstone must have his Audrey. For making this somewhat hasty and unequal alliance, he has been taken to task by some of his harsher critics, one of whom claps him forthwith into the dock and proceeds with the charge: 'He (Touchstone) does the contrary to Rosalind and Orlando: he misuses this natural life of retirement, in the intention of again casting off Audrey at a convenient season. He uses the opportunity which here presents itself, without possessing the fidelity which according to Lodge's romance should belong to the place. He seems equally devoid of the morality of either town or country.' Which shows us how dangerous it is to play the fool in some companies. The fact is that Touchstone cannot worm his way into the idyll; there is no conventional shepherdess, no lovely pink-and-white and entirely unreal Phebe, for him; he stays outside the pastoral and remains in this world, and so has to be content with an Audrey, that is, with the kind of damsel really to be found in the countryside, neither superlatively beautiful nor intelligent, but a great gawky country lass. With poor Audrey's unconscious aid, he contrives to stage a most adroit parody of pastoral love as it was depicted by the poets; his sceptical humour lets the east wind of reality into this great artificial palm-house that we call Arden.

He can indite verses as good as, if not better than, those of Orlando, and he certainly has more wit, but—alas!—his lady, being no Rosalind but a genuine creature of the countryside, can understand neither:

When a man's verses cannot be understood, nor a man's good wit seconded with the forward child, understanding, it strikes a man more dead than a great reckoning in a little room.—Truly, I would the gods had made thee poetical.

Audrey, good soul, cannot even pretend to poetry, and has, indeed, a most disarming knowledge of her own limitations, even confessing to a want of beauty, which may be joined in time, in Touchstone's opinion, by other defects, notably sluttishness. None of this, however, disturbs the ironist in motley for an instant: he revels in the incongruity of it all. And while the other lovers, triple-dyed in romance, are swearing eternal constancy, he is calmly welcoming a doubtful ceremony by a doubtful parson because 'he is not like to marry me well; and not being well married, it will be a good excuse for me hereafter to leave my wife.' But he is only seeing all round the question. Just as there is a possibility that, after all, the romantic lovers may not be true to one another for ever, so too it is possible that Touchstone may cleave to his Audrey a little longer than a couple of months or so. It is absurd that he should take up with her at all, waving aside, with the most delightful air of condescension, her faithful William; but then, what would you, surely it is all absurd, this business of courtship and marriage; rapid mating is in the air and reason has set behind a cloud and Audrey will do as well as another, nay, better than most, because she allows him more scope for his quips; and for the rest—'As the ox hath his bow, sir, the horse his curb, and the falcon her bells, so man hath his desires; and as pigeons bill, so wedlock would be nibbling.' The relation between Touchstone and his stolid mistress is really nothing but the reverse side, the unpoetical, comic, gross side, of the relation between Orlando and Rosalind, all ardour and bloom and young laughter, beyond the reach of disillusion. Shake them up together and out of them both could be fashioned the actual relations between most men and women in this world; and Shakespeare, who knew most things, knew this too, and so gave us both sides of the question. By the time he came to create Touchstone, his comic relief had become something more than buffoonery flung in at random, it had become comment, criticism.

That Touchstone's courtship of Audrey, as Hazlitt remarks, 'throws a degree of ridicule on the state of wedlock itself,' must be admitted, but both his vocation and his natural bent of mind urge Touchstone towards ridicule, and there is, in the last resort, more to be said about his queer courtship than this, more, indeed, than has apparently been said anywhere. That he is not seriously in love is obvious enough, but this is probably only because he cannot be entirely serious about anything. Even his surprisingly romantic devotion to his young mistress Celia, probably has a comical air: we have not heard him on the subject. Yet it is quite possible that a lapse of time that would find Oliver deserting Celia and taking to the forest again, to haunt the neighbourhood of Phebe, now the bored wife of Silvius, would also find Touchstone and Audrey still jogging along together, the gentleman still making mysterious jests and criticisms, and the lady fixing her stolid gaze upon the solid fruits of his jesting and not troubling her head about his whims and fancies. Geniuses, we are told, commonly find their mates among such peasant women, who alone can root them in the earth. For all their Martext and their mock marriage, these two, like the rest of the lovers, come in the end to face Hymen and are duly despatched—

> You and you are sure together,
> As the Winter to foul weather,

—a simile that in such a climate as this suggests a more than common security in their relation. And consider, before we leave him, Touchstone's introduction of his Audrey to the Duke: 'A poor virgin, sir, an ill-favour'd thing, sir, but mine own.' This, it will be said, is not the speech of a man in love; nor is it, but it might very well be the speech of a humorist, a dry, sceptical humorist, who is as near to being in love as he is likely to be. 'An ill-favour'd thing, sir, but mine own': the great romantic lovers could never have uttered this; Rosalind is not Orlando's 'ill-favour'd thing'; and yet the phrase, whose popularity is proved by its frequent misquotation, like a well-shot bolt goes hurtling home and we hear from far-away, faintly but unmistakably, the ringing bell that proclaims the truth of its aim. This world being what it is—and how well Motley knows the world—it describes with more accuracy than all the honeyed, golden speeches of our Romeos and Antonies the actual feelings that men and women, not poets and born lovers, ever ready to shower glittering words upon any newly found deity, but workaday men and women, have for one another; and as your mood runs, you may throw the emphasis upon 'the ill-favour'd thing' and laugh away the follies of youth; or, more justly, you may wait for the end of the phrase and see the significance, the odd pathos that somehow finds its way into all human relations, of the last three words, 'but mine own,' and so fall to wondering rather than laughing or perhaps to doing both at once. And no matter which colouring your mood takes on, you will find some correspondence in colour, some answer, in Touchstone, deep in Arden, for is he not parti-coloured, being in Motley? A rare fellow.

Originally published in J. B. Priestley.
(London: Bodley Head, 1928): 18–37.

SHAKESPEARE AND HIS PLAYS FROM A WOMAN'S POINT OF VIEW
Rosa E. Grindon
1930

"OTHELLO" is a tale of night, and night's darksome deeds. "As You Like It" scintillates with sunshine. After the first act, the scene is the lovely Forest of Arden, where all the time is "fleeted carelessly as in the golden world." To some approaching it heavy-hearted, weary of foot and hungry, it is an "uncouth" forest, a desert of inaccessible boughs. To those who know it well it is a beautiful wild wood. Lovely are its hills and hollows, the murmuring stream where the osiers grow, the lovely glades, oaks mossed with age, with ancient roots peeping out. There were caves where men could hide, venison and fruits that men could eat.

In this forest of Arden three distinct groups of fugitives, flying from wrong and oppression, find that "sweet are the uses of adversity."

In this exquisite "summer-time play" none of the oppressed have burdened themselves with bitterness; their life in the forest is altogether lovely, because they have remembered Hamlet's saying, "There's nothing good or bad, but thinking makes it so."

They themselves made the life sweeter than that of the painted courts from which they have been driven.

There are two distinct opposing forces that send these three groups of people into the forest, namely, a hate born of fear, and its exact opposite, the most self-sacrificing love.

The Duke is expelled by the ambition of his brother. But with him are the many lords, who give up house, lands, and home for a devotion to a man who can give them nothing in return.

Rosalind is driven away by the fear and hate of her uncle, but she is accompanied by the most truly loving friend that Shakespeare has depicted. Celia, out of her love, cheerfully gives up her exalted station, and her heirship to the dukedom.

Orlando, by the twin force of hate and fear, becomes a fugitive. But Adam, full of love, drops the "lean and slippered pantaloon" in a moment, offers the savings of a lifetime, and pleads that he, even at fourscore, may be allowed to limp the weary steps in pure love, ready to give up the home he has had for sixty-five years, and to face the world with his young master.

Thus the three groups have moved to the forest of Arden, having no material wealth but charged with a wealth of love. Well may we hear this in the opening song:—

> Under the greenwood tree,
> Who loves to lie with me
> And turn his merry note
> Unto the sweet bird's throat,
> Come hither, come hither, come hither;
> Here shall he see
> No enemy
> But winter and rough weather.

We all know that even the most harmonious combinations in the world have to strike some minor chords. However idyllic the life, an occasional note is struck portraying the infirmity of man.

In the novel by Dr. Lodge that Shakespeare has dramatised and renamed "As You Like It" the sombre tones are unpleasingly accentuated by a band of robbers. Shakespeare has a different mode, and one of his own invention.

Among the travellers to the forest of Arden are two who set off with mixed motives—Jaques and Touchstone.

Touchstone has been, and still is, devoted to Celia, and Celia's prophecy that he would go along o'er the wide world with her is justified. His motives, nevertheless, are mixed; for he wishes to please Celia and also to gratify his desire for travel.

When he arrives in the forest he says:—

Now am I in Arden, more fool I, when I was at home I was in a better place.

Seeing Rosalind at his elbow he adds:—

But travellers must be content.

Following Touchstone's personal career we shall see his quick wit. He knows how to take an oath and how to break it, yet not be forsworn; he knows to a nicety how far he can go in a quarrel without having to fight his way out and, finally, but for Jaques he would have deceived the innocent rustic maid, Audrey, with a false marriage.

Jaques has not gone to the forest for pure love of the Duke, and he tells us, as Touchstone does, his version of the life in the forest.

The lords have been singing the most beloved of songs, "Under the greenwood tree." But when they get to the lines:—

> Who doth ambition shun,
> And loves to live i' the sun,
> Seeking the food he eats,
> And pleased with what he gets,

it is too much for Jaques, and he gives them a verse which he says he wrote the day before:—

> If it do come to pass
> That any man turn ass,
> Leaving his wealth and ease,
> A stubborn will to please,
> There shall he see
> Gross fools as he.

There we have Jaques on himself, not for love had he left wealth and ease, and any man who does so turns ass.

Where we come across the two girls in Scene 2, Celia replies to Rosalind's suggestion that they fall in love, as follows:—

> Love no man in good earnest; nor no further in sport neither, when with safety of a pure blush thou may'st in honour come off again.

Rosalind thinks Celia is in earnest in not wishing her even to make sport of falling in love. She drops the suggestion at once and asks:—

> What shall be our sport then?

Celia suggests something very much tamer.

Some critics have said that they cannot understand why Shakespeare married Celia to Oliver at the close, and suggest that Shakespeare was at a loss in finding a husband for Celia; that he used Oliver as a makeshift.

Then misconception has arisen because much that takes place regarding Oliver is in the "still background." In other words we do not see the happenings with our own eyes. The events are described to us in narrative form, and to hear of a thing is not nearly so impressive as to see it.

At the same time, this cannot explain all the misconception of Oliver's character. To Orlando we give our hearts at once, and his enemies become ours. Orlando can do nothing wrong, whereas Oliver can do nothing right.

The old father, Sir Roland, has three sons, the eldest only lightly endowed by nature, the youngest a very paragon of youth, for whatever he undertakes he carries through. He is the image of his father, both in form and feature, mind and heart, and thus the valiant old man lives again in the child of his old age.

Says Oliver, "He's gentle; never schooled, and yet learned; full of noble device, of all sorts enchantingly beloved; and indeed, so much in the heart of the world, and especially of my own people, who best know him, that I am altogether misprised."

The very virtues of the lad have been his enemies. That the elder brother should become jealous is more a sign of human nature than of villainy.

The father had not thought so badly of him, or surely he would not have left the two younger sons in his charge. And we find that he had done his duty quite properly by the second son, Jaques, whom (as Orlando said) "he keeps at school, and report speaks goldenly of his profit thereby." But the younger brother he had utterly neglected through his jealousy.

When the story opens he has committed no act of villainy, but has simply left undone that which he ought to have done.

Orlando stands up for his rights. Sharp words are passed, and, taunted by being called "boy," young Orlando springs at Oliver's throat, and holds him in deadly grip, saying, "I would not take this hand from thy throat till the other had pulled out thy tongue, wert thou not my brother."

We may palliate the fury of Orlando, we may admire his pluck, and wonder at his strength and bravery. Yet he had, indeed, rashly thrown down the gauntlet, and he knew there was no more chance of help from his brother. Hence he will take his chance against the odds and try for the wrestling championship.

Seeing him come through with flying colours Oliver plans diabolical treachery, and sets fire to his lodgings in the night.

Orlando's attack upon his brother was caused by the latter's neglect, whereas Oliver's treacherous attack on Orlando was the immediate outcome of his own provocation.

At court, it was thought that Orlando had gone off with Rosalind and Celia, and the Duke tells Oliver that he must find Orlando, thinking in that way he will hear of his own daughter. Thus Oliver goes off in pursuit, and from his appearance as a "wretched ragged man o'er grown with hair" he must have suffered great hardships.

While in this dejected condition, he lies down under a tree and falls asleep. His treacherous plotting against Orlando is now to take effect, and poetical justice is righteously meted out to him. While asleep he is attacked by a snake which winds itself round his throat and threatens to strike his mouth, thus duplicating Orlando's attack upon his throat and the threat to wrench his tongue out. As Orlando approaches it glides away, but under a bush hard by crouches a hungry lioness ready to spring!

Orlando, seeing her, would have neglected his duty to Oliver, even as Oliver had neglected his duty towards him. Twice, we read, he turned away, but his better nature prompted him to give battle to the lioness, and risk his own life to save his brother.

This battle was no light matter. The beast seized him by the arm, and the encounter was so great that it woke the sleeping man. He woke to find Orlando, whose life he had attacked, risking everything to save him. Oliver was converted by this noble deed, and his jealousy died.

Then comes the test of Oliver's repentance. Orlando takes his brother to the Duke, and Oliver's wants are attended to. Food and clothing are given him, after which the two brothers go to Orlando's cave. Orlando, worn out with fatigue and loss of blood, drops unconscious to the ground.

How easy for Oliver to let his brother bleed to death! But he brought him back to consciousness, bound up his wounds, then departed on his errand to Rosalind and Celia, to whom he made an open and full confession of his sins and repentance.

Notice now the first sign of interest between Celia and Oliver that leads to love.

He addresses both with a question, but it is Celia who replies. His second question may also apply to both, or, if to one, it would be to Rosalind, the man, as owner of the cottage; yet Celia again replies.

Later when he says. "If you would know what man I am," etc., it is Celia who says, "I pray you tell it."

Finally, it is Celia who asks him to go with them to their cottage. The falling in love of Oliver and Celia is more natural than that of Othello and Desdemona.

Now let us turn to Jaques. Of all the characters introduced to us by Shakespeare the so-called "melancholy Jaques" most surely provokes a smile. This in itself is a good testimony to the fact that his melancholy is not real. It is assumed to give him licence to talk about himself. He has not the personal sympathy that is sad over the woes or wickedness of other people. He sums up the world as a thing of nought, and looks upon himself as a thing apart from the world. To Jaques there is but himself; all the rest are evil. As the prophet of old said, "I, even I alone, am left."

He thinks himself very wise, so that if he had his own way he could cleanse the whole world of error.

The Duke's character is one of great simplicity, but his outlook covers a wider field than that of Jaques. The one dwells upon the surface, the other goes deeper, and straight from the shoulder does he fire his rebuke.

"Fie on thee! I can tell thee what thou woulds't do. Most mischievous foul sin in chiding sin. To disgorge all the evil thoughts of evil things that thou thyself with license of free fool has caught in the life of the libertine that thou has lived; most mischievous foul sin, indeed, to disgorge that into the world."

After all, Jaques' remedy amounts to nothing but talk, and, as the Duke says, to talk of evil is not to remedy it.

Far better to let loose upon the world beautiful thoughts, such as those springing from the Duke's own mind, "Sweet are the uses of adversity," "Look to the running brook for our books," "Listen to what the trees have to say to us," etc.

For all the Duke's simplicity, Jaques is no match for him in argument. The Duke may search for Jaques, he may love to cope with him in his sullen fits, but Jaques does not like to cope with the Duke.

Later in the play there is a scene which some critics say is nothing but a stop-gap, a makeshift device to introduce another song. But it is really a striking commentary by Shakespeare himself on this supposed sympathy of Jaques for the wounded deer.

Jaques welcomes the men who return from the chase, bringing the spoils with them. He proclaims the man who killed the deer as a Roman conqueror, to be presented to the Duke with the horns of the deer on his head, and he closes the scene with a pæan of victory.

The old may possibly bear with a man like Jaques, but not so the young.

The Duke tries to convince Jaques by argument. Orlando gives him very short commons, and bluntly tells him that he'll find the image of a fool by looking into a brook. Jaques does not see the point, and he calmly remarks that he would see nothing there but himself! It had never dawned upon him that anybody could ever look upon him as a fool.

He is aghast! The talker has nothing to say in self-defence. All he can do is to flee, crying,

> I'll tarry no longer with you.
> Farewell, good senior.

He meets Rosalind in the forest and boasts of his melancholy. But she laughs at him, and scornfully declared that men like him are nothing short of abominable fellows, and worse than drunkards.

Never again does he try to teach the world, and in the final scene he is actually humble.

Let us touch upon a few ironies of fate occurring in the play.

Twice Rosalind patiently waits for one lover, and on both occasions fate offers another.

Rather a cruel irony comes to Celia. In the opening scene, Rosalind suggests that they shall fall in love, but Celia does not agree. The next thing Rosalind does is to fall in love, fathoms deep.

Celia gives up everything to go to the forest as a companion to Rosalind, and when she gets there she had to "play gooseberry" to Rosalind's lovemaking, a distasteful role.

When at court Rosalind is in trouble, Celia's sympathetic comfortings pass all description. But in the forest, so long as Orlando is there, Rosalind has never a word to throw to Celia, and immediately he is gone she will "find a shadow and sigh until he returns."

No wonder Celia is ready for the first lover that comes along.

There have been very different opinions as to the time of the year when these things happened. Mr. Grindon, in his book on Shakespeare's Flora, says that everything suggests the Autumn. Other writers say the play is redolent of the Spring. The young lioness with her cubs isn't any guide, as young lions are born all the year round.

Probably a long time elapsed while they were in the forest. But the spring song, "It was a lover and his lass" and "The Spring Time, the only pretty ring time" might suggest that the winter is over, and the Spring has come again.

A study of this play must enlarge our own outlook on life. Chiefly it shows us that, wherever we be, in town, court or countryside, in cottage or in ease, we are what we are, irrespective of our surroundings.

Originally published (Manchester: The Policy Holder Journal's Company, 1930): 65–72.

SHAKESPEARE'S WAY
Frederick C. Kolbe
1930

THERE is no more enlightening exercise in the study of dramatic art than to put side by side Shakespeare's *As You Like It* and Lodge's *Rosalind,* and note with a blue pencil in the latter where the former (1) adopts, (2) omits, (3) transposes, (4) changes, and (5) introduces new matter. Lovely as Lodge's pastoral story is, every difference is in favour of the drama. It is an enticing theme, but I must confine myself strictly to my thesis. There is some wonder expressed as to the meaning of the tide. Dowden suggests that it is borrowed from Lodge's dedication to his readers, —"If you like it, so." This is probable enough as far as the form is concerned, but it hardly accounts for the substance. Shakespeare generally did have a substantial meaning in his titles; and I think we shall find that this one is no exception.

I shall not this time begin with the enumerative induction, because there is a historical hint lying more clearly on the surface, though strangely enough it seems not to have caught the eye of the commentators. In 1598, the story goes, a young man named Ben Jonson offered to the Lord Chamberlain's Company a comedy named *Every Man in his Humour.* The play was submitted to Shakespeare and on his warm approval it was accepted and staged. This, they say, was the foundation of the friendship between the two dissimilar characters. The tradition is likely enough, though the evidence of it is characteristically elusive. It is not necessary to go further than the known fact that Shakespeare acted the part of Old Knowell, and thus became familiar with the artistic device which unified Jonson's comedy and is the real reason for its abiding success,— the idea, namely, of presenting each character in a distinctive peculiarity or "humour." In 1599 *As You Like It,* which might almost be renamed "Every Character in its own Caprice,"—which is precisely what "as you like it" means. The usurping Duke, with his strange fits and starts, not excluding his final conversion, is repeatedly called "the *humorous* Duke." Rosalind is the very embodiment of Caprice. Celia has unselfish and incalculable impulses which make her the most gracious figure in the play. Touchstone says: "A poor humour of mine, sir, to take that no man else will." Jaques is a mass of affected cynical melancholy. Orlando and Silvius are "slaves of love," one vauntingly, the other abjectly. Phebe affects the airs of a Lady Disdain. Oliver is as freakish in his hatred as afterwards in his love. Adam nobly exaggerates "the constant service of the antique world." Sir Oliver Martext is a caricature. Corin is the only perfectly normal character, and he is so self-conscious about it that it almost becomes a pose; asked if he has any philosophy in him, he replies:

"No more but that I know the more one sickens the worse at ease he is . . . that the property of rain is to wet, and fire to burn; that good pasture makes fat sheep, and that a great cause of the night is lack of the sun . . . . I am a true labourer: I earn that I eat, get that I wear, owe no man hate, envy no man's happiness; glad of other men's good, content with my harm; and the greatest of my pride is to see my ewes graze and my lambs suck"   (III, 2)

Surely his repudiation of philosophy is almost an affectation.

I think there can be no doubt of the historic connection between the two plays, and I submit it as a distinct and significant contribution to Shakespearian criticism. But even this was not enough. Shakespeare saw the linked variety of "humour" or caprice in Lodge's story, and added to it by the creation of Touchstone and Jaques. But he saw more. He got to the heart of things. Lodge's story was one of *Fortune,* with her uncertain and unstable *gifts,* the goddess of *caprice,* upsetting the order of *Nature* in a topsy-turvy *world.* That was the complex that showed itself in Shakespeare's original, and he brought it so to the surface of his mind to the exclusion of other groups of ideas, that it colours the whole of the play. The five ideas in the words italicised in the last sentence but one are those that force themselves on our attention: each of them occurs over 30 times. Not one of them, be it observed, prominent over the rest: the repetition is fivefold,—Fortune, gifts, caprice, Nature, world.

I must not too easily assume that I am taking my readers with me. Some of them perhaps, not caring to make the induction for themselves, may fancy that I am riding a hobby-horse to death. For their benefit I have pointed out that it is Shakespeare's habit in each play to throw enormous emphasis in one or more passages on his dominant idea or complex. Here is his tell-tale passage in the present play. (I italicise all the relevant words):

"*Cel.* Let us sit and mock the good housewife *Fortune* from her wheel, that her *gifts* may henceforth be bestowed *equally.*
Ros. I would we could do so, for her *benefits* are mightily *misplaced,* and the bountiful blind woman doth most *mistake* in her *gifts* to women.
Cel. 'Tis true; for those that she makes fair she scarce makes honest, and those that she makes honest she makes very ill-favouredly.

Ros. Nay, now thou goest from *Fortune's* office to *Nature's: Fortune* reigns in *gifts* of the *world,* not in the lineaments of *Nature.*

Cel. No! when *Nature* had made a fair creature, may she not by *Fortune* fall into the fire? Though *Nature* hath given us wit to flout at *Fortune,* hath not *Fortune* sent in this fool [Touchstone] to cut off the argument?

Ros. Indeed, there is *Fortune* too hard for *Nature,* when *Fortune* makes *Nature's natural* the cutter-off of *Nature's* wit.

Cel. Peradventure this is not *Fortune's* work neither, but *Nature's;* who, perceiving our *natural* wits too dull to reason of such *goddesses,* hath sent this *natural* for our whetstone: for always the dulness of the fool is the whetstone of the wits." (I, 2)

This passage, after all our argument, ought to be conclusive. We ought not to need to point out how Touchstone says:

"We that are true lovers run into strange *capers;* but as all is mortal in *nature,* so is all *nature* in love mortal in folly." (II, 4)

Again, we have that ever-quoted passage, whose full meaning, by the way, stands out more clearly in the light of this "complex":

> "*Duke.* This wide and universal theatre
> Presents more woful pageants than the scene
> Wherein we play in.
>   *Jaq.* All the *world's* a stage," etc.   (II, 7)

Rosalind certainly knew all about it:

"He was to imagine me his love, his mistress; and I set him every day to woo me: at which time would I, being but a moonish youth, grieve, be effeminate, changeable, longing and liking; proud, fantastical, apish, shallow, inconstant, full of tears, full of smiles, for every passion something, and for no passion truly anything." (III, 2)

One more example will suffice: it is Jaques' description of his own caprice, and if my readers will not believe me now, they will never believe anything:

"I have neither the scholar's melancholy, which is emulation; nor the musician's, which is fantastical; nor the courtier's, which is proud; nor the soldier's, which is ambitious; nor the lawyer's, which is politic; nor the lady's, which is nice; nor the lover's, which is all these: but it is a melancholy of mine own, compounded of many simples, extracted from many objects, and indeed the sundry contemplation of my travels, which, by often rumination, wraps me in a most humorous sadness." (IV, I)

Shakespeare, however, does not leave his world topsy-turvy. His theme is Fortune as the goddess of Caprice, with all her mistakes rectified and harmonised by Love.

(London: Steed & Ward, 1930): 81–86.

SHAKESPEARE AND PSYCHOLOGY
Cumberland Clark
1936

The chief motive for action of the comic character is self-love, its self-deception and attempts to deceive others: the discrepancy between real and feigned character. In *The Two Gentlemen of Verona* the self-love of Proteus is the central point. In *Love's Labour's Lost* self-love is patent in the vain desire for fame shown by the lords of Navarre and their associates. In *All's Well That Ends Well* the proud self-sufficiency of Bertram interferes with the comic character. In *The Merry Wives of Windsor* the gross side of Falstaff's egotism is the ground of comedy. In *Much Ado About Nothing* Claudio's sensitiveness about honour is based on self-love. Self-love, again, produces in Benedick and Beatrice contempt for the opposite sex and fickle abandonment of their own principle, which is the fruit of exaggerated pride. In *Twelfth Night*, above all, we see clearly how, in differing degrees, self-love holds the soul of the prominent characters, and how deeply it is interwoven with the main idea of the piece.

It was Shakespeare who originated, in *Love's Labour's Lost*, the idea of the comedy of manners, handled later in such masterly fashion by Molière. In *The Two Gentlemen of Verona* we have his earliest venture in the field of romantic comedy. His early plays may be regarded as preliminary sketches for the finished pictures of his maturity. Biron gives a foretaste of Benedick, and Julia is a forerunner of the more poetic Viola, just as the Nurse in *Romeo and Juliet* anticipates the rich humour of Falstaff.

In a more detailed consideration of the best-known comedies, we may note in *As You Like It* that the moral purpose of the play expresses itself simply in the praise of self-mastery, equanimity, and self-command, although it is a play of light and free action and conversation, a mere picture sketched for our contemplative faculties. Jaques shares with the Duke and his companions the propensity for drawing wisdom and philosophy from the smallest observations. But Shakespeare draws a contrast between the two men. Those who wish to derive enjoyment and advantage from this life must in themselves have a natural disposition for moderation and self-mastery. Another contrast in this play is that between Touchstone and Audrey, also psychologically illuminating.

Rosalind has a quick sense of humour as well as a bubbling wit. Obviously she enjoys the fun of the situation, and is unfailingly witty and ever entrancingly feminine. When Rosalind marries Orlando the characters of the semi-tragic underplot are transformed to semi-comic. The usurping Duke experiences a change of heart, the wicked elder brother repents and falls in love with Celia—a startling case of love at first sight on her part, almost as exceptional as the Duke's conversion—and all ends happily.

In *Twelfth Night* there is a delicious blend of sentiment and comedy. Viola's humour has a tender streak as becomes her experience of life. The more comic creations are sturdily English in their robust fun, even though they pretend to be living in Illyria, just as the very English Dogberry and Verges are set down in Messina.

Shakespeare again proves himself a master of the art of comedy by the manner in which he joins the pensive melancholy of Viola's love-story to the buxom merriment of Maria's trick upon Malvolio. A delightful fantasy is so cleverly interwoven with the infectious laughter of honest mirth that we are not aware of any incongruity. The jests of the humorous characters in *Twelfth Night* are no longer casual witticisms. They grow out of the situation itself, or are the ripe expression of character revealing itself in dialogue.

(London: Williams & Norgate Ltd., 1936).

SHAKESPEARIAN COMEDY AND OTHER STUDIES
George Gordon
1944

THE WORLD OF THE COMEDIES

THERE are two groups of characters in Shakespeare's comedies:

(1) The young men and women, who dwell in that romantically devised world, of youth, and dreams, and laughter, of which he possessed, and retains, the secret; and

(2) The workaday people, who keep things going—ploughmen, shepherds, servingmen, stewards, waiting-maids—with the unconverted drinkers, jesters, rogues, and odd fellows in a kind of limbo between the two regions—between upstairs and down—all plodding, stepping, tripping, and staggering along in a world of the four elements—of food and drink and sleep and labour. You may study this double world in any of these comedies: very fruitfully in *Much Ado* and *As You Like It*: most clearly, perhaps, in *Twelfth Night*. Like all these romantic comedies *Twelfth Night* is partly serious, and partly comic: a mixture of love and fun. The love story is the plot: it is serious, southern, and poetical. The comic story is the under-plot. It is not at all serious; it is anything but southern; and it is in prose. We don't at first know where we are when the play opens, and we very soon understand that it doesn't in the least matter. We are in the Utopia of lovers, where there is much despair, but no broken hearts.

All these plays are sweet with music: it is a part of this fairyland, the food of love. The Young Duke, being then in perfect health, sitting among his equally healthy lords, breathes out his luxurious agonies to the God of Love. It is a picture of eternal youth, framed in a setting of music, and poetry, and cushions, and flowers. What then, is the *climate* of these sweet tortures ? Do we care? Viola comes to land.

> *Viola.* What country, friends, is this?
> *Captain.* This is Illyria, lady.

We are on those Adriatic coasts where the East and West lie so neighbourly—in Illyria—one of the Elysiums of fiction—and to most of us even now—as to almost all Elizabethans—not much more real than Ruritania. We hear in a distant sort of way of Candy and Crete, and ships named the *Tiger* and the *Phoenix;* and of a place called Messaline, which by some trifling oversight of Nature seems never to have existed. It has been searched for (though you will hardly believe it) by scholars, and rechristened Metelin, for Mitylene—because, I suppose, Mitylene is a real place. As if that mattered! This game has rules: and really, as visitors, we must allow the dramatist to pour out his own tea, and pull his own curtains!

I receive almost annually, from America and Germany, printed attempts to discover the 'source', as it is called, of *The Tempest,* and to locate Prospero's island in the Mediterranean or the Atlantic. The authors of these investigations are gentlemen for whom Utopias were not intended. There is an entrance fee to this club of good Utopians, which they cannot pay; of which they do not even understand the currency. Their children (who, by the way, get in for nothing)—their children could teach them better. Because, if you think of it, to imagine, even if it could be shown to be true, that anything is gained by knowing that Prospero's island was Lampedusa, and lay between Malta and the African coast—or that it was Corcyra, as another critic is equally prepared to prove—is to declare the play, on the whole, a failure. If the Island does not convince us, and convince us without any argument, that it lies precisely nowhere, it has missed its purpose, and the ideal impression which the dramatist was all along attempting to make upon us has not been made. The island has neither latitude nor longitude, because Shakespeare gave it none: and this will still be true, even if the moles should triumph: if the lost story which Shakespeare read should be unearthed; and some paltry original island be produced with a name and a place on the map.

Being an *idle* world, this world of romantic Comedy of which I am speaking: there are therefore students in it—but no lectures. There are a number of university students in Shakespeare: it was one of the choices of Elizabethan youth:

> Some to the wars, to try their fortunes there:
> Some to discover islands far away
> Some to the studious Universities.

Young Walter Raleigh was so thorough an Elizabethan that he had done all three—fought, sailed, and studied—before he was twenty. The most notable of all the young students in Shakespeare, and, one would guess, by far the most studious, is Hamlet; but he is outside our range. The Prince and his friends in

Love's Labour's Lost are nearer our mark; or that bright spark Lucentio in *The Taming of the Shrew*. Lucentio was a graduate of the University of Rheims, and is supposed by his confiding relations to have entered on a post-graduate course at the University of Padua. I regret to say that there is no evidence that he even matriculated there, or, if he matriculated, that he ever did any work: unless you call it work disguising himself as a language-master, and teaching Bianca to misconstrue Ovid. 'Where left we last', says Bianca, coolly.

> *Luc.* Here, madam:
>   *Hic ibat Simois; hic est Sigeia tellus;*
>   *Hic steterat Priami regia celsa semis.*
> *Bian.* Construe them.
> *Luc. Hic ibat,* as I told you before, *Simois,* I am Lucentio, *hic est,* son unto Vincentio of Pisa, *Sigeia tellus,* disguised thus to get your love; *Hic steterat,* and that Lucentio that comes a wooing, *Priami,* is my man Tranio, *regia,* bearing my port, *celsa senis,* that we might beguile the old pantaloon.

A young puppy, you see!

> *Bian.* Now let me see if I can construe it: *Hic ibat Simois,* I know you not, *hic est Sigeia tellus,* I trust you not; *Hic steterat Priami,* take heed he hear us not, *regia,* presume not; *celsa senis,* despair not.

A nice pair! As Grumio says in the same play: 'See, to beguile the old folks, how the young folks put their heads together!' It has been the same since Menander. Lucentio's father, we are told, had his misgivings about his son, and they were not ill-founded. But the young man takes risks for love, and Shakespeare, therefore, sees him through.

In this climate of Romance, it is, of course, the rule that all the lovers shall love at once, and love absolutely. Nothing else, in this world, is to be permitted. One glance at Olivia, and no work need be expected from Orsino for some time to come. Olivia herself, *grande dame* though she is, succumbs in one interview: they are all struck from heaven. Only two of these couples have the temerity to stand off for a time, and assume, at any rate, the postures of defence—I mean Rosalind and Biron, and Benedick and Beatrice—and there are special reasons for that. This Utopian Love is what the Elizabethans called *Fancy:* bred neither in the head nor in the heart, but in the eyes. We call it 'love at first sight'—and, really, I have never heard that it wears worse than any other. The eyes are not the *least* intelligent agents either of the head or of the heart. It has, of course, some disadvantages, this remorseless way of loving, from the point of view of the performers: (1) it must be acknowledged to be extremely open to ridicule;

(2) if everybody did it, there would be an end of all society. The trouble is, that true love alone can never make a comedy. True love is serious, and Comedy should amuse. It is exclusive—most terribly so—and Comedy should be friendly. It is unsocial—it cannot be hidden from you how very unsocial two lovers can be!—but the subject of Comedy is Society. Comedy is a plump figure, and holds its sides; Love is lean, and holds a hand upon its heart.

What is to be done? Is *Romantic Comedy,* then, impossible? Must either the laughers or the sighers be given up? But which? *Not* the laughers, surely! Does true Comedy mean no more cakes and ale ? Shall there be no Comedy but Mr. Shaw's? But then—a play *all* laughter? What is to be done?

Shakespeare proceeded, as he always does, by compromise. If Comedy laughs, Romance is not to be offended; if Love sighs, Comedy promises to put up with it—to a point! to a point! If the jokes are good, and the sighs are true, there would appear, on this undertaking, to be no reason in literature why they should quarrel. In Romantic Comedy, therefore, the laughers and the sighers live side by side, like good neighbours: on only *one* condition: that neither shall commit excess, or compete for attention at the expense of the other. And this is sound. For what is more wearisome than the uninterrupted spectacle of lovemaking in which we have no share? Or more awful than the gravity which falls upon a company that has laughed too much, or giggled too intellectually ? The law, therefore, is one of decency and measure. The solemnity of Love is relieved by the generosity of Laughter, and the irresponsibility of Laughter by the seriousness of Love. This is the principle of Romantic Comedy, and for a compromise—how admirably it works! No one ever managed it so well as Shakespeare. The words of Mercury need not be harsh after the songs of Apollo.

I don't know a better or more convincing demonstration of this compact than to pass from Orsino and Viola in the first two scenes of *Twelfth Night* to Sir Toby and Maria in the third—from Illyria to the Buttery Hatch. The first two scenes pitch their language high. Romance is to be secured on her throne before Comedy comes in. Olivia being in mourning for her brother's death, Orsino has sent a messenger with kind inquiries. Maria very properly refuses to admit him, and informs him that her mistress does not intend either to put off mourning or go into society for seven years; This is how Valentine reports to Orsino:

> So please my lord, I might not be admitted;
> But from her handmaid do return this answer:
> The element itself, till seven years' heat,
> Shall not behold her face at ample view;
> But, like a cloistress, she will veiled walk,

And water once a day her chamber round
With eye-offending brine; all this, to season
A brother's dead love, which she would keep fresh
And lasting in her sad remembrance.

I am quite sure this is not how Maria said it, or anybody but an actor. The style goes on. Since Viola has escaped drowning herself, there is a hope that her brother may have escaped also, especially as the Captain saw him tied to a mast. This is how it is put:

Mine own escape unfoldeth to my hope,
Whereto thy speech serves for authority,
The like of him.

These are phrases neither of men nor of angels: only actors ever spoke them. Viola and the Captain now walk off: a door seems to open: we step into the Buttery: and a voice cries 'What a plague means my niece to take the death of her brother thus? I am sure care's an enemy to life.' With what a comfortable sense of shock we encounter this underworld. This is the very tune of unconverted man, and every ear is ready for it. It is the dialect of life. The etiquette of Romance is exacting: how pleasant it is to step downstairs! How snug it is. A different syntax controls the speech of these quarters. The air seems to change. It is Illyrian no longer. These strayed revellers, fools, and drinkers, who raise the owl at midnight, and burn sack to bring in the morning (because it is too late to go to bed), and talk of Puritans and weavers, and count the bells of St. Bennet—one, two, three—were never bred on the Adriatic. Every member of the audience, and every reader, knows that he is at home again—in the paradise of humorists and odd fellows—in England—among friends. The blood of the living Falstaff is in Sir Toby Belch; Sir Andrew might have sat on the same bench with Justice Silence; and Feste, the third man and best singer in the trio, is no other than Will Kempe, fool-in-ordinary to the company of the Chamberlain's Servants.

This was well understood by Shakespeare's audience: there was a tacit understanding at that time between the audience and the stage that the entrance of the comic characters indicated a temporary suspension of the romantic or historical fiction on which the serious action was based; that the assumption of a strange country or a different period of history had been dropped. This is the practical explanation of several liberties in more serious plays and even in Tragedies. Such was the Porter in *Macbeth,* with his jokes about Garnett the Jesuit and last year's harvest. No one supposed him to be a porter of ancient Scotland. Here was a primitive convention which Shakespeare maintained.

It is in his power over these two worlds, in his ostensible alternations between Nowhere and England, that Shakespeare's romantic comedies excel all others.

(Oxford: Oxford University Press, 1944): 45–51.

FACING THE MUSIC IN ARDEN: "'TWAS I, BUT 'TIS NOT I"
Margaret Maurer
1996

Pablo [Picasso] once remarked, when you make a thing, it is so complicated making it that it is bound to be ugly, but those that do it after you they don't have to worry about making it and they can make it pretty, and so everybody can like it when the others make it. (28)

from *The Autobiography of Alice B. Toklas*

Two versions of Shakespeare's *As You Like It* appeared in 1723. Charles Johnson's theatrical adaptation, *Love in a Forest* opened at the Drury Lane Theatre on January 9 and was published that same year. It is the first certainly recorded performance of any version of the play. Coincidentally, Alexander Pope's edition of Shakespeare began appearing, with 1723 seeing the first two volumes. *As You Like It* is the third play in Volume II.

As You Like It comes into focus in an interesting way around these two versions, the elements of the play they promote and the elements they suppress.[1] What directors and commentators today make of the play is related to the preoccupations of Johnson and Pope. This realization cannot but be

---

[1] Charles Johnson, *Love in a Forest*, 1723, has been reproduced in facsimile by the Cornmarket Press, 1969. References to it in my essay are to this facsimile edition. It is discussed by Edith Holding, "*As You Like It* Adapted: Charles Johnson's *Love In A Forest*," *Shakespeare Survey*, 32 (1979), 37–48. Pope's edition of Shakespeare has been reproduced in facsimile (New York: AMS Press, 1969), to which I also refer here. Quoting from both of these texts, I modernize slightly. There is a stage history of *As You Like It*, "The Play in Performance," in Alan Brissenden's edition of the play (Oxford: Clarendon Press, 1993), pp. 50–81. Unless otherwise noted, reference to the text of *As You Like It* in this essay will be to this edition, cited by act, scene, and line numbers. References to others plays by Shakespeare will be to the *The Complete Signet Classic Shakespeare*, gen. ed. Sylvan Barnet (New York: Harcourt, Brace, Jovanovich, 1972).

particularly poignant with respect to a play named *As You Like It*. It would be one thing if the play's fortunes since the early eighteenth century were a response to all the intricacies of its plot and language. It would be another if some of its elements had to be ignored if not mistaken before the play could widely please. Put interrogatively, the provocation of this essay is this: so what if the experience of *As You Like It* these days is closer to *Love in a Forest* than to anything the Elizabethan stage might have seen? Would we have it any other way?

In the forms in which we presently experience it, *As You Like It* generally pleases, exemplifying the virtues of the pastoral as neoclassicists defend the mode. For those who come to the theater for incidental amusements, it has singing, dancing, a witty fool, and fine set speeches proving the instructive and restorative powers of nature on the cultivated mind. Its hero, Orlando, is a fortunate youngest son temporarily frustrated to make his felicity in the end the sweeter; its heroine, Rosalind, invents a delightful masquerade to amuse herself and her lover before giving herself to him. For those who come to the theatre for doctrine as well as music, the play also embraces some provocative issues. Orlando's treatment by his brother reflects social problems newly acute in early modern England, and Rosalind's masquerade is an opportunity to examine early modern and contemporary attitudes toward gender.[2] In Shakespeare's day, no less than in Pope's and in our own, such larger concerns are welcome elements to a mode of poetry always liable to criticism for being artificial and frivolous. It is a criticism Sir Philip Sidney meets in *A Defence of Poetry*:

> Is it then the Pastoral poem which is misliked? (For perchance where the

---

[2] Recent important essays exploring the way the play reflects issues of class and gender in Shakespeare's society and our own include Louis Adrian Montrose, "'The Place of a Brother' in *As You Like It*: Social Process and Comic Form," *Shakespeare Quarterly*, 32 (1981), 28–54; Barbara Bono, "Mixed Gender, Mixed Genre in Shakespeare's *As You Like It*," in Barbara Kiefer Lewalski, ed., *Renaissance Genres: Essays on Theory, History, and Interpretation*, Harvard English Studies 14 (Cambridge, Mass.: Harvard U Press, 1986), 189–212; Richard Wilson, "'Like the old Robin Hood'": *As You Like It* and the Enclosure Riots," *Shakespeare Quarterly*, 43 (1992), 1–19; and Susanne L. Wofford, "'To You I Give Myself, For I Am Yours': Erotic Performance and Theatrical Performatives in *As You Like It*," in Russ McDonald, *Shakespeare Reread: The Texts in New Contexts* (Ithaca: Cornell U Press, 1994), 147–69. Classically appreciative comments on the play may be found in Harold Jenkins's lecture delivered to the Shakespeare Conference at Stratford-upon-Avon, August 18, 1953, printed in *Shakespeare Survey*, 8 (1955), 40–51.

hedge is lowest they will soonest leap over.) Is the poor pipe disdained, which sometime out of Meliboeus' mouth can show the misery of people under hard lords or ravening soldiers, and again, by Tityrus, what blessedness is derived to them that lie lowest from the goodness of them that sit highest; sometimes, under the pretty tales of wolves and sheep, can include the whole considerations of wrong-doing and patience; sometimes show that contentions for trifles can get but a trifling victory. (43)

The basis of this argument is that the pastoral world is an appropriate setting for examining society's ills, offering both the natural spectacles on which to moralize and leisure to do it. It is remarkable how Sidney's comments accord with the approach taken by many recently appreciative essays on *As You Like It*.[3]

Yet though *As You Like It* admits such a defense, the play is not wholly responsive to it. Sidney's comments recall the ruminations of *As You Like It*'s own melancholy Jaques, whose point of view is disputed by other characters. Indeed, one important strain of Elizabethan pastoral positively resists moralizing. Christopher Marlowe's provocative lyric "Come live with me and be my love" imagines pleasure in terms that are emphatically artificial and stubbornly nonreferential. Its delicate technical effects invite admiration, but its images defy interpretation. The no less notorious disputation of it attributed to Sir Walter Raleigh, "If all the world and love were young," fully appreciates this quality. The "Nymph's Reply" subjects the original poem's terms to the demands of life's realities. In its best known version, it does this by assuming, in its title, that the unspecified "love" is female (a nymph); then, point for point, it has her protest that what the shepherd offers cannot be found in the actual world.[4] Even at that, however, the "Nymph's Reply" does not reject the

---

[3] Stephen Gosson's *Schoole of Abuse,* to which Sidney's *Defence of Poesie* is allegedly a reply, does not deny that such activities as poetry and plays can have instructive potential. His condemnation of them depends on his conviction that "the sweetenesse of musicke, and pleasure of sportes" (B5) overwhelm any more thoughtful response. Sidney's *Defence* meets that argument. Sidney primarily, though not exclusively, defends these activities by discussing the interpretive process, as in the passage quoted above on the value of pastoral poetry.

[4] A four-stanza version of "Come live with me" appeared in *The Passionate Pilgrim* (1599), where it is followed by one stanza titled simply "Loves answere," approximately the first stanza of the "Nymph's Reply." The well-known six-stanza version appeared in *England's Helicon* (1600) where it is accompanied by two imitations, one of which is the whole "Nymph's Reply." There are other variations of the poem in manuscripts and books of the period.

shepherd's offer, concluding (much virtue in *if*) that the world imagined in the original is compelling on its own terms.

As You Like It's pastoral world resembles the world of Marlowe's lyric in being determinedly artificial, preoccupied with nothing so much as the techniques of its medium. Jaques's set piece on the world as stage (2.7.139–66) specifies the two notorious elements of that medium: the use of males to impersonate all characters regardless of gender ("all the men and women [are] merely players") and the casting of players in multiple roles within a play ("they have their exits and their entrances, / And one man in his time plays many parts"). Yet appreciating *As You Like It* technically, with attention to these elements, is not easy. Early texts offer few insights into the way the plays might have been enacted, and edited modern texts inevitably overwhelm what little evidence there is with the interpretive assumptions that have grown up around the play since the Restoration. In the case of *As You Like It,* the process begins with the Third Folio of 1663/4 and increases through the more systematically edited texts of the early eighteenth century. Elizabethan techniques have been recovered and are even incidentally practiced in the modern theatre; but the common consent of critics today, theatrical and literary, is that they are not crucial to a Shakespearean play's effect.[5] Just like Jaques in

---

See Christopher Marlowe, *The Complete Works,* ed. Fredson Bowers (Cambridge: Cambridge U Press, 1973), II, 519–33; 536–37; 541–42; William Griggs, *The Passionate Pilgrim, The First Quarto, 1599, a facsimile in photolithography* (London: W. Griggs, n.d.; and *England's Helicon, 1600, 1614,* ed. Hyder Edward Rollins, 2 vols. (Cambridge: Harvard U Press, 1935), I, 184–86, and II, 186–90. Bruce R. Smith, *Homosexual Desire in Shakespeare's England: A Cultural Poetics* (Chicago: University of Chicago Press, 1991), calls Marlowe's lyric "an exercise in soft pastoral" (93). I like Smith's terms, "hard" and "soft" pastoral, distinguishing between pastoral works that have their "real sights set on concerns beyond the boundaries of the shepherds' fields" and those that are "essentially escapist in spirit, celebrat[ing] the pleasures of the *locus amoenus*" (88). As he himself develops his discussion, however, particularly of Vergil's second eclogue (89–90), "hard" and "soft" become terms to describe, not so much two *kinds* of pastoral as two *approaches* to it. To be sure, the didactic impulse may be inherent in a piece; but even when it is not, it is often added when someone, a commentator or perhaps even the author in a later and more defensive mood, reflects on it. Marlowe's poem is remarkable for its resistance to this impulse.

[5] In his excellently full introduction to the new Oxford text, Alan Brissenden has sections on "metamorphosis," "doubleness," and "names and places" that discuss most of the elements of the play that are the focus of this essay. His comments on all these topics are suitably judicious and restrained, always careful to respect the right of the spectators not to be offended or confused. In

his speech, a critic who acknowledges them will generally do so only by the way, passing at once to more reflective considerations. As Jaques develops his conceit, he imagines a player playing himself throughout, only submitting in the tiring house to some physical alterations to convey the aging process. Such techniques might serve a player in the title role of *Everyman,* but he would need other skills to take a part (though perhaps not Jaques himself) in an Elizabethan *As You Like It.*

It is in an effort to imagine *As You Like It* with the dozen or so men of an Elizabethan company performing its twenty-odd speaking parts that Johnson's *Love in a Forest,* acted and printed a century after Shakespeare's play appeared in the First Folio, proves its value. This essay begins by describing Johnson's adaptation, relating the changes it makes in Shakespeare's play to the preoccupations of Pope's edition of that same year. It then examines a crucial moment in *As You Like It*—Oliver's meeting with Celia/Aliena and Rosalind/Ganymede—noting how the mysterious effect of the metamorphosis it represents would be deepened in an Elizabethan production where the players' taking multiple parts within a play would be part of the spectators' ordinary experience of theatre. The Ganymede device likewise presumes this practice; further, of course, it works out of the other notorious convention of the Elizabethan stage whereby male players represented women. The third major section of this essay discusses Rosalind's successive metamorphoses, undoing, in the process of this discussion, some of the revisions imposed on *As You Like It* since the Restoration. At last, however, I am as reflective as any other commentator. In my essay's epilogue, I consider the significance of all this to the likes of me.

i

While neither *Love in a Forest* nor Pope's edition of *As You Like It* commands much attention on its own in Shakespeare studies, taken together

---

his account of the "play in performance," he mentions a 1893 version done by a cast of women, some in false beards, Ben Greet's all-male version of 1920, and Clifford Williams's for the National Theatre at the Old Vic in 1967, remarking that such things are "more curious than satisfactory." He has praise, however, for Declan Donnellan's all-male production for Cheek By Jowl in 1991–92 (66–68). Michael Shapiro's *Gender In Play on the Shakespearean Stage: Boy Heroines and Female Pages* (Ann Arbor: University of Michigan Press, 1994) appeared after I wrote this essay. Shapiro's discussion of disguised-heroine plays, and particularly of *As You Like It* (chapter 6), does consider the effect of the actor's identity in his discussion of the play. My concern, though, with multiple casting in relation to the convention of the all-male company leads to a view of this play that is finally different from his.

they offer provocative insights into the interpretive fortunes of *As You Like It.*

Love in a Forest is an adaptation of one play, *As You Like It,* using speeches plundered from other plays—*Richard II, Much Ado About Nothing, A Midsummer Night's Dream, Love's Labour's Lost,* and *Twelfth Night.* Johnson's preoccupations with what in Shakespeare's works seems to him to be truth to human nature are first reflected in his dedication of the work to his Brethren in the Society of Freemasons, an organization that has

> . . . taught all Nations one Idiom, which, at the same Time that it gives a mutual Understanding, inspires a mutual Benevolence, removes every Prejudice of a distant Sun and Soil, and no Man can be a Foreigner who is a *Brother.* (vi)

The prologue describes the play as "Another Work from that great Hand":

> His Ore's refin'd, but not impar'd by Years.
> Those sacred Truths our Sages coldly tell
> In languid Prose; as *He* describes—we feel.
> He looks all Nature thro'; strikes at a Heat
> Her various Forms, irregularly Great . . . .

and concludes by describing the motive for changes:

> Forgive our modern Author's Honest Zeal,
> He hath attempted boldly, if not well:
> Believe, he only does with Pain, and Care,
> Presume to weed the beautiful Parterre.
> His whole Ambition does, at most, aspire
> To tune the sacred Bard's immortal Lyre;
> The Sceme [*sic*] from Time and Error to restore,
> And give the Stage, from SHAKESPEAR one Play more. (69–70)

Other plays by Shakespeare praised in this prologue indicate Johnson's interests. *Julius Caesar* is noted for its representation of an episode in the history of resistance to tyranny; *Timon of Athens* teaches the importance of distrusting flattery; *Othello* arouses passion in "the sympathising Mind"; and *Hamlet,* the story of the "pious Dane," figures "in one Character," a "Hero, Courtier, Patriot, and the Man." Johnson clearly knew the comedies to have drawn so heavily on passages from several of them for *Love in a Forest;* but, he mentions only one play in which "into lower Life his Pencil strays," *Merry Wives of Windsor.*

Love in a Forest seems, in fact, an attempt to elevate *As You Like It* to a plain of general truth and noble sentiment. Love is the emotion to which the good characters retreat until evil plays itself out; it is a restorative force in a corrupt society. In *Love in a Forest,* not only Duke Frederick's accusation against Rosalind, but also the charge of Oliver against his brother Orlando is an appeal of treason. Consequently, the wrestling match of *As You Like It* becomes a sword fight introduced by the challenging speeches of Mowbray (Charles) and Bolingbroke (Orlando) from *Richard II.* Oliver and Frederick are consistently evil threats to the well-being of others. This simplification of their characters serves *Love in a Forest's* most ingenious economy, which is to deny Oliver any role in the love action. Not Oliver but the third and, in *Love in a Forest,* youngest brother, Roberto du Bois, comes to the forest late in the play to be rescued from the lion by Orlando and to announce the death of the usurping Duke and the suicide of Oliver.

Removing Oliver as the match for Celia permits an expanded role for the melancholy Jaques, who, like the society at large, is restored to civility by love. Jaques is at first bemused by his attraction to the low, brown Aliena; and Johnson accordingly gives him some of the most delicious speeches of resistance that Shakespeare devised for Benedick and Berowne in their respective plays. Some of Touchstone's lines serve in this capacity, too, becoming Jaques's wooing scenes with Celia where she responds with Audrey's. Johnson eliminates both the clown and his country wench, along with other humorous characters—Silvius, Phoebe, William, and Sir Oliver Martext, though lines of Silvius and Phoebe survive in the love dialogue of the principals.

Instead of Touchstone's discourse on the degrees of the lie, *Midsummer Night Dream's* Pyramus and Thisbe play is added at the point where Rosalind and Celia leave the stage to revert to their female attire. There are no other scenes for the players who perform this interlude, but it is set up by references in the play to people who have "quit the Tyrant's Court, and hither / Resort in Crouds; Mechanics of all Sorts / Petition to delight and serve your Grace" (22). A bit later, Amiens takes advantage of the Duke's observation that "This wide and universal Theatre / Presents more woeful Pageants, than the Scene / Wherein we play" to announce that "Some Citizens from *Liege,* some of the many / Fled hither, Sir, for your Protection" are preparing "A *tedious brief Scene of young* Pyramus *and his Love* Thisby; very tragical Mirth." The Duke replies with Theseus's "Merry and Tragical, tedious and brief, / How shall we find the Concord of this Discord?"—and then continues, "Well, let them be ready before our Cave in the Evening; there they shall represent it; this Theatrical Performance will stir thy Gall, *Jaques"* (28).

Jaques's reply, though native to *As You Like It,* is introduced by lines that invite a comparison of *Pyramus and Thisby* to the fortunes of the lovers in *Love in a Forest*:

> Not at all;
> He that can reflect wants not these Mirrours:
> All the World's a Stage,
> And all the Men and Women meerly Players; . . . (28)

The success of the interpolation proves the degree to which Johnson's technique of pastiche still lingers in the prominence the speech enjoys out of its context. Translated to *Love in a Forest,* the amateur play of *Midsummer* suggests that Jaques's conceit should be understood as a two-way simile: the world is like the stage, the stage is like the world. The tale of Pyramus and Thisby has points of analogy to what Orlando and Rosalind experience in the forest, intimating that a violent fate shadows romantic happiness. The two actions are united by an image: Thisby's "Mantle good . . . stain'd with Blood" (63) in her encounter with a lion recalls the "bloody Handkerchief" (52) that Orlando, after his struggle with the lion, sends Ganymede to excuse his tardiness.

A "gallimaufry," as Alan Brissenden calls it, *Love in a Forest,* enjoyed six performances before "disappearing from the stage for ever" (52). Admirers of Shakespeare's genuine works usually disdain it; and if Pope knew the play he, too, was probably at least bemused. Many of the most conspicuous importations enlarge the part of Colley Cibber, who took the role of Jaques.[6]

Pope's admiration for Shakespeare's poetical achievement is, in one way, expressed in terms very unlike Johnson's impulse to conflate the plays. In his edition's preface, Pope observes that

> . . . every single character in *Shakespear* is as much an Individual, as those in Life itself; it is as impossible to find any two alike; . . . To this life and variety of Character, we must add the wonderful Preservation of it; which is such throughout his plays, that had all the Speeches been printed

---

[6] According to Pope's biographer Maynard Mack, Pope's antipathy to Cibber may have begun in 1717 or even earlier. See Mack, *Alexander Pope, A Life* (New Haven: Yale U Press, 1985), 774–81. Points of similarity between Johnson and Pope are generally discussed in Chapter 3, "Property and Propriety," of Michael Dobson's *The Making of the National Poet: Shakespeare, Adaptation and Authorship, 1660–1769* (Oxford: Clarendon Press, 1992), especially pp. 129–32.

without the very names of the Persons, I believe one might have apply'd them with certainty to every speaker. (I.iii)

This may seem an exaggerated claim, but in milder form it describes why one might perceive as incongruous the words of Touchstone in the mouth of Jaques.

Otherwise, there are significant points of contact between Johnson's and Pope's comments on Shakespeare. In the preface to his edition, Pope praises Shakespeare for conveying "*Sentiments* [that] are not only in general the most pertinent and judicious upon every subject; but by a talent very peculiar, something between Penetration and Felicity"; and he admires Shakespeare for knowing the world "by Intuition" and "look[ing] thro' humane nature at one glance" (I.iv). Like Johnson, he remarks especially on Shakespeare's knowledge of Roman history (I.x). When he must acknowledge errors and stylistic infelicities, he supposes how they might "have risen from one source, the ignorance of the Players, both as his actors, and as his editors" (I.xiv). He concedes also that Shakespeare's work is "Stage-Poetry of all other . . . more particularly levell'd to please the Populace, and its success more immediately depending upon the *Common Suffrage*" (I.v).

As editor, Pope is prepared to intrude where he can and still preserve the integrity of the play, excising or otherwise marking what he considers to be vulgar passages. If the offensive lines are unnecessary to the clarity of play's action, he degrades them to the bottom of the page (I.xxii); if they are necessary, he distinguishes them in the text with marks of "reprobation" (I.157 n.). Interested in conveying the text, however, and more tolerant of pastoral poetry, he is less aggressive in weeding than Johnson;[7] Pope's *As You Like It* has notably few negative intrusions. No lines are degraded, and only the dialogue between Celia and Rosalind in which Celia teases her cousin with the news that Orlando is in the forest (3.2.158–242), printed as a scene to itself, bears the reproving daggers.

Pope intervenes more often to indicate, "by comma's in the margin" (a single quotation mark at the start of each line) "Some of the most shining passages" (I.xxiii). *As You Like It* has good measure of these. Jaques on the

---

7 In the process of eliminating Touchstone, Corin, Phoebe, William, and Audrey, Johnson effectively reduces to a scant few any references to sheep and shepherds; and the effect of making the forest of Arden more the haunt of foresters than shepherds rationalizes the play's location, diminishes its pastoral elements, and incidentally includes (this is Holding's point, p. 43), in the "Mechanicks," or "Labourers in Handicraft," a nod to the Brotherhood of Freemasons who trace their origin to medieval craftsmen. Pope's efforts in pastoral poetry suggest more sympathy with the mode of rural life. See Mack, 213–18.

Seven Ages of Man (2.7.139–66) is so distinguished, along with Duke Senior on the uses of adversity (2.1.1–17), Adam on thrift (2.3.39–54), Jaques again on the fool he met in the forest (2.7.18–28), Orlando on the "if's" of true gentility (2.7.110–17), Corin on the dignity of a "true labourer" (3.2.69–73), even Rosalind on saying "a day without the ever" (4.1.133–43) and on the depth of her own love (4.1.194–98). Less expected perhaps is Pope's admiration for Silvius's lines on the pangs of love (2.4.30–39 and 5.2.78–94), Phoebe's description of the beauty of the beloved (3.5.121–24), and Touchstone's summary of his life as a courtier ("I have trod a measure," 5.4.42–46), but not his fortunes with Jane Smile (2.4.43–52) nor the seven degrees of the lie (5.4.66–78, 86–98). Particularly remarkable, for it is a passage more descriptive than sentimental or moral, is Pope's regard for Oliver's account of the snake and the lioness attacking the "wretched ragged man" (4.3.105–19).[8]

A writer given to pastiche might find Pope's edition useful for locating transportable generic poetry. Visually, Pope's approving marks seem to lift a speech out of its immediate context in the play and recommend its more universal application. The effect is to isolate the passage from any irony that the surrounding context might impart to it. It is indicative of the degree to which Pope's impulses persist in our perception of *As You Like It* that the effect of diminished irony may be apparent in some of the designated speeches but not in all. It may be most obvious to modern readers seeing the speeches of Silvius, Phoebe, and Touchstone so designated. These characters speak always to us in the humour of their roles—the lovesick shepherd and scornful nymph of pastoral convention and the professional fool. Few commentators today take straightforwardly the observations of such characters.

Rosalind/Ganymede's mocking advice to Orlando marked for special regard may elicit just the middle degree of ambivalence in agreeing with Pope's judgment about what is universally poetical in the play. The lines are manifestly delivered ironically, in the assumed person of Ganymede; and Shakespeare has Celia comment on the whole of Rosalind/Ganymede's conduct in this passage that she abuses women. Nonetheless, to many spectators and critics, Rosalind's impersonation of Ganymede is seen as a resort to a place where deeper truths can be experienced; and the speech is sometimes taken as Rosalind's rueful description of what she knows men, at heart, to be as much as it is understood as Ganymede's prescription to Orlando of the way he should

---

[8] Marking passages he disapproved of or particularly admired is by no means the full extent of Pope's editorial attention to *As You Like It*. See Mack, pp. 418–26. Very little of his work on the text survives in a modern edition like the new Oxford text. What do persist are some of the changes Pope made in the printing of verse as prose or prose as verse or the disposition of verse into lines.

behave. Interestingly, the second part of this speech, in which Rosalind/ Ganymede projects Rosalind's conduct as a wife, seems comically exaggerated, though Pope may well have not read it that way.

The effect will differ from reader to reader, but it is likely that many of the speeches singled out by Pope will be cases some commentator or other will appreciate for their expression of aphoristic truth. The speeches of Corin and Adam may seem old-fashioned, but the values of the legendary golden age have not lost their appeal; even Touchstone's wise-cracking cannot completely dismiss the dignity of the former, and Adam's integrity remains unimpeachable because of, rather than in spite of, the infirmity with which the player ought to utter the lines. We may notice the ironic effect of Amiens's flattery of Duke Senior for his sententious preference for the counsels of nature over those of his servile courtiers, but audiences never are led to laugh at the effect. Similarly, Orlando's speaking of gentility with a drawn sword in his hand seems nonetheless gentle. In other words, though perhaps not every reader would share Pope's regard for every one of these passages nor would these necessarily be the only places in the play that a given reader would absolve from the implications of dramatic context, Pope's technique warrants one of the most widely admired qualities of *As You Like It,* the disembodied power of its language. [9]

Confessing the extent to which we share this perception with Pope can lead us to wonder, however, about how much our liking of *As You Like It* depends on the sentiments its characters express. We might inquire what happens when we acknowledge the dramatic context of its fine speeches in something like Elizabethan terms. For this exercise, comparison of the plot of *As You Like It* to that of *Love in a Forest* helps to appreciate the play's peculiarly Elizabethan elements. In relation to those elements, one of the speeches singled out by Pope for special notice, Oliver's account of Orlando's rescue of him from the lioness, is a particularly useful site of contest.

---

[9] Moral sentiments expressed in highly crafted phrases are characteristic of euphuistic writing. This element of *As You Like It* shows Shakespeare to have been the beneficiary of his source, Thomas Lodge's *Rosalynde. Euphues golden legacie.* In his preface "To the Gentlemen Readers," Lodge identifies himself as "a souldier, & a sailer, that gives you the fruits of his labors that he wrought in the *Ocean,* when everie line was wet with a surge, & everie humorous passion countercheckt with a storme. If you like it, so" (160). In other words, Lodge seems content that his various readers take his work's moralizing tangents various ways. I am quoting here and slightly modernizing the text of *Rosalynde* printed in Geoffrey Bullough, *Narrative and Dramatic Sources of Shakespeare* (New York: Columbia U Press, 1958), II.158–256.

The dramatis personae of *Love in a Forest* lists ten speaking parts of "men," all assigned to men:

Frederick, the usurping Duke, ———————	Mr. *Williams.*
Alberto, the banish'd Duke, ———————	Mr. *Booth.*
Jaques, Amiens, two Friends to *Alberto,* ———	Mr. *Cibber,* Mr. *Cory.*
Oliver, Orlando, Roberto, three Brothers, ———	Mr. *Thurmond,* Mr. *Wilks,* Mr. *Roberts.*
Adam, an old Servant to *Orlando,* ———————	Mr. *Mills.*
Le Beu, ———————————————	Mr. *Theo. Cibber.*
Charles, Master of the Duke's Academy ———	Mr. *W. Mills.*

There are three of "women," all assigned to women:

Rosalind, ———————————————	Mrs. *Booth.*
Celia, ———————————————	Mrs. *Thurmond.*
Hymen, ———————————————	Miss *Linder.*

"In the Mock-Play," a third category of the list, men, women, and properties are intermingled; but only one part, Thisby, is assigned to an actress:

Pyramus, ———————————————	Mr. *Penkethman.*
Thisby, ———————————————	Mrs. *Miller.*
Wall, ———————————————	Mr. *Norris.*
Lion, ———————————————	Mr. *Wilson.*
Moonshine, ———————————————	Mr. *Ray.*

The early eighteenth-century disposition against men in women's roles apparently extended even to travesty. None of these eighteen actors doubles in a major speaking part, although possibly some of them reappear as Dennis, a Marshall, a lord, Silvius or a singing forester—the speaking roles among the "Lords, Foresters, Gentlemen, Guards, Singers and Dancers" listed in the *dramatis personae. Love in a Forest* occupies only Mr. Wilks (Orlando), Mrs. Booth (Rosalind), and Mrs. Thurmond (Celia) in their proper parts through the full course of its plot. The forest in *Love in a Forest* is a place where the harassed young people of the play's opening are introduced to a life that touches on their past troubles scarcely at all.

In terms of the action it represents, *As You Like It* does not differ much in this. The characters who retreat to the forest are Orlando, Oliver, Rosalind, Celia, and Touchstone. Touchstone, however, who does not appear in *Love in a*

Forest, articulates in *As You Like It* an attitude toward entrance into Arden that, in its preoccupation with memory and continuity, is unlike the simply liberated mood of the characters in *Love in a Forest*:

> Ay, now am I in Arden; the more fool I. When I was at home I was in a better place, but travellers must be content. (2.4.14–16)

His comment reflects on all his fellow travelers. For Orlando, whose change may consist of nothing more than different clothes (at seeing him for the first time, Rosalind/Ganymede addresses him as "forester," 3.2.288); for Celia, who puts herself in "poor and mean attire, / And with a kind of umber smirch[es her] face," but wants to maintain a sense of her self under the superficial changes, expressed in the choice of her new name, "a reference to [her] state . . . Aliena (1.3.110–11, 126–27); even perhaps for Rosalind, the most outwardly transformed of the group: for the characters of *As You Like It,* Arden is not a retreat, a temporary change of place and pace. Entering it is engagement with something more mysterious.

The concept of metamorphosis, as Shakespeare knew it from Ovid, explains changes, even spectacular ones, in terms of continuities.[10] The myths that Ovid assembles are explanatory tales of humans who experience monstrous transformations. Their stories are fantastic, pagan, not to be rationalized in Christian terms unless as instances of psychological deviation: the delicate Io, beloved of Jove, is transformed by him into a heifer to hide her from Juno, a state from which Io never altogether recovers (Book I); the proud Acteon, seeing the goddess Diana bathing, is turned to a stag and torn apart by his own dogs (Book III). In his final Book XV Ovid recounts the Pythagorean doctrine of metempsychosis or transmigration of the soul, an understanding of the continuities in all living things that would account for human beings being subject to impulses utterly foreign to their conscious memories and experiences. In the one passage that Pope marked as objectionable in the play,

---

[10] In his good book, *The Metamorphoses of Shakespearean Comedy* (Princeton: Princeton U Press, 1985), William C. Carroll discusses *As You Like It,* pp. 127–37, going in a direction rather different from mine here; his discussion of the Ovidian concept in this play does not involve speculation about stage effects. The penultimate paragraph of his appendix on "*Commedia dell-Arte* Transformations" (247–53) begins "It is also worth pondering for a moment what all this might have looked like on the stage" (252). He confines his comments, however, to stage properties. See also Jonathan Bate, in *Shakespeare and Ovid* (Oxford: Clarendon Press, 1993), for a good discussion of the importance of Ovid to Shakespeare and, pp. 157–62, for comments on the Ovidian references generally in *As You Like It.*

Rosalind/Ganymede alludes matter-of-factly to a metempsychotic experience, telling Celia/Aliena that the love poetry found on a palm tree (not yet known to be Orlando's) stirs some deep recollection:

> I was never so berhymed since Pythagoras' time that I was an Irish rat, which I can hardly remember. (3.2.170–172)[11]

In contrast to such mundane experiences of change as travel or maturation (two topics that preoccupy the melancholy Jaques), metempsychosis could be an explanation for the more disquieting dislocations of love, folly, poetry, and madness. An analogy to its process would also be the technique of "playing many parts" in the Elizabethan theatre. The player, taking on a succession of roles, is like the soul embodying *seriatim* a succession of bodies.[12]

---

[11] Charles Johnson retains the reference to Pythagoras but removes from it any insinuation of cross-species transmigration: "Look ye here, what I found on a Palm-Tree. I was never so Berhym'd since *Pythagoras*'s Time, which I can hardly remember!" (p. 32) The mention of Pythagoras in this passage may have been incidental to Pope's reasons for disapproving of it. He admired John Donne's satires, among which his "Metempsychosis, *Poema Satyricon*" or "The Progresse of the Soule" is often counted, and may have incorporated his memory of this *As You Like It* passage alluding to the idea into his "versifying" of Donne's Satire II, line 22. See the New Variorum *As You Like It*, ed. Horace Howard Furness (1890; New York: Dover, 1963), 155.

[12] All of the explicit references to metempsychosis in the plays of Shakespeare assume the movement of a soul from human to animal form or vice versa. In *As You Like It*, besides Rosalind's remark at 3.2.170, Duke Senior wonders if Jaques might have been "transformed into a beast, / For I can nowhere find him like a man" at the opening of 2.7; and just this transformation is actually accomplished in the play at the singing of the song "What shall he have that killed the deer?" in 4.2. Elsewhere in Shakespeare's plays, man-beast metempsychosis is alluded to by Gratiano at 4.1.130–38 of *Merchant of Venice* and Feste's catechism of Malvolio at 4.2.50–61 of *Twelfth Night*. Yet reference to what John Donne calls, in the prefatory letter to his "Metempsychosis," "man to man" (as opposed to "man to beast") transmigration is, in Shakespeare's day, a witty way to talk about the influence of the past on the present. Francis Meres alludes to it in his commendation of Shakespeare as "the sweet witty soul of Ovid" in *Palladis Tamia: Wit's Treasury* (1598). It also defines the character of Machiavel in Marlowe's *Jew of Malta*, and it is the basis of the conceit of Volpone's entertainment in 1.2 of Jonson's *The Fox*. Machiavel's Prologue and Volpone's masque seem to be asserting that "the opinion of Pythagoras" (*Twelfth Night*, 4.1.50) is essential to theatre; and it is a practice of theatre, playing parts other than himself, that would allow Malvolio to realize his

Merely knowing that Elizabethan companies used doubling begins to suggest how the effect of the players working their way through the plot of *As You Like It* could correspond to the characters' undergoing various kinds of metamorphosis upon entering Arden: each man in his time playing several parts perhaps (and even, as is likely the case with the player who presented Adam) undergoing transformations in the tiring house that aged or, in Adam's more metempsychotic case, rejuvenated him. Adam, who enters with Orlando in the first scene, reappears twice, his third scene being his last in that character. The players who impersonate Dennis, Charles, and Le Beau might shed their courtly attire fairly quickly. Court scenes after the third scene in the play are brief, and Duke Frederick requires only non-speaking attendants in them.

Duke Frederick himself reappears twice more before being absorbed into some other personage. While he persists in the story line (the forest party is informed in the last scene (5.4.149–60) of his military action against his brother and its dissipation in his conversion), the player who represents him has probably long since been made over. In some modern productions, he is Duke Senior, and it would be another kind of nice touch to make him Jaques de Boys, the messenger reporting his own fortunes. It is finally no matter, though, how he is recycled;[13] and in some ways, with respect to both the spectators' and the

---

fantasy of inhabiting a social state above his natural one in *Twelfth Night*. How the concern of Feste's catechism might accord with the Elizabethan staging of *Twelfth Night* is a subject I explore in a paper written for a 1989 Shakespeare Association Seminar on casting Shakespeare's plays, organized by Thomas Berger: "Coming of Age in Illyria: Doubling the Twins in *Twelfth Night*." As I have said above, to an appreciable extent commentators on Elizabethan drama seem to share Malvolio's "kind of Puritan" (2.3.140) reaction to Feste's plan. Thinking, no doubt, well of the soul and in no way approving Pythagoras's opinion, they are likewise reluctant to consider in any but the most rationalized way the effect of the doubling of roles in a play on the psychology of the players and the spectators.

[13] In his discussion of "doubleness" in the play, Brissenden answers Dr. Johnson's regret that Shakespeare misses an opportunity to represent the conversion of Duke Frederick ("a moral lesson in which he might have found matter worthy of his pen") by noting the "practical reason" for the omission: "Duke Frederick's part was doubled; on the modern stage it is sometimes doubled by the actor playing Duke Senior, which makes, at the very least, for a good family resemblance" (25). (In *Rosalynde,* Gerismond, the lawful king, and Torismond, the usurping king, are not brothers.) The doubling of Duke Senior with Duke Frederick would have to involve a very quick change: Senior exits at the end of 2.1 and Frederick enters at the opening of 2.2. If "family resemblance" were a desirable effect, however, the costume change might be simple. Analysis of the kinds of effects that doubling may have produced on the Elizabethan stage fall into two kinds. The casting of a single player in more

players' experience, the more insignificant the relationship between his parts the more the succession of them would mirror the disinterested process of nature that is the sublime comfort of the Pythagorean philosophy as Ovid has Pythagoras recount it.

And indeed, as the player of Frederick relinquishes his connection to that part, some choice opportunities are emerging to test his range: Amiens (if he can sing), Corin, Silvius, Audrey, Sir Oliver Martext, Phoebe, William, and Hymen. Some of these might themselves be combined with some of the others. The occasion of the song in 4.2 is an opportunity for a man-to-beast change with tiring house business accomplished on stage as some "lord" is outfitted with horns and a leather coat, becoming the deer he has killed. Imagining the effect of a production that confines the size of its company to not many more players than are given speaking roles in the last and largest scene of the play will emphasize the degree to which *As You Like It* conveys, structurally, the sense of Arden as the place of metamorphosis, opening up new categories of experience for the people, players, who enter it. The orderly way that Jaques

---

than one part may be considered simply pragmatically—as enabling a company to enact a play with more speaking parts than they have experienced players; or it may be discussed interpretively—as meaningful or patterned, reinforcing or even creating thematic or conceptual elements of the play. Most particular discussions of multiple casting assume it is meaningful and, even if they do not, they veer in that direction. See, for example, Richard Abrams, "The Double Casting of Cordelia and Lear's Fool: A Theatrical View," *Texas Studies in Language and Literature,* 27 (1985), 354–68; Stephen Booth, "Speculations on Doubling in Shakespeare's Plays," in *"King Lear," "Macbeth," Indefinition, and Tragedy* (New Haven: Yale U Press, 1983), 127–55; John C. Meagher, "Economy and Recognition: Thirteen Shakespearean Puzzles," *Shakespeare Quarterly,* 35 (1984), 7–21; and Thomas L. Berger, "Casting *Henry V,*" *Shakespeare Studies,* 20 (1988–89), 89–104. Of these, Meagher's and Berger's are more pragmatic, and, to my mind, more satisfying. Berger's also includes a very helpful review of earlier studies of this issue. Likewise pragmatic, and very attentive to early texts, is Giorgio Melchiori, "Peter, Balthazar, and Shakespeare's Art of Doubling," *Modern Language Review,* 78 (1983), 777–92; and exemplary in its method for imagining multiple casting possibilities is Gary Taylor, "'We Happy Few': The 1600 Abridgement," in Stanley Wells and Gary Taylor, *Modernizing Shakespeare's Spelling with Three Studies in the Text of* Henry V (Oxford: Clarendon Press, 1979), 72–123. His note 1, p. 73, summarizes the various points of view on how much time is sufficient time between the various identities of multiply cast characters, with five lines being the minimum found by David Bevington (*From Mankind to Marlowe* (Cambridge, Mass.: Harvard U Press, 1962), 91). I see myself as a pragmatist, but one who assumes that some of Shakespeare's plots exploit the likelihood that elements of multiple casting are tracked by sophisticated spectators and that Shakespeare manipulates the spectators' consciousness of this aspect of a play's construction.

develops his sententious pronouncements about the world as stage hardly begins to explore the wonder of it. To be sure the parts of one man comprise many ages in a lifetime; and Jaques's speech introduces what is, for the character of Adam, the "last scene of all" (2.7.163). In the theatre, however, a man's parts may encompass several identities, and the play of *As You Like It* is not even half over for the player in Adam's role when he makes his last entrance as Sir Rowland's aged retainer.

Imagining *As You Like It* enacted by only some dozen or thirteen players who must cover twenty-one speaking parts (not counting the singing pages) suggests another dimension to Oliver's speech when he, the last of the characters to do so in their original persons, enters the forest in the second half of the play (at 4.3.76). The player who opened the first scene as Oliver has not appeared in that person since the scene with Frederick just before the play's middle (3.1), though he might well have undertaken other small parts in the meantime. (Curiously, another Oliver, Martext, makes his only appearance at 3.3.57, on the line "Here comes Sir Oliver, leaving with the line "Ne'er a fantastical knave of them all shall flout me out of my calling" (3.3.96–97), not to be seen in the play again.)

When Oliver de Boys enters in 4.3, he is looking, he says, for "that youth that [Orlando] calls his Rosalind" (4.3.93) and his/her sister, people he can know only "by description. / Such garments, and such years" (4.3.85–86). Indeed, Oliver has never seen Rosalind nor Celia so far as the spectators know, though in an odd moment of the first scene he has asked Charles if "Rosalind, the Duke's daughter, be banished with her father" (1.1.100–01), as if there might have been romantic possibilities there. But even if he knows her, has either Rosalind or Celia seen him before? And if so, can the spectators expect them to recognize him? Does he look the same as he did? When do the spectators know who he is? The simplifications of *Love in a Forest* are useful here to underscore the technical problems attendant on Oliver's arrival in Arden in *As You Like It*. In Johnson's play, the brother who arrives is not Oliver but Robert, innocent and gentle as Orlando; and the actor playing him has no history with the spectators.

From the positioning of his inverted commas, it appears that Pope particularly admired the central part of Oliver's speech:

> When last the young *Orlando* parted from you,
> He left a promise to return again
> Within an hour; and pacing through the forest,
> Chewing the food of sweet and bitter fancy,
> Lo what befel! he threw his eye aside
> And mark what object did present it self

'Under an oak, whose boughs were moss'd with age,
'And high top bald, of dry antiquity;
'A wretched ragged man, o'er-grown with hair,
'Lay sleeping on his back; about his neck
'A green and gilded snake had wreath'd it self,
'Who with her head, nimble in threats approach'd
'The opening of his mouth; but suddenly
'Seeing *Orlando,* it unlink'd it self,
'And with indented glides did slip away
'Into a bush, under which bush's shade
'A Lioness, with udders all drawn dry,
'Lay couching head on ground, with cat-like watch
'When that the sleeping man should stir; for 'tis
'The royal disposition of that beast
'To prey on nothing that doth seem as dead:
This seen, *Orlando* did approach the man,
And found it was his brother, his elder brother.[14]

Pope seems to admire the speech's descriptive power. The lines he marks make the audience see with their ears the threatening wild life. But in the theatre, the spectators have eyes as well as ears to see; and the plot of *As You Like It* has the potential to make them do a double take at the last two lines of this passage.

The revelation unfolds as periodically as the movements of the snake and the lioness, though its surprises can be effected in various forms depending on the techniques of a given production. If Oliver looks precisely as he did in the first half of the play, the description he has just recounted of "a wretched, ragged man, o'ergrown with hair" (4.3.107) prevents the spectators from assuming that the "elder brother" of whom he speaks is himself. Orlando, the play has been careful to stress, like all the fortunate young men in old tales, has two elder brothers; but Celia does not seem to know that:

> O, I have heard him speak of that same brother,
> And he did render him the most unnatural
> That lived amongst men. (4.3.122–24)

---

[14] The passage is located at 4.3.99–121 in the new Oxford text. I have transcribed it here, however, slightly modernized, from Pope's edition. The modern text prints "with dry antiquity" instead of "of dry antiquity" at line 106. I continue my discussion of this scene quoting from the Oxford text.

The man she addresses replies as if he is not that brother, confirming that the brother in question is the evil, elder one:

> And well he might so do;
> For well I know he was unnatural. (4.3.124–25)

Rosalind/Ganymede interrupts, temporarily distracting Celia and the spectators from further puzzling:

> But to *Orlando.* Did he leave him there,
> Food to the sucked and hungry lioness? (4.3.126–27)

And now the trick is turned:

> Twice did he turn his back, and purposed so.
> But kindness, nobler ever than revenge,
> And nature, stronger than his just occasion,
> Made him give battle to the lioness,
> Who quickly fell before him; in which hurtling
> From miserable slumber I awaked. (4.3.128–33)

For the spectators, there may be no way to resolve the conflicting evidence of what their eyes have seen in fact and in imagination. Rosalind/Ganymede's and Celia/Aliena's questions reflect their relatively simple dismay that Oliver did not say earlier who he was and perhaps does not look so ragged and hairy as the man in his story; but for the spectators, they are questions to the player: "Are you his brother? Was't you he rescu'd? / Was't you that did so oft contrive to kill him?" (4.3.134–35)

Conceivably, if his appearance is identical to the one he assumed in the play's first scene, there are easy answers to these questions, obvious from the first moment of his entrance into the scene; but in the Elizabethan theatre, if he has changed his costume or the cut of his beard, his alteration is another instance of that species of metamorphosis that players continually undergo in this style of playing. And then these questions are pertinent not only to the spectators' experience of the action but to their experience of play. Could the turnabout have been anticipated? Can it be satisfactorily rationalized? What must we understand by it? Oliver's reply to these queries is a paradox: "'Twas I, but 'tis not I" (4.3.136). Is this fair play?

In any staging of this speech, the spectators must endure some suspense about the speaker's identity, including his relationship to Orlando and the ragged man. In some sense, it is the simplest and "fairest" staging to have the player be very recognizably the Oliver of the first scene. The spectators can then understand Oliver's psychology any way they can make sense of his description of his wretched raggedness and the strange way he suspends his self-revelation; their privilege is to know more than Celia/Aliena and Rosalind/Ganymede throughout most of the encounter. The extreme alternative to this approach, bringing Oliver on in a ragged, hairy condition, is also a possible strategy. In that case, the speaker would seem at first a stranger, coincidentally as wretched as the man he describes—maybe the middle brother, the spectators might surmise after the speaker says he knows the elder brother at 4.3.124–25. The identity of the speaker dawns on them and Celia/Aliena and Rosalind/Ganymede at once, though some of the spectators, expecting the unexpected, might anticipate the revelation. It is the most logical resolution, but it reintroduces Oliver in rags for the rest of the play. (To avoid this disadvantage to his actor, Mr. Roberts, Johnson has Robert du Bois describe himself as "A wretched Man, o'erpower'd with Sleep and Travel" (52) rather than as ragged and overgrown with hair.)

Some middle ground seems the most unfair of all, but it would be a good trick that way. Accomplishing it for the most intricate effect would require that Oliver at first be neither certainly himself from the first scene nor obviously the wretched man he describes. The near resemblance to the earlier Oliver is a positive invitation to the spectators to think of the third brother; and that impulse would throw into momentary relief Orlando's resentment at I.i.62 ff. that Oliver has taken advantage of his position to obscure Orlando's resemblance to the other de Boys boys.

Indeed, in this conception of the scene, *As You Like It* seems to be playfully flirting with the substitution that *Love in a Forest* makes, an impulse that might be tracked to Lodge's *Rosalynde* where fraternal resemblance is an issue in the episode. In *Rosalynde,* when Rosader (Orlando), dressed as a forester, encounters Saladyne (Oliver) and rescues him from a lion (not a lioness, and there is no snake), Rosader knows his brother but Saladyne does not know him until, after Saladyne protests his joy in doing "penaunce of my former follies" (219) and his desire to reconcile with Rosader, Rosader reveals his identity. The two brothers then rescue Aliena and Ganimede from "rascalls," both brothers being wounded in the process. Saladyne falls precipitously in love with Aliena, while Ganimede observes:

> All this while that he [Saladyne] spake, *Ganimede* lookt earnestly upon him, and said; Trulie *Rosader,* this Gentleman favours you much in the feature of your face. No mervaile (quoth hee) gentle Swaine, for tis my eldest brother *Saladyne.* Your brother? quoth Aliena (& with that she blusht) he is the more welcome . . . ." (223)

On the Elizabethan stage, establishing the identity of this newcomer to Arden, a question only momentarily perplexing to Celia/Aliena and Rosalind/ Ganymede, has wider implications for how the spectators interpret and will interpret other transformations they see the players sustain.

Is the resemblance they detect incidental to the theatre or an element of the play's fiction? "Are you his brother?" What relationship does each identity the player adopts have to his other roles? "Was't you he rescu'd?" How durable (it is Celia/Aliena who puts this question to Oliver in the play?) is this latest metamorphosis? "Was't you that did so oft contrive to kill him?"

> 'Twas I, but 'tis not I. I do not shame
> To tell you what I was, since my conversion
> So sweetly tastes, being the thing I am. (4.3.136–38)

The new Oliver recalls his old condition in his present being. In fact, he says, the sense of what he is is enhanced by the memory of what he was. The spectators' experience of him in the play's conclusion is to see his former wretchedness as a receding shadow on his reformed identity.

iii

The paradoxical configuration of the new Oliver is a useful guide for appreciating the major device of the play, the Ganymede disguise. As with Oliver, Ganymede can be easily rationalized. *As You Like It* is revised into a play about a girl Rosalind who enjoys an interlude dressed up as Ganymede. At every point in her actions, the spectators appreciate, justifying it with their sense of her plucky resistance to oppression, her efforts to pretend to male identity, how she grows and changes in masque, what she learns and teaches Orlando. In Charles Johnson's *Love in a Forest,* Rosalind was a breeches part, appealing to the delight spectators take in the spectacle of a woman dressed as a page. Johnson's production, like most modern ones of *As You Like It,* showcases the device by casting all female roles, even (in Johnson's case) that of Thisby, with actresses. Rosalind/Ganymede is then the only sexually ambiguous character on the stage. When the spectators have had time to contemplate her/him, she/he reverts in the final appearance of Rosalind to woman's attire. The handling of the Ganymede disguise in *Love in a Forest* corresponds to a prevailing strain in critical responses to *As You Like It.* Commentators discuss the play's relevance to women's experiences, focusing on the degree to which male apparel might permit a woman, in Shakespeare's day at least and for some commentators even in ours, to overcome if only temporarily the restrictions placed on her sex and perhaps, in some of the play's most optimistic interpretations, learn from the experience.[15]

In the Shakespearean theatre, however, where all the men and women were merely players and the effect of costume was to define everything about a character, including class and gender, the part of Rosalind offered a particular challenge. The player who took her on takes on a succession of parts, beginning as a woman and becoming, as the play proceeds, something else again. The plot of *As You Like It,* as it unfolds, is arranged so that it requires of the player an ability that, according to Ovid, existed in nature in creatures like the hyena:

> If all these things seem strange and marvellous,
> Well might we marvel at the hyena's change;
> A female lately mated with a male
> Becomes a male herself. (Met., XV. 408–10)[16]

---

[15] The best of such commentary, and there is a wealth of it, much of it good, acknowledges that Rosalind works within rather than challenges restrictive notions of female gender. See Jean Howard, "Crossdressing, The Theatre, and Gender Struggles in Early Modern England," *Shakespeare Quarterly,* 39 (1988), 418–40, for her useful comments on *As You Like It* (434–35) as well as for her comprehensive notes about other studies. Catherine Belsey, "Disrupting Sexual Difference: Meaning and Gender in the Comedies," in *Alternative Shakespeares,* ed. John Drakakis (New York: Methuen, 1985), 166–90, uses post-structuralist theory (Julia Kristeva) to explain how female transvestism in Shakespeare's comedies allows us to "glimpse a possible meaning, an image of a mode of being, which is not a-sexual, nor bisexual, but which disrupts the system of differences on which sexual stereotyping depends" (190). It is simpler, of course, to say that these plays employ images not of female but of male transvestism and that their appeal is homoerotic. See Lisa Jardine, "'As boys and women are for the most part cattle of this colour': Female roles and Elizabethan eroticism," in *Still Harping on Daughters: Women and Drama in the Age of Shakespeare* (Totowa, New Jersey: Barnes & Noble, 1983), 9–36; Stephen Orgel, "Nobody's Perfect: Or Why Did the English Stage Take Boys for Women?" *South Atlantic Quarterly,* 88 (1989), 7–29; and Smith, 144–51. Belsey's abrupt dismissal of the homoerotic readings of these plays (note 2, p. 235; she is "not entirely persuaded") puzzles me, and I find somewhat convoluted her explanation of how they might please those of us who should resent their misogyny. Nonetheless, readers of this essay may find my conclusion illustrative of just what she says the plays enable us to do.

[16] This is the translation of A. D. Melville (Oxford: Oxford U Press, 1987). The Latin of the Loeb Classical Library text, trans. Frank Justus Miller, rev. G. P. Goold, 2nd ed. (Cambridge: Harvard U Press, 1984), II, 392, is "Si tamen est

By 1599, the probable date of *As You Like It,* the turning of this trick on the Elizabethan stage was nothing new; Shakespeare's own company had doubtless exhibited it in several plays already. [17] *As You Like It* is special for its emphasis on the device; the appeal of the play, claimed for it by its title, would depend on the proficiency with which the players managed it. Its intricate working implicates them all.

The plot of *As You Like It* is structured to showcase the player in the part of Rosalind. Rosalind and Celia are introduced together as a pair of young women (two scenes are devoted to them in this condition) before Rosalind becomes Ganymede. After the costume changes to create Rosalind/Ganymede and Celia/Aliena, the plot of *As You Like It* keeps the pair together for a while,

---

aliquid mirae novitatis in istis, / alternare vices et, quae modo femina tergo / passa marem est, nunc esse marem miremur hyaenam." Melville seems closer to the Latin than Golding: "But if that any noveltye woorth woondring bee in theis / Much rather may we woonder at the *Hyen,* if we please, / Too see how interchaungeably it one whyle dooth remayne, / A female, and another whyle becommeth male againe." See *Shakespeare's Ovid,* ed. W. H. D. Rouse (London, 1904; rpt. 1961). Golding's translation suggests that the hyena moves back and forth between male and female. Melville's more literal translation suggests that the erotic encounter transforms the female to male. In *As You Like It,* as I will discuss below, the mock marriage of 4.1 is an important transitional point for Rosalind/Ganymede. Stephen Greenblatt, "Fiction and Friction," *Shakespearean Negotiations: The Circulation of Social Energy in Renaissance England* (Berkeley: University of California Press, 1988), 66–93, illustrates his discussion of the erotic effect of the "verbal friction" (90) of the comedies with Renaissance medical accounts of sex changes, noting that they are "almost always from female to male, that is, from defective [in the terms of Renaissance medical science] to perfect" (81). Orgel acknowledges this essay as he takes the argument to firmer conclusions than Greenblatt does about the homoerotic energy of the plays.

[17] Julia in *Two Gentlemen of Verona* and Jessica, Portia, and Nerissa of *Merchant of Venice* probably predate Rosalind. None gets the same amount of stage time in disguise. For the *Merchant* girls, it is literally, and in these terms interestingly, an interlude as it is not for Julia, who finishes the play as Sebastian. *Twelfth Night*'s sexually ambiguous twin, who also finishes the play in male attire, has, at the end, two aspects: as Sebastian he has married Olivia; as Cesario, he agrees to be Viola and change to female attire as soon as it can be recovered. This fabrication seems to be approximately contemporary with Rosalind, but most attempts to suggest a dating for Shakespeare's plays put it slightly later than *As You Like It.* Imogen, in the late play *Cymbeline,* once transformed, is Fidele to the end. For comments on the dating of *As You Like It,* see the new Oxford text, pp. 1–5.

moving them in and out of confrontations that alternate between privacy and exposure to others whom they are trying to delude. Alone with Celia and Touchstone, Rosalind is Rosalind/Ganymede, the player's original self in different attire; when these characters encounter strangers (Corin and Silvius, then Orlando on-stage and, off-stage, the spectators do not see it but are teased to imagine it, Rosalind's father), she/he must be Ganymede.

The first encounter of Ganymede with Orlando is literally climactic, occurring in the precise middle of the play's plot (3.2). When Rosalind/Ganymede heard that Orlando was in the forest, she/he had at first reverted to her Rosalind self (3.2.158–242). This passage, ending with the lines "Do you not know I am a woman? When I think, I must speak.—Sweet, say on," and including the reference to Pythagoras, is the one that Pope thought particularly vulgar. Rosalind/Ganymede then determines to "speak to him like a saucy lackey, and under that habit play the knave with him" (3.2.286–87). At last, as Ganymede, she/he complicates the masquerade to a new level by proposing to Orlando further encounters in which he will "call me Rosalind and come every day to my cot, and woo me" (3.2.405–06).

Seen in these terms, the second half of Shakespeare's plot offers the spectators increasingly ingenious situations in which to delight in the ability of the player. It is in this part of the play, that the Rosalind character is actually disengaged from the coupling with Celia and begins to encounter others unattended. The spectators see the trick in 3.5 without benefit of Celia/Aliena's foil. During this part of the play, Celia/Aliena is now no longer simply a second woman's part to set off Rosalind nor a properly costumed woman to set off the femininity of the cross-dressed Rosalind/Ganymede. Now when Celia/Aliena appears, she is there as the conventional alternative to the master-mistress Ganymede/Rosalind.

Again, a feature of Johnson's plot is comparatively helpful here. Interested in a second love action for Celia, Johnson constructs scenes (refurbished Touchstone-Audrey scenes) in which Celia appears, without Rosalind, to be wooed by Jaques. In contrast, Shakespeare's plot disposes of the business of Celia's love life only in report, using Celia/Aliena on stage exclusively as a foil to Rosalind/Ganymede/Rosalind. She reappears with Rosalind/Ganymede/ Rosalind significantly in the mock wedding scene (4.1), at first tentatively compliant in it and then, after Orlando's departure, critical of it, passing judgment in character as Rosalind's cousin and friend and also as player, in a more technical way:

> You have simply misused our sex in your love prate. We must have your doublet and hose plucked over your head, and show the world what the bird hath done to her own nest. (4.1.184–87)

The player in the role of Celia tells his fellow that the effect of his shenanigans is nearly to discover their essential mystery—male players counterfeit women on the stage. It is no matter though. The player of Rosalind/Ganymede/Rosalind is, by this point, no longer practicing that technique; and what he can convey now, he says, surpasses conventional representation of love:

> O coz, coz, coz my pretty little coz, that thou didst know how many fathom deep I am in love. But it cannot be sounded. My affection hath an unknown bottom, like the Bay of Portugal. (4.1.188–91)

As Rosalind/Ganymede moves more completely into the practice of Ganymede/Rosalind and particularly after the mock marriage of 4.1, she/he becomes, even without Orlando, Ganymede. Calling his sister Aliena (not Celia), he might almost (pace Pope) be mistaken for Berowne or Benedick:

> No, that same wicked bastard of Venus, that was begot of thought, conceived of spleen, and born of madness, that blind rascally boy that abuses everyone's eyes because his own are out, let him be judge how deep I am in love. I'll tell thee, Aliena, I cannot be out of the sight of Orlando. I'll go find a shadow and sigh till he come. (4.1.194–200)

The hilarity of this is the laugh of the hyena. That laugh is inspired, tradition has it, by knowing what it is to love and to be loved as both sexes.

Phoebe and Silvius, omitted by Johnson, are important components of the plot at this point, the former eliciting Ganymede/Rosalind's response to women (the effect depends on how the player playing Phoebe projects femininity), and the latter being the occasion of something like brotherly collusion. Silvius is also a significant foil to Orlando. Against Silvius's disinterest in Ganymede except as rival for Phoebe's love, Orlando's degree of involvement in the masquerade becomes a charged element in the play, and Rosalind/Ganymede's response to that involvement has implications for both of her/his aspects. If Orlando seems to find himself attracted in earnest to the creature he woos in jest, this is a complicated moment for both of them, never more so than when Orlando answers Ganymede/Rosalind's command that he produce love prate by saying he "would kiss before [he] spoke" (4.1.66).

Since her entry into Arden, Rosalind has been evolving before the eyes of the spectators into another self, as the increasing urgency of Orlando's dislocated desire fastens on, not Rosalind/Ganymede but Ganymede/Rosalind—not a woman masquerading as a man but a man with the aspect of a woman. Shakespeare probably did not need Christopher Marlowe's Leander to lead him to imagine this creature, but it is significant that Phoebe's response to first seeing the person she calls Ganymede is to vouch that the Dead Shepherd had it right: "now I find thy saw of might: / 'Who ever loved that loved not at first sight'" (3.5.82–83).[18] Love, in what is now for her the best sense, depends on the sheerly physical experience of seeing this desirable object. Phoebe is, of course, the most conspicuous casualty to the force that this creature exerts in the play, but, as noted above, Orlando himself (protesting all the while his devotion to his Rosalind) might not be immune; and the spectators may also be getting self-conscious of their reactions.

As the play moves into its final phase, an impulse to reduce and control the effect of Ganymede, already given voice in Celia/Aliena, takes concerted form in the new Oliver. His influence may be understood as a willful element of his character (his old spoiler self on the ascendancy), but it is not necessary to interpret it this way in order to acknowledge it. It may be said to be simply circumstantial to Shakespeare's use of him. He treats Ganymede/Rosalind in simplified, even crude terms. The speech in which he describes his rescue by Orlando makes a travesty of the Ganymede/Rosalind masquerade, using, as sexual travesties often do, mockery of women to define any degree of effeminacy as a risible condition. Oliver's story is alive with tantalizing physical details ("a green and gilded snake . . . approach[ing] / The opening of his mouth," "a lioness, with udders all drawn dry," 4.3.109–11, 115). He tells this story to explain an object, which he has produced and exhibited to the spectators—the bloody napkin, with its blatantly taunting feminine significance. In encounters with Ganymede/Rosalind, Oliver always reduces him/her to the feminine aspect of the role. When he/she swoons, Celia urges that Oliver "take him by the arm" (4.3.164), and Oliver, doing so, observes, "You a man? you lack a man's heart" (4.3.165–66);[19] and at his next meeting with Ganymede/Rosalind, he calls him/her "fair sister" (5.2.18).

Whether he is seen to be characterized as doing so or is simply understood

---

[18] The line is from Marlowe's *Hero and Leander,* line 176 of the "first sestyad" as Bowers prints it. Shakespeare's sonnets to the young man are helpful to describe Ganymede/Rosalind. Sonnet 20 is the explicit one, but sonnet 53 is interesting in this context for its emphasis on the idea that the beloved is an artificial rather than a natural phenomenon.

[19] The arm as a part of the body adjacent to the breast would permit Oliver's grasp of Ganymede to feel for the presence of that distinctive part of the female anatomy, which would be there in an actress and not there, except imaginatively or artificially, in the Elizabethan player. Ganymede/Rosalind uses a figure of speech based on the same proximity of breast to arm at 5.2.19 ff., when he/she says, "O, my dear Orlando, how it grieves me to see thee wear thy heart in a scarf," and he replies, "It is my arm."

as an agent for Shakespeare to achieve this effect, Oliver's appearance in Arden admits a strain to the play that suggests that it may be time for love-play with Ganymede/Rosalind to give way to more conventional romantic games. Prompted, he says, by envy of the happiness Oliver enjoys with Aliena/Celia, Orlando tells Ganymede that his heart is "Wounded . . . but with the eyes of a lady" (5.2.24) and asserts that he "can live no longer by thinking" (5.2.48). Later in the scene, he, Silvius, and Phoebe chant a litany to love, and Orlando's refrain is "Rosalind."

Yet as the play moves to its conclusion and the spectators anticipate, perhaps variously, the resolution they would like to see, Orlando's pining for Rosalind does not utterly displace Ganymede/Rosalind. Even as he chants Rosalind's name, he mistakes Ganymede/Rosalind for her, asking "why blame you me to love you?" (5.2.100). Orlando is, in fact, by this point in the play, in a lover's version of the spectators' dilemma: having flirted with a fascinating substitute for ordinary desires, they must wonder if and how they want the fantasy to end. For Orlando, in conventional romantic terms, there is only one way that his desire for Ganymede/Rosalind will not falsify his first love. Ganymede/Rosalind must be Rosalind after all. The stage is set for the final movement in the evolution of the part that was Rosalind and then undertook Ganymede to become by turns Rosalind/Ganymede and Ganymede/Rosalind. What is next? Where will it end? What would you like to see?

Ganymede/Rosalind responds to Orlando's desire for closure with the promise of magic:

> Believe then, if you please, that I can do strange things. I have since I was three year old conversed with a magician, most profound in his art, and yet not damnable. If you do love Rosalind so near the heart as your gesture cries it out, when your brother marries Aliena, shall you marry her. I know into what straits of fortune she is driven, and it is not impossible to me, if it appear not inconvenient to you, to set her before your eyes tomorrow, human as she is, and without any danger. (5.2.56–65)

It is not difficult for anyone, regardless of how uninitiated into the mysteries of theatre, to imagine a way to accomplish the trick Ganymede promises. The player must simply be returned in the tiring house to the condition of his first appearance in the play. What would be difficult to accept in the theatre, particularly by spectators who are anything but naive about theatre's conventions, is the sense of anticlimax produced by so simple an effect.[20]

---

[20] In her Arden edition of the play, Agnes Latham puts the ending of *As You Like It* in the context of the elaborate masques of the late plays. I concur with

As a final look at *Love in a Forest* suggests, even Charles Johnson saw the difficulty of the simple solution. The ingenious interpolation of the Pyramus and Thisby interlude significantly enhances his play's ending. Additionally, by its length, it allows ample time for Mrs. Booth to effect a spectacular return to her feminine condition. Johnson's text even specifies the interval, having Rosalind say at the opening of the last act, "And hence I go to make these Doubts all even / In half the Circle but of sixty Minutes" (57); and as the Duke replies to Orlando's agreeing with him that the boy Ganymede resembles the Duke's daughter, he turns to the projected entertainment with lines adapted from *A Midsummer Night's Dream*:

> Come, now what Entertainment shall we have
> To waste this half an Age, this long half Hour,
> When *Ganymede* has promis'd to perform
> These Miracles of Love. (58)

Something elaborate seems indicated, with Rosalind entering, so the *dramatis personae* records, accompanied by actresses in the roles of Celia and Hymen. In

---

the impulse of this comparison because it acknowledges that *As You Like It* is promising its audience "greater wonders" (5.2.27) at the end than anything seen earlier. I am not so anxious, however, as she is to see the masque as utterly solemn in its effect, with "sacramental or symbolic value" (xxii). Depending on how it is staged, it might also be precisely what Latham says it is not, "frivolous, idle and unreal" (xxiii). For that matter, metatheatrical playing around might well attend even the elaborate *coup de grace* of *The Winter's Tale*. In the late play, as in *As You Like It*, a woman apparently lost to the hero is to be restored by magic to him in the final scene. An unnamed gentleman releases news of a statue, "which is in the keeping of Paulina—a piece many years in doing and now newly performed by that rare Italian master, Julio Romano, who, had he himself eternity and could put breath into his work, would beguile Nature of her custom, so perfectly he is her ape: he so near to Hermione hath done Hermione, that they say one would speak to her and stand in hope of answer. Thither with all greediness of affection are they gone, and there they intend to sup" (5.2.97–105). What ingenious effect a given modern production accomplishes to pay off on this promise often depends on an actress doubling in the roles of Hermione and Perdita. In Shakespeare's theatre, however, the effect is at least projected to be much more wondrous. The crucial ingredient is conveyed by the name Julio Romano, not a sculptor but a painter, notorious, R. B. McKerrow reminds us in annotating Thomas Nashe's *Pierce Penilesse* (4.149–50), for drawings accompanied by Pietro Aretino's *Sonetti Lussuriosi*. A nude or semi-nude statue, especially if the spectators expect it to be represented by a player, is something to look forward to, on the Shakespearean stage at least.

contrast to *As You Like It, Love in a Forest* makes Rosalind's beauty, not her gender, an issue in her last entrance.

Shakespeare's plot separates Rosalind/Ganymede's and Celia/Aliena's exit from their reentrance by only as much time as Touchstone needs to explain and rehearse the degrees of the lie and has "Rosalind and Celia," attended by Hymen, variously costumed male players, enter announced or accompanied by *"Still Music."*[21] As to how the player of Rosalind appears in this last entrance, the play's text is silent. Oliver's paradox is, however, useful—"'Twas I, but 'tis not I": if these are the terms of Rosalind's final appearance, the creature must appear to be what he/she has been, yet be, in some sense, not anything the spectators have seen before. Given the length of the interval taken up by Touchstone's discourse, the metamorphosis must also be relatively simple to accomplish in the tiring house. The pre-Restoration Folio texts of the play, in contrast to most of their successors, are provocative in what they say and what they do not.[22] They are consequently unusually open to a wide range of

---

[21] In the Oxford text, this part of the direction precedes "Enter Hymen with Rosalind and Celia as themselves" after 5.4.102. Brissenden describes its position in First Folio in a note: "F places the stage direction ['Still Music.'] after the entry." It is actually on a separate line, centered over the song. Brissenden continues, noting that the First Folio position of the notice of music "creat[es] some ambiguity, as it could accompany [the entrance] then continue as Hymen speaks." The ambiguity is compounded by the potential of "still" to function verbally (signifying that the music ceases as Hymen speaks) or adverbally (suggesting that the music continues through Hymen's recital of the song). Brissenden's gloss implies that he assumes the music continues, but reveals that he takes "still" adjectivally (denoting "quiet, serious" music, as he takes it to mean in the direction "Still music of recorders" in 5.3 of *The Two Noble Kinsmen*); but "quiet" and "serious" could not describe the sense of "still" in the more obviously analogous "storm still" through the heath scenes of the third act of *King Lear*. See also Brissenden's note to this moment for some descriptions of how directors elaborate Hymen's entrance, including "garlands and wreaths, boys and girls strewing flowers, a kind of temple erected on stage" (Macready, Drury Lane, 1842) and "a descending cloud machine which opened to reveal the god" (Trevor Nunn, RSC, 1977). Theatrically, if Rosalind is not a wonder, something else must be.

[22] Maura Slattery Kuhn, "Much Virtue in If," *Shakespeare Quarterly,* 28 (1977), 40–50, suggests "What if . . . Rosalind and Celia come in very much as they went out—that is, instead of a gowned Rosalind, we have a shepherd with, perhaps, a clean face, long hair, and no hat who might walk like a girl instead of having a swashing and martial air?" (42) My own speculations are of this order of simplicity, but I would look to the player to make good on his promise of 5.2.65 in some, as Ganymede/Rosalind says, "magical" way. I am also indebted to Kuhn's essay for the impulse to look closely at the First Folio text.

possible effects out of which a company might select, in a given production, what would best please the spectators in that place.

In the First Folio, Hymen's speech implies a stage direction:

> Then is there mirth in heaven,
> When earthly things made even
> Atone together.
> Good Duke, receive thy daughter,
> Hymen from heaven brought her,
> Yea, brought her hither,
> That thou mightst join his hand with his
> Whose heart within his bosom is. (5.4.103–10)

The Third Folio, the first one printed after the Restoration, changes the penultimate line. Apparently eager to have the lovers join hands, the printer emends "his hand with his" to "her (hir) hand with his," in effect bidding the Duke to join Orlando's hand with Rosalind's rather than Orlando's with Hymen's or with that of a Rosalind who might be considered, because that is how, to some extent, she appears, a he.[23] Subsequent editors concur with the emendation of F3, often going further in stage directions. Nicholas Rowe adds "Rosalind in Woman's Cloths." Pope follows both of these changes.

The Third Folio editor presses on with the importance of Orlando and Rosalind joining hands by having the next two lines, which in the First Folio are assigned to Rosalind,

> To you I give myself, for I am yours.
> To you I give myself, for I am yours. (5.4.111–12)

spoken in turn, the first by Rosalind and the second by Orlando. Rowe restores them both to Rosalind and adds directions that specify that the first is spoken "To the Duke" and the second "To Orl." Again Pope follows Rowe as do most

---

[23] In Hymen's song quoted above, I have silently replaced "her" with "his," in otherwise quoting the new Oxford text. In the discussion below, I likewise remove from the new Oxford text the stage directions that have been added by editors after the First Folio and are accepted in that text. In the *Textual Companion,* the new Oxford editors say, of the pronoun in Hymen's song, that "Rosalind's next line, 'To you I giue myselfe, for I am yours,' may support F1's reading" (394). In pastoral romances of Shakespeare's day, Sidney's *Arcadia* and Lodge's *Rosalynde,* for example, characters disguised as people of the opposite sex are referred to, in the narration, by the pronoun appropriate to the sex of their disguises. In this song as printed in the First Folio, the pronouns seem to describe shifting perspectives on Rosalind's aspect.

modern editors. Since there are three characters who speak after Rosalind's
double bequest of herself, the Duke, Orlando, and Phoebe—

> *Duke Senior.* If there be truth in sight, you are my daughter.
> *Orlando.* If there be truth in sight, you are my Rosalind.
> *Phoebe.* If sight and shape be true,
> Why then, my love adieu!

and Rosalind responds to all three—

> *Rosalind.* I'll have no father if you be not he,
> I'll have no husband if you be not he,
> Nor ne'er wed woman if you be not she. (5.4.113–19)

there is no textual reason not to allow Rosalind to offer herself to both Orlando
and Phoebe. Phoebe seems to want to reconsider (what she sees seems to have
undergone a change); but Rosalind persists, saying Phoebe is the only woman
she *would* marry, as at 5.3.107–09, Ganymede/Rosalind did promise Phoebe to
"marry you if ever I marry woman, and I'll be married tomorrow" and at
5.4.21–21, had enjoined her, "Keep your word, Phoebe, that you'll marry me, /
Or else refusing me to wed this shepherd." Phoebe's further reply at this point
is prevented by Hymen's next words, "Peace, ho, I bar confusion / 'Tis I must
make conclusion / Of these most strange events. / Here's eight that must take
hands / To join in Hymen's bands, / If truth holds true contents" (5.4.120–25).
It is for the god to decide who, in the group, gets whom.

Editors are busy about all aspects of the play's final disposition of joys,
preventing all but the most conventional possibilities. In 1765, Dr. Johnson
apportioned Hymen's blessings—

> You and you no cross shall part;
> You and you are heart in heart.
> You to his love must accord,
> Or have a woman to your lord.
> You and you are sure together
> As the winter to foul weather. (5.4.126–31)

in order, to Orlando and Rosalind ("no cross shall part"), Oliver and Celia ("are
heart and heart"), Phoebe ("to his love [Silvius's] love must accord"), and the
clown and Audrey ("sure together, / As the winter to foul weather"). Only the
third, however, certainly goes to anyone and that is to Phoebe, reminding her
that if she reneges on her promise to marry Silvius, she will be married to

FACING THE MUSIC IN ARDEN   505

Rosalind. At 5.4.144–45, saying "I will not eat my word. Now thou art mine, / Thy faith my fancy to thee doth combine," she makes her choice. (The alternative to what she must do may have always been unthinkable; but since Capell's 1765 edition, the Variorum notes, lines 144–45 are marked "to Silvius.") Having Touchstone and Audrey addressed in the coupling of two "sure together / As the winter to foul weather" is reasonable, but it disappoints the clown, who had no wish to be married well (3.3.81–84); and why editors prefer that Hymen address Orlando and Rosalind before Oliver and Celia is puzzling since it confers a negative blessing on them rather than a positive one. It is consistent, however, with interpretations of the play that wish to stress its fairy-tale operation of reversing the social status of the elder and younger brother.

In these last moments, a "second brother" has entered, announcing that he is "the second son of old Sir Rowland" (5.4.147) and bringing news that Duke Frederick has become a hermit and Duke Senior's dukedom is restored to him. This announcement Duke Senior converts to political terms:

> To one [brother] his lands withheld, and to the other
> A land itself at large, a potent dukedom. (5.4.163–64)

The lines refer respectively to Oliver, whose lands were confiscated by Duke Frederick in 3.1 (though it is not explained in the play how that is communicated to Duke Senior) and Orlando, whose marriage to Duke Senior's daughter would bring with it some potency, if not a dukedom.

Yet in the Elizabethan theatre, Oliver and Orlando's relative rank and power is not the only thing resolved by the second brother's entry. Since 1.1.5, the spectators have known that there are three brothers, and at 2.1.26, they register that the middle brother has the same name as the old Duke's friend. In *Love in a Forest*, Johnson eliminates the redundancy by renaming the other brother Robert; and commentators on the play usually note the repetition with an eye to explaining it or saying that it does not matter. [24] The fussiness testifies to the success of Shakespeare's sustained play with the curiosity he has aroused about these brothers, preoccupied as it is likely to be with fraternal resemblance and thus with the endlessly amusing glance at women inherent in jokes about paternity. Throughout all the incidents of characters being transformed to enter

---

[24] See Brissenden's introduction, p. 38, "Names and Places," for some good conjectures, including Helen Gardner's that Shakespeare meant Jaques to be the middle brother and then changed his mind, and a reference to a reviewer who actually became confused by a production into thinking the melancholy Jaques was the middle brother.

Arden, there are likely to be some among the spectators who are expecting a final little bit of tidying up around the character of the melancholy Jaques, an event that is finally, certainly prevented by the entrance of someone never seen before (in this person), saying he is "the second son of old sir Rowland" (5.4.147).

So after all there is one in Arden who is resistant to its transforming power. Duke Senior's sententious friend is not the middle brother, grown to an age that disguises him so that Orlando did not recognize him. He is only what he has seemed all along, Monsieur Melancholy, playing his last scene as himself, making his bequests:

> You to your former honour I bequeath;
> Your patience and your virtue, well deserves it.
> You to a love that your true faith doth merit;
> You to your land, and love, and great allies;
> You to a long and well-deserved bed;
> And you to wrangling, for thy loving voyage
> Is but for two months victualled. (5.4.181–87)

Rowe marked these lines to be delivered respectively to the Duke, Orlando, Oliver, Silvius, and Touchstone, a reasonable disposition though by no means the only one; and it is a shame to settle the lines so conclusively when the speaker's habitual perversity might be further illustrated by passing around different combinations.

In fact, the play is not conclusive about what any of the characters will take from what they have experienced; and some, like the second brother, will take nothing at all. The only certain detail is the context for the final arrangement of the stage:

> Play, music, and you brides and bridegrooms all,
> With measure heaped in joy to th' measures fall. (5.4.173–74)

A dance to conclude the play's action is an ingenious device, creating social distinction and dissolving it and conceivably allowing the player of Rosalind a final opportunity to exhibit the prescribed graces of both genders, each in turn or in some proportion, before coming to rest as Orlando's lady.

iv

It has become something of a minor theme in criticism of the play these days to consider whether *As You Like It* is informed by or open to a feminist vision. I will say that I think there is no question. The play is indifferent to women, except as they might offer occasions for men to interact with one another. At points in the play, notably at Oliver's long speech about the snake and the lioness in Act IV, the play mocks woman outright. There may be something of value to learn from this mockery about the origins of patriarchy or its consequences; and it may be true as well that, in this comedy, Shakespeare's misogyny is benign enough that it can be subverted in production; but it is there, and feminism is best served by facing that aspect of the play without pretense.

Yet the play has always delighted me. "All the world's a stage" was the first Shakespearean speech I learned by heart. The strange, metempsychotic experience of finding my way inside someone else's language until its vocabulary and syntax became extensions of my own occurred first for me with the realization that "pipes" was a verb. It was a line with curious relevance to my state: "and his big manly voice, turning again to childish treble, pipes and whistles in his sound" (2.7.161–63). When I took my seven-year-old daughter to see the play, she was at the age where she had chosen another name—Frederick it was, of all things, so she started with delight every time the name was mentioned. (Two ladies behind us took this reaction for precocity when it occurred during the speech in the last act, 5.4.149, describing the bad duke's conversion.) The fantasy of having been or possibly becoming some absolute other may be one of the things that take us out of the world we actually inhabit and into the world that is the stage.

Rosalind was the part I played at school, a woman's college, so the men in the cast came to rehearsal in a bus. Our little production ended with the epilogue: "If I were a woman" (Ep. 16–17), a line that I was pleased to realize amused the audience as I said it. A boy I knew dated me for a while after that. He said he liked the way my legs looked in black tights and the way I talked to Orlando as Ganymede. He stopped calling me when I would not spend the night with him: "I can live no longer by thinking" (5.2.48), I guess.

In other words, I have made this play, at various points in my life, what I need it to be. This is why I feel no disdain for *Love in a Forest* nor for Alexander Pope's desire to wish away certain passages while marking the ones he took most to heart. It is why I value the play most for the variety of incidental fantasies it can sustain. This essay brings me to the conclusion that the play's essential conceit, embodied in the elements of the stylized theatre for which it was created, is unusually open to anything those who play with it can imagine, finally all but indifferent to what is or what should be.

Fortunately, this means *As You Like It* can be taken, among other ways, seriously. As a play representing customary diversions in polite society, it eventually found the stage after the Restoration and has frequented it ever since. Its early editors supported its sober uses; and they have never quite released their hold on it, in something like the way that the "Nymph's Reply" has become the companion piece to Marlowe's lyric in anthologies. As we take advantage of this circumstance, it may be important to consider why we would not have these things any other way.

(New York, 1996)

III REVIEWS

On two Italian *Dancers*

An intimate Friend desired that I would go with him to *Drury-Lane*
Playhouse to see the celebrated Comic Dancers, Signior and Signiora *Fausan,*
who were become the Topic of all polite Conversations from their
Performances, which are as extraordinary as they are new.

I was surpriz'd on my entring into the Pit to find it almost full, but was
inform'd by my Friend, the House had been crowded ever since *Shakespear's*
Play of, *As you like it,* had been acted, and these Dancers had perform'd. I
could not but with Pleasure reflect on the just Taste of the Publick, who had
receiv'd so fine a Piece with such universal Approbation: But then I knew not
how to reconcile, that those polite Audiences, who gave a judicious Applause to
every beautiful sentiment of *Shakespear,* should at the same time be delighted
with the Gesticulations and Capers of a Forcing Mimic. At the End of the third
Act these Foreign dancers were to perform a Comic Dance call'd, *Le Buffoon,*
or the *Idiot:* My Expectation was rais'd to the height; but at their Entrance on
the Stage, they alarm'd me by an inexpressive Agility and descriptive Action,
look and Motion, which was all perform'd with such mimic Variety, that I defy
the most severe Cynick to say that they wou'd not at least raise in him an
agreeable Surprize, to see all the Attitudes, oddities, and mock gesticulations of
the two Idiots, who may be suppos'd to be in Love with one another. It is not
any Distortion of Body or unnatural transposition of the Limbs which they
exhibit to the View, but the extravagant Idiotry, which the Passions of Love,
Disdain, Joy, Resentment, would on a regal Occasion actuate on the personages
they represent: Nor do they so manage their Dance that it is ungraceful; they
take opportunities to shew by Actions and Movements, that in their Comic
Humour they have an Elegancy. This Performance therefore, on Reflection,
appear'd to me, instead of an unnatural Extravaganza, to be founded on the
nicest Observations of human Nature, and prove Signior and Signiora to be
Persons of good Judgment, as well as great Agility. At the End of the Play they

danced another Comic Dance, call'd the *Swedish Gardiners,* where there is a Courtship in low life, describ'd with much Humour and Expression of the Passions; for the Variations of their Countenances are so new, so comic, and at the same time so excellently adapted to the Story, that no spectator can be so dull, as not to know what they intend should be meant, as well as if it were express'd in Words.

After the Play was over I went into some Company, where the chief of the Conversation turn'd upon these *Italian* Dancers manner of performance: Mr. Classic imagin'd that these People gave the best idea that we cou'd have form'd of the *Roman Pantomime;* for the Mime, or Dancing Actor of the Antients is thus describ'd by Claudian:

> *Qui Nutu manibusque loquax.*
> Who by his *Nod* and *Hands* expressive speaks.]

Nor indeed is this Conjecture to be disapprov'd, for other Reasons than the Significancy of their comick Motion and Action, which excite laughter and Approbation: I doubt not but this kind of Dancing, in which the *Italians* only are excellent, was originally taken from the *Roman Pantomime;* and tho' the Modern Artists may not be equal to the Antient, and there may be a great difference in the power of each, yet it is not absurd to think, the natural humour of the People, and their Love of the Diversion, have, thro' several Ages, still retain'd some Remains of this old *Roman Entertainment,* as of the Arts and Sciences of their Ancestors.

(*The Gentleman's Magazine,* 1741) Vol. 11: 28–29

THE TIMES
7 February 1786

THEATRE

As You Like It, the most beautiful of the beautiful pieces of the immortal Shakespeare, was performed yesterday evening at *Covent Garden,* with two material alterations in the cast, *Mrs. Wells* being the *Rosalind,* and *Mrs. Brown* the *Audrey.*

Rosalind is certainly the best character, out of the line of low and simple nature, that *Mrs. Wells* has yet attempted; but it will not bear the strict test of criticism. The beauty of her face is not expressive of the vivacity which is the characteristic of *Rosalind;* nor has her person, though finely formed, the elegance and ease of a woman bred in the high fashion of court.

Mrs. Brown looked *Audrey* better than she played it, yet she played it well, though not as well as little Wilson.

Though *Quick's* performance of *Touchstone* is not so chaste in its stile as we have seen it, yet, as the manner is original, and the effect produced loud approbation and vociferous laughter, it has our ample approbation—and indeed, though *chastity* in the acting of his character has been praised, we have our doubts if a little *outre* colouring is not proper ornament to a court jester wearing a pied fool's coat.

Orlando by *Lewis* had its usual merit and applause, and the acting of Adam by Hull was truly pathetic.

Jaques is a character of great difficulty—it was played by *Aicken,* and it is but justice to say he did it every possible justice—in our memory it has not been better played.

LONDON GAZETTE
18 February 1786

THEATRICALS
(BY a Correspondent)

Drury Lane

If the applause of Saturday's audience was the criterion—and that applause *real*—"As You Like It" could not be too oft repeated; but appearances are often deceitful—the applause we now advert to—a perfect *Tempest*—was merely the figure for a more violent storm of disapprobation—a storm that totally wrecked Kemble's fondest hopes of dramatic fame.

The Siddons—in despite of critics—those tyrants of the stage—the Siddons—was *herself* in Rosalind—and in the sublime Asiatic conclusion, "what can we say more."

Kemble's Orlando was given with a delicacy of colouring—in some parts with new *reading*—most of them with sufficient *emphasis*—and one not with perfect good *discretion*—we mean where Rosalind questions Orlando as to the *height* of his mistress—"just as high as my heart,"—is the answer—in our opinion Kemble gave it too trippingly o'er the tongue.

Packer—and well has the veteran been termed the *Pack-house* of the drama—Packer, though the elder brother of Orlando—is much too old a representative of one with whom the Princess Celia is to be *struck* with at first sight.

Palmer's Jaques ought not to pass without observance—his reflections on the wounded deer, and delivery of the seven ages—what in the ark could have been better?

Of Kemble's "Projects" the less that's said the better—they have failed— the lion wars not with the dead.

Of *Cobb's* prologue too much cannot be said—the earlier in print the better—then shall it *speak* for itself.

THE TIMES
12 December 1788

Theatre

Drury Lane

The Comedy of "As You Like It" announced last week, but deferred on account of the absence of Mr. *King* and his TOUCHSTONE, was yesterday evening presented at the Theatre, in order to introduce *Mrs Goodall,* from the Bath theatre, in the arduous part of *Rosalind*—we say *arduous*—for though there are not any very trying scenes—yet is so much discrimination—*archness* and pleasantry—with no inconsiderable share of *feeling* are required that it must be considered as a very trying character for a first appearance.

Mrs Goodall, of whom we have now to speak—discovered so much *sensibility* on her entré, that must have totally disarmed the critic, not devoid himself of sensibility, from forming any judgment of what presented itself in the first act of her *Rosalind*—for so infinitely depressed was Mrs. *Goodall* by her fears, that it was not till the third act that she gave her comic powers the full scope—from that period we were happy to perceive much progressional improvement—and the curtain was not suffered to close on her actions without the most warm and unfeigned testimonies of approbation.

This Lady, as we are informed, is the daughter of a Mr. *Staunton,* Manager of the Stafford, Newcastle and Litchfield companies—her person is not inelegant, and her breeches figure though not equal to Mrs. *Jordan's,* far from indifferent—Mrs. *Goodall's* voice, though not remarkable for strength—is not unlike Miss *Brunson's*—it has at times much sweetness, and seems well calculated for the arch playfulness, peculiar sprightly Comedy.

We do not mean to assert that Mrs *Goodall's* Rosalind had the *real town make,* but with practice assiduity, and attention, we have no doubt of its receiving the true *polish.*

PALMER surprised us agreeably, considering it was got up on the *spur* of the *occasion,* with a very pleasant portrait of the *motley* fool,—his next appearance will render it an unexceptionable performance.

THE TIMES
23 September 1789

Drury Lane

Last night Shakespeare's much admired comedy of As You Like It, was performed to a good house, which, indeed, at half price was crouded.

This Play was in general well cast—*Sweet* for the first time in Touchstone went through the character with much credit—*Wroughton* in Jaques was nervous and impressive.

Barrimore, we have often mentioned as an improving Actor, nor was we disappointed in *Orlando,* which he went through with great spirit.

We must not omit the Justice due to *Aickin,* whom we ever behold with pleasure, in the characters he sustains.

The MANAGER has acted with great judgment during the NATURAL absence of Mrs. *Jordan,* and GREAT indisposition of Miss *Farren,* to bring forward into notice the talents of Mrs. *Goodall,* whom it would be injustice not to notice as the most promising actress which has appeared on the boards of Old Drury for many years. Her memory is retentive, her person pleasing, and her action in general easy.

If she keeps to the study of her genius, and does not let the applause she merits, betray her into affectation, we pronounce her an acquisition to the entertainment of the public. If she will profit from our opinion, she will lay aside the bandeau on her hair, when she expires in the last scene. We think them no ornament in the paraphernalia of dress.

THE TIMES
21 November 1789

THEATRE

Covent Garden

To the liberality of Mr. *Harris,* the public are indebted for the re-appearance of their old friend TOM KING—and for both their sakes we are happy to remark his TOUCHSTONE had all the *magnetism* it deserved.

Our old favourite was welcomed by a brilliant and crouded audience, with that kind of applause which must have been highly gratifying to his feelings—of his excellence in TOUCHSTONE and SIR JOHN TROTLEY it would be needless to enlarge—it will be sufficient to observe, that in both he truly merited the plaudits so warmly and frequently bestowed.

Harley gives a rough brutality to JAQUES not intended by the Author—in the first act his stern malignity of countenance indicated more of the villainous plottings of the tyrant RICHARD—than the calm observation of the moralizing noble—his laugh in describing the motley fool was injudicious and strained—the latter part of the SEVEN AGES was most ably delivered—and the miseries attending second childhood finely conceived—and pathetically enforced.

Mr. *Harley* has resources within himself—and if he suffers them to evaporate in a vile imitation of something better we have seen before—or a wretched drawl, most studiously to be avoided—it is his own fault—for it is most certain, that in some characters where the perfection of form and feature is not demanded—he may—if he will—defy criticism.

The *Orlando* of Mr. *Holman* was throughout given too trippingly o'er the tongue—the ardent love and distresses of Sir Rowland's youngest son was totally put to flight by a pert insignificant levity that destroyed the interest of the character—for who can feel for those who are not disposed to feel for themselves?

Mrs. Pope's ROSALIND had weight sufficient without every line being enforced by the thumping of their spear,—We hope she will forgive our remarking this fault,—when we confess at the same time, it was the only one we could perceive in her ROSALIND.

Miss *Chapman* played the Duke's daughter prettily enough,—but till she can read better, we would advise her to leave out as many of Orlando's lines as possible.

From Miss *Stuart's* appearance we should be apt to presume the *Forest of Arden* was well stocked with hair-dressers, and that Shepherdesses were dressed for love, not money. We were in hopes the Dukes would have found better representatives than *Powel* and *Gardiner,*—who, though well enough in their way,—were here quite out of their way.

Johnstone laughed heartily in Amiens,—and in return, the audience laughed as heartily at his singing.

THE TIMES
3 October 1842

Drury Lane Theatre

Mr. Macready commenced his second season here on Saturday, to all appearances received to carry it on in the same spirit and to steer the same course as in the former one. Revivals both of plays and music invested with all the charms of Stanfield's scenery and every accessory to stage effect which can be devised and intrusted to a most complete company, now enriched from the ruins of the former rival management with names of Mr. and Mrs. Mathews. Mrs. Nisbett and Mr. Stratton will, it seems, form the staple motive of attraction and from the extreme friendliness, not to say enthusiasm, of Mr. Macready's reception, at the outset, by an almost crowded audience, he has not, we think, miscalculated the public. Immediately after "God Save the Queen," executed by the *corps d'opera,* and loyally encored by the audience, a loud shout was raised on all sides for Mr. Macready, who after a short time obeyed, and came forward in the dress of Jaques, to receive the good wishes of his audience and stand a fire of bouquets from the more zealous of his supporters.

The cast of *As You Like It,* as it was played on Saturday night, certainly justified the anticipation of a performance in every respect complete; such, however, it did not prove. Of Mr. Macready's Jaques it is needless to enter into a detailed criticism, as well known must it be. Though not of equal goodness throughout, he is in certain expressions of the character most happy. His delivery of the celebrated passage "All the world's a stage" was particularly forcible and free from that overstriving at light and shade which is the prevailing blemish of his acting. Mrs. Nisbett's Rosalind, though agreeable enough, and great applause was conceded to it, did not certainly fulfill every requisite of the character. Joyous indeed she was and merry, it was not the joy and merriment of the banished Duke's daughter; it betrayed an inward heaviness of heart, it was thoughtless when it should have been thoughtful. In short, there was an absence of that graceful sensibility which is the very soul of the character, and without which it loses all its poetry. Mrs. Stirling's Celia was all that could be desired—full of feeling and playfulness most naturally expressed. This and the part of Orlando by Anderson were the most satisfactorily acted in the whole play. The frank and manly bearing of the latter, his affection for old Adam (Phelps), the sage and good humour of his scenes with the women, made up altogether a most pleasing piece of acting, and its merits were frequently acknowledged by the audience. We must not omit to mention the acting of Hudson, in M. Le Beau, the extreme absurdity of which provoked an immense deal of laughter. Of the Touchstone and Audrey, respectively played by Keeley and his wife, we cannot speak in very high terms; in fact, we never saw either to so much disadvantage. Keeley wanted the pompous fluency and oracular pedantry which are essential to the character, and without which much of the dialogue must lose its effect. Audrey, on the other hand, was hardly wild enough in her rusticity, and there was far too much intelligence in Mrs. Keeley's eye for the hard uncouth mind of the forest wench. Both created laughter in their own way, however,—as when did they ever fail to do so! The songs interspersed in the place, of which not one was omitted, were all most effectively executed. The principal singers were Allen Philips, Stretton, Miss Horton, and Miss Gould. The first song, "Under the Greenwood Tree," sung in the first instance as a solo by Allen, and afterwards as a glee, with the rest of the male singers, was particularly successful. And now let us say a word about one of the greatest features of the performance— namely, the scenery and "getting-up," than which nothing could be more admirable, and, in the minutest particular, complete. Every scene was a complete picturesque study, and above all the wrestling scene deserves mention, in which the new effect was introduced of including the space where the wrestlers encounter with ropes and staves round which the courtiers and spectators stand pressing eagerly forward, watching every movement of the combatants. The effect of this was most vivid, and the natural manner of the two wrestlers through every vicissitude of the struggle elicited shouts of applause.

At the conclusion of the play Mr. Macready was again called for, and appeared with Mrs. Nisbet, when they were received with the most tumultuous waving of hats and handkerchiefs that ever agitated a crowded pit. The farce of *The Attic Story* which was brought out at the end of last season concluded the entertainments.

THE ATHENAEUM
July 1890

A somewhat conventional representation of 'As You Like It' by the Daly company was lifted into popularity by the beauty of Miss Rehan's Rosalind. A revelation such as dawned upon us when her Katharine was first seen was not to be expected in the case of Rosalind. Comedy and poetry are both present in Miss Rehan's great performances, but comedy prevails. In her Rosalind we see a bright, mirthful, and bewitching creature, whom Orlando might well worship, as against her lures it is impossible for masculine humanity to strive. It is, however, a woman that he adores, a passionate enchanting, volatile creature, whose voice is all music, and whose movements are all grace. Enjoyment is her prime aim. She seeks to communicate to others the animal spirits by which she is carried away, and she succeeds. Of the princess we see little. Whether Shakespeare, could he see the present exposition, and realize its variety and beauty, would refuse to recognize it as an embodiment of his conception is doubtful. His modern followers have, however, dwelt upon a Rosalind more ethereal than is now seen. Miss Rehan assigns the character nothing of Miranda, or even of Perdita. None the less her performance is irresistible, and as accomplishment in art is magnificent. Mr. John Drew is an earnest and a picturesque Orlando, Mr. Lewis an acceptable Touchstone. So far as regards the other characters and the *mise en scene* the performance is not to be told from an average English representation.

SHAW ON SHAKESPEAR

George Bernard Shaw

1897

As You Like It

I never saw Miss Ada Rehan act without burning to present Mr. Augustin Daly with a delightful villa in St. Helena, and a commission from an influential committee of his admirers to produce at his leisure a complete set of Shakespear's plays, entirely rewritten, reformed, rearranged, and brought up to the most advanced requirements of the year 1850. He was in full force at the Islington Theatre on Monday evening last with his version of As You Like It just as I dont like it. There I saw Amiens under the greenwood tree, braving winter and rough weather in a pair of crimson plush breeches, a spectacle to benumb the mind and obscure the passions. There was Orlando with the harmony of his brown boots and tunic torn asunder by a piercing discord of dark volcanic green, a walking tribute to Mr. Daly's taste in tights. There did I hear slow music stealing up from the band at all the well-known recitations of Adam, Jaques, and Rosalind, lest we should for a moment forget that we were in a theatre and not in the forest of Arden. There did I look through practicable doors in the walls of sunny orchards into an abyss of pitchy darkness. There saw I in the attitudes, grace, and deportment of the forest dwellers the plastique of an Arcadian past. And the music synchronized with it all to perfection, from La Grande Duchesse and Dichter und Bauer, conducted by the leader of the band, to the inevitable old English airs conducted by the haughty musician who is Mr. Daly's special property. And to think that Mr. Daly will die in his bed, whilst innocent presidents of republics, who never harmed an immortal bard, are falling on all sides under the knives of well-intentioned reformers whose only crime is that they assassinate the wrong people! And yet let me be magnanimous. I confess I would not like to see Mr. Daly assassinated: St. Helena would satisfy me. For Mr. Daly was in his prime an advance man relatively to his own time and place, and was a real manager, with definite artistic aims which he trained his company to accomplish. His Irish-American Yank-German comedies, as played under his management by Ada Rehan and

Mrs. Gilbert, John Drew, Otis Skinner and the late John Lewis, turned a page in theatrical history here, and secured him a position in London which was never questioned until it became apparent that he was throwing away Miss Rehan's genius. When, after the complete discovery of her gifts by the London public, Mr. Daly could find no better employment for her than in a revival of Dollars and Cents, his annihilation and Miss Rehan's rescue became the critic's first duty. Shakespear saved the situation for a time, and got severely damaged in the process; but The Countess Gucki convinced me that in Mr. Daly's hands Miss Rehan's talent was likely to be lost not only to the modern drama, but to the modern Shakespearean stage; that is to say, to the indispensable conditions of its own fullest development. No doubt starring in Daly Shakespear is as lucrative and secure as the greatest of Duse's achievements are thankless and precarious; but surely it must be better fun making money enough by La Dame aux Camelias to pay for Heimat and La Femme de Claude, and win the position of the greatest actress in the world with all three, than to astonish provincials with versions of Shakespear which are no longer up even to metropolitan literary and dramatic standards.

However, since I cannot convert Miss Rehan to my view of the position, I must live in hope that some day she will come to the West End of London for a week or two, just as Réjane and Sarah Bernhardt do, with some work of sufficient novelty and importance to make good the provincial wear and tear of her artistic prestige. Just now she is at the height of her powers. The plumpness that threatened the Countess Gucki has vanished: Rosalind is as slim as a girl. The third and fourth acts are as wonderful as ever—miracles of vocal expression. If As You Like It were a typical Shakespearean play, I should unhesitatingly declare Miss Rehan the most perfect Shakespearean executant in the world. But when I think of those plays in which our William anticipated modern dramatic art by making serious attempts to hold the mirror up to nature—All's Well, Measure for Measure, Troilus and Cressida, and so on—I must limit the tribute to Shakespear's popular style. Rosalind is not a complete human being: she is simply an extension into five acts of the most affectionate, fortunate, delightful five minutes in the life of a charming woman. And all the other figures in the play are cognate impostures. Orlando, Adam, Jaques, Touchstone, the banished Duke, and the rest play each the same tune all through. This is not human nature or dramatic character; it is juvenile lead, first old man, heavy lead, heavy father, principal comedian, and leading lady, transfigured by magical word-music. The Shakespearolators who are taken in by it do not know drama in the classical sense from "drama" in the technical Adelphi sense. You have only to compare Orlando and Rosalind with Bertram and Helena, the Duke and Touchstone with Leontes and Autolycus, to learn the difference from Shakespear himself. Therefore I cannot judge from Miss

Rehan's enchanting Rosalind whether she is a great Shakespearean actress or not: there is even a sense in which I cannot tell whether she can act at all or not. So far, I have never seen her create a character: she has always practised the same adorable arts on me, by whatever name the playbill has called her— Nancy Brasher (ugh!), Viola, or Rosalind. I have never complained: the drama with all its heroines levelled up to a universal Ada Rehan has seemed no such dreary prospect to me; and her voice, compared to Sarah Bernhardt's *voix d'or,* has been as all the sounds of the woodland to the chinking of twenty-franc pieces. In Shakespear (what Mr. Daly leaves of him) she was and is irresistible: at Islington on Monday she made me cry faster than Mr. Daly could make me swear. But the critic in me is bound to insist that Ada Rehan has as yet created nothing but Ada Rehan. She will probably never excel that masterpiece; but why should she not superimpose a character study or two on it! Duse's greatest work is Duse; but that does not prevent Cesarine, Santuzza, and Camille from being three totally different women, none of them Duses, though Duse is all of them. Miss Rehan would charm everybody as Mirandolina as effectually as Duse does. But how about Magda? It is because nobody in England knows the answer to that question that nobody in England as yet knows whether Ada Rehan is a creative artist or a mere virtuosa.

(London: *Saturday Review.* 9 October 1897.)

The irony of Fate prevails at the St. James's Theatre. For years we have been urging the managers to give us Shakespear's plays as he wrote them, playing them intelligently and enjoyingly as pleasant stories, instead of mutilating them, altering them, and celebrating them as superstitious rites. After three hundred years Mr. George Alexander has taken us at our words, as far as the clock permits, and gives us As You Like It at full four hours' length. And, alas! it is just too late: the Bard gets his chance at the moment when his obsolescence has become unendurable. Nevertheless, we were right; for this production of Mr. Alexander's, though the longest, is infinitely the least tedious, and, in those parts which depend on the management, the most delightful I have seen. But yet, what a play! It was in As You Like It that the sententious William first began to openly exploit the fondness of the British Public for sham moralizing and stage "philosophy." It contains one passage that specially exasperates me. Jaques, who spends his time, like Hamlet, in vainly emulating the wisdom of Sancho Panza, comes in laughing in a superior manner because he has met a fool in the forest, who

> Says very wisely, It is ten o'clock.
> Thus we may see [quoth he] how the world wags.

Tis but an hour ago since it was nine;
And after one hour more twill be eleven.
And so, from hour to hour, we ripe and ripe;
And then, from hour to hour, we rot and rot;
And thereby hangs a tale.

Now, considering that this fool's platitude is precisely the "philosophy" of Hamlet, Macbeth ("Tomorrow and tomorrow and tomorrow," etc.), Prospero, and the rest of them, there is something unendurably aggravating in Shakespear giving himself airs with Touchstone, as if he, the immortal, ever, even at his sublimest, had anything different or better to say himself. Later on he misses a great chance. Nothing is more significant than the statement that "all the world's a stage." The whole world *is* ruled by theatrical illusion. Between the Caesars, the emperors, the Christian heroes, the Grand Old Men, the kings, prophets, saints, judges, and heroes of the newspapers and the popular imagination, and the actual Juliuses, Napoleons, Gordons, Gladstones, and so on, there is the same difference as between Hamlet and Sir Henry Irving. The case is not one of fanciful similitude but of identity. The great critics are those who penetrate and understand the illusion: the great men are those who, as dramatists planning the development of nations, or as actors carrying out the drama, are behind the scenes of the world instead of gaping and gushing in the auditorium after paying their taxes at the doors. And yet Shakespear, with the rarest opportunities of observing this, lets his pregnant metaphor slip, and, with his usual incapacity for pursuing any idea, wanders off into a grandmotherly Elizabethan edition of the advertisement of Cassell's Popular Educator. How anybody over the age of seven can take interest in a literary toy so silly in its conceit and common in its ideas as the Seven Ages of Man passes my understanding. Even the great metaphor itself is inaccurately expressed; for the world is a playhouse, not merely a stage; and Shakespear might have said so without making his blank verse scan any worse than Richard's exclamation, "All the world to nothing!"

And then Touchstone, with his rare jests about the knight that swore by his honor they were good pancakes! Who would endure such humor from anyone but Shakespear!—an Eskimo would demand his money back if a modern author offered him such fare. And the comfortable old duke, symbolical of the British villa dweller, who likes to find "sermons in stones and good in everything," and then to have a good dinner! This unvenerable impostor, expanding on his mixed diet of pious twaddle and venison, rouses my worst passions. Even when Shakespear, in his efforts to be a social philosopher, does rise for an instant to the level of a sixth-rate Kingsley, his solemn self-complacency infuriates me.

And yet, so wonderful is his art, that it is not easy to disentangle what is unbearable from what is irresistible. Orlando one moment says:

> Whate'er you are
> That in this desert inaccessible
> Under the shade of melancholy boughs
> Lose and neglect the creeping hours of time,

which, though it indicates a thoroughly unhealthy imagination, and would have been impossible to, for instance, Chaucer, is yet magically fine of its kind. The next moment he tacks on lines which would have revolted Mr. Pecksniff:

> If ever you have looked on better days,
> If ever been where bells have knolled to church,
>   [*How perfectly the atmosphere of the rented pew is caught in*
>   *this incredible line!*]
> If ever sat at any good man's feast,
> If ever from your eyelids wiped—

I really shall get sick if I quote any more of it. Was ever such canting, snivelling, hypocritical unctuousness exuded by an actor anxious to shew that he was above his profession, and was a thoroughly respectable man in private life? Why cannot all this putrescence be cut out of the play, and only the vital parts—the genuine story-telling, the fun, the poetry, the drama, be retained? Simply because, if nothing were left of Shakespear but his genius, our Shakspearolaters would miss all that they admire in him.

Notwithstanding these drawbacks, the fascination of As You Like It is still very great. It has the overwhelming advantage of being written for the most part in prose instead of in blank verse, which any fool can write. And such prose! The first scene alone, with its energy of exposition, each phrase driving its meaning and feeling in up to the head at one brief, sure stroke, is worth ten acts of the ordinary Elizabethan sing-song. It cannot be said that the blank verse is reserved for those passages which demand a loftier expression, since Le Beau and Corin drop into it, like Mr. Silas Wegg, on the most inadequate provocation; but at least there is not much of it. The popularity of Rosalind is due to three main causes. First, she only speaks blank verse for a few minutes. Second, she only wears a skirt for a few minutes (and the dismal effect of the change at the end to the wedding dress ought to convert the stupidest champion of petticoats to rational dress). Third, she makes love to the man instead of waiting for the man to make love to her—a piece of natural history which has kept Shakespear's heroines alive, whilst generations of properly governessed young ladies, taught to say "No" three times at least, have miserably perished.

The performance at the St. James's is in some respects very good and in no respect very bad or even indifferent. Miss Neilson's Rosalind will not bear criticism for a moment; and yet the total effect is pardonable, and even pleasant. She bungles speech after speech; and her attacks of Miss Ellen Terry and Mrs. Patrick Campbell are acute, sudden, and numerous; but her personal charm carries her through; and her song is a great success: besides, who ever failed, or could fail, as Rosalind? Miss Fay Davis is the best Celia I ever saw, and Miss Dorothea Baird the prettiest Phoebe, though her part is too much cut to give her any chance of acting. Miss Kate Phillips is an appallingly artificial Audrey; for, her style being either smart or nothing, her conscientious efforts to be lumpish land her in the impossible. And then, what is that artistically metropolitan complexion doing in the Forest of Arden?

Ass as Jaques is, Mr. W. H. Vernon made him more tolerable than I can remember. Every successive production at the St. James's leaves one with a greater admiration than before for Mr. Vernon's talent. That servile apostle of working-class Thrift and Teetotalism (O William Shakespear, Esquire, you who died drunk, WHAT a moral chap you were!) hight Adam, was made about twenty years too old by Mr. Loraine, who, on the other hand, made a charming point by bidding farewell to the old home with a smile instead of the conventional tear. Mr. Fernandez impersonated the banished Duke as well as it is in the nature of Jaques's Boswell to be impersonated; Mr. H. B. Irving plays Oliver very much as anybody else would play Iago, yet with his faults on the right side; Mr. Vincent retains his lawful speeches (usually purloined by Jaques) as the First Lord; and Mr. Esmond tries the picturesque, attitudinizing, galvanic, Bedford Park style on Touchstone, worrying all effect out of the good lines, but worrying some into the bad ones. Mr. Wheeler, as Charles, catches the professional manner very happily; and the wrestling bout is far and away the best I have seen on the stage. To me, the wrestling is always the main attraction of an As You Like It performance, since it is so much easier to find a man who knows how to wrestle than one who knows how to act. Mr. Alexander's Orlando I should like to see again later on. The qualities he shewed in it were those which go without saying in his case; and now that he has disposed of the really big achievement of producing the play with an artistic intelligence and practical ability never, as far as my experience goes, applied to it before, he will have time to elaborate a part lying easily within his powers, and already very attractively played by him. There are ten other gentlemen in the cast; but I can only mention Mr. Aubrey Smith, whose appearance as "the humorous Duke" (which Mr. Vincent Sternroyd, as Le Beau, seemed to understand as a duke with a sense of humor, like Mr. Gilbert's Mikado) was so magnificent that it taxed all his powers to live up to his own aspect.

The scene where the two boys come in and sing It was a lover and his lass to Touchstone has been restored by Mr. Alexander with such success that I am inclined to declare it the most delightful moment in the whole representation. Mr. Edward German has rearranged his Henry VIII music for the masque of Hymen at the end. Hymen, beauteous to gorgeousness, is impersonated by Miss Opp.

The production at this Christmas season could not be more timely. The children will find the virtue of Adam and the philosophy of Jaques just the thing for them; whilst their elders will be delighted by the pageantry and the wrestling.

(London: *The Saturday Review.* 5 December 1896.)

I have been for some time waiting for an opportunity of saying a word about Mrs. Langtry's revival of As You Like It at the St. James's Theatre. I submit that the play is spoiled by the ruthless cutting to bits of the last half of it. This has been forced on the management by want of skill and want of thought on the part of the actors. The problem is to get through a play of so many lines between eight o'clock and eleven. Any fool can solve this in the fashion of Alexander (I allude to the man who stopped a hole to keep the wind away, and not to the lessee of the Avenue Theatre) by cutting out a chunk here and a scrap there until the lines are few enough to fit. But, somehow, the shorter you make your play in this fashion, the more tedious it becomes. The proper way is to divide your play into movements like those of a symphony. You will find that there are several sections which can be safely taken at a brisk *allegro,* and a few that may be taken *pretissimo:* those, for instance, which serve only to explain the mere mechanism of the plot. Each *allegro* will improve the representation if it is judiciously chosen and managed. Mr. Benson has introduced one or two in Hamlet with the happiest effect. Of course the thing must be honestly done: the familiar star system trick of making the minor characters slur their work in order to leave plenty of time for the mock pregnant pauses, head waggings, and elaborate business of the leading actor, is vile, and shows a pitiful ambition in the fool that uses it. The star must not take a minute more than his lines are worth, or put off the third murderer with a minute less. Under these conditions, I believe it would be quite feasible to play As You Like It right through in a little over three hours without sacrificing a point.

However, it would be necessary to get another Jaques than Mr. Bourchier, or else to rudely shake his conviction that the secret of effective elocution is to pause at every third word and look significantly out of the corners of his eyes at anybody who happens to be in that direction before letting out the fourth. Mr.

Bourchier can easily make himself a competent Jaques; but he may take it from me that he is at present as bad a one as London has seen for some years. Mrs. Langtry makes a very womanly Rosalind, and succeeds better than any other actress within my recollection in making her love for Orlando the keynote of the part. I may remark that in spite of the beauty of the verse and the deep feeling for sylvan and pastoral scenery which pervades the play, the human part of it is excessively conventional, and might almost have been planned by Tom Taylor. Like Henry V, it belongs to that moment of sympathy with the common morality and thought of his time which came between the romanticism of Shakespear's early plays and the independent thought of his later one; and this is why it is so easily played by any company with a fair share of sense and skill. There is no confounded insight required in the business.

(London: *The Star.* 18 April 1890.)

. . . Just at present I am more anxious about Miss Dorothea Baird, whom I did see, as Rosalind. Rosalind is to the actress what Hamlet is to the actor—a part in which, reasonable presentability being granted, failure is hardly possible. It is easier than Trilby up to a certain point, though it will of course hold much more acting. Miss Baird plays it intelligently and nicely; and this, to such a very pretty Ganymede, is enough to secure success. How far the niceness and intelligence of the pretty young lady will develop into the passion and intuition of the artist, or whether the prettiness will develop into the "handsome is as handsome does" fascination which holds the stage for many years against Time, remains to be seen. All that can be said at present is that Miss Baird's Rosalind is bright and pleasant, with sufficient natural charm to secure indulgence for all its shortcomings. Of these the most serious is Miss Baird's delivery of the lines. Everybody by this time knows how a modern high-schoolmistress talks—how she repudiates the precision, the stateliness, the awe-inspiring oracularity of the old-fashioned schoolmistress who knew nothing, and cloaks her mathematics with a pretty little voice, a pretty little manner, and all sorts of self-conscious calineries and unassumingnesses. "Poor little me! what do *I* know about conic sections?" is the effect she aims at. Miss Baird's Rosalind has clearly been to the high school and modelled herself upon her pet mistress, if not actually taught there herself. But that dainty, pleading, narrow-lipped little torrent of gabble will not do for Shakespeare. It is so unintelligible across the footlights that even I, who knows As You Like It almost as well as I know Beethoven's Pastoral Symphony, could not always catch what she was saying. This being so, it may safely be taken that Camberwell did not catch more than a very small conic section of it. For even an expert cannot make sense of Elizabethan blank verse at a first hearing when it is delivered at the rate of 200 words a minute and upwards. Besides, its lyrical flow, if such a tiny ladylike patter can be credited with so broad a quality, is not that of Shakespear's verse. The effect is like a canary trying to sing Handel.

The scenes from As You Like It included nothing of Jaques except the few scraps of dialogue between the pessimist and Orlando; and no exception can be taken to the way in which these were handled by Mr. Irving. He dressed and looked the part well.

The best bit of work was Mr. Bernard Gould's Orlando; the worst, Mr. Ben Greet's Touchstone. Mr. Greet put himself out of the question before he had been two minutes on the stage by the profound stroke of picking one of Orlando's sonnets from a tree, and reading from it the impromptu burlesque:

> If a hart do lack a hind,
> Let him seek out Rosalind, etc.

This was a new reading with a vengeance. He was not much more successful as executant than as Shakespearean student. He completely missed the piled-up climax of the speech to William, and was, in short, as bad a Touchstone as a critic could desire to see. It is no disgrace to an actor to be unable to play Touchstone; but why, under these circumstances, and being a manager, he should cast himself for it, passes my understanding. Mr. Rawson Buckley played Oliver very well, but persisted, as usual, in dressing himself smartly, and then describing himself as "a wretched ragged man, o'ergrown with hair." Mr. Gould managed his part, especially the difficulties of the sham courtship with Ganymede, better than I can remember having seen it managed before; and some of his lines were finely spoken; but he was not Orlando. Orlando's intelligence is the intelligence of the heart: he always comes out best as an amiable, strong, manly, handsome, shrewd-enough-to-take-care-of-himself, but safely stupid and totally unobservant young man. Now, Mr. Gould plays with his head; his intelligence is always on the alert; and he is so observant that in spite of his many valuable stage qualities he almost disqualifies himself as an actor by his draughtsman's habit of watching himself and everyone else so keenly and interestedly that he is more apt to forget his part than to forget himself in it. The born actor looks in: Mr. Gould looks on. He acts like a good critic, and probably represses his tendencies—if he has any—to the maudlin self-sympathy, the insane egotism, the bottomless folly, the hysterical imaginative mendacity which—with the help of alcohol—make acting easy to some men who are for all other purposes the most hopeless wastrels. However, I do not object: I recognize the fact that the ascendency of the sentimental amorphous actor means the ascendency of the sentimental amorphous drama, and that the critical actor, like Mr. Gould is indispensable to a drama with any brains in it. Still, the critical actor need not be also a draughtsman actor. I once elaborately explained to Mr. Gould a part of which I was myself the author. He paid me the closest attention; retired to ponder my utterances; and presently returned with a perfectly accurate and highly characteristic drawing of me, which I shall probably never live down. And if I had been Shakespear explaining Orlando, it would have been just the same.

(London: *The Saturday Review.* 2 May 1896.)

THE STAGE SHAKESPEÀRE
Austin Brereton
1908

INTRODUCTION.

Literary History.

THIS serene pastoral play followed the more brilliant comedy, "Much Ado About Nothing," and preceded the more farcically inclined "Twelfth Night." Although founded on a serious interest, and possessing its purely dramatic moments, it is a comedy admirably even throughout, and without a jarring note. Commencing with what might easily have been a tragedy, it concludes in an atmosphere of soft beauty, forgiveness, and peace. As usual, Shakespeare found the source of his story elsewhere than in his own fertile brain. For the outline of his plot he went to Lodge's romance—which in itself recalled "The Tale of Gamelyn," attributed to Chaucer—entitled "Rosalynde: Euphues Golden Legacie: found after his death in his cell, at Silexedra. Bequeathed to Philautus Sonnes, noursed up with their Father in England." It was first published in 1590, and again in 1592, and, in his introduction, the author states that he wrote the story in order to while away the time during a voyage to the island of Terceras and the Canaries—"every line was writ with a surge, and every humorous passion counter-checkt with a storme. If You Like It, so; and yet I will be yours in duty, if you will be mine in favour." Here, as will be seen, Shakespeare found the suggestion for his title, and he followed the original story closely. But he created three absolutely original characters—Touchstone, the first of Fools; the cynical, melancholy Jaques; and the country wench, Audrey.

It is also to be noted that, in Lodge, Rosalind and Celia represent themselves as a lady and her page. Shakespeare's poetical instinct may have induced him to make Rosalind pass for a boy in the forest scenes, or he may have made the alteration in order to facilitate the impersonation of the character, for, be it remembered, there were no actresses in his day. So that

Rosalind, being played by a real boy, would appear perfectly natural in the greater part of the comedy. In any case, it was a happy thought, and, as our literature has been indebted by the alteration, so, many an actress has been enabled to create an effect which otherwise would have been impossible. When Rosalind speaks the epilogue and comes to the words, "If I were a woman, I would kiss as many of you as had beards that pleased me," etc., one often notices a titter in the audience, because the spectators know that the Rosalind before them is in reality a woman, and they laugh at the qualifying "If." When it is considered that the part was originally played by one of the boy-actors of Shakespeare's day, the reason for the qualification becomes apparent.

"As You Like It" was written at the end of 1599, or early in 1600, five years after the appearance of another volume from which Shakespeare derived further ideas. This was a book on the art of self-defence, called "Saviolo's Practise," the work of an Italian fencing-master in the employ of the Earl of Essex. Hence came suggestions for the wrestling scene between Orlando and Charles, and for Touchstone's well known description, in the fifth act, of "a lie seven times removed." The historic period of the play is the fourteenth century. "As You Like It," so far as we know, was first printed, with many imperfections and various indications of carelessness and haste, in the Folio of 1623.

THE CHARACTERS.

The Forest of Arden is not, as some ingenious chroniclers assert, the district lying between the rivers Sambre and Maas and Meuse, and Moselle. Arden is not Ardennes, save only in the suggestion of the name. It is a bit of the Warwickshire which Shakespeare knew and loved so well. Here, in this lovely bit of old England, the banished Duke and his companions "fleet the time carelessly, as they did in the golden world." Here, "nursed in solitude, 'under the shade of melancholy boughs,'" says Hazlitt, "the imagination grows soft and delicate, and the wit runs riot in idleness, like a spoiled child that is never sent to school. Caprice and fancy reign and revel here, and stern necessity is banished to the court. The mild sentiments of humanity are strengthened with thought and leisure; the echo of the cares and noise of the world strikes upon the ear of those 'who have felt them knowingly,' softened by time and distance. 'They hear the tumult and are still.' The very air of the place seems to breathe a spirit of philosophical poetry, to stir the thoughts, to touch the heart with pity, as the drowsy forest rustles to the sighing gale. Never was there such beautiful moralising, equally free from pedantry or petulance—

> 'And this our life, exempt from public haunt,
>   Finds tongues in trees, books in the running brooks,
>   Sermons in stones, and good in every thing.'

"Jaques is the only purely contemplative character in Shakespeare. He thinks and does nothing. His whole occupation is to amuse his mind, and he is totally regardless of his body and his fortunes. He is the prince of philosophical idlers; his only passion is thought: he sets no value upon anything, but as it serves for food for reflection. He can 'suck melancholy out of a song, as a weasel sucks eggs'; the motley fool, 'who morals on time,' is the greatest prize he meets with in the forest. He resents Orlando's passion for Rosalind as some disparagement of his own passion for abstract truth; and leaves the Duke as soon as he is restored to his sovereignty, to seek his brother out who has quitted it and turned hermit."

In the character of Rosalind, Shakespeare has depicted the deep, steadfast love of a true woman, and, under all Rosalind's joyousness, lies this sincere attachment, this passionate love and devotion. Rosalind's comedy scenes are instinct with gaiety, but the more serious side of her character should never be lost sight of by her stage impersonator. One of the most celebrated of our English players, the late Helen Faucit (Lady Theodore Martin), pointed this out in her admirable summary of the character—"At the core of all that Rosalind says and does, lies a passionate love as pure and all-absorbing as ever swayed a woman's heart. Surely it was the finest and boldest of all devices, one on which only a Shakespeare could have ventured, to put his heroine into such a position that she could, without revealing her own secret, probe the heart of her lover to the very bottom, and so assure herself that the love which possessed her own being was as completely the master of his. Neither could any but Shakespeare have so carried out this daring design, that the woman, thus rarely placed for gratifying the impulses of her own heart, and testing the sincerity of her lover's, should, come triumphantly out of the ordeal, charming us, during the time of probation, by her pretty, womanly waywardness playing like summer lightning over her throbbing tenderness of heart, and never in the gayest sallies of her happiest moods losing one grain of our respect. No one can study this play without seeing that, through the guise of the brilliant-witted boy, Shakespeare meant the charm of the high-hearted woman, strong, tender, delicate, to make itself felt. Hence it is that Orlando finds the spell, which 'heavenly Rosalind' had thrown around him, drawn hourly closer and closer, he knows not how, while at the same time he has himself been winning his way more and more into his mistress's heart. Thus, when at last Rosalind doffs her doublet and hose, and appears arrayed for her bridal, there seems nothing strange or unmeet in this somewhat sudden consummation of what in truth has been a lengthened wooing."

STAGE HISTORY.

The history of "As You Like It" on the stage, differs in one respect from Mr. Weller's knowledge of London, inasmuch as it is not "extensive." On the other hand, it is certainly "peculiar," for tragic actresses and comediennes have alike played Rosalind successfully, Sarah Siddons and Dora Jordan, not to mention their predecessors, Mrs. Pritchard and Peg Woffington, having competed for supremacy in the character. The early history of the play is a blank. It is not even on record that it was acted during the Restoration period; but, in view of its delicacy, it is no matter for wonderment that no room could be found for it in the riotous, debauched days of Charles II. Indeed, it is not until 1723 that we find any mention of its production in a theatre, and then it was only done in a sorry, mutilated adaptation. This was entitled "Love in a Forest," and was the work of one Charles Johnson, who was "famous for writing a play every year, and being at Buttons" [the celebrated Coffee-house, in Great Russell Street near Covent Garden] "every day." The sapient Johnson entirely omitted the characters of Touchstone, Audrey, William, Corin, Phebe, and Sylvius, except that the latter, in the second act, spoke some eighteen lines properly belonging to Corin. Johnson also interpolated passages from some other of Shakespeare's works, and added a very little of his own composition.

The adaptation was, in truth, a marvellous conglomeration. Here is an authentic account of the curious mixture: "Act I.—The wrestling between Orlando and Charles is turned into a regular combat in the lists. Charles accuses Orlando of treason, and several speeches are introduced from 'Richard II.' Act II.—When Duke Alberto enters with his friend, the speech about the wounded stag is taken from the First Lord and given to Jaques; in the next scene between the same parties, notwithstanding Touchstone is omitted, yet Jaques gives his description of meeting with a fool; much, however, of his part in this scene is left out very injudiciously. Act III.—The verses which Celia ought to read are omitted, and Touchstone's burlesque verses are given her instead. When Orlando and Jaques enter, they begin their conversation as in the original, and end it with part of the first act of 'Much Ado.' Jaques speaking what Benedick says about women; when Rosalind and Celia come forward, Jaques walks off with Celia. Rosalind omits the account of Time's different paces. Jaques returns with Celia and makes love to her, after which he has a soliloquy patched up from Benedick and Touchstone, with some additions from C. Johnson. Act IV. begins with a conversation between Jaques and Rosalind, in which he tells her of his love for Celia. In the scene between Orlando and Rosalind, considerable omissions are made, and Viola's speech ('she never told her love') is inserted, the act concluding with the second scene of Shakespeare's fifth act, in which Rosalind desires all the parties on the stage to meet her to-morrow. Act V. consists chiefly of the burlesque of Pyramus and Thisbe from 'Midsummer Night's Dream;' this is represented before the Duke, while Rosalind is changing her dress, instead of Touchstone's description of the quarrel. When Rosalind returns, the play ends much as in the original, except that Jaques marries Celia, instead of going in quest of Duke Frederick, and that the epilogue is omitted." This "preposterous pasticcio," as it has been aptly called, was dedicated to the Worshipful Society of Freemasons.

"As You Like It" was restored to the stage on December 20, 1740, when it was acted with great success at Drury Lane. James Quin was the Jaques, Mrs. Pritchard the Rosalind. Two years later, the play was revived at Covent Garden, Mrs. Pritchard being again the Rosalind. Five years later, Margaret Woffington represented the character at Drury Lane. Mrs. Pritchard (1711–1768) was of common origin and very illiterate to boot. She was a great Lady Macbeth, nevertheless, but she can hardly have been satisfactory as Rosalind, although she frequently acted the part. Peg Woffington, however, made the character entirely her own for the ten years which preceded here death, and it was when playing Rosalind that she was stricken with paralysis and was removed from the stage, to which she never returned. This was on May 3, 1757, at Covent Garden. The occasion was characteristic of the proverbial charity which is ingrained in the heart of the stage player. Some fellow performers were in need of a benefit, and Peg Woffington insisted upon giving her services, although she had been in indifferent health for some time. An eye-witness actor, an actor who had offended the "lovely Peggy" by churlish behaviour, thus recorded the tragic scene. He watched the performance from the side of the stage. Mrs. Woffington "went through Rosalind for four acts without my perceiving she was in the least disordered; but in the fifth, she complained of great indisposition. I offered her my arm, the which she graciously accepted. I thought she looked softened in her behaviour and had less of the *hauteur*. When she came off, at the quick change of dress, she again complained of being ill; but she got accoutred, and returned to finish the part. When in the epilogue she arrived at, 'If I were among you, I would kiss as many as had beards that pleased me,' her voice broke, she faltered, endeavoured to groan, but could not; then, in a voice of terror, screamed, 'God! O God!' and tottered to the stage-door" [the door which formerly stood, at the side of the stage, in the proscenium, through which the players passed in order to take their calls] "speechless, where she was caught. The audience, of course, applauded until she was out of sight, and then sank into awful looks of astonishment, both young and old, before and behind the curtain, to see one of the most handsome women of the age, a favourite principal actress, and who had, for several seasons given high entertainment, struck so suddenly by the hand of death, in such a situation of time and place, and in her prime of life." Such was the tragic ending of Peg Woffington. She lingered, a helpless invalid, until 1760, passing much of her time at Teddington, where she was buried. But she did not die there, as many people think. That event occurred on March 28 of the year named, at number six, Queen Square, Westminster. One of the most interesting events in the history of Rosalind on the stage was the appearance of Mrs. Siddons in the character at Drury Lane on April 30, 1785. Less than three months previously—on February 2, to be precise—the great actress had startled London by her vivid rendering of Lady Macbeth, and, naturally, her Rosalind attracted great attention. Naturally, also, opinions differed as to her interpretation. Thomas Campbell, in his "Life of Mrs. Siddons," says: "After a successful transition from the greatest to the gentlest parts of tragedy" [alluding to her Lady Macbeth and Desdemona] "it would have been but one step further, in the versatility of genius, to have been at home in the enchanting Rosalind; and as the character, though comic, is not broadly so, and is as romantic and poetical as anything in tragedy, I somewhat grudgingly confess my belief that her performance of it, though not a failure, seems to have fallen equally short of a triumph. . . . Here alone, I believe, in her whole professional career, Mrs. Siddons found a rival who beat her out of a single character. The rival Rosalind was Mrs. Jordan, but those who best remember Mrs. Jordan will be the least surprised at her defeating her great contemporary in this one instance. Mrs. Jordan was, perhaps, a little too much of the romp in some touches of the part; but, altogether, she had the *naivete* of it to a degree that Shakespeare himself, if he had been a living spectator, would have gone behind the scenes to have saluted her for her success in it."

The Rosalind of Mrs. Siddons is, however, praised by her other biographer, James Boaden, who considered it "one of the most delicate achievements of Mrs. Siddons. The common objection to her comedy, that it was only the smile of tragedy, made the express charm of Rosalind; her vivacity is understanding, not buoyant spirits; she closes her brilliant assaults upon others with a smothered sigh for her own condition. . . . Mrs. Siddons put so much soul into the raillery of Ganymede as really to cover the very boards of the stage. She seemed, indeed, brought up by a deep magician, to be forest-born. But the return to the habiliments of Rosalind was attended by that happy supplement to the poet's language, where the same terms are applied to different personages, and the meaning is expanded by the discrimination of look and tone and action—

'To you I give myself, for I am yours.'"

It will interest the curious in these matters, to know that the salary of Mrs. Siddons at this period was twenty-five pounds a week. During the season in question she performed seventy-one times, acting seventeen characters. She played Lady Macbeth thirteen times, Desdemona five, and Rosalind on four occasions.

Dora Jordon, who outshone Mrs. Siddons as Rosalind, was, from all accounts, a delightful actress until the end of her career. Born at Waterford, in

1762, she made her first appearance in London in 1785, at Drury Lane, as Peggy in "The Country Girl." Two years later, on April 13, 1787, she acted Rosalind, for her benefit, and with enormous success. Hazlitt says that it was not as an actress, but as herself that she charmed every one. "Nature had formed her in her most prodigal humour; and when nature is in the humour to make a woman all that is delightful, she does it most effectually. Her face, her tones, her manner, were irresistible; her smile had the effect of sunshine, and her laugh did one good to hear it; her voice was eloquence itself, it seemed as if her heart were always at her mouth. She was all gaiety, openness, and good nature; she rioted in her fine animal spirits, and gave more pleasure than any other actress, because she had the greatest spirit of enjoyment in herself." In our own day, Miss Ellen Terry has many of the qualities which helped Mrs. Jordan to success—that same irresistible joyousness of life, for instance; and Mrs. Jordan, like Miss Terry, could touch the pathetic stop when it was necessary. Hence, she was excellent as Ophelia and Rosalind, and her Viola, in "Twelfth Night," was a tender and exquisite performance, combining feeling with sportive grace, and creating as much effect by the "music of her melancholy as the music of her laugh." When she was fifty, she played Rosalind, we are assured, "perfectly." In her earlier days, wrote Charles Lamb, her voice "sank, with her steady, melting eye, into the heart. Her joyous parts, in which her memory now chiefly lives, in her youth were outdone by her plaintive ones. There is no giving an account how [as Viola] she delivered the story of her love for Orsino. . . . She used no rhetoric in her passion; or, it was nature's own rhetoric, most legitimate then, when it seemed altogether without rule or law."

"As You Like It" was revived by Macready at Drury Lane on October 1, 1842. Macready was the Jaques, Mrs. Nisbett the Rosalind. But this was not one of his most successful productions. Helen Faucit played Rosalind with fine feeling and great intelligence. "It is clear that she has entered into the soul of Rosalind," wrote a contemporary, "nor realised that alone, but all the life of the woman, and her surroundings as well. Rosalind's words, therefore, sparkle upon her lips as if they were the offspring of the moment, or deepen into tenderness as if her very Orlando were thrilling her heart with tones that are but faint echoes of her own emotion. All she says and does seems to grow out of the situation, as if it were seen and heard for the first time."

In more recent days, Mrs. Kendal appeared—in 1875, at the Opera Comique, and in 1885, at the St. James's Theatre—as Rosalind. But this splendid actress is not fitted to such a character. On February 25, 1880, a poetical revival of "As You Like It" was given at the Imperial Theatre by the late Miss Marie Litton. The manageress appeared as Rosalind, Mr. Hermann Vezin was the Jaques, Mr. Lionel Brough the Touchstone, Mr. Kyrle Bellew the Orlando. Incomparably the best of all Rosalinds of the later half of the nineteenth century was Lilian Adelaide Neilson, an actress who, to great personal charms—including a most musical voice—added a depth of feeling and a power to which the stage of to-day is largely a stranger. Mr. George Alexander revived the comedy at the St. James's Theatre on December 2, 1896. He was the Orlando, Miss Julia Neilson was the Rosalind, Miss Dorothea Baird the Phebe, and Mr. H. V. Esmond the Touchstone. One hundred and fifteen performances were given.

AUSTIN BRERETON.

(London: 1908): v-xix.

THE STORY OF MY LIFE
Ellen Terry
1908

Iolanthe was one of Helen Faucit's great successes. I never saw this distinguished actress when she was in her prime. Her Rosalind, when she came out of her retirement to play a few performances, appeared to me more like a *lecture* on Rosalind, than like Rosalind herself: a lecture all young actresses would have greatly benefited by hearing, for it was of great beauty. I remember being particularly struck by her treatment of the lines in the scene where Celia conducts the mock marriage between Orlando and Ganymede. Another actress, whom I saw as Rosalind, said the words, "And I do take thee, Orlando, to be my husband," with a comical grimace to the audience. Helen Faucit flushed up and said the line with deep and true emotion, suggesting that she was, indeed, giving herself to Orlando. There was a world of poetry in the way she drooped over his hand.

(London, 1908)

THE TIMES
April 23, 1919

OPENING OF STRATFORD FESTIVAL
"As You Like It" At Memorial Theatre
(From Our Special Correspondent.)

Stratford, April 22

The fine weather of the holiday time and the resumption of the Shakespeare Festival have combined to fill Stratford-on-Avon fuller than I have ever seen it at this season of the year, and the crowds, though mainly English, included more than one nationality, omitting of course one which used to be represented here years ago. There have been American officers quartered in Stratford for some time, and the trains have been bringing many more from London and elsewhere to enjoy this rare opportunity of seeing Shakespeare's town on Shakespeare's birthday, and Shakespeare's plays acted in the Shakespeare Memorial Theatre. Bridge-Street is already gay with the flags which will be a feature of to-morrow's restored ceremony of the birthday; and Bridge-street is also gay with huge red motor-omnibuses from Birmingham, which have brought crowds of tourists to enjoy the sunshine on the river or in the gardens and streets of the old town.

The Stratford Shakespeare Festival opened yesterday under the brightest conditions and promises to be for several reasons memorable among its kind. As the afternoon wore on to a golden evening the motor-omnibuses and motor-cars and motor-bicycles bore back to Birmingham, Leamington, and elsewhere the crowds of day visitors. But when the curtain rang up at the Memorial Theatre on *As You Like It* the little white house was so full that one could not help wondering whether even Stratford could find beds for all these people. Many familiar faces were to be seen in the audience and many familiar faces also will be seen no more, but old habitués and newcomers from England and from foreign countries joined in giving a hearty welcome to Sir Frank Benson as he came in with his party and took his place not on the stage of footlights where Stratford knows him so well, but in the front row of the stalls. He and Lady Benson will have their day to-morrow.

Tonight the stage is occupied by Mr. Nigel Playfair and his company from Hammersmith, who are representing *As You Like It* in a setting that will be novel to the Stratford revenants, but is certainly interesting. The basis of the staging is obviously some illuminated manuscript of the early 15th century, perhaps not altogether unaffected by the Omega style in drawing. The forest, for instance, is ruthlessly simplified, while the costumes are all 15th century, and very brilliant and exciting they are, even in the dim lighting affected by the modern stage artist. Mr. C. Lovat Fraser, who has designed it all, has, at any rate, vigour, and his daring mixture of styles certainly throws up the player against the scene. And, after all the play is the thing.

Mr. Playfair's company is composed of experience and of youthful ardour in about equal proportions. Here is Mr. Gilbert Hare, as Adam, and we know that Mr. Hare has been trained in a school where the speaking of poetry is not neglected. And here is Miss Marjory Holman as Celia, and, if Miss Holman has not had that training, she has at least the youthful spirit which gets at the heart of the matter in its own rough-and-tumble way. Mr. Geoffrey Kerr, who plays Orlando, has not been trained in that school, but there is a fine manly abruptness about him that is not unpleasing. And Miss Athene Seyler has both qualifications, the training and the spirit, and her Rosalind is tingling with life and humour and femininity from start to finish. The Touchstone of Mr. Nigel Playfair, the Jacques of Mr. Herbert Marshall, the singing of Mr. Bertram Binyon, and the acting of the company as a whole made up a production which if it is of a kind unfamiliar to Stratford is full of life and direction. A word too, must be said for the effort to give the play almost complete without the cuts which usually rob us of the interesting lines. And the Elizabethan music performed upon stringed instruments by players in appropriate costumes rather as a part of the play than as a mere interlude of decoration is a very delightful feature.

A DEFINITION OF ARDEN
Bamber Gascoigne
1961

As You Like It. (Stratford-upon-Avon.)

Shakespeare gets the best of every world in *As You Like It*. His source, Thomas Lodge's *Rosalynde,* was a popular romance which had run through four editions in the eight years since 1590. Lodge took the pastoral frolics of his courtly characters with complete seriousness, but Shakespeare widens the perspective. To the courtiers playing at rustics he adds Audrey and William, genuine lumpish rustics, Touchstone, a clown playing the courtier, and Jaques, a courtier whose cynicism cuts through the fake rusticity. In Lodge the swains carve love sonnets to their shepherdesses on the trees. When Shakespeare's Orlando does the same, Jaques is on hand with a cutting rebuke. Touchstone even has the effrontery to criticise the economy of the pastoral utopia, the new Eden which is the antidote to the harsh world of Ambition and Pride, of getting and spending. The glories of capitalism were still deeply shocking to the Elizabethans—Dekker described a usurer as 'a bawd to his own money bags, taking a fee that they may engender together.' But now Touchstone applies Dekker's criterion to the goodly shepherds. When Corin has smugly listed the quiet joys of his perfect rustic life, ending with '. . . and the greatest of my pride is to see my ewes graze and my lambs suck,' Touchstone counters: 'That is another simple sin in you . . . to offer to get your living by the copulation of cattle.'

So, on one level, *As You Like It* is a discussion play, each scene bringing a new perspective to the topics of ambition, of life at court, of the pastoral convention and of real country life. But this discussion is a sub-plot. Shakespeare has taken over from Lodge more than he has rejected, and the play is first of all a romance. Rosalind's joy and laughter in the forest are truly delightful, the long, happy ending is magical, the recuperative effect of Arden acts quicker and more completely than that of Malvern or Leamington Spa. If a production misses this romance, or makes it laughable, the sub-plot discussions seems mere pedantry and a bore.

At Stratford Richard Negri, Michael Elliot and Vanessa Redgrave feast us with delight. Negri's set is a steep green breast of a hill; from its top a mighty tree soars up and out of sight; branches jest from it like elephant tusks, supporting flat palletes of leaves. For the first scene or two I found the steepness of the rake distracting—actors would need at least a Stem Christie to change course, one felt—but soon the set began to reveal its remarkable possibilities. For scene changes, patterns could be projected on to the background; the grille of a gate in a courtyard, the dappled pattern of sunlight through the leaves of the forest. Superb groupings could be formed without any blatant use of 'levels.' And characters could converse on their backs—which (quite apart from its theatrical novelty) is precisely what one does in a forest glade. By the end of the evening I was in no doubt that, from Epping to the Schwartwald, this was the knoll where I would pitch my ideal picnic. And what better definition could there be of Arden?

Michael Elliot's direction is crisp and intelligent. He knows precisely the pulse of Shakespeare's changing perspectives, and he adds one particularly telling touch: he stages the implicit hunt which leads up to Jaques's question, 'Which is he that killed the deer?' In the excitement of the chase these courtly foresters show a streak of savagery which is out of keeping with the spirit of Arden. With a shudder one's mind is jerked back to the obscene ferocity with which Michael Elliot's court ladies had cheered on the wrestlers and to Jaques's earlier complaint that the nobles in the forest are just as much usurpers and tyrants

> To fright the animals and to kill them up
> In their assigned and native dwelling place

as is the wicked Duke to drive *them* into hiding in the forest. Yet Elliot, like Shakespeare, is not wholly on melancholy Jaques's side. For he has directed Vanessa Redgrave as Rosalind.

Her performance is a triumph. For the first few scenes it looked as if she was going to seem gawky in the part, but I suspect she intended it. Her Rosalind, very properly, is mewed up in court clothes. As soon as she gets into the forest, she expands, throws her arms wide to the air and frolics up and down Negri's hill like one of shepherd Corin's long-legged lambs. Between leaps she pants out Rosalind's euphuistic conceits with all the excitement of someone who has just found that she too can play the game of fashionable wit. In every way the forest of Arden is a place of discovery for her. Once or twice my tight English soul winced at her exuberance because methought, the lady did protest too much. But in fact, the lines cry out for this interpretation rather than for the usual more lady-like version. Miss Redgrave has done the most alarming admirable thing—she has thrown herself so fully into her role that, if it goes wrong, she will merely look foolish. Max Adrian plays Jaques with the calmest precision, and Ian Bannen's Orlando seems palely romantic beside Miss Redgrave, that is partly Orlando's fault. The tree-spoiler is a conventional wooer unworthy of the girl.

The Spectator, July 14, 1961: 59.
Reprinted with permission of *The Spectator.*

SHAKESPEAREAN COMEDY AND SOME EIGHTEENTH-CENTURY ACTRESSES
Jeanne Addison Roberts
1983

In 1776, the year of David Garrick's retirement from the stage, Mrs. Thrale entered in her diary a vignette of the household of Bennet Langton, Sr., father of Dr. Johnson's friend. Dr. Johnson had visited the Langton family estate near Spilsby in Lincolnshire in 1764, and Thrale's description reports anecdotes of his visit. Langton had three daughters, wild, strong-minded, and eccentric "dowdies," to use Johnson's word, over whom their father was unable to exercise any authority. Thrale identifies the cause of this "disorder" in the household. The guilty party, as any modern analyst would guess, was Langton's wife. Not only had she spawned free-spirited daughters, she had also failed with the housekeeping—and all because of an addiction to the theater. She was, Thrale tells us,

a *London Lady,* always teizing her husband to go to Town, and never regulating her Family for twenty Years, never buying a Cow, never putting up a Fowl to feed,—never repairing their Furniture or house in Lincolnshire where they always lived because they were to go to London next Year forsooth and see the Players, who made all the Subject of her Conversation, settling the Merits of Mrs. Cibber and Mrs. Pritchard in the midst of a Family ruined by Mismanagement, and running to speedy Decay; and in a Neighborhood of Country Gentlewomen who had never seen nor were like to see them.

I confess to considerable sympathy for the slovenly Mrs. Langton in her protracted exile from the center of human felicity, but I also find her particularly interesting as a symptom of her time. It seems to me significant that she wants to go to London, not to see plays but players, and that at the very height of the Garrick years her theatrical interest is focused not on the brilliant Garrick or the romantic Spranger Barry, but on two leading female players, Susanna Maria Cibber and Hannah Pritchard. I should like to use Mrs.

Langton's longing as a clue to the roles of women, both actresses and audiences, in the middle of the eighteenth century and in particular, to suggest that female influences were crucial in one of the most striking developments on the stage of this period—the revival of Shakespeare's comedies.

I will argue that the emergence of first-rate actresses who were neither dependent courtesans nor social pariahs but affluent and respected professionals was an unprecedented development in the social history of women; that these actresses, truly extraordinary individuals, would have found in the spirited, self-reliant heroines of Shakespearean comedy roles that expressed their characters much more fully than did the limp, tearful ladies of popular comedies. These actresses unquestionably had the power to influence repertory choices: and, in both private and stage roles, their influence on the theater public, male as well as female, was significant. I will examine in particular the careers of Hannah Pritchard, Kitty Clive, and Peg Woffington as they impinge on Shakespearean comedy, and I shall also glance briefly at Susanna Maria Cibber.

The contributions of these women have not been ignored, but they have suffered a partial eclipse as the result of an insistent male emphasis. This emphasis started, of course, with a theatrical structure that was in its origins entirely male. It was carried on by the male theatrical managers, actors, and reviewers of the period who strongly influenced public opinion, but it has been perpetuated by scholars. The tendency to ignore women is strongly apparent in G. C. D. Odell's pioneer work, *Shakespeare from Betterton to Irving* (2 vols.. New York: Scribner's. 1920. repr. 1963), with its major divisions named for actors and its merely passing references to Cibber, Pritchard, Clive, and Woffington. Odell grants that *As You Like It* was "saved to the stage" by a succession of great Rosalinds, but he is less generous in claiming that *Much Ado About Nothing* and *Cymbeline* were constantly revived because of Garrick's "supreme success" in the leading roles (1:339). In fact, the praise accorded to Pritchard's Beatrice during the long run of *Much Ado* almost exactly matches (and sometimes surpasses—see below) that given to Garrick as Benedick; and since Garrick ceased playing Posthumus after two seasons, the remarkable success of *Cymbeline* can hardly be due solely to his performance. Much progress has been made since Odell, but a male bias persists.

James J. Lynch (*Box, Pit, and Gallery* [Berkeley: University of California Press, 1953]) lists the great Shakespearean roles of the Garrick period: in tragedy, Pritchard as Lady Macbeth, Garrick as Hamlet, Barry as Othello, Quin as Falstaff, Cibber as Juliet: in comedy, Pritchard as Beatrice, Clive as Portia, Theophilus Cibber as Pistol, Garrick as Benedick (p. 161). But in pointing out important factors in the Shakespeare revival he mentions only actors, specifically Garrick, Macklin, and Quin (p. 194). In another context, assigning credit for the Shakespeare revival of 1740–41, he mentions some of the revised plays—*As You Like It, Twelfth Night, The Winter's Tale, The Merchant of Venice, Alls Well that Ends Well*—and concludes that though these revivals cannot be attributed to Garrick, since they precede his career, some credit may be assigned to Charles Macklin (p. 95). Lynch's disregard of female contributions in dealing with these particular plays, with their strong female roles, seems especially striking. Lynch notes that midcentury audiences came to see stars rather than plays, but he specifies only Garrick and Barry (p. 139). He emphasizes the importance of Garrick in the 1744 revival of *Macbeth,* quoting Thomas Davies on the "indescribable excellence" of the actor in the banquet scene (p. 103). Lynch neglects to mention, however, that Davies specifically includes Pritchard, insisting "I will not separate these performers for the merits of both were transcendent." In fact, his description of the banquet scene includes two lines on Garrick and seventeen lines on Pritchard. Garrick himself felt Pritchard's importance so strongly that he retired from the part of Macbeth when she retired from the stage. All discussions of acting styles emphasize as innovative Garrick's great naturalness, but this observation is rarely linked in modern criticism with the praise of the great natural acting credited to Pritchard, Clive, and Woffington, all of whom preceded Garrick on the stage. Finally, Arthur Scouten, in looking for influences other than Garrick's to account for new interest in Shakespeare in the early 1740s, lists the importance of editions of the plays, the reaction of licensing, the Shakespeare Ladies Club, and Theophilus Cibber—again without recognition of the possible impact of female stars.

The lives and careers of the female stars demonstrate their personal and professional stature. Spiritual descendants of Aphra Behn and the actresses of the Restoration and early eighteenth century, but no longer the first pioneers on the new frontiers of female professionalism, Clive, Cibber, Woffington, and Pritchard enjoyed security, affluence, and independence remarkable for their time. Each of them displayed in pursuit of her career a high degree of courage and determination but admirably combined these qualities with generosity and personal integrity.

Daughter of an impoverished Dublin lawyer, Kitty Clive was married at age twenty-two to a barrister, but within two years she had separated from him. She was already a successful actress, and with her earnings she supported herself and her aged father and provided a home for her brother. She was able to retire relatively early and comfortably, devoting time and energy to her friends— especially Horace Walpole and Jane Pope, a younger actress with whom she sustained a long and mutually supportive correspondence.

Susannah Cibber, daughter of a London upholsterer and sister of the musician Thomas Arne, was reluctantly propelled first into marriage with Theophilus Cibber and then, by her husband's avarice, into the arms of a lover.

With the lover she took her stand, surviving two stormy lawsuits and bearing him two children. In spite of her adulterous situation, she established herself as a respected "wife" and mother; and in the midst of the strong pressures of a Protestant milieu she remained a devoted Catholic. Neither dubious social status nor religious discrimination prevented her from making and controlling her own fortune.

Peg Woffington grew up in Dublin in extreme poverty but early won attention as a professional actress. The most sexually adventurous of the four, she remained unmarried, preferring freedom to compromise. After a prolonged affair with Garrick, during which she shared quarters with him for perhaps five years and was visited by such notables as Dr. Johnson, she broke off the relationship before Garrick's marriage and steadfastly refused to return to Drury Lane while he was manager. Excluded from proper society herself, she nonetheless succeeded in educating her sister and marrying her advantageously to the second son of a lord. She gave up Roman Catholicism in order to qualify for an inheritance from an admirer, but most of the considerable fortune she left to her sister was the reward of a disciplined and dedicated dramatic career.

Hannah Pritchard was the child of a prosperous London staymaker. To all appearances her life was the most conventional of the four, but she added new dimensions to convention. Fortunate in having a supportive husband, she maintained a long marriage, successful motherhood, and an elevated social station without compromising her distinguished acting career. She must have been one of the first women in English history to perform such an impressive balancing act.

All four of these women made choices, made money, and made their way astonishingly well in a male-dominated society where they were often legally helpless. My particular interest in them here is that all four were also important in the revival of Shakespeare's comedies in the early 1740s. It is significant that the comedies revived were those with strong female leads, multiple female roles, and provocative examples of women moving, often helped by male disguise, with a freedom rare either in actual society or in the popular drama of the day. In the years of midcentury most often thought of as the Garrick years, female forces need to be reckoned with.

I have no wish whatever to denigrate Garrick. His importance in every aspect of theatrical production is beyond question. And indeed he deserves special credit for his recognition of female talent and his able success in sustaining frequently difficult relationships with his leading ladies. However, his influence in the revival of Shakespeare's comedy was actually negative. We know that he had, understandably, a strong interest in the plays in which he acted, and that only three of his established Shakespearean roles were in the comedies. Of these—Benedick, Leontes, and Posthumus—only Benedick can be considered major, since Leontes has only a small part in Garrick's adaptation of *The Winter's Tale,* and since Posthumus was played by others after two seasons. During the period of Garrick's management of Drury Lane, twenty-seven percent of all the tragedies produced there were Shakespearean, as opposed to only sixteen percent of the comedies. Among the revivals of the comedies specifically initiated by Garrick, only that of *Cymbeline* in 1759 was a close approximation of Shakespeare's play, and even that suffered from a weakening and shortening of the role of Imogen. Managerial impetus for the numerous comic revivals of 1740–46 was supplied by other entrepreneurs, and the three most frequently performed comedies of that period (see table) owed very little to Garrick.

Performances of Shakespeare's Comedies. Seasons 1739–40 through 1760–61*

The Merchant of Venice	134
As You Like It	121
The Merry Wives of Windsor	94
The Tempest	87
Much Ado About Nothing	79
The Taming of the Shrew	58
A Midsummer Night's Dream	48
The Winter's Tale	44
Measure for Measure	39
All's Well that Ends Well	30
Twelfth Night	27
Cymbeline	10
The Comedy of Errors	5

*Includes adaptations, some musical.

Audiences at midcentury were more heterogeneous than they had been in the Restoration period, and tensions between classes and sexes were frequently projected onto the stage. The aristocrats in the boxes and the bourgeoisie in the pit often disagreed. A good example is the flap over *The Foundling* in 1748 (*The London Stage, Part 4,* vol. 1, pp. 30–35), when Lord Hubbard formed a party to hiss the play off the stage in protest against its protracted run. When *As You Like It* was proposed as a successor, the pit rose and insisted on a continuation of *The Foundling,* a play in the sentimental tradition, which, though well acted appealed more because of its middle-class values than its artistic standards. Judged by this incident, Shakespeare's comedy was regarded as a suitable pacifier for the upper class, but its appeal extended to the middle class and especially to women—both those in the audience and those on the stage.

The presence and power of women in the audience at midcentury is well attested. The existence of a club connected with Covent Garden, (made up of some of the most intelligent and fashionable ladies of the time), whose purpose was to foster Shakespeare on the stage, is regularly noted. If it is a little disappointing to discover that the three revivals known to have been sponsored by the club in 1737–38 were of *King John, Richard II* and *1 Henry* VI (none of them very memorable for their female characters), it is worth noting that the production of an adaptation of *Much Ado About Nothing* called *The Universal Passion* was as mounted at Drury Lane in 1737, within a week of Covent Garden's *King John*, with a prologue specifically addressed to the "*noble Fair*" who now "*to* Shakespear's *Sense attend.*" It concludes with a plea to women as "*the ablest Judges of this Play*," entreating that they "To their *Protection* Shakespear's *Offspring take, And save the* Orphan for the Father's *Sake.*" The production was repeated for four nights (with Clive as Liberia-Beatrice, and Pritchard, later to become the great Beatrice of the century, as Delia-Margaret) and seems to have stimulated a four-night revival of the original play at Covent Garden in the same year.

Women on the stage were also active in promoting Shakespeare. Pritchard and Clive, who maintained a close friendship during almost forty years, played together constantly until Clive followed Pritchard into retirement in 1768, even though she might have continued longer on the stage. Their partnership frequently extended into other Shakespearean comedies featuring two women. As early as 1735 they were playing in *A Cure for a Scold,* an adaptation of *The Taming of the Shrew,* with Clive as Peg-Katherine and Pritchard as Flora-Bianca. Later, in 1754, when Garrick's *Catherine and Petruchio* was mounted at Drury Lane, both actresses played the lead, though it was Clive who finally "owned" the part. In *As You Like It* Clive played Celia to Pritchard's Rosalind many times, beginning with the Drury Lane production of 1740–41, designed to challenge Woffington's success in two "breeches roles" at Covent Garden. In a reversal of role priority in *The Merchant of Venice,* Pritchard played Nerissa to Clive's Portia, and then, exchanging precedence again in *Twelfth Night,* Clive was Olivia to Pritchard's Viola. It is very difficult indeed to avoid the conclusion that these good friends discovered in the mid-thirties that they played well together, and, considerably before Garrick, fostered the production of the Shakespearean comedies with interesting dual roles.

The unflagging mutual support of Clive and Pritchard reflects on the small scale a rather surprising system of female reinforcement in the larger theatrical world. In spite of some notorious quarrels among actresses, we are repeatedly told of friendship and generosity within the profession and of impressive support from female audiences, especially the aristocracy. George Anne Bellamy says that she dates her theatrical advancement from the notice given her by the duchess of Montague. She also recounts how Mrs. Butler, a patroness in Dublin, supplied her with diamonds for her elaborate costumes, and how the same lady kept down the house for Garrick's *King John* when Bellamy was denied the role of Constance. The duchess of Queensberry on one occasion took 250 tickets and all but one of the boxes for a Bellamy benefit. Similar benefits sponsored by women for women were apparently a regular feature of the Dublin stage. Davies repeatedly describes the esteem in which actresses were held by members of their own sex of "the most distinguished wealth and character." Complaining publicly of her difficulties with managers, Clive appealed to audiences, concluding "I have in consideration of these hardships been promised the protection of many ladies to whom I have the honour to be personally known. . . ." Theophilus Cibber speaks in his "Serio-Comic Apology" of his efforts to comply with the "ladies who are desirous to see" his wife act, and we are reminded of the longings of Mrs. Bennet Langton. Finally, in a footnote reference to a comment on the power of managers in a letter from Mrs. Abington to Garrick, James Boaden, editor of Garrick's correspondence, has added, "The power of a manager indeed! what is it to an actress of powerful talent backed by half the women of fashion in the metropolis." This kind of female solidarity certainly suggests a strong identification between women in the audience and actresses and helps to explain the appeal of Shakespeare's comedies.

Shakespeare's comedies were among the most popular of the period. They were enacted with about the same frequency as the "humane comedies" of Farquhar, Vanbrugh, Colley Cibber, Congreve and Steele. Shakespeare shared with these writers an underlying insistence on sexual morality and the sanctity of marriage, and, above all their pervasive good humor, tolerance, and optimism about human nature. To some critics his women seemed similar. Colley Cibber says that in writing female roles for boys, Shakespeare knew that he could not expect much and therefore emphasized simplicity, innocence, and virtue. Even such female characters as Celia. Portia, and the merry wives were, somewhat incongruously, admired for being tender, modest, and delicate. Davies speaks more perceptively (*Dr. Misc.* 2: 237), however, when he praises the "abundant and varied originality" of Shakespeare's women. In fact, the most striking difference between Shakespeare and the writers of "humane comedy" is their characterization of women. Whereas the later writers, with a few exceptions, tended to create good women who were weak, humorless, and passive, Shakespeare's heroines combine goodness with aggressive intelligence and wit. For eighteenth-century as for Elizabethan audiences, they continued to bridge both class and sex barriers. They pleased the aristocrats with their wit and high spirits, but they also gratified the middle class with their lack of aristocratic pretension. John Upton observes that "Shakespeare seems . . . not to have known such a character as a fine lady; nor does he ever recognize their dignity. . . . Instead of the Lady Bettys, and Lady Fannys, who shine so much in modern comedies, he brings you on the stage plain Mrs. Ford and Mrs. Page, two honest good-humored wives of two plain country gentlemen." In the comedies revived (in adaptations and in the original) in the late thirties and early forties, Rosalind, Portia, Beatrice, Isabella, Viola, and Helena presented a stunning array of females uniquely qualified to satisfy both the middle-class demand for virtue and the interest of the discriminating of all classes in subtlety and spirited characterization. Audiences could enjoy the beauty, charm, and occasional giddiness of these heroines and at the same time find horizons stretched by their display of female enterprise and determination. The stage characters must also have delighted the actresses, themselves risen from middle-class backgrounds through energy and talent to an artistic aristocracy. These powerful women surely did as much as actors to shift critical attention from dramatic structure to character and personality. Regrettably this fortunate conjunction of commanding actresses and roles that gave them scope was part of a rear-guard action. By the end of the century (with the help of the novel), the duller, more sentimental heroines of contemporary plays had triumphed: and a new generation of actresses either modified or played down the more unmaidenly aspects of the women in comedies.

At midcentury, however, the struggle to define the role of women and to analyze male-female relationships seemed to be at its height. Attitudes toward marriage in the popular comedies of the early part of the century have already been perceptively analyzed, and these comedies continued to dominate the stage. The titles alone are eloquent: *The Provok'd Wife, The Careless Husband, The Modern Husband, The Provok'd Husband, The Distressed Wife, The Jealous Wife,* etc. Although the popular Shakespeare comedies are special in that they focus primarily on the brief heady period of courtship, where female freedom generates a particular excitement, heightened perhaps by its ephemeral nature, they still point up the perennial conflict between the sexes that was obviously of absorbing interest to midcentury audiences. From the exhilarating dominance of Rosalind, Portia, and the merry wives to the tenacious devotion of Viola and Helena, the comic heroines offered an intriguing spectacle that male and female observers could use to test the varying shades of their own feelings.

Restoration and eighteenth-century adaptations of *The Taming of the Shrew* reflect the vicissitudes of fashion on this compelling subject. All of them keep Petruchio's accurate but offensive announcement to his new wife:

I will be master of what is mine own;
She is my goods, my chattels: she is my house,
My household stuff, my field, my barn,
My horse, my ox, my ass, my any thing. . . .

[3. 9. 299–32]

But in other ways they temporize. *Sauny the Scot,* the 1667 version, in general a vicious and sadistic play, still gives Margaret-Kate lines like "I'll make Petruchio glad to wipe my shoes or walk my horse ere I have done with him," although in the end she apologizes and utters a speech greatly shortened from the original, conceding "They are our lords." Petruchio is given a mollifying last word, however, with a prophecy:

I've tamed the shrew, but will not be ashamed
If next you see the very tamer tamed.

In 1735 James Worsdale's *Cure for a Scold,* in which Peg-Kate was played by Clive, duly prescribes for its heroine two final lines of wifely submission but then cancels them out with an epilogue where Clive reveals:

Well, I must own, it wounds me to the Heart
To act, unwomanly—so mean a Part.
What—to submit, so tamely—so contented.
Thank Heav'n I'm not the Thing I represented.

Her final word is to the women in the audience who knows that in real life they make the "Monsters tame." She pleads,

Ye Fair, who form the radiant Circle here,
Approve that Censure, which you cannot fear. . . .

Garrick's version, *Catherine and Petruchio,* is closer to the original, but it too offers some slight compromise. Though Catherine has six final lines of total submission, Petruchio has already promised to "doff the lordly husband" and live in "mutual love, compliance, and regard." A great attraction of Garrick's adaptation seems to have been that it was enjoyed as a reflection of real-life antagonism between its principals, Clive and Henry Woodward (one of Drury Lane's major comedians). On this level it was a contest between equals.

Kitty Clive was a comic genius. By 1756, the year of maximum popularity of *Catherine and Petruchio,* she had already been a favorite of the English stage for more than twenty years. Her range in comedy was extensive, including, says Davies (*Memoirs,* 2:192), "country girls, romps, hoydens, and dowdies, superannuated beauties, viragoes, and humourists." Her special forte was "sprightliness of humour." Boswell quotes Johnson as saying, "she was a better romp than any I ever saw in nature." Offstage, Clive was famous for direct speech and a no-nonsense temperament. It was she who, after a notorious battle with Mrs. Cibber in 1736 (during which she was dubbed in a popular ballad, "a Green-Room (Scold"), won back the role of Polly in *The Beggar's Opera* from Cibber who had been briefly slated to play the part. Samuel Foote said that Clive's forcible manner was assumed in order "to procure a more decent Entertainment," and obviously she was a force not to be ignored (*Biographical Dictionary,* 3:344–59).

Garrick valued Clive enough to beg her to postpone her retirement, and a mutual respect seems to have tempered their frequently stormy relationship. Davies says that Garrick dreaded altercations with her and was happy to get a draw because she was so "true game" that she "would have died upon the spot rather than have yielded the field of battle to any body" (*Memoirs,* 2:190–98). Clive's most famous comic role was Portia in *The Merchant of Venice,* and yet ironically it was also the role that drew the most critical attack, since she apparently played the courtroom scene in a style recognizable as a parody of a local judge.

Obviously an influential figure, Clive was also delightfully capable of self-parody. She wrote a farce in imitation of *The Rehearsal* called *Boys in Petticoats,* which, though not a dramatic triumph, is full of revealing personal references. Her female lead, Mrs. Hazard, is an actress who has written a play. Mrs. Hazard's male "friend," appropriately named Witling, warns her that "there is not ten women in the Creation that have sense enough to write a consistent *N. B.*" (i.e., compose a sensible footnote). This satirically drawn male chauvinist is balanced by a laughing denigration of the "conceited, and insolent Mrs. Clive who has been scheduled to act in the play-within-the-play but sends word that she cannot come because she is busy with "Ladies about her Benefit." The author is careful to note that the actress makes £800 a year, but still she refers to her alter ego as a "poor Lady . . . ignorant as Dirt." Clive's self-portrait comes close to some of the criticisms made of her, and she clearly enjoys the joke of her own caricature.

In the same vein Clive could enjoy the role of Kate in *Catherine and Petruchio.* During her struggle with Cibber, Woodward, now her Petruchio, had called her in a rhyme a "Fierce Amazonian Dame" and an anonymous pamphlet had described her as a "little Gypsy" whose natural Temper is inclined to be Shrewish" (*Biographical Dictionary,* 3:346, 349). Even though she is finally tamed in the drama, personality and role merged in a way to give actors maximum opportunity and audiences maximum pleasure. Witnessing Clive and

Woodward in action must have been as fascinating as watching Elizabeth Taylor and Richard Burton in the parts on the modern screen. Clive seems to have reinstituted an epilogue, and it is interesting to speculate whether Garrick's own feelings or his accurate gauging of the temper of his audience was responsible for his tipping the sexual equilibrium in his text slightly to the male side. In any case *Catherine and Petruchio* was extremely popular, and Clive's early experience of the play and her special suitability for the role made it a logical choice for adaptation.

Clive deserves major credit for the success of *The Shrew* in two versions and some notice for her Portia, whether or not it conformed to Shakespeare's intention. She also should be credited with long and successful support of Pritchard in her roles in *As You Like It* and *Twelfth Night*. Her virtue was well rewarded. She lived to enjoy long and prosperous golden years in a cottage on Horace Walpole's Strawberry Hill estate. She carried on a lively correspondence and moved frequently in the highest circles. Dr. Johnson said to Boswell, "Clive, sir, is a good thing to sit by: she always understands what you say" (*Biographical Dictionary,* 3:360). And Davies praised her power to "raise admiration" and "excite mirth," thus uniting, he announces (without any sense of hyperbole), the qualities of Milton and Samuel Butler (*Memoirs,* 2:195).

Katherine in *The Shrew* is only one example of the female freedom and female aggressiveness, sometimes to the point of dominance, that characterize all the popular Shakespearean comedies played repeatedly without adaptation in the middle of the century. This freedom is pointed up emblematically in *As You Like It, The Merchant of Venice, Twelfth Night,* and *Cymbeline* by the presence of women who assume male disguises that free them from the conventional confines of feminine activity and enable them to experience social relationships from new perspectives.

Although the importance of the ascension of female players after the Restoration to the roles of Shakespeare's women characters is regularly noted, the impact of the change has never been sufficiently appreciated. There is a vast difference between watching "women" behave as men when the watcher is secure in the knowledge that they really are male, and in seeing women in these roles—the effect must have been all the more powerful when the audience knew that the women on the stage were also confidently and competently assuming "male" roles in real life. The popularity of breeches roles has been explained in terms of the delectable opportunities they provided for male appraisal of the usually discreetly shrouded female leg. Certainly I would not deny this attraction, but I suggest that a different fascination must have exerted itself far more strongly, not only especially for the female audience, but indeed for all—the revolutionary prospect of actually witnessing a sort of female emancipation acted out with applause in a public place.

As we have seen, the female emancipation in life that was played off against male-female characters on the stage is a strong characteristic of all the great Shakespearean actresses of the period. There is no precedent in English culture for a class of self-made women of such stature, and their impact must have been electrifying, inspiring, and perhaps frightening.

The greatest contrast between stage roles and private life is in the case of Susanna Cibber. I mention her chiefly as an example of a woman who created for herself a central role in the theater, perhaps in spite of her natural inclinations. After leaving her husband, she kept control of her very considerable funds (her husband, who complained that in losing her he had been deprived of income, said she was making a salary of £1200 a year at Drury Lane in 1744–45, for less than six months' work; *Biographical Dictionary*, 3:267–72). Mrs. Cibber was widely respected and admired by both sexes—especially for her great tragic roles—Juliet, Desdemona, Cordelia, Ophelia, and Constance in *King John*. In comedy she regularly played Isabella in *Measure for Measure* and Perdita in adaptations of *The Winter's Tale*. Arthur Murphy wrote that on seeing her as Isabella he was moved to make excuses for Angelo because, "when I saw Mrs. Cibber before him on her knees: the elegance of her figure, the musical plaintiveness of her voice, and the gentleness of her manners [were] sufficient to make any one fall in love with her." But her tenderness, sweetness, and pathos on stage were complemented offstage by the tenacity and strongmindedness of a real-life Isabella. Although she and Garrick were said to be "formed by nature for the illustration of each others talents" (Davies, *Memoirs*, 1:116), that were not perfectly harmonious in daily life. In 1745 the idea of buying the patent for Drury Lane seems to have been Susanna Cibber's, but in the end Garrick consummated the deal without her. She reputedly had a contract that gave her the privilege of choosing new roles, and "illness" more than once prevented her appearance in a role she did not fancy. After Cibber's death in 1766 Garrick lamented that tragedy had expired with her. But also added,

she was the greatest female plague belonging to my house. I could easily parry the artless thrusts and despise the coarse language of some of my other heroines. . . . but she was always sure to counterpoint by the acuteness of her invective and the steadiness of her deliverance. (*Biographical Dictionary*, 3:281, 279.)

Breeches roles were not for Cibber (she was slight in stature and girlish in figure until the end of her career), but the aura of power that singled her out from other females was fundamental to her image.

Much more closely related to the revival of Shakespearean comedy is the career of Peg Woffington. All accounts agree that she was breathtakingly beautiful. John Rich's initial reaction to her is typical. He described her as "an amalgamated Calypso, Circe, and Armida . . . as majestic as Juno, as lovely as Venus and as fresh and charming as Hebe." This ravishing feminine beauty was uniquely combined with a lack of affectation and an extraordinary dedication to freedom and independence. In her *Apology,* George Anne Bellamy plaintively describes the outrage of her elegant patroness, the duchess of Queensberry, when Bellamy, hoping to demonstrate the wit and polish of actors, took the duchess on a long-anticipated visit to the Green Room after a benefit performance of *All For Love,* and they were greeted by Woffington in Cleopatra costume drinking porter and crying "Confusion to all order! Let Liberty thrive" (Bellamy, *An Apology,* 2:51–53). Woffington was, in fact, famous for her wit, frequently displayed in interchanges with the militantly chaste Clive, who once complained that "a pretty face . . . excuses a multiplication of sweethearts," only to be answered by Woffington, "And a plain one insures a vast overflow of unmarketable virtue" (Daly, *Woffington,* p. 46). Woffington liked men (she was elected president of the all-male Beef Steak Club in Dublin [Davies, *Memoirs,* 1:341]) and her unconventional sexual morality was notorious (a popular ballad praising her pointedly conceded "one fault" [Daly, *Woffington,* p. 107]), yet this did not prevent her carrying off such virginal roles as Isabella, Cordelia, and Ophelia with great success. Indeed she was particularly praised by a Dublin newspaper that marveled, "You each character so close pursue/We think the author copied it from you" (ibid. p. 122).

And yet actor and role were finally inseparable. Woffington seems to have found a way, particularly in comedy, of joining her own personal freedom of spirit with projections of stage character so intriguing and irresistible to her audiences that her name virtually guaranteed financial success. Her greatest gift was for comedy, but she was more versatile than Clive or Cibber and also more wideranging in her career, which included professional residence in Dublin and Paris as well as at Drury Lane and Covent Garden. Her contribution to the revival of Shakespearean comedy was both direct and indirect. During her London career she played Rosalind, Adriana (in *The Comedy of Errors*), Helena (in *All's Well that Ends Well*), Portia, Nerissa, Isabella, Beatrice, Viola, and Mistress Ford. Her indirect influence is linked with the particular kind of versatility that made possible her astounding success in breeches roles, both in those, such as Sylvia in *The Recruiting Officer* that featured women in male disguise and in the actual male role of Sir Harry Wildair in *The Constant Couple.*

Woffington prided herself on avoiding female company (because women spoke only of silks and scandal), and she seems never to have enlisted the female patronage that benefited other actresses (perhaps because of her great success with males), but women as well as men admired her (Davies, *Memoirs,* 1:341). When she first played Wildair in Dublin, the Green Room was packed afterwards with both sexes, and several popular ballads record her "universal conquest" as the result of roles in *The Beggar's Opera* and *The Constant Couple.* All agree that

> Her charm resistless, conquers all—
> Both sexes vanquished lie
> And who to Polly scorned to fall,
> By Wildair, ravaged, die.

> [Daly, *Woffington,* p. 18]

Charles Macklin described Woffington's male-female performances as showing "an ease and elegance of deportment that seemed almost out of the reach of female accomplishments." She was acclaimed widely as "a creature uncommon,/Who's both man and woman/And the chief of the belles and the beaux!"

The usual account of Woffington's sensational arrival on the stage as Sylvia in *The Recruiting Officer* in 1740 attributes the idea of the role to Rich and to the Prince of Wales who "commanded" the performance (at Rich's instigation), but there is little doubt that the moving spirit behind this and other breeches roles was Woffington herself. At the Aungier Street Theatre Royal in Dublin she had in 1734 played the part of Rose in *The Recruiting Officer* to the Sylvia of Mrs. Bellamy (Sr.), and from that time she was ambitious to try the leading role. It was she who suggested the production there of *The Female Officer,* in which she made her transvestite debut, and it was she who urged the revival of *The Recruiting Officer* in 1738, in which she was Sylvia. In 1739, when Quin was playing to packed houses at Smock Alley, Woffington conceived the idea of launching her career as Sir Harry Wildair in competition. Predictably, her huge success in Dublin prepared the path for her triumphant conquest of London as Sylvia and Wildair at Covent Garden in the fall of 1740. It was these Woffington triumphs that led to the Drury Lane counterattack in the form of the revival of those Shakespeare's comedies that had breeches roles and women in male disguise (*Twelfth Night, As You Like It,* and in *The Merchant of Venice*), providing new scope for the team of Clive and Pritchard and elevating Pritchard as Rosalind to a stardom that she maintained during her long and distinguished Shakespearean career. Woffington herself went on to later success as Rosalind, and Clive was alternately Celia to the one or the other of the two leads. The winning androgyny of Rosalind suited Woffington well. It seems especially appropriate that her last lines on the stage were from the epilogue of *As You*

Like It. Following an "unapproachable performance" as Rosalind, she collapsed after the words, "If I were among you [note the necessary change from "If I were a woman"], I would kiss as many of you as had beards that pleased me." John Hoole, in a monody on her death, describes Shakespeare as the first of many grateful poets bending "o'er his favorite's tomb" (Daly, *Woffington*, pp. 146, 172).

Whatever Shakespeare's ghost may have felt for Woffington, however, the poet's greatest debt to a Shakespearean actress at midcentury was to Hannah Pritchard. Her most famous role was Lady Macbeth, and we need only look at a contemporary illustration to see how the commanding figure of Pritchard, towering over the diminutive Garrick, must have helped to shape their interpretation of the play. Similarly, her dignity and presence and her distinctively "articulate harmonious voice," combined with striking command of stage business, gave a rare importance to her Gertrude (Davies, *Dram. Misc.*, 3:116–17). Pritchard lacked the beauty of Woffington. In fact, Mrs. Thrale, though admiring her *Mind,* concedes the "supreme Ugliness of her person (Vaughan, *Born to Please,* pp. 112, 130). Endowed with a figure that made her an impressive and convincing male in her earlier years, Pritchard grew heavy at the end of her career, a disability that she managed to offset by sheer force of dramatic skill. *The Theatrical Examiner* of 1757 records that "though [she was] not the girl Beatrice, her performance was such that she compensated for all the advantages of 18" (Vaughan, *Born to Please,* p. 126). She seems to have had a genius for body language, and even in Garrick's truncated version of *The Winter's Tale,* where she spoke "hardly 10 words" as Hermione, the *Universal Museum,* 1762 (Vickers, *Shakespeare,* 4:462) describes her rendering of the statue as "truly great," elaborating, "While she descends from the temple her face is a perfect picture, and her countenance so serene and composed, so expressive of that part that perhaps the whole theatre cannot produce so remarkable an instance."

In other Shakespearean comedies Pritchard was Imogen, Mistress Ford, both Portia and Nerissa, Helena and the Countess of Roussillon (abdicating the lead in favor of her daughter), and most successfully Viola, Rosalind, and Beatrice. These three roles, with their dramatic force and their scope for female versatility, provided her and her audience with opportunities, all too rare in the theater of the period, to realize on the stage the fulfillment of female potentialities that Pritchard had regularly demonstrated in her own life. A devoted mother of three daughters and a successful wife, she was obviously the chief support of her family. Her husband's will disposes of "my worldly affairs received through the bounty of God and the greater part being through industry of my dear and loving wife . . . whom I do hereby constitute my whole and sole executrix." Her social importance is documented by the fact that she was appointed dresser to Princess Charlotte of Mecklenberg on the occasion of her wedding and coronation as queen (Vaughan, *Born to Please,* pp. 92, 84). Pritchard's theatrical success considerably predates Garrick's. John Hill recollects her debut as Rosalind noting that at first her modesty inhibited her, and that she did not put forth all her talent until she received great applause for her rendering of the "Take the cork out of thy mouth" speech. Then, he adds, "She was applauded throughout and for ever after" as "the best actress of the British Stage" (ibid. p. 19). Davies admired her independence in playing Constance in Colley Cibber's *Papal Tyranny* (an adaptation of *King John*) when only she ignored Cibber's directorial advice and gained approval and applause (*Dram. Misc.,* 1:23). Samuel Foote in 1747 awarded her his ultimate accolade: "I would, were I a Pattentee, rather have her in my service than any Woman in England" (Vaughan, *Born to Please,* p. 123).

Pritchard's partnership with Garrick was legendary, and her crowning achievement as Beatrice was perfectly complemented by his Benedick. Arthur Murphy and Davies conferred credit on the two equally, suggesting that every scene was a struggle in which the audience could determine no victor. Mrs. Thrale and Horace Walpole gave the edge to Pritchard on the basis of "spirit and originality" (ibid., pp. 54, 130). Certainly these qualities, embodied in Shakespeare's comic heroines made Pritchard, like Cibber, Clive, and Woffington, mind-stretching models of female possibility for the audiences of midcentury. Their achievements were neatly celebrated in verse in *A Letter of Compliment* (with lines on Cibber, Woffington, Clive, and Pritchard, respectively):

> Four ladies in one happy Era born,
> Did once the English Stage adorn;
> THE FIRST assumed the moving tragick part
> And drove successful Pity to the Heart:
> THE NEXT, beside the Magick of her Face,
> Had softness, Air, Gentility and Grace:
> THE THIRD in Comick Pleasantry surpass'd:
> In ev'ry Character, in all THE LAST:
> The Force of Nature cou'd no further flee,
> To make a Fourth, she join'd the former THREE.
>
> [Vaughan, *Born to Please.* p. I.]

After her death admirers erected a white marble slab in honor of Pritchard next to Shakespeare's monument in Westminster Abbey (ib pp. 1, 104), but it was later removed to a less prominent spot, her demotion is symbolic. As the century waned, women like Pritchard were pushed from center stage in the public imagination. In the last quarter of the century the feminine ideal was narrowed and diminished. By the end of 1768, Woffington, Cibber, and Pritchard were dead and Clive was in retirement. A new vision of womanhood, epitomized in the passive romantic victims of the novels, began to dominate popular literature. Something of the spirit of their revivers lived on in the Portias, Violas, Rosalinds, and Beatrices of younger actresses (none as distinguished as those of midcentury), but increasingly Shakespearean comic heroines were either divorced from life or modified to conform with new standards. Their virtue but not their versatility was to be imitated. In doubtful cases, texts were altered, and as a result Imogen, Hermione, Paulina, and Helena survived only in Garrick's amputated versions. Victor advised actresses against male roles because they required something beyond the propriety of their sex (3:5), and toward the end of the century the decorous Sarah Siddons covered the breeches of her Rosalind with an abbreviated skirt. Meekness and modesty were celebrated in sermons on female character, and a learned doctor said to his daughters, "I am sorry to say there are few English comedies a lady can see without a shock to delicacy."

With the passing of the principal players in the drama of female self-discovery and the changing of social and literary values, the briefly glorious convergence of Shakespeare's comic heroines with the superwomen of the mid-eighteenth-century stage faded from the memory of a new era. A generation of giants had vanished from the land.

K. Muir, J. Halio, D. J. Palmer, eds. *Shakespeare: Man of the Theater.*
(Newark: University of Delaware Press, 1983): 212–30.
Reprinted with permission of University of Delaware Press.

PLAYERS OF SHAKESPEARE
Philip Brockbank, ed.
1985

ORLANDO IN *AS YOU LIKE IT*
John Bowe

BEFORE joining the Royal Shakespeare Company in 1978, John Bowe had played a variety of parts, including Dunois in the Prospect production of *Saint Joan* and Iago in the New Shakespere Company's *Othello*. At Stratford, his parts have ranged from Corporal Taylor in *The Churchill Play,* Jack Skipper in *Captain Swing,* and Black Will in *Arden of Faversham* (all, initially, at The Other Place) to his Shakespearean roles at the Royal Shakespeare Theatre. Between 1978 and 1983 he has appeared there as Gratiano, Orlando, Laertes, Mowbray, Ratcliffe, the King of France (in *King Lear*) and Tranio, repeating many of these roles in seasons at Newcastle, the Aldwych, the Warehouse and the Barbican. He has also arranged fights for some Royal Shakespeare Company productions. He first played Orlando in the 1980 season, with Susan Fleetwood as Rosalind and Sinead Cusack as Celia. The production, designed by Farrah, was directed by Terry Hands.

From the outset *As You Like It* was to be a fairy tale. A boy, Orlando, meets a girl, Rosalind, and each falls instantaneously in love with the other. The boy undergoes a trial of his manhood against the champion of the wicked Duke, and wins. Both are the children of enemies of the Duke and out of fear for their lives each runs away to the comparative safety of the forest, where eventually they discover each other again, marry and supposedly live happily ever after. This was Terry Hands's guideline for our production.

My initial problems in attempting to make my Orlando a part of this fairy tale were weight, age and innocence. I lost a stone in weight, gave up smoking (at last!), shaved off my beard and worked hard at raising the range of my voice. So much for the exterior, but what about the way this earthy young man saw the world? Terry helped me to discover this when he took us to see an old silent movie called *Tramp, Tramp, Tramp* starring Harry Langdon. I think he wanted us to see just how far you can go and yet still retain the sympathies of an audience. Here was the perfect example, Harry Langdon, with white face and baby-like mannerisms, making us laugh, and quite beautifully moving us to tears. He was outrageous and yet truthful, coy and cheeky, but charmingly so. Just as, in a cartoon, animators can make us willingly suspend our disbelief in a talking mouse, so an actor can make an audience willingly suspend their disbelief in a make-believe world of wicked dukes and boys dressed up as girls, or was it the other way round?

So I had this energetic but shy young man, suppressed by his eldest brother, Oliver, since his father's death. No bad thing, perhaps, since it meant his life was spent nearer to Nature. Throughout rehearsal and performance I felt more and more that this was of importance to the balance of Rosalind and Orlando's relationship. She, from the court, well-mannered, well-educated, with hands no doubt perfumed with civet; he, rustically kept, ill-educated, and condemned to a life of servitude. Indeed, the comparisons of a life at court to a life in the country run through the play; in the first forest-lord scene:

> Now my co-mates and brothers in exile,
> Hath not old custom made this life more sweet
> Than that of painted pomp? Are not these woods
> More free from peril than the envious court? (2.1.1–4)

And in Touchstone's debate with Corin:

TOUCHSTONE Why, if thou never wast at court, thou never saw'st good manners; if thou never saw'st good manners, then thy manners must be wicked, and wickedness is sin, and sin is damnation. Thou art in a parlous state, shepherd.

CORIN Not a whit, Touchstone. Those that are good manners at the court are as ridiculous in the country as the behaviour of the country is most mockable at the court. You told me you salute not at the court, but you kiss your hands: that courtesy would be uncleanly if courtiers were shepherds.

(3.2.40–51)

The interaction of their backgrounds serves as an education for the two lovers. Although Rosalind mocks the uneducated Orlando's verses—'Some of them had in them more feet than the verses would bear'—she learns much from his simple faith and sincerity, after she has abused them. He in turn learns sophistication from her. He grows up, and he grows out of games. This contrast, indeed conflict, was echoed in the design. Farrah startlingly offset the beauty of the multicoloured forest with a monochromatic court. The court scenes were set on a white floor with white walls and steel bars, with actors in black velvet Jacobean-type costumes. On the other hand, the forest scenes were on a raised stage, rather like a log raft, out of which grew pines that soared to the heavens, and as spring moved into summer so the foliage appeared to grow and adorn the stage. The set often reminded me of scenes I had imagined when reading *Lord of the Rings*.

Opening a play is always difficult. In *As You Like It,* as in many of Shakespeare's plays, the action starts in the middle of a conversation, but in this instance Orlando's speech takes on the form of a prologue. We decided it was to this that Rosalind refers at the end of the play: 'It is not the fashion to see the lady the epilogue; but it is no more unhandsome to see the lord the prologue.' So Terry put Adam down-centre on an upturned bucket and I delivered the exposition through him to the audience. In rehearsals and early performances this was delivered at breakneck speed. Like an egg Orlando is hatching, and his rebellion is the outburst of the prologue in which he justifies to himself his feelings of frustration and injury. Wise old Adam can only observe for the moment. The play starts at a climactic point in Orlando's life, a fine vehicle for gripping an audience; hence the fast, pressured delivery. Later in the run of the play we compromised a little and I slowed my speech down without, I hope, losing any of the pressure.

The wrestling scene was vital to the production and to my character. Losing weight and visiting a gym three times a week paid dividends. Ian McKay was the fight arranger. I had worked with him before, which meant he knew my limitations. Terry Wood was a marvellous Charles, the wrestler—six feet five inches and approximately twenty stone. I have nightmares about facing lunatic actors in stage fights, but Terry Wood dispelled any fears and I hope I did the same for him. Right from the start there was total trust, always the emphasis was on taking care of each other, and as a result of all this Ian was able to devise a fight that was both spectacularly entertaining and apparently dangerous; so much more difficult to do in unarmed combat than it is with weapons. This proved to be essential to the production. In keeping with the fairy tale idea we had a fight that was reminiscent of professional wrestling at the local town hall between opponents grossly mismatched. It had moments of hilarity mixed with moments of alarming brutality. It was generally at this point that audiences loosened up and sometimes joined in. There were often boos, cheers and rounds of applause. At my suggestion we incorporated a move in which I was hurled headlong into the front row of the audience. This often took me out of the vision of the upper circles and invariably brought them all to their feet, a reaction an actor rarely achieves in a long career. The front row into which I was hurled often produced reactions most actors never see. Old ladies wielding handbags yelled abuse at Charles and pin-stripe-suited stockbroker types bemoaned the fact that, now the leading actor had killed himself, their ticket money and evening out were lost. I am sorry for all the shopping bags and picnic boxes I smashed as I crashed to the feet of the front row, but it was good theatre, and I never met a member of any audience that didn't think it had happened only on their night.

It was this particular move that caused the only serious accident during the run at Stratford. In a performance just before Christmas I had a bad fall. I was on my way into the front row and I landed right on the point of my right shoulder, separating my acromio-clavicular joint. I love the sound of that part of my anatomy, verbal, not actual. I slumped to the floor at the feet of the front row, and lay there grimacing. Occasionally a member of the audience would help me back on to the stage, but not this time. I assumed I had broken something in my shoulder, and decided the best thing to do was to stay there. Charles, my opponent, had other ideas. To my utter horror Terry Wood appeared over the edge of the stage and bent down to help me up. In the true spirit of the theatre yours truly scrambled to his feet and managed one more desperate flying drop-kick before Duke Frederick, appreciating the agony I was in, mercifully came out with the words, 'No more, no more.' But there was more. Having scraped through the rest of the scene, I left the stage to be greeted by the Company Manager Nick Jones, who had miraculously found a doctor in what seemed like seconds. If I thought the pain I was already suffering was bad, this doctor was about to prove me wrong. Out of earshot of the audience and the other actors a needle the size of a knitting needle was plunged into my shoulder and waggled about until it found the appropriate cavity, where it delivered its painkiller. The relief was instantaneous, and although it began to wear off after an hour or so, it got me through the show. But I shall never forget that needle, and Nick Jones will never forget the agony it caused me. So I was out of the show for a couple of months. I remember one amusing incident. I was walking my dog around the gardens by the theatre one day, my arm in a sling, when I bumped into another member of the company, David Suchet, and another actor, Bernard Lloyd. After talking together for a few minutes it occurred to David that here were three actors, each of whom had played the part of Orlando, and each of whom had suffered in playing it, Bernard with his back and David, like me, with his shoulder. But my injury was simply the result of a stupid mistake. I hadn't been concentrating, I wasn't prepared and I fell incorrectly. There was only myself to blame.

A main character and influence in the story of Orlando is Adam. Although he has reached the seventh age of man, he is the 'venerable' Adam. He is the one who is closest to Orlando throughout the first half of the play. He is the one who warns Orlando of Oliver's murderous intentions. He is the one who suggests Orlando should run away. He even gives Orlando all his savings. It is a truly sympathetic part, and one that they say that Shakespeare played himself. In our production Adam was played by Jimmy Gardner, a great friend and a warm and generous man.

Returning home from the wrestling I was confronted with this tiny old man loaded down with several pieces of luggage and a huge two-handed sword. Terry suggested that this sword had been handed down to Adam. Rusty and blunt, it was the only weapon the old man could lay his hands on, but one he could hardly lift. Adam was discovered like this at the beginning of the scene, marching up and down like a sentry on duty, waiting for his master to come home. When we next appeared, in our first forest scene, I, of course, was carrying the sword, all the luggage, and, by the end of the scene, old Adam as well. I asked Terry if I could use the sword to smash my way into the forest lords' camp, and he agreed. I felt that Orlando was surrounded by enemies at court and here in an alien world his initial and now in-bred reaction was offensive. The stronger the violation of the foresters' camp the greater his surprise when they offer charity and the more poignant his lesson. In response to their gentleness and offers of succour he can think only of Adam, in many ways his saviour, and he rushes off to fetch him. Terry wanted to make the most of the juxtaposition of 'Sans teeth, sans eyes, sans taste, sans everything' with Adam's entrance, so he had me carry Adam like a baby in my arms, and we arrived bang on the end of the line right next to Jaques.

Both Rosalind and Orlando had arrived safely in the forest, and here Terry wanted to end the first half. During the singing of 'Blow, blow, thou winter wind' (another stunning arrangement by Guy Woolfenden) I fondled and kissed the necklace given me by Rosalind after the wrestling—a little touch to relate the two lovers and to put into the audience's mind the prospect of their meeting.

After the interval our fairy tale blossomed, as did our forest set, as did indeed the relationship between Orlando and Rosalind, in the guise of Ganymede, played by Susan Fleetwood. I was often asked if Orlando realized that it was Rosalind with whom he was playing in the forest. It never crossed my mind once. I had only seen her briefly at the wrestling, and although I fell in love with her, trying to recall her face was not easy. Certainly there was a resemblance, and I talk of it to the Duke, her father:

> My lord, the first time that I ever saw him,
> Methought he was a brother to your daughter. (5.4.28–9)

But to mark that would only have been a distraction in the scenes between Rosalind and Orlando in our second half. Orlando is overflowing with love. He bounces on, swirling about the stage, carving up the trees and advertising his love by hanging his terrible poems on every available branch. He is infatuated with the memory of a girl he only saw for a few minutes when he was fighting for his life in the wrestling match.

Terry's simple solution to lovers' games was circles: histories and tragedies have straight lines, comedies and romances have circles. If you had a map of our footprints in the two major scenes of the second half, you would have a picture of spirals all over the stage. And so the first antagonistic contest of a meeting between Orlando and Rosalind swirls and whirls to a feverish climax and an exhausted collapse at the foot of a tree, where Rosalind professes she can cure Orlando of his love by pretending to be his love. Being a gambler at heart I could always appreciate Orlando's willingness to accept this dare. After all, he has nothing to lose. He doesn't think for a moment that this boy can cure him of his love, but these games may pleasingly pass the time.

It transpires that time is of the essence to Rosalind as she complains of Orlando's late arrival into their second forest scene. In our production the preceding Jaques-Rosalind scene was played as a seduction by the melancholic intellectual of the vibrant youth (perhaps in an effort to complement his personality). So at the moment Orlando enters, Ganymede is on the verge of being devoured by Jaques and his cloak. No wonder she reprimands him. For me there was a definite shape to this, the second of the forest scenes. The games reach a crescendo when Rosalind gets Celia to marry them. 'I take thee Rosalind for wife', says Orlando in play and almost collapses in grief, as the despair of his unrequited love looms in his face. He looks at Ganymede and sees Rosalind. This happens again at the end of the scene. Rosalind encourages pretend bed-games based on their discussion of fidelity, and as Orlando makes to go, she rises and, pretending that she is naked, drops Celia's shawl, which they have been using as a bedspread. Orlando is so involved in the game, he almost imagines he sees his love's body. This is too much, the games must cease and he must leave, but Rosalind torments him and makes him promise to return at two o'clock, which he does, 'With no less religion than if thou wert indeed my Rosalind'. He has been wounded deeply, and the next time they meet he has been wounded physically. Rosalind is cruel and he counters her curtly. She goads him and teases him about his love until he can bear it no longer: 'I can live no longer by thinking.' We all felt that it was at this point that Rosalind and Orlando learn their greatest lesson. He realizes that the dream is no substitute for the reality, and she realizes that she has been very wrong to play with Orlando's emotions. Together with Phoebe and Silvius they (Orlando unknowingly) intone their devotion to each other in the quartet at the end of Act 5, Scene 3. Terry tended to leave this scene alone, hoping that when we had become familiar with the lines, we would naturally catch each other's tune as we said the lines. When this happened it made it easy for me to break down on 'To her that is not here, nor doth not hear'.

And so with the stage adorned with colourful blossom and foliage a cart appears, pulled by the forest lords, chariot-style. On board are Corin, commandeered to play Hymen in this pageant (with terrible verse supplied), Celia and Rosalind, dressed as a girl again. All is resolved and all presumably live happily ever after, as in all fairy tales. To celebrate the cast dance and sing. It's a sort of fertility dance, rather like a Morris dance on the local village green, the audience clap to the beat and finally Rosalind delivers her epilogue to a sea of smiling, happy faces. I think they've had a good time.

I hope this has given a taste of the production, how we worked on it and how we reached various decisions and attitudes to scenes. I cannot remember enjoying a production so much. Even when I was depressed, after a few scenes the depression would lift. I believe Terry Hands's concept for the piece was excellent, and it was this more than anything that bound the company together and made the work so enjoyable. The production had so much panache and vigour, it was irresistibly entertaining. Entertainment was the key word. I hope Orlando provided a little of it.

(Cambridge: Cambridge University Press, 1988): 67–76.
Reprinted with permission of Mrs. Philip Brockbank.

WATCHING SHAKESPEARE
Anthony R. Dawson
1988

A moment that catches the full flavour of *As You Like It* occurs toward the end of the second scene. A wrestling-match, itself a highly theatrical display, has just ended. If the production is at all exciting, the audience has been caught up in the athletic dazzle of this event, as well as in the success of the hero, Orlando, in foiling the plot against him by beating both the odds and Charles, the Duke's wrestler. The wrestling-match is one example among many of Shakespeare's larding of the play with spectacular, witty or musical 'numbers'. *As You Like It* has some of the characteristics of a first-rate variety show. But, as in the present instance, the different numbers are subtly integrated into the whole texture. For the acrobatic bravado of the wrestling-match leads immediately to a series of sharp intimate exchanges, which together create a complex effect. The shape and feeling of the scene shift rapidly. Upon Orlando's victory, the usurping Duke Frederick asks the victor his name. The simple reply, 'Orlando, my liege, the youngest son of Sir Rowland de Boys', falls coldly on the ears of the Duke and his careful court. For Sir Rowland has been a close friend of the former duke, now banished, who is the brother of the present one and father of Rosalind, Frederick's distrusted niece. Orlando then is the son of a man who has been Frederick's mortal enemy. In John Dexter's 1979 production at the National Theatre in London, at Orlando's words 'the puppet court froze into attitudes of obsequious horror'.

The choice to emphasize the court reaction, and hence to draw attention to the dangerously sycophantic nature of Frederick's milieu, meant that the social and political background behind the love story was being taken seriously. The court's potential for harm, which bursts out into the open in the following scene with the banishment of Rosalind, was thus strongly signalled. More commonly, however, these scenes are skimmed over rather quickly—indeed, the whole of the first act is played more for plot and spectacular effect than for meaning.

If the danger of the court is played as real, then Rosalind's position in it will be the more precarious. And our attention will be directed not only to her budding love, but also to her response to the political pressures of her situation. At the beginning of I.ii, she has appeared sad and uncomfortable in the court of her usurping uncle, mindful of her banished father, yet witty and cheerful in her conversation with Celia, especially when their talk has turned to love—in the abstract, of course. Suddenly Orlando the wrestler makes his appearance and Rosalind's knees begin to wobble. She watches the wrestling with unwonted keenness and is naturally relieved by its outcome. When Orlando subsequently reveals his identity, her feelings are reinforced—he is the son of Sir Rowland, *her* father's friend. Her budding love is therefore justified, legitimized. But, given the response of the rest of the court, the danger of her present circumstances becomes apparent; she must, therefore, conceal from the court, though not from Celia, her delight at Orlando's distinguished parentage.

Other directors have treated Duke Frederick's court more humorously or more softly than Dexter did. In a jazzed-up modern-dress version directed by Buzz Goodbody for the RSC in 1973, the Duke appeared as 'an elderly playboy in a black eyepatch', while his dinner-jacketed guests smoked and circulated under a showy chandelier. The wrestling-match was a stagy TV affair introduced by Charles's finger-stretching exercises and a histrionic fist punched wickedly into the palm of his other hand. Charles was actually played by a professional wrestler. A different atmosphere was created at the New York Shakespeare Festival, where Joseph Papp set his open-air version amid a grove of ghostly silver-white branches. They were there for both court and forest, contributing to the gentle, elegantly melancholy tone that prevailed throughout. One reviewer commented that in this production the emotions as well as the costumes were in pastel. Neither of these versions could quite uncover the sense of menace conveyed by the strict, unnatural formality of Frederick's court in Dexter's interpretation. His costumes and style were high Elizabethan, with ruffs, jewelled brocade and curled wigs. But the decorative function of this style was subordinated to its power to trap and fix the 'puppets' within it, and force them into collusion with Frederick.

What with evil dukes, heroic younger sons, love blossoming in the midst of complicated familial hatreds and alliances, we are likely to be reminded here of the typical procedures of fairy tales or romances, and there is much in *As You Like It,* especially in the early scenes, which will give us that impression. In I.i, for example, the arbitrarily cruel behaviour of older brother to younger brother, and in I.iii the equally unjustified and equally cruel behaviour of the Duke toward Rosalind, seem deliberately contrived to challenge our realistic expectations.

It is precisely this quality of contrivance which has led to the general tendency to de-emphasize Act I in both productions and criticism of the play. The common view has been that the initial scenes, given their rather arbitrary and unrealistic mode, exist primarily to get the main characters into Arden so that the real fun can begin. On the stage this has often meant hurried and superficial treatment aimed at laying down the lines of the plot while the audience settle into their seats. But it is important to discover and to register the truth under the contrivance. The play as a whole enjoys its own artificiality, but it has too a keenness of insight and a sharpness of observation that is never far below the surface. Indeed, one mark of a superior production may well be the sense that, from the very outset, the play is being seriously and fully scrutinized.

In the opening scene, Orlando complains that his brother, Oliver, keeps him 'rustically at home' without proper education. The reality of this was underlined in Dexter's production by having Orlando working the fields with the peasants, tying sheaves of grain in a 'Millet-like tableau'. His strength was suggested a moment later when he took his brother by the throat and hurled him to the ground in fury. Oliver is an arbitrarily villainous older brother, a fairy-tale figure, but the deliberate artificiality of that kind of characterization was tied in this production to a firm naturalistic rendering. This approach drew out an important implication of the text itself: that the actual practice of Shakespeare's time—the tradition of primogeniture and the real injustice that often derived from it—could easily have harsh and ominous consequences for those affected by it; but modern productions and audiences can easily miss the relevance of this.

The full flavour of *As You Like It* is thus one that includes a blend of different tastes: elements of variety show, love story, and fairy tale are mixed together with close psychological observation and acute social awareness. During the central part of the play, an artificial convention, this time the 'pastoral', is offset by a sharply realistic set of attitudes toward *love*—the central subject of *As You Like It,* as it is of much pastoral literature. The play continually brings together the differing effects wrought by conventional forms and realistic presentation. In doing so, it uses widely various theatrical means, such as athletic displays, elaborate set-pieces, disguises, mock debates, songs, recitations, parodies and a masque. The essential problem, and it is one that any director must contend with, is that, once we are through with the fairy-tale twists and turns of Act I, there is practically no *plot* whatever. Different energies must keep the play afloat.

The play is a pot-pourri, and the performers must catch a style that will make sense of it all and yet retain the play's humour, lightness of touch and *charm*. There is no mistaking that charm, and a production that lacks it is sure to founder. Rosalind is its exemplar, the play's animating spirit; the audience, like Orlando, should fall in love with her at first sight. But the other characters must be worthy of her. Orlando, who complains that his brother's mistreatment has deprived him of education and refinement, is nevertheless no boor. Still less is he a pretty boy. He needn't even be handsome, but he does need to be attractive, vigorous, manly. Rosalind, after all, falls in love with *him* at first sight too. He is extravagant, earnest, impulsive, he takes himself too seriously, but he retains the winning smile of the youngest child. Celia, so often played in the shadow of Rosalind, actually has as much vivacity, and a gentler heart. It is she, not Rosalind, who develops the plan to flee the court, and she who is rewarded with a trouble-free love, after enduring for a time the disconsolate but ironic role of fifth wheel. Even the more 'literary' characters, such as Silvius and Phebe, parodies of types from pastoral literature, are not without their charm: Silvius's naïveté, for instance, or Phebe's amusing inconsistency.

Charm, however, does not preclude either scepticism or irony. The best Rosalinds combine delight with comic detachment, and Orlandos that are too sentimental are bound to drag. Although the mooning, love-struck youth is still frequently to be seen, Orlandos in recent years have begun to change, often bringing, as in Simon Callow's performance in Dexter's National Theatre production, an unexpected power to the role, a power that in his case was combined with impish humour (for example, the trick of doing the obviously expository speeches in I.i directly to the audience) and with naïve earnestness (as in his habit of constant reading as though to catch up on his education). In New York in 1973, Raul Julia played the part as a high-energy youth 'straight out of West Side Story'. Walter Kerr praised his 'feline command' and a knowing, insinuating quality that cast sceptical doubt on what was said and done—especially the play-acting with Rosalind. At one point during the false wooing, he backed off shocked after Rosalind-Ganymede kissed him on the mouth, and he responded warily when Ganymede said with a knowing smile that he could do 'strange things'.

It has been said that the essential thing in a production is to highlight the intense and ironic, warm and amusing, ultimately *real* relationship between the two principals, Orlando and Rosalind, by underlining the artifice of everything else. This may have been the impulse behind a lavishly baroque, operatic version of the play that Trevor Nunn mounted in 1977. He provided, among other things, an allegorical prologue starring Hymen, Fortune and Nature, a large ensemble piece that turned 'It was a lover and his lass' into a choral celebration of spring, and a final masque with Hymen entering on a 'baroque cloud which opened and shut, attended by cherubs with absurd wings'. Critics differed as to whether the essential combination of powerful erotic charge and ironic detachment was present in the central relationship, though one remarked that the intent of the production seemed to be to celebrate the baroque while at the same time suggesting its limitations in terms of human values.

The usual approach to the play has indeed been to stress the 'reality' of

Orlando and Rosalind in opposition to the unreality of the play's other elements, which accounts for its susceptibility to productions in which artifice is allowed to flower as in a greenhouse. One revival that I saw (at the Vancouver Playhouse, 1980) portrayed Duke Senior and his men as a bunch of left-over hippies, complete with benign young women with shawls, ineffable smiles and a baby (they looked always on the verge of saying, 'Have a good day!'); there was even a Hare Krishna adept in this forest, and Jaques, huge and bearded, looked like a graduate-student drop-out in search of hallucinogenic enlightenment. Touchstone was a new-wave Las Vegas-style master of ceremonies, Phebe appeared in a skin-tight scarlet jumpsuit on roller skates, and Rosalind and Celia were a pair of gum-chewing adolescents on the loose, their ears glued to transistor radios. The production substituted the humour generated by surprise for the necessary charm, and thus ended up being funny but trivial.

There is no doubt that the relationship between Orlando and Rosalind is the primary thing, and that their interplay in Acts III and IV is the very centre of the play's interest and idea, as well as its chief delight. It is also true that the extensive background—sub-plots, set-pieces and all—is more consciously artificial than the central relationship. A successful production can therefore be mounted which makes a clear distinction between foreground and background. Central to any version, however, will be the two scenes, III.ii and IV.i, in which Orlando wooes the disguised Rosalind, thinking she is only a young man pretending to be Rosalind. (The artifice of the situation here does not take away from the reality of the interplay; in fact the scenes provide the best example in the play of Shakespeare's deriving human significance out of conventional materials.) Rosalind's disguise affords her a wonderful opportunity for ironic deflation but it doesn't completely cover her deep and growing feelings. The dramatic result is a constantly shifting movement from mockery to rapture, which both captivates and confuses Orlando.

In the National Theatre production to which I have already referred several times, Sara Kestelman gave Rosalind a dynamic, fast-talking power, as well as a persuasive 'androgynous eroticism' that fit in exactly with the overall approach. The conception was first of all serious. It was also passionate, sincere and, at the same time, formal (as revealed not only by the acting-style but also by the costumes, which reminded more than one reviewer of Nicholas Hilliard miniatures). Kestelman perhaps missed the softness and tenderness of the part, its sweeter and gentler tonalities, but this was in keeping with Dexter's emphasis on courtly Elizabethan style and rich country rites. The empty, even menacing, ritual played out at Duke Frederick's court was replaced in Arden by a hard-won spring, symbolized especially in the ritual slaying of a deer. Arden first appeared as a wind-swept and wintry tundra that was gradually tickled into life. 'After the interval a slender tree with white blossoms rose up centre stage ... and later expanded into an umbrella of cascading leaves, the focus for country rituals, garlanded with flowers, and in the finale becoming a Maypole.' Some critics felt that *The Golden Bough,* quoted in the programme, was putting in a too-obtrusive appearance, though others saw the seasonal associations as integral to the serious purpose.

The high point of anthropological reference came in IV.ii, a tiny, usually unnoticed scene, where, instead of a modest hunters' song and a stuffed deer head, the Dexter production invented an elaborate ritual. William, almost always presented as a comic yokel in other revivals, was conceived of as a local country boy who had succeeded in killing the deer and who was therefore initiated and rewarded (in the text he is not even in IV.ii). The plump deer was cut open on stage; William was smeared with its blood and given an antlercrown, as other members of the exiled court group gathered around wearing deer masks. Some of the entrails, as well as a red garland, were hung on the central, sacred tree. For the final masque, William again appeared, this time as Hymen (recruited by Rosalind), an antlered, rustic god surrounded again by figures in deer masks. Against this background, the Rosalind-Orlando scenes were played out with both wit and intensity; they probably ended up being slightly less gay, less delightfully mocking, less tender, than in more conventional productions, but at the same time they came across as more deeply erotic.

The love scenes culminate in V.ii, where the complications introduced by the Silvius-Phebe plot and the ambiguity of Phebe's love for Rosalind-Ganymede come to a head. In the famous 'quartet', as it has come to be called, the four as-yet unmatched lovers intone in a highly formal, rhetorical way what it means to love:

> SILVIUS. It is to be all made of sighs and tears;
>   And so am I for Phebe.
> PHEBE. And I for Ganymede.
> ORLANDO. And I for Rosalind.
> ROSALIND. And I for no woman.
> SILVIUS. It is to be all made of faith and service;
>   And so am I for Phebe.
> PHEBE. And I for Ganymede.
> ORLANDO. And I for Rosalind.
> ROSALIND. And I for no woman ...

(V.ii.84–93)

Despite Rosalind's high-spirited irony—she ends the recital with 'Pray you no more of this; 'tis like the howling of Irish wolves against the moon'—there is an important sense here that her and Orlando's love is parallel to, and continuous with, that of Silvius and Phebe. There is a sense of community, of shared values. The quartet is indeed just that—a quartet in which each member has an important voice, though Rosalind's is the first violin. It is also deliberately formal and therefore a challenge to modern, naturalistic production techniques.

The scene can certainly be played ironically—mocking or 'guying' both character and situation and refusing to take the romanticism seriously. An alternative strategy would be to seek a style that suits this scene not only to the Rosalind-Orlando dialogues, but to various aspects of the 'background' as well. In Dexter's production, the quartet was ritualized, each lover, as he or she spoke, touching hands against the sacred tree. At the same time, the powerful eroticism of the production was evoked in Rosalind's promise to Orlando, just after the quartet and right on the heels of her ironic remark about Irish wolves: 'leaning against that tree among those white flowers and fixing her dark, piercing eyes upon Orlando . . . she filled "I will satisfy you if ever I satisfied man" with fierce, urgent desire'. One can readily see how other elements of the play—the songs, for instance, concerned as they are with country life, with weather, love and fertility might fit into this sort of conception.

All this may sound a little heavy for so gentle a play as this one, but handled with delicacy, and not forgetting the subversive ironies, such an approach could give both depth and seriousness to a production without eliminating the charm. No doubt a certain gravity is likely to characterize the kind of production that Dexter mounted. But the advantage of taking the *whole* play seriously, including the early scenes (which Dexter emphasized rather than hurried over), can compensate for any loss of gaiety.

Shakespeare derived the basic plot and situation of *As You Like It* from a prose romance called *Rosalynde,* published in 1590 and written by Thomas Lodge. Two of the play's most memorable characters, Touchstone and Jaques, do not, however, appear in Lodge's work but are Shakespeare's own creations. Touchstone, inventive, parodic, cheerful, and realistic, may owe part of his character to the personality and capabilities of Will Kemp, the clown of Shakespeare's company till about 1599, who probably created the role, though the sharper voice of Robert Armin, who replaced Kemp, can also be heard in the part. Touchstone's function is often to deflate the romantic pretensions of his betters, but his 'love' for Audrey leads him to join in with the other 'country copulatives', as he calls them, in the final festive rites. Mockery and celebration, the two poles of the play's attitudes, are neatly combined in him. Audrey, who since at least 1825 has been seen wandering barefoot around the stage peeling and eating a turnip or, more recently, munching an apple, seems inevitably and incorrigibly a wench. Touchstone, by contrast, has been played in many colours, including the traditional motley, but his outward guise hardly affects his essentially ironic, corrective and, at the same time, complementary role.

Jaques is a more difficult case. He has been played in a hundred different ways, often with a minimum of attention to the style of the rest of the production. There is a tendency for the lead actor of a troupe to take the role, with the result that it can get a trifle overweighted. It is, after all, a minor, though mysterious, part, whose main function is tonal. Still, tone can be important, especially in such a play as *As You Like It,* and one can understand the appeal of the role. A further difficulty, or challenge, is that Jaques has become famous for a single speech (the 'seven ages'), which has frequently been taken out of context and now presents something of a hurdle to the actor. It is, of course, a set-piece, akin to Touchstone's comic disquisition on the various 'degrees of the lie' in the final scene. Both provide entertainment, and both fill in time between an important character's exit and subsequent re-entry (Orlando with Adam in the first instance, Rosalind with Hymen in the second— she needs the time for a quick costume change). But of course Jaques' speech is much better known, and the actor has to get through it somehow, without having half the audience mouthing a *sotto voce* accompaniment. In the New York production mentioned earlier, Frederick Coffin, dressed in black against the predominantly white surroundings, bounced back quickly in answer to the Duke's clichéd comment about 'this wide and universal theatre', treating 'All the world's a stage' as an 'almost idiotically obvious explanation of the Duke's proposition'. He thus bypassed 'that awful split-second pause in which the actor steadies himself for a bout with what he feels to be a bromide'. This type of approach allows the actor to play the elaborations in the speech as variations or improvisations on his performance, discovered as he goes along.

The basis of the character is a posture, parallel to the poses of Silvius, Phebe, and even Duke Senior with his praise of the value of country life and his rapid return to the court once conditions allow it. Jaques' posture is melancholy, a fashionable Elizabethan malady, indicative supposedly of profundity and complexity of character. His view of the world is therefore satiric, even cynical—i.e. he imagines he sees farther than others do; he distrusts pleasure, perhaps because, as we are told, he has once been a 'libertine' himself; and he enjoys the special place that his role as a malcontent and the eloquence with which he performs it create for him in the Duke's circle. Some actors prefer to see Jaques as ironically aware of the role he is playing. In the Dexter production, Michael Bryant's performance seemed to extend its cynical observation of the world to the fashion of melancholy that he himself had adopted. Other actors have treated the melancholy as less of a pose, and more the result of Jaques' thirst for experience (as he claims it is in IV.i).

Whatever the approach, Jaques is clearly the centre of the Duke's exiled retinue. When he is not there, the others talk about him, and, when he is, they defer to him. One critic commented about Richard Pasco's Jaques in Goodbody's modern-dress version of the play that 'the party was never complete when he wasn't there, and never at ease when he was'. There were reticent indications of a 'tensely loving relationship' between himself and the Duke, the latter enjoying Jaques' talk but always a bit nervous about what he might say. Pasco's conception of the part was built around the textual hints that he has been a libertine and a scholar. He 'had the air of a man faced with the alternative of alcoholism or indigestion' and knew, like a character out of Graham Greene, that 'every smile can accompany an unpleasant memory'. After the 'seven ages' speech, 'left alone at the dining table, [he] wheezed his way into a long belly-laugh—at the Duke, at life, at us—which became, in effect, the beginning of the interval.' The same derisive attitude toward sentiment appeared at the end, when Jaques' departure to join the converted Duke Frederick was edged with bitterness. The wedding had been staged with rock music and modern dancing which Jaques had watched from the side. He spat out, 'So to your pleasures/I am for other than for dancing measures', in a way that clearly disconcerted the Duke. A shadow thus fell over the little sequence that follows:

> DUKE. Stay, Jaques, stay.
> JAQUES. To see no pastime I. What you would have
>   I'll stay to know at your abandon'd cave (*Exit*).
> DUKE. Proceed, proceed. We'll begin these rites
>   As we do trust they'll end, in true delights.

(V.iv.93–7)

Here, as so often, Shakespeare gives no hint of his intentions. Critics who argue that the text should be played 'straight' forget that much of Shakespeare is made up of just such moments as this. Pasco didn't hesitate before leaving. He was aloof and misanthropic, and, as an uncomfortable hush settled over the crowded stage, the Duke had trouble recovering enough poise to restart the dancing.

The importance of Jaques' role in the play can thus be measured by the effect that he can have on the ending. The most common approach to his decision to leave is to have it easily accepted, his exit only a brief comma in the action, the return to 'delights' genuine and normal. But, given a performance such as Pasco's, the predominantly festive tone of the marriage celebrations is a little soured by Jaques' harshness and Duke Senior's disappointment. If, on the other hand, Jaques is primarily an absurd *poseur,* his refusal to take part in the final festivities will be no great loss, and the tone of the ending will be uninterrupted by melancholy. A production that adds a concluding tinge of sadness—and to do so with the comedies is rather in fashion these days—will usually prepare for it by giving real weight to Jaques' weariness, or scepticism, or restlessness, earlier in the action. The tonality established near the beginning by the winter and rough weather, metaphorical or literal or both, will thus be carried through to the end, despite the indications of a general clearing. On the other hand, a more satirical or comic conception of Jaques will reduce his importance throughout the play, making him the butt of Touchstone's, Rosalind's and even Orlando's wit, and revealing his final exit as yet another self-deluding pose.

The complexity of the ending is elaborated by two other noteworthy elements. One is the masque of Hymen; the other, Rosalind's epilogue. The high formality and solemnity of the one, and the witty informality of the other, bespeak the play's delight in contrasts. The masque—at least in our time, when deliberate artifice is so much suspected—has generally fared worse in the hands of directors than the epilogue. It has been cut, sidestepped, curtailed or performed with a certain amount of embarrassment. But it has also been met head-on: highlighted, as at Ashland in 1979, by the descent on a trapeze of an eight-foot golden god, backed by a golden monstrance, who provided a sonorous benediction; or integrated into the country rituals, as at the National Theatre. Like the other 'variety' elements, the masque is partly a 'number' in itself, partly a figure to be woven into the overall tapestry. However it may be done, it requires subtlety and tact to fit it in. The epilogue depends entirely on Rosalind and, unlike the masque, is hard to spoil, though it loses something in the post-Elizabethan theatre, since women's parts are no longer played by boys. (Nor will all-male productions really serve to resurrect lost stage conditions.) Playing ironically with the differences between men and women, and the ambiguity she herself embodies, Rosalind ends the play with that combination of wit and charm, mockery and celebration, which has characterized it, and her, throughout.

(New York: St. Martin's Press, 1988): 39–50.
With permission of St. Martin's Press, Inc.

ON DIRECTING SHAKESPEARE
Ralph Berry
1989

Robin Phillips (II)

Ralph Berry You've directed something like half the Shakespeare canon and I know that in the last few years you've revisited three or four plays. I can think of *Antony and Cleopatra, Twelfth Night, As You Like It,* the *Dream* that you've returned to. Is there something in the process of revisiting Shakespeare that you find especially beneficial?

Robin Phillips Although to direct seems to become more difficult each year, it is certainly easier to be simple—to do things more simply when you come back to the plays. One needs less visual aid the second time around. Of course, that may also mean that I have become a little more mature and have learned to trust the text more.

I have learned to trust the text in a special way. One becomes aware of the enormity of truth *beyond* the text, and that truth becomes more and more clear as one revisits the plays. It becomes much more obvious to you how the evening's communication is not, *in truth,* the text; in *fact,* but not in truth; The text is the means to the end. The end is a spontaneous communication of whatever lies beyond the text, beyond the subtext, the cumulative effect of thought and feeling. That's much more apparent when you revisit the play, because why else is it different? Why does it mean something different this time, why does the play appear to be saying something different? How can it be saying something entirely different when the text is exactly the same? We refer to a play as 'speaking' to us and so believe that the communication (or perhaps the communicator) is the text, the voice. But then we are aware that the play 'says something different to me tonight'. How is that possible? It is possible because we sense a truth beyond the accumulation of fact that is clearly presented by the text. We are aware of an elemental truth and yet can only sense it, feel it, experience it. The feelings of the moment seem to link backwards and forwards in time, recalling past emotions and pointing towards an enlightenment still to come.

RB You're talking about something that goes far beyond a mere restaging. Can you give me an instance or two of a play that you've redirected that seems to throw up a substantially different meaning?

RP I was certainly most fearful of attempting a new production of *As You Like It,* having done it twice before.

The first production was with Maggie Smith as Rosalind and Jack Wetherall as Orlando. It was alarming to come back to a play when, rarely for me, it was one of the productions of mine that I happened to like. But it proved not to be so very difficult. It was very interesting to see what had so clearly, *textually* appeared to be a wise and more mature Rosalind leading a less experienced Orlando towards love, teaching him; guiding him towards experience and understanding. It was a divine performance by Maggie Smith of aching beauty and wisdom, totally supported by the text. How could a new performance differ radically from this original?

In the new production an entirely different relationship emerged, from exactly the same text and imagery with a Rosalind (in the Nancy Palk version) who discovered freedom in disguise, personal freedom. This was not so much in her relationship with Orlando, but you saw a girl who, disguised as a man, stepped into her own enlightenment and self-discovery.

As we moved into the new production of *Twelfth Night,* we made new discoveries, prompted by the proximity of the two plays. Now Nancy's Viola was in disguise for her life. I hadn't noticed this as clearly the first time round because with Patricia Conolly it was an older Viola. It was because this (later) Viola and this Rosalind happened to be in the same season with the same company, the same actress, that one saw very clearly the suffocating covering that disguise created for Viola and the pain she experienced of having love held in . . .

Can we talk about the text itself? You have,—I think, certain reservations about the limitations of the word alone.

RP I'm sure that the text is purely a series of signposts. It's the map that will lead us to the truth that is to be communicated. Because it is a very well-defined and accurate map, drawn by an experienced craftsman, we must follow it with immense care. It's a complicated and tricky one, and like all maps there will be many pitfalls if you veer from the prescribed route. Nevertheless, if you follow the route, the text, it leads you to the hidden truth. Truth, that reaches beyond the intellect to the heart, to the emotions, feelings and responses.

It's the same with many writing or language arts. The best journalism is about giving you facts in a straightforward sequence as honestly as is possible, but usually because the journalist believes the more clearly they are placed the more they will reveal behind the accumulation of facts a truth that is of greater importance than the sum of the facts themselves. That's why editorials used to be called 'leaders': it was to guide us towards this truth, this knowledge, this understanding, that should not be put into words because it would diminish its scope and its size, and its personal acceptance for each reader. It led us there and left us to do the rest of the work personally.

RB But always for the director choices have to be made. Another example from your work: Arden is, of course, a country of the mind, the absolute rural idyll of our dreams. It's got to be located somewhere, in the text itself perhaps. It might be mid-Warwickshire, with this talk of sheepcotes, forests, woods and so on. In your recent *As You Like It* it was a Mennonite community, which is something that means a good deal to many people in North America. They have some basis of knowledge, perhaps experience, to relate to your ordering of this idyllic community.

RP Not only is the work you're going to do connected with the artists you work with, the actors and the designers, it's also being presented in a specific place and communicated to a specific group of people. Within that community you have to be prepared to make choices that make the response personalised for them. I was amazed to discover some Mennonite poetry that was so close to the banished Duke's description of where he and the forest lords were living, and what they thought they could achieve in their new community, that it was hard to believe that the author had not read *As You Like It*. Textually, Shakespeare and the Mennonite society matched very well. I will never forget the first public performance of *As You Like It* here, in Stratford. As we went into the first forest-lord scene with Mennonite dress, there was a gasp, a sigh of recognition that was one of the most amazing sounds I've ever heard. The audience knew that mere design could not have revealed to them. I was a combination of text, sound, light, costume, colour and the very rhythm of movement that the actors had acquired. Something was shared that was beyond the sum of all those things put together. That's precisely what Shakespeare expects us to do.

Adrian Noble

AN In particular. I suppose the person to whom most directors owe most, this century, is Tyrone Guthrie, who created the idea of staging as we have received that idea and as we now challenge that idea. He was a man who rewrote the agenda for most theatre directors of this country. After him, of course, came Brook and he adjusted the agenda. For most English directors nowadays I would imagine that we look more to Europe for influence than to our contemporaries—to Patrice Chéreau, to Giorgio Strehler, to Peter Stein— for excitement in the theatre these days.

RB This may seem too simplifying a question, but what is your sense of the agenda—the agenda as you receive it now?

AN I think Tyrone Guthrie stepped into the shoes that used to be worn by the leading actor of the company. In other words, he would set the time and place of the production; he would give relative value, production value, to different characters and scenes. He would actually, by doing these things, create an interpretation above and beyond—probably in sympathy with, but certainly above and beyond—that of just the leading actors. That was massively important in the twentieth century. It has roots of course in the nineteenth century, in the Meiningen company. That agenda has been rewritten since the Second World War, by Brook in the first instance, possibly by others like Devine, whereby the director as circus master was revalued and the director became more of a collaborator with a group of people, including the designer. And you would get situations whereby in the Sixties someone like Brook would go into rehearsals without a concept, without possibly a design, sometimes without even a script, and would make theatre. That's the particular branch of that inheritance that I've picked up most of all, those productions at the end of the Sixties.

RB May I take up what you were saying about the design and the concept. Isn't there a hard, practical point here? Is it possible for the director of Shakespeare to go into rehearsal without a concept? I mean, that design itself may involve a commission, may involve a great deal of practical work to be done, which has a timetable that extends back from the actual first night. And that it may therefore be impossible for director not to have a design, and a concept, before rehearsals begin.

AN That's true, particularly of the modern theatre, whereby sets, costumes, props are very expensive, and the earlier they are designed, the cheaper they become. You get more for your money. This is a serious problem for modern theatre—for any theatre, ancient or modern. Actors find this very limiting. This is a modern problem, though, because for centuries actors turned up and received last year's costumes; it was perfectly normal. Directors find this a great limitation on their exploration. One hears this sometimes in the rehearsal room, with an actor looking at his costume and saying, 'Ah, that's my character, is it?' Every production requires a different approach, and different approaches occur according to where one is in one's life and one's career, what relationships one has with one's leading actors. For example, when I did *Macbeth,* I worked for eight months with Jonathan Pryce, before we started rehearsals, and for the first four months the designer wasn't even appointed, let alone involved in that process of discussion and debate. When I did *As You Like It,* we had not designed that production on the first day of rehearsals. We designed it during rehearsals. And that wasn't a totally successful concept.

RB It was a fascinating concept, though. What I and I'm sure everyone remembers is that billowing dust sheet that first swathed the furniture, and then became some kind of emblem for Arden.

AN It also became a mantrap. Not only was it extremely slippery, which meant that you would find yourself physically in danger, but it became a bit of a worry for everyone. The very point of it became its problem. We wanted something that was genuinely plastic, that would change shape according to what the actors did, according to the moment in the play, because the Forest of Arden in *As You Like It* changes shape, dimension, character, according to the perception of each person. At one point it's a friendly place with bunny rabbits, at another point it's a dangerous place with lions. And we thought we had the solution. The problem was that while physically it was a bit dangerous, the actors would never know what it was going to do next, which meant that you would walk into the wings during that production and continually see the actors anxiously peering on to the stage to see how they were going to make their entrance. Not how they were going to do that scene or what their character was feeling like, but physically how they were going to get downstage, which is the kind of worry you don't want.

(London: Hamish Hamilton, 1989): 151–59, 162–64.
Reprinted with permission of Ralph Berry.

AS YOU LIKE IT AND THE PERILS OF PASTORAL
J. C. Bulman
1988

"*As You Like It* was the catalyst that precipitated the plan to televise the whole canon of Shakespeare's plays for the BBC." In retrospect, given the reception of that production, this statement may read like a bad joke. The BBC Shakespeare was the brainchild of Cedric Messina, and the story of its birth is worth recounting. Messina was directing Barrie's *The Little Minister* at Glamis Castle and grew enchanted with both the castle and its surroundings. "I went for the bum walk, and it seemed to be the most wonderful sort of forest," he recalls. "It occurred to me that if one were to do a location production of *As You Like It*, then this was the place to do it." Do it he did, in June of 1978; and that production inaugurated the series. But the *if* clause proved to be the problem. For most who saw the production, the location that appealed to Messina as "wonderful" seemed far too earthbound, too specific for the elusive joys of the Forest of Arden.

In principle, pastoral poses problems for producers of Shakespeare. In both ethos and form, pastoral is highly artificial: it signifies retreat to an ideal; it is a state of mind. At its most romantic (as in Lodge's *Rosalynde*), the green world is a world of play and game, not a place where shepherds tend sheep and maidens milk goats; at its most political (as in Spenser's "Shepheardes Calender"), it depicts an allegorical world of good government. Contemporary theater has sought various ways to present pastoral artifice. Perhaps taking its cue from Peter Brook's minimalist *Midsummer Night's Dream*, the RSC's staging of *As You Like It* in 1980 used mere poles for trees, and sheepskins stretched between them suggested shelter; The Acting Company's postmodernist staging of 1985 used parti-colored umbrellas to suggest the play world of Arden, and they were rolled about to suggest another part of the forest. In such productions, the conventions of pastoral romance are something to which we can willingly surrender—the love at first sight, the miraculous conversions, the theophany of Act 5.

Television, however, makes its own demands on a Shakespeare text. Chief among them is the demand for realism. Audiences unused to modern theatrical productions and nurtured instead on films shot "on location" are skeptical of stage conventions—indeed, sometimes downright derisive. Thus the directors of Shakespeare's comedies for the BBC, including Basil Coleman, who directed *As You Like It* for Messina, have had difficulties knowing how to stage obviously unrealistic situations (women playing men, male and female mistaken for identical twins, middle-aged courtiers living happily in the woods) for a medium in which the camera reveals each blemish, exposes each fake, and destroys romantic fictions that might be easily tolerated in the theater.

Other BBC directors came to terms with this problem in ways different from Coleman. Jane Howell, for example, chose to stage the pastoral scenes of *Winter's Tale* in a bare, white studio to evoke a feeling of endless space, broken only by a blasted tree and a rock—a set evocative of *Waiting for Godot*. By making the set so minimal and artificial, she directed our attention to the poetry, where the true pastoral vision resides, and thereby encouraged us to participate in creating an imaginary world. With perhaps more success, Elijah Moshinsky conceived of the Renaissance canvas as an apt analogue for the television screen and thus invited us to expect artifices similar to those used by Rembrandt, Vermeer, and others. At its most allusive, his *Dream* recreates Rembrandt's *Danae in Her Bower* for Titania; and his set for the Athenian woods—dominated by a pool of water through which characters pass to effect their metamorphoses, and by a moon ever smiling on their inconstancy—richly employs the contrasts of Renaissance chiaroscuro. Moshinsky's iconographic method of preserving pastoral artifice may have been more sophisticated than Howell's reliance on the empty space, but we would do well to remember that both directors were, in a sense, responding to what was widely regarded as the failure of *As You Like It* and to Messina's belief that pastoral romance could be played "on location."

What was Coleman to do when Messina instructed him to translate the green world of pastoral into the great outdoors? The more realistic the setting, the more we are inclined to apply the criteria of naturalistic drama to the action. Thus, inevitably, we begin to question the logic of the play. How can callow Orlando beat the professional wrestler Charles? Why do Celia and Rosalind so gleefully decide to "waste" their time in a wilderness? Can't Orlando see through Ganymede's disguise? Isn't it absurd for a duke and his middle-aged courtiers to live like Robin Hood and his band of merry men? How can we credit the instantaneous conversions of Oliver and Duke Frederick? And where the hell does Hymen come from?

Before one attacks the BBC production for violating the spirit of the play, however, one must recall that *As You Like It* contains much mockery of the pastoral ethos within itself. Touchstone, for one, ridicules the excesses of pastoral romance by courting Audrey with barnyard manners, and Silvius himself stands as a ludicrous exhibit of such excess. Jaques chides the political presumption of pastoral retreat: for him, the courtiers have fled from one corrupt civilization only to corrupt another. Even Rosalind, in the voice of Ganymede, speaks of wedded love and fidelity with a seasoned skepticism. In these ways satire balances pastoral, just as it did in ancient Greece, and keeps us from being fully engaged with the artifice of the play. Shakespeare took pains to achieve a tonal balance that allows us both to participate in a celebration of love and, at the same time, to consider the more serious implications of pastoral. These pains were not wasted on Coleman, who praised *As You Like It* as "an anti-materialist play . . . about rediscovering Nature and our dependence on it. . . . It touches on our responsibility to the environment, questions the need for courts and armies and self-protection. It rediscovers natural freedom." These may sound suspiciously like the sentiments of a director straining to fit the fashion of the times; nonetheless, one should note his reluctance to mention the love, the romance, and all that makes the play a "festive" comedy.

Coleman, I suggest, made a virtue of necessity. Bound by Messina's decision to film on location and yet determined to have the play speak intelligently to a modern audience, he put quotation marks around the pastoral artifice. He played up the satire, he let us in on the game, he allowed "reality" to hold idealism at bay, as if assuming that only the skepticism inherent in the play could allow us to credit *As You Like It* as a serious exploration of love and society. Numerous examples illustrate how he used the camera's eye to catch a comic reality. It shows us Rosalind brushing away a fly that interrupts her first encounter with Orlando in Arden. It shows her straining to be heard over a very real wind. It shows us Orlando's verses hanging absurdly on real trees, and Orlando himself embracing an oak. As the duke's men carry off a bloody carcass in IV.ii, the camera reveals that buck season has come to Arden. And in response to Corin's question, "And how like you this shepherd's life, Master Touchstone?" (lll.ii), Touchstone steps in sheep dung. There are indeed real sheep in this green world: Coleman insists on them.

The wooing of Ganymede by Orlando is likewise played to strain our belief in the pastoral fiction. Orlando, for one thing, is rather slight and understated: his defeat of the wrestler Charles is patently absurd. And Helen Mirren's Rosalind, buxom and beautiful, is clearly no male Ganymede. The camera does not disguise her femininity—indeed, exploits it when, in IV.iii Ganymede faints at seeing Orlando's bloody handkerchief. As Oliver stoops to undo Ganymede's doublet, Aliena stops his hand and cries, "There is more in it!" The joke, made at the expense of preserving the artifice, glances wryly at the bosom that we, and perhaps Oliver, are meant to appreciate.

Ganymede's femininity is readily apparent to Orlando, too; and in the course of the wooing scene (IV.i), they both show through knowing smiles that they are playing a game, perpetuating a fiction, fully aware of the rules. At the outset, Rosalind is shown to feel real disappointment that Orlando is late: it is as clear to him as it is to us that she is not feigning a passion. A bit later, when she bids him to "woo me, woo me" in most seductive tones, he, who has been looking admiringly at her bosom, teasingly tries to steal a kiss from her on the line "I would kiss before I spoke." We assume either that he knows who she is or that he is gay, and the latter is unlikely. Further along, when he lounges suggestively on an old chestnut tree, she, "in a more coming-on disposition," kneels before him, fumbles with her hat, acts coy, and doesn't try to hide her true feelings; nor does he when, in the mock wedding scene, he seems to take his vows in earnest. The camera takes advantage of facial close-ups to indicate that these lovers know precisely what they are doing. They are playing with each other—and they play in a vein more knowing, more ironic than pastoral would ever allow. The effect of the scene finally is to detach us from the artifices of pastoral romance. Rosalind and Orlando indulge in a game that neither mistakes for reality; they see through one another's poses—and both are aware of that; they become self-conscious actors in a pastoral play. What Coleman achieves, I suggest, is a kind of alienation effect.

Coleman strains our belief in pastoral most comically in the appearance of Hymen. Stage productions have dealt with Hymen in a number of ways, ranging from the full-fledged theophanies of nineteenth-century productions to the more realistic accounts rendered by more recent productions, where, for example, as in the RSC's 1980 staging, Corin dresses as Hymen and enters atop a wagon bursting with the fruits of harvest. In either case, the pastoral fiction is preserved, either through the magic of *deus ex machina* or in the rustic celebration of harvest home. In Coleman's version, Hymen is neither god nor rustic. He is a fey figure dressed in gossamer—a ballet skirt, with a laurel wreath about his temples—who looks vaguely like a young man painted on a Greek vase. He is not a member of the Duke's entourage recruited by Rosalind to join her game, nor is he from Arden: his effete Oxbridge intonation and demeanor give the lie to that. And as he appears from atop a hill overlooking a beechwood grove, holding hands with Rosalind and Celia, we may well ask, Where did he come from? His appearance (and worse, his voice) is simply absurd. No one believes it is magic: the Duke's mystified look when ethereal music begins, and his greater astonishment when he sees the trio tripping down the hill, are deliberately funny. They confirm the idea that what we are watching is beyond belief. And that is just the point: Coleman bids us to laugh *at* pastoral artifice and *with* the characters who are themselves as detached from that artifice as we are.

If the pastoral romance is undercut by devices that alienate us from the action and prevent our suspension of disbelief, then the more serious pastoral plot involving the banished Duke is likewise darkened by the force of Jaques's cynicism. Coleman cast Richard Pasco, one of the RSC's finest tragic actors, as Jaques; and Pasco plays him as a melancholic, alcoholic, almost tragic visionary. This Jaques is alienated as much from the Duke as from the lovers, and his railing against the world has more bitterness in it than is usually the case. An examination of what I think is the strongest scene in this production, II.vii, will illustrate Coleman's bias.

The scene was filmed in a grove of yew trees at night. (Nighttime pastoral? The idea is as unconventional as it is sinister.) The Duke and his men sit around a blazing fire eating and drinking as Jaques, shrouded in smoke, delivers his seven ages of man speech. Cup of wine in hand, he speaks in a guttural voice and his face registers disgust. At his ultimate line about old age—"Sans teeth, sans eyes, sans taste"—his eyes light on old Adam, who enters with the aid of Orlando; and Jaques's disgust turns to sneer—"sans everything." To be sure, Adam cuts a silly and pathetic figure, his face (with apologies to Arthur Hewlett, who plays him) resembling nothing more than that of an aging basset hound. Once this venerable burden is set down, Amiens begins to sing in a rich baritone, "Blow, blow, thou winter wind;" but the melody and the singer alike are as melancholy as Jaques. There is no levity in them. But there *is* satire: as the camera backs away from Amiens, it reveals a whole consort surrounding him, viols and hautboys. We smile at the foolishness of a chamber orchestra in Arden; and as we do so, we join in Jaques's skepticism. The camera moves to him as the song continues, and there it lingers: he sits alone, still shrouded in smoke, drinking, and looking scornfully on the sentimental scene of Adam licking food from his master's fingers (and looking all the more basset-like for doing so). Lest we miss the satirical "angle" on such sentimentality, the camera keeps Jaques firmly in view, in the center background, during the final exchange between the Duke and Orlando. Their assurances of good will and familial love are mocked by Jaques's looking on. We see through his eyes, whose cynical vision clouds any optimism we may feel in this restoration of civility.

Jaques's satiric perspective sets the tone for much of the production. Take, as a final instance, his farewell in Act 5. The union of lovers there, as we have seen, is a bit too silly to be credited, and Coleman has allowed us to feel as alienated from the proceedings as Jaques does. With tragic sobriety, then, Jaques passes judgment on all the couples and, rejecting the Duke's entreaty to stay, vows to await him at his "abandon'd cave." He then begins a slow exit up the same hill that Hymen has earlier descended; and the camera, placed where the group of lovers stands, follows him up. But when the Duke bids the couples to "proceed, proceed" with their dance, the camera suddenly spies them from atop the hill—from the very position in which Jaques has just stood. We regard them as he does, looking down on them as they form a circle: we may note that the camera here repeats an earlier joke, when (in II.v) Amiens asks Jaques what "Ducdame" means, and, as the courtiers circle about him for an answer, Jaques explains that "'tis a Greek invocation, to call fools into a circle." As Jaques departs for the Duke's cave, he leaves behind him a circle of fools.

I do not suggest that Coleman's *As You Like It* is a successful production. Indeed, as most viewers agree, it is far too dark and self-conscious to do justice to the spirit of festive comedy. Other approaches to pastoral, such as Howell's and Moshinsky's, might better have preserved the play's balance between artifice and skepticism, belief and disbelief. I hope, however, that I have helped to rescue this *As You Like It* from accusations that it is naive or ill-considered, as if Coleman, like Messina, simply miscalculated in trying to equate pastoral with love in the woods. Coleman, it seems to me, knew what he was doing: his choices, even if we disagree with them, were both intelligent and consistent. Taking his cue from satirical qualifications of pastoral inherent in the play, he apparently decided that no television audience could swallow pastoral artifices straight, especially when they are played out in a "location" that by tradition demands realism. Thus he chose to alienate us from the fiction, to make the retreat to Arden seem a game that the players play only to keep from acknowledging the darker lessons of human nature that Jaques insists on. This is a peculiarly contemporary bias. As a response to Shakespeare's comedy, we may find it inadequate or discomforting. But find it so, we ought not to dismiss it before considering how it reflects, or speaks to, our age.

J. C. Bulman & H. R. Coursen, eds. *Shakespeare on Television*.
(Hanover, NH: University Press of New England, 1988): 174–79.
Reprinted with permission of University Press of New England.

REFLECTIONS ARISING FROM RECENT PRODUCTIONS OF
LOVE'S LABOUR'S LOST AND *AS YOU LIKE IT*
Glynne Wickham
1989

In a short article for *Shakespeare Quarterly* I suggested that a source, hitherto lacking, for *Love's Labour's Lost* was to be found in *The Four Foster Children of Desire; or, The Castle of Perfect Beauty,* edited for printing by Henry Goldwell from verses by Philip Sidney and published shortly after the entertainment that Sidney himself and three other chivalrically minded courtiers presented to Queen Elizabeth I and the French ambassadors in the tiltyard at Whitehall Palace in 1581.

This entertainment had been devised in the most courtly and diplomatic style to inform the duc d'Alencon—duke of Anjou and Brabant, and heir to the throne of France—who was at that time seeking, through his ambassadors, the queen's hand in marriage, that he was wasting his time. Shakespeare, as I argued in that article, when writing *Love's Labour's Lost,* had a copy of Goldwell's edited text of this notorious entertainment before him. From it he took his own "four foster children of desire"—Navarre, Berowne, Dumaine, and Longaville and then substituted for the figure of Queen Elizabeth I and her maids of honor (the impregnable "castle of perfect beauty") the Princess of France and her three maids of honor, Rosaline, Katherine, and Maria.

To alert the play's first audience to these allusions, he then proceeded to arrange for Rosaline and Katherine to claim in the dialogue of act 2, scene 1, that it was in Brabant, and more specifically at a dance given by the duc d'Alencon, that they had first met Berowne and the young Dumaine. Lest this broad hint toward a recognition in the auditorium of the original state occasion that he was about to parody in his comedy miss its mark, Shakespeare allows Don Armado, when embarrassed by his unworthy passion for Jaquenetta, to lament the fact that he cannot "take desire prisoner and ransom him to any French courtier for a new devis'd curtsey" (I .2.56–63).

Directing this play again for a third time this summer (1986) in an open-air production at the University of the South, Sewanee, Tennessee, I was struck by other peculiarities in this text that, once again, help as I believe to unravel the mystery of how this highly sophisticated play first came to be written and performed.

The most singular of these peculiarities is the "antic," or "bergomask," of *Hiems* and *Ver,* winter and spring, respectively represented on the stage by the owl and the cuckoo. This charming musical epilogue is stuck onto the end of the play with a view to translating the pathos of the final farewells between the departing princess and the chastened young men left behind at Navarre's court for a year and a day to ponder their mistakes into a jollier and more lighthearted atmosphere befitting a comedy before the audience exchanges the world of the play for the real world. But why "Winter" and "Spring"? Why "a twelvemonth and a day"?

This deliberate contrast of winter with spring, heightened and made visible in song and costume, strongly suggests a need on the author's part to take note of a particular calendar festival traditionally associated with the winter solstice; in other words, a need to link a festive comedy to the no less festive occasion responsible for the commissioning and writing of the play—the twelve-day feast of Christmas. If this premise is granted, then the Princess's choice of a year and a day as the penitential period to be imposed upon Navarre before he may challenge her by his gift of diamonds to marry him not only ceases to be arbitrary and whimsical but fixes the date of the calendar festival in question as New Year's Eve, or Twelfth Night.

This deduction, while it cannot be proved, at least has the virtues of tradition and precedent behind it stretching back into the past to John Lydgate's *Mumming at Hertford,* ca. 1425. In that courtly disguising, presented to the young King Henry VI when he was spending the Christmas holiday at Hertford Castle in Essex, six lusty tradesmen complain to the king through the poet-presenter about the rough treatment each has received, on returning home from his labors, from his wife; they demand that a law be placed on the statute book guaranteeing them "maistry" in their own homes. The six wives then retaliate by delivering a spirited reply through one of their own number to justify their conduct. The piece concludes with an appeal to the king to grant them "the maistry," the king's "sentence and iugement" on "þe complaynte of þe lewed husbands with þe cruwell aunswers of þeyre wyves." This is delivered on the king's behalf by a pursuivant (a junior herald) who states that the matter in question, being too serious to permit an instant verdict, is to be passed to a committee for rigorous "examynacyoun" and "inquysicyoun": this committee will then report back to the king who will deliver his verdict to the husbands and their wives if they will return to receive it at the same time next year. Thus, where both playmaker and actors are concerned, the poet's formula has provided neatly for a return visit to court at this same calendar feast a year hence. This formula, moreover, accords appropriately with the winter solstice when life itself appears to be precariously balanced between decline and renewal, death and rebirth, malevolence and goodwill.

Within this context, it strikes me as particularly significant that Berowne, in *Love's Labour's Lost*, when referring to the treatment accorded by the Princess to his own Masque of Muscovites (5.2) should say to Navarre that it had been "dashed like an old Christmas comedy": for this, of course, is exactly the fate that is to overtake Don Armado's and Holofernes's *Pageant of the Nine Worthies*. Such boisterous, if ill-mannered, audience participation was thus something that actors had learned to anticipate as a normal occurrence during the twelve-day feast of Christmas, presided over throughout by a Lord of Misrule, himself a vestigial survivor from the Feast of Fools (1 January).

In *Love's Labour's Lost* Shakespeare has cleverly protected himself and his actors from this fate by using the "Pageant of the Nine Worthies" as a lightning conductor to abstract such mockery as they might otherwise fear would be visited upon them by an arrogant, if sophisticated, audience fortified in its sense of its own cleverness and self-esteem by wine: "not generous, not gentle; not humble" (5.2.626). as Holofernes so succinctly observes.

The fortunate survival of the *Gesta Greyorum* provides us with a full account of how the festive Christmas holiday period, with its insistence upon inversion of normal social order, was celebrated at the Inns of Court in London in Shakespeare's own lifetime. The case argued by Leslie Hotson for regarding *Twelfth Night* as a play commissioned for and presented on Twelfth Night in Middle Temple Hall is a strong one. The case I am now arguing for *Love's Labour's Lost* likewise to have been first presented before a highly sophisticated audience of lawyers and young courtiers at one of the Inns of Court is at least as strong as his. In that environment all the allusions to *The Four Foster Children of Desire* of 1581 would have been instantly picked up and greatly enjoyed. Moreover, anticipation by author and actors of such an audience at once justifies and explains the emphasis placed by Shakespeare within this text upon oaths, perjury, and the highly legalistic twisting of patent vice into apparent virtue exemplified by the recourse taken to the entry of a plea of "necessity." That word, first dropped by Navarre in the opening scene, is seized upon by Berowne as an expedient loophole to extract him, should this become desirable, from the oath to which he is being asked by Navarre to sign his name. Yet so preoccupied has the young king been with his own dream of a utopian Platonic Academy established within his own Court (itself a mirror image of the Inns of Court) that he has failed to remember, when issuing his proclamation forbidding cohabitation or consort with women, the imminent arrival of the Princess of France on a diplomatic mission concerning the future of the adjacent Duchy of Acquitaine.

Navarre. What say you, lords? Why this was quite forgot.
Berowne. So study evermore is overshot.

. . . .

Navarre. We must of force dispense with this decree:
　　She must lie here on mere necessity.

(1.1.139–40, 145–146)

Berowne immediately leaps upon this word as offering the escape clause that he and his fellows need to protect themselves against the consequences of their rash vow.

Berowne. Necessity will make us all forsworn
　　Three thousand times within this three year space;

. . . .

　　If I break faith, this word shall speak for me:
　　I am forsworn on mere necessity.

(1.1.147–48, 151–52)

On this explicit understanding, he signs.

This idea then lies dormant until after all four young men have exposed their own hypocrisy in their private dealings with the Princess and her ladies in the sonnet scene (4.3). The king appeals directly to Berowne.

Navarre . . . . good Berowne, now prove
　　our loving lawful, and our faith not torn.

(4.3. 280–8

This is a direct appeal to an able barrister to enter a plea that black is white and white black—a brilliantly calculated device to whet the appetite of an Inns of Court audience both for the case that is to be pleaded and the manner in which the orator will handle it. For the next seventy-six lines—a speech of quite exceptional length by Shakespeare's standards—Berowne settles to his task. Step by logical (if emotional) step, he leads his case to the desired conclusion.

Berowne. Then fools you were these women to forswear
　　Or, keeping what is sworn, you will prove fools
　　For wisdom's sake, a word that all men love;
　　Or for Love's sake, a word that loves all men:
　　Or for men s sake, the authors of these women;
　　Or women's sake, by whom we men are men
　　Let us once lose our oaths to find ourselves
　　Or else we lose ourselves to keep our oaths.

> It is religion to be thus forsworn;
> For charity itself fulfils the law,
> And who can sever love from charity?

(4 3.351–61)

As a peroration designed to sway the sympathy of the jury in the defendant's favor, little could be better judged—or, indeed, better calculated to win applause from spectators at the back of the Court.

From here I move on to more speculative territory—to that of the sequel to *Love's Labour's Lost,* the return visit of the company with the supposed *Love's Labour's Won* which, as the company had itself suggested, might follow to celebrate the same Christmas festival a year later. *Much Ado About Nothing* has proved to be a favorite candidate among critics; and, indeed, Beatrice and Benedict, in the swift thrust and parry of their bouts of wit, do provide some grounds for this supposition, granted the more mature versions of Rosaline and Berowne that the play contains. Dogberry too, with his pretentious use of his own illiteracy, bears some resemblance to the earlier Costard; but there is little else to support this contention. In my own view, *As You Like It* makes a much stronger candidate.

This is a view I have reached while directing this play for the Hartke Theatre in Washington, D.C. Both *Love's Labour's Lost* and *As You Like It* share predominantly woodland settings. In the latter, here again most strikingly we find the four girls and the four young men central to the former—this time decked out as Rosalind, Celia, Audrey, and Phebe, and as Orlando, Oliver, Touchstone, and Silvius. They are all very different from the original "four foster children of desire" and their matching ladies; but in their own ways they are all nevertheless love's victims and love's prisoners: moreover, in *As You Like It,* love's labors are finally won for all eight of them. As Duke Senior puts it in the closing moments of the final scene,

> First, in this forest let us do those ends
> That here were well begun and well begot;
> And after, every of this happy number
> That have endured shrewd days and nights with us
> Shall share the good of our returned fortune,
> According to the measure of their stakes.
> Meantime forget this new fall'n dignity
> And fall into our rustic revelry.
> Play, music, and brides and bridegrooms all,
> With measures heaped in joy, to the measures fall.

(5.4. 16673)

Here, then, is a faithful fulfillment of a promise to translate a festive Christmas comedy in which four "Jacks" failed to win their "Jills" (to use Berowne's terminology) into one in which all eight Jacks and Jills are led by Hymen into wedlock. Can this be attributed merely to coincidence? If so, there are other striking similarities of structure, characterization, and dialogue to be accounted for.

The first among these is the lively reduction (if not repetition) of the famous sonnet scene in *Love's Labour's Lost* (4.3) in the form of the sonnets addressed to Rosalind that Orlando hangs on forest trees and which are read aloud by Orlando himself, Rosalind, and Celia (3.2). The closing bergomask of *Love's Labour's Lost* is also repeated in *As You Like It,* where it is now fully incorporated into the fabric of the final scene as part of the "rustic revelry" ordered by Duke Senior to celebrate the quadruple wedding ceremony; and it is to Jaques that the final valedictory lines are given, just as in *Love's Labour's Lost* they are entrusted to Don Armado.

These correspondences are further reinforced by the dramatization in both plays of the winter solstice with its message of renewal in the songs provided within the texts. For the owl and the cuckoo as the representatives of winter nights and summer days of *Love's Labour's Lost* we are offered, "Blow, blow thou winter wind" with its contradictory refrain of "Then heigh-ho the holly/This life is most jolly," and "It was a lover and his lass" with its complementary refrain of "Sweet lovers love the spring."

Against this, it may be objected that where *Love's Labour's Lost* contains five female parts, *As You Like It* provides only four; but here, we must remember, Shakespeare had a practical problem to contend with that critics tend to overlook or to forget. Unlike most plays written today, Shakespeare's were carefully planned to fit the talents of a company whose membership was known to him before he set pen to paper and whose skills and talents played a major part in his thinking about the number of roles and the individual personalities of his stage characters. The one serious variable year by year was the time at which a trained boy actor's voice might break, thereby depriving the company of his services in female roles. Thus where in *Love's Labour's Lost* he had been able to count on the availability of five trained boys—two of exceptional ability who could be trusted with the taxing roles of Rosaline and the Princess—by the time he began to write *As You Like It* there were only four. When the cast lists of the two plays are set side by side it is fairly easy to judge what had happened. The boy whose voice had broken, and who could no longer be used (at least where female roles were concerned), was the one who played the Princess of France. Take her/him away and the use of the other four can readily be discerned. Rosaline becomes Rosalind; Katherine and Maria graduate to the larger roles of Celia and Phebe; and that leaves Jaquenetta free to take on Audrey. This raises the interesting question of the two Pages attendant on Duke Senior in *As You Like It* who appear in a single scene (5.3) with two lines each and as singers of a single song. Are these two new apprentices being given their first chance to appear in public and thus groomed to replace the boy already lost and the boy expected to drop out next?

This strictly theatrical problem may have sufficed in itself to deter Shakespeare from scripting a *Love's Labour's Won* for the same group of characters that had peopled *Love's Labour's Lost;* but it is also hard to imagine how the later could have been spun out into another full-length play ending with a quadruple wedding without any obvious narrative source material out of which to fashion it. Thomas Lodge's romance, *Rosalynde, Euphues's Golden Legacy* of 1590 supplied an alternative that offered an equally rich and varied group of stage characters and the possibility of the desired quadruple wedding.

While that, however, can at best only be regarded as hypothetical, there is much firmer evidence to support this case within the text of *As You Like It* and to prove that *Love's Labour's Lost* was still vividly alive in Shakespeare's mind as he was writing it. This is at its clearest in the characterizations of Jaques, Le Beau, and Audrey.

Jaques is so much himself as to be a role still greatly coveted by actors. Yet Jaques unmistakably carries within himself much of Don Armado and a touch or two of Holofernes, just as Sir Oliver Martext echoes Sir Nathaniel in his inadequacy to his priestly pretensions. Duke Senior retains Jaques as an amusing companion in whose company to spend leisure time just as Navarre employs Armado. Both are gentlemen born but having fallen on hard times have become dependent on a wealthy patron; both are said to have been great travelers and, like all tourists, to possess as a result a fund of strange and amusing anecdotes, both are bachelors and singular in their appearance, deportment, and language. This singularity, combined with their respective affectations and pretentions, makes them vulnerable to attack as laughing stocks to others who are more confident and secure in their knowledge of themselves and of their status in society. It is surely no coincidence that both Armado and Jaques should, in their isolation from the mainstream of daily working occupations, fall back on singers and music for solace and comfort— Armado on Moth, Jaques on Amiens. Armado never makes any pretensions to being a philosopher and professional cynic; nor does Jaques claim to have been an army officer or to be well versed in the latest literary fashions. They are thus interestingly different; yet both are clearly grafted of the same stock.

The only repetition of Don Armado's linguistic gymnastics in *As You Like It* is given to Touchstone in conversation with William.

William. Which he sir?

Touchstone. He, sir, that must marry this woman. Therefore, you clown, abandon—which in the vulgar is leave—the society—which in the boorish is company—of this female—which in the common is woman—which together is: abandon the society of this female: or, clown, thou perishest: or, to thy better understanding, diest. . . .

(5.1.42–49)

Similar affinities link Le Beau in *As You Like It* to Boyet in *Love's Labour's Lost;* for while Le Beau disappears from the text of the former by the end of act 1, never to reappear, he serves the same purpose at Duke Frederick's court as does Boyet in the household of the Princess of France—a highly placed official whose foppishness is matched by the precision of his wit and his diplomatic skills. Both, it is to be assumed from the dialogue, are bachelors and ladies' men. Le Beau is drawn as no more than an echo of Boyet; but all viewers seeing *As You Like It* who had already seen *Love's Labour's Lost* would instantly recognize where they had met him before.

Audrey, likewise, is a recognizable redaction of Jaquenetta, cut down from a figure appearing in five scenes to a character confined to three scenes in the latter half of the play. Both are farm girls—Jaquenetta a dairy maid, Audrey a keeper of goats; both are as spirited and robust in their fleshy femininity as the sun-kissed harvest wenches depicted in the paintings of Peter Paul Rubens; and both are as sharply perceptive in recognizing a situation that they can exploit to their own advantage as they are naïve and illiterate in their command of language. Shakespeare even equips Audrey with the same joke about Touchstone's physical appearance as he had previously given to Jaquenetta concerning Don Armado's.

> *Armado.* I do betray myself with blushing. Maid!
> *Jaquenetta.* Man!
> *Armado.* I will visit thee at the lodge.
> *Jaquenetta.* That's hereby.
> *Armado.* I know where it is situate.
> *Jaquenetta.* Lord how wise you are!
> *Armado.* I will tell thee wonders.
> *Jaquenetta.* With that face?

(1.2.126–33)

In *As You Like It* it recurs as,

> *Touchstone.* And now, Audrey, am I the man yet?
> Doth my simple feature content you?
> *Audrey.* Your features, Lord warrant us. What features?

(3.3.2–4)

The conclusions I have drawn from the chances given me to direct *Love's Labour's Lost* and *As You Like It* in sequence and within six months of each other persuade me forcibly that the latter play proved to be the fulfillment of the promise made in the concluding scene of the former to supply the same audience with a *Love's Labour's Won* after an interval of "a twelvemonth and a day." Some readers may feel that this is just so much moonshine; but I remain confident that directors, actors, and actresses who have become aware of these structural parallels, correspondences of characterization, and even direct repetition of snatches of dialogue, are more likely to wish to hang onto them than to reject them.

In Marvin & Ruth Thomson, eds. *Shakespeare and the Sense of Performance.* (Newark: University of Delaware Press, 1989): 210–18.
Reprinted with permission of University of Delaware Press.

STAGING SHAKESPEARE: SEMINARS ON PRODUCTION PROBLEMS
Suzanne Bloch
1990

MUSIC AND SHAKESPEARE

Outside of *Midsummer Night's Dream,* is there a comedy with more than two songs?

THOMSON:

As You Like It doesn't have many either, but they are very famous ones. Anyway, as you have more offstage trumpet calls in the tragedies, in the comedies you have virtually no offstage anything that really functions. You do have a few more songs, but they are limited. The comedies are not "musicals" in the modern sense. Shakespeare was firm about this in his built-in arrangements. Of course, a comedy is a looser structure than a tragedy, and the Shakespearian comedies are not heavily timed like modern comedies—not tightly timed. They are very loose in timing and structure, and you can always take time out to sing a song, if it has reasonable function.

After all, Shakespeare's contemporaries were not just foolishly sticking in interpolated numbers without dramatic purpose, but Shakespeare was by far the strictest of them in economizing music and limiting it, to prevent the Establishment from moving in on his theatre, which they could have done easily when the theatre troupe gave royal performances. They wouldn't have had to move over to Southwark to do it. They could just say, "Well, Queen Elizabeth, now what about us? We've had lovely ideas for this production you're going to have at the house."

Shakespeare pretended a great love for music. I sometimes think he didn't even like it, because he called it dirty names all the time: "The food of love." You play music to rats—they stay awake for days and do nothing but make love. The food of love is what rats consume, as music. On another occasion, he referred to it as "a concourse of sweet sounds." I don't know how much Establishment anger that brought down, but if anybody had referred in

Shakespeare's hearing to poetry as a concatenation of lovely words, I think they would have heard from papa. Music is constantly considered as a thing valued for its sentiment, and chiefly its softness as sentiment, you see, in Shakespearean accounts of it.

At the same time, whether or not he liked the stuff, he certainly wrote words very beautifully for music. He knew the difference between a text for reading and text for singing. A great many composers have written operas to plays by Shakespeare. Those who have used the English text, however cut it may be, have practically all fallen on their faces, because Shakespeare's verse is much too strong as image. Blank verse, in any case, does not lend itself to music; it does not ask for music; it does not like music. The successful operas that have been written to Shakespeare's plays have all been written in French, German, or Italian, in which case, they tightened up the play a little bit, and got rid of the Shakespeare. You acquire verses or a text of some kind in the language you're going to use, and you're not stuck with the sacred liturgy of the Shakespeare lines in *Hamlet, Othello, Falstaff.* And you get any number of successful operas in the continental languages.

Now, Shakespeare knew what to do if he had to deal with music. This is a little book that I brought along called *Words for Music,* by V. C. Clinton Baddeley, published in Cambridge in 1941. He actually put his finger on a piece of text which proves that there were in Shakespeare's time, or very close to it, two styles of writing poetry: one for reciting, and another for singing. This is a poem by John Donne called "Love's Infiniteness." Unfortunately, the other example is not by Donne, but it's from a poet of his time and is a translation of Donne's poem into singable verses. The Donne goes—and imagine singing this:

> Thou cans't not every day give me thy heart,
> If thou cans't give it, then thou never gavest it:
> Love's riddles are, that though they heart depart,
> It stays at home, and thou with losing savest it:
> But we will have a way more liberal
> Than changing hearts, to join them, so we shall
> Be one and one another's All.

You see, it moves in jumps. You have to stop and think about the grammar all the time, and there are means which explode in the middle of it. The version for singing goes:

> You cannot every day give mee your hart
> For merit;

Yet if you will, when yours doth goe
You shall have still one to bestow,
For you shall mine, when yours doth part,
Inherit.
Yet if you please, weele find a better way
Then change them,
For so alone (dearest) wee shall
Bee one and one another all;

Let us so joyne our harts, that nothing may
Estrange them.

There's a predominance of long vowels and virtually a complete absence of pictorial symbols—all the specifications that are suited to music, plus irregular line lengths. Musicians don't like four-by-four, you know. The author of this book says "In these two arrangements of language, the same ideas and even the same words have been framed in two separate designs; the one is a poem: the other is words for music." Then he brings up—and I would have brought it up, if he hadn't—the supreme lyric for music in the entire English-language repertory, which is out of *Measure for Measure.* You can't say it without taking off into song. Shakespeare knew exactly what he was doing there, and he didn't do it for the actors:

Take, O take those lips away:
That so sweetly were forsworn;
And those eyes, the break of day,
Lights that do mislead the morn:
But my kisses bring again,
bring again,
Seals of love, but seal'd in vain,
seal'd in vain.

Glenn Loney, ed.
Staging Shakespeare: Seminars on Production Problems
(New York: Garland, 1990): 191–93
Reprinted with permission of Garland Publishing Company, Inc.

TAINT NOT THY MIND—PROBLEMS AND PITFALLS IN STAGING PLAYS AT THE GLOBE
Alan C. Dessen
1990

The two richest overlaps or juxtapositions are to be found in *King Lear,* 2.3 and *As You Like It,* 2.6. Consider the latter where editors and critics continue to puzzle over Duke Senior's "banquet" that, according to the dialogue, is set up on stage in 2.5 (see lines 26–7, 95–6) and then enjoyed in 2.7 with no indication that it is removed for the brief 2.6 (the first appearance of Orlando and Adam in Arden). After reviewing various options (e.g., use of an "inner stage," transposition of scenes) the New Variorum editor (Richard Knowles) concludes: "the early setting of the table seems to me thoroughly puzzling; it is totally unnecessary, for the banquet could have been carried on, as banquets usually were, at the beginning of scene 7" (109). Directors have therefore developed their own strategies for dealing with this anomaly: some transpose 2.5 and 2.6; some cut the offending lines in 2.5 so that the banquet first appears in 2.7; some play the Folio lines and sequence but darken the stage so that neither Orlando or the playgoer can "see" the banquet during 2.6.

As most editors and critics would agree, Shakespeare did not have to introduce a banquet into 2.5. Yet he did. The result, moreover, is a clear example of the kind of simultaneous staging often found in earlier English drama that yields for the playgoer a strong sense of overlap or juxtaposition comparable to that produced by early entrances or by bodies, scrolls, or leafy screens not removed from the stage. What we should be asking, especially given the availability of the new Globe as testing ground, is: what are the advantages of having such a banquet in full view during the speeches that constitute 2.6?

As one possible answer, consider how the presence of such food affects our reaction to Adam's "O, I die for food" and Orlando's subsequent "if" clauses: "If this uncouth forest yield anything savage, I will either be food for it or bring it for food to thee . . . I will here be with thee presently, and if I bring thee not something to eat, I will give thee leave to die; but if thou diest before I come, thou art a mocker of my labor . . . thou shalt not die for lack of a dinner if there live anything in this desert." What is the effect of such speeches if the food Orlando eventually finds in 2.7 is indeed visible to us while we are hearing these words? What seems anomalous or unrealistic to a reader nurtured upon our theatrical idiom could, in their vocabulary, be one of the striking moments or images in the show (as perhaps with Blunt's body) if the playgoer somehow gains from the juxtaposition an understanding of the distinctive nature of Arden. To what extent has our sense of "forest" or our resistance to simultaneous staging eclipsed a major signifier in Shakespeare's theatrical vocabulary?

Here, moreover, is where my strictures about variable lighting and modern sense of design become especially important. If we can transcend our own theatrical reflexes, we may be able to imagine a Forest of Arden in this instance defined for us not by onstage greenery but by the presence of food in the background while two figures are starving. Through such juxtapositional staging or signifying, that sense of an option available to be exercised or a potential there (under the right circumstances) to be fulfilled could emerge as the point of the sequence and a major building block for the final three acts. A director in a modern theatre who does introduce the banquet in 2.5 and does not remove it during 2.6 may still be tempted to darken part of the stage and highlight Orlando and Adam (as is usually done with Kent in the stocks during Edgar's speech that constitutes *King Lear*, 2.3). But in a New Globe where that option is not available (and where the whole concept of controlling the playgoer's sense of events by means of variable lighting is thwarted), the rationale behind this moment and its potential richness—in their terms—could be realized.

(New York: 1990).
Reprinted by permission of Peter Lang Publishing.

THE TELEVISED SHAKESPEARE CANON
Susan Willis
1991

The director's care in melding text camera work, an essential conjunction for televised Shakespeare, shows in the productions of Miller, Moshinsky, and Howell. Their choices differ, but their individual styles reveal how potent an interpretive device televised production can be. The series is richer, in fact, for their very diversity of approach, their particular technical interests, which are more easily seen when considering their plays collectively. Certainly no single method of televising Shakespeare is guaranteed to bring success; stylization can be exciting as in the controlled effects of the RSC televised tragedies and the BBC *Henry VI-Richard III* sequence or distracting as in parts of *King John,* and a representational or realistic emphasis can be enriching as in *All's Well That Ends Well* or *The Merry Wives of Windsor* or irrelevant and intrusive as in *As You Like It.* Nonetheless, the visual element of the productions was a major concern of the directors working with this visual medium; some directors considered creating the world of the play their essential interpretive contribution.

With the two on-location productions the first season, there was admittedly a bias toward realism or the representational early in the series. But this exploration was not limited to the initial productions; directors throughout the series were drawn to representing reality, to attempting *trompe-l'oeil* studio work. Nonetheless, these productions vary in their approach to and definition of reality, for some are more obviously studio-bound or stagey than others. Even filming reality itself varies in effectiveness, as *Henry VIII* and *As You Like It* demonstrate.

One major difference between *Henry VIII* and *As You Like It* is that, despite the elegance of the settings chosen for filming locations, *Henry VIII* did not become a production about castles, whereas *As You Like It* very nearly became a production more about Mother Nature than about Rosalind, Orlando, or the dukes. The characters in Arden were dwarfed by their green environs as members of the Tudor court were not by Leeds, Hever, or Penshurst, although *Henry VIII*'s director Kevin Billington thought the location work was a vital part of the production: "I don't think the play would work in a studio. . . . I wanted to get away from the idea that this is some kind of fancy pageant. I wanted to feel the reality: I wanted great stone walls." (Compare the walls of *Henry VIII* to the walls in *King John* to survey the difference in effect between real stone and stylization.)

Billington, his designer Don Taylor, and his production manager chose historically apt sites for taping: "We shot at Hever Castle, where Anne Bullen lived; at Penshurst, which was Buckingham's place; and at Leeds Castle, where Henry was with Anne Bullen," Billington explained. Moreover, Billington found opportunities to use place to clarify narrative, as when we see the King and his party of maskers arriving by barge at Wolsey's palace (I.4) rather than simply hearing a drum and a trumpet offstage. Television also solves some practical problems, as script editor Alan Shallcross pointed out; the only scene cut was the one with the commoners preceding infant Elizabeth's christening: "You have to have the scene in the theatre if for no other reason than that people have to change clothes," a need taping obviates.

Henry VIII greatly benefited from being taped on location. In the hands of the BBC, the history closest to Shakespeare's own time, his only work treating Renaissance historical figures, proved how effective reality itself can be. In the context of the Shakespeare series, several small details exemplify the difference. From the opening shot of *Henry VIII,* for instance, we see the ceilings in the castle rooms, and only by registering their presence are we aware of how often rooms are ceilingless in the rest of the series, since ceilings would block out lighting in the studio. In *All's Well* the camera had to shoot through a pane of painted glass to provide the appearance of a ceiling in the French king's hall, and in *The Comedy of Errors* any shot from the piazza up into the second story of the Phoenix had to be very carefully arranged to avoid shooting off the set and into the lighting grid because there was no roof over the structure.

Moreover, because *Henry VIII* was taped in winter (late November until early January), it was cold, and we often see the characters' condensed breath as they speak, both outdoors as in I.1, the arrest of Buckingham, and indoors, as in II.4, the divorce trial. This effect is lost in the studio, for while one might easily shiver in a BBC control room since all that equipment likes to be frigid, the studio lights and activity usually keep anyone from getting a chill on the floor; Imogen and others play several scenes of *Cymbeline* in studio snow, but we never see their condensed breath. The climatic realities of *Henry VIII* were not just visual grace notes, however, but sometimes serious impediments to the production, since frozen cameras cause major problems and production expense.

Surrounded by Tudor architecture and sporting elegant costumes that look like Britain's National Portrait Gallery on parade, the actors succeed in bringing the political intrigues of this Tudor court to life, the whisperings of lords, the observations of gentlemen and commoners, the grantings, the public rituals and private confrontations. Billington's cast gave fine performances: the exercise of will in both Henry and Wolsey matches Katherine's firm dignity, Anne's willing but thoughtful acquiescence, and Cranmer's un-Wolseyian humility in their reactive roles. Billington knew the production was a success because this neglected, musty play proved exciting before the cameras: "It's a play that deserves looking at again. I'm hoping that this production will set people off trying to see how they can do it in the theatre. That would be a wonderful thing for television to do." The ability to capture both physical detail or surroundings and psychological detail of character portrayal proved the advantage of televising Shakespeare, though the expense of this production prompted the BBC to mandate the rest of the series as studio-based, a victory for the play but something of a defeat for the options of putting Shakespeare on television. In the rest of the histories, Giles's selective stylization and frequent representationalism and Howell's carefully planned stylizations are responses to taping in the studio.

As You Like It, on the other hand, by literalizing the pastures of the pastoral mode, diminished Shakespeare's effect, his playfulness with conventions and attitudes. If *Henry VIII* ran into winter chills, the gnats of summer plagued *As You Like It*'s actors—realism with a vengeance. The idea of doing the play on location was producer Cedric Messina's; as he pointed out, "Ninety-five per cent of it takes place in the forest," so using real woods seemed perfect, and he thought "*As You Like It* fitted completely beautifully into the bucolic setting." Basil Coleman does get the benefits of nature's rich colors, the estate's wooded vistas, and beautifully dappled summer sunlight, but planning for location work differs from designing for studio work because instead of building to order or to concept, one uses the locale. As director Coleman explained, "Everything tends to begin from the location." Oak woods, beech woods, an ancient chestnut tree became taping sites, but there were no meadows for grazing sheep at Glamis, and they had to construct a shepherd's cottage (twice, since cows ate the first one). The location often determines the effect, for, as set designer Don Taylor added, "normally what is there dictates, or heavily influences, the way things get done."

In location work there are explorations, discoveries, compromises, rethinkings, and even surprises, as when the pine woods, selected months ahead for the scenes with the banished Duke because of their wintry quality, were three feet deep in ferns when taping occurred in June. Consequently, the hardship and inclemency mentioned in the text never threaten these woodland visitors; their time in the forest appears to be more an upscale camping expedition than exile, as when chic campfire entertainment is provided by two cellos, a flute, and a zither and later an impromptu masque poses no difficulties.

Being set in a real park prompts an audience to ask questions and make demands of the action that would never occur in a theatre because there an audience accepts the limits of theatrical realism. The acting had trouble getting momentum; though Rosalind and Touchstone had moments and Richard Pasco's Jaques was eloquently morose, the overall production never quite sparked into sustained life in its woodland setting.

In the studio, along with Elijah Moshinsky's efforts, both John Gorrie and David Jones also sought to create realistic worlds for the camera and the plays. Consider Gorrie's work. His productions, *Twelfth Night* and *The Tempest,* are based on the belief that the places shown need to have a real geography, that spaces need a definite physical relationship visible on camera. Hence in *The Tempest* we see the trees on one side of the island's cliff face and the shore on the other, and in *Twelfth Night* we could draw a blueprint of Olivia's house. The *Twelfth Night* set for the country manor was especially lovely; years later those involved with the series still fondly recalled that vine-covered estate. Gorrie developed the viewer's familiarity with the house and its forecourt and then capitalized on it. Not only do scenes go back and forth through the gate and the doors, but when she is inside, Olivia helps the viewer be aware of the outside by looking for Cesario out the window.

In many scenes Gorrie was careful to show the environs, using long shots of the courtyard or the main hall with its fireplace, and often pulled the camera back at the end of a scene as the characters exited. At least once Gorrie played off that geographic familiarity; he divided the long III.4 into five smaller scenes yet took care to relate them. Olivia sees the newly cross-gartered Malvolio in a side room, then leaves to greet Cesario in the courtyard. Malvolio lingers in self-satisfaction, then proceeds the length of the corridor to the main hall. There is a cut to action with Sir Toby in the hall, into which Malvolio strides. Since the audience just saw him approach that room from the other angle, his appearance binds the scene and establishes simultaneity. The rest of III.4 is united in a similar manner as Sir Toby and Fabian incite the unwilling combatants to a duel; the composite set lets camera cuts suggest parallel action on each side of the wall.

In this production Gorrie also used point-of view shots quite well, especially regarding Malvolio. When the steward makes his yellow-stockinged entrance to Olivia, the shot cuts from her amazed face to pan up his body from feet to head, following the angle of her gaze. The most complicated shots, however, are in Malvolio's letter scene. Theatrical eavesdropping scenes are notoriously difficult for television, but Gorrie succeeded admirably in this comedy.

(Chapel Hill: University of North Carolina Press, 1991): 84–85, 187–90.
Reprinted with permission of University of North Carolina Press.

AS YOU LIKE IT—PERFORMANCE AND RECEPTION
Michael Jamieson
1995

Come the millennium *As You Like It*[1] will be some four hundred years old, so that an essay of this length on the ways it has been performed and how it has been received must be selective. Three broad movements in its performance history can be discerned. First comes a long, blank period from 1600 to 1723 when (a) there is no hard evidence that the play was ever performed in Shakespeare's lifetime, and (b) in the much more fully documented years from 1660 there is every indication that the old comedy was totally ignored in the playhouses of London and the provinces. Next comes a span, ending in the 1890s, when versions of *As You Like It* were performed with increasing frequency in the English-speaking theatres of Britain and North America, most memorably by star actresses who were applauded in the great role of Rosalind but who often had to appear under the restrictive, even resentful régime of male managers—especially when these gentlemen were themselves leading actors. This era saw Shakespeare consolidated as England's national poet, and towards its end, especially in London and New York, technological and cultural changes

---

[1] Much information about the performance-history and the treatment of the text on the stage can be found in The New Variorum Edition of *As You Like It* by Richard Knowles (New York: The Modern Language Association of America, 1977). Full of details about old theatrical customs and traditions is Arthur Colby Sprague, *Shakespeare and the Actors: The Stage Business in His Plays, 1660–1905* (Cambridge, MA: Howard U Press, 1945). Sprague was co-author with J. C. Trewin of a book which stands as a sequel, *Shakespeare's Plays Today: Some Customs and Conventions of the Stage* (London: Sidgwick and Jackson, 1970). Two surveys of Shakespearean production are Robert Speaight, *Shakespearian Performance* (London: Collins, 1973) and Dennis Kennedy, *Looking at Shakespeare: A Visual History of Twentieth-Century Performance* (Cambridge: Cambridge U Press, 1993). Both authors take an admirably international outlook and their books are splendidly illustrated. In discussing productions from 1952 onwards I have drawn on my own experience—sadly Anglophone—as a playgoer.

allowed theatrical productions to be much more spectacular and scenic so that the imagination of playgoers and journalists was sometimes focussed on the visual contribution of the managers and the scene-painters. From the mid-nineties onwards the situation is bewildering and complex. *As You Like It* may not have exercised the Western imagination in quite the same way as *Hamlet* or *King Lear,* but the proliferation of performances in schools and colleges, the establishment of institutions in England and North America dedicated mainly to the staging of Shakespeare, the international advent of the director as the authoritative interpreter of theatrical texts, and the impact of radio, film, TV and video all contributed to the regular presentation of this once neglected romantic comedy. Actresses (and on occasion actors) still aspire to play Rosalind; and especially since World War I there have been innovative or conceptual interpretations often in foreign translations. There have also been curious *lacunae.* Two marvellous English actresses (Dame Ellen Terry, Dame Judi Dench) never played Rosalind, and, amongst British directors generally regarded as notable Shakespeareans, at least five have never directed the play: William Poel, Harley Granville Barker, Tyrone Guthrie, Peter Brook and Peter Hall. The list of foreign directors who never did an *As You Like It* would be much longer.

As often with Elizabethan and Jacobean texts there is no record of the first performance of *As You Like It* which most scholars assume was first acted around 1600, perhaps at the recently erected Globe Playhouse on Bankside—to which Jaques' set speech 'All the world's a stage' may stand as a precise metatheatrical allusion. A comedy based so closely on the much-reprinted pastoral romance *Rosalind* (1590) is likely to have proved as popular with audiences as Thomas Lodge's prose narrative already had become with readers. Touchstone, like Jaques, is a Shakespearean invention; and it is possible that the part was created to accommodate the skills of the company's new clown, Robert Armin. That Shakespeare himself played old Adam is a Stratford tradition recorded as a faint local memory as late as 1774. Deductions made from the Folio text have greater interest. The unknown youth who first played Rosalind must have been a talented and resourceful performer.[2] Not only does the heroine dominate and even control the action, but this is the longest woman's part Shakespeare ever wrote (736 lines as against Orlando's 321). Furthermore, this is the only script in the canon in which the boy-actor speaks the epilogue.

---

[2] See Michael Jamieson, "Shakespeare's Celibate Stage: The Problem of Accommodation to the Boy-Actors" in G. E. Bentley, ed., *The Seventeenth-Century Stage: A Collection of Critical Essays* (Chicago & London: The University of Chicago Press, 1968), 70–93.

Another tradition about *As You Like It* was recorded as late as 1865. William Cory, poet, scholar and Eton master, wrote in his journal of a visit to Wilton House

> The house (Lady Herbert said) is full of interest: . . . we have a letter, never printed, from Lady Pembroke to her son, telling him to bring James I from Salisbury to see *As You Like It;* 'we have the man Shakespeare with us.'[3]

Cory never saw the alleged letter, nor could it be produced for E. K. Chambers in 1898.[4] However, a document first transcribed by Peter Cunningham in 1842 does record a payment to the company for a single performance at Court on 2 December 1603. In this time of plague the Court is known to have been at Wilton from around 20 October to 12 December 1603 and the King did visit Salisbury. Nothing supports the idea that the play paid for was *As You Like It,* or even by Shakespeare, but scholars of a romantic bent like to fancy a performance—possibly out of doors—of a comedy which celebrates the sylvan pleasures of the hunt to which King James was passionately devoted.

When the playhouses were reopened in 1660 those middle comedies of Shakespeare which centre on disguise, love and courtship were not revived. Dramatic historians have variously conjectured that *As You Like It* was lacking in downright comic power or was too fresh and clean for the jaded appetites of Restoration rakes. A major reason for the neglect may well be that its male characters did not offer much scope to Restoration actors. The comedy first emerges from obscurity as *Love in a Forest,* an adaptation by Charles Johnson acted at Drury Lane in January 1723. This 'improvement' was explained in a prologue:

> In Honour to his Name, and this learn'd Age,
> Once more your much lov'd SHAKESPEAR treads the Stage.
> Another Work from that great Hand appears,
> His Ore's refin'd, but not impar'd by *Years.*

And later:

> Forgive our modern Author's Honest Zeal,
> He hath attempted boldly, if not well:

---

[3] Quoted from the edition by F. W. Cornish in the New Variorum *As You Like It,* 633.

[4] E.K. Chambers, *William Shakespeare: A Study of Facts and Problems* 2 vols. (Oxford: Clarendon Press, 1930), vol.2, 239.

Believe, he only does with Pain and Care,
Presume to weed the beautiful Parterre.[5]

Johnson's weeding of the Shakespearean garden was ruthlessly correct: his excisions include Touchstone and all the shepherds and shepherdesses, with Bottom and his mechanicals brought in at the close to act 'Pyramus and Thisbe' to the restored Duke. The adaptation was played for only six nights. The part of Jaques, acted by Colley Cibber, was built up by transforming the First Lord's report in II.i. into a recollection by Jaques himself. This long remained a theatrical tradition.

On 20 December 1740 *As You Like It* was billed at Drury Lane as 'Not Acted these Forty Years' (over a hundred being more likely). There was a strong cast and three of Shakespeare's songs were given new settings by Thomas Arne. The Rosalind was Hannah Pritchard, then twenty-nine, who got off to a bad start. In those more boisterous days, when the auditorium remained illuminated, a performer's 'points' were applauded. It was only when Pritchard, given an unbecoming gown by the management, reached the line "Take the cork out of thy mouth that I may drink thy tidings" that she was applauded loudly for her spirited delivery. The performance not only brought her to the top of her profession but created a vogue for other Shakespearean comedies. It was acted twenty-eight times in the season, and Francis Hayman's painting of the wrestling scene, which is now in the Tate Gallery, probably depicts Pritchard (better gowned) as Rosalind with Kitty Clive and Celia.[6]

Pritchard's Rosalind was soon challenged by others, notably the more alluring Peg Woffington, who had earlier made an impact in what were called 'breeches parts'. From the Restoration onwards actresses had been encouraged to expose themselves to the male gaze, and one of the ways they could be sexually provocative was to reveal their ankles and legs in the roles of rakes and gallants. Rosalind (*pace* Jan Kott[7]) is not really a breeches part, since the actress does not have to play a man but a girl masquerading as one. Some of the notable later players of Rosalind/Ganymede had previously excelled in such parts. In the neo-classical era tragic and comic roles, especially female ones, were sharply differentiated. Yet the great Sarah Siddons was determined to

---

[5] Quoted in Michael Dobson, *The Making of the National Poet: Shakespeare, Adaptation and Authorship, 1660–1769* (Oxford: Clarendon Press, 1992), 131–2.

[6] See Anthony Vaughan, *Born to Please: Hannah Pritchard, Actress, 1711–1768* (London: The Society for Theatre Research, 1979), 18–20 and pl 2.

[7] Jan Kott, "The Gender of Rosalind," *Interpretations: Shakespeare, Buchner, Gautier* (Evanston, Ill.: Northwestern U Press, 1992), 39 n 13.

essay Rosalind. When she did so at Drury Lane in 1785, she muffled herself up as Ganymede, concealing her limbs, and was ridiculed in the press. In the years 1787 to 1814 the unsurpassable Rosalind was the enchanting Mrs Jordan, a mischievous, infectious player with a voice which reminded Siddons' brother, J. P. Kemble, of a phrase in Sterne: "like the natural notes of some sweet melody which drops from it whether it will or no."[8] She played Rosalind for twenty-seven years at Covent Garden, at Drury Lane and in the provinces. She played her in sickness and in health, often in the advanced stages of pregnancy. For Little Pickle (as the much-loved Dora was called after one of her breeches parts) lived openly with the Duke of Clarence, the future King William IV, and bore him ten FitzClarences, first cousins to the legitimate Victoria, who duly succeeded their father as sovereign. In the years before her widowhood, Queen Victoria was a great playgoer and several times quizzed Lord Melbourne about Dora Jordan, on one occasion when they were contemplating the memorial statue by Chantrey. The royal diary records:

> "She was beautifully formed", Lord M said, "her legs and feet were beautifully formed, as this statue is; and she used to be fond of acting in men's clothes; she used to act . . . Rosalind in *As You Like It*"; "a lovely play", said Lord M, "the prettiest play in the world; and her acting in that was quite beautiful." "She had a beautiful enunciation," he added. She was an Irish girl.[9]

Weightier critics like William Hazlitt and Leigh Hunt agreed. Dora has recently been restored to her place in cultural and social history in Claire Tomalin's biography, which reproduces in colour William Beechey's portrait of the young actress in yellow knee-breeches and wide lace collar as Rosalind.[10] More theatrically telling is a scene engraved by Henry Bunbury in 1795 in which Dora in boots, breeches and wide-brimmed, feathered hat contemplates Silvius wooing Phoebe. The disguise as Ganymede would fool nobody; this Rosalind is deliciously feminine even *en travestie*.

From the 1780s onwards playgoers thronged to see their favourite players in their best parts. Rehearsals, especially in the provinces, were slipshod and

---

[8] William Robson, *The Old Playgoer* (London, 1845; repr. with intro by Robert Gittings, London: Centaur Press, 1969), 141.

[9] Quoted by George Rowell, *Queen Victoria at the Theatre* (London: Paul Elek, 1978)

[10] *Mrs. Jordan's Profession: The story of a great actress and a future King* (London: Viking, 1994), colour plate opposite p. 320, black and white between pp. 72 and 73.

perfunctory, and even at Covent Garden and Drury Lane players, hired by the season, resumed old roles or inherited new ones in which they reproduced traditional 'lines'. The schoolmaster William Robson—who recalled in *The Old Playgoer* (1845) having often received "a passing nod and smile from the window of the royal-coronetted carriage of Jordan"—watched *As You Like It* so often that past evenings coalesced in memory into one ideal cast: John Philip Kemble as Jaques; Charles Kemble as Orlando; Mrs Jordan as Rosalind; "dear old Murray" as Adam, etc.[11] *As You Like It* was increasingly liked; *Much Ado* had half as many performances; *Twelfth Night* about two thirds. It was first done in New York in 1786 and was more frequently performed there than in London. The acting text was by tradition heavily cut. Among the customary deletions were: Jaques' parody of Amiens' song and the exiled Duke's recollection of Jaques' libertinism; Sir Oliver Martext's appearance; Rosalind's exchange with Jaques; the epiphany of Hymen. Subsequent Bowdlerian excisions concentrated on seeming indelicacies. Cuts reduced running time, but they were sometimes necessitated by such interpolations as songs from other plays. Mrs Jordan was not the only Ganymede to tease Orlando by singing "Cuckoo" from *Love's Labour's Lost*. Stage custom also dictated certain details of costume and stage business. The low comedian playing Touchstone tended to commandeer some of Le Beau's lines in the wrestling scene and often fussily supervised the removal of the insensate Charles.

The presentation of *As You Like It* by William Charles Macready in October 1842 at Drury Lane, then under his management, must rank as the first which gave one man's vision of the play.[12] For a start Macready had restored much of the Folio text and the players had been thoroughly rehearsed. Great attention and much expense had been given to the scene-painting, which was by Charles Marshall. The fair-copy of the prompt-book has an enthusiastic note: "the most wonderfully perfect representation of Court and pastoral life was witnessed on the English stage." There were ten settings, mostly backcloths, but two scenes exploited the full depth of the Drury Lane stage, the wrestling bout and the finale. A surviving drawing shows the former: the painted backcloth depicts a French château with a forested landscape while in front, centre stage, on a terrace is the wrestling space. There were seventy-three supers (or extras) in

---

[11] *The Old Playgoer,* 15, 53–4.

[12] The account of Macready's production draws on Alan Downer, *The Eminent Tragedian, William Charles Macready* (Cambridge, Mass.: Harvard U Press, 1966), 215–6, 223, 243–4, 251, and on Charles H Shattuck's *Mr Macready Produces As You Like It: a Prompt-book Study* (Urbana, IL: Illinois Phi Mu, 1962).

this spectacle. Macready's biographer has recreated the scene from prompt-book and text:

> Groups of Courtiers and Ladies, enter up terrace steps, L and move upon the scene, as if awaiting the wrestling. Attendts enter, and begin to place chairs, and prepare the ring, with ropes and pillars. As the Courtiers catch sight of Celia, or Rosalind, they salute them respectfully. As the Duke and Suite enter—Rosalind, Celia &c retire towards R 2 E, where attendts are placing seats, many of the Courtiers and Ladies, are crowding round Charles, as if congratulating him,—he is, apparently, full of confidence,—other courtiers are talking together, all in high glee, in regarding Charles, and, occasionally, glancing sneeringly at Orlando, who stands, modestly apart at back L 3 E—speaking to Dennis;—The Ring is formed as rapidly as possible, but the L entrances are not closed—the Court are grouped without and within—the Duke, LeBeau, and 2 or 3 of the Courtiers have Merlins on their wrists.
>
> [Orlando: "When I have made it empty."] Duke and Court move to leave the ring.
>
> [Rosalind: "Pray heaven, I be deceived in you."] As the Duke moves down to his seat, R—the Attendants clear and close the ring.—All are arranged, without, around.
>
> [Orlando: "Ready, sir."] takes off cloak—gives it to Dennis, at back R.
>
> [Orlando: "But come your ways."] Great anxiety and interest among the bystanders, with cries of encouragement, fear &c commencing in a whisper, and as the parties close to struggle, become most vehement.
>
> [*Charles is thrown*] Gen shout and applause, from all on the stage—As the Duke rises, the Attendts on his signal take up the ropes &c. and exit down terrace—the Courtiers &C crowd round in eager congratulations to Orl:—the Duke adv to Orl, Courtiers giving way.
>
> [As the Duke speaks] Courtiers, &c, become grave, and look with timid distrustful glances at Duke and Orl. They exeunt diversely—some foll'g Duke R U E—others L U E. Others, the terrace steps—All as if speak'g of Orlando.

Macready himself played Jaques in what he later regarded as the favourite among his splendid revivals. He came to regret that he had cast the lively and beautiful comic actress, Louise Nisbett (later Lady Boothby), as Rosalind, for she played the part in the old hoyden tradition, which was not quite to Victorian taste. Subsequently Rosalind was played by the cooler, more elegant Helen Faucit (later Lady Martin), who in retirement wrote several essays on 'Shakespeare's Female Characters by One Who Has Impersonated Them'. When, in 1843, Macready gave up the management of Drury Lane, the Queen commanded a performance of *As You Like It* and an afterpiece, rather to his displeasure, for The Eminent Tragedian would have preferred to appear in a greater role. Again the royal diary is revealing:

> Macready acted the part of Jacques and pronounced the famous speech about the Ages beautifully but what surprised me most of all was the really beautiful acting of Miss H. Faucit as "Rosalind". She looked pretty in male attire and was lively and "naive".[13]

Macready's production remained a landmark, but actresses continued to covet the role of Rosalind. Charlotte Cushman, the American actress who liked taking men's parts in Shakespeare, played Rosalind rather broadly in London in 1845 and often in New York between 1849 and 1857. Helena Modjeska, whose frail, lady-like Rosalind spoke with Polish inflections, regularly acted coast-to-coast. Playing opposite her was one of the few men ever to have made much of Orlando, the virile and muscular Maurice Barrymore—founder of a theatrical dynasty—who sparred with a professional prize-fighter as Charles the Wrestler. Hermann Vezin, the American actor and elocutionist, virtually appropriated the role of Jaques in London between 1875 and 1900. From 1871 to 1902 the most distinguished theatre in London was the Lyceum under Henry Irving, whose charming leading lady, Ellen Terry, was the best-loved actress since Jordan and the highest paid woman in England. But, though she played opposite him in nine sumptuous Shakespearean revivals, Terry was never allowed to play Rosalind. When one of Irving's advisers urged that she must get to play Rosalind while in her prime, the actor-manager (who had been Silvius and Orlando in his long apprentice years) was not enthusiastic about taking on Touchstone.[14]

Terry must have had mixed feelings when she heard rumours of a surprising *As You Like It* which, for a few summer afternoons in 1884 and 1885 united the worlds of high society and of the Aesthetic Movement in a woodland glade in Surrey.[15] Lady Archibald Campbell, a high priestess of aestheticism, who had been painted by Whistler and published by Wilde, had recently done a portrait of the beautiful American actress, Eleanor Calhoun, as Rosalind, using as

---

[13] *Queen Victoria at the Theatre.*

[14] The adviser in 1882 was Squire Bancroft, the first actor to be knighted after Irving. See *The Bancrofts: Recollections of Sixty Years* (London: John Murray, 1909) 326–7.

[15] This section is based on "Aesthetic Theatre: The Career of E. W. Godwin in John Stokes, *Resistible Theatres: Enterprise and experiment in the late nineteenth century* (London: Paul Elek, 1972), 31–68.

background the wood of Coombe Warren, the Duke of Cambridge's country estate near Kingston-upon-Thames. She now invited E. W. Godwin, the architect and designer, to supervise an open-air charity performance of the forest scenes in *As You Like It*. Godwin had been the lover of Ellen Terry and, after he deserted her and their two children, he provided designs and counsel to other theatre people. He had also made himself a scholar of the historical costumes appropriate to Shakespeare. Apart from Miss Calhoun as Rosalind and the irreplaceable Hermann Vezin, specially engaged for Jaques, the company consisted mainly of Lady Archie's fashionable friends. Godwin chose the period of the late-fifteenth century. The men wore costumes of rough materials and those characters who had spent longer in Arden were kitted out with well-worn garments. In all this Godwin had the cooperation of Arthur Lazenby Liberty of Regent Street. Both Lady Archie, who herself played Orlando, and Miss Calhoun in her disguise as Ganymede, wore doublet and hose and thigh-high leather boots; the former's costume was dark green plush, the latter's warm-coloured russet and cinnamon. The Duke, Commander-in-Chief of the British Army and first cousin of the Queen, refused to lend his estate for such theatricals, but the adjoining woodlands of Dr MacGeagh's hydropathic establishment provided what all judged to be an ideal pastoral setting. Oddly in this Edenic landscape both a proscenium and a curtain were deemed necessary. The acting area was a grove of lime trees with views stretching beyond. It faced a raked stand draped in sage-green, with chairs for three hundred spectators. A green curtain was strung between two trees and lowered into a hidden trench by two foresters to signal the start of the performance. A slain stag was carried in the distance in the hunting scene and deer and goats grazed on the fringes of the action. The experiment was so successful that an extra performance was attended by the Prince of Wales and there was much discussion in the journals about the amazing naturalism of the performance which had made some spectators feel like eavesdroppers.

The gentlemanly actor-managers continued the attempt to cram a convincing Arden within the picture-frames of their West End playhouses. When John Hare and W. H. Kendal collaborated on a production at the civilised St James's Theatre in 1885 the setting included real grass, real ferns, a real waterfall—and Hermann Vezin as Jaques. The master of this mode of presentation, which involved a good deal of textual rearrangement and interpolation of songs and business, was the American impresario Augustin Daly, who managed theatres named after him in both New York and London. Although purists objected to the 'Dalyised' approach, everyone applauded his leading lady, the spirited, red-headed Irishwoman, Ada Rehan, one of the great Rosalinds of all time. Daly died in 1899 and Rehan's withdrawal from her triumphant career suggested to some that he had been Svengali to her Trilby. In

1897 she brought a company to play *As You Like It* out of doors one afternoon at Stratford, but rain drove the players into the new Shakespeare Memorial Theatre, which would later become the centre of the Shakespeare Industry.

By the turn of the century a bewildering amount of scholarly, cultural and institutional attention was being focussed on the staging of Shakespeare, though on the whole *As You Like It* was conventionally treated. William Poel, who pioneered a return to Elizabethan modes of presentation, never directed the comedy, which obviously figured prominently in the repertory of the extrovert Ben Greet, who for some thirty years led companies of young aspirants round the gardens of England and the campuses of North America giving pastoral performances. The Shakespeare Memorial Theatre had been built at Stratford in 1879, endowed by the local brewing firm of Flowers. At first it presented only a week's season in April in honour of the Bard's birthday. More significantly, a former melodrama houses the Old Vic on the Waterloo Road, was converted by the philanthropist Emma Cons into a centre of temperance entertainment; by 1914 it had evolved into a theatre for low-budget seasons of Shakespeare. *As You Like It* figured in the repertories of both organisations. The Stratford seasons from 1888 to 1916 featured the hard-worked touring company of F. R. Benson. Athletically handsome in his younger days, he excelled as Orlando, especially at that moment when he tossed in the air the hefty Oscar Asche as Charles. Benson's settings, after much touring, became notoriously shabby; for Arden artificial branches adorned the set and the stage was strewn with leaves. When Asche mounted his own lush Edwardian production for a London run at the fashionable His Majesty's, the characters strolled through bracken in places two feet high (two thousand pots of fern in all).[16] Asche himself slowly peeled and ate an apple as he recited 'All the world's a stage'.

Granville Barker, for all his influence, directed only four Shakespeare plays in London. He wrote briefly in a preface of Rosalind and the boy actor. It was left to Nigel Playfair, who had acted for Poel and Barker, to release *As You Like It* from dreary stage traditions and to animate it with all the resources of modern design.[17] The Memorial Theatre had been closed for the last years of the war and in 1919 Playfair was invited to bring a guest company to the April festivities in *As You Like It.* His actors played a very full text, speaking briskly

---

[16] J. C. Trewin, *The Edwardian Theatre* (Oxford: Basil Blackwell, 1976), 119.

[17] Sir Nigel Playfair gave witty accounts of his *As You Like It* in two works of reminiscence, *The Story of the Lyric Theatre Hammersmith* (London: Chatto and Windus, 1925), and *Hammersmith Hoy* (London: Faber & Faber, London, 1930), 203–7, the former of which contains designs by Fraser reproduced in colour and black and white.

and lightly. The highly intelligent Athene Seyler played Rosalind with wit and verve and Playfair himself was Touchstone. But the revelation (and—to Benson's loyal followers—the horror) was the designs. Playfair, with a limited budget, had engaged the brilliant young illustrator Claud Lovat Fraser, whose bright, boldly-coloured costumes and sharply stylised settings were based on fourteenth century French missals. They had the clarity of illustrations for children's books. What shocked Stratfordians most, however, was the Londoner's failure to observe an immemorial local tradition. As far back as 1879, when *As You Like It* graced the first festival, H. S. Lucy of Charlecote Park had shot and presented a stag from the very estate on which Shakespeare was supposedly apprehended for poaching deer. That day the trophy of the chase was slowly borne across the stage by the Lucy retainers with their dogs. The stag was stuffed and was carried on-stage—progressively moth-eaten—in all subsequent performances of *As You Like It*. Fraser's designs were thought by some to be subversively Cubist. They had the same brightness of colour and boldness of line that had excited comment in Barker's productions; the ultimate influence was probably the stunning *decors* brought to London in Diaghilev's Russian ballets. The original sketches were much reproduced in the art magazines, although production photographs tell more about the scenography. The production was later revived at Playfair's own playhouse, the Lyric, Hammersmith. Gordon Crosse, looking back on sixty-two years of Shakespeare playgoing, recalled the performance as eccentric only in the sense that it was *not* traditional—"all jolly and delightful, and rather free and easy".[18] Playfair was later invited by the Oxford University Dramatic Society to re-direct the comedy with male undergraduates and guest actresses in the gardens of Wadham College, when Fraser's costumes were re-used. At Cambridge in the twenties Terence Gray ran a company at the Festival Theatre where his iconoclastic versions of Shakespeare shocked dons but intrigued students. In *As You Like It* in 1928, Rosalind fled to Arden dressed as a Boy Scout with Celia as a Girl Guide.[19]

In the twenties and thirties at Stratford and the Old Vic, *As You Like It* was given frequent, fairly conventional revivals. Fabia Drake made a big local reputation as a spirited Rosalind at Stratford, where the seasons now ran for five weeks, first in 1930 and then in 1932, when the new Memorial Theatre was opened. The Vic, with its much longer seasons and its responsive audience of locals, students and dedicated playgoers, was the greater nursery of talent, and

---

[18] Gordon Crosse, *Shakespearean Playgoing, 1890–1952* (London: A. R. Mowbray, 1953), 155.

[19] Norman Marshall, *The Other Theatre* (London: John Lehmann, 1947), 58. Marshall also gave an account of Playfair's production.

its productions got reviewed in the national press. Even the established actress Edith Evans volunteered to work south of the river to stretch herself in a range of Shakespearean parts, including Rosalind in 1926. The Vic also made stars. The radiant and lyrical Peggy Ashcroft, then twenty-five, did her first Rosalind there in 1932 when she was sketched by Sickert putting the chain around Orlando's neck. She was trounced by the reigning drama critic, James Agate, for "taking away the poetry, the depth of feeling and what I should like to call the lineage of the part."[20]

Edith Evans's later Rosalind sheds light on Agate's phrase. She was invited for a season of three plays in 1936 by the brilliant, occasionally maverick director, Tyrone Guthrie, who was determined to improve production values at the Old Vic. There was a problem. Evans wanted to play Rosalind for the last time. Guthrie was blunt: at forty-nine she was too old. He assigned the direction to the actress and teacher of drama, Esmé Church, who in partnership with the designer, Mollie MacEwen decided on pastoral settings *a la* Watteau. Michael Redgrave, then twenty-eight, was Orlando. Evans triumphed by sheer force of will and by her remarkable vocal technique. Never conventionally beautiful, she had the capacity to assume glamour on stage, and she came back to Rosalind after playing some of the witty, independent women of Restoration comedy, including Millamant. She brought wit, style and impeccable timing to speaking the marvellous cadences of Shakespeare's prose. Her performance may have been given added radiance by the fact (disclosed much later in a biography) that she and her young leading man had enjoyed what Dame Edith in old age referred to as "my five-minute love".[21] Reviewing the production for *The Manchester Guardian,* Alan Dent noted that it seemed October in this Arden, but found the Rosalind "a Meredithian lady rich in mind." Praising the wit and romance of Evans's performance he concluded: "in the end the audience is made one Orlando."[22] The production transferred to the West End where within two years Edith Evans first played her definitive Lady Bracknell.

Two notions of Rosalind seemed to co-exist in the thirties: the Congrevian or Meredithian witty woman and the *gamine*—Millamant and Peter Pan. Several actresses who acted Rosalind, especially on the greensward of the Open Air Theatre in Regent's Park, also played the Boy Who Did Not Wish to Grow

---

[20] *Brief Chronicles: A Survey of the Plays of Shakespeare and the Elizabethans in Actual Performances* (London: Jonathan Cape, 1943), 60–61.

[21] Bryan Forbes, *Ned's Girl: The Authorised Biography of Dame Edith Evans* (London: Elm Tree Books/Hamish Hamilton, 1977), 183–8. See also James Forsyth, *Tyrone Guthrie: A Biography* (London: Hamish Hamilton, 1976), 153, 157.

[22] Alan Dent, *Prelude and Studies* (London: Macmillan, 1942), 111–2.

Up. Almost contemporaneous with Evans's performance was the refugee Dr Paul Czinner's lavish Anglo-American film of 1936, conceived as a vehicle for his internationally famous wife, Elisabeth Bergner. The Viennese star had played Rosalind in German at Zürich in 1920 and at Berlin a couple of years later under the great Max Reinhardt. The film tended to be reviewed as a film version of Shakespeare rather than as a movie in its own right. The palace of Duke Frederick recalled the set for an Astaire-Rogers dance routine and the studio artificiality of the forest was made especially noticeable by the presence of bleating sheep and grazing deer.[23] Although Laurence Olivier, who had decided Orlando was a bit mad, made a good impression, Bergner herself—tiny and elfish and given to turning somersaults—was judged to be too cloying, too arch, too coy; and her palpably thirties make-up tempted one journalist to dub the film 'Lost in the Forest of Elizabeth Arden'. Nor did Bergner's foreign accent make Rosalind's cadenced prose intelligible to filmgoers. The dialogue, over which her great fan Sir James Barrie was consulted, was pruned of all sexual innuendoes and the running time was cut to 97 minutes. William Walton composed his first Shakespearean score for this film, which now has an archival fascination in that several British actors of the old school are preserved on celluloid and on the sound-track. Henry Ainley (born 1879), playing the exiled Duke, had been a dashingly handsome Orlando in 1902. Leon Quartermaine (born 1876) was especially praised for his measured delivery of 'All the world's a stage'.

Foreign productions often had a freshness and freedom stemming from the fact that directors were not bound by precedent. Two stagings in Paris in 1934 took diametrically opposed approaches.[24] The first, admirably translated by Jules Supervielle, was an elaborate affair starring the film actress Annabella at the big Théâtre des Champs-Elysées. It featured real sheep grazing, which seems odd as the designer was the painter Balthus. More resonant was the conception of Jacques Copeau, theorist, teacher and reformer of French theatre, who often chose to work on Elizabethan texts because the stage conventions liberated him from French academicism. His production at the intimate Théâtre de l'Atelier was based on a free adaptation entitled *Rosalinde* and it marked his return to Paris after a ten-year period of study and experimentation with a small group of young actors, Les Copains, in rural Burgundy. The music was by Georges Auric. The ascetic-looking director himself was Jaques, and the young Jean-Louis Barrault played small parts including Hymen. Later he took over at short notice as Touchstone, conceived as a circus clown who conjured

---

[23] James Agate, *Around Cinemas* (London: Horne & Van Thal, 1946), 173–7.

[24] Speaight, *Shakespeare on the Stage,* 190–3.

innumerable properties from the recesses of his garments. (Years later in the early sixties Barrault presented *Comme il vous plaira* at the Odéon in Supervielle's text.) In the summer of 1938 Copeau was invited to recreate his production with Italian actors in the baroque Boboli gardens in Florence. He arranged the action on various fixed locations, simultaneously visible to the audience. One was a specially built rustic hillock built round a real tree. Copeau added some striking effects of light and shadow to the Tuscan dusk, and at the close he brought on the hermit, the agent of Duke Frederick's conversion, to bless the participants in the wedding masque.

The most amazing production of the comedy in the immediately post-war years was the *Rosalinda* staged in Rome in 1948 by Luchino Visconti, who envisaged it as "a fantasy, a dream, a fairy-tale verging on ballet".[25] Accordingly he secured designs from Salvador Dali. Although their production was later dismissed, sight unseen, as a half-hearted attempt at a surrealist staging, the truth was more complex and more intellectually valid, for Dali and Visconti took as their starting-point the extraordinary and mysterious *boschetto* at Bomarzo, a cryptically allegorical grove created around 1560 by an aristocratic humanist and filled with gnomic inscriptions and grotesque sculptures. Dali designed two emblematic rococo backcloths—one Court, one Forest—and costumes of extraordinary richness and elaborateness. On the stage were two elephants bearing obelisks like Bernini's sculptures and a Palladian temple which opened into four sections. The music was by Shakespeare's English contemporaries. Visconti's usual leading lady Rita Morelli was Rosalind, the darkly handsome Vittorio Gassman played Orlando, and a young Roman called Marcello Mastrionni made his début as one of Jaques' foresters. The fact that the veteran Ruggero Ruggeri, who had created major roles for Pirandello, spoke 'All the world's a stage' must have evinced an authentic metatheatrical *frisson* amongst older playgoers. Visconti's abandonment of his habitual *neorealismo* astonished some admirers; and as a Marxist he was privately berated by Party members for working with a designer who had not denounced Franco. Dali's work had an afterlife amongst book-collectors in that several of his designs were reproduced as colour plates in the Folio Society's edition of *As You Like It* which was published in 1953 with a preface by Peter Brook, who had been fascinated by the art-work at a Roman exhibition but had never seen the production. Four years later Brook expressed his dislike of the comedy as "far too hearty . . . unpoetic, and frankly not very funny". He asked:

---

[25] Visconti's production is briefly described by Monica Stirling in *A Screen of Time: A Study of Luchino Visconti* (New York: Harcourt Brace Jovanovich, 1976), 81–2, and in Gaia Servadio in *Luchino Visconti: A Biography* (London: Weidenfeld & Nicolson, 1982), 120, 235.

"Could the fact that I did *As You Like It* for School Certificate have anything to do with it?" [26]

Things were perhaps tamer in the English-speaking theatre. Katharine Hepburn appeared as Rosalind at the Cort Theatre in New York in 1950 and later made a hugely successful coast-to-coast tour of the States. This was a lavishly spectacular production by The Theatre Guild, with an imported English director and designer, Michael Benthall and James Bailey, and several London actors. Brooks Atkinson in *The New York Times* complained about the "heavily accented" and "singularly busy" direction, which was:

> ... equipped with bird songs, owl hoots, a snow-storm, garlanded processionals, wood smoke, choruses, a fine chamber orchestra, and ... spiced with several episodes of egregious horse-play.

The scholarly stage-historian Arthur Colby Sprague was annoyed by the cuts, transpositions and additions, and by the fact that "the cuckoo and the owl songs from *Love's Labour's Lost* were thrust in for good measure just as they used to be in Victorian times".[27] But, of course, the whole *raison d'etre* of the production was the sprightly star's return to the theatre from Hollywood in her first classical rôle. Several iconic photographs show Hepburn seated against a tree trunk stretching her shapely legs in what look like sheer nylon tights. Benthall duly returned to London where he was director of the Old Vic between 1953 and 1961 when he supervised the staging of all the plays in the First Folio, often with such emerging stars as Richard Burton, John Neville and Claire Bloom; but in 1955 and 1958, when *As You Like It* was revived, he delegated the actual direction to others. The high level of casting is indicated by the fact that in 1958 Barbara Jefford's tall and well spoken Rosalind was supported by Maggie Smith as Celia, Judi Dench as Phebe and Moyra Fraser as Audrey.

Some reviewers and academics preferred productions of Shakespeare which did not carry the imprint of strong directorial interpretation. Professor Dame Helen Gardner claimed that in the fifties when Glen Byam Shaw was directing at Stratford no-one spoke of Byam Shaw's *As You Like It* but of Peggy

---

[26] "An Open Letter to William Shakespeare," *The Sunday Times,* September 1, 1957, reprinted in *The Shifting Point, 1946–1987* (London and New York: Harper & Row, 1987), 72–5.

[27] Arthur Colby Sprague and J. C. Trewin, *Shakespeare's Plays Today: Some Customs and Conventions of the Stage* (London: Sidgwick and Jackson, 1970), 79. Sprague quoted Brooks Atkinson, but did not even mention Katharine Hepburn.

Ashcroft's 'heavenly Rosalind'.[28] This self-effacing director had himself been an actor, and his earliest *As You Like It* was done for the touring group the Young Vic, mostly recent graduates from the short-lived Old Vic School. Its innovation was to start with an Arden in winter. Byam Shaw twice directed the comedy at Stratford. In 1952 the lovers were played by Margaret Leighton and Laurence Harvey (who subsequently got married). Kenneth Tynan thought the production first rate: "the shift in mood from wintry discord to summery consonance was perfectly reflected in the settings". He found Leighton a little too much the head girl but marvelled at Michael Hordern—"a magical Jaques, proud and sorrowful as the White Knight, and daft as Don Quixote".[29] Byam Shaw mounted his third version in 1957, when Dame Peggy Ashcroft, nearing fifty, played her last Rosalind with blazing sincerity and romantic feeling, though she complained in a letter to her mentor George Rylands, the Shakespearean don and director: "Rosalind is a wonderful girl but I wish she didn't talk *quite* so much".[30]

Stratford audiences saw a landmark *As You Like It* in 1961—a radiant production by Michael Elliott for the reorganised Royal Shakespeare Company which made a star of Vanessa Redgrave, daughter of Dame Edith's Orlando. This marked the happiest coming together of director, designer and player. Richard Negri's memorable set was dominated by a vast tree and the whole sloping stage was carpeted in green. Sombre in the early scenes, the stage came alive later with dappled sunshine in the Forest. This was probably the first occasion when most reviewers mentioned the lighting, some even naming the lighting designer, Richard Pilbrow. The magic was Redgrave's. More than common tall, she played Ganymede barefoot, with a working-man's cap pulled down over her eyes. When she finally came running round the great tree in her wedding dress, the audience gasped. Max Adrian may have been the first actor to tinge the sardonic Jaques' melancholy with homosexual desire. The interpretation was totally humanist: Corin haltingly recited Hymen's lines. Redgrave repeated her Stratford triumph at the Aldwych in London and the production was redirected on film for BBC TV which took 138 minutes. Peter Hall, head of the RSC, recalled in his memoirs taking a reluctant playgoer Jean Renoir to the theatre and placing him for a few minutes at the back of the stalls:

---

[28] Helen Gardner, "Shakespeare in the Director's Theatre", chap. 3 of *In Defence of the Imagination* (Oxford: Clarendon Press, 1982), 67.

[29] *Curtains: Selections from the Drama Criticism* (London: Longmans, 1961) 34–5.

[30] Michael Billington, *Peggy Ashcroft* (London: John Murray, 1988), 170.

After a short time I took his arm to show him the way out, but he resisted and stayed, his eyes alight. On stage was a girl like a rush of sunlight. He was watching the twenty-four year old Vanessa Redgrave play Rosalind, her first unqualified triumph.[31]

The Redgrave/Elliott inhibited successors. It seemed to encapsulate that view of Shakespearean comedy put forward by Northrop Frye and C. L. Barber. But in the late sixties theatre people began to think of Arden less as The Green World or The Great Good Place and more as some sort of metaphor for the alternative life-style of youth culture and the flower people. A precursor seems to have been Word Baker's modern-dress revival at Stratford, Connecticut, in which Kim Hunter played Rosalind; Orlando was barefoot and in overalls and Sir Oliver Martext was a bicycling vicar. Peter Dews' production at the Birmingham Rep in 1967 with a young cast including Brian Cox as Orlando was graced with Carnaby Street costumes and pop music.

Even before this flower-power As You Like It had briefly transferred to the Vaudeville in London, John Dexter, a brilliant and acerbic Associate Director of the National Theatre, then still at the Old Vic, had been working for over a year on an up-to-date and all-male version with music by Donovan, the folk singer. But the National Theatre's director Laurence Olivier, soon to be made a Life Peer, unexpectedly vetoed the project, fearing public hostility to a drag show.[32] He offered Rosalind to one of the National's leading ladies, Maggie Smith, whose dazzling success in the company had not entirely pleased him.[33] Then in 1971 he suddenly entrusted an all-male production to a safer pair of hands, Clifford Williams, a director with a strongly visual sense on loan from the RSC. Dexter's project was influenced by Jan Kott's essay 'Shakespeare's Bitter Arcadia', especially as regards notions of sexuality and homo-eroticism explored through the concept of the original boy-actor playing the woman Rosalind disguised as the youth Ganymede. Though Kott was copiously quoted in the National Theatre programme, Williams added a note distancing himself from such problematic theories. The intellectual basis of his dazzlingly successful production was perhaps a little fuzzy. (Olivier was reported as having wondered aloud at rehearsals whether the men playing women should perhaps wear false bosoms and shave their legs.) Ralph Koltai designed an

---

[31] Peter Hall, *Making an Exhibition of Myself* (London: Sinclair-Stevenson, 1993), 123–4.

[32] John Elsom and Nicholas Tomalin, *The History of the National Theatre* (London: Jonathan Cape, 1978), 195–6.

[33] Michael Coveney, *Maggie Smith: A Bright Particular Star* (London: Victor Gollancz, 1992), 130.

almost abstract set which could have been used for other plays. In the Forest scenes Plexiglass tubes and cloud-shaped transparencies descended to suggest trees and foliage; kaleidoscopic lighting enhanced the dappled shadows; and Marc Wilkinson's pop-style music seemed almost to emanate from the abstract tubes. The mood was celebratory and festive, and the players, most of whom had been together for several seasons, formed a marvellous *ensemble*. The costumes of the young folk were Unisex from the King's Road, sometimes made of plastic in the style of Courrèges. The four women were acted in different conventions. Ronald Pickup played Rosalind with neutral tact in a trouser-suit, chiffon scarf and jaunty cap. Charles Kay was a watchful, waspish Celia in granny glasses and mini-skirted frock. Richard Kay as Phebe played more in the sixth-form, serious schoolboy mode, while Antony Hopkins as Audrey was a bit like a Welsh rugby player in drag. Derek Jacobi was genuinely funny as a young, rather camp Touchstone. And in the final epiphany Hymen was sung in the asexual tones of a counter-tenor. The production was kept in the repertory, and toured four continental cities.

The very success of this controversial all-male production provoked strong reactions from other directors. The earliest was the production in 1973 at Stratford by the young Buzz Goodbody, the first woman to be given a permanent directorial appointment at the RSC, hitherto a male oligarchy. A feminist and a Communist, she strove to reclaim the text for women. The setting by Christopher Morley consisted of metal tubes hanging round a circular playing space—an allusion to Koltai. The court was Edwardian, with Touchstone as a cheeky chappie from the Music Hall. In Arden the banished Duke and his followers seemed like gentry weekending in the country, with Richard Pasco's detached Jaques acknowledging kinship with Chekov's doctors. Eileen Atkins, who as Ganymede wore long hair, headband and flared jeans was, according to Richard David, self-doubting and inward in the Edith Evans tradition.[34] The production left Goodbody disillusioned with the big space of the Stratford stage. She went on, before her too early death, to found the smaller, more intimate Other Place, but the RSC has never explored *As You Like It* there nor at its third playhouse, the Swan.[35] Being a popular play, much studied for A-levels, it crops up almost too often and successive directors at the RSC seem to feel challenged to make it different. Trevor Nunn's production in the main house in 1977 turned the comedy, especially in its last act, into a sort of baroque opera with arias for Celia and Orlando and with Hymen descending

---

[34] Richard David, *Shakespeare in the Theatre* (Cambridge: Cambridge U Press, 1978), 134–8.

[35] Colin Chambers, *Other Spaces: New Theatre and the RSC* (London: Eyre Methuen, 1980), 32–3.

in a throne of two-dimensional clouds. Terry Hands' production in 1980 was a direct response to his boss's operatic interpretation. For it Farrah designed a monochromatic Jacobean court that was mechanically transformed into a forest in which, as Spring moved into Summer, the pine trees seemed to sprout foliage. Suzanne Fleetwood was a tall and resilient Rosalind; and Sinead Cusack was an observant, rather alarmed Celia. John Bowe, the tough and likeable Orlando, later wrote that Farrah's Arden reminded him of scenes he had imagined when reading *Lord of the Rings*.[36] Terry Hands had indeed returned the action to The Green World.

The elegant Regency version of *As You Like It* staged at Stratford, Ontario, in 1977 and 1978 by the British director Robin Phillips was perhaps some compensation to Maggie Smith for the deliberate snub by Lord Olivier at the National Theatre. Notoriously a nervous, brittle performer in comedy, she can occasionally go over the top with swooping vowels and wild wrist-flapping. She played four seasons in Canada with Phillips and, when rehearsals for this play began, he encouraged her at first to clown outrageously as Rosalind and then helped her to modify and control her performance.[37] Like Dame Edith in 1936 Maggie Smith came to Rosalind by way of Millamant and other witty women of high comedy. She also came to the part a little late, but at forty-two she did not have to assume glamour. The British public was denied the joy of seeing her in the part, but North American and British reviewers were ecstatic. Bernard Levin continues to regard her performance as one of the most moving and powerful memories of his life, especially the flourish at the end:

> She spoke the epilogue like a chime of bells; but what she looked like as she did so, I cannot tell you, because I saw it through eyes curtained with tears.[38]

The Orlando was a strapping Canadian actor Jack Wetherall, and Phillips later recalled "a wise and more mature Rosalind leading a less-experienced Orlando towards love." When he came to direct the play again at Stratford in 1987 with Nancy Polk in a Victorian setting he was not inhibited by memories of Smith's "divine performance," for he found the younger actress, with equal fidelity to the text, established a new dimension which had to do with a girl disguised as a man discovering personal freedom.[39]

---

[36] In Philip Brockbank, ed., *Players of Shakespeare: Essays in Shakespearean Performance by Twelve Players with the RSC,* 1 (Cambridge: Cambridge U Press, 1985), 67–76.

[37] Coveney, *Maggie Smith,* 178–84.

[38] *The Times,* 30 December, 1994, quoting his earlier review.

[39] Ralph Berry, *On Directing Shakespeare: Interviews with Contemporary*

Maggie Smith's starry Rosalind was seen on the relatively compact thrust stage of the Festival Theatre and the only scenery was a gnarled tree. The most ambitious and costly *As You Like It* of the century must have been the great German director Peter Stein's seminal production for the Schaubühne in West Berlin.[40] This had its origins in an independent project in 1971, when the *dramaturg* and playwright Botho Strauss conducted a series of seminars and workshops with the permanent company in an attempt to recover the social, political and cultural elements of Shakespeare's world. Subsequently long sessions under Stein himself led to the presentation over two evenings in December 1976 in a big film studio at Spandau miles from the centre of Berlin of an extraordinary assemblage of materials from the popular and the high culture of Elizabethan England to which an English title was given: *Shakespeare's Memory.* Research had taken the group to Warwickshire. This kaleidoscope was performed to a promenade audience of about 360, who sometimes had to choose between two items simultaneously staged in separate spaces. Only then did the ensemble choose the actual Shakespeare text they would now rehearse: *As You Like It,* which eventually opened at the same distant film studios in December 1977. The audience, again over 300, had first to assemble as promenaders in a long, high hall. The actors in elaborate Elizabethan costumes sat immobile on various platforms; once the play began the early scenes were juxtaposed almost cinematically. The wrestling match was the climax of the first part with a professional wrestler in the non-speaking part of Charles. Then came a chase to the Forest in which the spectators had to follow the actors. They proceeded single-file through a tunnel to a second, bigger space in which Arden had been recreated in almost realistic detail—a pool, tree-trunks, a cottage, a farm, cat-walks. The audience sat on three sides while on the fringes of the action various denizens of the Forest wandered: Robin Hood, Robinson Crusoe, a hermit, a witch. Costumes were well-worn and timeless—Rosalind, played by Jutta Lampe, arrived in fur hat and jerkin, later changing into a shirt and cotton trousers and sporting a painted moustache. 'All the world's a stage' was delivered, very much as a set speech, *in English.* There were invented sequences as when, after the gory skinning of the deer, Orlando was seen wrestling with a figure in the deerskin as if with the lioness. Duke Frederick's court actually arrived in armour in the forest towards the end of the performance, which ran well over four hours with production costs of DM.700,000 at a time when the West Berlin theatre was hugely subsidised by

---

Directors (London: Hamish Hamilton, 1989), 153.

[40] There is an extended description and analysis of this whole enterprise in Michael Patterson's *Peter Stein: Germany's Leading Theatre Director* (Cambridge: Cambridge U Press, 1981), chapter 7.

the Federal Republic. It has been noted that in a divided city during the Cold War the notion of escape from a constricting urban world to a sylvan space (together perhaps with the necessity to return) had a special resonance for West Berliners. The idea of a double acting space must have been with Stein from the beginning, but the Rumanian director Andrei Serban worked in France for several months in the summer of 1977 on an experimental fun-fair *As You Like It* in the Ardennes which invited spectators to walk from their village to see the later scenes acted in the depths of the woods. Serban re-staged his version indoors for La Mama in New York in 1980.

By the time John Dexter was invited in 1979 to stage *As You Like It* at the National Theatre that organisation had moved to its new complex of three playhouses on the South Bank. Dexter was allocated the huge, awkward saucer of the Olivier stage and he used it as simply as possible to focus attention on the activities taking place on the white raked stage of the court and the green one of the forest. The production emphasised the back-breaking labour of harvesting in the opening scene. Dexter, now more influenced by *The Golden Bough* than by *Shakespeare Our Contemporary,* discovered (or imposed) a savage cruelty in Arden. A young man, naked to the waist and blooded from the chase, was paraded in the hunting scene. Later he turned out to be William and eventually he spoke for a pagan Hymen. The costume designs were richly Elizabethan, and Sara Kestleman as the disguised Rosalind looked as if she had stepped from a miniature by Hilliard. Simon Callow, who was cast, rather against type, as a stubby and endearing Orlando, later wrote in *Being An Actor* (1984) of the dictatorial, bullying methods of the director and said he gave Dexter's performance of Orlando not his own. Michael Bryant as Jaques spoke the famous speech while peeling and eating an apple. After the first night Sir Peter Hall, who had succeeded Olivier as supremo of the National Theatre, dictated a note for his diary:

> ". . . slightly slow, slightly tense, but you feel the whole of the Elizabethan mind laid out before you. I have seen the play better performed but never better directed."[41]

He was disappointed that the London reviewers found the three hours the play took too long. What would they have made of Stein's production, rumours of which must have influenced Dexter?

Five British productions in three different media revealed varying degrees of political or directorial interpretation. The BBC TV/Time-Life *As You Like It*

---

[41] John Goodwin, ed., *Peter Hall's Diaries* (London: Hamish Hamilton, 1983), 455.

(150 minutes), seen on video in innumerable classrooms, remains a monument to the lost cause of canonical Shakespeare. Shot in colour on location in and around Glamis Castle in Scotland in 1978, it never quite reconciles the stylistic clash between the real settings in formal gardens and woodlands and the theatrical-looking, rather picture-book medieval costumes.[42] There are good performances by Helen Mirren as Rosalind and Richard Pasco as Jaques. Adrian Noble's much more considered stage production for the RSC in 1985 encouraged the leading actresses (Juliet Stevenson as Rosalind; Fiona Shaw as a distinctly taller Celia) to take a feminist approach to their sisterly relationship.[43] The design by Bob Crowley—considerably simplified at the Barbican in 1986—presented an Arden which was not a specific location but an almost dream-like or Jungian space for self-discovery. When Fiona Shaw proceeded to play Rosalind herself in a production by Tim Albery at the Old Vic in 1989 she looked marvellously androgynous as Ganymede. The court scenes were played against heavy metal walls which later opened to reveal an immense, fairly realistic Arden which was yet some sort of imaginary world. At Stratford in the same year for John Caird's rather superficial production with the RSC the over-ingenious designer Ultz set the court scenes in a thirties corridor—a direct architectural reference to the foyer of the Shakespeare Theatre. The wooden floor was ripped up in a protracted scene by the exiled Duke's henchmen to reveal green turf underneath. Later Rosalind, played by the tiny Sophie Thompson, timidly opened the doors in the back wall to reveal a threatening Arden beyond. All these three stage productions seemed to envisage the Forest as an alternative through-the-looking-glass world. Very different was Christine Edzard's film (1992; 114 minutes) which was conceived as a State of the Nation commentary. There was a deliberate disjunction between the Elizabethan text and the up-to-the-minute social context. The Duke's court was an echoing municipal office peopled by executives, while Arden was a blighted urban wasteland near the Thames inhabited by drop-outs. On film Andrew Tierney was able to play both Orlando and his brother Charles; he carried an aerosol can with which he sprayed the love-poems on

---

[42] The text, illustrated with production photographs in colour and black and white was published (London: BBC Publications, 1978). It is divided into 28 scenes which stress location and time of day, e.g. "SCENE 10. *Exterior. A Pine Wood in the Forest of Arden. Day*" or "SCENE II. *Exterior. A Grove of Yew Trees in the Forest of Arden. Day*." This is close to the old editorial "*Another part of the Forest.*"

[43] Shaw and Stevenson wrote of their collaborative project in Russell Jackson and Robert Smallwood, eds., *Players of Shakespeare* 2 (Cambridge: Cambridge U Press, 1988), 55–71. Alan Rickman, the young and sardonic Jaques, also contributed, 73–80.

walls as graffiti. Audrey kept a mobile snack-bar. The film, however, never caught on and was quickly withdrawn from general release. Deconstruction pleased not the multitude.

No other production of *As You Like It* can have been seen by more people in more cities with more acclaim than Cheek by Jowl's between 1991 and 1995. This radical and innovative group, founded in 1981 by the director Declan Donnellan and his partner the designer Nick Ormerod, began by playing one-night stands and developed into an exciting venture, touring internationally under the auspices of the British Council. The company is committed to integrated casting and it recruits versatile players with physical, vocal and musical skills. Productions are visually resourceful but conceived to be stageable in playing-spaces of all shapes and sizes. Music, always by Paddy Cunneen, is performed live by members of the company. Their *As You Like It* which opened in July 1991 had the first professional all-male cast since 1967. Donnellan confessed later that during the early rehearsals four actresses were on the pay-roll, in case the performers could not avoid what he called the mysogynies of camp. [44] He was much more aware than Clifford Williams of the problematics of an all-male staging; and many in his audiences must have been familiar with current theories about sexuality and gender—Marjorie Garber's *Vested Interests: Cross-Dressing and Cultural Anxiety* was published late in 1991. The adaptable basic set was of white canvas. Fourteen actors trooped in wearing black pants, white collarless shirts, and braces. Jaques, played by a black actor Joe Dixon, spoke the first lines of 'All the world's a stage'. At 'And all the men *and women* merely players' two men (soon to be Rosalind and Celia) stepped aside. Seconds later the play began. There was no attempt at illusion. Lighting was brilliant and bright. The actors in the one scene usually entered before those in the previous scene had left; sometimes they froze onstage until their next scene, with marvellous, almost cinematic effects of irony or parallelism. The playing was spirited with extraordinarily creative doubling—not just Duke Frederick and his brother played by one actor but Charles the Wrestler/Jaques, Adam/Phebe, Le Beau/Corin. Amiens was Hymen in the masque. Rosalind was dazzlingly played by Adrian Lester, a young black Londoner of six-foot two, clearly never a French princess but always a male actor. Rosalind's character by some alchemy became more feminine once Lester was doubly disguised as Ganymede, with a straw hat pulled over a headscarf. Tom Hollander, recently down from Cambridge, played Celia in his own long curly hair. Green streamers descended to suggest the Forest, largely created by lighting. The whole production built up to a final scene of dizzying ambiguities, and the conclusion was extraordinarily joyous and celebratory.

---

[44] Interview with Dominic Cavendish, *The Independent* 4 January 1995, 21.

Jaques was overtly gay, but rescued from solitariness with a kiss from Amiens. Cheek by Jowl printed on the programme a list of the places this production played at in 1991/92, which reads like a litany: Adelaide, Belfast, Brasilia, Breda, Bury St. Edmunds, Buxton, Cambridge, Coventry, Derry, Dublin, Farnham, Hammersmith, Luxembourg, Madrid, New York, Recife, Rio de Janeiro, Rotterdam, São Paulo, Stratford-upon-Avon, Tokyo, Wellington, Winchester, Worthing and York.

In September 1994 Cheek by Jowl joyously recreated this production. Adrian Lester was irreplaceable; David Hobbs once more played both Dukes; and Peter Needham again came very close to ad-libbing as Touchstone. Some of the newcomers were challenged by different doubling: Paul Kissaum was Charles/Corin; Rhasan Stone was Amiens/William; and Richard Cant, originally a double-jointed, skinny Audrey added an aged, doddery automaton of an Adam. The new version was as remarkable as the old and toured for five months: Barcelona, Brooklyn, Bucharest, Craiova, Düsseldorf, Jerusalem, Manchester, Moscow, Norwich, Paris, Pilsen, Princeton, St. Petersburg, Sofia and Tel Aviv. Finally the company played for three weeks early in 1995 to full houses at the Albery in London. The most magical moment came when, during the final music-making and dancing, the house lights came up and Adrian Lester stepped forward, removing his head-dress, to speak the epilogue. The Albery was formerly called the New Theatre. Possibly a few elderly playgoers could recall Edith Evans speaking those very words there almost sixty years ago from the same stage-position. All the world, after all, *is* a stage.